MEDIEVAL ENGLISH LITERATURE

THE OXFORD ANTHOLOGY OF ENGLISH LITERATURE
General Editors: Frank Kermode and John Hollander

Medieval English Literature
J. B. TRAPP, Librarian, Warburg Institute, London

The Literature of Renaissance England
JOHN HOLLANDER, Hunter College;
and FRANK KERMODE, University College London

The Restoration and the Eighteenth Century
MARTIN PRICE, Yale University

Romantic Poetry and Prose
HAROLD BLOOM, Yale University;
and LIONEL TRILLING, Columbia University

Victorian Prose and Poetry
LIONEL TRILLING and HAROLD BLOOM

Modern British Literature
FRANK KERMODE and JOHN HOLLANDER

Medieval English Literature

J. B. TRAPP
Warburg Institute, London

New York OXFORD UNIVERSITY PRESS
London Toronto

Library of Congress Catalogue Card Number: 72–92353
printing, last digit: 20 19

Selections from the following works were made possible by the kind permission of their respective publishers and representatives:

An Anthology of Old English Poetry, translated by Charles W. Kennedy, copyright © 1960 by Oxford University Press, Inc.; reprinted by permission.
Beowulf: The Oldest English Epic, translated by Charles W. Kennedy, copyright 1940 by Oxford University Press, Inc.; renewed 1968 by Charles W. Kennedy; reprinted by permission.
Sir Gawain and the Green Knight, translated by Brian Stone, copyright © 1959, 1964, 1973 by Brian Stone; reprinted by permission of Penguin Books Ltd.
The Oxford Book of Ballads, edited by James Kinsley, copyright © 1969 by Oxford University Press; reprinted by permission of The Clarendon Press, Oxford.
The Romance of the Rose, translated by F. S. Ellis, reprinted by permission of J. M. Dent & Sons Ltd.

Printed in the United States of America

General Editors' Preface

The purpose of the Oxford Anthology is to provide students with a selective canon of the entire range of English Literature from the beginnings to recent times, with introductory matter and authoritative annotation. Its method is historical, in the broadest sense, and its arrangement, commentary, and notes, both analytic and contextual, have benefited not only from the teaching experience of the several editors, but from a study of the virtues and shortcomings of comparable works. A primary aim has been to avoid the insulation of any one section from the influence of others, and more positively, to allow both student and instructor to come to terms with the manner in which English literature has generated its own history. This aim has been accomplished in several ways.

First, a reorganization of chronological phases has allowed the Tudor and Stuart periods to be unified under the broad heading of the English Renaissance, with two editors collaborating over the whole extended period. Similarly, the nineteenth century has two editors, one for the poetry of the whole period, and one for the prose. This arrangement seemed appropriate in every way, especially since neither of these scholars could be called a narrow specialist in "Romantic" or "Victorian," as these terms are used in semester- or course-labels.

Every contributing editor has worked and taught in at least one period or field outside the one for which he is, in this anthology, principally responsible, and none has ever allowed specialization to reduce his broader commitment to humane studies more largely considered. Thus we were able to plan a work which called for an unusual degree of cross reference and collaboration. During a crucial phase in the preparation of the text, the editors held daily discussions of their work for a period of months. By selection, allusion, comparison, by direction and indirection, we contrived to preserve continuity between epochs, and to illuminate its character. At the same time, the close co-operation of the various editors has precluded the possibility of common surrender to any single dominating literary theory; and the teacher need have no fear that he must prepare to do battle with some critical Hydra showing a head on every page.

The method of selecting text was consistent with these principles. In the eighteenth- and nineteenth-century sections it was our general policy to exclude the novel, for obvious reasons of length; but in the twentieth, where short fiction becomes more prominent and more central, we have included entire works of fiction, or clearly defined parts of them—for example, *Heart of Darkness,* "The Dead," the "Nausicaa" episode of *Ulysses,* and *St. Mawr.* On the other hand we were persuaded, after much reflection, that a different principle must apply in the cases of Spenser and Milton, where we waived the requirement of completeness. To have given the whole of one book—say, the First of *The Faerie Queene*—would have been a solution as easy as it is, no doubt, defensible; but it is asking a great deal of students to see that portion of the poem as an epitome of the rest, which is often so delightfully different; and we decided that we must provide selections from the whole poem, with linking commentary. We did the same for *Paradise Lost* though without abandoning the practice of providing complete texts when this was both possible and desirable; for example, *Comus* is reprinted entire, and so is a lesser-known but still very important masque, Jonson's *Pleasure Reconciled to Virtue,* which is interesting not only in relation to *Comus* but as an illustration of the part poetry can play in political spectacle and—more generally—in the focusing of the moral vision. Minor texts have been chosen for their exemplary force and their beauty, as well as to embody thematic concerns. If the teacher wishes, he or she may work, both within and across periods, with recurrent patterns as large as the conception of the Earthly Paradise, or with sub-genres as small but as fascinating as the Mad Song. It will also be evident from certain patterns of selection—*The Tempest* as the Shakesperean play, the very large amount of Blake, the emphasis given to D. H. Lawrence's poems as well as his fiction—that a genuinely modern taste, rather than an eager modishness, has helped to shape our presentation of the historical canon. It is also hoped that the unusually generous sampling of material in certain sections—notably the Renaissance, eighteenth century, and the Romantics—will allow the teacher to use secondary or minor works, if he so chooses, to highlight these newer concerns or to fill in contextual background.

As for the annotations, the editors have never been afraid to be lively or even speculative. They have consistently tried to avoid usurping the teacher's role, as providing standard or definitive readings might do. On the other hand, the commentary goes beyond merely providing a lowest common denominator of information by suggesting interpretive directions and levels along which the teacher is free to move or not; and of course he always has the freedom to disagree. The editors have been neither prudish nor portentous in their tone, nor have they sought—in the interests of some superficial consistency, but with leaden effect—to efface their personal styles.

Texts have all been based on the best modern editions, which happen quite often to be published by the Oxford University Press. Spelling and punctuation have been modernized throughout, save in three instances: portions of the medieval period, and the texts of Spenser and Blake, two poets whose spelling and punctuation are so far from idiosyncrasies to be silently normalized that they constitute attempts to refashion poetic language. In the medieval section, modern verse translations of *Beowulf* (by C. W. Kennedy) and of *Gawain* (by Brian Stone) have been adopted. Glossaries of literary and historical terms in all periods have been provided, sometimes keyed to the annotations, sometimes supplementing the larger headnotes. These, it will be noticed, seek to illuminate the immediate contexts of the literature of a period rather than to provide a dense précis of its social, political, and economic history. Similarly, the reading lists at the end of each volume are not exhaustive bibliographies; in the happy instance where a teacher finds an extensive bibliography advisable, he or she will want to supply one.

A word about the pictures. They are not to be thought of simply as illustrations, and certainly not as mere decorations, but rather as part of the anthologized material, like the musical examples and the special sections (such as the one on Ovidian mythology in the Renaissance and on the Urban Scene in the eighteenth century). Throughout, the reader is introduced to the relations between poem as speaking picture, and picture as mute poem. Aside from contextual and anecdotal illustration, of which there is indeed a good deal, the pictorial examples allow teachers, or students on their own, to explore some of the interrelations of texts and the visual arts in all periods, whether exemplified in Renaissance emblems or in contemporary illustrations of Victorian poems.

Finally, an inevitable inadequate word of acknowledgment. To the English Department of Dartmouth College the editors are deeply indebted for having so generously and hospitably provided a place in which to work together for a sustained period. The staff of the Dartmouth College Library was extraordinarily helpful and attentive.

All of the editors would like to extend a note of gratitude to the many academics throughout the United States who willingly made suggestions as to what should be included as well as excluded. A special note of thanks to Jim Cox of Dartmouth College and Paul Dolan of the State University of New York at Stony Brook for their challenging and always helpful comments.

And finally to the entire staff of the New York branch of the Oxford University Press who have done more than could be humanly expected in connection with the planning and execution of this book. We would especially like to thank our editor John Wright, as well as Leona Capeless and her staff, Mary Ellen Evans, Patricia Cristol, Joyce Berry, Deborah Zwecher, and Jean Shapiro. An unusual but very deserved note of thanks to the Production people, especially Gerard S. Case and Leslie Phillips and to the designer, Frederick Schneider, whose excellent work speaks for itself.

Frank Kermode
John Hollander

New York
September 1972

BRITISH ISLES
10°W
5°W
0°
60°N
60°N
N
Atlantic Ocean
North Sea
SCOTLAND
Clyde
Glasgow
Edinburgh
55°N
55°N
Belfast
LAKE DISTRICT
YORKSHIRE
York
Hull
Blackpool
Leeds
Irish Sea
Manchester
Sheffield
Liverpool
Shannon
IRELAND
Dublin
MERCIA
Trent
Nottingham
Norwich
EAST ANGLIA
Birmingham
Avon
WALES
ENGLAND
Severn
Oxford
Thames
Bristol
London
Southampton
KENT
WESSEX
50°N
English Channel
FRANCE
Miles
0
50
100
150
10°W
5°W

Contents

* An asterisk indicates that a work does not appear in its entirety.

MEDIEVAL ENGLISH LITERATURE

Medieval English Literature

HISTORICAL BACKGROUND

Britain's first experience of a literate civilization came in 55 B.C., when Julius Caesar's military expedition from across the Channel initiated the Romanization of this part of the known world. Settled by Celtic tribes from Gaul in the fifth century B.C., Britain had hitherto been, for Rome, the remotest of countries, known only from traders' reports and garbled accounts. Caesar's two brief forays in successive years established Roman dominion and opened up the island. "Corn, cattle, gold, silver and iron; also hides, slaves and clever hunting dogs" were the British commodities that could help to maintain the Roman standard of living, while in return British chieftains received food, drink, furniture, and household equipment of a luxury never before available to them.

For nearly a century Britain remained a trading outpost of the Roman Empire. Not until after 43 A.D., under the Emperor Claudius, did the island come fully under Roman political and military domination. Even then, remoter areas in Scotland retained independence, and Ireland, never conquered by Rome, was free to continue its Celtic tradition.

Roman conquest meant that Roman civic organization created an urban civilization on the Roman model within the conglomeration of small local Celtic tribal units. The Romans encouraged the chiefs and leading families to adopt their way of life and to have their sons educated in the Roman manner. Walled towns were laid out in the Roman style, some at the old tribal centers, some outside the walls of Roman fortresses, some as settlements of discharged veterans. In the countryside, villas replaced older farm complexes and served as rural centers.

Roman civilization in Britain managed to weather the first raids of Saxon pirates in the late third century, but once the Roman forces were withdrawn (c. 410) it soon collapsed under the impact of much larger armed migration. During the first half of the fifth century the Angles, Saxons, and Jutes descended on the country in great numbers from northern Germany and Jutland or the Jutish Peninsula. The initial wave of this migration is dated 449 by many Anglo-Saxon writers, on the basis of a statement by the Venerable Bede (c. 673–735), the first historian of the English church and people. According to Bede, the Britain of his time comprised four nations—English, British (Welsh), Picts, and Scots—each having its own language yet united in the study of God's truth by the fifth—Latin. When the English invasion began, the Picts inhabited the northernmost parts of the island, the modern Scotland, the Scots (confusingly) occupied Ireland, and the Britons held possession of all the island of Britain to the south of the Firth of Forth. The invaders, according to race, settled in the South-East (the Jutes, in Kent and on the Isle of Wight); in Essex (north of Kent: "East Saxony"), Sussex (south of Kent: "South Saxony," and Wessex (South-West as far as Gloucestershire and Devon, "West Saxony"); and in the North-East (East Anglia), North (Northumbria) and North-West (Mercia), these last three being occupied by the Angles.

While Bede's division corresponds too closely to the political divisions of his day to be entirely reliable, it is a useful guide. It is valuable particularly as suggesting the disunity within unity of these pagan Germanic invaders, a disunity reflected in the cultural differences that continued throughout the Anglo-Saxon and Middle English periods. It is important to remember that despite centralizing influences English provincial cultures remained vigorous. Canterbury, in Kent, the town from which Roman Christianity spread from the sixth century, is today the primatial Anglican see of England and was throughout the Middle Ages a notable literary and artistic center, besides being later a place of pilgrimage. Winchester, the chief town of the Anglo-Saxon kingdom of Wessex, was highly influential in both the visual and the verbal arts during the later Anglo-Saxon period, as well as being a city where Norman kings held court. Superb manuscripts were produced in later medieval East Anglia, and manuscript writing and illumination and wood and stone carving, as well as literary studies, flourished in late seventh- and early eighth-century Northumbria. Later, in the fourteenth century, poems in the West Midland dialect and plays in the Northern sustained the standard of provincial culture in regions remote (by medieval reckoning) from the capital. A pilgrim to Canterbury took four days to cover the sixty miles from London; the West Midland area where *Sir Gawain and the Green Knight* was written was more than twice as far from the metropolis.

In the fifth century this flourishing England provincial and metropolitan culture was of course far in the future. The invaders were a hardy, warlike race, their characteristics still resembling those of the Germans as described by Tacitus (see Headnote to *Beowulf,* below). An index of their success is the degree to which the Celtic languages were supplanted: only a very few words of Celtic origin survived to find their way into later medieval and modern English. The English drove the Britons from their land and brought much more of the land under the plow; basically, however, like Tacitus's Germans, they were not prone to group themselves into large social organisms—let alone urban societies—or to maintain the quite elaborate communications system between groups that would have been possible if they had taken over existing towns with their connecting Roman roads.

A centralized urban society developed only very slowly among the small, oligarchic, local units of the various English kingdoms. For long, chieftains and petty kings moved with their courts from one royal estate to the other, expecting and receiving generous hospitality. Their counselors, chosen by them and not elected by any democratic process, served one month in three and retired to their estates for the other two. Gradually, more permanent establishments evolved, kingdoms grew in size and strength, and learning and the arts of peace began to flourish. The kingdoms of Northumbria, Mercia, and Wessex rose to a dominant position in the seventh, eighth, and ninth-tenth centuries respectively.

During the eighth century the nascent civilization of the English was already menaced by the Norwegian sea-raiders, who sacked the Northumbrian monastery of Lindisfarne in 793. The Danes made great inroads into England during the next two hundred years. In 870 they came down by land to attack the southwestern kingdom of Wessex; when later defeated by King Alfred the Great they retired, to be confined by treaty to the territory in the North and East Midlands known as the Danelaw. A century and a half later, a Danish king, Canute, succeeded to the throne of Wessex and ruled a great part of England.

Throughout the Anglo-Saxon period and for centuries thereafter, the Church remained the most powerful force in the written culture of the English nation. Since St. Augustine's mission from Rome had landed in Canterbury in 597, the English church had flourished, although the Roman Christianity represented by Augustine had been in doctrinal conflict with Celtic Christianity, which had earlier evangelized the North and the South-West. The two were notably at loggerheads about the date of Easter, and their differences were not settled until the Synod held at Whitby Abbey in Northumbria in 664, when Canterbury won the day. Later during the same century, Englishmen began to evangelize heathen Germany, and finally in the eighth brought that entire territory to Christianity.

The importance of the Church and of its monastic, predominantly Latin, culture for the cultural life of Anglo-Saxon England can hardly be overemphasized. In the development of a beautiful script for the writing of texts, in the decoration and illumination of manuscripts, as well as in scholarship and the arts of architecture and sculpture, Church patronage was paramount. This was especially so of monastic patronage: a monastic community was a small town in itself, in this respect a kind of equivalent of the country villa of Roman times, with a community existing on the fruit of its own toil and on charitable benefactions.

THE NORMAN CONQUEST AND LATER

The men who followed Duke William of Normandy to England in 1066, to assert his right to the West-Saxon throne, were the descendants of Scandinavians who had landed on the north coast of France a century and a half before. Nominally subjects of the French king and speaking the French language, the Normans comprised virtually an independent state, with territorial ambitions and a Viking joy in war. During the same century in which they conquered England they founded states in South Italy and Sicily.

These invaders, like the Romans before them, were a compact, efficient army, many of them mercenaries, rather than half a nation on the move like the Angles, Saxons, and Jutes. Immediately on landing, William won the decisive Battle of Hastings, to become—by right of conquest as well as by family—King of England and Duke of Normandy. For four hundred years, until the end of the Hundred Years' War between England and France (1453), this dual kingdom was the most powerful state in Europe. Its territories on the French side of the Channel were greatly extended by William the Conqueror's successors. The kings of England gave at least as much of their time and attention to their French dominions as to their English, held their court at least as often in France as in England, and regularly engaged in military operations on French soil.

The Normans brought to England their northern dialect of the French language, and their social and political dominance imposed this dialect on the almost exclusively Germanic (with borrowings from Latin) language of the conquered English as the norm of educated and aristocratic communication. Latin remained the language of learning, and Old English continued to be spoken and written; but the machinery of government and the law functioned in French. Throughout the Middle Ages, French taste in literature and the arts prevailed, especially in southern English noble and royal circles. The language that grew up in this situation was an amalgam known as Middle English: its syntax and grammar largely remained English while its vocabulary was greatly augmented by French.

Before the coming of the Normans the English had created a society remarkable for a degree of civilization that had continued to flourish in spite of Danish invasions. After the Danish wars of the ninth century the Kingdom of Wessex had established a military and cultural ascendancy over the whole country, but the kingdoms of Mercia and Northumbria, as well as the Norse kingdom of York, survived in a shadow form in 1066. Despite the ascendancy of Wessex, and the existence of a consistent and workable system of law, local government, and taxation throughout the land, England before the Norman Conquest was by no means a close-knit unity. The Frenchmen, as the conquered called the conquerors, imposed themselves on England, driving the older English aristocracy from the court and to a lower position in society in general, and creating one kingdom from many.

William the Conqueror's method of asserting his power (binding on the whole realm) was orderly, simple, autocratic—and novel to the English. Every inch of the land was declared to be the king's; retaining great estates for himself, he distributed the remainder among his followers, who held it as his tenants only in return for the performance of exactly defined services. Within this feudal system the Norman barons were free to govern and exploit their lands as they wished. They were encouraged to build strongholds, and William himself saw to it that a castle, with a constable (a noble vassal of the king), was erected in every county town and at strategic points throughout the country. These great stone fortresses, on ground naturally or artificially elevated, with moats around them and stockades for an outer defense, became the symbol of Norman power. The English had never seen anything like them.

William also took care to know, by means of a systematic enquiry made in the 1080's and recorded in Doomsday Book, the feudal obligation of each of his vassals. He also took care to strengthen the towns already established during the Anglo-Saxon period, as centers of trade, justice, and administration in peace, and defense in war. Ports such as Southampton on the south coast and London on the navigable River Thames gradually came into greater prominence because of their advantages in these respects. London, already a major town in Roman days, had become by the beginning of the thirteenth century a community strong and rich enough to turn the scale in a dispute—according as it supported the barons against the king (as in 1215 against King John) or vice versa. It was by far the largest, wealthiest, and most powerful town in England, and the administrative and cultural hub of the country as well.

By the fourteenth century the English kingdom—in the British Isles and in France—was at the height of its political strength and economic prosperity. The power of Edward III (*d.* 1377), the military exploits of his eldest son the Black Prince, and the political and cultural influence of his fourth son, John of Gaunt, are among the outstanding features of English life at the time. Even though social unrest and political strife were prevalent during the reign of Richard II (deposed 1399), these did not destroy the social and economic conditions in which literature and the arts could flourish.

Though the power and influence of the King of England tended to concentrate itself in the south, both because of its proximity to the French territories of the king and because of the metropolis of London and the ports of the south coast, mercantile centers in the provinces also came to prosper. The Yorkshire farms and towns in the north grew rich on the production of wool, and the eastern and western counties, on weaving and the export trade. The rising well-to-do bourgeois society of London and of these provincial towns began to exert an influence on taste. The most obvious example in literature is the fourteenth-century mystery play in the north and the Midlands. The exactions of great landowners in pursuit of more profitable means of farming became a staple source of the literature of social complaint.

One of the most distinctive features of the later Middle Ages in England and in Europe was the change that came about in institutions of education. The first universities were founded in Europe during the twelfth century. Their curricula included civil and canon (ecclesiastical) law, the Latin classics, the newly revived Aristotelian philosophy, especially logic (in Latin translation), mathematics, and medicine. Until the late twelfth century an English boy acquired his education either in a school—perhaps attached to a cathedral but in any case licensed by the bishop of the diocese, or in a royal or noble household whose life he shared, or an abbey or monastery, where he was trained by the monks. Little care was taken for the education of girls. The late twelfth century saw the beginnings of the University of Oxford (its constituent colleges were not founded until later); and Cambridge was founded during the early thirteenth century. These two remained the only English universities for more than five hundred years.

After elementary schooling in cathedral, court, or abbey, a boy would enter university at the age of about fourteen, and spend seven years or so equipping himself for a career in the church or the administration of the realm. From the last years of the thirteenth century onward, he had another choice. During the reign of Edward I (1272–1307) the laws of England became the object of serious study and definition and at about the same time the "common" or civil lawyers began to group themselves into societies known as Inns of Court. In these "Inns" the senior members lived, studied, and taught; and there a boy could be sent as an alternative to university or for post-university education.

In the thousand years between the coming of the Anglo-Saxons in the fifth century and the waning of the Middle Ages in the fifteenth, England had advanced from a land conquered and sparsely populated by a alien race to a civilization in full flower. From a country divided among many petty rulers, she had become one powerful kingdom, commercially prosperous, with a unified legal system and the beginnings of parliamentary government by two houses, Lords and Commons. At various times architecture, sculpture, painting, and the minor arts had all been brought to a point where they excelled what the rest of Europe had to offer. By the end of the fifteenth century, however, she was beginning to lag behind in the arts and in scholarship. Italy, in particular, was now the leader: when Gothic was still the style of England, Italian Renaissance painters, sculptors, and architects were producing the masterpieces that set the standard for the next three hundred years. In learning, too, England was retardataire. But vernacular literature, both popular and courtly, was still her great glory, and she had already produced, in Geoffrey Chaucer, a great European poet who united both French and English traditions, as well as other English masters working in a poetic that was the lineal descendant of Old English verse techniques.

ANGLO-SAXON (OLD ENGLISH) LITERATURE

It is no accident that the entire Old English section of this anthology is in verse. All cultures find their first verbal artistic expression in rhythmic utterance, the organization into less free, more formal repetitive patterns of the basic prosodic structures of language. These patterns are first used in ritual, that is to say, in the oral realization of a solemn or joyful effect, involving the raising and fulfilling of an exalted expectation, sometimes with the aid of music, sometimes without. This often occurs at a preliterate stage, since poetry depends less than prose on the written word. Nevertheless, all poems seek and some are felt to have—or else they would never be written down at all—a validity beyond the single performance, as well as a dimension and an influence that go beyond the merely verbal and either imitate or command some basic and universal pattern or harmony.

While any artistic utterance seeks the condition of permanence, oral poetry always retains something of the occasional quality of performance. Chief among the accidents of time as they affect the transmission of literature, especially medieval literature, is the point in its development at which a text was committed to writing. Sometimes the act of writing down crystallized and solidified the text; sometimes it allowed it an existence of continued change as spoken art—as in the popular ballads. To a certain extent this is true of all literature: the form in which we read a modern poem or novel is the form in which the author was finally obliged to give it to the publisher—which may or may not be "final." Its transmission, even in a literate society that produces multiple copies of books by mechanical means—Western society as it has been since the invention of printing—is not entirely straightforward. Still, modern texts are comparatively stable and the range of variant conditions remains relatively narrow, growing narrower the nearer we approach our own times.

Of many of the poems that make up the first part of this anthology, we can say little with certainty about date of composition or authorship. We have more information about the poets and other authors of the later Middle Ages, but never as much as we should like—and it is surprising how frequently we are unable to give even the name of an author to some of the most remarkable works of the fourteenth century.

To go back to the time when the earliest poetry of the English people is thought to have been composed, we must pick an arbitrary date, say about 500 A.D., when the migration of the Germanic tribes was more or less complete. The written records we possess from that time amount only to a handful of inscriptions, serving a no longer definable magical function, expressed in pagan characters known as runes. Runes continue to appear on Christian monuments, such as the Ruthwell Cross (Fig. 23), on which a portion of the poem *The Dream of the Rood* is carved, and on such objects as the Franks Casket (Fig. 22); yet with very few exceptions they are not used in the transcription of any extant manuscript texts. The vernacular manuscripts originating in the seventh century used an alphabet based on the Latin script of the Irish missionaries to England, with a few extra characters for Anglo-Saxon sounds having no equivalent in Latin (Fig. 4).

By the seventh century the physical means for recording texts and enough trained scribes to write them were in existence, particularly in Northumbria. The Lindisfarne Gospels (Fig. 5), now in the British Museum, are only one witness to the skill and sophistication exercised at the end of the seventh century and the beginning of the eighth. On the other hand, the manuscripts in which Old English poetry is preserved are almost all unique, and almost none of them were written until the end of the tenth century. Scribal effort, in other words, had been expended on the new learning in the new language of culture—Latin—rather than on what we now think of as the earliest monuments of our literature, the heroic poetry of the Anglo-Saxon people. This means that many poems, in the form in which we have them, were not written down until perhaps two and one-half centuries after their composition. On the other hand, certain works, such as *The Battle of Maldon,* which commemorates a historical event of 991, must have been copied into a manuscript almost as soon as composed Most scholars think that earlier manuscripts of the earlier poems must have existed, and that they were probably transcribed in various dialects rather than only in the literary West Saxon in which the tenth-century versions are expressed. We cannot be sure, but it seems likely that *Beowulf,* for example, was given a form approximating that which we know, by a singer or singers at some time during the eighth century. The poet was probably binding together materials from an earlier time and adding to them. During the Anglo-Saxon period, however, it looks as though the transcription of works which were predominantly secular, or only indirectly didactic—especially those based on pagan materials and pagan codes of value and behavior—must have taken a very secondary place to the writing of sacred works.

Throughout the Middle Ages, in all Europe, the Bible was by far the most frequently copied text, either in itself or in the many liturgical books for which it formed the basis. Without the Christian missionaries from Ireland and Rome, the impulse toward a written culture in England would have come far later; yet the culture that the missionaries brought with them and in which they educated their converts was primarily a sacred one, Latin not English, learned rather than popular. Those who came under its influence were more likely to busy themselves with Latin verse and prose (especially Christian) than with the vernacular. Since Latin was the common language of learned Europe, Englishmen could make a European reputation in that language: St. Aldhelm of Malmesbury (640–709), in Wessex; the Venerable Bede (c.653–735) scholar, grammarian, poet, encyclopedist, Scripture commentator, hagiographer, and historian, monk of Jarrow in Northumbria; and Alcuin of York (735–804) did exactly that. After a distinguished career in his native York, Alcuin spent most of the last twenty years of his life as principal educator to the Emperor Charlemagne and the Frankish court.

By translation from the Latin, too, the most beneficial works of the new faith could be made available—the Bible itself, the *Pastoral Care* and the *Dialogues* of St. Gregory the Great, the *Consolation of Philosophy* of Boethius (a pagan philosopher, d. c.524, then thought to be Christian). This was the ambition of King Alfred, in Wessex during the later ninth century; and though there is evidence that he was an admirer of *Beowulf,* there is stronger evidence that he was more an admirer of piety and learning, which he wished to see flourish in a kingdom at peace and secure from the attacks of Scandinavian marauders.

The further development of the Alfredian program during the late tenth- and early eleventh-century movement which goes under the name of the Benedictine Revival is associated especially with the name of St. Dunstan, Archbishop of Canterbury from 959 to 988, whose program of monastic reform brought education, learning, and the arts into still closer contact than ever before in England. In its beginnings the Benedictine Revival was primarily Latin in character, but in its wake was produced some of the greatest vernacular work of the entire medieval period, in both the visual and the verbal arts. The inspiration is classical and Mediterranean, the finished product characteristically English. With a writer such as Ælfric (955–1020), it is no longer a matter of saving oneself for Latin or of producing a stiff rendering of Latin into Old English, but rather of a highly conscious, fully mastered rhetorical art in Old English prose. So too, in the manuscript illumination of the century preceding the Norman Conquest: in the Benedictional of St. Æthelwold, St. Dunstan's collaborator (Fig. 6), a Mediterranean model has been assimilated into a style recognizably national and entirely independent and self-assured. A later example still, with influences from Byzantium, is seen in Fig. 7, from the St. Albans Psalter of the first quarter of the twelfth century.

The Benedictine Revival was the summing up and crowning of a process that had begun in the sixth century and had produced a large body of English prose by the time of the Norman Conquest in 1066. Much of this prose consists of sermons or of works of devotion or morality, private and public. Some is legal and administrative, some annalistic, like the sometimes lively (and often dull) narrative of the *Anglo-Saxon Chronicle*. Some pieces, like the translations of the Greek romance of *Apollonius of Tyre* and of the *Marvels of the East,* seem to exist for the sake of the tale alone. Most of it would have been intended for reading aloud, since only a small proportion of the population could read and write; and some of the sermons, in particular, must have been delivered with a sense of performance almost as great as that of poetry. But it is unlikely that such prose was intended to be memorized to the same extent as verse, even in an age when men's verbal memories were more exercised and more tenacious than they are today. It is recorded of King Alfred that as a boy he received a coveted book of poetry as a reward for memorizing its entire contents after having them read to him.

By comparison with the mass of prose writings, the amount of Old English verse that survives is small. Some of it is religious: *The Dream of the Rood,* brief and highly wrought, is perhaps its high point. Much consists of what is loosely described as heroic: that is to say, it takes as its basic assumptions the older Germanic pagan insistence on the virtues of courage in battle and endurance in the face of all the ills that beset a man as he passes from youth to old age. Its greatest monument is *Beowulf,* its most perfect epitome *The Battle of Maldon*—a late, fully crystallized statement of the heroic ideal which is also a memorial for an aged English leader against the Danes.

Though it is probable that poetry, the older literary form, took second place in the monastic scriptoria to English and Latin prose, the poetic gift was always held in high esteem among the English. The singer of tales, the *scop,* with a repertoire part memorized and part improvised, and accompanying his verses on the harp, was an important member of a noble household. He could expect his stock-in-trade to command a receptive audience, his listeners themselves versed in, and hence appreciative of, his poetic skills. Performances by such trained and (so to speak) professional minstrels, as well as by the guests themselves in turn, were an important feature of any feast.

While we have the names of many scholars and prose writers of the Anglo-Saxon period, and even considerable biographical information about a good number, we can name only three poets, all of them Christian and active in a monastic ambience. Cædmon is one, Aldhelm another; six lines of vernacular poetry survive from one, none at all from the second. Of the third, Cynewulf, we know little, except that he has left us about twenty-six hundred lines of verse, including a long poem, *Elene* (on St. Helena and the finding of the True Cross). More survives from what is known as the school of Cynewulf, all of it seemingly written by ecclesiastics during the late eighth and early ninth centuries. Its subject matter is religious—saints' lives, Gospel stories, and Christian allegory. Works such as *The Phoenix,* adapted from pseudo-Lactantius (see the section The Other World: Paradise), and *The Dream of the Rood,* the latter chiefly because of resemblance to *Elene* in subject, are often called Cynewulfian. Though the *Dream* has a depth and richness and is of a quality that sets it above the other work of Cynewulf and his "school," there are enough resemblances between the two in style and diction to make the comparison useful.

The remainder of the Old English poetic corpus is anonymous and untitled. In a very few cases, such as the Riddles, to have given a title would have been to destroy the point of the game, which was to describe a familiar object in language as figurative and impenetrable as possible, provoking admiration for poetic skill in the making and surprised pleasure at the solution. This delight in figurative diction is one of the chief characteristics of Old English poetry—as indeed of medieval literature in general. For the medieval poet, richness and difficulty of language were not to be avoided, but rather to be cultivated. Rhetoric and ornament were not the terms of abuse that they have become in modern times. Old English poetry, naturally, does not bear the strong impress of Latin rhetorical theory and practice that marks later English medieval verse and prose. But it loves ornament, repeated in patterns—just as Anglo-Saxon art did (Figs. 5–6, 21). It preserves a careful balance between what is strange and what is familiar and it orders its rhythms and effects according to metrical and structural principles that are strict in operation. Particularly in a heroic epic like *Beowulf,* but also in shorter elegiac poems, it achieves an effect of carefully contrived and ordered ceremonial performance. Like oral poetry in general, it is essentially an art of preservation rather than of innovation, using and re-using traditional materials. The hearer or reader is made to feel that he is on familiar ground as he recognizes the highly conventional—the word is again not one of abuse in medieval times—figurative vocabulary, with its formulaic repetitions and fossilized poetic terms, and the poet's use of one incident to convey the parallel implications of another.

One of the chief marks distinguishing the literature of medieval and Renaissance Europe from that of our day is its profound belief in the didactic and exemplary value of the verbal work of art. *Beowulf* is a poem of praise punctuated, in a manner typical of Old English poetry, by passages of Christian and pagan moralizing. In one sense it can be very loosely called an allegory of the perpetual struggle of light against dark, good against evil. Over and above the pleasure it was undoubtedly expected to give its audience, the weight of the poem is thrown into the attempt to move and persuade this audience that Beowulf's example is one that it would be admirable to follow if one wished for fame in this generation and the generations to come.

MIDDLE ENGLISH LITERATURE

This belief survives the changes in both the language itself and the forms of English literature as they develop during the centuries succeeding the Norman Conquest. If anything, it becomes stronger, as influences from other literatures, especially French, begin to assert themselves. The language of English poetry and prose becomes more recognizably our own. Both are refined and augmented by contact with and imitation of the French language and the new narrative and lyrical poetic that came into being in France during the twelfth century. Latin culture continues to play a large part in the formation of English literature, but for at least four centuries France becomes the dominant outside influence. Its power is greater for the fact that for so much of the time England was first of all a province of the Dukes of Normandy and later the ruler of large tracts of France. The influence of France on England was often direct, but often, and in some respects more significantly, it was indirect, acting as the intermediary between English and Latin or Italian literature. Frequently, instead of going to originals for translation or adaptation, an English writer went to a French version.

From the century or so after the Norman Conquest we now possess comparatively little literature in English. The works written at the beginning of what historians call the Middle English period—from a little before 1200 to the end of the fifteenth century—suggest, however, that the tradition of vernacular writing was continuous and that there was constant interaction between Latin, French, and English. English prose works of religious instruction have a continuous tradition from Anglo-Saxon times to the end of the Middle Ages—the late twelfth-century *Ancrene Riwle* (a manual for women religious recluses) is an early example of devout impulse and sophisticated performance. In secular literature the Latin and French form of verse debate is naturalized in the lively late-twelfth-century rhyming poem *The Owl and the Nightingale,* in which the two birds put the case respectively for the solemn and the joyous ways of life. Layamon, at about the same time, is the first writer to give substance in English to what becomes one of the most potent myths of the English Middle Ages and Renaissance: the legendary history of King Arthur and his ancestor Brutus, eponymous founder of Britain, and descendant of Aeneas, the Trojan hero and founder of Rome. Layamon writes in an alliterative measure that is the intermediary between Old English poetic and the verse of the alliterative revival in the West and North-West Midlands in the fourteenth century (Langland and the *Gawain*-Poet).

During the twelfth century the English poet and the English writer of devotional prose, in particular, came to have at their disposal, either directly or through French, a much larger range of classical literature and literary theory—and, increasingly, of medieval adaptations of them—than ever before. Their enlarged education gave them access to the sources of knowledge contained in the liberal arts—the *trivium* (grammar, rhetoric, and logic) and the *quadrivium* (astronomy, arithmetic, geometry, and music)—as well as to the poets and rhetoricians of Rome. The development of the Latin liturgy and of the literature of devotion and religious instruction, in both verse and prose, enormously enlarged their sacred range.

France provided a recognized classification of the materials of secular story. The "matter of France," less important for England, yielded the stories of Charlemagne, Roncevaux, Roland, and the rest; the "matter of Britain" (i.e. Brittany) comprised the Arthurian legend and the so-called Breton lays, of which Chaucer's *Franklin's Tale* is an adaptation; and the "matter of Rome," including the Troy story (Rome being a Trojan foundation), the story of Thebes, and the stories of Alexander the Great, was the largest in scope and most influential of all. While many of these stories, especially those of the "matter of Rome," were available in Latin, it was their French versions that made them the narrators' basic material, the inexhaustible well from which they could draw. It was never thought to be the poet's task to make it new: these stories were worth the telling again and again. They are the tales that displace the Germanic heroic legends.

The romances—ancestors of the novel—that are made from them differ from the oral epic poetry which they supplant almost as much in the manner of their telling as in their matter. They reflect a different society from the earlier Germanic variety, and a new valuation of social activity. Bravery in battle becomes less an end in itself, less the prime opportunity to win reputation, so that it occupies relatively less space in the social experience and consequently in literature. As the institution of chivalry comes into being, warlike courage begins to function, still importantly but less prominently, as part of a larger and more sophisticated pattern of social activity. The virtues of chivalry were in part an elaboration and refinement of the older pagan heroic ideals of the conduct befitting a man of good birth. Courage and generosity, the keeping of an oath remained, as they still remain, part of the groundwork of virtuous behavior, but they were incorporated in a system of values radically transformed by Christian ethics and a philosophy of love. True courtesy, honor, the practice of the ideal of knighthood, implied the exercise in their various aspects of the "cardinal" virtues of prudence, fortitude, temperance, and justice, controlled and enriched by the "theological"—faith, hope, and charity. All these words and concepts had a much wider and less institutionalized application than they do today; they embraced such other virtues as generosity, honor, good temper, friendliness, truth, and their various manifestations. In the world of the romances and, at a lower pitch, in the real world, fame and life everlasting were to be won by the practice of these virtues in the service of the Christian faith and of both a heavenly lady—the Virgin Mary—and an earthly.

The matter of Britain, especially, and the matter of Rome are deployed to tell stories of true lovers, to explore the nature of their thoughts and actions, in a context of martial adventure and fairy magic, and often at great length. The nature of love itself, religious and profane, becomes a subject for exploration by philosophers and poets, who picked up some of what had been written about its theory and practice by Plato and by the Latin and Arabic authors through whom Plato became known to the Middle Ages; and by the love poets of ancient Rome, especially Ovid. In philosophy, the investigation is carried on most remarkably during the twelfth century by the school of Chartres in the north; in poetry by the Provençal poets of the south, who shape the new genre of love lyric. The first of these secular poets of France known to us by name is William, Duke of Aquitaine (1071–1127), who already had behind him a tradition of classical and medieval love poetry in Latin and Arabic-Spanish for which there are no more than one or two parallels in the earlier Germanic languages. The troubadour poets, in their exploration of love's nature and transforming power and of the anguish of love-longing, evolve the notion of *fin' amors:* gracious love, noble and ennobling, love-worship, for which nineteenth-century scholars coined the term "courtly love." Nothing illustrates better the change from an old Germanic to a typical European medieval society than this complex of ideas in which women, love, and praise of women occupy a dominant position.

The same change in values is apparent in the songs that deal less with love as a state of being than with imagined love-encounters: the *alba*—the song of lovers' prearranged secret meeting by night and their despairing parting at dawn, and the *pastourelle*—the song of lovers' chance meeting by day and what comes of it, as well as in the other varieties of love lyric. The lyrical stanzaic form in which many of these songs are expressed had already been developed in Latin religious poetry of the ninth century. Rhyme, too, is first to be found in Latin poetry and is transferred from that to the vernacular. Throughout the early development of medieval lyric poetry there is constant interplay between Latin and vernacular, sacred and secular. Religious poetry, in particular, exploits the notion of *figura,* either in its narrower typological sense or in the broader and universal, in which Eve or the Maiden in the Moor can stand for all women, all humanity.

Some of the developing poetic genres reflect the growing taste, in a society where women were assuming a considerable role, for what much later came to be called polite literature. The *carole* is one example: a dance-song in which the leader sang the verse and the rest of the dancers, men and women, the refrain. It was a graceful musical diversion for a festival, a winter evening, or a summer afternoon; and typical of its age in that it was inseparable from its musical accompaniment. The *fabliau* is another example, wittier, more polished than the popular prose "merry tale." The longer comic beast fable or poem—the ironic, satiric counterpart of the chivalric romance, as in the cycle of stories concerned with Reynard the Fox—is a third. More important, often longer still, and most characteristic is the allegorical poem, such as the *Romance of the Rose,* exploring the nature of love and of many other philosophical matters, by means of a story whose characters are personifications of the qualities of a lover and his mistress, of Nature herself, of Fortune, and of the other abstractions which preside over a systematic view of human life.

At the same time as these French poetic forms and modes of thought were passing into currency in England, a huge body of prose was being produced, particularly in the field of moral instruction and exhortation—treatises, sermons, meditations. A vast increase in these works came with the thirteenth-century rise of the friars, the Mendicant Orders, vowed to poverty. Prayer, penance, and (for the Dominicans) the preaching of God's word was their major obligation; and the volume of their (and others') sermons continues to expand throughout the Middle Ages.

Another form that seems to have developed earlier in France than in England was the religious drama, which emerged into vigorous life in northern provincial centers of England—York, Wakefield, Coventry and Chester—in the fourteenth century. The drama was the vehicle of bourgeois piety and religious instruction in a half-secular context. It displayed the whole scheme of salvation, from the Creation and the Fall of Man to the Resurrection and the Harrowing of Hell, its production being under the control of the tradesmen's guilds and the solemnity of its message tempered with the beginnings of dramatic comedy. Later still, dramatized moral instruction was presented in morality plays.

When French literary genres passed into English they underwent changes of various kinds. Romances, for example, tended to be shorn of their speculative and spiritualized dimensions, and the Arthurian stories of *Sir Gawain and the Green Knight* or Malory's *Morte Darthur* are more down-to-earth than their French counterparts.

Some fourteenth-century English works have no French equivalent. One is *Piers Plowman,* which preserves the older English verse technique of the alliterative long line and conducts its investigation of the nature of goodness and of the ordering of a truly Christian society in such a way as to leave no room for doubt in the reader's mind that this is what the poem is really about. We can be sure of this, as we cannot be quite sure what the author of *Sir Gawain and the Green Knight* intended us to take from his poem.

Even taking into account exceptions like *Piers Plowman* and allowing for the changes wrought by English variations on originally French forms and themes, English medieval literature is strongly tinctured with French. It is the measure of Chaucer's greatness that he has assimilated the French tradition and made it his own. His shorter lyrics can deal with the values of "courtly love" seriously or satirically; his *Troilus and Criseyde,* the greatest romance in our language, investigates the experience of love in depth and at length; his *Book of the Duchess, Parliament of Fowls,* and *House of Fame* show his self-assurance in handling the allegorical vision; his Franklin's Tale is a perfectly balanced work of art in its transformation of the fairy "matter of Britain" into an exploration of love and its obligations; his Miller's Tale is a perfectly judged *fabliau;* his Pardoner's Tale and Nun's Priest's Tale are literary transformations of sermons, exactly adjusted to the characters of their tellers. The Nun's Priest's Tale holds in equilibrium the animal-story-for-moral-instruction of the *Bestiary,* the sermon, and the rhetorical mode, in a magnificently managed parody of genres and of manner.

At the other end of the scale of sophistication are some of the short lyrics of moral and religious instruction. These, and their less direct and simple companions in the lyric genre, emphasize the fact that by far the largest part of what was written during the Middle Ages was intended for instruction, direct or indirect. This is true of all medieval fiction—or at least of most of it:

> St. Paul saith that all that written is
> To our doctrine it is ywrit, iwis . . .

If a fourteenth-century Englishman had been asked to defend himself against the old Platonic or the Christian-ascetic charge leveled at the artist—that he made fictions that were lies—he might have replied (as one in fact did) that St. Paul did not mean that everything that is written for our "doctrine" (teaching) is or need be true. He meant that, if we take it aright, everything that is written can give us useful instruction. If what we feign in our fictions has some signification and is not merely empty, then it is not a lie but indeed a figure of the truth.

The same Englishman would not have doubted that if his treatise or his fiction was to be fully effective it ought to be constructed with true rhetorical decorum, employing the tropes—the figures of thought and of speech inherited by medieval authors from the classics—to bring home story and lesson with all its force. He would have been especially concerned that his language should be rich and strong enough to support the weight of the doctrine and the richness of the effect that he wished it to carry. It would never have occurred to him to speak of "mere rhetoric" or "mere ornament." Only the greatest poet of the English Middle Ages, Chaucer himself, can afford to demonstrate his independence of a tradition he respects.

The generations following Chaucer's saw an increasing concern with richness of diction and—at its best as in the work of the "Scottish Chaucerians"—an exuberance of rhetoric that were to help the English language toward its triumph in the sixteenth century. Didactic and exemplary verse and prose flourished as perhaps never before during the reign of the pious Henry VI (1422–61). In the turbulent period of the Wars of the Roses (1455–85), when the throne of England was being battled for—the twilight of the Middle Ages—two literary figures stand out: the reprobate knight, Sir Thomas Malory, author of the *Morte Darthur,* and the thriving bourgeois, William Caxton.

Caxton not only brought printing to England but moreover was Malory's first printer. Both were deeply concerned with the values of an aristocratic, chivalric social system that was already in decline. For a hundred years the English archer had displaced the mounted knight as the architect of England's military strength. The commercial and professional men of the cities were thrusting themselves forward to form the beginnings of the English urban middle class, while the smaller landowners were also rising in power and wealth. Malory chose to write of the legendary, knightly King Arthur and his followers, providing the last medieval expression of the myth that was to serve the Tudor dynasty (1485–1603, founded by Henry VII) so well and to reach its finest expression in Edmund Spenser's *Faerie Queene*. Caxton, too, concerned himself with chivalric codes and practices, but still more with the provision of entertaining and edifying literature in a strengthened, refined, and uniform English. The printing press made more copies of a given work available to more people than had ever before been possible: a whole culture changed with the end of the era of the hand-produced book. The process by which the writer's audience became a reading, rather than a read-to, public had begun.

VERSIFICATION

The reader coming to Old and Middle English poetry for the first time will find a great deal that is unfamiliar and disconcerting in its verse techniques. He has been led, by his reading in the verse of the sixteenth to the twentieth century, to expect that poetry will be written in a regular series of lines, rhyming or not rhyming, with regularly alternating stresses and a strict attention to form. Modern free-verse techniques will have done something to prepare him for what he will find in this selection from poets who wrote before Chaucer, and from two of Chaucer's contemporaries; yet the close-knit accentual patterns of Old English verse are much firmer and stricter in their requirements than the modifications of such patterns that have been used by modern poets.

The Old English poets built their poems of single-line units of accentual verse, each single line divided at its center by a pause or caesura. Rhyme, either to link two half-lines or to hold together single lines in couplets, stanzaic forms, or verse paragraphs, is almost unknown among them. Instead of rhyme they developed alliteration—that is, the choice of words beginning with the same sound.

A song I sing   of sorrow unceasing

is a translation of one typical line in an Old English poem. Such a line contains four main stresses, two on either side of the caesura, here marked by a space. The line is welded into a unit by the fact that both stressed words of the first half begin with the same sound as the first stress of the second half. Further, the same sound is picked up again in the second element of the second stressed word of the second half-line.

This is only one of the line patterns used by Old English poets. The poet had the further option that any vowel could alliterate with any other vowel. But he was strictly limited as to the number of the patterns of half-line that he could employ, by the number of unstressed syllables that he was allowed and by the patterns in which they might be placed, and by other prescriptions.

The metrical effect of Old English poetry is of a disciplined series of dignified (though not slow-moving), single utterances in a regular and very marked rhythm, taut and carefully timed. Heightened and pointed by being sung or chanted to the accompaniment of a harp, Old English verse must have achieved in recitation—for it was predominantly oral in character, like most vernacular poetry written throughout the Middle Ages—a tone equal to that of the best of its kind.

After the Norman Conquest, French literary models came to supplant the older English tradition of unrhymed alliterative verse. The chief differences between the two were that French verse employed rhyme, and later stanza form, and was written in a pattern of metrical feet—that is, with alternating stressed and unstressed syllables. But the older tradition was not immediately and entirely supplanted by the new. What happened was that its patterns of alliteration became looser and more permissive of extra syllables and more accents to the line. Rhyme is still not employed, though some poets combine the rhymed and the alliterative techniques and there is still a strongly marked caesura in the middle of each line. To either side of the break there are deviations and license. Often, the line consists of the basic four stresses, but as often it has five or six or even more. The alliteration may be the bare minimum—one stress in each half-line; or it may run through almost every stress in the line. There are no norms for the number of unstressed syllables, so that short lines like

> And had leave to lie   all their life after

may occur next to lines like

> To each a tale that they told   their tongue was tempered to lie.

The effect of control that a poet such as Langland can give the alliterative measure is exceptional—and even Langland slips into formlessness from time to time. When Langland came to use the alliterative meter it was already out of fashion: it was his achievement to give it new life. The same may be said of the poet of *Sir Gawain and the Green Knight,* also writing in a center of provincial culture remote from the capital and, as far as can be told, making a conscious effort to revive the form. In his other poems the *Gawain* poet uses rhyme; and even in *Sir Gawain* he organizes the poem into unrhymed blocks, each of them marked off and in a sense summed up by the "bob" (a two- or three-syllable half-line) rhyming with one of the rhymes of the four-line "wheel" that follows it. So he gives an impression of a tighter and more organized form to his poem, especially since these little comments form a kind of synopsis-commentary to the whole. Rhetorically as well as metrically he holds his poem together in the large unit, however free his treatment of the single alliterating line.

Both before and after Chaucer there is much rhymed verse in Middle English in which the meter is irregular and shambling and seemingly constructed after no metrical principle except a rough approximation to an uneven rhythm. But there is a good deal of sophistication in stanzaic form; and even a poem that appears to be largely imitating the rhythms of common speech (such as the *Second Shepherd's Play*), keeps a firm and regular stanza. But one cannot have the same expectation of disciplined variety in regularity that is to become the norm in the sixteenth century, nor the feeling of deliberate and rhetorically controlled irregularity that one has from John Skelton—as will be illustrated later in this volume.

When one comes to Chaucer's verse, however, the situation changes. There were, in his day, poets who could handle with entire competence the meters and stanzaic forms of the French tradition, even the very forms and meters that Chaucer uses. But none have his variety, whether in the octosyllabic couplets (already naturalized in English) that he adopted from his French models; or the lyric forms also taken over from French; or the various stanzaic patterns, especially the rhyme royal (iambic pentameters, rhyming *ababbcc* in a seven-line stanza) of *Troilus and Criseyde* and the *Parliament of Fowls.* Chaucer's greatest achievement was with a verse form that he may have introduced into England and certainly naturalized there—the heroic couplet in which most of the *Canterbury Tales* are written. To state that this basic unit consists of ten- or eleven-syllable iambic pentameters rhyming in twos

> In Flaundres whilom was a compaignye
> Of yonge folk that haunteden folye . . .

gives no notion of the variations, the force, and the richness Chaucer imparts to it. He is able to give an effect of even greater metrical fluidity and variety than if he were using a stanzaic form, maintaining the metrical units of line and couplet while building the large unit of sentence and paragraph from it, playing off sentence structure against the rhythm of the verse. The rhythms of speech provide a constant counterpoint to the accentuation of the meter, the verse running in the smooth, rising rhythm of the iambic pentameter, always varied, never monotonous. It is incomparable poetry for reading aloud.

Old English Poetry

Cædmon's Hymn

Cædmon, a layman to whom the gift of poetry came late in life, was received into the abbey of Whitby in Northumbria, where he composed a great deal of religious verse. The nine lines given below are all of what survives that can reasonably be attributed to him.

All that we know of Cædmon's life, we know from the greatest English scholar of the next generation, the Venerable Bede, monk of Jarrow (c. 673–735), who tells his story in *The Ecclesiastical History of the English People* (completed in 731). When St. Hilda ruled Whitby Abbey (which she had founded)—between 658 and 680—there was brought to her one day a layman who was employed on the abbey's estates. The night before, at a feast, he had seen that his turn to sing to the harp and entertain the others was approaching and, as he always did from bashfulness, he had escaped and taken himself off to tend the farm animals. His bed was in their quarters and, as he lay asleep there, he dreamed that someone came to him, commanding: "Cædmon, sing me something." Cædmon excused himself, saying "I cannot sing; and it was for just this reason that I left the feast when I saw that my turn was coming." His visitor was not to be put off and ordered him to sing "the beginning of created things," which he did. On waking, he remembered what he had composed and could—we must suppose—recite it to the Abbess or dictate it to a scribe.

Cædmon's new gift never deserted him, Bede tells us, but it remained an oral one and could be devoted to sacred subjects only—a kind of metrical prayer. He never learned to read, his method being to make, very rapidly, a verse paraphrase of the sacred writings that were read to him. Bede gives a long list of his writings, but we cannot certainly identify any of them with surviving Old English works and have to be content with this, his first brief effort.

Old English verse is nowadays printed in lines composed of two half-lines, the caesura being indicated by an extra space between the halves; with modern punctuation and in a modern English alphabet. Three Old English letters are used: æ (*aesc*, pronounced ash), which is either a short sound (a) or a long (open e long); þ (*thorn*) and ð (*eth*), which are both pronounced *th*.

This is not the way that Old English poetry was written down in manuscripts. There it appears as if it were continuous prose, without caesura markings; without line divisions; without punctuation, except the period; and with some other no-longer-used letter forms (long ſ, for example, for *s*; ƿ (*wynn*) for *w*; ꞃ for *r*); and with scribal contractions (e.g. ⁊ for *ond* [and]). A few lines from the manuscript of *Beowulf* are shown in Figure 4.

Cædmon's Hymn is here given in a West Saxon version, with a literal prose translation.

Cædmon's Hymn

Nu sculon° herigean   heofonrices weard,°
metodes meahte   and his modgeþanc,°
weorc wuldorfæder,   swa he wundra° gehwæs,
ece drihten,   or onstealde.
He ærest sceop°   eorðan° bearnum°
heofon to hrofe,   halig scyppend;
þa middangeard°   moncynnes weard,
ece drihten,   æfter teode
firum foldan,   frea° ælmihtig.
658–680

Now must we praise   of heaven's kingdom the Keeper
Of the Lord the power   and his Wisdom
The work of the Glory-Father,   as he of marvels each,
The eternal Lord,   the beginning established.
He first created   of earth for the sons
Heaven as a roof,   the holy Creator.
Then the middle-enclosure   of mankind the Protector
The eternal Lord,   thereafter made
For men, earth   the Lord almighty.

Beowulf

The finest surviving long poem in Old English has come down to us in a single manuscript, now MS. Cotton Vitellius A.XV in the British Museum, transcribed in the West Saxon dialect at the end of the tenth century, at least two centuries after its composition. We still do not know the name of its author, and it was not given the title *Beowulf* until 1805 and not printed until 1815.

We need not be surprised at this. Almost all Old English poetry is untitled and anonymous: we know the names of only two poets whose work survives—Cædmon and Cynewulf, and of Cædmon's poetry we possess only the few lines presented at the head of the present selection. Almost all Old English poems survive in a single manuscript, often in a copy that includes other texts composed at an earlier or a later date. Most of these manuscripts were written down in the West Saxon dialect at about the end of the tenth century, when the full force of the monastic revival had made itself felt and the literary culture of England had reached its high point.

It is not clear just how far the fact that most of the Old English poetry we possess was transcribed about this time and in this dialect reflects a conscious program aimed at preserving, in a written "literary standard" language, what was thought to be best.

sculon the modern "shall," in its old meaning "must"
weard mod. "ward," "guard(ian)"
modgeþanc compound noun: heart, mind plus thought, intention
wundra mod. "wonders" (poss. case)
sceop lit. shaped
eorðan the reading of later manuscripts; earlier have *ielda*, of men
bearnum See Scots *bairns*, children (poss. case).
middangeard the dwelling or enclosure in the middle—between heaven above and hell below—therefore the earth. *Geard* is modern "yard."
frea chief, leader

We know that *Beowulf* was admired in the ninth century, by King Alfred among others, and that poets then used it to strengthen their own work. The author of *The Battle of Maldon,* at the end of the tenth century, borrowed from *Beowulf,* and an anonymous sermon-writer used the description of Grendel's mere.

Nor is it clear how much Old English poetry, for want of such copying down, has been lost. It is generally assumed that a great deal has perished without trace, leaving a remainder of a scant 30,000 lines—about the length of some single poems of a few centuries later. There must have been other manuscripts of many, if not all, of the poems, often earlier and in other dialects.

We possess *Beowulf* only because the unique manuscript survived the fire of 1731, which destroyed or damaged much of the remarkable library of Sir Robert Cotton (1571–1631), in which the *Beowulf* manuscript then was. But the scorching that it then received caused its edges to crumble, so that some of the text was already lost when the Icelandic scholar G. J. Thorkelin came to make the transcriptions which were completed in 1787. All modern editions of the poem use Thorkelin's transcripts to reconstruct, as far as possible, the words and letters that are missing from the manuscript as it is today. The text is divided into forty-three fitts or sections, with line-endings and, less frequently, half-line endings, indicated by punctuation. The arrangement of the text as verse is the work of modern editors.

Scholars agree that the Cotton manuscript of *Beowulf* does not represent the first occasion on which the poem was written down. Its reputation suggests that there must have been earlier manuscripts, perhaps transcribed in West Mercia, the modern West Midlands, or further north, in Northumbria, where the poem may well have been composed. We do not know the date of the first of these, though archaic verbal forms suggest that a written version existed by the middle of the eighth century.

No evidence so far, however, is conclusive for date and place of composition. Some have put the composition earlier than the eighth century, but most agree that the Christian coloring of the diction and of some of the subject matter of the poem reflects an audience and a poet to whom Christianity and the usages of the church have been familiar long and thoroughly enough for the one to use and the other to catch allusions to the Bible and Christian literature—to Cain, to the giants, to the Devil as the "old enemy" or the "enemy of mankind." This can hardly have been before the eighth century. By 664, the date of the Synod of Whitby, at which important differences between the Celtic church and the Roman church in England were settled, Christianity was the dominant religion in the country—but thirty years later bishops still found it necessary to prescribe penance for those who sacrificed to devils (i.e. the Germanic pagan gods). Moreover, the poem can hardly be earlier than the work of the Northumbrian poet Cædmon, which must have been dictated between 658 and 680 and which established many of the modes of Christian heroic poetry. It may be of a specific poem by Cædmon that the *Beowulf* poet is thinking when he makes Hrothgar's *scop* or minstrel sing of the Creation of the World. Some scholars feel that *Beowulf* would fit best the Christian culture of Northumbria at this time, the golden age of the Venerable Bede (c. 673–735), one of the greatest European scholars of the early Middle Ages. This was the civilization that produced the superb Lindisfarne Gospels, now in the British Museum (Fig. 5), and the Northumbrian crosses of Ruthwell (Fig. 23) and Bewcastle. Such monuments are Christian in a sense in which *Beowulf* is not: a fairer comparison with the poem is the whalebone box in the British Museum known as the Franks Casket—a more provincial work, on which scenes from Germanic legend mingle with Christian scenes: the Germanic smith of the gods, Weland, and the Adoration of the Magi side by side (Fig. 22).

Other scholars, now in the majority, argue for a West Mercian origin for the poem, which may imply a date sometime in the eighth century. Strong support for West Mercia as *Beowulf*'s place of composition comes from the supposition that the poem was written for the court of Offa the Great, king of Mercia from 757 to 796. This Offa's ancestor, Offa the Angle, is especially praised by the *Beowulf* poet in an episode whose structural function seems to be to commend Queen Hygd, Hygelac's consort, by comparing her with the cruel queen of the earlier Offa.

Beowulf, the longest surviving Old English poem, is a somber masterpiece, the first great English work in the oral, primary epic mode. English as it is in language, and written in English as it must have been, it makes mention only twice, or perhaps three times, of an Englishman. It must have been written when English and Scandinavian events were of enough mutual interest for an English audience to grasp their implications, perhaps a time when the Germanic tribes still retained a consciousness of common origins and history. Scholars agree that, as far as can be told from other evidence, including the archaeological, the *Beowulf* poet has got his Swedish history—for example—right. English-Scandinavian relations must still have been close in the eighth century: we find at Sutton Hoo, dating from about 670, a mixture of English and Scandinavian cultures in both the manner of the burial and the goods in the burial mounds.

The hero of the poem is a Geat, a prominent member of a tribe known by that name from only a few other sources, but said by the poet to be ancient and powerful. Earlier scholarship identified the Geats with the Jutes (whose name in Old English was Eotan), who came either from Jutland or from the country east of the Lower Rhine. Modern opinion more strongly favors their being the Gautar, who seem to have lived in what is now southern Sweden. It is also possible that they are the Getae, believed in late classical and medieval times to inhabit southern Scandinavia, a land as remote and forbidding as Scythia, thought to have been their original home. These Getae, founding fathers of the Germanic nations as legend made them out, would be a fitting people to be the heroes of a poem set in a remote and indefinite Germanic heroic past. (See map, Fig. 2.)

Identification cannot be pressed too far nor historical consistency demanded in a poem which relies so much on indirectness and allusion, on the atmosphere of far away and long ago, shaded, deliberately darkened, and misty—a time when men still fought the evil creatures of the dark which they believed to threaten and beset them hard. An English poet is writing about the common heroic past of the Germanic race: the tribes who take part in the action are out there somewhere, distant in time and space. This is an essential assumption of the poet's art.

Nevertheless, a kind of historical and geographical frame for *Beowulf* clearly exists. The Danes, neighbors of the Geats, inhabit the island which is now Zealand: that is historical fact. The Geats come to their aid, led by Beowulf, from what is now southeast Sweden. North of the Geats are the Swedes and other tribes—again historical fact. South of the Danes, on the European mainland, are the Heathobards, sworn enemies, while farther to the west, at the extreme edge of the Merovingian domain, in Frisia, are the Hetware, the Atuarii, raided by Hygelac the Geat, who finds defeat and death among them.

This raid is the one piece of hard history in *Beowulf*. According to Frankish historians such as Gregory of Tours (c. 540–594), one Chlochilaicus was killed on such a raid in about 520. But the mode of the poem is such that this may mean that all Hygelac's doings—even much of the poem's action—have a historical basis, or it may not: we cannot tell. We can safely say that Grendel and his dam are fabulous monsters of the night—and so is the dragon, though sober historical sources record a dragon in England as late as the end of the eighth century, and men went on believing in the physical existence of such creatures for many centuries after. The supernatural elements might belong to almost any age. The incidents of the digressions, elliptically and allusively told, clearly cannot all be referred to the same limited portion of time. If we ask the date of the events of *Beowulf,* rather than the date at which the poem was composed, the best answer is that some belong to the early sixth century and others are probably older, while others again are fabulous. To expect a more exact answer is as pointless as to try to fix the direction and distance of Beowulf's swimming match with Breca, or how many suits of armor Beowulf actually carried as he swam home after the fatal conclusion of Hygelac's raid. We are dealing with a poem, not a piece of history.

Nevertheless, the poem embodies and takes as the basis of its characters' actions a social system and a set of behavioral assumptions which were common to the Germanic peoples of history. These were set out in their earliest, simplest, and most clearly recorded form by the first-century Roman historian Tacitus, in his *Germania.* These Germans, Tacitus says, are a warrior race, fierce and cruel, setting courage above all the other virtues, finding their deepest shame in cowardice, ready to use any end to gain the victory: "To retreat, provided that you return to the attack, is thought to be cunning, not cowardly." They choose their leaders for courage and demand that they continue to set a courageous example. They have a profound belief in Fate and in casting lots to foresee the future. Their warlike character is seen in the fact that all come to their assemblies and transact their business fully armed—and a young men enters manhood when he is publicly equipped (after due proof of valor), with spear and shield. Young and old group themselves round the chief as his retinue, the companions or *comitatus.* Their numbers and their bravery lend him power. He holds their allegiance by courage and generosity: his keenest disgrace is to be outdone by retainer or enemy. The companions, having sworn him allegiance, must not fall short: they must die on the battlefield rather than leave it—especially once the chieftain is killed (cf. the praise of Wiglaf in *Beowulf* and the close of *The Battle of Maldon*). "The chieftain battles for victory, the companions fight for their chief," Tacitus goes on. If the young men find no fighting at home, they seek it abroad, for they have no taste for peace. They are grasping and demanding, which encourages war and plunder to maintain the supply of what they value—horses, arms and armor, jewelry, collars. They live not in cities, but in scattered houses, each house a community. Monogamous, reverencing their women for the gift of holiness and prophecy they find in them, the men bring the dowry. Women bring men weapons, and their exchange of gifts symbolizes the holiest of bonds, the sharing of burdens. Germanic reverence for women is mirrored in their recognition of an especially close tie between a man and his sister's son—a tie as close as that between father and son.

Everyone is bound to continue the feuds and the friendships of his father and his family. Feuds are often concluded by payment of tribute, and even murder can be paid for, in money and goods (*wergild*), so that—for a time—the dishonor is wiped out.

The Germans love to feast and entertain, holding it sinful to turn a man from the door. If a host cannot continue to give the visitor the hospitality he deserves, he sends him on to another. Drinking bouts of a day and a night are commonplace and the quarrels they engender are settled by blows. Banquets have peaceful, ceremonial functions, too: they are the setting to discuss truces, form marriage alliances, make new chiefs, decide for peace or war. Feasts are chosen as a time for making such decisions because the heart is then open and exalted. At these feasts a sort of "juice extracted from barley or grain" washes down plain food: there is no excess in their eating. Their addiction to gambling may lead them to gamble away their freedom; if this happens, they go uncomplainingly into slavery, as a point of "honor." Slaves are agricultural serfs rather than household or body servants, and even when freed seldom rise to positions of influence. Usury is unknown. The land is tilled communally and shares in it are allotted according to rank.

Death is attended by no pomp, though their great men are cremated, after the pagan usage, on a pyre on which arms and armor, and sometimes also horses, are placed. Over the body is raised a barrow, a high mound of earth. Excessive mourning is frowned on: women are permitted to express their grief, but men hide it in their hearts.

Physically, these men are hardy, tough and trained, savage and vigorous, placing their trust in courage, the one thing they see as sure, though like all that is mortal, it is subject to fortune and chance. Some are hardy, sea-going people, their ships, oar-propelled, having a prow at each end for easier putting into land. Some tribes wear the images of boars for protection (Fig. 20).

Tacitus is writing of the Germanic tribes of the end of the first century A.D., three hundred and fifty years before some of them migrated to England, nearly five hundred before Pope Gregory the Great sent St. Augustine of Canterbury to bring Roman Christianity to the country, nearly six hundred before it can be said that England was Christian, and perhaps a little more before *Beowulf* was written down. Nevertheless, Tacitus tells us much about the world of *Beowulf* and of heroic poetry in general. His picture of warrior societies close-knit in small units by the ties of blood and of mutual duty between lord and retainer, finding in the ethos of the *comitatus* the most effective of social bonds and in courage the only possible stance in response to the harsh and inescapable decrees of fate and the duties of life—this picture is closely relevant to the poem. The virtues of such a society, like its vices, are fierce and combative. There is dignity, but it is martial dignity: renown can be won in battle and nowhere else. Age is more poignant in that it lessens appetite for battle and chances of success in it. Ancestry counts for much, for this is an aristocratic society, but each generation must confirm by its own courage the family's title to consideration.

This was the society to which Roman Christianity came with the arrival of St. Augustine in England in 597. The progress of the new religion was sporadic. Areas like Essex were notably slow to accept conversion, and there especially pagan practices and much of the pagan flavor of everyday life must have long remained. *Beowulf,* at least in the form in which we have it, reflects the usages of a pagan society of an indeterminate period before the Christian conversion and perhaps a time near the migration of the Angles, Saxons, and Jutes to England about the middle of the fifth century, with later accretions. The poet, almost certainly a Christian, is perhaps, like a less sophisticated Virgil, recalling to his people a past which is heroic but legendary, indeterminate, undifferentiated, and therefore ever present.

The poet's allusive, apparently unstructured technique—regular in oral poetry—

seems to expect an audience conversant with its own legendary past, with details of this and other stories. He is touching on the known to awaken resonances which will enhance what he is saying. The digressions concerning the feud between Danes and Heathobards, the Fight at Finnsburg, Hygelac's fatal expedition against the Frisians and the Hetware, the story of Sigemund and the dragon, in addition to the story of Offa and his cruel queen—are all intended not to stop the march of the narrative but to reinforce its episodic, disjointed progress. The poet counts on his audience to apply the associations of these to the other events of the poem. All tragic in their outcome, they prepare the hearers, singly and cumulatively, for the tragic outcome, in human terms, of *Beowulf.* The allusions are planted with skill to bring home the transitoriness of human glory and human life, the forward seeping of the menacing dark. At the height of exultation, the poet will slip in the hint of deadliness that lurks in all actions—often in an understatement that strikes us as flat or banal, but achieves its strong effect from the narrowness of its ironic range. Hrothgar's high hall, Heorot, glitters with gold—but its future destruction in the Heathobard feud is foretold within the first hundred lines of the poem and recalled seven hundred lines later. Hrothgar's brother, Hrothulf, who will be the betrayer of his blood, breaker of loyalty, instigator of civil war in Denmark, usurper, sits enthroned in Heorot with Hrothgar—but an allusion to his future treachery will be taken up later by Queen Wealhtheow's poignant expression of trust and confidence in her brother-in-law. These are two of the lesser digressions. The greater episodes operate in the same way. Hygelac's piracy is frequently referred to after its first mention about a third of the way through the poem.

On that first occasion, a pang of mortality strikes Beowulf as he looks at the splendid neck-ring he has been given by Hrothgar as part of his reward for victory over Grendel. It reminds him of the magic necklace of the fire dwarfs which Hygelac took with him on his last raid. Later, just before Beowulf's own fatal last encounter with the dragon, his own behavior at the time of the raid is recounted—his superhuman feat of swimming back with thirty suits of armor, his punctilious refusal of the throne, his protection of Hygelac's widowed queen and of the rightful heir, the young Heardred, as well as his own final ascent of the throne when Heardred had been killed in fighting against the Swedes. He has fulfilled all that a hero should do—and the audience is intended to have in mind at this moment that heroic as he has been, magnanimous and good, especially by contrast with Hrothulf's behavior in a similar situation, he has now grown old and his end is near. Nor is it only his destruction that the audience is aware to be looming, but the annihilation of the whole Geatish race at the hands of the Swedes, once Beowulf, the protector hero of the Geats, has been taken from them. The poet manages to deal even-handed justice to Beowulf the hero and Beowulf the mortal, exalting him only to deepen the tragedy.

So, too, he throws into relief by example and counter-example the qualities of spirit and action in which the heroic society found its fulfillment, the duties that it enjoined upon its members. The lay that the *scop* (bard) sings in Heorot of the Fight at Finnsburg and the story of the strife between Danes and Heathobards mirror the overriding necessity for vengeance to be taken by a member of the *comitatus* for the killing of the lord—a necessity that justifies dissemblance and treachery, as it overrides any attempt to compose the feud. The power of social obligation is too strong for single human instance: strife and violence, restrained for a time by material or spiritual generosity, hasten the death which is every man's lot. The details of these two stories parallel each other, foreshadowing the strife between Geats and Swedes with its fatal outcome.

These digressions, by which the poet binds his poem together, throwing the reference forward and backward, seem to modern taste to slow the pace. Meditative, moralizing passages from the poet himself, or from such characters as Hrothgar, also deepen the elegiac tone. The language—formalized, traditional, often arranged in elaborately parallel double statement—and the steady dignity of the style keep the movement of the poem deliberate and exalted. To this effect the mode of performance—chanting aloud to the accompaniment of a stringed instrument—must have greatly contributed.

The poetic vocabulary of *Beowulf* is remarkable for the large number of words it contains of the same or very similar meaning—words for "warrior," for example—which could be brought into play according to the demands of expressing a precise meaning or to the more mechanical needs of rhythm and alliteration. Compound nouns and adjectives are also plentiful and are found, like many of the simple words, only in poetry, the more exalted medium than prose: rain-hard, shower-hard, enmity-hard, fire-hard, iron-hard; ring-bestower, battle-flasher (for sword) are examples. They are one way in which the poet sustains the promise of a performance arresting and rich made with the opening word of his poem: "Hwæt!", "Lo!", the formulaic call to silence and attention. Still more characteristic and important are the condensed metaphors (Old English is not rich in the conventional metaphor or simile and has no equivalent of the extended Homeric simile) known as *kennings* (an Old Norse word).

The stateliness of the language, its tonal resources—we must always imagine it as it would have sounded—enhance and justify the slowness of the action and drive home the realization that *Beowulf* is essentially a poem of praise, elegiac only because its hero is human. Its mode is the superlative. Essentially it is a poem in praise of earthly life and the glory that a man may win in it by courage, and magnanimity—*lof* (reputation) is one of its key words—even as he realizes that life is short, passing, and often bitter.

There is no trace of any confidence in a greater triumph, in a life after death, such as raises even the simplest narratives of the passions of saints to a kind of epic level and is characteristic of the literature of Christian heroism. Nevertheless, scholarly opinion agrees to call *Beowulf* a Christian poem in that it was written by a Christian and many parts of it would be intelligible only to a Christian audience—particularly its Christian moralizing and many of its allusions. But given the relatively short time that had elapsed since Christianity had come to Britain, and given the firm structure of social institutions and ethical and religious assumptions already existing, we could hardly expect that a heroic poem of such a time would be permeated with the spirit of the New Testament. *Beowulf* is not a poem of Grace, but of the Law: its morality is nearer that of the Old Testament, partly perhaps because of direct influence, partly owing to a joint participation in the epic genre. All the biblical references that it contains are to the Old Testament. It is the power and glory of God the Creator that move the poet and his characters to joy in the Creation or to at least sporadic recognition of his will as equivalent to Fate, just as they are moved to fear of judgment, to certainty that the souls of giants and monsters, Grendel and his dam, will fall to Hell and the Devil while those of believers will go to God. The bloodthirsty monster Grendel is made the descendant of Cain, the first murderer, and the sword which Beowulf catches up to kill Grendel's mother has its blade decorated with the destruction of the Old Testament giants by the Flood. None of these allusions, nor even the moralizing sermon of Hrothgar, give us any reason to suppose that the poet thought of Beowulf as passing to immortality in a Christian Heaven.

Beowulf is a tragedy, as it must be: a gigantic elegy for its hero in which the moments of glory serve only to emphasize the completeness and inevitability of his end. In its broadest dimension, it is a tragedy of the human predicament: more narrowly, of the warrior's situation. A Germanic hero's fulfillment is not reached in victory alone, but in unflinching courage in all circumstances, most of all when the odds—adversaries, conditions, age, and the rest—are stacked against him and he must die. A glorious death is the only fitting close to a glorious life. We are meant to feel the contrast between Hrothgar, a good king, generous and firm, but now old and lacking the true heroic spirit which would send him out to battle with this enemy of his land (at the beginning of the poem), and Beowulf, Hrothgar's rescuer, who dies in his moment of triumph over the enemy of his people, at the poem's end. The hero knows that his fate has long been decided and he knows it at every moment of his life, with every successive battle. He can only trust, as encounter follows encounter, that his doom is not yet written and that therefore his courage will suffice for one more occasion. These occasions, with the shadow of the human condition lengthening as the hero passes from fierce and aggressive youth to fierce and unyielding old age, are the stuff of the poem.

The poet who produced *Beowulf* and the audience which heard it recited were aristocratic and of considerable literary and artistic cultivation. Of their standard of material culture, the frequent reference to splendor of ornament is witness enough, even if we did not have from the poem's period the masterpieces of Northumbrian stone sculpture and manuscript illumination (Figs. 23, 5), the earlier jewelry and other objects from Sutton Hoo (Figs. 9, 11, 13–17, 19), and the richly decorated metal work of other centers (Figs. 18, 21). We can get some idea, too, of what the musical instrument ment to which the poem was later recited probably looked like—from manuscripts (Fig. 10) and from the present reconstruction of the Sutton Hoo instrument (Fig. 11). Some notion of the arms and armor of the period 650–1050 can be got from surviving fragments and from manuscripts (Figs. 8, 9, 18–21).

Of the level of literary culture little need be added to what has already been said in the General Introduction. Poet and audience may well have known Virgil's *Aeneid* and there are many allusions which would be lost on those unfamiliar with the writings of the Fathers of the Church and the Bible itself. The audience that enjoyed *Beowulf* must have had a considerable body of heroic verse to compare with it, as well as a body of other verse of great skill in the handling of feeling and incident, of the formal, exalted, "distanced" language and the narrow though varied metrical range which are the media of Old English poetry.

The translation used here is by Charles W. Kennedy, and appears below as it was first published in 1940, with the exception of the numbering of lines. The line numbers are not those of the original poem but serve merely as a guide.

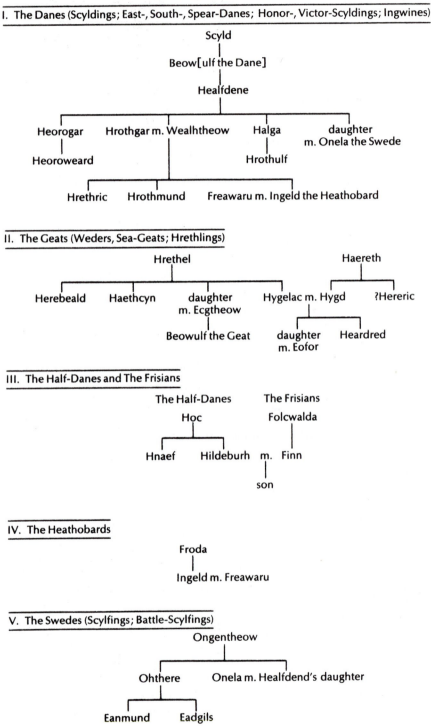

I. The Danes (Scyldings; East-, South-, Spear-Danes; Honor-, Victor-Scyldings; Ingwines)

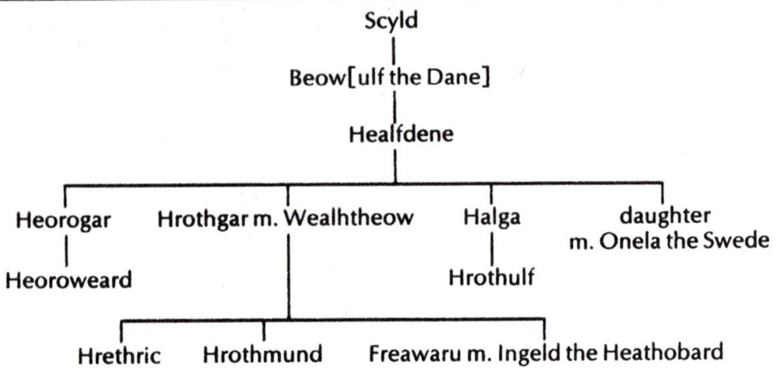

II. The Geats (Weders, Sea-Geats; Hrethlings)

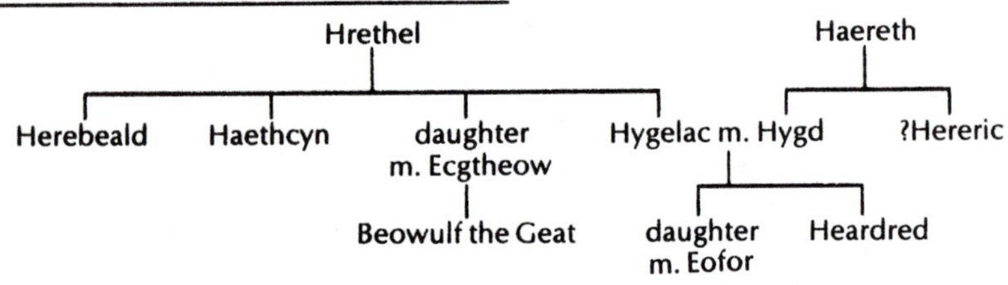

III. The Half-Danes and The Frisians

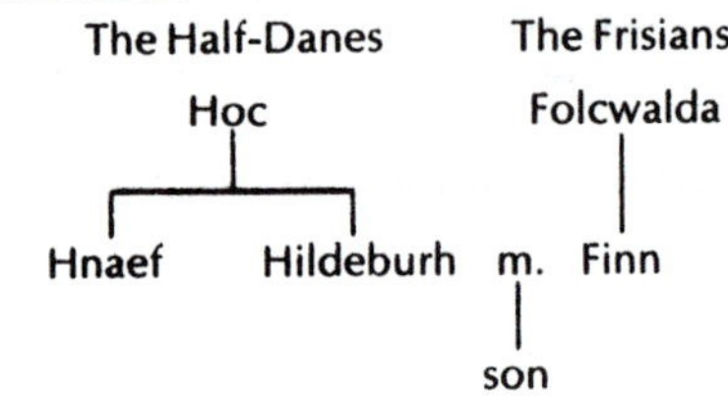

IV. The Heathobards

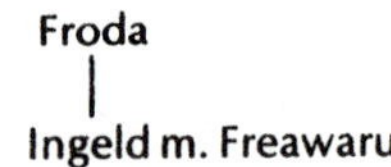

V. The Swedes (Scylfings; Battle-Scylfings)

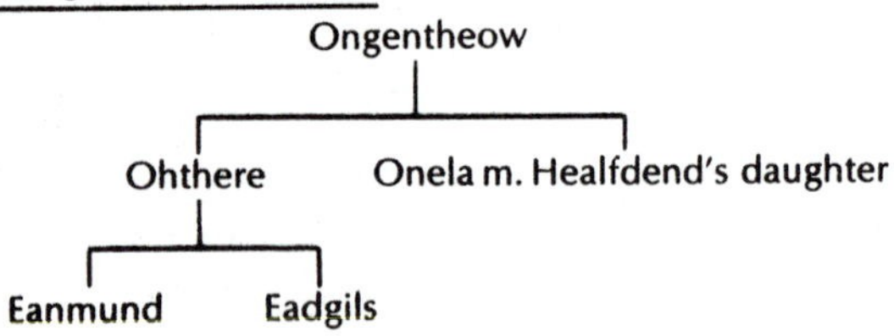

Beowulf

[*The Danish Court and the Raids of Grendel*]

Lo! we have listened to many a lay
Of the Spear-Danes'° fame, their splendor of old,
Their mighty princes, and martial deeds!
Many a mead-hall° Scyld,° son of Sceaf,
Snatched from the forces of savage foes.
From a friendless foundling, feeble and wretched,
He grew to a terror as time brought change.
He throve under heaven in power and pride
Till alien peoples beyond the ocean
Paid toll and tribute. A good king he!
    To him thereafter an heir was born,
A son of his house, whom God had given
As stay to the people; God saw the distress
The leaderless nation had long endured.
The Giver of glory, the Lord of life,
Showered fame on the son of Scyld;
His name was honored, Beowulf° known,
To the farthest dwellings in Danish lands.
So must a young man strive for good
With gracious gifts from his father's store,
That in later seasons, if war shall scourge,
A willing people may serve him well.°
'Tis by earning honor a man must rise
In every state. Then his hour struck,
And Scyld passed on to the peace of God.
    As their leader had bidden, whose word was law
In the Scylding° realm which he long had ruled,
His loving comrades carried him down
To the shore of ocean; a ring-prowed ship,°
Straining at anchor and sheeted with ice,

Spear-Danes The Danes are given various epithets in the course of the poem—perhaps partly to help out alliteration, partly as an aid to characterization—e.g. Bright-, Half-, Ring-, Spear-, North-, East-, South- and West-Danes.
mead-hall rather "mead-bench," i.e. he conquered other tribes and took away the symbol of the independence of the chief, the high bench in the hall from which he dispensed gifts and justice
Scyld The arrival and departure of the mysterious Scyld, eponymous hero of the Danes (Scyldings: men of the shield, sons of Scyld), form a prologue to the poem, and Scyld's life is perhaps intended to be a parallel to the career of Beowulf in capsule form. Scyld is well known in Scandinavian tradition: the poet's account of how he came, young, weak, and friendless to the coast of Denmark and founded a mighty dynasty is, however, unique and makes Scyld into a figure frequent in folktale: the apparently poor foundling, whose royalty is revealed by his later deeds (cf. Theseus and Arthur). The poet is also planting at the beginning a sense of the dignity and antiquity of the Danish race, drawing out, by suggestion, its genealogies and at the same time implying that this great and ancient people, in all its strength and power, will be found to be helpless against the attacks of the monster Grendel, against whom only the greater hero from outside, Beowulf, can deliver Hrothgar and his Danes. Beowulf's stature is thus magnified.
Beowulf not Beowulf the Geat, who is the hero of the poem, but a Danish king whom most now agree to call Beow or Beo, the Dane, grandfather of Hrothgar
So . . . well (ll. 19–22) the first of the poet's moralizing comments, pauses in the motion of the poem, statements of the heroic virtues which its action exemplifies
Scylding Danish
ring-prowed ship It is not quite certain what "ring-prowed" means. Ships were broad, with a tall prow and stern, and of shallow draft, so that they could easily be beached and dragged up on land (Fig. 12).

Rode in the harbor, a prince's pride.
Therein they laid him, their well-loved lord,
Their ring-bestower, in the ship's embrace,°
The mighty prince at the foot of the mast
Amid much treasure and many a gem
From far-off lands. No lordlier ship
Have I ever heard of, with weapons heaped,
With battle-armor, with bills and byrnies.°
On the ruler's breast lay a royal treasure
As the ship put out on the unknown deep.
With no less adornment they dressed him round,
Or gift of treasure, than once they gave
Who launched him first on the lonely sea
While still but a child. A golden standard
They raised above him, high over head,
Let the wave take him on trackless seas.
Mournful their mood and heavy their hearts;
Nor wise man nor warrior knows for a truth
Unto what haven that cargo came.
    Then Beowulf ruled o'er the Scylding realm,
Beloved and famous, for many a year—
The prince, his father, had passed away—
Till, firm in wisdom and fierce in war,
The mighty Healfdene held the reign,
Ruled, while he lived, the lordly Scyldings.
Four sons and daughters were seed of his line,
Heorogar and Hrothgar, leaders of hosts,
And Halga, the good. I have also heard
A daughter was Onela's consort° and queen,
The fair bed-mate of the Battle-Scylfing.
    To Hrothgar was granted glory in war,
Success in battle; retainers bold
Obeyed him gladly; his band increased
To a mighty host. Then his mind was moved
To have men fashion a high-built hall,
A mightier mead-hall than man had known,
Wherein to portion to old and young
All goodly treasure that God had given,
Save only the folk-land,° and lives of men.°

ship's embrace The sea burial of Scyld reflects earlier pagan Scandinavian practice, but by the time *Beowulf* was written ship burials on land, with the dead chieftain surrounded by rich possessions and a barrow, or burial-mound, heaped above, were common.

bills and byrnies swords and coats of ring-mail

Onela's consort The text being defective at this point we can only conjecture that Onela the Swede is referred to, and we are not given the name of Healfdene's daughter, Onela's wife. Onela was son of Ongentheow (ll. 2750 ff.), His nephews Eadgils and Eanmund rebelled against him (ll. 2466 ff.) and took refuge at the Geatish court. Onela pursued them there and killed the young Geatish king Heardred. Eanmund was also killed. Later, Beowulf helps Eadgils in a punitive expedition against Onela, who is slain (ll. 2261 ff.).

folk-land public common land, which Germanic law gave by inalienable right to be held by the community at large for grazing

men i.e. men's bodies; the reference is unclear

His word was published to many a people
Far and wide o'er the ways of earth
To rear a folk-stead richly adorned;
The task was speeded, the time soon came
That the famous mead-hall was finished and done.
To distant nations its name was known,
The Hall of the Hart;° and the king kept well
His pledge and promise to deal out gifts,
Rings at the banquet. The great hall rose
High and horn-gabled,° holding its place
Till the battle-surge of consuming flame
Should swallow it up; the hour was near
That the deadly hate of a daughter's husband
Should kindle to fury and savage feud.°
Then an evil spirit who dwelt in the darkness
Endured it ill that he heard each day
The din of revelry ring through the hall,
The sound of the harp, and the scop's° sweet song.
A skillful bard sang the ancient story
Of man's creation;° how the Maker wrought
The shining earth with its circling waters;
In splendor established the sun and moon
As lights to illumine the land of men;
Fairly adorning the fields of earth
With leaves and branches; creating life
In every creature that breathes and moves.
So the lordly warriors lived in gladness,
At ease and happy, till a fiend from hell
Began a series of savage crimes.
They called him Grendel, a demon grim
Haunting the fen-lands, holding the moors,
Ranging the wastes, where the wretched wight
Made his lair with the monster kin;
He bore the curse of the seed of Cain°
Whereby God punished the grievous guilt
Of Abel's murder. Nor ever had Cain

Hart Heorot, probably situated near modern Lejre, on the north coast of Zealand, not far from Roskilde, the ancient seat of Danish kingship. The royalty of the hall is emphasized by its name, Hart or Stag, a symbol of kingship—see the stag on the Sutton Hoo scepter (Fig. 17).

horn-gabled rather "wide-gabled"

consuming flame . . . feud (ll. 80–83) Heorot stood until it was burned to the ground, probably during an attack by Ingeld, king of the Heathobards, on Hrothgar, which the poet later describes (ll. 1893 ff). The poet is using his characteristic device of "tragic anticipation" for an audience already familiar with the story: the contrast is made between the present magnificence of Hrothgar's mead-hall and its later fate.

scop's the singer of tales, the bard chanting stories in verse at the feast to the sound of the harp

creation i.e. all created good (cf. "Cædmon's Hymn"), and man, sinless and perfect.

seed of Cain The first murderer—Genesis 4:8 ff. The giant race before Noah's flood (Genesis 6:4) is taken by the Biblical commentators, from very early times, to be not merely strong but also cruel and cunning—cf. Genesis 6:5: "And God saw that the wickedness of man was great in the earth." The giants were thought to spring from the union of the descendants of Cain the wrongdoer with the descendants of the righteous Seth.

Cause to boast of that deed of blood;
God banished him far from the fields of men;
Of his blood was begotten an evil brood,
Marauding monsters and menacing trolls,
Goblins and giants who battled with God
A long time. Grimly He gave them reward!
Then at the nightfall the fiend drew near
Where the timbered mead-hall towered on high,
To spy how the Danes fared after the feast.
Within the wine-hall he found the warriors
Fast in slumber,° forgetting grief,
Forgetting the woe of the world of men.
Grim and greedy the gruesome monster,
Fierce and furious, launched attack,
Slew thirty spearmen asleep in the hall,
Sped away gloating, gripping the spoil,
Dragging the dead men home to his den.
Then in the dawn with the coming of daybreak
The war-might of Grendel was widely known.
Mirth was stilled by the sound of weeping;
The wail of the mourner awoke with day.
And the peerless hero, the honored prince,
Weighed down with woe and heavy of heart,
Sat sorely grieving for slaughtered thanes,
As they traced the track of the cursed monster.
From that day onward the deadly feud
Was a long-enduring and loathsome strife.
Not longer was it than one night later
The fiend returning renewed attack
With heart firm-fixed in the hateful war,
Feeling no rue for the grievous wrong.
'Twas easy thereafter to mark the men
Who sought their slumber elsewhere afar,
Found beds in the bowers,° since Grendel's hate
Was so baldly blazoned in baleful signs.
He held himself at a safer distance
Who escaped the clutch of the demon's claw.
So Grendel raided and ravaged the realm,
One against all, in an evil war
Till the best of buildings was empty and still.
'Twas a weary while! Twelve winters' time
The lord of the Scyldings had suffered woe,
Sore affliction and deep distress.

slumber The mead-hall was the place of honor and of communal living for the lord's close companions, the *comitatus*, who also slept there. This was a mark of the lord's generous hospitality and of the companions' acceptance of their honorable vassalage.

bowers the small separate rooms elsewhere in the building complex rather than the central hall

And the malice of Grendel, in mournful lays,
Was widely sung by the sons of men,
The hateful feud that he fought with Hrothgar—
Year after year of struggle and strife,
An endless scourging, a scorning of peace
With any man of the Danish might.
No strength could move him to stay his hand,
Or pay for his murders;° the wise knew well
They could hope for no halting of savage assault.
Like a dark death-shadow° the ravaging demon,
Night-long prowling the misty moors,
Ensnared the warriors, wary or weak.
No man can say how these shades of hell
Come and go on their grisly rounds.
With many an outrage, many a crime,
The fierce lone-goer, the foe of man,
Stained the seats of the high-built house,
Haunting the hall in the hateful dark.
But throne or treasure he might not touch,
Finding no favor or grace with God.°
Great was the grief of the Scylding leader,
His spirit shaken, while many a lord
Gathered in council considering long
In what way brave men best could struggle
Against these terrors of sudden attack.
From time to time in their heathen temples
Paying homage they offered prayer
That the Slayer of souls° would send them succor
From all the torment that troubled the folk.
Such was the fashion and such the faith
Of their heathen hearts that they looked to hell,
Not knowing the Maker, the mighty Judge,
Nor how to worship the Wielder of glory,
The Lord of heaven, the God of hosts.
Woe unto him who in fierce affliction
Shall plunge his soul in the fiery pit
With no hope of mercy or healing change;
But well with the soul that at death seeks God,
And finds his peace in his Father's bosom.
The son of Healfdene° was heavy-hearted,
Sorrowfully brooding in sore distress,

pay . . . murders i.e. pay *wergild,* lit., "man-money," the money payment which Germanic law prescribed for a killer to buy peace from the dead man's family; payable only for the life of a free man, it varied according to the social status of the victim

death-shadow The word is used elsewhere of Satan, but Grendel throughout preys on bodies, not, like the Devil (l. 176), on souls.

Finding . . . God The sense is difficult, but seems to apply to Grendel and mean that, since he does not obey the laws of God or of man he cannot share in either human or divine gifts.

Slayer of souls the Devil. The Danes are here pointedly thought of as pagan idolaters.

son of Healfdene Hrothgar

Finding no help in a hopeless strife;
Too bitter the struggle that stunned the people,
The long oppression, loathsome and grim.

[*The Coming of Beowulf*]

Then tales of the terrible deeds of Grendel
Reached Hygelac's thane° in his home with the Geats;
Of living strong men he was the strongest,
Fearless and gallant and great of heart.°
He gave command for a goodly vessel
Fitted and furnished; he fain would sail
Over the swan-road to seek the king
Who suffered so sorely for need of men.
And his bold retainers found little to blame
In his daring venture, dear though he was;
They viewed the omens, and urged him on.
Brave was the band he had gathered about him,
Fourteen stalwarts seasoned and bold,
Seeking the shore where the ship lay waiting,
A sea-skilled mariner sighting the landmarks.
Came the hour of boarding; the boat was riding
The waves of the harbor under the hill.
The eager mariners mounted the prow;
Billows were breaking, sea against sand.
In the ship's hold snugly they stowed their trappings,
Gleaming armor and battle-gear;
Launched the vessel, the well-braced bark,
Seaward bound on a joyous journey.
Over breaking billows, with bellying sail
And foamy beak, like a flying bird
The ship sped on, till the next day's sun
Showed sea-cliffs shining, towering hills
And stretching headlands. The sea was crossed,
The voyage ended, the vessel moored.
And the Weder° people waded ashore
With clatter of trappings and coats of mail;
Gave thanks to God that His grace had granted
Sea-paths safe for their ocean-journey.
Then the Scylding coast-guard watched from the sea-cliff
Warriors bearing their shining shields,
Their gleaming war-gear, ashore from the ship.
His mind was puzzled, he wondered much
What men they were. On his good horse mounted,

Hygelac's thane Beowulf the Geat, hero of the poem. The word "thane," originally meaning "servant," by this time meant "a royal vassal of some consequence." Beowulf was bound to Hygelac by his obligation both as a companion and as an especially close kinsman. He was Hygelac's sister's son and would therefore be regarded as in a special relationship with his uncle.

Of living . . . heart For the poet, Beowulf's heroic magnanimity is sufficient reason for his going to Hrothgar's help.

Weder Weder-Geats or "Storm-loving" Geats—Beowulf's people

Hrothgar's thane made haste to the beach,
Boldly brandished his mighty spear
With manful challenge: 'What men are you,
Carrying weapons and clad in steel,
Who thus come driving across the deep
On the ocean-lanes in your lofty ship?
Long have I served as the Scylding outpost,
Held watch and ward at the ocean's edge
Lest foreign foemen with hostile fleet
Should come to harry our Danish home,
And never more openly sailed to these shores
Men without password, or leave to land.
I have never laid eyes upon earl on earth
More stalwart and sturdy than one of your troop,
A hero in armor; no hall-thane° he
Tricked out with weapons, unless looks belie him,
And noble bearing. But now I must know
Your birth and breeding, nor may you come
In cunning stealth upon Danish soil.
You distant-dwellers, you far sea-farers,
Hearken, and ponder words that are plain:
'Tis best you hasten to have me know
Who your kindred and whence you come.'
    The lord of the seamen gave swift reply,
The prince of the Weders unlocked his word-hoard:
'We are sprung of a strain of the Geatish stock,
Hygelac's comrades and hearth-companions.°
My father was famous in many a folk-land,
A leader noble, Ecgtheow° his name!
Many a winter went over his head
Before death took him from home and tribe;
Well nigh every wise man remembers him well
Far and wide on the ways of earth.
With loyal purpose we seek your lord,
The prince of your people, great Healfdene's son.
Be kindly of counsel; weighty the cause
That leads us to visit the lord of the Danes;
Nor need it be secret, as far as I know!
You know if it's true, as we've heard it told,
That among the Scyldings some secret scather,
Some stealthy demon in dead of night,
With grisly horror and fiendish hate
Is spreading unheard-of havoc and death.
Mayhap I can counsel the good, old king
What way he can master the merciless fiend,

no hall-thane i.e. not merely splendid-looking on ceremonial occasions, but tough and powerful in battle

hearth-companions the *heorthwerod,* the close companions of the lord

Ecgtheow Nothing is known of Beowulf's father.

If his coil of evil is ever to end
And feverish care grow cooler and fade—
Or else ever after his doom shall be
Distress and sorrow while still there stands
This best of halls on its lofty height.'
Then from the saddle the coast-guard spoke,
The fearless sentry: 'A seasoned° warrior
Must know the difference between words and deeds,
If his wits are with him. I take your word
That your band is loyal° to the lord of the Scyldings.
Now go your way with your weapons and armor,
And I will guide you; I'll give command
That my good retainers may guard your ship,
Your fresh-tarred floater, from every foe,
And hold it safe in its sandy berth,
Till the curving prow once again shall carry
The loved man home to the land of the Geat.
To hero so gallant shall surely be granted
To come from the swordplay sound and safe.'
Then the Geats marched on; behind at her mooring,
Fastened at anchor, their broad-beamed boat
Safely rode on her swinging cable.
Boar-heads° glittered on glistening helmets
Above their cheek-guards, gleaming with gold;
Bright and fire-hardened the boar held watch
Over the column of marching men.
Onward they hurried in eager haste
Till their eyes caught sight of the high-built hall,
Splendid with gold, the seat of the king,
Most stately of structures under the sun;
Its light shone out over many a land.
The coast-guard showed them the shining hall,
The home of heroes; made plain the path;
Turned his horse; gave tongue to words:
'It is time to leave you! The mighty Lord
In His mercy shield you and hold you safe
In your bold adventure. I'll back to the sea
And hold my watch against hostile horde.'

[*Beowulf's Welcome at Hrothgar's Court*]

The street had paving of colored stone;
The path was plain to the marching men.
Bright were their byrnies, hard and hand-linked;
In their shining armor the chain-mail sang

seasoned *scearp*, more likely "acute, keen-witted." The sentry is courteously apologizing for his challenge.
loyal friendly
Boar-heads images of boars placed on Germanic helmets as a protection to the wearers in the material sense—giving extra protection against a blow at the head or upper part of the face—and to invoke the strength and cunning of the boar for the wearer

As the troop in their war-gear tramped to the hall.
The sea-weary sailors set down their shields,
Their wide, bright bucklers along the wall,
And sank to the bench. Their byrnies rang.
Their stout spears stood in a stack together
Shod with iron and shaped of ash.
'Twas a well-armed troop! Then a stately warrior°
Questioned the strangers about their kin:
'Whence come you bearing your burnished shields,
Your steel-gray harness and visored helms,
Your heap of spears? I am Hrothgar's herald,
His servant-thane. I have never seen strangers,
So great a number, of nobler mien.
Not exiles,° I ween, but high-minded° heroes
In greatness of heart have you sought out Hrothgar.'
Then bold under helmet the hero made answer,
The lord of the Weders, manful of mood,°
Mighty of heart: 'We are Hygelac's men,
His board-companions; Beowulf is my name.
I will state my mission to Healfdene's son,
The noble leader, your lordly prince,
If he will grant approach to his gracious presence.'
And Wulfgar answered, the Wendel° prince,
Renowned for merit° in many a land,
For war-might and wisdom: 'I will learn the wish
Of the Scylding leader, the lord of the Danes,
Our honored ruler and giver of rings,
Concerning your mission, and soon report
The answer our leader thinks good to give.'
He swiftly strode to where Hrothgar sat
Old and gray with his earls about him;
Crossed the floor and stood face to face
With the Danish king; he knew courtly custom.°
Wulfgar saluted his lord and friend:°
'Men from afar have fared to our land
Over ocean's margin—men of the Geats,
Their leader called Beowulf—seeking a boon,
The holding of parley, my prince, with thee.
O gracious Hrothgar, refuse not the favor!

stately warrior a proud-hearted and haughty—rather than stately—warrior, who is later named as Wulfgar
exiles i.e. you do not come seeking a new lord and protector because you have lost or been dismissed by your old one; cf. "The Wanderer" below
high-minded brave
mood mind, heart
Wulfgar . . . Wendel perhaps a Vandal, but more likely a man from Vendel in Sweden or Vendill in Jutland, Denmark (where the Vandals may have left pockets of settlement); he is a foreign prince serving Hrothgar—like Beowulf, and recognizing the likeness—from heroic magnanimity and love of adventure, not from necessity
merit courage
courtly custom the usage of the *comitatus*
friend This emphasizes the close but not carefully defined nature of the relationship. The obligations of allegiance and friendship are the ties that bind lord and man together, not, as in the later feudal system, a more exactly set-out complex of legal obligation.

In their splendid war-gear they merit well
The esteem of earls;° he's a stalwart leader
Who led this troop to the land of the Danes.'
Hrothgar spoke, the lord of the Scyldings:
'Their leader I knew when he still was a lad.
His father was Ecgtheow; Hrethel° the Geat
Gave him° in wedlock his only daughter.
Now is their son come, keen for adventure,
Finding his way to a faithful friend.
Sea-faring men who have voyaged to Geatland
With gifts of treasure° as token of peace,
Say that his hand-grip has thirty men's strength.
God, in His mercy, has sent him to save us—
So springs my hope—from Grendel's assaults.
For his gallant courage I'll load him with gifts!
Make haste now, marshal the men to the hall,
And give them welcome to Danish ground.'
Then to the door went the well-known warrior,°
Spoke from the threshold welcoming words:
'The Danish leader, my lord, declares
That he knows your kinship; right welcome you come,
You stout sea-rovers, to Danish soil.
Enter now, in your shining armor
And vizored helmets, to Hrothgar's hall.
But leave your shields and the shafts of slaughter
To wait the issue and weighing of words.'
Then the bold one rose with his band around him,
A splendid massing of mighty thanes;
A few stood guard as the Geat gave bidding
Over the weapons stacked by the wall.
They followed in haste on the heels of their leader
Under Heorot's roof. Full ready and bold
The helmeted warrior strode to the hearth;°
Beowulf spoke; his byrny glittered,
His war-net woven by cunning of smith:
'Hail! King Hrothgar! I am Hygelac's thane,
Hygelac's kinsman. Many a deed
Of honor and daring I've done in my youth.
This business of Grendel was brought to my ears
On my native soil. The sea-farers say
This best of buildings, this boasted hall,
Stands dark and deserted when sun is set,

earls originally men of the higher class of society; later use, in poetry, gives it the sense of "warriors"

Hrethel king of the Geats, father of Hygelac, grandfather of Beowulf

him Ecgtheow, Beowulf's father

gifts of treasure The giving of gifts to followers and to equals was the obligation and the pleasure of Germanic chieftains, see Tacitus, *Germania*, 15.

warrior Wulfgar

strode . . . hearth rather "took up his stand inside the hall"

When darkening shadows gather with dusk.
The best of my people, prudent and brave,
Urged me, King Hrothgar, to seek you out;
They had in remembrance my courage and might.
Many had seen me come safe from the conflict,
Bloody from battle; five foes I bound
Of the giant kindred, and crushed their clan.
Hard-driven in danger and darkness of night
I slew the nicors° that swam the sea,
Avenged the woe they had caused the Weders,
And ended their evil—they needed the lesson!
And now with Grendel, the fearful fiend,
Single-handed I'll settle the strife!
Prince of the Danes, protector of Scyldings,
Lord of nations, and leader of men,
I beg one favor—refuse me not,
Since I come thus faring from far-off lands—
That I may alone with my loyal earls,
With this hardy company, cleanse Hart-Hall.
I have heard that the demon in proud disdain
Spurns all weapons; and I too scorn—
May Hygelac's heart have joy of the deed—
To bear my sword, or sheltering shield,
Or yellow buckler, to battle the fiend.
With hand-grip only I'll grapple with Grendel;
Foe against foe I'll fight to the death,
And the one who is taken must trust to God's grace!
The demon, I doubt not, is minded to feast
In the hall unaffrighted, as often before,
On the force of the Hrethmen,° the folk of the Geats.
No need then to bury the body he mangles!
If death shall call me, he'll carry away
My gory flesh to his fen-retreat
To gorge at leisure and gulp me down,
Soiling the marshes with stains of blood.
There'll be little need longer to care for my body!
If the battle slays me, to Hygelac send
This best of corselets that covers my breast,
Heirloom of Hrethel, and Wayland's work,°
Finest of byrnies. Fate goes as Fate must!'
　　Hrothgar spoke, the lord of the Scyldings:
'Deed of daring and dream of honor
Bring you, friend Beowulf, knowing our need!
Your father once fought the greatest of feuds,

nicors water monsters

Hrethmen Perhaps a name for the Geats; it may not be a proper name at all but a compound noun meaning "glorious warriors."

Wayland's work i.e. a mail-shirt which is both ancient and excellent. Wayland or Weland, the cunning smith of the gods in Germanic legend, was a magician in his own right; see "Deor's Lament" below.

Laid Heatholaf° low, of the Wylfing line;°
And the folk of the Weders refused him shelter
For fear of revenge.° Then he fled to the South-Danes,
The Honor-Scyldings beyond the sea.
I was then first governing Danish ground,
As a young lad ruling the spacious realm,
The home-land of warriors. Heorogar° was dead,
The son of Healfdene no longer living,
My older brother, and better than I!
Thereafter by payment composing the feud,
O'er the water's ridge I sent to the Wylfing
Ancient treasure; he° swore me oaths!
It is sorrow sore to recite to another
The wrongs that Grendel has wrought in the hall,
His savage hatred and sudden assaults.
My war-troop is weakened, my hall-band is wasted;
Fate swept them away into Grendel's grip.
But God may easily bring to an end
The ruinous deeds of the ravaging foe.
Full often my warriors over their ale-cups
Boldly boasted,° when drunk with beer,
They would bide in the beer-hall the coming of battle,
The fury of Grendel, with flashing swords.
Then in the dawn, when the daylight strengthened,
The hall stood reddened and reeking with gore,
Bench-boards wet with the blood of battle;
And I had the fewer of faithful fighters,
Beloved retainers, whom Death had taken.
Sit now at the banquet, unbend your mood,
Speak of great deeds as your heart may spur you!'
Then in the beer-hall were benches made ready
For the Geatish heroes. Noble of heart,
Proud and stalwart, they sat them down
And a beer-thane° served them; bore in his hands
The patterned ale-cup, pouring the mead,°
While the scop's sweet singing was heard in the hall.
There was joy of heroes, a host at ease,
A welcome meeting of Weder and Dane.

Heatholaf not otherwise known
Wylfing line lit. "Wolves' sons"—Germanic tribe which lived on the southern shores of the Baltic
revenge i.e. Ecgtheow could not pay the necessary *wergild,* so that Heatholaf's people would have the obligation to take revenge; fear of this caused the Geats to refuse Beowulf's father leave to stay with them.
Heorogar Danish king, elder brother of Hrothgar
he Ecgtheow; Hrothgar had composed the feud by sending ancient prized treasure to the Wylfings, and Ecgtheow presumably swore an oath of friendship and good conduct.
boasted formal boasting, especially of future exploits, protestations of what would be done: a prominent feature of Germanic warriors' feasting
beer-thane the cup-bearer, the butler of later chivalric society—an important person in the household of the chieftain
mead a drink made from fermented honey; but the Old English word used here means literally "sweet drink," which may be beer

[*Unferth Taunts Beowulf*]
Then out spoke Unferth,° Ecglaf's son,
Who sat at the feet of the Scylding lord,
Picking a quarrel—for Beowulf's quest,
His bold sea-voyaging, irked him sore;
He bore it ill that any man other
In all the earth should ever achieve
More fame under heaven than he himself:
'Are you the Beowulf that strove with Breca°
In a swimming match in the open sea,
Both of you wantonly tempting the waves,
Risking your lives on the lonely deep
For a silly boast? No man could dissuade you,
Nor friend nor foe, from the foolhardy venture
Of ocean-swimming; with outstretched arms
You clasped the sea-stream, measured her streets,
With plowing shoulders parted the waves.
The sea-flood boiled with its wintry surges,
Seven nights you toiled in the tossing sea;
His strength was the greater, his swimming the stronger!
The waves upbore you at break of day
To the stretching beach of the Battle-Ræmas;°
And Breca departed, beloved of his people,
To the land of the Brondings, the beauteous home,
The stronghold fair, where he governed the folk,
The city and treasure; Beanstan's son°
Made good his boast to the full against you!
Therefore, I ween, worse fate shall befall,
Stout as you are in the struggle of war,
In deeds of battle, if you dare to abide
Encounter with Grendel at coming of night.'
Beowulf spoke, the son of Ecgtheow:
'My good friend Unferth, addled with beer
Much have you made of the deeds of Breca!
I count it true that I had more courage,
More strength in swimming than any other man.
In our youth we boasted—we were both of us boys—
We would risk our lives in the raging sea.
And we made it good! We gripped in our hands
Naked swords, as we swam in the waves,
Guarding us well from the whales' assault.
In the breaking seas he could not outstrip me,

Unferth Hrothgar's courtier, a type of the "wicked counsellor," sets out to mock Beowulf, but is put down by the hero. His name means "Peace-spoiler" and he here tries to cast doubt on Beowulf's ability to deal with Grendel.
Breca Tales of swimming matches and other such trials of strength occur in later Germanic literature: they usually involve endurance rather than speed. Breca's name may mean "rush, storm": he is known from other Germanic myths. His people, the Brondings, are not.
Battle-Ræmas Heatho-Ræmas, a tribe living in Norway, north of modern Oslo
Beanstan's son Breca

Nor would I leave him. For five nights long
Side by side we strove in the waters
Till racing combers wrenched us apart,
Freezing squalls, and the falling night,
And a bitter north wind's icy blast.
Rough were the waves; the wrath of the sea-fish
Was fiercely roused; but my firm-linked byrny,
The gold-adorned corselet that covered my breast,
Gave firm defense from the clutching foe.
Down to the bottom a savage sea-beast
Fiercely dragged me and held me fast
In a deadly grip; none the less it was granted me
To pierce the monster with point of steel.
Death swept it away with the swing of my sword.
    The grisly sea-beasts again and again
Beset me sore; but I served them home
With my faithful blade as was well-befitting.
They failed of their pleasure to feast their fill
Crowding round my corpse on the ocean-bottom!
Bloody with wounds, at the break of day,
They lay on the sea-beach slain with the sword.
No more would they cumber the mariner's course
On the ocean deep. From the east came the sun,
Bright beacon of God, and the seas subsided;
I beheld the headlands, the windy walls.
Fate often delivers an undoomed earl°
If his spirit be gallant! And so I was granted
To slay with the sword-edge nine of the nicors.
I have never heard tell of more terrible strife
Under dome of heaven in darkness of night,
Nor of man harder pressed on the paths of ocean.
But I freed my life from the grip of the foe
Though spent with the struggle. The billows bore me,
The swirling currents and surging seas,
To the land of the Finns.° And little I've heard
Of any such valiant adventures from you!
Neither Breca nor you in the press of battle
Ever showed such daring with dripping swords—
Though I boast not of it! But you stained your blade
With blood of your brothers,° your closest of kin;

Fate . . . undoomed earl i.e. a warrior not singled out for death by Fate. Fortune favors the brave, but only as Fate preordains: Fate is inescapable. This concept permeates the entire poem. It is typically pagan Germanic and especially typical of Old English poetry.

land of the Finns often identified with Finnmarken, in northern Norway, but probably the territory of the Lapps (frequently called Finns in Old English poetry) in southwest Sweden

you stained . . . brothers Beowulf turns Unferth's taunts in a devastating way: if this Danish spokesman is a boaster and a fratricide, Grendel has nothing to fear from the people he represents. Unferth might have retorted that his fratricide was the result of the *comitatus* system, where a brother serving one lord might have to fulfill his obligation to that lord by killing a brother serving another. But the blood-tie was always very strong—and the poet leaves Beowulf in possession of the field.

And for that you'll endure damnation in hell,
Sharp° as you are! I say for a truth,
Son of Ecglaf, never had Grendel
Wrought such havoc and woe in the hall,
That horrid demon so harried your king,
If your heart were as brave as you'd have men think!
But Grendel has found that he never need fear
Revenge from your people, or valiant attack
From the Victor-Scyldings; he takes his toll,
Sparing none of the Danish stock.
He slays and slaughters and works his will
Fearing no hurt at the hands of the Danes!
But soon will I show him the stuff of the Geats,
Their courage in battle and strength in the strife;
Then let him who may go bold to the mead-hall
When the next day dawns on the dwellings of men,
And the sun in splendor shines warm from the south.'
Glad of heart was the giver of treasure,
Hoary-headed and hardy in war;
The lordly leader had hope of help
As he listened to Beowulf's bold resolve.
There was revel of heroes and high carouse,
Their speech was happy; and Hrothgar's queen,
Of gentle manners, in jewelled splendor
Gave courtly greeting° to all the guests.
The high-born lady first bore the beaker
To the Danish leader, lord of the land,
Bade him be blithe at the drinking of beer;
Beloved of his people, the peerless king
Joined in the feasting, had joy of the cup.
Then to all alike went the Helming° lady
Bearing the beaker to old and young,
Till the jewelled queen with courtly grace
Paused before Beowulf, proffered the mead.
She greeted the Geat and to God gave thanks,
Wise of word, that her wish was granted;
At last she could look to a hero for help,
Comfort in evil. He took the cup,
The hardy warrior, at Wealhtheow's hand
And, eager for battle, uttered his boast;
Beowulf spoke, the son of Ecgtheow:
'I had firm resolve when I set to sea
With my band of earls in my ocean-ship,
Fully to work the will of your people

sharp keen-witted
courtly greeting The Queen's social graces are emphasized: she knows what is due to each person according to his rank and attainments.

Helming the ruling family of the Wylfings—of which Helm was the founder—to which Hrothgar's queen, Wealhtheow, belongs

Or fall in the struggle slain by the foe.
I shall either perform deeds fitting an earl
Or meet in this mead-hall the coming of death!'
Then the woman was pleased with the words he uttered,
The Geat-lord's boast; the gold-decked queen
Went in state to sit by her lord.

[*Beowulf Slays Grendel*]

In the hall as of old were brave words spoken,
There was noise of revel; happy the host
Till the son of Healfdene would go to his rest.
He knew that the monster would meet in the hall
Relentless struggle when light of the sun
Was dusky with gloom of the gathering night,
And shadow-shapes crept in the covering dark,
Dim under heaven. The host arose.
Hrothgar graciously greeted his guest,
Gave rule of the wine-hall, and wished him well,
Praised the warrior in parting words:
'Never to any man, early or late,
Since first I could brandish buckler and sword,
Have I trusted this ale-hall save only to you!
Be mindful of glory, show forth your strength,
Keep watch against foe! No wish of your heart
Shall go unfulfilled if you live through the fight.'
Then Hrothgar withdrew with his host of retainers,
The prince of the Scyldings, seeking his queen,
The bed of his consort. The King of Glory
Had stablished a hall-watch, a guard against Grendel,
Dutifully serving the Danish lord,
The land defending from loathsome fiend.
The Geatish hero put all his hope
In his fearless might and the mercy of God!
He stripped from his shoulders the byrny of steel,
Doffed helmet from head; into hand of thane
Gave inlaid° iron, the best of blades;
Bade him keep well the weapons of war.
Beowulf uttered a gallant boast,
The stalwart Geat, ere he sought his bed:
'I count myself nowise weaker in war
Or grapple of battle than Grendel himself.
Therefore I scorn to slay him with sword,
Deal deadly wound, as I well might do!
Nothing he knows of a noble fighting,
Of thrusting and hewing and hacking of shield,
Fierce as he is in the fury of war.

inlaid "engraved," "patterned"; the reference is not necessarily to the blade, but may be to hilt or pommel

In the shades of darkness we'll spurn the sword
If he dares without weapon to do or to die.
And God in His wisdom shall glory assign,
The ruling Lord, as He deems it right.'
Then the bold in battle bowed down to his rest,
Cheek pressed pillow; the peerless thanes
Were stretched in slumber around their lord.
Not one had hope of return to his home,
To the stronghold or land where he lived as a boy.
For they knew how death had befallen the Danes,
How many were slain as they slept in the wine-hall.
But the wise Lord wove them fortune in war,
Gave strong support to the Weder people;
They slew their foe by the single strength
Of a hero's courage. The truth is clear,
God rules forever the race of men.
Then through the shades of enshrouding night
The fiend came stealing; the archers slept
Whose duty was holding the horn-decked hall—
Though one was watching—full well they knew
No evil demon could drag them down
To shades under ground if God were not willing.°
But the hero watched awaiting the foe,
Abiding in anger the issue of war.
From the stretching moors, from the misty hollows,
Grendel came creeping, accursed of God,
A murderous ravager minded to snare
Spoil of heroes in high-built hall.
Under clouded heavens he held his way
Till there rose before him the high-roofed house,
Wine-hall of warriors gleaming with gold.
Nor was it the first of his fierce assaults
On the home of Hrothgar; but never before
Had he found worse fate or hardier hall-thanes!
Storming the building he burst the portal,
Though fastened of iron, with fiendish strength;
Forced open the entrance in savage fury
And rushed in rage o'er the shining floor.
A baleful glare from his eyes was gleaming
Most like to a flame. He found in the hall
Many a warrior sealed in slumber,
A host of kinsmen. His heart rejoiced;
The savage monster was minded to sever
Lives from bodies ere break of day,
To feast his fill of the flesh of men.
But he was not fated to glut his greed

God . . . willing Here it is God, not Fate, who has pre-decided the issue.

With more of mankind when the night was ended!
The hardy kinsman of Hygelac waited
To see how the monster would make his attack.
The demon delayed not, but quickly clutched
A sleeping thane in his swift assault,
Tore him in pieces, bit through the bones,
Gulped the blood, and gobbled the flesh,
Greedily gorged on the lifeless corpse,
The hands and the feet. Then the fiend stepped nearer,
Sprang on the Sea-Geat lying outstretched,
Clasping him close with his monstrous claw.
But Beowulf grappled and gripped him hard,
Struggled up on his elbow; the shepherd of sins
Soon found that never before had he felt
In any man other in all the earth
A mightier hand-grip; his mood was humbled,
His courage fled; but he found no escape!
He was fain to be gone; he would flee to the darkness,
The fellowship of devils. Far different his fate
From that which befell him in former days!
The hardy hero, Hygelac's kinsman,
Remembered the boast he had made at the banquet;
He sprang to his feet, clutched Grendel fast,
Though fingers were cracking, the fiend pulling free.
The earl pressed after; the monster was minded
To win his freedom and flee to the fens.
He knew that his fingers were fast in the grip
Of a savage foe. Sorry the venture,
The raid that the ravager made on the hall.
There was din in Heorot. For all the Danes,
The city-dwellers, the stalwart Scyldings,
That was a bitter spilling of beer!°
The walls resounded, the fight was fierce,
Savage the strife as the warriors struggled.
The wonder was that the lofty wine-hall
Withstood the struggle, nor crashed to earth,
The house so fair; it was firmly fastened
Within and without with iron bands
Cunningly smithied; though men have said
That many a mead-bench gleaming with gold
Sprang from its sill as the warriors strove.
The Scylding wise men had never weened
That any ravage could wreck the building,
Firmly fashioned and finished with bone,
Or any cunning° compass its fall,

bitter . . . beer the characteristic Old English grimly allusive poetic understatement: i.e. that was no feast, such as the hall had been built for

cunning skill

Till the time when the swelter and surge of fire
Should swallow it up in a swirl of flame.
Continuous tumult filled the hall;
A terror fell on the Danish folk
As they heard through the wall the horrible wailing,
The groans of Grendel, the foe of God
Howling his hideous hymn of pain,
The hell-thane shrieking in sore defeat.
He was fast in the grip of the man who was greatest
Of mortal men in the strength of his might,
Who would never rest while the wretch was living,
Counting his life-days a menace to man.
Many an earl of Beowulf brandished
His ancient iron° to guard his lord,
To shelter safely the peerless prince.
They had no knowledge, those daring thanes,
When they drew their weapons to hack and hew,
To thrust to the heart, that the sharpest sword,
The choicest iron in all the world,
Could work no harm to the hideous foe.
On every sword he had laid a spell,
On every blade; but a bitter death
Was to be his fate; far was the journey
The monster made to the home of fiends.
Then he who had wrought such wrong to men,
With grim delight as he warred with God,
Soon found that his strength was feeble and failing
In the crushing hold of Hygelac's thane.
Each loathed the other while life should last!
There Grendel suffered a grievous hurt,
A wound in the shoulder, gaping and wide;
Sinews snapped and bone-joints broke,
And Beowulf gained the glory of battle.
Grendel, fated, fled to the fens,
To his joyless dwelling, sick unto death.
He knew in his heart that his hours were numbered,
His days at an end. For all the Danes
Their wish was fulfilled in the fall of Grendel.
The stranger from far, the stalwart and strong,
Had purged of evil the hall of Hrothgar,
And cleansed of crime; the heart of the hero
Joyed in the deed his daring had done.
The lord of the Geats made good to the East-Danes
The boast he had uttered; he ended their ill,
And all the sorrow they suffered long
And needs must suffer—a foul offense.

ancient iron a sword, sometimes with a name, which was of especially good quality and strength and would be handed down as a prized heirloom from generation to generation

The token was clear when the bold in battle
Laid down the shoulder and dripping claw—
Grendel's arm—in the gabled hall!

[*The Joy of the Danes and the Lay of Sigemund*]

When morning came, as they tell the tale,
Many a warrior hastened to hall,
Folk-leaders faring from far and near
Over wide-running ways, to gaze at the wonder,
The trail of the demon. Nor seemed his death
A matter of sorrow to any man
Who viewed the tracks of the vanquished monster
As he slunk weary-hearted away from the hall,
Doomed and defeated and marking his flight
With bloody prints to the nicors' pool.
The crimson currents bubbled and heaved
In eddying reaches reddened with gore;
The surges boiled with the fiery blood.
But the monster had sunk from the sight of men.
In that fenny covert the cursed fiend
Not long thereafter laid down his life,
His heathen spirit; and hell received him.
Then all the comrades, the old and young,
The brave of heart, in a blithesome band
Came riding their horses home from the mere.°
Beowulf's prowess was praised in song;
And many men stated that south or north,
Over all the world, or between the seas,
Or under the heaven, no hero was greater,
More worthy of rule. But no whit they slighted
The gracious Hrothgar, their good old king.
Time and again they galloped their horses,
Racing their roans° where the roads seemed fairest;
Time and again a gleeman° chanted,
A minstrel mindful of saga and lay.
He wove his words in a winsome° pattern,
Hymning the burden of Beowulf's feat,
Clothing the story in skillful verse.
All tales he had ever heard told he sang of Sigemund's° glory,
Deeds of the Wælsing° forgotten, his weary roving and wars,

mere pond, lake
roans horses of mixed color
gleeman *scop*, bard
winsome pleasing, beautiful
Sigemund Germanic hero, son of Wæls, well known from the Old Norse *Volsungasaga* and the German *Nibelungenlied.* The Old Norse tradition makes him father of Fitela. Here he slays the dragon who guards the treasure: in the other two versions his son Sigurd or Siegfried does so. The story is meant to set up resonances—of Sigurd-Siegfried-Sigemund's dragon-slaying, taking away of the treasure, of the curse that was on the treasure, and of his tragic fate—which the audience will apply to Beowulf. The parallel with Beowulf's past and future life, the proleptic reference to his death in battle with the dragon and the melancholy sense that even the greatest and bravest of heroes must grow old and meet death, would all be present in the minds of the listeners.
Wælsing son of Wæls, Sigemund-Sigurd

Feuds and fighting unknown to men, save Fitela° only,
Tales told by uncle to nephew when the two were companions,
What time they were bosom-comrades in battle and bitter strife.
Many of monster blood these two had slain with the sword-edge;
Great glory Sigemund gained that lingered long after death,
When he daringly slew the dragon that guarded the hoard of gold.
Under the ancient rock the warrior ventured alone,
No Fitela fighting beside him; but still it befell
That his firm steel pierced the worm,° the point stood fast in the wall;
The dragon had died the death! And the hero's daring
Had won the treasure to have and to hold as his heart might wish.
Then the Wælsing loaded his sea-boat, laid in the breast of the ship
Wondrous and shining treasure; the worm dissolved in the heat.
Sigemund was strongest of men in his deeds of daring,
Warrior's shield and defender, most famous in days of old
After Heremod's° might diminished, his valor and vigor in war,
Betrayed in the land of the Jutes to the hands of his foemen, and slain.
Too long the surges of sorrow swept over his soul; in the end
His life was a lingering woe to people and princes.
In former days his fate was mourned by many a warrior
Who had trusted his lord for protection from terror and woe,
Had hoped that the prince would prosper, wielding his father's wealth,
Ruling the tribe and the treasure, the Scylding city and home.
Hygelac's kinsman had favor and friendship of all mankind,
But the stain of sin sank deep into Heremod's heart.
Time and again on their galloping steeds
Over yellow roads they measured the mile-paths;
Morning sun mounted the shining sky
And many a hero strode to the hall,
Stout of heart, to behold the wonder.
The worthy ruler, the warder of treasure,
Set out from the bowers with stately train;
The queen with her maidens paced over the mead-path.°
Then spoke Hrothgar; hasting to hall
He stood at the steps, stared up at the roof
High and gold-gleaming; saw Grendel's hand:
'Thanks be to God for this glorious sight!
I have suffered much evil, much outrage from Grendel,
But the God of glory works wonder on wonder.
I had no hope of a haven from sorrow
While this best of houses stood badged with blood,
A woe far-reaching for all the wise

Fitela nephew and son of Sigurd, by his sister Signy, who had seduced her brother in disguise in order to bear a true Volsung son who could revenge the wrongs done to her and to her family

worm dragon; the word once meant reptile, serpent, of any kind

Heremod See ll. 1596 ff. The intention is to contrast the savagery and tyranny of this king, his early goodness and later evil-doing and failure, with Beowulf, who has already been exalted by the comparison with Sigemund-Sigurd.

paced . . . mead-path i.e. walked from their apartments to the mead-hall

Who weened that they never could hold the hall
Against the assaults of devils and demons.
But now with God's help this hero has compassed
A deed our cunning could no way contrive.
Surely that woman may say with truth,
Who bore this son, if she still be living,
Our ancient God showed favor and grace
On her bringing-forth! O best of men,
I will keep you, Beowulf, close to my heart
In firm affection; as son to father
Hold fast henceforth to this foster-kinship.°
You shall know not want of treasure or wealth
Or goodly gift that your wish may crave,
While I have power. For poorer deeds
I have granted guerdon,° and graced with honor
Weaker warriors, feebler in fight.
You have done such deeds that your fame shall flourish
Through all the ages! God grant you still
All goodly grace as He gave before.'
Beowulf spoke, the son of Ecgtheow:
'By the favor of God we won the fight,
Did the deed of valor, and boldly dared
The might of the monster. I would you could see
The fiend himself lying dead before you!
I thought to grip him in stubborn grasp
And bind him down on the bed of death,
There to lie straining in struggle for life,
While I gripped him fast lest he vanish away.
But I might not hold him or hinder his going
For God did not grant it, my fingers failed.
Too savage the strain of his fiendish strength!
To save his life he left shoulder and claw,
The arm of the monster, to mark his track.
But he bought no comfort; no whit thereby
Shall the wretched ravager racked with sin,
The loathsome spoiler, prolong his life.
A deep wound holds him in deadly grip,
In baleful bondage; and black with crime
The demon shall wait for the day of doom
When the God of glory shall give decree.'
Then slower of speech was the son of Ecglaf,°
More wary of boasting of warlike deeds,
While the nobles gazed at the grisly claw,
The fiend's hand fastened by hero's might
On the lofty roof. Most like to steel

foster-kinship tie regarded as equivalent to the bond of blood
guerdon reward
then slower . . . Ecglaf Unferth, now discomfited and unable to taunt Beowulf at all

Were the hardened nails, the heathen's hand-spurs,
Horrible, monstrous; and many men said
No tempered sword, no excellent iron,
Could have harmed the monster or hacked away
The demon's battle-claw dripping with blood.

[*The Feast and the Lay of Finnsburg*]

In joyful haste was Heorot decked
And a willing host of women and men
Gaily dressed and adorned the guest-hall.
Splendid hangings with sheen of gold
Shone on the walls, a glorious sight
To eyes that delight to behold such wonders.
The shining building was wholly shattered
Though braced and fastened with iron bands;
Hinges were riven; the roof alone
Remained unharmed when the horrid monster,
Foul with evil, slunk off in flight,
Hopeless of life. It is hard to flee
The touch of death, let him try who will;
Necessity urges the sons of men,
The dwellers on earth, to their destined place
Where the body, bound in its narrow bed,
After the feasting is fast in slumber.
Soon was the time when the son of Healfdene
Went to the wine-hall; he fain would join
With happy heart in the joy of feasting.
I never have heard of a mightier muster
Of proud retainers around their prince.
All at ease they bent to the benches,
Had joy of the banquet; their kinsmen bold,
Hrothgar and Hrothulf,° happy of heart,
In the high-built hall drank many a mead-cup.
The hall of Hrothgar was filled with friends;
No treachery yet had troubled the Scyldings.
Upon Beowulf, then, as a token of triumph,
Hrothgar bestowed a standard of gold,
A banner embroidered, a byrny and helm.
In sight of many, a costly sword
Before the hero was borne on high;
Beowulf drank of many a bowl.
No need for shame in the sight of heroes
For gifts so gracious! I never have heard
Of many men dealing in friendlier fashion,
To others on ale-bench, richer rewards,
Four such treasures fretted with gold!

Hrothulf Danish prince, nephew of Hrothgar, son of his brother Halga. Hrothulf seems to have usurped the throne after Hrothgar's death.

On the crest of the helmet a crowning wreath,
Woven of wire-work,° warded the head
Lest tempered swordblade, sharp from the file,
Deal deadly wound when the shielded warrior
Went forth to battle against the foe.
Eight horses also with plated headstalls
The lord of heroes bade lead into hall;
On one was a saddle skillfully fashioned
And set with jewels, the battle-seat
Of the king himself, when the son of Healfdene
Would fain take part in the play of swords;
Never in fray had his valor failed,
His kingly courage, when corpses were falling.
And the prince of the Ingwines° gave all these gifts
To the hand of Beowulf, horses and armor;
Bade him enjoy them! With generous heart
The noble leader, the lord of heroes,
Rewarded the struggle with steeds and with treasure,
So that none can belittle, and none can blame,
Who tells the tale as it truly happened.
    Then on the ale-bench to each of the earls
Who embarked with Beowulf, sailing the sea-paths,
The lord of princes dealt ancient heirlooms,
Gift of treasure, and guerdon of gold
To requite his slaughter whom Grendel slew,
As he would have slain others, but all-wise God
And the hero's courage had conquered Fate.
The Lord ruled over the lives of men
As He rules them still. Therefore understanding
And a prudent spirit are surely best!
He must suffer much of both weal and woe
Who dwells here long in these days of strife.
    Then song and revelry rose in the hall;
Before Healfdene's leader the harp was struck
And hall-joy wakened; the song was sung,
Hrothgar's gleeman rehearsed the lay
Of the sons of Finn when the terror befell them:

Hnæf° of the Scyldings, the Half-Dane, fell in the Frisian slaughter;
Nor had Hildeburh cause to acclaim the faith of the Jutish folk,

crowning . . . wire-work rather, as on the Sutton Hoo helmet, which is Swedish work, a metal ridge adorned with wire-work running from the top of the head to the nose (Fig. 19)

Ingwines lit. "friends of Ing," i.e. Danes

Hnæf Hnæf, king of the Danes, who had succeeded his father, King Hoc, had gone with his retainers on a visit to his sister Hildeburh and her husband Finn, king of the Frisians (or Jutes) at their home, Finnsburg. During the festivities, Jutish treachery—according to the poet—provoked a fight in which Hnæf and his sister's son, his closest kinsman, though half Jute, were killed. They were cremated on the same pyre and a truce was made. Hengest, the new Danish king, stayed the winter with Finn, meditating revenge for the death of Hnæf. Two Danish warriors then provoked another battle, in which Finn was killed. The Danes returned home, taking plunder and Hildeburh with them.

The *scop*'s version, since he is a Dane singing to his fellow Danes, lays the blame for the initial bloodshed on the Jutes. He tells it as a piece of old Danish lore, a story that would be familiar to his hearers, in an oblique and highly allusive manner, designed to set up reso-

Blameless, bereft of her brothers in battle, and stripped of her sons
Who fell overcome by their fate and wounded with spears!
Not for nothing Hoc's daughter bewailed death's bitter decree,
In the dawn under morning skies, when she saw the slaughter of kinsmen
In the place where her days had been filled with the fairest delights
of the world.
Finn's thanes were slain in the fight, save only a few;
Nor could he do battle with Hengest or harry his shattered host;
And the Frisians made terms with the Danes, a truce, a hall for their dwelling,
A throne, and a sharing of rights with the sons of the Jutes,
And that Finn, the son of Folcwalda, each day would honor the Danes,
The host of Hengest, with gifts, with rings and guerdon of gold,
Such portion of plated treasure as he dealt to the Frisian folk
When he gladdened their hearts in the hall. So both were bound by the truce.°
And Finn swore Hengest with oaths that were forceful and firm
He would rightfully rule his remnant, follow his council's decree,
And that no man should break the truce, or breach it by word or by will,
Nor the lordless in malice lament they were fated to follow
The man who had murdered their liege; and, if ever a Frisian
Fanned the feud with insolent speech, the sword should avenge° it.
Then a funeral pyre° was prepared, and gold was drawn from the hoard,
The best of the Scylding leaders° was laid on the bier;
In the burning pile was a gleaming of blood-stained byrnies,
The gilded swine° and the boar-helm hard from the hammer,
Many a warrior fated with wounds and fallen in battle.
And Hildeburh bade that her son be laid on the bier of Hnæf,
His body consumed in the surging flame at his uncle's shoulder.
Beside it the lady lamented, singing her mournful dirge.°
The hero was placed on the pyre;° the greatest of funeral flames
Rolled with a roar to the skies at the burial barrow.
Heads melted and gashes gaped, the mortal wounds of the body,
Blood poured out in the flames; the fire, most greedy of spirits,
Swallowed up all whom battle had taken of both their peoples.
Their glory was gone! The warriors went to their homes,
Bereft of their friends, returning to Friesland,° to city and strong-hold.
Then Hengest abode with Finn all the slaughter-stained winter,
But his heart longed ever for home, though he could not launch on the sea

---

nances in the minds of his hearers. We should know far less of the background if we did not have the story in the much more straightforward narrative of the independent fragment known as the Fight at Finnsburg.

Some think that the allusiveness is carried still further and that the Finnsburg lay is a kind of forecast of the treachery by which Hrothulf, Hrothgar's nephew, usurped the Danish throne from the rightful heirs, Hrothgar's sons, after the death of the old king.

truce This involved Hengest's taking service with the man who had killed his lord—a crime against the Germanic code and only to be justified because it served the final end of revenge.

avenge i.e. settle the dispute

pyre According to the older pagan custom the dead man's precious possessions were burned with him.

best . . . leaders i.e. Hnæf

swine boar-image on the helmet

dirge This was the pagan custom; cf. the woman at Beowulf's funeral, below; and Tacitus, *Germania*, 27.

hero . . . pyre probably a reference to Hildeburh's son

Friesland i.e. Frisian or Jutish country

His ring-stemmed ship, for the billows boiled wtih the storm,
Strove with the wind, and the winter locked ocean in bonds of ice;
Till a new Spring shone once more on the dwellings of men,
The sunny and shining days which ever observe their season.
The winter was banished afar, and fair the bosom of earth.
Then the exile longed to be gone, the guest from his dwelling,
But his thoughts were more on revenge than on voyaging over the wave,
Plotting assault on the Jutes, renewal of war with the sword.
So he spurned not° the naked hint when Hunlafing laid in his lap
The battle-flasher, the best of blades, well known to the Jutes!
In his own home death by the sword befell Finn, the fierce-hearted,
When Guthlaf and Oslaf° requited the grim attack,
The woe encountered beyond the sea, the sorrow they suffered,
Nor could bridle the restive spirits within their breasts!
Then the hall was reddened with blood and bodies of foemen,
Finn killed in the midst of his men, and the fair queen taken.
The Scylding warriors bore to their ships all treasure and wealth,
Such store as they found in the home of Finn of jewels and gems.
And the noble queen they carried across the sea-paths,
Brought her back to the Danes, to her own dear people.
So the song was sung, the lay recited,
The sound of revelry rose in the hall.
Stewards poured wine from wondrous vessels;
And Wealhtheow, wearing a golden crown,
Came forth in state where the two were sitting,
Courteous comrades, uncle and nephew,
Each true to the other in ties of peace.°
Unferth, the orator,° sat at the feet
Of the lord of the Scyldings; and both showed trust
In his noble mind, though he had no mercy
On kinsmen in swordplay; the Scylding queen spoke:
'My sovereign lord, dispenser of treasure,
Drink now of this flagon, have joy of the feast!
Speak to the Geats, O gold-friend of men,
In winning words as is well-befitting;
Be kind to the Geat-men and mindful of gifts
From the gold you have garnered from near and far.°
You have taken as son, so many have told me,
This hardy hero. Heorot is cleansed,
The gleaming gift-hall. Rejoice while you may

So . . . not This passage can be interpreted in several ways. As translated it seems to mean that the son of Hunlaf the Dane, who had taken part in the Danish-Frisian feud, placed a naked sword in Hengest's lap, as a token of allegiance and a reminder that the deaths of Hnæf and of Hunlaf in the fight at Finnsburg are still unavenged. The action is also a pledge that the son of Hunlaf will take part in the revenge, when it is taken. "Battle-flasher" may be the name of a special sword or a *kenning* (condensed metaphor) for any sword.

Guthlaf . . . Oslaf These two Danish warriors, brothers of Hunlaf, seem to have begun the second fight at Finnsburg.

peace perhaps a reference by ironic contrast to the usurpation and strife after Hrothgar's death

orator spokesman, counsellor, again represented as sitting in the place of honor

Be kind . . . far an incitement to generosity: the best sense that can be made of this obscure and difficult passage; the text may be corrupt

In lavish bounty, and leave to your kin
People and kingdom when time shall come,
Your destined hour, to look on death.
I know the heart of my gracious Hrothulf,
That he'll safely shelter and shield our sons
When you leave this world, if he still is living.
I know he will favor with gracious gifts
These boys of ours, if he bears in mind
The many honors and marks of love
We bestowed upon him while he still was a boy.'
She turned to the bench where her boys were sitting,
Hrethric and Hrothmund,° the sons of heroes,
The youth together; there the good man sat,
Beowulf of the Geats, beside the two brothers.
Then the cup was offered with gracious greeting,
And seemly presents of spiraled gold,
A corselet, and rings, and the goodliest collar°
Of all that ever were known on earth.
In the hoarding of heroes beneath the sky
I have never heard tell of a worthier treasure
Since Hama bore off to the shining city
The Brosings' jewel,° setting and gems,
Fled from Eormanric's cruel craft
And sought the grace of eternal glory.
Hygelac,° the Geat, grandson of Swerting
Wore the ring in the last of his raids,
Guarding the spoil under banner in battle,
Defending the treasure. Overtaken by Fate,
In the flush of pride he fought with the Frisians
And met disaster. The mighty prince
Carried the ring o'er the cup of the waves,
The precious jewel, and sank under shield.
Then his body fell into Frankish hands,
His woven corselet and jewelled collar,
And weaker warriors plundered the dead
After the carnage and welter of war.
The field of battle was covered with corpses
Of Geats who had fallen, slain by the sword.
The sound of revelry rose in the hall;
Wealhtheow spoke to the warrior host:
'Take, dear Beowulf, collar and corselet,
Wear these treasures with right good will!

Hrethric and Hrothmund sons of Hrothgar and Wealhtheow
collar torc, neck-ring, of gold
Brosings' jewel This was a necklace, which had, according to Old Norse legend, been made for the goddess Freyja, wife of Odin and goddess of love, fecundity, and death, by the Brisingas. The legend of how Hama, apparently, stole the necklace from Eormanric, king of the Ostrogoths—the historical Eormanric died about 375—is not otherwise known. In Norse legend Freyja loses the necklace through the treachery of Loki.
Hygelac cf. ll. 194 ff. and ll. 2222 ff., 2742 ff.

Thrive and prosper and prove your might!
Befriend my boys with your kindly counsel;
I will remember and I will repay.
You have earned the undying honor of heroes
In regions reaching as far and wide
As the windy walls that the sea encircles.
May Fate show favor while life shall last!
I wish you wealth to your heart's content;
In your days of glory be good to my sons!
Here each hero is true to other,
Gentle of spirit, loyal to lord,
Friendly thanes and a folk united,
Wine-cheered warriors who do my will.'

[*The Troll-Wife*° *Avenges Grendel*]

Then she went to her seat. At the fairest of feasts
Men drank of the wine-cup, knowing not Fate,
Nor the fearful doom that befell the earls
When darkness gathered, and gracious Hrothgar
Sought his dwelling and sank to rest.
A host of heroes guarded the hall
As they oft had done in the days of old.
They stripped the benches and spread the floor
With beds and bolsters. But one of the beer-thanes
Bowed to his hall-rest doomed to death.
They set at their heads their shining shields,
Their battle-bucklers; and there on the bench
Above each hero his towering helmet,
His spear and corselet hung close at hand.
It was ever their wont to be ready for war
At home or in field, as it ever befell
That their lord had need. 'Twas a noble race!
Then they sank to slumber. But one paid dear
For his evening rest, as had often happened
When Grendel haunted the lordly hall
And wrought such ruin, till his end was come,
Death for his sins; it was easily seen,
Though the monster was slain, an avenger survived
Prolonging the feud, though the fiend had perished.
The mother of Grendel, a monstrous hag,
Brooded over her misery, doomed to dwell
In evil waters and icy streams
From ancient ages when Cain had killed
His only brother, his father's son.
Banished and branded with marks of murder
Cain fled far from the joys of men,
Haunting the barrens, begetting a brood

Troll-Wife i.e. woman evil-spirit

Of grisly monsters; and Grendel was one,
The fiendish ogre who found in the hall
A hero on watch, and awaiting the fray.
The monster grappled; the Geat took thought
Of the strength of his might, that marvelous gift
Which the Lord had given; in God he trusted
For help and succor and strong support,
Whereby he humbled the fiend from hell,
Destroyed the demon; and Grendel fled,
Harrowed in heart and hateful to man,
Deprived of joy, to the place of death.
But rabid and raging his mother resolved
On a dreadful revenge for the death of her son!
She stole to the hall where the Danes were sleeping,
And horror fell on the host of earls
When the dam of Grendel burst in the door.
But the terror was less as the war-craft is weaker,
A woman's strength, than the might of a man
When the hilted sword, well shaped by the hammer,
The blood-stained iron of tempered edge,
Hews the boar from the foeman's helmet.
Then in the hall was the hard-edged blade,
The stout steel, brandished above the benches;
Seizing their shields men stayed not for helmet
Or ample byrny, when fear befell.
As soon as discovered, the hag was in haste
To fly to the open, to flee for her life.
One of the warriors she swiftly seized,
Clutched him fast and made off to the fens.
He was of heroes the dearest to Hrothgar,
The best of comrades between two seas;
The warrior brave, the stout-hearted spearman,
She slew in his sleep. Nor was Beowulf there;
But after the banquet another abode
Had been assigned to the glorious Geat.
There was tumult in Heorot. She tore from its place
The blood-stained claw. Care was renewed!
It was no good bargain when both in turn
Must pay the price with the lives of friends!
Then the white-haired warrior, the aged king,
Was numb with sorrow, knowing his thane
No longer was living, his dearest man dead.
Beowulf, the brave, was speedily summoned,
Brought to the bower; the noble prince
Came with his comrades at dawn of day
Where the wise king awaited if God would award
Some happier turn in these tidings of woe.
The hero came tramping into the hall

With his chosen band—the boards resounded—
Greeted the leader, the Ingwine lord,
And asked if the night had been peaceful and pleasant.
    Hrothgar spoke, the lord of the Scyldings:
'Ask not of pleasure; pain is renewed
For the Danish people. Æschere° is dead!
Dead is Yrmenlaf's elder brother!
He was my comrade, closest of counsellors,
My shoulder-companion as side by side
We fought for our lives in the welter of war,
In the shock of battle when boar-helms crashed.
As an earl should be, a prince without peer,
Such was Æschere, slain in the hall
By the wandering demon! I know not whither
She fled to shelter, proud of her spoil,
Gorged to the full. She avenged the feud
Wherein yesternight you grappled with Grendel
And savagely slew him because so long
He had hunted and harried the men of my folk.
He fell in the battle and paid with his life.
But now another fierce ravager rises
Avenging her kinsman, and carries it far,
As it seems to many a saddened thane
Who grieves in his heart for his treasure-giver.
This woe weighs heavy! The hand lies still
That once was lavish of all delights.
    Oft in the hall I have heard my people,
Comrades and counsellors, telling a tale
Of evil spirits their eyes have sighted,
Two mighty marauders who haunt the moors.
One shape, as clearly as men could see,
Seemed woman's likeness, and one seemed man,
An outcast wretch of another world,
And huger far than a human form.
Grendel my countrymen called him, not knowing
What monster-brood spawned him, what sire begot.
Wild and lonely the land they live in,
Wind-swept ridges and wolf-retreats,
Dread tracts of fen where the falling torrent
Downward dips into gloom and shadow
Under the dusk of the darkening cliff.
Not far in miles lies the lonely mere
Where trees firm-rooted and hung with frost
Overshroud the wave with shadowing gloom.
And there a portent appears each night,
A flame in the water; no man so wise

Æschere not otherwise known

Who knows the bound of its bottomless depth.
The heather-stepper, the horned stag,
The antlered hart hard driven by hounds,
Invading that forest in flight from afar
Will turn at bay and die on the brink
Ere ever he'll plunge in that haunted pool.
'Tis an eerie spot!° Its tossing spray
Mounts dark to heaven when high winds stir
The driving storm, and the sky is murky,
And with foul weather the heavens weep.
On your arm only rests all our hope!
Not yet have you tempted those terrible reaches
The region that shelters that sinful wight.
Go if you dare! I will give requital
With ancient treasure and twisted gold,
As I formerly gave in guerdon of battle,
If out of that combat you come alive.'
        Beowulf spoke, the son of Ecgtheow:
'Sorrow not, brave one! Better for man
To avenge a friend than much to mourn.
All men must die; let him who may
Win glory ere death. That guerdon is best
For a noble man when his name survives him.
Then let us rise up, O ward of the realm,
And haste us forth to behold the track
Of Grendel's dam. And I give you pledge
She shall not in safety escape to cover,
To earthy cavern, or forest fastness,
Or gulf of ocean, go where she may.
This day with patience endure the burden
Of every woe, as I know you will.'
Up sprang the ancient, gave thanks to God
For the heartening words the hero had spoken.

[*Beowulf Slays the Troll-Wife*]

Quickly a horse was bridled for Hrothgar,
A mettlesome charger with braided mane;
In royal splendor the king rode forth
Mid the trampling tread of a troop of shieldmen.
The tracks lay clear where the fiend had fared
Over plain and bottom and woodland path,
Through murky moorland making her way
With the lifeless body, the best of thanes
Who of old with Hrothgar had guarded the hall.

eerie spot lit. "that is no pleasant spot." There are general resemblances to the visit to the underworld in the sixth book of Virgil's *Aeneid* and to the apocryphal *Vision of St. Paul,* but there are many features here for which the poet seems to have drawn on a typically Northern winter scene. There are also parallels with the Old Norse saga of Grettir. Later, an English sermon, perhaps of the ninth or earlier tenth century, draws on this passage in *Beowulf* for a description of an icy Hell.

By a narrow path the king pressed on
Through rocky upland and rugged ravine,
A lonely journey, past looming headlands,
The lair of monster and lurking troll.
Tried retainers, a trusty few,
Advanced with Hrothgar to view the ground.
Sudden they came on a dismal covert
Of trees that hung over hoary stone,
Over churning water and blood-stained wave.
Then for the Danes was the woe the deeper,
The sorrow sharper for Scylding earls,
When they first caught sight, on the rocky sea-cliff,
Of slaughtered Æschere's severed head.
The water boiled in a bloody swirling
With seething gore as the spearmen gazed.
The trumpet sounded a martial strain;
The shield-troop halted. Their eyes beheld
The swimming forms of strange sea-dragons,
Dim serpent shapes in the watery depths,
Sea-beasts sunning on headland slopes;
Snakelike monsters that oft at sunrise
On evil errands scour the sea.
Startled by tumult and trumpet's blare,
Enraged and savage, they swam away;
But one the lord of the Geats brought low,
Stripped of his sea-strength, despoiled of life,
As the bitter bow-bolt pierced his heart.
His watery-speed grew slower, and ceased,
And he floated, caught in the clutch of death.
Then they hauled him in with sharp-hooked boar-spears,
By sheer strength grappled and dragged him ashore,
A wondrous wave-beast; and all the array
Gathered to gaze at the grisly guest.
    Beowulf donned his armor for battle,
Heeded not danger; the hand-braided byrny,
Broad of shoulder and richly bedecked,°
Must stand the ordeal of the watery depths.
Well could that corselet defend the frame
Lest hostile thrust should pierce to the heart.
Or blows of battle beat down the life.
A gleaming helmet guarded his head
As he planned his plunge to the depths of the pool
Through the heaving waters—a helm adorned
With lavish inlay and lordly chains,
Ancient work of the weapon-smith
Skillfully fashioned, beset with the boar,

richly bedecked "Strongly made" is more accurate.

That no blade of battle might bite it through.
Not the least or the worst of his war-equipment
Was the sword° the herald of Hrothgar° loaned
In his hour of need—Hrunting° its name—
An ancient heirloom, trusty and tried;
Its blade was iron, with etched design,
Tempered in blood of many a battle.
Never in fight had it failed the hand
That drew it daring the perils of war,
The rush of the foe. Not the first time then
That its edge must venture on valiant deeds.
But Ecglaf's stalwart son was unmindful
Of words he had spoken while heated with wine,
When he loaned the blade to a better swordsman.
He himself dared not hazard his life
In deeds of note in the watery depths;
And thereby he forfeited honor and fame.
Not so with that other undaunted spirit
After he donned his armor for battle.
Beowulf spoke, the son of Ecgtheow:
'O gracious ruler, gold-giver to men,
As I now set forth to attempt this feat,
Great son of Healfdene, hold well in mind
The solemn pledge we plighted of old,
That if doing your service I meet my death
You will mark my fall with a father's love.
Protect my kinsmen, my trusty comrades,
If battle take me. And all the treasure
You have heaped on me bestow upon Hygelac,
Hrothgar beloved! The lord of the Geats,
The son of Hrethel, shall see the proof,
Shall know as he gazes on jewels and gold,
That I found an unsparing dispenser of bounty,
And joyed, while I lived, in his generous gifts.
Give back to Unferth the ancient blade,
The sword-edge splendid with curving scrolls,
For either with Hrunting I'll reap rich harvest
Of glorious deeds, or death shall take me.'
After these words the prince of the Weders
Awaited no answer, but turned to the task,
Straightway plunged in the swirling pool.
Nigh unto a day he endured the depths
Ere he first had view of the vast sea-bottom.
Soon she found, who had haunted the flood,
A ravening hag, for a hundred half-years,

sword The text calls it "gleaming with venom twigs," which may mean that the blade had a serpentine pattern.

herald of Hrothgar Unferth

Hrunting perhaps meaning Thruster

Greedy and grim, that a man was groping
In daring search through the sea-troll's home.
Swift she grappled and grasped the warrior
With horrid grip, but could work no harm,
No hurt to his body; the ring-locked byrny
Cloaked his life from her clutching claw;
Nor could she tear through the tempered mail
With her savage fingers. The she-wolf bore
The ring-prince down through the watery depths
To her den at the bottom; nor could Beowulf draw
His blade for battle, though brave his mood.
Many a sea-beast, strange sea-monsters,
Tasked him hard° with their menacing tusks,
Broke his byrny and smote him sore.
Then he found himself in a fearsome hall
Where water came not to work him hurt,
But the flood was stayed by the sheltering roof.
There in the glow of firelight gleaming
The hero had view of the huge sea-troll.
He swung his war-sword with all his strength,
Withheld not the blow, and the savage blade
Sang on her head its hymn of hate.
But the bold one found that the battle-flasher
Would bite no longer, nor harm her life.
The sword-edge failed at his sorest need.
Often of old with ease it had suffered
The clash of battle, cleaving the helm,
The fated warrior's woven mail.
That time was first for the treasured blade
That its glory failed in the press of the fray.
But fixed of purpose and firm of mood
Hygelac's earl was mindful of honor;
In wrath, undaunted, he dashed to earth
The jewelled sword with its scrolled design,
The blade of steel; staked all on strength,
On the might of his hand, as a man must do
Who thinks to win in the welter of battle
Enduring glory; he fears not death.
The Geat-prince joyed in the straining struggle,
Stalwart-hearted and stirred to wrath,
Gripped the shoulder of Grendel's dam
And headlong hurled the hag to the ground.
But she quickly clutched him and drew him close,
Countered the onset with savage claw.
The warrior staggered, for all his strength,
Dismayed and shaken and borne to earth.

Tasked him hard i.e. tore at him

She knelt upon him and drew her dagger,
With broad bright blade, to avenge her son,
Her only issue. But the corselet's steel
Shielded his breast and sheltered his life
Withstanding entrance of point and edge.
Then the prince of the Geats would have gone his journey,
The son of Ecgtheow, under the ground;
But his sturdy breast-net, his battle-corselet,
Gave him succor, and holy God,
The Lord all-wise, awarded the mastery;
Heaven's Ruler gave right decree.
Swift the hero sprang to his feet;
Saw 'mid the war-gear a stately sword,
An ancient war-brand of biting edge,
Choicest of weapons worthy and strong,
The work of giants,° a warrior's joy,
So heavy no hand but his own could hold it,
Bear to battle or wield in war.
Then the Scylding warrior, savage and grim,
Seized the ring-hilt and swung the sword,
Struck with fury, despairing of life,
Thrust at the throat, broke through the bone-rings;
The stout blade stabbed through her fated flesh.
She sank in death; the sword was bloody;
The hero joyed in the work of his hand.
The gleaming radiance shimmered and shone
As the candle of heaven shines clear from the sky.
Wrathful and resolute Hygelac's thane
Surveyed the span of the spacious hall;
Grimly gripping the hilted sword
With upraised weapon he turned to the wall.
The blade had failed not the battle-prince;
A full requital he firmly planned
For all the injury Grendel had done
In numberless raids on the Danish race,
When he slew the hearth-companions of Hrothgar,
Devoured fifteen of the Danish folk
Clasped in slumber, and carried away
As many more spearmen, a hideous spoil.
All this the stout-heart had stern requited;
And there before him bereft of life
He saw the broken body of Grendel
Stilled in battle, and stretched in death,
As the struggle in Heorot smote him down.
The corpse sprang wide as he struck the blow,
The hard sword-stroke that severed the head.
Then the tried retainers, who there with Hrothgar

work of giants i.e. huge, old, and powerful

Watched the face of the foaming pool,
Saw that the churning reaches were reddened,
The eddying surges stained with blood.
And the gray, old spearmen spoke of the hero,
Having no hope he would ever return
Crowned with triumph and cheered with spoil.
Many were sure that the savage sea-wolf
Had slain their leader. At last came noon.
The stalwart Scyldings forsook the headland;
Their proud gold-giver departed home.
But the Geats sat grieving and sick in spirit,
Stared at the water with longing eyes,
Having no hope they would ever behold
Their gracious leader and lord again.
Then the great sword, eaten with blood of battle,
Began to soften and waste away
In iron icicles, wonder of wonders,
Melting away most like to ice
When the Father looses the fetters of frost,
Slackens the bondage that binds the wave,
Strong in power of times and seasons;
He is true God! Of the goodly treasures
From the sea-cave Beowulf took but two,
The monster's head and the precious hilt
Blazing with gems; but the blade had melted,
The sword dissolved, in the deadly heat,
The venomous blood of the fallen fiend.

[*Beowulf Returns to Heorot*]

Then he who had compassed the fall of his foes
Came swimming up through the swirling surge.
Cleansed were the currents, the boundless abyss,
Where the evil monster had died the death
And looked her last on this fleeting world.
With sturdy strokes the lord of the seamen
To land came swimming, rejoiced in his spoil,
Had joy of the burden he brought from the depths.
And his mighty thanes came forward to meet him,
Gave thanks to God they were granted to see
Their well-loved leader both sound and safe.
From the stalwart hero his helmet and byrny
Were quickly loosened; the lake lay still,
Its motionless reaches reddened with blood.
Fain of heart men fared o'er the footpaths,
Measured the ways and the well-known roads.
From the sea-cliff's brim the warriors bore
The head of Grendel, with heavy toil;
Four of the stoutest, with all their strength,

Could hardly carry on swaying spear
Grendel's head to the gold-decked hall.
Swift they strode, the daring and dauntless,
Fourteen Geats, to the Hall of the Hart;
And proud in the midst of his marching men
Their leader measured the path to the mead-hall.
The hero entered, the hardy in battle,
The great in glory, to greet the king;
And Grendel's head by the hair was carried
Across the floor where the feasters drank—
A terrible sight for lord and for lady—
A gruesome vision whereon men gazed!
Beowulf spoke, the son of Ecgtheow:
'O son of Healfdene, lord of the Scyldings!
This sea-spoil wondrous, whereon you stare,
We joyously bring you in token of triumph!
Barely with life surviving the battle,
The war under water, I wrought the deed
Weary and spent; and death had been swift
Had God not granted His sheltering strength.
My strong-edged Hrunting, stoutest of blades,
Availed me nothing. But God revealed—
Often His arm has aided the friendless—
The fairest of weapons hanging on wall,
An ancient broadsword; I seized the blade,
Slew in the struggle, as fortune availed,
The cavern-warders. But the war-brand old,
The battle-blade with its scrolled design,
Dissolved in the gush of the venomous gore;
The hilt alone I brought from the battle.
The record of ruin, and slaughter of Danes,
These wrongs I avenged, as was fitting and right.
Now I can promise you, prince of the Scyldings,
Henceforth in Heorot rest without rue
For you and your nobles; nor need you dread
Slaughter of follower, stalwart or stripling,°
Or death of earl, as of old you did.'
Into the hand of the aged leader,
The gray-haired hero, he gave the hilt,
The work of giants, the wonder of gold.
At the death of the demons the Danish lord
Took in his keeping the cunning craft,
The wondrous marvel, of mighty smiths;
When the world was freed of the ravaging fiend,
The foe of God, and his fearful dam

stalwart or stripling i.e. member of the *duguth*, the tried and seasoned warriors; or the *geogoth*, the young retainers

Marked with murder and badged° with blood,
The bound hilt passed to the best of kings
Who ever held sceptre beside two seas,
And dealt out treasure in Danish land!
Hrothgar spoke, beholding the hilt,
The ancient relic whereon was etched
An olden record of struggle and strife,
The flood that ravaged the giant race,°
The rushing deluge of ruin and death.
That evil kindred were alien to God,
But the Ruler avenged with the wrath of the deep!
On the hilt-guards, likewise, of gleaming gold
Was rightly carven in cunning runes,
Set forth and blazoned, for whom that blade,
With spiral tooling and twisted hilt,
That fairest of swords, was fashioned and smithied.
Then out spoke Hrothgar, Healfdene's son,
And all the retainers were silent and still:
'Well may he say, whose judgment is just,
Recalling to memory men of the past,
That this earl was born of a better stock!
Your fame, friend Beowulf, is blazoned abroad
Over all wide ways, and to every people.
In manful fashion have you showed your strength,
Your might and wisdom. My word I will keep,
The plighted friendship we formerly pledged.
Long shall you stand as a stay to your people,
A help to heroes, as Heremod° was not
To the Honor-Scyldings, to Ecgwela's° sons!
Not joy to kindred, but carnage and death,
He wrought as he ruled o'er the race of the Danes.
In savage anger he slew his comrades,
His table-companions, till, lawless and lone,
An odious outcast, he fled from men.
Though God had graced him with gifts of strength,
Over all men exalting him, still in his breast
A bloodthirsty spirit was rooted and strong.
He dealt not rings to the Danes for glory;
His lot was eternal torment of woe,
And lasting affliction. Learn from his fate!
Strive for virtue! I speak for your good;
In the wisdom of age I have told the tale.
'Tis a wondrous marvel how mighty God°

badged marked, distinguished by
The flood . . . race Noah's flood, which overwhelmed the wicked race of giants
Heremod see above, ll. 841 ff. His name means "Warlike disposition." King of the Danes before Scyld, he seems to have given promise of being a splendid king, but he turned out to be cruel, avaricious, and oppressive.
Ecgwela's a Danish king, otherwise unknown: his name means "Sword-wealth"
'Tis . . . God Hrothgar seizes the occasion to moralize the encounter—cf. the earlier Heremod digression above—in terms of spiritual attack and defense, the transitoriness of human life and happiness.

In gracious spirit bestows on men
The gift of wisdom, and goodly lands,
And princely power! He rules over all!
He suffers a man of lordly line
To set his heart on his own desires,
Awards him fullness of worldly joy,
A fair home-land, and the sway of cities,
The wide dominion of many a realm,
An ample kingdom, till, cursed with folly,
The thoughts of his heart take no heed of his end.
He lives in luxury, knowing not want,
Knowing no shadow of sickness or age;
No haunting sorrow darkens his spirit,
No hatred or discord deepens to war;
The world is sweet, to his every desire,
And evil assails not—until in his heart
Pride overpowering gathers and grows!
The warder slumbers, the guard of his spirit;
Too sound is that sleep, too sluggish the weight
Of worldly affairs, too pressing the Foe,
The Archer who looses the arrows of sin.
    Then is his heart pierced, under his helm,
His soul in his bosom, with bitter dart.
He has no defense for the fierce assaults
Of the loathsome Fiend. What he long has cherished
Seems all too little! In anger and greed
He gives no guerdon of plated rings.
Since God has granted him glory and wealth
He forgets the future, unmindful of Fate.
But it comes to pass in the day appointed
His feeble body withers and fails;
Death descends, and another seizes
His hoarded riches and rashly spends
The princely treasure, imprudent of heart.
Beloved Beowulf, best of warriors,
Avoid such evil and seek the good,
The heavenly wisdom. Beware of pride!
Now for a time you shall feel the fullness
And know the glory of strength, but soon
Sickness or sword shall strip you of might,
Or clutch of fire, or clasp of flood,
Or flight of arrow, or bite of blade,
Or relentless age; or the light of the eye
Shall darken and dim, and death on a sudden,
O lordly ruler, shall lay you low.
    A hundred half-years I've been head of the Ring-Danes,
Defending the folk against many a tribe
With spear-point and sword in the surges of battle
Till not one was hostile 'neath heaven's expanse.

But a loathsome change swept over the land,
Grief after gladness, when Grendel came,
That evil invader, that ancient foe!
Great sorrow of soul from his malice I suffered;
But thanks be to God who has spared me to see
His bloody head at the battle's end!
Join now in the banquet; have joy of the feast,
O mighty in battle! And the morrow shall bring
Exchange of treasure in ample store.'
Happy of heart the Geat leader hastened,
Took seat at the board as the good king bade.
Once more, as of old, brave heroes made merry
And tumult of revelry rose in the hall.
Then dark over men the night shadows deepened;
The host all arose, for Hrothgar was minded,
The gray, old Scylding, to go to his rest.
On Beowulf too, after labor of battle,
Came limitless longing and craving for sleep.
A hall-thane graciously guided the hero,
Weary and worn, to the place prepared,
Serving his wishes and every want
As befitted a mariner come from afar.
The stout-hearted warrior sank to his rest;
The lofty building, splendid and spacious,
Towered above him. His sleep was sound
Till the black-coated raven, blithesome of spirit,
Hailed the coming of Heaven's bliss.°

[*The Parting of Beowulf and Hrothgar*]

Then over the shadows uprose the sun.
The Geats were in haste, and eager of heart
To depart to their people. Beowulf longed
To embark in his boat, to set sail for his home.
The hero tendered the good sword Hrunting
To the son of Ecglaf,° bidding him bear
The lovely blade; gave thanks for the loan,
Called it a faithful friend in the fray,
Bitter in battle. The greathearted hero
Spoke no word in blame of the blade!
Arrayed in war-gear, and ready for sea,
The warriors bestirred them; and, dear to the Danes,
Beowulf sought the high seat of the king.
The gallant in war gave greeting to Hrothgar;
Beowulf spoke, the son of Ecgtheow:
'It is time at last to tell of our longing!
Our homes are far, and our hearts are fain
To seek again Hygelac over the sea.

Heaven's bliss i.e. the sun　　**son of Ecglaf** Unferth

You have welcomed us royally, harbored us well
As a man could wish; if I ever can win
Your affection more fully, O leader of heroes,
Swift shall you find me to serve you again!
If ever I learn, o'er the levels of ocean,
That neighboring nations beset you sore,
As in former days when foemen oppressed,
With thanes by the thousand I will hasten to help.
For I know that Hygelac, lord of the Geats,
Prince of the people, though young in years,
Will favor and further by word and deed
That my arm may aid you, and do you honor,
With stout ash-spear and succor of strength
In the press of need. And if princely Hrethric°
Shall purpose to come to the court of the Geats,
He will find there a legion of loyal friends.
That man fares best to a foreign country
Who himself is stalwart and stout of heart.'
Hrothgar addressed him, uttered his answer:
'Truly, these words has the Lord of wisdom
Set in your heart, for I never have harkened
To speech so sage from a man so young.
You have strength, and prudence, and wisdom of word!
I count it true if it come to pass
That point of spear in the press of battle,
Or deadly sickness, or stroke of sword,
Shall slay your leader, the son of Hrethel,
The prince of your people, and you still live,
The Sea-Geats could have no happier choice
If you would be willing to rule the realm,
As king to hold guard o'er the hoard and the heroes.
The longer I know you, the better I like you,°
Beloved Beowulf! You have brought it to pass
That between our peoples a lasting peace
Shall bind the Geats to the Danish-born;
And strife shall vanish, and war shall cease,
And former feuds, while I rule this realm.
And many a man, in the sharing of treasure,
Shall greet another with goodly gifts
O'er the gannet's° bath. And the ring-stemmed ship
Shall bear over ocean bountiful riches
In pledge of friendship. Our peoples, I know,
Shall be firm united toward foe and friend,
Faultless in all things, in fashion of old.'
Then the son of Healfdene, shelter of earls,
Bestowed twelve gifts on the hero in hall,

Hrethric eldest son of Hrothgar
The longer . . . you lit. "The temper of your heart pleases me more the more I see of it . . ."
gannet's sea-bird's

Bade him in safety with bounty of treasure
Seek his dear people, and soon return.
The peerless leader, the Scylding lord,
Kissed the good thane and clasped to his bosom
While tears welled fast from the old man's eyes.
Both chances he weighed in his wise, old heart,
But greatly doubted if ever again
They should meet at council or drinking of mead.
Nor could Hrothgar master—so dear was the man—
His swelling sorrow; a yearning love
For the dauntless hero, deep in his heart,
Burned through his blood. Beowulf, the brave,
Prizing his treasure and proud of the gold,
Turned away, treading the grassy plain.
The ring-stemmed sea-goer, riding at anchor,
Awaited her lord. There was loud acclaim
Of Hrothgar's gifts, as they went their way.
He was a king without failing or fault,
Till old age, master of all mankind,
Stripped him of power and pride of strength.

[*Beowulf Returns to Geatland*]

Then down to the sea came the band of the brave,
The host of young heroes in harness of war,
In their woven mail; and the coast-warden viewed
The heroes' return, as he heeded their coming!
No uncivil greeting he gave from the sea-cliff
As they strode to ship in their glistening steel;
But rode toward them and called their return
A welcome sight for their Weder kin
There on the sand the ring-stemmed ship,
The broad-bosomed bark, was loaded with war-gear,
With horses and treasure; the mast towered high
Over the riches of Hrothgar's hoard.
A battle-sword Beowulf gave to the boatwarden
Hilted with gold; and thereafter in hall
He had the more honor because of the heirloom,
The shining treasure. The ship was launched.
Cleaving the combers of open sea
They dropped the shoreline of Denmark astern.
A stretching sea-cloth, a bellying sail,
Was bent on the mast; there was groaning of timbers;
A gale was blowing; the boat drove on.
The foamy-necked plunger plowed through the billows,
The ring-stemmed ship through the breaking seas,
Till at last they sighted the sea-cliffs of Geatland,
The well-known headlands; and, whipped by the wind,
The boat drove shoreward and beached on the sand.
Straightway the harbor-watch strode to the seashore;

Long had he watched for the well-loved men,
Scanning the ocean with eager eyes!
The broad-bosomed boat he bound to the shingle
With anchor ropes, lest the rip of the tide
Should wrench from its mooring the comely craft.
From the good ship Beowulf bade them bear
The precious jewels and plated gold,
The princely treasure.° Not long was the path
That led to where Hygelac, son of Hrethel,
The giver of treasure, abode in his home
Hard by the sea-wall, hedged by his thanes.
Spacious the castle, splendid the king
On his high hall-seat; youthful was Hygd,°
Wise and well-born—though winters but few
Hæreth's daughter had dwelt at court.
She was noble of spirit, not sparing in gifts
Of princely treasure to the people of the Geats.

Of the pride of Thryth,° and her crimes, the fair folk-queen was free;
Thryth, of whose liegemen none dared by day, save only her lord,
Lift up his eyes to her face, lest his fate be a mortal bondage,
Seizure and fetters and sword, a blow of the patterned blade
Declaring his doom, and proclaiming the coming of death.
That is no way of a queen, nor custom of lovely lady,
Though peerless her beauty and proud, that a weaver of peace°
Should send a dear man to his death for a feigned affront.
But the kinsman of Hemming° at last made an end of her evil.
For men at the drinking of mead tell tale of a change,
How she wrought less ruin and wrong when, given in marriage
Gleaming with jewels and gold, to the high-born hero and young,
Over the fallow° flood she sailed, at her father's bidding
Seeking the land of Offa, and there while she lived,
Famed for goodness, fulfilled her fate on the throne.
She held high love for her lord, the leader of heroes,
The best, I have heard, of mankind or the children of men

treasure A gift to Beowulf would have at least to be formally offered to his lord, who could remit it to him.

Hygd Hygelac's queen, a young woman, daughter of Hæreth, is suddenly introduced into the narrative. She may have married Beowulf after Hygelac's death. Later, she offers the Geat throne to Beowulf in place of her young son Heardred.

Thryth "Strength." Some investigators take the name to be Modthryth. Thryth seems to be a version of the cruel queen who puts to death all except one who look at her. She is the equivalent of Brunhild in another Germanic romance, the *Nibelungenlied.* The male exception, in such tales, is sometimes the father of the cruel woman, or the hero who conquers her (for another, in the case of Brunhild). The digression is probably meant to throw Hygd's virtues into high relief by comparison with Thryth's evil nature.

weaver of peace a woman, one of whose functions it would be to heal differences—or, more specifically, a king's daughter given in marriage to seal a peace or alliance

kinsman of Hemming King Offa, husband of Thryth. According to an Anglian legend, he was the ancestor of another ruler, named Offa: the king of Mercia, one of the Anglo-Saxon kingdoms. Nothing more is known of his kinsman, Hemming. The use of Thryth to praise Hygd *per contrariam* modulates into a praise by direct comparison of the reformed Thryth, after her marriage to Offa, with Hygd. A version of the legend of Offa and Thryth (the Constance legend), with the cruelties reversed, is later told by Chaucer's Man of Law. Offa and his kinsmen are the only Englishmen mentioned in the poem.

fallow gray-brown

Between the two seas; for Offa, the stalwart, was honored
For his gifts and his greatness in war. With wisdom he governed;
And from him Eomær descended, Hemming's kinsman, grandson of Garmund,°
Stalwart and strong in war, and the helper of heroes.

Then the hero strode with his stalwart band
Across the stretches of sandy beach,
The wide sea-shingle. The world-candle shone,
The hot sun hasting on high from the south.
Marching together they made their way
To where in his stronghold the stout young king,
Ongentheow's slayer,° protector of earls,
Dispensed his treasure. Soon Hygelac heard
Of the landing of Beowulf, bulwark of men,
That his shoulder-companion had come to his court
Sound and safe from the strife of battle.
The hall was prepared, as the prince gave bidding,
Places made ready for much travelled men.
And he who came safe from the surges of battle
Sat by the side of the king himself,
Kinsman by kinsman; in courtly speech
His liege lord greeted the loyal thane
With hearty welcome. And Hæreth's daughter
Passed through the hall-building pouring the mead,
With courtesy greeting the gathered host,
Bearing the cup to the hands of the heroes.
In friendly fashion in high-built hall
Hygelac questioned his comrade and thane;
For an eager longing burned in his breast
To hear from the Sea-Geats the tale of their travels.
'How did you fare in your far sea-roving,
Beloved Beowulf, in your swift resolve
To sail to the conflict, the combat in Heorot,
Across the salt waves? Did you soften at all
The sorrows of Hrothgar, the weight of his woe?
Deeply I brooded with burden of care
For I had no faith in this far sea-venture
For one so beloved. Long I implored
That you go not against the murderous monster,
But let the South Danes settle the feud
Themselves with Grendel. To God be thanks
That my eyes behold you unharmed and unhurt.'
Beowulf spoke, the son of Ecgtheow:
'My dear lord Hygelac, many have heard°

Eomær . . . Garmund Little or nothing is known of these two.

Ongentheow's slayer Hygelac did not kill Ongentheow with his own hands, though he led the Geats in their attack on Ongentheow's people, the Scylfings. The full story is told below (ll. 2749 ff.).

many . . . heard lit. "from many it is not concealed"

Of that famous grapple 'twixt Grendel and me,
The bitter struggle and strife in the hall
Where he formerly wrought such ruin and wrong,
Such lasting sorrow for Scylding men!
All that I avenged! Not any on earth
Who longest lives of that loathsome brood,
No kin of Grendel cloaked in his crime,
Has cause to boast of that battle by night!
First, in that country, I fared to the hall
With greeting for Hrothgar; Healfdene's kinsman
Learned all my purpose, assigned me a place
Beside his own son. 'Twas a happy host!
I never have seen under span of heaven
More mirth of heroes sitting at mead!
The peerless queen, the peace-pledge° of peoples,
Passed on her round through the princely hall;
There was spurring of revels, dispensing of rings,
Ere the noble woman went to her seat.
  At times in the host the daughter of Hrothgar
Offered the beaker to earls in turn;
Freawaru men called her, the feasters in hall,
As she held out to heroes the well-wrought cup.
Youthful and gleaming with jewels of gold
To the fair son of Froda° the maiden is plighted.
For the Scylding leader, the lord of the land,
Deems it wise counsel, accounting it gain,
To settle by marriage the murderous feud,
The bloody slaughter! But seldom for long
Does the spear go ungrasped when a prince has perished,
Though the bride in her beauty be peerless and proud!
Ill may it please the Heathobard prince
And all his thanes, when he leads his lady
Into the hall, that a Danish noble
Should be welcomed there by the Heathobard host.
For on him shall flash their forefathers' heirlooms,°
Hard-edged, ring-hilted, the Heathobards' hoard
When of old they had war-might, nor wasted in battle
Their lives and the lives of their well-loved thanes.
  Then an aged spearman° shall speak at the beer-feast,
The treasure beholding with sorrow of heart,
Remembering sadly the slaughter of men,

peace-pledge i.e. her marriage had been part of a peace settlement between nations

son of Froda Froda was king of the Heathobards, an unidentified Germanic tribe. Freawaru, Hrothgar's daughter, had been betrothed to Ingeld, Froda's son, in pledge of peace between the Danes and the Heathobards. The poet's purpose in putting the story of the Danish-Heathobard feud into the mouth of Beowulf is much debated: it may be intended as a sort of prophecy or as a display of political wisdom on the part of the Geat, who can see the dangers of Hrothgar's attempt to settle the feud by marriage.

heirlooms Armor and ornaments that had been Heathobard property before they were captured by the Danes; they will remind the Heathobards of vengeance untaken.

spearman a Heathobard

Grimly goading the young hero's spirit,
Spurring to battle, speaking this word:
"Do you see, my lord, the sword of your father,
The blade he bore to the last of his fights,
The pride of his heart as, under his helmet,
The Scyldings slew him, the savage Danes,
When Withergyld° fell, and after the slaughter,
The fall of heroes, they held the field?
And now a son of those bloody butchers,
Proud in his trappings, tramps into hall
And boasts of the killing, clothed with the treasure
That is yours by your birthright to have and to hold?"
    Over and over the old man will urge him,
With cutting reminders recalling the past
Till it comes at last that the lady's thane,°
For the deeds of his father, shall forfeit his life
In a bloody slaughter, slain by the sword,
While the slayer goes scatheless knowing the land.
On both sides then shall sword-oaths be broken
When hate boils up within Ingeld's heart,
And his love of his lady grows cooler and lessens
Because of his troubles. I count not true
Heathobard faith, nor their part in the peace,
Nor their friendship firm to the Danish folk.
    I must now speak on, dispenser of treasure,
Further of Grendel, till fully you know
How we fared in that fierce and furious fight!
When the jewel of heaven had journeyed o'er earth,
The wrathful demon, the deadly foe,
Stole through the darkness spying us out
Where still unharmed we guarded the gold-hall.
But doom in battle and bitter death
Were Handscio's° fate! He was first to perish
Though girded with weapon and famous in war.
Grendel murdered him, mangled his body,
Bolted the dear man's bloody corpse.
No sooner for that would the slaughterous spirit,
Bloody of tooth and brooding on evil,
Turn empty-handed away from the hall!
The mighty monster made trial of my strength
Clutching me close with his ready claw.
Wide and wondrous his huge pouch° hung
Cunningly fastened, and fashioned with skill
From skin of dragon by devil's craft.
Therein the monster was minded to thrust me

Withergyld a Heathobard warrior
lady's thane a Dane attendant on Freawaru
Handscio's a Geat warrior companion of Beowulf's
pouch lit. "glove"; a huge glove is carried by trolls in Old Norse stories

Sinless and blameless, and many beside.
But it might not be, when I rose in wrath,
And fronted the hell-fiend face to face.
Too long is the tale how I took requital
On the cursed foe for his every crime,
But the deeds I did were a lasting honor,
Beloved prince, to your people's name.
He fled away, and a fleeting while
Possessed his life and the world's delights;
But he left in Heorot his severed hand,
A bloody reminder to mark his track.
Humbled in spirit and wretched in heart
Down he sank to the depths of the pool.
When the morrow fell, and we feasted together,
The Scylding ruler rewarded me well
For the bloody strife, in guerdon bestowing
Goodly treasure of beaten gold.
There was song and revel. The aged Scylding
From well-stored mind spoke much of the past.
A warrior sang to the strains of the glee-wood,°
Sometimes melodies mirthful and joyous,
Sometimes lays that were tragic and true.
And the great-hearted ruler at times would tell
A tale of wonder in fitting words.
Heavy with years the white-haired warrior
Grieved for his youth and the strength that was gone;
And his heart was moved by the weight of his winters
And many a memory out of the past.
All the long day we made merry together
Till another night came to the children of men,
And quickly the mother of Grendel was minded
To wreak her vengeance; raging with grief
She came to the hall where the hate of the Weders
Had slain her son. But the hideous hag
Avenged his killing; with furious clutch
She seized a warrior—the soul of Æschere,
Wise and aged, went forth from the flesh!
Not at all could the Danes, when the morrow dawned,
Set brand° to his body or burn on the bale°
Their well-loved comrade. With fiendish clasp
She carried his corpse through the fall of the force.°
That was to Hrothgar, prince of the people,
Sorest of sorrows that ever befell!
For your sake the sad-hearted hero° implored me
To prove my valor and, venturing life,°

glee-wood harp
brand i.e. firebrand
bale funeral pyre
force waterfall, cascade
hero Hrothgar
venturing life lit. "by your life," perhaps "for your sake"

To win renown in the watery depths.
He promised reward. Full well is it known
How I humbled the horrible guard of the gulf.
Hand to hand for a space we struggled
Till the swirling eddies were stained with blood;
With cleaving sword-edge I severed the head
Of Grendel's hag in that hall of strife.
Not easily thence did I issue alive,
But my death was not fated; not yet was I doomed!
Then the son of Healfdene, the shelter of earls,
Gave many a treasure to mark the deed.
The good king governed with courtly custom;
In no least way did I lose reward,
The meed° of my might; but he gave me treasure,
Healfdene's son, to my heart's desire.
These riches I bring you, ruler of heroes,
And warmly tender with right good will.
Save for you, King Hygelac, few are my kinsmen,
Few are the favors but come from you.'
Then he bade men bring the boar-crested headpiece,
The towering helmet, and steel-gray sark,°
The splendid war-sword, and spoke this word:
'The good king Hrothgar gave me this gift,
This battle-armor, and first to you
Bade tell the tale of his friendly favor.
He said King Heorogar,° lord of the Scyldings,
Long had worn it, but had no wish
To leave the mail to his manful son,
The dauntless Heoroweard, dear though he was!
Well may you wear it! Have joy of it all.'
As I've heard the tale, he followed the trappings
With four bay° horses, matched and swift,
Graciously granting possession of both,
The steeds and the wealth. 'Tis the way of a kinsman,
Not weaving in secret the wiles of malice
Nor plotting the fall of a faithful friend.
To his kinsman Hygelac, hardy in war,
The heart of the nephew was trusty and true;
Dear to each was the other's good!
To Hygd, as I've heard, he presented three horses
Gaily saddled, slender and sleek,
And the gleaming necklace Wealhtheow gave,
A peerless gift from a prince's daughter.
With the gracious guerdon, the goodly jewel,
Her breast thereafter was well bedecked.

meed reward
sark shirt of mail
Heorogar Hrothgar's brother and predecessor as king of the Danes
bay lit. "apple-fallow"—bright brown

So the son of Ecgtheow bore himself bravely,
Known for his courage and courteous deeds,
Strove after honor, slew not his comrades
In drunken brawling; nor brutal his mood.
But the bountiful gifts which the Lord God gave him
He held with a power supreme among men.
He had long been scorned,° when the sons of the Geats
Accounted him worthless; the Weder lord
Held him not high among heroes in hall.
Laggard they deemed him, slothful° and slack.
But time brought solace for all his ills!
Then the battle-bold king, the bulwark of heroes,
Bade bring a battle-sword banded with gold,
The heirloom° of Hrethel; no sharper steel,
No lovelier treasure, belonged to the Geats.
He laid the war-blade on Beowulf's lap,
Gave him a hall and a stately seat
And hides° seven thousand. Inherited lands
Both held by birth-fee, home and estate.°
But one held rule o'er the spacious realm,
And higher therein his order and rank.

[*The Fire-Dragon and the Treasure*]

It later befell in the years that followed
After Hygelac sank in the surges of war,
And the sword slew Heardred° under his shield
When the Battle-Scylfings, those bitter fighters,
Invaded the land of the victor-folk
Overwhelming Hereric's nephew in war,
That the kingdom came into Beowulf's hand.
For fifty winters he governed it well,
Aged and wise with the wisdom of years,
Till a fire-drake° flying in darkness of night
Began to ravage and work his will.
On the upland heath he guarded a hoard,
A stone barrow lofty. Under it lay
A path concealed from the sight of men.
There a thief broke in on the heathen treasure,
Laid hand on a flagon all fretted with gold,

scorned We have no other information on Beowulf's younger, feebler days. The scorned weakling who grows into a mighty hero is a frequent figure in folktales.
slothful weak
heirloom i.e. inherited by Hrothgar from his father
hides a huge tract of land. A hide was basically the area of land required for the subsistence of one free peasant family and its dependents, or, alternatively, as much land as could be worked by one plow in one year. Thus the size varies with the peasant's standard of living in different parts of the country from 40 to 120 acres. The gift to Beowulf is a princely one.
Inherited . . . estate Both Hygelac and Beowulf had inherited land, a house, and the estate that went with it.
Heardred The story is told more fully below. Heardred, Hygelac's son, succeeded his father as king, but was killed by the Swedes (Battle-Scylfings) on his own territory. Hereric was probably his maternal uncle, Hygd's brother.
fire-drake a fiery dragon, such as the *Anglo-Saxon Chronicle* records as having been seen in the late 8th century.

As the dragon discovered, though cozened in sleep
By the pilferer's cunning. The people soon found
That the mood of the dragon was roused to wrath!°
Not at all with intent, of his own free will,
Did he ravish the hoard, who committed the wrong;
But in dire distress the thrall° of a thane,
A guilty fugitive fleeing the lash,
Forced his way in. There a horror befell him!
Yet the wretched exile escaped from the dragon,
Swift in retreat when the terror arose.
A flagon he took. There, many such treasures
Lay heaped in that earth-hall where the owner of old
Had carefully hidden the precious hoard,
The countless wealth of a princely clan.
Death came upon them in days gone by
And he who lived longest, the last of his line,
Guarding the treasure and grieving for friend,
Deemed it his lot that a little while only
He too might hold that ancient hoard.
A barrow new-built near the ocean billows
Stood cunningly° fashioned beneath the cliff;
Into the barrow the ring-warden bore
The princely treasure, the precious trove
Of golden wealth, and these words he spoke:
'Keep thou, O Earth, what men could not keep—
This costly treasure—it came from thee!
Baleful slaughter has swept away,
Death in battle, the last of my blood;
They have lived their lives; they have left the mead-hall.
Now I have no one to wield the sword,
No one to polish the plated cup,
The precious flagon—the host is fled.
The hard-forged helmet fretted with gold
Shall be stripped of its inlay; the burnishers sleep
Whose charge was to brighten the battle-masks.
Likewise the corselet that countered in war
'Mid clashing of bucklers the bite of the sword—
Corselet and warrior decay into dust;
Mailed coat and hero are moveless and still.
No mirth of gleewood, no music of harp,
No good hawk swinging in flight through the hall;
No swift steed stamps in the castle yard;
Death has ravished an ancient race.'
So sad of mood he bemoaned his sorrow,

There . . . wrath (ll. 2087–91) The manuscript is badly damaged at this point; so it is possible only to guess at the precise meaning of the text.

thrall a slave escaping from his master

cunningly lit. "made difficult of access"

Lonely and sole survivor of all,
Restless by day and wretched by night
Till the clutch of death caught at his heart.
Then the goodly treasure was found unguarded
By the venomous dragon enveloped in flame,
The old naked night-foe flying in darkness,
Haunting the barrows; a bane that brings
A fearful dread to the dwellers of earth.
His wont is to hunt out a hoard under ground
And guard heathen gold, growing old with the years.
But no whit for that is his fortune more fair!
For three hundred winters this waster of peoples
Held the huge treasure-hall under the earth
Till the robber aroused him to anger and rage,
Stole the rich beaker and bore to his master,
Imploring his lord for a compact of peace.
So the hoard was robbed and its riches plundered;
To the wretch was granted the boon that he begged;
And his liege-lord first had view of the treasure,
The ancient work of the men of old.
Then the worm awakened and war was kindled,
The rush of the monster along the rock,
When the fierce one found the tracks of the foe;
He had stepped too close in his stealthy cunning
To the dragon's head. But a man undoomed
May endure with ease disaster and woe
If he has His favor who wields the world.
Swiftly the fire-drake sought through the plain
The man who wrought him this wrong in his sleep.
Inflamed and savage he circled the mound,
But the waste was deserted—no man was in sight.
The worm's mood was kindled to battle and war;
Time and again he returned to the barrow
Seeking the treasure-cup. Soon he was sure
That a man had plundered the precious gold.
Enraged and restless the hoard-warden waited
The gloom of evening. The guard of the mound
Was swollen with anger; the fierce one resolved
To requite with fire the theft of the cup.
Then the day was sped as the worm desired;
Lurking no longer within his wall
He sallied forth surrounded with fire,
Encircled with flame. For the folk of the land
The beginning was dread as the ending was grievous
That came so quickly upon their lord.
Then the baleful stranger belched fire and flame,
Burned the bright dwellings—the glow of the blaze
Filled hearts with horror. The hostile flier

Was minded to leave there nothing alive.
From near and from far the war of the dragon,
The might of the monster, was widely revealed
So that all could see how the ravaging scather
Hated and humbled the Geatish folk.
Then he hastened back ere the break of dawn
To his secret den and the spoil of gold.
He had compassed the land with a flame of fire,
A blaze of burning; he trusted the wall,
The sheltering mound, and the strength of his might—
But his trust betrayed him! The terrible news
Was brought to Beowulf, told for a truth,
That his home was consumed in the surges of fire,
The goodly dwelling and throne of the Geats.
The heart of the hero was heavy with anguish,
The greatest of sorrows; in his wisdom he weened
He had grievously angered the Lord Everlasting,
Blamefully broken the ancient law.
Dark thoughts stirred in his surging bosom,
Welled in his breast, as was not his wont.
The flame of the dragon had levelled the fortress,
The people's stronghold washed by the wave.
But the king of warriors, prince of the Weders,
Exacted an ample revenge for it all.
The lord of warriors and leader of earls
Bade work him of iron a wondrous shield,
Knowing full well that wood could not serve him
Nor linden defend him against the flame.
The stalwart hero was doomed to suffer
The destined end of his days on earth;
Likewise the worm, though for many a winter
He had held his watch o'er the wealth of the hoard.
The ring-prince scorned to assault the dragon
With a mighty army, or host of men.
He feared not the combat, nor counted of worth
The might of the worm, his courage and craft,
Since often aforetime, beset in the fray,
He had safely issued from many an onset,
Many a combat and, crowned with success,
Purged of evil the hall of Hrothgar
And crushed out Grendel's loathsome kin.
Nor was that the least of his grim engagements
When Hygelac fell, great Hrethel's son;
When the lord of the people, the prince of the Geats,
Died of his wounds in the welter of battle,
Perished in Friesland, smitten with swords.
Thence Beowulf came by his strength in swimming;
Thirty sets of armor he bore on his back

As he hasted to ocean. The Hetware° men
Had no cause to boast of their prowess in battle
When they gathered against him with linden shields.
But few of them ever escaped his assault
Or came back alive to the homes they had left;
So the son of Ecgtheow swam the sea-stretches,
Lonely and sad, to the land of his skin.
Hygd then tendered him kingdom and treasure,
Wealth of riches and royal throne,
For she had no hope with Hygelac dead
That her son could defend the seat of his fathers
From foreign foemen. But even in need,
No whit the more could they move the hero
To be Heardred's liege,° or lord of the land.
But he fostered Heardred with friendly counsel,
With honor and favor among the folk,
Till he came of age and governed the Geats.
Then the sons of Ohthere° fleeing in exile
Sought out Heardred over the sea.
They had risen against the lord of the Scylfings,
Best of the sea-kings, bestower of rings,
An illustrious prince in the land of the Swedes.
So Heardred fell. For harboring exiles
The son of Hygelac died by the sword.
Ongentheow's son,° after Heardred was slain,
Returned to his home, and Beowulf held
The princely power and governed the Geats.
He was a good king, grimly requiting
In later days the death of his prince.
Crossing the sea with a swarming host
He befriended Eadgils,° Ohthere's son,
In his woe and affliction, with weapons and men;
He took revenge in a savage assault,
And slew the king. So Ecgtheow's son
Had come in safety through all his battles,
His bitter struggles and savage strife,
To the day when he fought with the deadly worm.
With eleven comrades, kindled to rage
The Geat lord went to gaze on the dragon.
Full well he knew how the feud arose,
The fearful affliction; for into his hold

Hetware men i.e. the Atuarii
Heardred's liege Beowulf, though free to do so, refused to usurp the Geatish throne which rightfully belonged to Hygelac's son Heardred. Instead, he acted as the young king's counsellor and protector.
sons of Ohthere the Swedes Eanmund and Eadgils, driven into exile by their uncle Onela, who had usurped the throne of Ohthere and made himself king of the Scylfings (Swedes). Heardred took them into the protection of the Geat court and was attacked by Onela for this act of hospitality, and killed, along with Eanmund. Beowulf then ruled the kingdom, and acted as Eadgils's protector.
Ongentheow's son Onela
befriended Eadgils Beowulf helped Eadgils to get back the Swedish throne from Onela. It is not clear whether it is Eadgils or Beowulf who kills Onela.

From hand of finder the flagon had come.
The thirteenth man in the hurrying throng
Was the sorrowful captive who caused the feud.
With woeful spirit and all unwilling
Needs must he guide them, for he only knew
Where the earth-hall stood near the breaking billows
Filled with jewels and beaten gold.
The monstrous warden, waiting for battle,
Watched and guarded the hoarded wealth.
No easy bargain for any of men
To seize that treasure! The stalwart king,
Gold-friend of Geats, took seat on the headland,
Hailed his comrades and wished them well.
Sad was his spirit, restless and ready,
And the march of Fate immeasurably near;
Fate that would strike, seek his soul's treasure,
And deal asunder the spirit and flesh.
Not long was his life encased in the body!
    Beowulf spoke, the son of Ecgtheow:
'Many an ordeal I endured in youth,
And many a battle. I remember it all.
I was seven winters old when the prince of the people,
The lord of the treasure-hoard, Hrethel the king,
From the hand of my father had me and held me,
Recalling our kinship with treasure and feast.
As long as he lived I was no less beloved,
As thane in his hall, than the sons of his house,
Herebeald and Hæthcyn and Hygelac, my lord.
For the eldest brother the bed of death
Was foully fashioned by brother's deed
When Hæthcyn let fly a bolt from his horn-bow,°
Missed the mark, and murdered his lord;
Brother slew brother with bloody shaft—
A tragic deed and beyond atonement,
A foul offense to sicken the heart!
Yet none the less was the lot of the prince
To lay down his soul and his life, unavenged.°
    Even so sad and sorrowful is it,
And bitter to bear, to an old man's heart,
Seeing his young son swing on the gallows.°
He wails his dirge and his wild lament
While his son hangs high, a spoil to the raven;
His aged heart can contrive no help.
Each dawn brings grief for the son that is gone

horn-bow Either a bow tipped with a horn or curved like a horn; the bow was not a common Anglo-Saxon weapon.
unavenged The crime could not be wiped out by *wergild* or by vengeance since it was unwitting and the king was father of both parties.
gallows Similarly, since no *wergild* or vengeance could be exacted for an executed criminal, his father could only mourn.

And his heart has no hope of another heir,
Seeing the one has gone to his grave.
In the house of his son he gazes in sorrow
On wine-hall deserted and swept by the wind,
Empty of joy. The horsemen and heroes
Sleep in the grave. No sound of the harp,
No welcoming revels as often of old!
He goes to his bed with his burden of grief;
To his spirit it seems that dwelling and land
Are empty and lonely, lacking his son.
So the helm of the Weders° yearned after Herebeald
And welling sadness surged in his heart.
He could not avenge the feud on the slayer
Nor punish the prince for the loathsome deed,
Though he loved him no longer, nor held him dear.
Because of this sorrow that sore befell
He left life's joys for the heavenly light,
Granting his sons, as a good man will,
Cities and land, when he went from the world.
Then across the wide water was conflict and war,
A striving and struggle of Swedes and Geats,
A bitter hatred, when Hrethel died.
Ongentheow's sons° were dauntless and daring,
Cared not for keeping of peace overseas;
But often around Hreosnabeorh° slaughtered and slew.
My kinsmen avenged the feud and the evil,
As many have heard, though one of the Weders
Paid with his life—a bargain full bitter!
Hæthcyn's° fate was to fall in the fight.
It is often recounted, a kinsman with sword-edge
Avenged in the morning the murderer's deed
When Ongentheow met Eofor. Helm split asunder;
The aged Scylfing° sank down to his death.
The hand that felled him remembered the feud
And drew not back from the deadly blow.
For all the rich gifts that Hygelac gave me
I repaid him in battle with shining sword,
As chance was given. He granted me land,
A gracious dwelling and goodly estate.
Nor needed he seek of the Gifths,° or the Spear-Danes,
Or in Swedish land, a lesser in war

helm . . . Weders protector (helmet) of the Geats, i.e. Hrethel
Ongentheow's sons Onela and Ohthere, of the Swedish royal family
Hreosnabeorh a hill in Geat territory
Hæthcyn a prince of the Geats, second son of Hrethel, who had accidentally killed his elder brother Herebeald with an arrow and therefore succeeded his father on the throne. Hæthcyn was killed by Ongentheow, the Swedish king (see below) in battle at Ravenswood and was succeeded by Hygelac. Eofor avenged Hæthcyn's death by killing Ongentheow.
aged Scylfing Ongentheow
Gifths an East Germanic tribe, the Gepidae, having affinities with the Goths. They originally lived near the delta of the Vistula, but moved in the third century down to Hungary. Here they still seem to be thought of as a Baltic people.

To fight for pay; in the press of battle
I was always before him alone in the van.
So shall I bear me while life-days last,
While the sword holds out that has served me well
Early and late since I slew Dæghrefn,°
The Frankish hero, before the host.
He brought no spoil from the field of battle,
No corselet of mail to the Frisian king.
Not by the sword the warden of standards,
The stalwart warrior, fell in the fight.
My battle-grip shattered the bones of his body
And silenced the heart-beat. But now with the sword,
With hand and hard blade, I must fight for the treasure.'

[*Beowulf and Wiglaf Slay the Dragon*]

For the last time Beowulf uttered his boast:
'I came in safety through many a conflict
In the days of my youth; and now even yet,
Old as I am, I will fight this feud,
Do manful deeds, if the dire destroyer
Will come from his cavern to meet my sword.'
The king for the last time greeted his comrades,
Bold helmet-bearers and faithful friends:
'I would bear no sword nor weapon to battle
With the evil worm, if I knew how else
I could close with the fiend, as I grappled with Grendel.
From the worm I look for a welling of fire,
A belching of venom, and therefore I bear
Shield and byrny. Not one foot's space
Will I flee from the monster, the ward of the mound.
It shall fare with us both in the fight at the wall
As Fate shall allot, the lord of mankind.
Though bold in spirit, I make no boast
As I go to fight with the flying serpent.
Clad in your corselets and trappings of war,
By the side of the barrow abide you to see
Which of us twain may best after battle
Survive his wounds. Not yours the adventure,
Nor the mission of any, save mine alone,
To measure his strength with the monstrous dragon
And play the part of a valiant earl.
By deeds of daring I'll gain the gold
Or death in battle shall break your lord.'
Then the stalwart rose with his shield upon him,
Bold under helmet, bearing his sark
Under the stone-cliff; he trusted the strength

Dæghrefn a Frankish (Huga) warrior, standard bearer, and perhaps slayer of Hygelac on his last expedition; killed by Beowulf at that time

Of his single might. Not so does a coward!
He who survived through many a struggle,
Many a combat and crashing of troops,
Saw where a stone-arch stood by the wall
And a gushing stream broke out from the barrow.
Hot with fire was the flow of its surge,
Nor could any abide near the hoard unburned,
Nor endure its depths, for the flame of the dragon.
Then the lord of the Geats in the grip of his fury
Gave shout of defiance; the strong-heart stormed.
His voice rang out with the rage of battle,
Resounding under the hoary stone.
Hate was aroused; the hoard-warden knew
'Twas the voice of a man. No more was there time
To sue for peace; the breath of the serpent,
A blast of venom, burst from the rock.
The ground resounded; the lord of the Geats
Under the barrow swung up his shield
To face the dragon; the coiling foe
Was gathered to strike in the deadly strife.
The stalwart hero had drawn his sword,
His ancient heirloom of tempered edge;
In the heart of each was fear of the other!
The shelter of kinsmen stood stout of heart
Under towering shield as the great worm coiled;
Clad in his war-gear he waited the rush.
In twisting folds the flame-breathing dragon
Sped to its fate. The shield of the prince
For a lesser while guarded his life and his body
Than heart had hoped. For the first time then
It was not his portion to prosper in war;
Fate did not grant him glory in battle!
Then lifted his arm the lord of the Geats
And smote the worm with his ancient sword
But the brown° edge failed as it fell on bone,
And cut less deep than the king had need
In his sore distress. Savage in mood
The ward of the barrow countered the blow
With a blast of fire; wide sprang the flame.
The ruler of Geats had no reason to boast;
His unsheathed iron, his excellent sword,
Had weakened as it should not, had failed in the fight.
It was no easy journey for Ecgtheow's son
To leave this world and against his will
Find elsewhere a dwelling! So every man shall
In the end give over this fleeting life.
    Not long was the lull. Swiftly the battlers

brown lit. "bright," "shining"

Renewed their grapple. The guard of the hoard
Grew fiercer in fury. His venomous breath
Beat in his breast. Enveloped in flame
The folk-leader suffered a sore distress.
No succoring band of shoulder-companions,
No sons of warriors aided him then
By valor in battle. They fled to the forest
To save their lives; but a sorrowful spirit
Welled in the breast of one of the band.
The call of kinship can never be stilled
In the heart of a man who is trusty and true.
His name was Wiglaf,° Weohstan's° son,
A prince of the Scylfings, a peerless thane,
Ælfhere's° kinsman; he saw his king
Under his helmet smitten with heat.
He thought of the gifts which his lord had given,
The wealth and the land of the Wægmunding line
And all the folk-rights his father had owned;
Nor could he hold back, but snatched up his buckler,
His linden shield and his ancient sword,
Heirloom of Eanmund, Ohthere's son,
Whom Weohstan slew with the sword in battle,
Wretched and friendless and far from home.
The brown-hued° helmet he bore to his kinsmen,
The ancient blade and the byrny of rings.
These Onela° gave him—his nephew's arms—
Nor called for vengeance, nor fought the feud,
Though Weohstan had slaughtered his brother's son.°
He° held the treasures for many half-years,
The byrny and sword, till his son was of age
For manful deeds, as his father before him.
Among the Geats he gave him of war-gear
Countless numbers of every kind;
Then, full of winters, he left the world,
Gave over this life. And Wiglaf, the lad,

Wiglaf The passage seems at first contradictory about the origins of Wiglaf in that he is said to be both Swede (Scylfing) and Geat (the Wægmundings were the Geat family to which Beowulf belonged). But the poet may mean that the young Wiglaf is of Swedish royal blood and now under the protection of Beowulf, as one of his household. This system of putting children, sometimes as young as seven years old, to be brought up in another family was common among Germanic peoples.

Weohstan's Wiglaf's father, a Swede, may also have changed his allegiance and become a vassal of Beowulf's. Previously, he had taken part in Swedish King Onela's attack on Heardred, king of the Geats, and himself killed Eanmund, whom Heardred was protecting, receiving Eanmund's sword and armor as the spoils of war. Wiglaf had inherited Eanmund's sword from his father and was now using it against the dragon.

Ælfhere not otherwise known

brown-hued lit. "shining bright"

Onela All the spoils of war belonged by right to the lord, who apportioned them among his followers.

Nor called . . . brother's son The remark has nothing to do with *wergild*: in the heroic age the normal thing would have been for Eanmund's killing to be avenged in blood by his uncle Onela, but Eanmund, having fought against his uncle, has forfeited this family right and Onela is, on the contrary, grateful to Weohstan for killing his kinsman, so that he rewards Weohstan instead of demanding retribution from him.

he Weohstan

Was to face with his lord the first of his battles,
The hazard of war. But his heart did not fail
Nor the blade of his kinsman weaken in war,
As the worm soon found when they met in the fight!
    Wiglaf spoke in sorrow of soul,
With bitter reproach rebuking his comrades:°
'I remember the time, as we drank in the mead-hall,
When we swore to our lord who bestowed these rings
That we would repay for the war-gear and armor,
The hard swords and helmets, if need like this
Should ever befall him. He chose us out
From all the host for this high adventure,
Deemed us worthy of glorious deeds,
Gave me these treasures, regarded us all
As high-hearted bearers of helmet and spear—
Though our lord himself, the shield of his people,
Thought single-handed to finish this feat,
Since of mortal men his measure was most
Of feats of daring and deeds of fame.
Now is the day that our lord has need
Of the strength and courage of stalwart men.
Let us haste to succor his sore distress
In the horrible heat and the merciless flame.
God knows I had rather the fire should enfold
My body and limbs with my gold-friend and lord.
Shameful it seems that we carry our shields
Back to our homes ere we harry the foe
And ward the life of the Weder king.
Full well I know it is not his due
That he alone, of the host of the Geats,
Should suffer affliction and fall in the fight.
One helmet and sword, one byrny and shield,
Shall serve for us both in the storm of strife.'
Then Wiglaf dashed through the deadly reek
In his battle-helmet to help his lord.
Brief were his words: 'Beloved Beowulf,
Summon your strength, remember the vow
You made of old in the years of youth
Not to allow your glory to lessen
As long as you lived. With resolute heart,
And dauntless daring, defend your life
With all your force. I fight at your side!'
    Once again the worm, when the words were spoken,
The hideous foe in a horror of flame,
Rushed in rage at the hated men.
Wiglaf's buckler was burned to the boss

comrades a typical *comitatus* speech

In the billows of fire; his byrny of mail
Gave the young hero no help or defense.
But he stoutly pressed on under shield of his kinsman
When his own was consumed in the scorching flame.
Then the king once more was mindful of glory,
Swung his great sword-blade with all his might
And drove it home on the dragon's head.
But Nægling° broke, it failed in the battle,
The blade of Beowulf, ancient and gray.
It was not his lot that edges of iron
Could help him in battle; his hand was too strong,
Overtaxed, I am told, every blade with its blow.
Though he bore a wondrous hard weapon to war,
No whit the better was he thereby!
    A third time then the terrible scather,
The monstrous dragon inflamed with the feud,
Rushed on the king when the opening offered,
Fierce and flaming; fastened its fangs
In Beowulf's throat; he was bloodied with gore;
His life-blood streamed from the welling wound.
    As they tell the tale, in the king's sore need
His shoulder-companion showed forth his valor,
His craft° and courage, and native strength.
To the head of the dragon he paid no heed,
Though his hand was burned as he helped his king.
A little lower the stalwart struck
At the evil beast, and his blade drove home
Plated° and gleaming. The fire began
To lessen and wane. The king of the Weders
Summoned his wits; he drew the dagger
He wore on his corselet, cutting and keen,
And slit asunder the worm with the blow.
So they felled the foe and wrought their revenge;
The kinsmen together had killed the dragon.
So a man should be when the need is bitter!
That was the last fight Beowulf fought;
That was the end of his work in the world.

[*Beowulf's Death*]

The wound which the dragon had dealt him began
To swell and burn; and soon he could feel
The baneful venom inflaming his breast.
The wise, old warrior sank down by the wall
And stared at the work of the giants of old,°
The arches of stone and the standing columns
Upholding the ancient earth-hall within.

Nægling Beowulf's sword
craft skill in battle
plated or ornamented
work . . . old ancient buildings, usually taken to be Roman ruins

His loyal thane, the kindest of comrades,
Saw Beowulf bloody and broken in war;
In his hands bore water and bathed his leader,
And loosened the helm from his dear lord's head.
Beowulf spoke, though his hurt was sore,
The wounds of battle grievous and grim.
Full well he weened that his life was ended,
And all the joy of his years on earth;
That his days were done, and Death most near:
'My armor and sword I would leave to my son
Had Fate but granted, born of my body,
An heir to follow me after I'm gone.
For fifty winters I've ruled this realm,
And never a lord of a neighboring land
Dared strike with terror or seek with sword.
In my life I abode by the lot assigned,
Kept well what was mine, courted no quarrels,
Swore no false oaths. And now for all this
Though my hurt is grievous, my heart is glad.
When life leaves body, the Lord of mankind
Cannot lay to my charge the killing of kinsmen!
Go quickly, dear Wiglaf, to gaze on the gold
Beneath the hoar stone. The dragon lies still
In the slumber of death, despoiled of his hoard.
Make haste that my eyes may behold the treasure,
The gleaming jewels, the goodly store,
And, glad of the gold, more peacefully leave
The life and the realm I have ruled so long.'
Then Weohstan's son, as they tell the tale,
Clad in his corselet and trappings of war,
Hearkened at once to his wounded lord.
Under roof of the barrow he broke his way.
Proud in triumph he stood by the seat,
Saw glittering jewels and gold on the ground,
The den of the dragon, the old dawn-flier,
And all the wonders along the walls.
Great bowls and flagons of bygone men
Lay all unburnished and barren of gems,
Many a helmet ancient and rusted,
Many an arm-ring cunningly wrought.
Treasure and gold, though hid in the ground,
Override man's wishes, hide them who will!
High o'er the hoard he beheld a banner,°
Greatest of wonders, woven° with skill,
All wrought of gold; its radiance lighted
The vasty ground and the glittering gems.

banner The word may mean a standard, not a flag.

woven "Worked" is more accurate.

But no sign of the worm! The sword-edge had slain him.
As I've heard the tale, the hero unaided
Rifled those riches of giants of old,
The hoard in the barrow, and heaped in his arms
Beakers and platters, picked what he would
And took the banner, the brightest of signs.
The ancient sword with its edge of iron
Had slain the worm who watched o'er the wealth,
In the midnight flaming, with menace of fire
Protecting the treasure for many a year
Till he died the death. Then Wiglaf departed
In haste returning enriched with spoil.
He feared, and wondered if still he would find
The lord of the Weders alive on the plain,
Broken and weary and smitten with wounds.
With his freight of treasure he found the prince,
His dear lord, bloody and nigh unto death.
With water he bathed him till words broke forth
From the hoard of his heart and, aged and sad,
Beowulf spoke, as he gazed on the gold:
'For this goodly treasure whereon I gaze
I give my thanks to the Lord of all,
To the Prince of glory, Eternal God,
Who granted me grace to gain for my people
Such dower of riches before my death.
I gave my life for this golden hoard.
Heed well the wants, the need of my people;
My hour is come, and my end is near.
Bid warriors build, when they burn my body,
A stately barrow on the headland's height.
It shall be for remembrance among my people
As it towers high on the Cape of the Whale,°
And sailors shall know it as Beowulf's Barrow,
Sea-faring mariners driving their ships
Through fogs of ocean from far countries.'
Then the great-hearted king unclasped from his throat
A collar of gold, and gave to his thane;
Gave the young hero his gold-decked helmet,
His ring and his byrny, and wished him well.
'You are the last of the Wægmunding line.
All my kinsmen, earls in their glory,
Fate has sent to their final doom,
And I must follow.' These words were the last
The old king spoke ere the pyre received him,

Cape of the Whale Hrones-næs, a headland on the coast of Geatland. The almost literal parallel with the make-up and position of the funeral pyre here with that of Achilles and Patroclus in the *Odyssey* (XXIV. 80 ff.) has often been noticed. Earlier, cremation of Germanic chieftains was less elaborate; see Tacitus, *Germania*, 27.

The leaping flames of the funeral blaze,
And his breath went forth from his bosom, his soul
Went forth from the flesh, to the joys of the just.
Then bitter it was for Beowulf's thane
To behold his loved one lying on earth
Suffering sore at the end of life.
The monster that slew him, the dreadful dragon,
Likewise lay broken and brought to his death.
The worm no longer could rule the hoard,
But the hard, sharp sword, the work of the hammer,
Had laid him low; and the winged dragon
Lay stretched near the barrow, broken and still.
No more in the midnight he soared in air,
Disclosing his presence, and proud of his gold;
For he sank to earth by the sword of the king.
But few of mankind, if the tales be true,
Has it prospered much, though mighty in war
And daring in deed, to encounter the breath
Of the venomous worm or plunder his wealth
When the ward of the barrow held watch o'er the mound.
Beowulf bartered his life for the treasure;
Both foes had finished this fleeting life.
Not long was it then till the laggards in battle
Came forth from the forest, ten craven in fight,
Who had dared not face the attack of the foe
In their lord's great need. The shirkers in shame
Came wearing their bucklers and trappings of war
Where the old man lay. They looked upon Wiglaf.
Weary he sat by the side of his leader
Attempting with water to waken his lord.
It availed him little; the wish was vain!
He could not stay his soul upon earth,
Nor one whit alter the will of God.
The Lord ruled over the lives of men
As He rules them still. With a stern rebuke
He reproached the cowards whose courage had failed.
Wiglaf addressed them, Weohstan's son;
Gazed sad of heart on the hateful men:
'Lo! he may say who would speak the truth
That the lord who gave you these goodly rings,
This warlike armor wherein you stand—
When oft on the ale-bench he dealt to his hall-men
Helmet and byrny, endowing his thanes
With the fairest he found from near or from far—
That he grievously wasted these trappings of war
When battle befell him. The king of the folk
Had no need to boast of his friends in the fight.
But the God of victory granted him strength

To avenge himself with the edge of the sword
When he needed valor. Of little avail
The help I brought in the bitter battle!
Yet still I strove, though beyond my strength,
To aid my kinsman. And ever the weaker
The savage foe when I struck with my sword;
Ever the weaker the welling flame!
Too few defenders surrounded our ruler
When the hour of evil and terror befell.
Now granting of treasure and giving of swords,
Inherited land-right and joy of the home,
Shall cease from your kindred. And each of your clan
Shall fail of his birthright when men from afar
Hear tell of your flight and your dastardly deed.
Death is better for every earl
Than life besmirched with the brand of shame!'

[*The Messenger Foretells the Doom of the Geats*]

Then Wiglaf bade tell the tidings of battle
Up over the cliff in the camp of the host
Where the linden-bearers° all morning long
Sat wretched in spirit, and ready for both,
The return, or the death, of their dear-loved lord.
Not long did he hide, who rode up the headland,
The news of their sorrow, but spoke before all:
'Our leader lies low, the lord of the Weders,
The king of the Geats, on the couch of death.
He sleeps his last sleep by the deeds of the worm.
The dreadful dragon is stretched beside him
Slain with dagger-wounds. Not by the sword
Could he quell the monster or lay him low.
And Wiglaf is sitting, Weohstan's son,
Bent over Beowulf, living by dead.
Death watch he keeps in sorrow of spirit
Over the bodies of friend and foe.

Now comes peril of war when this news is rumored abroad,
The fall of our king known afar among Frisians and Franks!
For a fierce feud rose with the Franks when Hygelac's warlike host
Invaded the Frisian fields, and the Hetware vanquished the Geats,
Overcame with the weight of their hordes, and Hygelac fell in the fray;
It was not his lot to live on dispensing the spoils of war.
And never since then of the Franks had we favor or friend.
And I harbor no hope of peace or faith from the Swedish folk,
For well is it known of men that Ongentheow° slew with the sword
Hæthcyn, the son of Hrethel, near Ravenswood, in the fight

linden-bearers shield-bearers, warriors
Ongentheow See ll. 2342 ff. for the battle at Ravenswood.

When the Swedish people in pride swept down on the Geats.°
And Ohthere's aged father,° old and a terror in battle,
Made onslaught, killing their king, and rescued his queen,°
Ohthere's mother and Onela's, aged, bereft of her gold.
He followed the flying foe till, lordless and lorn,
They barely escaped into Ravenswood. There he beset them,
A wretched remnant of war, and weary with wounds.
And all the long hours of the night he thundered his threats
That some on the morrow he would slay with the edge of the sword,
And some should swing on the gallows for food for the fowls!°
But hope returned with the dawn to the heavy-hearted
When they heard the sound of the trumpets and Hygelac's horn,
As the good king came with his troops marching up on their track.
Then was a gory meeting of Swedes and Geats;
On all sides carnage and slaughter, savage and grim,
As the struggling foemen grappled and swayed in the fight.
And the old earl Ongentheow, crestfallen and cowed,
Fled with his men to a fastness, withdrew to the hills.
He had tasted Hygelac's strength, the skill of the hero in war,
And he had no hope to resist or strive with the sea-men,
To save his hoard from their hands, or his children, or wife.
So the old king fled to his fortress; but over the plain
Hygelac's banners swept on in pursuit of the Swedes,
Stormed to the stronghold's defenses, and old Ongentheow°
Was brought to bay with the sword, and subject to Eofor's will!
Wulf, son of Wonred, in wrath then struck with his sword,
And the blood in streams burst forth from under the old man's hair.
Yet the aged Scylfing was all undaunted and answered the stroke
With a bitter exchange in the battle; and Wonred's brave son
Could not requite the blow, for the hero had cleft his helmet,
And, covered with blood, he was forced to bow; he fell to the earth.
But his death was not doomed, and he rallied, though the wound was deep.
Then Hygelac's hardy thane,° when his brother lay low,
Struck with his ancient blade, a sturdy sword of the giants,
Cut through the shield-wall, cleaving the helmet. The king,
The folk-defender, sank down. He was hurt unto death.
Then were many that bound Wulf's wounds when the fight was won,
When the Geats held the ground of battle; as booty of war
Eofor stripped Ongentheow of iron byrny and helm,
Of sword-blade hilted and hard, and bore unto Hygelac

Swedish . . . Geats The Swedes had perhaps first provoked a battle—now the Geats had made an expedition in revenge.
father Ongentheow
queen The Geats, under their king, Hæthcyn, are at first successful and capture Ongentheow's queen. Then Ongentheow rescues her and kills Hæthcyn, after which he drives the Geatish forces into Ravenswood. Then Hygelac, Hæthcyn's brother and successor, arrives with reinforcements, and Ongentheow in his turn is driven to take refuge and is killed. The next stages in the Geat-Swedish war have already been told at ll. 2464 ff. and 2246 ff.
fowls carrion birds
Ongentheow Ongentheow first fells, but does not kill, Wulf, one of the sons of Wonred, who has wounded him. Wonred's other son, Eofor, then kills Ongentheow and strips him of his armor and ornaments.
thane Eofor

The old man's trappings of war. And Hygelac took the treasures,
Promising fair rewards, and this he fulfilled.
The son of Hrethel, the king of the Geats, when he came to his home,
Repaid with princely treasure the prowess of Eofor and Wulf;
Gave each an hundred thousand° of land and linked rings,
And none could belittle or blame. They had won the honor in war.
He gave to Eofor also the hand of his only daughter
To be a pledge of good will, and the pride of his home.

This is the fighting and this the feud,
The bitter hatred, that breeds the dread
Lest the Swedish people should swarm against us°
Learning our lord lies lifeless and still.
His was the hand that defended the hoard,
Heroes, and realm against ravaging foe,
By noble counsel and dauntless deed.
Let us go quickly to look on the king
Who brought us treasure, and bear his corpse
To the funeral pyre. The precious hoard
Shall burn with the hero. There lies the heap
Of untold treasure so grimly gained,
Jewels and gems he bought with his blood
At the end of life. All these at the last
The flames shall veil and the brands devour.
No man for remembrance shall take from the treasure,
Nor beauteous maiden adorn her breast
With gleaming jewel; bereft of gold
And tragic-hearted many shall tread
A foreign soil, now their lord has ceased
From laughter and revel and rapture of joy.
Many a spear in the cold of morning
Shall be borne in hand uplifted on high.
No sound of harp shall waken the warrior,
But the dusky raven despoiling the dead
Shall clamor and cry and call to the eagle
What fare he found at the carrion-feast
The while with the wolf he worried the corpses.'°
    So the stalwart hero had told his tidings,
His fateful message; nor spoke amiss
As to truth or telling. The host arose;
On their woeful way to the Eagles' Ness°
They went with tears to behold the wonder.

hundred thousand If this meant 100,000 hides or measures of land (see above), it would equal the size of Geatland itself: probably the meaning is "the value of 100,000 (coins) in land and gold."

Lest . . . us The point of the Ravenswood story: the messenger fears that, once the death of Beowulf becomes known, the Swedes will renew their attacks on the Geats, now without their protector.

eagle . . . corpses See "The Wanderer" (ll. 74–75).

Eagles' Ness Earna-næs, perhaps modern Swedish Ornäs—the promontory near the scene of Beowulf's battle with the dragon

They found the friend, who had dealt them treasure
In former days, on the bed of death,
Stretched out lifeless upon the sand.
The last of the good king's days was gone;
Wondrous the death of the Weder prince!
They had sighted first, where it lay outstretched,
The monstrous wonder, the loathsome worm,
The horrible fire-drake, hideous-hued,
Scorched with the flame. The spread of its length
Was fifty foot-measures! Oft in the night
It sported in air, then sinking to earth
Returned to its den. Now moveless in death
It had seen the last of its earthly lair.
Beside the dragon were bowls and beakers,
Platters lying, and precious swords
Eaten with rust, where the hoard had rested
A thousand winters in the womb of earth.
That boundless treasure of bygone men,
The golden dower, was girt with a spell
So that never a man might ravage the ring-hall
Save as God himself, the Giver of victory—
He is the Shelter and Shield of men—
Might allow such man as seemed to Him meet,
Might grant whom He would, to gather the treasure.
　　His way of life, who had wickedly hoarded
The wealth of treasure beneath the wall,
Had an evil end, as was widely seen.
Many the dragon had sent to death,
But in fearful fashion the feud was avenged!
'Tis a wondrous thing when a warlike earl
Comes to the close of his destined days,
When he may no longer among his kinsmen
Feast in the mead-hall. So Beowulf fared
When he sought the dragon in deadly battle!
Himself he knew not what fate was in store
Nor the coming end of his earthly life.
The lordly princes who placed the treasure
Had cursed it deep to the day of doom,
That the man who plundered and gathered the gold
Might pay for the evil imprisoned in hell,
Shackled in torment and punished with pain,
Except the invader should first be favored
With the loving grace of the Lord of all!
　　Then spoke Wiglaf, Weohstan's son:
'Often for one man many must sorrow
As has now befallen the folk of the Geats.
We could not persuade the king by our counsel,
Our well-loved leader, to shun assault

On the dreadful dragon guarding the gold;
To let him lie where he long had lurked
In his secret lair till the world shall end.
But Beowulf, dauntless, pressed to his doom.
The hoard was uncovered; heavy the cost;
Too strong the fate that constrained the king!
I entered the barrow, beholding the hoard
And all the treasure throughout the hall;
In fearful fashion the way was opened,
An entrance under the wall of earth.
Of the hoarded treasure I heaped in my arms
A weighty burden, and bore to my king.
He yet was living; his wits were clear.
Much the old man said in his sorrow;
Sent you greeting, and bade you build
In the place of burning a lofty barrow,
Proud and peerless, to mark his deeds;
For he was of all men the worthiest warrior
In all the earth, while he still might rule
And wield the wealth of his lordly land.
Let us haste once more to behold the treasure,
The gleaming wonders beneath the wall.
I will show the way that you all may see
And closely scan the rings and the gold.
Let the bier be ready, the pyre prepared,
When we come again to carry our lord,
Our leader beloved, where long he shall lie
In the kindly care of the Lord of all.'

[*Beowulf's Funeral*]

Then the son of Weohstan, stalwart in war,
Bade send command to the heads of homes
To bring from afar the wood for the burning
Where the good king lay: 'Now gleed° shall devour,
As dark flame waxes, the warrior prince
Who has often withstood the shower of steel
When the storm of arrows, sped from the string,
Broke over shield, and shaft did service,
With feather-fittings guiding the barb.'
Then the wise son of Weohstan chose from the host
Seven thanes of the king, the best of the band;
Eight heroes together they hied to the barrow
In under the roof of the fearful foe;
One of the warriors leading the way
Bore in his hand a burning brand.
They cast no lots who should loot the treasure

gleed fire

When they saw unguarded the gold in the hall
Lying there useless; little they scrupled
As quickly they plundered the precious store.
Over the sea-cliff into the ocean
They tumbled the dragon, the deadly worm,
Let the sea-tide swallow the guarder of gold.
Then a wagon was loaded with well-wrought treasure,
A countless number of every kind;
And the aged warrior, the white-haired king,
Was borne on high to the Cape of the Whale.
    The Geat folk fashioned a peerless pyre
Hung round with helmets and battle-boards,°
With gleaming byrnies as Beowulf bade.
In sorrow of soul they laid on the pyre
Their mighty leader, their well-loved lord.
The warriors kindled the bale° on the barrow,
Wakened the greatest of funeral fires.
Dark o'er the blaze the wood-smoke mounted;
The winds were still, and the sound of weeping
Rose with the roar of the surging flame
Till the heat of the fire had broken the body.
With hearts that were heavy they chanted their sorrow,
Singing a dirge for the death of their lord;
And an aged woman with upbound locks
Lamented for Beowulf, wailing in woe.°
Over and over she uttered her dread
Of sorrow to come, of bloodshed and slaughter,
Terror of battle, and bondage, and shame.
The smoke of the bale-fire rose to sky!
    The men of the Weder folk fashioned a mound
Broad and high on the brow of the cliff,
Seen from afar by seafaring men.
Ten days they worked on the warrior's barrow
Inclosing the ash of the funeral flame
With a wall as worthy as wisdom could shape.
They bore to the barrow the rings and the gems,
The wealth of the hoard the heroes had plundered.
The olden treasure they gave to the earth,
The gold to the ground, where it still remains
As useless to men as it was of yore.
Then round the mound rode the brave in battle,°
The sons of warriors, twelve in a band,
Bemoaning their sorrow and mourning their king.

battle-boards i.e. shields
bale pyre, bonfire
And . . . woe (ll. 2948–49) The manuscript is damaged at this point, but the word "Geatish" has been deciphered as describing the woman. Some take this to mean that Beowulf had married Hygelac's widow, Hygd.
round . . . battle See the account in the sixth-century Gothic historian Jordanes of the funeral of Attila the Hun; and Virgil's *Aeneid* XI.182–212.

They sang their dirge and spoke of the hero
Vaunting his valor and venturous deeds.
So is it proper a man should praise
His friendly lord with a loving heart,
When his soul must forth from the fleeting flesh.
So the folk of the Geats, the friends of his hearth,
Bemoaned the fall of their mighty lord;
Said he was kindest of worldly kings,
Mildest, most gentle, most eager for fame.

8th century 1815

Deor's Lament

This poem and "The Wanderer," which follows it here, are preserved in the Exeter Book, a manuscript collection of Anglo-Saxon poetry transcribed at the end of the tenth century and given to the chapter of Exeter Cathedral, in Devon, by its Archbishop, Leofric, in the middle of the eleventh. The book is still kept in the chapter library at Exeter. None of the poems in it has a title: the titles by which the poems are now known have all been supplied by modern editors.

Nothing is known of the bard who names himself *Deor* (Brave or Excellent) in line 35. We do not know, either, when he wrote his poem. It cannot (by reason of the references to Theodoric the Ostrogoth) be earlier than the sixth century in origin; it may belong to the eighth; and there is evidence that it existed in King Alfred's time (reigned 871–99). Perhaps the most likely date is the late ninth century.

The mood of "Deor's Lament" is elegiac, and its genre that of the *consolatio,* the topics of which go back at least as far as Homer. The Roman poets use them often—Horace, for example:

> Dead too is the sire of Pelops, the guest of the gods
> And Tithonus, carried off into air,
> And Minos, party to Jove's secrets. Now Tartarus
> Keeps Panthous' son . . .

All these great men had to die: their greatness could not save them from the greatest misfortune of all. We who remain must take what consolation we can from the realization that our lot is common to all. What must happen must happen. We can hope for better in this life than its misfortunes, but the ways of the gods are inscrutable.

When Christian writers took over the topics of the *consolatio*, they could add a dimension: God's ways were mysterious, but there was the promise of eternal life, vindication, and happiness for the good man. But though "Deor's Lament" is a poem written by a Christian, it can hardly be called a Christian poem: hope is for the passing of sorrow in this world, not in the world to come. The quality of that hope can be read as stoical resignation toward, or as heroic defiance of, the lot of Deor. The refrain which drives home the moral and separates the single *exempla* of misfortune one from another can be read in either sense. In the conventional consolatory mode, the poem proceeds by these *exempla* of misfortune, its structure a set of such units, its movement punctuated by the refrain. In this it is unusual, almost unique in Anglo-

Saxon poetry: only one other poem, and that a late one, uses a stanza division, and only one other any kind of refrain.

Though the poet is using a genre that was popular in the Latin poetry of the early Middle Ages, his *exempla* are all drawn from Germanic legend. His characters would be well known to his audience. Weland, Beadohild, and Mæthhild are entirely mythological; Theodoric and Eormanric were historical characters around whom legend grew. But though all but Mæthhild are familiar figures, no coherent or convincing explanation of their presence together in the poem has yet been offered.

The translations of this poem and the three that follow ("The Wanderer," *The Battle of Maldon,* and *The Dream of the Rood*) are those of C. W. Kennedy, published in his *An Anthology of Old English Poetry,* 1960. The lines have been numbered here merely as a guide.

Deor's° Lament

Weland° knew fully°   affliction and woe,
Hero unflinching   enduring distress;
Had for companionship   heart-break and longing,
Wintry exile   and anguish of soul,
When Nithhad bound him,   the better man,
Grimly constrained him   with sinewy bonds.°

That evil ended.°   So also may this!

Nor was brother's death   to Beadohild
A sorrow as deep   as her own sad plight,
When she knew the weight   of the child in her womb,
But little could know   what her lot might be.

That evil ended.°   So also may this!

Many have heard   of the rape of Hild,°
Of her father's affection   and infinite love,
Whose nights were sleepless   with sorrow and grief.

That evil ended.   So also may this!

Deor's This poet is mentioned nowhere else and nothing is known of him beyond the poem's implication that he was an exile; the name is probably a persona adopted by the poet.

Weland or Wayland or Welund, whose name means "maker" or "workman," the smith of Germanic legend, a supernatural being corresponding to the Vulcan of classical mythology. He had been captured by Nithhad, set to work, and hamstrung to prevent his escape. But he managed to escape, after all, killing the two sons of Nithhad and raping his daughter Beadohild. Weland is shown on the whalebone reliefs of the Franks Casket (Northumbria, *c.* 700) in the British Museum (Fig. 22).

fully a fill-in for two words in the Old English for which no one has yet suggested a suitable translation

sinewy bonds bonds imposed by cutting the sinews

That . . . ended Weland got away (by flying, in one form of the story).

That . . . ended (l. 12) As a result of the rape, Beadohild bore the hero Widia; the poet considers that to be the mother of a hero is sufficient compensation for her.

Hild Beadohild. This translation takes this and the obscure next two lines to be a restatement of Beadohild's plight as it affected her father. The reference may rather be to an unidentified Hild or Mæthhild and an unidentified Geat, her lover, so that **affection . . . love** should be rendered "passion," and **sorrow and grief** as "bitter love."

For thirty winters Theodoric° held,
As many have known, the Mæring's stronghold.

That evil ended. So also may this!

We have heard of Eormanric's° wolf-like ways,
Widely ruling the realm of the Goths;°
Grim was his menace, and many a man,
Weighted with sorrow and presage of woe,
Wished that the end of his kingdom were come.

That evil ended. So also may this!

He who knows sorrow, despoiled of joys,
Sits heavy of mood; to his heart it seemeth
His measure of misery meeteth no end.
Yet well may he think how oft in this world
The wise Lord varies His ways to men,
Granting wealth and honor to many an eorl,°
To others awarding a burden of woe.

And so I can sing of my own sad plight
Who long stood high as the Heodenings'° bard,
Deor my name, dear to my lord.
Mild was my service for many a winter,
Kindly my king till Heorrenda° came
Skillful in song and usurping the land-right°
Which once my gracious lord granted to me.

That evil ended. So also may this!

Late 9th century

The Wanderer

"The Wanderer," anonymous, untitled, and elegiac, is preserved in the Exeter Book along with the group of poems usually known as the *Elegies:* "The Ruin," "The Seafarer," "The Husband's Message," and "The Wife's Lament." All deal with exile, solitariness, separation, loss—generally the loss of fellow warriors and protectors. Anglo-Saxon literature has little to say about the pangs of lovers, almost nothing that can be called love-poetry.

Theodoric probably Theodoric the Great, 454–526, king of the Ostrogoths, lord of Italy, who murdered Odoacer, the barbarian mercenary who had made himself Emperor of the West in 493; the reference is not clear. Others have suggested that Theodoric the Frank (Wolfdietrich), who also suffered exile and defeat, may be meant. The Mæring (l. 18) may be Theodoric.

Eormanric's the historical Eormanric, or Ermanric, king of the Ostrogoths, who died about 375, having made himself ruler from the Baltic to the Black Sea; later legend made him a cruel tyrant.

Goths the Ostrogoths, who originated in southern Russia and held Italy during the late fifth and early sixth century

eorl The word means either a nobleman, man of the upper class (as it does here), or a warrior: by this time its use was largely confined to poetry.

Heodenings' ruling family, descended from Heoden

Heorrenda Nothing is known of this bard, either.

land-right estate granted to Deor as a reward for his poetry

No trace of love between man and woman is found in "The Wanderer," the finest of the elegiac lyrics. Its poignancy, its desolate chill, the atmosphere of physical and mental suffering it conveys, spring from the loss of the lord, protector of and provider for his household, from the loss of companions-at-arms, of the joys of feasting, drinking, of song and story and boast in the mead-hall, from the transitoriness of what is glorious and desirable in this world. The lord's death is the greatest of tragedies: it casts a man, old and unprotected when he most needs protection, on a hostile world, where all is perpetual winter.

The poem is a difficult one. Its language presents many problems, and the exact connotations that the poet intends us to catch are elusive. In genre it is an elegiac *consolatio,* written by a Christian poet who had some familiarity with Latin literature, as well as being steeped in the traditions of the Anglo-Saxon poetic craft. For some, the poem is an allegory: the exile it portrays is the spiritual exile from God of the Christian, while he is still in the world—so that the exile's journey is a kind of *Pilgrim's Progress,* by sea and not by land, the sea being the chosen road of the early Germanic peoples. The difficulty about this view is that such a specifically Christian allegory is not found elsewhere in Anglo-Saxon poetry, except in the set forms of the *Bestiary* or *The Phoenix,* both of which are, significantly, translations. The poem is perhaps best read as a moralization on the theme of the vanity of worldly things and worldly joy.

The Wanderer's opening statement of his faith that, after all the weariness and bitter cold of his life on earth, he will at last find comfort (ll. 1–7), is taken up again to round off the poem (ll. 103 ff.). Between, he tells of the tribulations of the man who must seek a new lord and new comrades, and the desolation he endures when, frozen and weary upon a freezing sea, he falls asleep, to dream of the warmth and happiness of companionship and feasting, only to wake and find it all a dream (ll. 8–53). Then, in the second section of the poem, he turns to meditate on his experience, to apply its lessons. Some have assumed that this second part of the poem is spoken by a third person, the sage who (l. 103) takes up the argument after the poet has provided the framework (ll. 6–7 and other occasional remarks) and the Wanderer has made his catalogue of wretchedness.

Of the poet who wrote "The Wanderer" we know nothing, not even an approximate date of birth or death. The most likely date of composition is the early tenth century.

The Wanderer°

Oft to the Wanderer,   weary of exile,
Cometh God's pity,   compassionate love,
Though woefully toiling   on wintry seas
With churning oar   in the icy wave,
Homeless and helpless   he fled from Fate.°
Thus saith the Wanderer   mindful of misery,
Grievous disasters,   and death° of kin:

Wanderer "Wanderer" is the translator's choice for words that literally would be "man alone" (l. 1) and "earth-walker" (l. 6).

Fate The translation of *wyrd* as "Fate" deserves comment because of basic etymologic differences. "Fate" is from a Latin root connected with speaking: that which has been decreed by the gods; *wyrd* is connected with the word for "become," and so literally means "what comes to pass" in the broadest context or, applied to men or to a single man, "the human lot," the state of change to which all are subject except God and the angels.

death by violence

'Oft when the day broke, oft at the dawning,
Lonely and wretched I wailed my woe.
No man is living, no comrade left,
To whom I dare fully unlock my heart.
I have learned truly the mark of a man
Is keeping his counsel° and locking his lips,
Let him think what he will! For, woe of heart
Withstandeth not Fate; a failing° spirit
Earneth no help. Men eager for honor
Bury their sorrow deep in the breast.
'So have I also, often in wretchedness
Fettered my feelings, far from my kin,
Homeless and hapless, since days of old,
When the dark earth covered my dear lord's face,
And I sailed away with sorrowful heart,
Over wintry seas, seeking a gold-lord,°
If far or near lived one to befriend me
With gift in the mead-hall and comfort for grief.
'Who bears it, knows what a bitter companion,
Shoulder to shoulder, sorrow can be,
When friends are no more. His fortune is exile,
Not gifts of fine gold; a heart that is frozen,
Earth's winsomeness dead. And he dreams of the hall-men,
The dealing of treasure, the days of his youth,
When his lord bade welcome to wassail and feast.
But gone is that gladness, and never again
Shall come the loved counsel of comrade and king.
'Even in slumber his sorrow assaileth,
and, dreaming he claspeth his dear lord again,
Head on knee, hand on knee, loyally laying,
Pledging his liege° as in days long past.
Then from his slumber he starts lonely-hearted,
Beholding gray stretches of tossing sea,
Sea-birds bathing, with wings outspread,
While hailstorms darken, and driving snow.
Bitterer then is the bane of his wretchedness,
The longing for loved one: his grief is renewed.
The forms of his kinsmen take shape in the silence;
In rapture he greets them; in gladness he scans
Old comrades remembered. But they melt into air
With no word of greeting to gladden his heart.
Then again surges his sorrow upon him;
And grimly he spurs his weary soul

keeping . . . counsel According to Tacitus, in his *Germania*, the Germanic peoples held that "a woman may decently express her grief in public; a man should nurse his in his heart."
failing Another translation is "fierce," to make a contrasting pair—i.e. neither sorrow nor anger will avail—rather than a repetitive pair.
gold-lord a generous giver of gold and gifts, who would take him into his household
Head . . . liege kneeling before the lord and making his profession of allegiance

Once more to the toil   of the tossing sea.
'No wonder° therefore,   in all the world,
If a shadow darkens   upon my spirit
When I reflect   on the fates of men—
How one by one   proud warriors vanish
From the halls that knew them,   and day by day
All this earth ages   and droops unto death.
No man may know wisdom   till many a winter
Has been his portion.   A wise man is patient,
Not swift to anger,   nor hasty of speech,
Neither too weak,°   nor too reckless, in war,
Neither fearful nor fain,°   nor too wishful of wealth,
Nor too eager in vow°—   ere he know the event.
A brave man must bide   when he speaketh his boast
Until he know surely   the goal of his spirit.
'A wise man will ponder   how dread is that doom
When all this world's wealth   shall be scattered and waste
As now, over all,   through the regions of earth,
Walls stand rime-covered   and swept by the winds.
The battlements crumble,   the wine-halls decay;
Joyless and silent   the heroes are sleeping
Where the proud host fell   by the wall they defended.
Some battle launched   on their long, last journey;
One a bird° bore   o'er the billowing sea
One the gray wolf° slew;   one a grieving eorl°
Sadly gave   to the grave's embrace.
The Warden of men   hath wasted this world
Till the sound of music   and revel is stilled,
And these giant-built structures°   stand empty of life.
'He who shall muse   on these mouldering ruins,
And deeply ponder   this darkling life,
Must brood on old legends   of battle and bloodshed,
And heavy the mood   that troubles his heart:
'Where now is the warrior?°   Where is the war horse?
Bestowal of treasure,   and sharing of feast?
Alas! the bright ale-cup,   the byrny-clad warrior,
The prince in his splendor°   —those days are long sped
In the night of the past,   as if they never had been!'

No wonder Some scholars see a break here, with a second speaker, not the Wanderer but the sage or wise man of l. 103, taking up the tale. A case can be made for this reading of the poem, but it is not necessary to make the division.
weak unreliable
fain probably fawning, servile
vow boastful promise
bird No completely convincing explanation has yet been offered of the bird; perhaps it is the eagle or the raven, feeding on corpses, a common occurrence in the battle scenes of Anglo-Saxon literature.
wolf perhaps, again, feeding on the dead in battle
eorl warrior
giant-built structures usually taken to be Roman ruins, buildings of the great men of far-off times
Where . . . warrior This brief *ubi sunt* lament, a further variation on the theme of transitoriness, on which the poem turns, is an echo of Latin homiletic and other works, applied to the things that the warrior prizes most.
splendor i.e. as the center of the heroic community

And now remains only, for warriors' memorial,
A wall wondrous high with serpent shapes° carved.
Storms of ash-spears° have smitten the eorls,
Carnage of weapon, and conquering Fate.
'Storms now batter these ramparts of stone;
Blowing snow and the blast of winter
Enfold the earth; night-shadows fall
Darkly lowering, from the north driving
Raging hail in wrath upon men.
Wretchedness fills the realm of earth,
And Fate's decrees transform the world.
Here wealth is fleeting, friends are fleeting,
Man is fleeting, maid is fleeting;
All the foundation of earth shall fail!'
Thus spake the sage in solitude pondering.
Good man is he who guardeth his faith.
He must never too quickly unburden his breast
Of its sorrow, but eagerly strive for redress;
And happy the man who seeketh for mercy
From his heavenly Father, our Fortress° and Strength.

? 10th century

The Battle of Maldon

This poem must have been written not long after the battle itself, which took place in 991. In this year, the terse prose narrative of the *Anglo-Saxon Chronicle* tells us, the Danes descended on the southeast coast of England. They came "with ninety-three ships to Folkestone, plundered the neighborhood and sailed on to Sandwich, whence they went to Ipswich, overran the whole countryside, and then proceeded to Maldon. Ealdorman Byrhtnoth came against them with the *fyrd* (the home levies) and fought them, but they killed the Ealdorman there and had possession of the battlefield . . ." Another version gives the information that "in this year it was decided for the first time to pay tribute to the Danes, because of the great terror they spread along the coast." This first time the amount was 10,000 pounds in gold and silver, but it was more later.

The annalists' bare little paragraphs set down the dismal facts, telling us nothing about the Battle of Maldon itself and next to nothing about the English leader, Byrhtnoth, except that he was a great nobleman. Nothing is said of how his noble qualities showed in the battle. Humiliation fills the scene, obliterating or crowding out everything else.

There had been for some years past plenty to be ashamed of. Scandinavian raiders had first attacked England in the late eighth century, and the contest between them

serpent shapes No architecture survives which would answer to this description; the nearest approaches are in Celtic minor art, the interlace patterns of Anglo-Saxon cross-shafts, metal work such as the Sutton Hoo buckle, or the Fetter-Lane sword pommel, all of which are on a much smaller scale.

ash-spears *æsc*, from the wood of which the shaft was made, one of the two normal names for a spear

Fortress See Proverbs 18:10, Psalms 17:2 for the notion of God as a fortress; Luther's *feste Burg* is a later example.

and the English had not finally been settled in England's favor until the early years of the tenth century, in spite of King Alfred's considerable victories. Since the Battle of Brunanburh in 937, there had been peace. Within a couple of years of the accession of King Ethelred II, the Unready (noble-counsel-no-counsel would be a way to render the Anglo-Saxon pun in his name and nickname), who reigned ignominiously from 978 to 1016, Danish raiders had begun again to harry the English coasts. They continued to do so throughout Ethelred's reign: countermeasures were sporadic, ill-organized, and unsuccessful. Treachery and betrayal were common among the nobility who ought to have been leading the resistance, and the payments by which the raiders were bought off became, later in Ethelred's reign, an annual and growing imposition (the tax was known as Danegeld). At Ethelred's death in 1016, a Dane, Canute, was finally crowned king of England.

Histories of Ethelred's reign chronicle warfare, misery, and defeat. Beside their grim story and spare language, the poem's depictions of Byrhtnoth's heroic qualities in stately and formal diction stand in marked contrast. The tale of his final battle emphasizes both the courage of other resistances and the cowardice of capitulations.

The poet's hero, Byrhtnoth, was at this time a man well over sixty, white-haired but still strikingly handsome, of giant height and strength. From a family of great landowners near Cambridge, he had himself been made (in 956) *ealdorman* ("earl" would be a good modern equivalent) of the East Saxons (Essex), that is to say, a kind of sub-king, the king's deputy in all the functions of government. He was a man of great power in his district, high in the king's favor, a great respecter and patron of monastic foundations, as well as a great scourge of the Danes. Byrhtnoth's legend was still alive in the twelfth century, when most others had been forgotten. The poet's celebration of the Christian Earl's fruitless courage against the pagan raiders, glorifying the heroic ideal, with contempt—not less strongly felt for being formally expressed—for cowardice and breaking of allegiance, must have contributed substantially to the legend.

The poem, as we have it, lacks a beginning and an end; both were already missing when the poem perished in the fire of 1731 that damaged the manuscript of *Beowulf*. We have the text only from a transcript which had fortunately been made. It is probable that the fragment preserved is, in fact, almost the whole of the work and that the poet intended to plunge us immediately into the middle of the action—bringing us, as in so much oral poetry, quickly to the heart of its significance. We, like the original audience, are expected to know something of the events previous to the mutual and ceremonial tauntings of the two sides that precede the battle itself.

The Danish raiders had sailed up the estuary of the River Blackwater and established a base on Northey Island from which they could set out, by land or sea, in search of fresh plunder. The arm of the river that lay between them and the mainland was good protection from attack by land, but it had the disadvantage of being navigable only in a narrow channel at its center, so that ships could not be used to help them make raids further inland. Their only way across was by a ford, the *brycg*, with a causeway at water level, and this *brycg* was also the only means by which the English force could arrive at a hand-to-hand battle with the Vikings. At the landward end of the causeway the English force was stationed. In this position of stalemate, one side had to give, if there was to be any contest. Since it was essential to the English that the issue be decided, Byrhtnoth withdrew, placing his men to best tactical advantage at the head of a slope—and lost the battle (see map, Fig. 3).

Byrhtnoth had had little choice, but we should not assume that tactical considerations alone determined his action in allowing the raiders to cross. There is a strong element of heroic pride in his action, and the *Maldon* poet emphasizes this dimension. The word that he uses to characterize it—*ofermod*—is generally translated "rashness," but it more likely means "magnanimity," noble warrior's pride, scorning expediency, relying on fate and force of arms to settle the matter. The poem is, indeed, from first to last a presentation, the most richly compact and striking in Anglo-Saxon literature, of the heroic ideal of the Germanic peoples and its implications: the acceptance by the lesser nobility of the obligation of service to the lord, whose responsibility it was to provide the materials of combat, generous gifts of clothing, ornament and property, entertainment and protection, in return for unflinching service in peace and war. In this code, defeat was shame, even though it had involved no drawing back: cowardice, consequently, was an abomination. It is perfectly summed up in the words of Byrhtwold at the end of the poem:

> Heart must be braver, courage the bolder,
> Mood the stouter, as our strength grows less.

The poet's theme turns on this narrow Germanic convention of honor and loyalty. The heroic dimension to what was essentially a local battle, between marauding and experienced pirates and a largely untrained local force led by the small aristocratic retinue of the Ealdorman, is imparted by a rigorous restraint in language and in incident. Concentration and severity are the keynotes of the style, and a deliberate avoidance of richness in vocabulary and rhetoric. The battle resolves itself into a series of formal exchanges of insults, followed by descriptions of single combat. Nowhere in the whole corpus of Anglo-Saxon poetry is there such a complete and satisfying artistic success.

The Battle of Maldon

. . . . was broken.
He° bade a warrior° abandon his horse°
And hurry forward to join the fighters,
Take thought to his hands and a stout heart.
Then Offa's kinsman° knew that the eorl°
Would never suffer weakness or fear;
And he let from hand his beloved hawk
Fly to the forest, and made haste to the front;
By which one could know the lad would never

He Byrhtnoth
a warrior Offa's kinsman, see below
abandon . . . horse Cavalry was not much used in battle by the English at this period: the horses, having served for travel and transport, would be turned off for the duration of the fighting, partly to get them out of the way, partly as a deterrent from flight. On the terrain over which the Battle of Maldon was fought, horses would have been especially useless. The contest was one of bow, arrow, throwing-spear, and later, a hand-to-hand affair with sword, thrusting-spear, and axe (Figs. 8, 18, 21). Byrhtnoth is the last to dismount, having used his horse to make his battle dispositions.
Offa's kinsman Offa was one of Byrhtnoth's chief followers, but we do not know the name of his young kinsman, who is made to realize that the serious business of battle is afoot.
eorl In this poem the word means "noble warrior" when used of Byrhtnoth's followers; as applied to Byrhtnoth himself it carries the additional meaning of a nobleman of the highest class, an *Ealdorman*, as he is called in other sources.

Weaken in war when he seized a sword.
Eadric° also stood by his lord,
His prince, in the battle; forward he bore
His spear to the fight; he had firm resolve
While he could hold in hard hand-grip
Broad sword and buckler; he made good his boast
That he would battle beside his lord.
Byrhtnoth began to hearten his fighters;
He rode and gave counsel, instructing the men
How they should stand and defend the spot.°
He bade that they hold their bucklers aright
Firm in their hands, and be not afraid.
When he had fairly mustered the folk
He lighted down where it liked him well,°
Where he knew his retainers° were truest and best.
Then stood on the strand and boldly shouted
The Viking herald, boastfully° hurled
To the eorl on the shore the shipmen's message:
'These dauntless seamen have sent me to you,
Bade me say you must quickly send
Riches for ransom;° better for you
That you buy off with tribute a battle of spears
Than that we should wage hard war against you.
Nor need we waste strength if you will consent;
But we for the gold will confirm a peace.
If you will agree, who are greatest here,
To ransom your people and promise to pay
On their own terms unto the shipmen
Gold for goodwill, and have peace at our hands,
We with the treasure will take to our ships,
Put to sea, and observe the peace.'
Byrhtnoth addressed him; brandished° his shield;
Shook pliant ash-spear; speaking with words
Enraged and resolute, gave him answer:
'Hear you, sea-rover, what my people say?
The tribute they'll send you is tribute of spears,
Ancient sword-edge and poisoned point,
Weapons availing you little in war!
Pirate messenger, publish this answer,
Proclaim to your people tidings more grim:
Here stands no ignoble eorl with his army
Guarding my lord Æthelred's° country and coast,

Eadric another of Byrhtnoth's followers
the spot They had been drawn up at the head of a slope, in a position of advantage.
liked him well seemed good to him
retainers the *heorthwerod* or *comitatus*, the picked men of Byrhtnoth's own household, who need no instructions from Byrhtnoth, unlike the *fyrd*, the troops levied locally
boastfully rather "threateningly"
ransom i.e. to buy peace
brandished The Anglo-Saxon word more likely means "raised," to call for silence while formal reply is made.
Æthelred's King Ethelred II, the Unready

His land and his folk. The heathen shall fall
In the clash of battle. Too shameful it seems
That you with our tribute should take to your ships
Unfought, when thus far you've invaded our land.
You shall not so easily take our treasure,
But sword-edge and spear-point first shall decide,
The grim play of battle, ere tribute is granted.'
Then he bade bear buckler, warriors advance
And form their ranks on the river's edge;
Not yet, for the tide, could either attack.
The flood-tide was flowing after the ebb,
And the currents locked.° Too long it seemed
Till men to battle might bear their spears.
Near Panta River° in proud array
Stood the East Saxon host° and the Viking horde;
Nor could either army do harm to the other
Except who through arrow-flight found his death.
Then the flood-tide ebbed; the raiders stood ready,
The pirate army eager for war.
The lord commanded a war-hardened man
To defend the ford, Wulfstan° his name,
Brave among kinsmen, Ceola's son.
He wounded with weapon° the foremost man
Who first there fiercely set foot on the ford.
At Wulfstan's shoulder stood fearless fighters,
Ælfere and Maccus, a mighty pair.
Never would such take flight at the ford!
But they bravely defended against the foe
What time they were able to wield their weapons.
When the pirates perceived and clearly saw
That they had been met by bitter bridge-wardens,
The Viking shipmen began to dissemble,
Asked for permission to make approach,
To fare over ford and take their troops.
It was then the eorl disdainfully granted
Too much ground to the hostile host.
Across cold° water Byrhthelm's° son
Shouted reply, and the shipmen hearkened:
'Now way is made open, come quickly to us,
Warriors to the onset; God only knows
Who shall hold sway on the field of slaughter.'
The war-wolves advanced, heeded not water,
West across Panta; the Viking host

locked i.e. the tide came up the estuary to meet the current of the river
Panta River the Blackwater River
East Saxon host the men of Essex
Wulfstan A relative of Byrhtnoth's, a local man; nothing more is known of him or his companions.
weapon lit. spear; etymologically, Frankish spear, barbed and long-headed
cold dire, baleful
Byrhthelm's Byrhtnoth's father, not otherwise known

Over shining water carried their shields.
Among his warriors Byrhtnoth stood bold
Against the grim foe; bade form with shields
The war-hedge° for battle, hold firm the folk
Against the foemen. Then fighting was near,
Honor in battle. The hour was come
Doomed men must fall. A din arose.
Raven and eagle were eager for carnage;
There was uproar on earth. Men let from their hands
File-hard° darts and sharp spears fly.
Bows were busy, shield stopped point,
Bitter was the battle-rush. Warriors fell
In both the armies. Young men lay dead.
Wulfmær was wounded; Byrhtnoth's kin,
His sister's son,° was savagely butchered
Choosing the slaughter-bed, slain with the sword.
Then to the seamen requital was made.
I have heard that Eadweard° slew one with sword,
Withheld not the blow; the fated fighter
Fell at his feet. And for that the prince
Thanked his retainer when later was time.
So resisted the stout of heart,
Young men in battle; boldly strove
Who first with spear, warrior with weapon,
Could visit death on life that was doomed.
There was slaughter on earth; steadfast they stood,
And Byrhtnoth heartened them, bidding each man
Take thought to the war who would win° from the Danes.
The battle-hard brandished his weapon for war,
His shield for defense, and stormed at the foe;
Even so bold went eorl against churl.°
Both purposed evil, each for the other.
Then the shipman cast a southern spear°
And the lord of warriors suffered a wound.
He thrust° with his shield so the shaft was shattered,
The lance was broken, the parts fell back.
The prince was angered; he stung with his spear
The arrogant Viking who gave him the wound.
He fought with skill driving his dart

war-hedge a close defensive formation, a wall of shields (l. 236), the front rank with shields overlapping in front of their bodies, the rank behind holding shields above their heads to protect both themselves and the front rank
File-hard The file was used to test the temper of the blade.
Wulfmær . . . sister's son The bond between a man and his sister's son was especially close in Germanic society. See *Beowulf* ll. 194 ff.
Eadweard may or may not be the same as the Eadweard the Long, of l. 267.
win i.e. win glory
eorl . . . churl a poetic formula: noble against base
southern spear A spear made in a country south of the Viking lands, for example in England or France; such weapons seem to have been highly prized.
thrust Byrhtnoth swept the spear aside with his shield, from the point where it had struck him, and broke it into pieces. He could have done this only to the light throwing-spear; the thrusting-spear had a deep socket to prevent its being hacked or splintered with sword or shield.

Through the pirate's throat; he thrust with hand
So he touched the life of the savage foe.
Then most quickly he cast another
And the byrny° burst. He was wounded in breast
Through his woven mail, and the poisoned point
Bit at his heart. The eorl was the blither;
The proud man laughed, gave thanks to God
For that day's work which the Lord had granted.
But one of the shipmen hurled from his hand
A flying spear; and the speeding dart
Pierced through Æthelred's princely thane.°
A stripling lad stood at his shoulder,
A boy in the battle, who bravely drew
The bloody spear from the warrior's side,
Wulmær the youthful, Wulfstan's son.
Back he hurled the battle-hard dart;
The point pierced in and he sank to earth
Whose hand had given the grievous hurt.
Then a pirate warrior went to the eorl;
Soon would he seize his jewels and gems,
His armor of rings, and his well-wrought sword.
But Byrhtnoth snatched his sword from the sheath,
Broad and brown-edged,° and struck at his byrny.
Too speedily one of the shipmen hindered,
Striking aside the arm of the eorl;
And the gold-hilted sword fell to the ground,
Nor might he hold longer the hard blade,
Or wield his weapon. Once more he spoke;
The aged ruler rallied his men,
Bade them go forward and bear them well.
No more could he stand firm on his feet,
But he looked to heaven. . . .
'I give Thee thanks, O God of men,
For all the joys I have had on earth.
O Lord of mercy, I have most need
That now Thou wilt grant me good to my soul,
That my spirit may come into Thy kingdom,
O Prince of angels, departing in peace
Into Thy power. To Thee I pray
No fiend of hell may have hold upon me.'
Then the heathen scoundrels hacked him down
And both the fighters who stood at his side.
Ælfnoth and Wulmær both were fallen;
They laid down their lives beside their lord.

byrny shirt of ring-mail
thane The word originally meant "servant," but as the dignity of the king advanced with the passing of time, so the dignity of his servants went up. A king's thane was a considerable person, a great nobleman.
brown-edged shining, bright-edged

Then fled from the battle   who feared to be there:
The sons of Odda   were first in flight,
Godric from battle,   leaving his lord
Who had given him many   a goodly steed;
He leaped on the horse   that belonged to his leader,
Rode in the trappings   that were not his right,
And his brothers with him   both galloped off.
Godrinc° and Godwig   recked not of war,
But turned from the fighting,   took to the wood,
Fled to the fastness,   and saved their lives;
And more of men   than was any way right
If they had remembered   the many gifts
Their lord had given them   to their good.
As Offa once said,   at an earlier time
In the meeting-place   when he held assembly,
That many were there   making brave boasts°
Who would never hold out   in the hour of need.
Then was fallen   the lord of the folk,
Æthelred's eorl;   and his hearth-companions
All beheld   that their lord lay dead.
Forward they pressed,   the proud retainers,
Fiercely charged   those fearless thanes.
Each of them wished   one thing of two:
To avenge his leader   or lose his life.
Ælfric's° son   spurred them to battle,
A warrior young;   in words that were bold
Ælfwine spoke,   undaunted of spirit:
'Take thought of the times   when we talked at mead,
Seated on benches   making our boasts,
Warriors in hall,   concerning hard battle.
Now comes the test   who truly is bold!
I purpose to prove   my lineage to all men:
That in Mercia° I come   of a mighty clan;
Ealhelm° the name   of my aged father,°
A powerful ealdorman   wealthy and wise.
None shall reproach me   among that people
That I was willing   to slink from the strife,
Hastening home   when my lord lies dead,
Slain in the battle.   Of all disasters

Godrinc The name may be, rather, Godrine or Godwine.
boasts Formal boasting of deeds to be done, rather than of past achievements, was characteristic of Germanic social custom, especially at feasts (see l. 285 below).
Ælfric's probably the Ælfric who became ealdorman of Mercia in 983 and was banished in 986. This is perhaps the reason why his son Ælfwine does not boast of him as he does of his grandfather. Ælfwine was with Byrhtnoth because of his father's banishment: he needs the protection of another lord.
Mercia the Midland territory originally occupied by the Mierce, "boundary people." The kingdom of Mercia rose to great power in the eighth century, being supreme over England south of the Humber, but declined in the ninth and became partially subject to the Danes, from whom it was liberated later in the same century.
Ealhelm ealdorman of Mercia (*c.* 940–*c.* 951) frequently mentioned in records of the period
aged father The word so translated more likely means "grandfather."

That to me is the greatest of griefs,
For he was my kinsman; he was my lord.'
Then he dashed forward, took thought of the feud;
One of the shipmen he stabbed with spear
Among the folk, and he fell to earth
Slain with weapon. He encouraged his comrades,
Friends and companions to press to the front.
Offa spoke and brandished his ash-spear:
'Now hast thou, Ælfwine, heartened us all
In the hour of need. Now our lord lies dead,
Our eorl on earth, there is need that we all,
Each of us here embolden the others,
Warriors to combat, while hand may bear
Good sword and spear, and hold hard blade.
This sneaking Godric, Odda's son,
Has betrayed us all; for when he rode off
Sitting on horse, on our lord's proud steed,
Many men weened that it was our lord.
On the field of fate now the folk is divided,
The shield-hedge is shattered; cursed be his deed
That he caused so many to flee from the fight.'
Leofsunu spoke, lifted his buckler,
His board° for protection, making his boast:
'I promise you here I will never turn hence
Or flee one foot, but I'll fight in the front,
In the bitter strife, and avenge my lord.
Steadfast warriors by the River Stour°
Shall never have need of words to reproach me,
Now my lord is fallen, that lordless I fled,
Turned back from the battle and went to my home;
But weapon shall take me, sword-edge and spear.'
Then in rage he rushed to the fighting
Despising to flee.
Dunnere shook spear,
The aged churl,° called out to them all,
Bidding take vengeance for Byrhtnoth's fall:
'He may not weaken who thinks to avenge
His lord on this folk, nor fear for his life.'
Then they rushed forward, recked not of life,
Household-retainers fierce in the fight,
Bitter spear-bearers beseeching God
They might work revenge for their friendly lord
In death and destruction upon the foe.
Then a hostage° began to give them help,

board shield
Stour a river near by in Essex, near which Leofsunu lived
churl yeoman, free commoner. The word here does not, as it does in l. 125, imply baseness, but merely non-noble birth.
hostage A noble hostage, living in the household of a nobleman, would receive the privileges of other members of the household and accept their obligations, such as that of serving the lord in battle.

Of Northumbrian° race and hardy kin,
A son of Ecglaf, Æscferth his name.
He wavered not in the midst of the war-play
But forward pressed to the arrow-flight,
Now shooting on shield, now piercing a shipman,
But oft and often dealing a wound,
While he could wield his weapon in war.
In front line still stood Eadweard the Long,
Skillful and eager; he spoke his boast:
That he would not flee foot-measure of ground
Nor turn from the battle where his better lay dead.
He shattered the shield-wall and fought with the Danes.
Upon the shipmen he stoutly avenged
His gracious lord ere he sank in the slaughter.
So did Ætheric, excellent comrade,
Sibyrht's brother; he boldly strove
Eager and ready; and many another
Stood their ground and shattered the shields.
Bucklers broke, and byrnies sang
A song of terror. Then Offa smote
One of the shipmen and laid him low;
But Gadd's kinsman also fell in the fight.
Quickly in battle was Offa cut down.
But he had performed what he promised his lord,
When he made his boast to his bracelet-bestower,°
That both unharmed they would ride to the borough,°
Back to their homes, or fall in the fight
And perish of wounds in the place of slaughter.
Thane-like° he lay beside his lord.
Then was breaking of bucklers, shipmen advanced
Bold to the battle; sharp spears pierced
Life-house of doomed men. Wistan hastened,
Thurstan's son, and strove with the Danes.
Three he slew in the stress of battle
Ere Wigelm's son was slain in the war.
The strife was stern, warriors were steadfast,
Bold in battle; fighters fell
Weary with wounds. Death covered earth.
Oswold and Ealdwald all the while,
Both the brothers, marshalled their men;
Bade friend and kinsman endure in combat
And never weaken, but wield the sword.
Byrhtwold encouraged them, brandishing buckler,

Northumbrian The kingdom of Northumbria extended to the Lowlands of Scotland north from the River Humber; its time of greatest glory was the seventh and eighth centuries. The Danes had begun to settle there in the ninth century. It is not clear why a Northumbrian hostage was with Byrhtnoth's forces.

bracelet-bestower lord, giver of gifts

borough Fortified town, administrative center, where the lord lived and dispensed justice; or the meaning may simply be "manorhouse."

Thane-like i.e. having fulfilled his obligation of service

Aged companion   shaking ash-spear;
Stout were the words   he spoke to his men:
'Heart must be braver,°   courage the bolder,
Mood the stouter   as our strength grows less!
Here on the ground   my good lord lies
Gory with wounds.   Always will he regret it
Who now from this battle   thinks to turn back.
I am old in years;   I will never yield,
But here at the last   beside my lord,
By the leader I love   I think to lie.'
And Godric to battle   heartened them all;
Æthelgar's son   hurled many a spear
At the Viking horde.   First in the front
He hacked and hewed   till he fell in the slaughter.
He was not the Godric   who fled from the fight.°. . .

? End of 10th century

The Dream of the Rood

The Dream of the Rood was written, probably at the end of the seventh century, in Northumbria, the northernmost of the Anglo-Saxon kingdoms, by a poet whose name we do not know. We have the text from the collection of Anglo-Saxon poetry and sermons known as the Vercelli Book, written down in the second half of the tenth century and preserved for centuries in the cathedral library at Vercelli, in north Italy. Certain passages are carved, in runic script, on the sculptured stone cross at Ruthwell in Dumfriesshire, Scotland, probably erected in the early eighth century, the golden age of Northumbria (Fig. 23).

The poem, standing out from the rest of Anglo-Saxon poetry in its graphic intensity, its richly visual quality, and its firmly integrated structure, seems to owe little to any known particular source. There are analogies with and reminiscences of Latin hymns, but they are not many or important. Though the biblical narrative of Christ's Passion naturally stands behind it, the poem's imaginative achievement is far beyond that of the common Anglo-Saxon poetic form of biblical paraphrase. It is built with great skill round the co-existence in the Passion of the human suffering and divine triumph of Christ. Giving the Cross (the Rood) a share in each, and using its degradation and glorification as a figure of Christ on Golgotha, the poet is probably echoing the doctrinal disputes of his day.

In the prelude, he describes how the glorious Cross, glittering with gold and gems (compare the late fourth-century mosaic picture in Sta. Pudenziana at Rome of the jeweled Cross), changes its appearance to the Cross unadorned and bloodied by Christ's Passion, and then becomes again the figure of his triumph. Then, when the Cross itself, by the rhetorical device known as *prosopopeia,* is made to speak, it is

Heart . . . braver the perfect statement of the heroic code of battle, "Heart" being "warrior's pride"

He . . . fight ironic, rhetorical understatement, not naïveté. Great shame was attached to leaving a battlefield alive if one's lord had been killed —cf. Tacitus, *Germania,* 6.

transformed into a figure of Christ's suffering, its own tortures detailed: as it is hewn from the forest and dragged to become a gallows for criminals, sadly bends to receive Christ, feels his wounds and his agony with him, is itself cut down and buried. Then, in a parallel to the resurrection of Christ, it is discovered, adorned and worshiped, triumphant in the triumph of Christ as he harrows Hell, breaking down the gates and elevating the just to heaven (Fig. 7). Similarly, Christ the divine warrior, hastening boldly and willingly to mount the Cross, confident in divine victory but suffering for a time in his human nature, rises triumphant at his Resurrection and comes again to triumph over Hell and the Devil. The figure of Christ as warrior-hero voluntarily accepting the contest with the forces of evil is an example of both the Anglo-Saxon convention of restating a Christian subject in terms of its own heroic code and the borrowing of a notion of Christ as warrior-contestant that goes back to Greek patristic sources. (A visual expression can be seen in the figure of the imperial, victorious Christ in the Chapel of the Palace of the Archbishop at Ravenna.)

Throughout the poem, the paradoxes of the Passion, its extremes of suffering and glory, of darkness and light, alternate with each other, and culminate in the final triumphant image.

The Dream of the Rood

Lo! I will tell the dearest° of dreams
That I dreamed in the midnight when mortal men
Were sunk in slumber. Me-seemed I saw
A wondrous Tree towering in air,
Most shining of crosses compassed with light.
Brightly that beacon was gilded with gold;
Jewels adorned it fair at the foot,
Five on the shoulder-beam,° blazing in splendor.
Through all creation the angels of God
Beheld it shining— no cross of shame!
Holy spirits gazed on its gleaming,
Men upon earth and all this great creation.
Wondrous that Tree, that Token of triumph,°
And I a transgressor soiled with my sins!
I gazed on the Rood arrayed in glory,
Shining in beauty and gilded with gold,
The Cross of the Saviour beset with gems.
But through the gold-work outgleamed a token
Of the ancient evil of sinful men
Where the Rood on its right side° once sweat blood.
Saddened and rueful, smitten with terror

dearest most splendid
Five . . . shoulder-beam i.e. either on the cross-beam or at the intersection of the beams, symbolizing the five wounds of Christ
triumph The Cross is often called the Tree of Triumph in Latin hymns.
right side In art the wound in Christ's side is usually shown (especially before the later seventeenth century, but often later as well) on the right of his body.

At the wondrous Vision,   I saw the Cross
Swiftly varying   vesture and hue,
Now wet and stained   with the Blood outwelling,
Now fairly jeweled   with gold and gems.
Then, as I lay there,   long I gazed
In rue and sadness   on my Saviour's Tree,
Till I heard in dream   how the Cross addressed me,
Of all woods worthiest,   speaking these words:
'Long years ago   (well yet I remember)
They hewed me down   on the edge of the holt,°
Severed my trunk;   strong foemen took me,
For a spectacle wrought me,   a gallows for rogues.
High on their shoulders   they bore me to hilltop,°
Fastened me firmly,   an army of foes!
'Then I saw the King   of all mankind
In brave mood hasting   to mount upon me.
Refuse I dared not,   nor bow nor break,
Though I felt earth's confines   shudder in fear;
All foes I might fell,   yet still I stood fast.
'Then the young Warrior,°   God, the All-Wielder,
Put off His raiment,   steadfast and strong;
With lordly mood   in the sight of many
He mounted the Cross   to redeem mankind.
When the Hero clasped me   I trembled in terror,
But I dared not bow me   nor bend to earth;
I must needs stand fast.   Upraised as the Rood
I held the High King,   the Lord of heaven.
I dared not bow!   With black nails driven
Those sinners pierced me;   the prints are clear,
The open wounds.   I dared injure none.
They mocked us both.   I was wet with blood
From the Hero's side   when He sent forth His spirit.
'Many a bale°   I bore on that hillside
Seeing the Lord   in agony outstretched.
Black darkness° covered   with clouds God's body,
That radiant splendor.   Shadow went forth
Wan° under heaven;   all creation wept°
Bewailing the King's death.   Christ was on the Cross.
'Then many° came quickly,   faring from far,
Hurrying to the Prince.   I beheld it all.
Sorely smitten with sorrow   in meekness I bowed

holt forest
hilltop i.e. of Calvary
Warrior The Old English word is parallel to Greek *athlētēs*.
bale torment
darkness the eclipse at the Crucifixion, as Christ died; see Matthew 27:45; Luke 23:44–5
Wan dark
creation wept See the Norse story of the lament of all nature, save only one giantess, for the death of Baldr, the young and beautiful. Christ was thought to be thirty, or thirty-three, years old at the Crucifixion, and to have been surpassingly handsome.
many presumably Joseph of Arimathea and Nicodemus—see John 19:38–39; perhaps with the three Maries and St. John, who were already present—John 19:25–27. In medieval art, all are sometimes shown as taking part in the Deposition.

To the hands of men.   From His heavy and bitter pain
They lifted Almighty God.   Those warriors left me
Standing bespattered with blood;   I was wounded with spears.
Limb-weary they laid Him down;   they stood at His head,
Looked on the Lord of heaven   as He lay there at rest
From His bitter ordeal all forspent.°   In sight of His slayer°
They made Him a sepulcher   carved from the shining stone;
Therein laid the Lord of triumph.   At evening tide
Sadly they sang their dirges   and wearily turned away
From their lordly Prince;   there He lay all still and alone.
'There at our station   a long time we° stood
Sorrowfully weeping   after the wailing of men
Had died away.   The corpse grew cold,
The fair life-dwelling.   Down to earth
Men hacked and felled us,   a grievous fate!
They dug a pit   and buried us deep.°
But there God's friends   and followers° found me
And graced me with treasure   of silver and gold.
'Now may you learn,   O man beloved,
The bitter sorrows   that I have borne,
The work of caitiffs.°   But the time is come
That men upon earth   and through all creation
Show me honor   and bow to this sign.
On me a while   God's Son once suffered;
Now I tower under heaven   in glory attired
With healing for all   that hold me in awe.°
Of old I was once   the most woeful of tortures,
Most hateful to all men,   till I opened for them
The true Way of Life.   Lo! the Lord of glory,
The Warden of heaven,   above all wood
Has glorified me   as Almighty God
Has honored His Mother,   even Mary herself,
Over all womankind   in the eyes of men.
'Now I give you bidding,   O man beloved,
Reveal this Vision   to the sons of men,
And clearly tell   of the Tree of glory
Whereon God suffered   for man's many sins
And the evil that Adam   once wrought of old.
'Death He suffered,   but our Saviour rose
By virtue of His great might   as a help to men.
He ascended to heaven.   But hither again
He shall come unto earth   to seek mankind,

forspent utterly wearied
slayer i.e. the Cross
we the Cross of Christ and the crosses on which the two thieves had been crucified
buried us deep i.e. in shame for what had passed
God's . . . followers St. Helena, the mother of the Emperor Constantine, was said by 4th-century writers to have discovered the True Cross at Jerusalem on her visit there in 326. Other accounts, including Old English, speak of her adornment of it.
caitiffs villains, evil-doers
Now . . . awe The mosaic cross in the apse of Sta. Pudenziana at Rome towers from earth to heaven—see Headnote; such a cross would be always before the eyes of the faithful at worship, and promise salvation.

The Lord Himself   on the Day of Doom,°
Almighty God   with His angel hosts.
And then will He judge,   Who has power of judgment,
To each man according   as here on earth
In this fleeting life   he shall win reward.
'Nor there may any   be free from fear
Hearing the words   which the Wielder shall utter.
He shall ask before many: Where is the man
Who would taste bitter death   as He did on the Tree?
And all shall be fearful   and few shall know
What to say unto Christ.   But none at His Coming
Shall need to fear   if he bears in his breast
This best of symbols;   and every soul
From the ways of earth   through the Cross shall come
To heavenly glory,   who would dwell with God.'
Then with ardent spirit   and earnest zeal,
Companionless, lonely,   I prayed to the Cross.
My soul was fain of death.   I had endured
Many an hour of longing.   It is my life's hope
That I may turn   to this Token of triumph,
I above all men,   and revere it well.
This is my heart's desire,   and all my hope
Waits on the Cross.   In this world now
I have few powerful friends;   they have fared hence
Away from these earthly gauds   seeking the King of glory,
Dwelling now with the High Father   in heaven above,
Abiding in rapture.   Each day I dream
Of the hour when the Cross of my Lord,   whereof here on earth
I once had vision,   from this fleeting life may fetch me
And bring me where is great gladness   and heavenly bliss,
Where the people of God   are planted and stablished for ever
In joy everlasting.   There may it lodge me
Where I may abide in glory   knowing bliss with the saints.
May the Lord be gracious   who on earth of old
Once suffered on the Cross   for the sins of men.
He redeemed us, endowed us with life   and a heavenly home.
Therein was hope renewed   with blessing and bliss
For those who endured the burning.°   In that great deed
God's Son was triumphant,   possessing power and strength!
Almighty, Sole-Ruling   He came to the kingdom of God
Bringing a host of souls   to angelic bliss,
To join the saints   who abode in the splendor of glory,
When the Lord, Almighty God,   came again to His throne.

Late 7th century

Day of Doom Day of Judgment (Fig. 50)
those . . . burning This is a reference to the Harrowing of Hell, when Christ, the King of Glory, descended after his death to break down the gates of Hell, and bring out of it the souls of those (including Adam and Eve, the patriarchs and prophets) who have awaited this manifestation of his victory and his mercy. The chief biblical basis for the Descent into Hell is Matthew 27:52 ff.

GEOFFREY CHAUCER

c. 1343–1400

Geoffrey Chaucer was born into a well-to-do bourgeois family, in London, about 1343. Of his life he himself tells us almost nothing in his poetry, but from the documents, by which it has been possible to piece together the career of moderately distinguished public service which he made for himself, we know a good many details.

His family name goes back to the thirteenth century in the London area, and the Chaucers were already prosperous members of the rising commercial class in the days of Geoffrey's grandfather. Chaucer's father, a wine merchant, was a member of the growing number of men in the commercial centers of England, especially in London, who were beginning to exert a powerful effect on the structure of English society. They were commoners who were advancing in wealth, office-holding, and social prestige to a position above the ordinary, but were excluded from the aristocracy by birth, and from the country gentry by their city occupations. They were somewhere in between: the beginnings of the English middle class.

There was no place in their thinking—or in Chaucer's—for the leveling doctrines of John Ball, the fourteenth-century social agitator: ". . . matters cannot go well in England and never will until all things be in common, and there shall be neither serfs nor gentlemen, but we shall all be equal. . . ." A father from Chaucer's stratum of society would wish to advance his son's interests. He would send him first to school and then either to the University (which would often mean that the son was intended for the priesthood, the third order of English society); or he would place him in a noble household, where he might have the chance to continue his education in a less formal and devout way. In his early teens, Geoffrey Chaucer was made a page in the household of one of England's most considerable noblemen, Prince Lionel, third son of King Edward III, and later Duke of Clarence. The connections he made there must have served him well in later life and we know that his talents kept him in association with members of the aristocracy. His first great patron was John of Gaunt, fifth son of the king and the most powerful noble in England, who may also have been his friend. From the successive kings, Edward III, Richard II, and Henry IV, Chaucer received offices, grants of money, and other privileges for his services in various capacities. He married well; his wife Philippa was a member of the households of both Queen Philippa and of the third wife of John of Gaunt, and was probably the daughter of a knight. A Thomas Chaucer, probably their son, rose to public prominence and Alice Chaucer, possibly their granddaughter, married into the aristocracy not once but twice. From this tangle of connections, it emerges that the family was steadily rising in its social position.

Geoffrey Chaucer was the chief agent in this rise. The fact that his family had money and had been able to give him certain advantages obviously helped greatly, but his abilities also kept him on the road to advancement. In 1359 he went on one of Edward III's many expeditions against the French, was taken prisoner, and ransomed the following year; he then probably spent some time in study of the law, was made "valet" to the King in 1367 (an honor, not a servant's position), went on diplomatic missions to France several times, to Flanders in 1377 and to Italy in 1372–73 and 1378. In 1374 he was given a rent-free London house and made Controller of the Customs and Subsidies on Wool, Skins, and Hides for the Port of London. This was a lucrative office, for the wool trade was England's most important at the time. Other Customs appointments followed, but in 1386 Chaucer seems to have fallen on less good times and gone to live in Kent—perhaps only at Greenwich, now a suburb of London, a little way down the river. He had meantime become a public man of modest importance, being Justice of the Peace for Kent in 1385 and Knight of the Shire (representative in parliament) for Kent in 1386. After a short time in apparently rather straitened circumstances, he received in 1389 the office of Clerk of the King's Works, which put him in charge of the buildings and their repair at ten of the royal residences, of preparing places for tournaments, and of the walls, ditches, and sewers along a stretch of the Thames. There were later appointments, grants of wine, of money, and of privileges. In 1399, he rented a house in London again, near Westminster Abbey. He died the following year.

These bare facts about Chaucer's career indicate that he was given considerable responsibilities and, presumably, that he discharged them well. But they are the record, in the main, of a public servant's career, not a poet's. This is hardly surprising, since official documents are not the most obvious place to look for critical remarks on poetry, but it is significant because it indicates that the professional man-of-letters has not yet begun to emerge. The functioning of such a person depended upon the growth of a much larger reading public (even in 1533, Sir Thomas More estimated that fewer than four people in ten in England could read), the establishment of a system of printing and publishing, and an enlarged demand for dramatic performance. On the other hand, Chaucer provides a pattern of the writer which will serve for England for two centuries after his lifetime: the poet, whether a cleric or not, who holds ecclesiastical or secular office as a means to gain the leisure to write. A further—and often the most important—source of livelihood would be the dedication of poems to rich or noble patrons, and we know that Chaucer did just that with his first major poem, *The Book of the Duchess,* written in 1369–70 to commemorate the death of Blanche, Duchess of Lancaster, wife of John of Gaunt.

This position of the writer in his society is also a European one, especially in France and Italy. The new status that poets were now claiming is reflected in the ceremony—which Chaucer and all Europe knew about—performed on the Capitol at Rome in 1341, when Francesco Petrarca ("Francis Petrarch, the laureate poet," as Chaucer calls him) had himself formally crowned as a poet with a laurel garland. Petrarch thought he was reviving an ancient Roman custom, admirable because ancient and Roman and therefore pointing the way to the resuscitation of Roman virtue and glory. He also made a speech on the occasion, proclaiming the nobility and dignity of poetry and therefore of the poet, who was necessary to society because he could confer immortality on others as well as upon himself by his verses, and because beneath what seemed poetic fancies and dreams there lurked profound truth. The poet, indeed, was a moral philosopher, as Petrarch held: what he wrote would tend toward the inculcation of virtue in all its aspects.

Petrarch's Coronation Oration has been called "the first manifesto of the Renaissance," and the influence of the concept of the poet that it embodies is clear through to Sir Philip Sidney and even to the last English Renaissance poet, John Milton. But it has, in its serious statement of the poet's role, relevance to Chaucer, the first English poet to write in a manner that is as self-aware as it is self-assured and controlled. Petrarch's example as a poet meant much, consciously and unconsciously, to Chaucer. The first translation of a Petrarch sonnet into English (see below) is embedded in Chaucer's *Troilus and Criseyde,* and there are other indications in his work of his admiration for his Italian mentor. This is not to say that Chaucer would agree with all Petrarch's solemn claims: he was too much the satirist for that. Nor would he hold Petrarch's beliefs about the moral value of poetry as simply and directly as did Petrarch. His poetic method of slipping into and out of one of his characters—especially in *The Canterbury Tales*—often makes it difficult to hold in the mind exactly where he himself stands. We must balance his statement in the Retraction of the *Tales,* where he specifically disowns all in his work which tends toward the encouragement of sin, against the superb, controlled irony of the Clerk's Tale of patient Griselda; she endures in resignation and obedience to her husband all the trials he puts upon her, even to having her children taken from her and given up for dead, and to being put away by him. For Petrarch, this story was an exhortation to the Christian to be as steadfast for God as Griselda had been for her husband under her tribulations. Chaucer, by his very inclusion of the tale in his dramatic framework, has already lowered the story's tone and mode. But, fully in control of his manipulation, he raises the tone of the story again by giving it to the unworldly, idealist Clerk (see the General Prologue, ll. 287 ff.), who reiterates Petrarch's point and then goes on to concede that such absolute patience is a thing of the past and we must now do the best we can with what we have. Chaucer himself adds his ironic comment: a man should not try his wife's patience as hard as that "in trust to finde / Grisildis, for in certein he shall faile."

The Clerk's Tale operates at several levels: for the Clerk it is a moral tale, of trials and their endurance, turned so that it is also a hit at the Wife of Bath and her termagant ways, but it is capped by Chaucer's final encouragement—ironical, too—to sturdy wives to stand no nonsense from husbands. We must here, as always, make up our own minds as to how far we can identify anything that Chaucer says in *The Canterbury Tales* with Chaucer's own views, and judge for ourselves the extent of his irony and detachment. His intention is basically serious, even in the comic tales, but this is not to say that his poems are all moral allegories, lessons as directly applied as Petrarch would apply the Clerk's Tale.

Of the great Italians besides Petrarch, Chaucer was most indebted to Boccaccio and to Dante, but it is now becoming clear that much, though not all, of the influence on him that was formerly thought to be directly from the Italian, came via the French. This is natural: English culture for nearly three centuries before Chaucer and for nearly a century after him, relied heavily on France as a model. For a good part of those centuries, the two countries were, if not one kingdom, at least intimately connected in friendship or enmity. French was still the language of the English court, and in the manners and courtesies of polite society, especially in literature and in music, French practice was still the norm for imitation and modification.

Chaucer's youth, passed in a court milieu where such matters would be taken for granted, must have exposed him to French models, but in attempting to say just what these were and when and how he read and used them, we come up against one of our major difficulties with the poet: we simply do not know, except by inference, when exactly he wrote most of his works, major and minor. In general, his translations and direct imitations are reckoned to be early—the part of the incomplete English translation of the *Roman de la Rose* which is thought to be his, and some short poems, are given to the 1360's. The *Roman de la Rose* was a vast French poem of the thirteenth century, its first half a dream exploration of the process of falling in love according to the approved courtly canons, which had made of human love a deeply refining and ennobling influence on the spirit. This part was the work of Guillaume de Lorris (see below, The Other World: Paradise). To this was added, by Jean de Meun, an immense encyclopedic continuation, dealing with matters such as love, women, nobility, society and its foundations, the clergy, providence, fortune, the nature of dreams, sorcery, and the physical sciences. Chaucer frequently drew on these materials.

The Book of the Duchess (which can be dated exactly to 1369–70), uses a traditional English octosyllabic meter but often borrows directly from Jean Froissart, the French historian and poet who was Chaucer's almost exact contemporary, and from the French poet and musician Guillaume de Machaut (c. 1300–1377). It is an elegy and a dream vision at once. Sleepless, as the dreamer in such visions so often pictures himself, he reads and re-tells Ovid's story of Ceix and Alcyone from the *Metamorphoses* (the legend of how the kingfisher came into being), falls asleep, and dreams of a May morning encounter in the forest with a Man in Black, who tells his sorrow. Such dream visions were a highly fashionable literary form at the time. They allowed the poet to distance his illusion from his reader; they prepared the reader for the unrealities he might encounter, notably the personification of abstract qualities used to explore the nature of an experience or emotion; and they vouched, in one sense, for the validity of the vision. (See below, the Nun's Priest's Tale.)

The Book of the Duchess is an exquisitely turned evocation of grief at the death of Blanche "who every day hir beauté newed," already an assured and skillful poem combining French material with the literature of the ancient world. Of the classical writers who must have formed a part of Chaucer's education, by far the most important for him was Ovid, as both the poet of love and the poet of mythology, even the ancient poet most resembling him in temperament, with his characteristic blend of tenderness and satire, his love of a story. On no other classical author does Chaucer draw so heavily for material and for suggestions. He knew his Virgil, too, especially the *Aeneid,* but the *Eclogues* and the *Georgics* as well. Lucan and Statius (see below, the epilogue to *Troilus and Criseyde*), who were much admired in the Middle Ages, he knew and used also, but it seems probable that much of his knowledge of the Roman poets came from French translations and adaptations.

In the 1370's or early 1380's, again using a French version to help him, Chaucer translated the Latin work which influenced him most profoundly. This was the *Consolation of Philosophy* of Boethius, the Roman statesman, philosopher, and polymath put to death by the Emperor Theodoric in 524 A.D. Boethius wrote influential works on music, on geometry, on arithmetic—which became standard textbooks in medieval education for three of the four subjects of the quadrivium (see Glossary)—and on the philosophy of Aristotle. But his chief work, for the Middle Ages and for Chaucer, was the *Consolation,* a work of Stoic doctrine, teaching detachment from the troubles and difficulties of daily life and the patient bearing of adversity, which had the greater reputation because it was thought that Boethius was a Christian. Cast in the form of a vision, in alternate verse and prose, it tells how Boethius, in prison, was visited by the Lady Philosophy, who showed him how the afflictions of life—from which one must not try simply to escape—were transitory and could be borne once one had determined to put one's trust in absolute good and not allow oneself to come under the domination of Fortune, worldly good. Evil itself, Philosophy taught, could have no existence, since it has no part in absolute good: the evil of the world is therefore illusory. (See below, the Nun's Priest's Tale, ll. 472 ff.). The use Chaucer made of the *Consolation* to construct the philosophical framework for his *Troilus and Criseyde* makes it clear that Boethius's thought had for him the status of philosophic explanation as well as a guide to conduct and consolation in adversity.

At some time before he translated Boethius, Chaucer had tried his hand at a poem which one can already call typically Chaucerian, but which remains fragmentary: *The House of Fame.* The work owes much to many writers—Macrobius on dreams (see below, the Nun's Priest's Tale, ll. 353 ff.), Ovid and Virgil—but especially to Dante. It contains some of the best and most moving lines that Chaucer ever wrote and it has many echoes of Dante, transformed by the lively Chaucerian technique. Indeed, it has elements of burlesque Dante; and it may well be that Chaucer left it off because he did not feel himself equal to the *tour de force* he was attempting. Later, using Dante's words in the conclusion to *Troilus and Criseyde,* he was to show that he could intermittently rise, in all seriousness, to something like Dante's grave exaltation. But he could not keep it up.

Though it is true that Chaucer often used Italian literature, through French versions, it was only during the 1370's that it came to be a major influence on his poetry. Certainly his interest must have derived in part from his visits to Italy. The Italian author who most influenced him was Giovanni Boccaccio (1313–75), best known among his contemporaries for his Latin collections of exemplary lives, *The Falls of Princes* and *Of Famous Ladies,* but also a poet and prose writer of genius in Italian. To Boccaccio, directly or indirectly, Chaucer is indebted for a long passage in *The Parliament of Fowls.* This extended poem is a debate about the nature of love (a *demande d'amours*) in dream allegory form, as argued by birds with the intervention of Dame Nature, on St. Valentine's day. More importantly, Boccaccio provided the plot for one of the greatest love poems in the language, Chaucer's Troy-romance, *Troilus and Criseyde,* which is based, perhaps via the French *Roman de Troyle,* on Boccaccio's *Il Filostrato.* Chaucer never acknowledges this; indeed he never anywhere acknowledges that he has taken anything from Boccaccio, though the debt is enormous. But his poem is far more than Boccaccio, good as Boccaccio's story is. Chaucer transformed it into a more profound work—partly because of the Boethian philosophic character which he gave it, partly because of the depth and subtlety of his insight, and partly because of the unforgettable trio of characters he created from the much more conventional figures of Boccaccio's poem: Pandarus, Troilus, and Criseyde. Like *The Parliament of Fowls* the poem is also an exploration of the nature of earthly love, but played out this time by human actors, not personified abstractions or birds. Troilus has put himself on the wheel of Fortune through love of Criseyde and, through her fickleness, he comes to see the falseness of earthly love: this is his final vision. We, however, cannot forget the glory and the sweetness that have gone before—and Chaucer does not mean us to.

THE CANTERBURY TALES

There is no way of avoiding the feeling that all that has gone before in Chaucer's poetic career merely leads up to *The Canterbury Tales.* Chronologically, the *Tales* are his final achievement, though it looks as if he had long before worked out drafts of some of the stories which he proposed to use (the "tragedies" of the Monk's Tale, the Second Nun's Tale of St. Cecilia, an early version of the Knight's Tale—for the plot of which he was again indebted to Boccaccio). In terms of artistry the *Tales* represent the peak of his gigantic and varied talent, his fullest and most mature production. Chaucer seems to have given to this great poem the major part of his poetic time for the last fifteen or so years of his life. The only interruptions seem to have been his *Treatise on the Astrolabe* and, quite early in the period, a somewhat half-hearted attempt, in *The Legend of Good Women,* at a poem on the Ovidian model concerning women who were martyrs to their faithful love.

The *Tales* are certainly the expression of Chaucer's fully matured genius; yet even if he had never written them he would have done enough to make it clear that he has no superior as an English poet except Shakespeare. He dwarfs his contemporaries —and the poets of the next hundred and fifty years—in the same way as Shakespeare dwarfs his. The isolation of Chaucer's performance, indeed, makes it all the more astonishing. Nothing in the tradition of English poetry prepares us for him, and it appears, though he obviously knew a good deal of what had been written in English before and around him, that he did not find it very helpful. He acknowledges a debt to his older London contemporary, John Gower, "moral Gower"—or rather he dispatches his *Troilus and Criseyde,* perhaps ironically, to Gower for "correction." But he does not seem, anywhere, really to owe anything to any other writer in English—and the kind of poem that he can produce is entirely beyond the reach of any other writer of the time, let alone of the careful, often charming, but pedestrian Gower. It is easy to exaggerate the picture either way and to see—for example, in his mockery of the jog-trot of English romances in his own virtuoso piece, the Tale of Sir Thopas—more knowledge of English poetry than in fact he possessed. Throughout his life his models seem to have been French. His genius was to transform those models and naturalize them in English as thoroughly as he did—verse forms, meters, literary modes and all—to absorb influences from a number of literatures and make himself the first English poet fit to stand with the best that the rest of Europe could produce.

There were many respects in which he shared European preoccupations, one of the most important being the conscious artistry of his verse. As with any great poet, this is partly a matter for which instinct must account. But it is also partly a matter of self-awareness in the handling of subject and verse, so as to produce the maximum effect of "sentence and solas": profit and delight. One means of doing this was to imitate the ancient poets, to show oneself truly worthy to be in their company, inheritor of their poetic. This is one of the things that Petrarch was asserting in his Coronation Oration: Chaucer proclaims it in the epilogue to *Troilus and Criseyde,* with his humble recommendation of the book to the great classical poets. They represent the solid block of tradition behind any true poet. Remembrance of the past, constant remaking of its great stories—stories of Troy, Alexander, Rome, Thebes, Britain—was the essential task of the poet—and this, not any slavish desire for simple support, is the reason for the stress constantly laid on the necessity for authority and example in medieval literature—"auctoritee" and "ensaumple": "And if that olde bokes weren aweye, / Yloren were of remembrance the keye."

Chaucer's sense of the imperfections of his language and his treatment of the stories is not a modesty topos (see Glossary), still less mock modesty: it is the index of a deep concern for literary art: "The lyf so short, the craft so long to lerne," as he says in *The Parliament of Fowls.* Similarly, his conscious parodies of rhetoric (see Glossary) and rhetoricians are the index of his concern for the effects and effectiveness of language. Even when they mock, they mock something which is conceded to be necessary: "The dayes honour and the hevenes ye, / The nyghtes foo. . . ." Chaucer means us to recognize these rhetorical *traductiones* ("conceits"), piled up in *frequentatio* (repetition of the same structure) and with *polysyndeton* (use of the same syntactical scheme). The joke that he then springs on us, "al this clepe I the sonne," is a kind of double-take: he pretends to be amazed that he has been writing rhetoric all the time, mocking himself too for seeing that he is doing so. So too in the famous lament for "black Friday" in the Nun's Priest's Tale, where Chaucer, in the character of the Nun's Priest, is parodying a famous rhetorical set piece without implying that all such set pieces are pompous and useless. Chaucer is a profoundly rhetorical poet, with an explicit concern for his craft. Some of his uses of it are self-mocking, but for every one of these we can discover a hundred where the ordinary devices recommended by the rhetoricians—for beginning an argument, inventing arguments or incidents, varying a theme, making it both effective and pleasant—are being deployed. It is important to remember that rhetoric, for Chaucer, meant effective writing, not bombast, and that when he called a fellow poet "rhetor," it was a compliment.

The question of Chaucer's rhetoric—now taking the word in its widest sense—is much complicated in *The Canterbury Tales* by the dramatic illusion of the tellers within a framework of tales, the double fiction being simultaneously maintained. There was nothing new in the notion of framing a set of stories by putting them into the mouths of different tellers, and collections of such stories were composed from the fifth century A.D. onward. They were common enough in later medieval times. Boccaccio had arranged the hundred tales of his *Decameron* among ten men and women who had left the city for fear of the plague. Each told a tale on ten successive days. Boccaccio's fellow countryman Giovanni Sercambi, probably about 1374, also put together a set of such tales, told by one narrator on a journey and sometimes varied to fit the locality the travelers had reached at a given stage of their journey. We do not know whether Chaucer knew either Boccaccio's or Sercambi's collection—though he certainly knew an analogous use of the framing device by Gower in his *Confessio Amantis* (The Lover's Confession). His exploitation of the device is a brilliant variation on other uses: unlike Boccaccio, he fits tale to teller; unlike Sercambi and Gower, he provides more than one narrator. It is possible that Chaucer's pilgrim-framework was the result of what he could see himself at any moment, especially from his house at Greenwich, where he was living when he began the *Tales* in earnest—a party of pilgrims on the road to the shrine of St. Thomas Becket at Canterbury, England's most famous and most frequented place of pilgrimage, within easy reach of London. Such pilgrimages were well known, even notorious, for the convoys in which they were made, and the diversions and tale-telling that went on by the way. (Fig. 35)

As he tells us, through the Host in the Prologue, Chaucer had originally planned some one hundred and twenty tales, two for each pilgrim on the way to Canterbury and two more for the way back. Like many ambitious plans, this was severely curtailed in the execution. Before his death at age fifty-seven—which was considered advanced in Chaucer's day—he had completed only twenty-two, had left two more uncompleted, and had done a certain amount of shuffling of tales from those for whom they were originally intended. The result, especially after the addition of the links between tales, with the backchat between pilgrims, the tensions, anger, insults, alliances, and friendships these reveal between teller and teller, tale and tale, is the richest and most complex collection of its kind in any language.

The cheerful, lively General Prologue, with its descriptions of all the pilgrims and the relationships that exist between them before the beginning of the pilgrimage, is followed by the grave, chivalric tale of the Knight—a story of Athens long ago, and the knightly contest of Palemon and Arcite for the love of Emily, a tale perfectly proportioned to its teller. So too, is the Miller's *fabliau* (see Headnote and Glossary) about a stupid carpenter cuckolded by his dapper young lodger, told with force and gusto and rousing the anger of the Reeve, himself a carpenter by trade and resenting the implication that one of his fellow workmen should be treated in this way. The Reeve's turn comes immediately, and he takes advantage of it to tell another *fabliau* about a miller who is outwitted by two students whom he has tried to cheat. Not only do they get back their bread which the miller has stolen, but they manage to lay both his wife and daughter. Later, the Friar and the Summoner also quarrel and each tells a tale against the profession of the other. These are single examples of pairing, but there is one instance where something more seems to have been intended. This occurs in the group of tales known as the Marriage Group: the Wife of Bath, with her militant feminism and aggression and her curious tale of faery love and "maistry," begins it. Then, in the usual order of the *Tales,* we have the disagreement between Summoner and Friar and their opposing tales—and then, to counter the Wife and to calm the atmosphere, the gentle, cool, placid tale of the Clerk, about the patient Griselda and obedience in marriage—followed, to keep the tone from staying too cool, by Chaucer's ironic *envoi* (see Glossary). There follows the Merchant's Tale about the old man, January, who married a young wife, May, and was cuckolded for it—another *fabliau* of cleverness and quick-thinking, its pace much quicker than the Clerk's. Finally comes the moving, sober, simple tale of the Franklin. Since we do not know the exact order of tales that Chaucer had in mind, we cannot be sure that his intention was that these particular tales should function as a close-knit group or should run through the series as a kind of counterpoint, or thematic unifier.

The problem about discovering thematic unity in *The Canterbury Tales* is that we cannot be sure that this was what Chaucer meant us to find. The headlinks give us some clues, but the unfinished state of the work makes it impossible to know whether the sequence is due to chance or design. In the manuscripts the tales are grouped into a number of blocks or fragments, but the order of these is far from invariable. The General Prologue and the tales of the Knight, Miller, Reeve, and Cook (unfinished) are always a beginning; the Parson's Tale and the Retraction always come last. Within that framework, order varies. Here the General Prologue and the tales of the Miller, Nun's Priest, Pardoner, Wife of Bath, and Franklin are presented; this corresponds with the grouping of some manuscripts. It presents the general introduction, followed by two comic tales, one a *fabliau,* one a burlesque beast fable with a final serious "morality." Then comes the self-portrait of the much-married Wife of Bath, and her tale; and the deeply serious and affecting tale of the Franklin; with the dark moral apologue of the Pardoner, preceded by the teller's devastating self-portrait, for a finale.

Of all Chaucer's works, *The Canterbury Tales* has always been the most popular. We can only guess at when exactly most of the tales were composed, for neither Chaucer nor his scribes give us any help. The more than eighty manuscripts, mostly of the fifteenth century, and Caxton's two editions of about 1478 and 1484, besides many other early printings, are indications of how well the poet's successors thought of his great poem.

CHAUCER'S ENGLISH

Chaucer gave both prestige and currency to the English spoken in London at his time, but this was not the only dialect of the language in which works of literature were composed during the fourteenth century. In particular, the regional dialects of the West and North of England and the North-West Midland of the time had a literature of their own, in a language which would often have been next to unintelligible to a Southern reader. This literature is often of great stature—Langland's *Piers Plowman* was originally written in the dialect of the West; the works of the *Gawain*-poet were written in North-West Midland. In the fourteenth and fifteenth centuries, too, the cycles of mystery plays were composed in the Northern dialect (Chaucer makes one of the students speak it in the Reeve's Tale). The comic scenes in *The Second Shepherds' Play* use the difference to set the affected Southern speech of the character Mak against the plain, blunt Northern outspokenness of the shepherds. The difficulty that one part of the country had in understanding another was still present in Caxton's day (see below, his Preface to the *Aeneid*). These two fifteenth-century examples of dialect difference indicate the continuance of the problem: despite Chaucer, London English was not established as the English norm overnight—and considerable dialect differences remain, even today. (The longer Middle English texts in this volume which are not written in the London dialect have been modernized or translated.)

Chaucer, along with John Gower and other London authors of the fourteenth century, took the English of London just at a time when it was beginning to assert itself as the major dialect and carried it farther along the road. Their use of it represents the true beginning of modern standard English. Hitherto, French had been the language of cultured entertainment, and Latin the language of scholarly instruction—and up to a point remained so until the sixteenth century. Gower, in fact, wrote in French and Latin as well as in English. The fifteenth and sixteenth centuries see a conscious effort on the part of poets, prose writers, and their printers alike to bring English to a level of richness and expressive subtlety where it can compete with both French and Latin on equal terms (see Caxton's Prefaces below).

The London English that Chaucer used was a composite, made up of the dialects of the neighboring counties, chiefly of the East Midlands, but with some South-Eastern (Kentish) features and a few South-Western. It is so much the ancestor of modern English that there is comparatively little in vocabulary, syntax, and grammar that is not easily recognizable to a modern reader. The elaborate system of inflections which had characterized Old English and earlier Middle English was being leveled, and unstressed final -e was becoming a silent letter. Most of Chaucer's vocabulary is still recognizable, even though the spelling often differs considerably from the modern: *dayeseye* for "daisy," for example; or *defaute,* a French spelling for "default." Spelling is not uniform, and the same word may be spelled in different ways: thus, *mone, moone,* for "moon." About a third of Chaucer's vocabulary is French. There are differences in sense between Chaucer's vocabulary and ours: *parcel,* for example, for "part"; *chalange* for "claim"; *lust* for "pleasure." *"Him thoughte," "me thoughte"* do not mean "he (or I) thought" but "it seemed to him/me."

The best way to understand Chaucer is to read him aloud. Though we cannot hope to recover the exact manner in which his language was spoken, we can achieve a reasonably good notion of it. Reading aloud minimizes the difficulties of understanding Chaucer, which lie in the different meanings of much of his vocabulary and the subtlety of his poetry, rather than in his grammar or syntax. The merest skeleton of these two is therefore given below, but the pronunciation is dealt with rather more fully.

PRONUNCIATION

The chief points to note about Chaucerian pronunciation are:

Vowels

Stressed short vowels are pronounced as in Modern English, with the exception of a, which is open, i.e. a "rounder" sound than in modern "man," as in Modern French *patte,* and *u* (often spelled *o* as in *love*), which has only the sound of modern *put.* A vowel is always short when it is followed by two consonants. Otherwise, it may be short or long: modern pronunciation is a good guide.

Long vowels are pronounced as they are in modern Italian or French. A long vowel can be recognized as long if it is doubled in spelling (*maad, reed, wood*); or if it occurs in a stressed position at the end of a word (*he, mo, wisly*). *A,* e, o are long if followed by a single consonant plus -e (*made, rede, wode*).

a as in Modern English "father": *fader, maad.*

e as in Modern English "air": *ese, heed;* or as in Modern French "été": nede, theef.

(A practical guide here is modern spelling: Chaucer's words with the open sound as in modern "air" tend to be spelled today with ea: *ease; head;* those with the close sound to be spelled with *ee* or *ie: need, thief.* In the early stages of familiarizing oneself with Chaucerian pronounciation, it may be best to ignore the distinction and use only the pronunciation as in "air.")

i(y) as in Modern English "machine": *sire, slyde.*

o as in Modern English "note": *oo, stoon;* or as in Modern French "chose": *do, good.*

(Modern English sometimes spells the open sound *oa: boat;* and the closed *oo.* Again, the best advice to the beginner is to ignore the distinction and use only the pronunciation as in *boat.*)

u generally spelled *ou, ow* as in Modern English "rude": *luce.* (In words of French origin, such as *aventure,* the French pronunciation of *u* is kept.)

Diphthongs combine the two elements, as given above:

ai (ay), *ei* (ey) are midway between Modern English "play" and "aisle": *fair, way, veines, wey.*

au (aw) as in Modern English "house": *baume, bawd.* (In words of French origin, such as *daunce,* it is pronounced as in *haunt.*)

eu (ew) as in Modern English "few": *newe, knew;* or as in Modern English "lewd": *fewe, lewed.*

Unstressed vowels (chiefly final -e).

as in Modern English "about."

By Chaucer's time, final unstressed -e was probably not sounded in everyday speech, but in verse it is sounded or not, according to the demands of the meter. It is usually elided, i.e. merged into the following word, if that word begins with a vowel. It is usually sounded before the caesura or at the end of a line.

Consonants

All consonants are pronounced, except the initial *h-* in some words of French origin: *honour.* Both elements of initial *gn, kn, wr* are pronounced *g-naw, g-nof, k-nyt, k-now, w-rap, w-recche.* Similarly both elements of *lk, lf, lm: folk, half, palmer.* The combination *gh* is pronounced gutturally like German *-ch.*

GRAMMAR

The features of Chaucerian grammar on which the modern reader needs most guidance are:

Nouns and adjectives. Almost all older case-endings have disappeared, and those that remain are similar to those surviving in Modern English. The plural of most nouns ends in *-es* or *-s;* with an occasional *-en* plural (*eyen,* or *yën* for "eyes") and an occasional uninflected plural (*pound, yeer*). The possessive case ends in *-es* or *-s.* Adjectives add -e to their final consonant in certain circumstances.

Pronouns. Both *thou* and *you* are used, *you* sometimes to signify respectful or formal use of language. The third person singular uses *his* for the possessive of *it;* and the plural uses *hem, here, hir*(e) for the objective and possessive of they.

Adverbs are formed from adjectives by adding -e, or *-lich*(e), *-ly.*

Verbs. Infinitives end in -e or -en.

Present participles usually end in -ing(e), *-yng*(e), with an occasional *-and.*

Past participles end in *-en* or -e and often begin with *y-*. Chaucer uses several different forms: *sworn, swore, ysworn, yswore, comen.*

Present indicative ends in -e, *-est, -eth* for the first three persons of the singular, and all these endings may be contracted after a final vowel or final *-d* or *-t. Lith, lieth, lyeth,* and *last, laste, lasteth* may all be found. All persons of the plural end in -e(*n*).

Past definite. The plural usually ends in -e or -en. *Goon* (go) has two forms for the past: *yede* and *wente.*

SYNTAX

Chaucer's syntax is often oral syntax, sometimes tortuous and inverted, full of omissions and with occasional superfluous words and constructions, but not difficult. One major point to note is that in Chaucer, as in Middle English in general, negatives do not cancel each other out as they do in Modern English. They intensify, so that "That nevere . . . / Ne sholde upon him take no maistrie" is a strong negative. Another important point is the frequent use of impersonal constructions: *him list* for "it pleased him," *me thoughte* for "it seemed to me." Another is the frequent use of auxiliary verbs: *gan* is used to form a simple past tense: *gan slyde* means "did slide," or "slid," and it may be used also to express a sense of beginning. *Do* is used in the sense of "make"—*do me lyve:* "make me live"; go in the sense of "let us"—*go we soupe:* "let us have supper."

The text is based on that of W. W. Skeat, first published in 1894–97, with readings introduced from other sources. For the General Prologue, the helpful text of Phyllis M. Hodgson, 1969, has been much drawn upon. As an aid to the reader, an e which has now become silent has been printed e where the meter requires it to be pronounced as a syllable; an acute accent indicates an e pronounced like modern French é; and accentuation which differs from Modern English is marked thus: *àppearence.*

It is hoped that this will encourage the reader to recite Chaucer's verse aloud, following the indications for pronunciation given above. This was the way in which many of Chaucer's contemporaries would have made their acquaintance with his works, for they were composed with recitation in mind (Fig. 24).

The Canterbury Tales

General Prologue

With the General Prologue, as with all Chaucer's works, the difficulty is to know art from nature, and to see how Chaucer, from the mass of conventions in which he worked, achieved an utterly unconventional and original masterpiece, the first and the greatest of its kind in our literature. We cannot say what gave him the idea of building his great poem out of a slice of society which is typical but not entirely representative. We do not know whether he began with the notion of a set of tales told by pilgrims, or whether he had written a number of stories before deciding to link them together in this way. We do not know whether the General Prologue, as we have it, is a final version or only the draft for one: we can only say that it was probably written in the 1380's.

The Prologue opens with a rhetorical passage which at once poses a problem. It is a hymn to the regenerative power of the sun and to the rise of the sap in nature, the rebirth of the dead year that sends men and women to seek spiritual regeneration at a place of pilgrimage and physical and mental recreation during the journey. It is often praised as a miracle of naturalistic description: this *is* how it happens. Yet it is thoroughly conventional in two ways. First, a hymn to Spring was a recognized literary commonplace, especially for beginning a poem. Second, it is not, as is so often claimed, utterly lifelike: for example, March is not a dry month in England and the description of it as such is part of a literary convention that, far from being English, goes back to classical literature. Yet the life and vigor are undoubtedly there, in this perfectly wrought, eighteen-line verse paragraph, the striking beginning recommended by rhetorical theory which at once engages the reader and then modulates gently into the lower rhetorical mode of the portraits that are to follow.

The portraits themselves are as difficult to characterize as the opening passage. They are types, without doubt, and intended in their total to represent contemporary English society, with the exception of the higher nobility, who would go on pilgrimage with their own train and not in a company. If we were dealing with an attempt at naturalistic description, we should expect to find more than one representative of each profession or each rank. Yet the characters are so individual that they seem to ride out of the pages. Are we to conclude that they are portraits drawn from life? So many exact details are given for so many of them that Chaucer must, at the very least, be making some reference to existing persons, the point of which is now lost to us but would have been understood by his listeners or his readers. It may be that there is more to it than that: the Host has been identified with an actual innkeeper, and people living in Chaucer's day have been found whose characters would certainly fit the characters that Chaucer gives in the Prologue. He may have taken hints from contemporary men and women who were known to him personally or by repute to diversify the types he was drawing.

Once more our difficulty is to know what is convention and what is not. The tender and delicate portrait of the Prioress, for example, plays with the tension between the heavenly love to which she is vowed and the earthly love which shows in her love of small, delicate, pretty things, and on the ambiguities of applying a single language to both. She is described in terms that fit a heroine of romance—some of her features are a direct imitation of the features of Leisure/Idleness in the *Roman de la*

Rose, and the description of her table manners is derived from the same text. The ambiguities of her character are typical human ambiguities. Her own gentleness is matched by the gentleness of the portrait: the satire is light, controlled, unwounding. She is individual and type in one, lovingly and gently yet satirically placed in relation to the other ecclesiastics of the pilgrimage. Later, Chaucer will intensify the portrait by means of her pitiful tale of the murdered little boy, Hugh of Lincoln, just as he will poke gentle fun at the young, modest, learned Clerk—the type of the earnest young scholar—in his tale. Here the irony and satiric method are quiet, caressing, indirect. For the "noble ecclesiast" who is the Pardoner, or the worldly Monk and begging Friar, much harsher ironic treatment is reserved. As types, they are set against what a religious man ought to be; as characters they are set against what the other religious characters in the Prologue actually are. We are intended to see both how they fall short of what should be—that is, of their profession—and of the example they might take from the pious, decent Parson.

In the Parson and the Plowman, his brother, Chaucer has taken stock types from another sort of literature. In the contemporary prose and poetry of social complaint and criticism, the Plowman in particular figures as critic and as the example of the true laborer, against whose simple piety, scrupulousness in performing his allotted task, poverty, and oppressed condition may be measured the surface devotion, cynicism, neglect of duty, money-grubbing, and love of power of those who profess to be his betters. The same holds true, to a lesser extent, of the country priest—whom Chaucer significantly makes the Plowman's brother.

In presenting his characters Chaucer—like a modern author drawing on present-day psychology—frequently uses the psychological theory of his time, which gave the planets in a man's horoscope at birth, and their positions at different times during his life, an influence on the kind of man he was. Similarly, the bodily fluids, or humors, of which he was composed—blood, phlegm, choler (bile), and melancholy (black bile)—with their "qualities" of hot, cold, dry, and moist, according to their mixture in him, would determine character and behavior. One could, too, according to the theory of the time, read the signs of character in the face (physiognomy, physiognomics) or the outward bodily characteristics (see Fig. 37). The Wife of Bath's horoscope would predispose her to the lasciviousness she glories in. The description of the Miller's physical traits can be interpreted to mean that he is bold, angry, shameless, and talkative. The Summoner's appearance is both the result and the expression of his lecherous temperament. The Pardoner's spiritual degeneracy is partly due to his physical state: he is a eunuch born. The Franklin's love of rich food and wine and hospitality might be deduced from the combination of humors which make up his temperament: blood predominates, so that he is red-faced, outgoing, confident, generous, quick to anger.

Yet to say this about the kind of detail from all sources that Chaucer uses for his descriptions of the pilgrims is not to arrive at the heart of his mystery. It is merely an indication of how incomparably rich were the materials on which he was able to draw and how remarkably he handles them. The poet William Blake has the last word: "Of Chaucer's characters . . . some of the names or titles are altered by time, but the characters themselves remain forever unaltered."

General Prologue

Here biginneth the Book of the Tales of Caunterbury.

When that Aprille° with hise shourės> sote> *showers / sweet*
The droghte of March hath percėd> to the rote, *pierced*
And bathėd every veyne° in swich licour
Of which vertu engendrėd is the flour;
Whan Zephirus° eek> with his sweetė breeth> *also / breath*
Inspirėd hath in every holt> and heeth> *wood/ field*
The tendre croppės,> and the yongė sonne° *shoots*
Hath in the Ram his halfė cours yronne,> *run*
And smalė fowlės> maken melodye *birds*
That slepen al the night with open iye°
(So priketh hem> Nature in hir corages)>: *them / their hearts*
Thanne longen> folk to goon> on pilgrimages, *long / go*
And palmeres° for to seken straungė strondes,> *foreign shores*
To fernė halwės, couthe in sondry londes;°
And specially from every shirės ende
Of Engėlond to Caunterbury° they wende,> *go*
The holy blisful> martir for to seeke, *blessed*
That hem hath holpen> whan that they were seke.> *helped / sick*
  Bifel> that in that seson> on a day, *It happened / season*
In Southwerk° at the Tabard as I lay
Redy to wenden> on my pilgrimage *go*
To Caunterbury with ful devout corage,
At nyght was come into that hostelrye> *inn*
Wel nine and twenty in a companye,
Of sondry folk, by aventure> yfalle *chance*
In felawship,> and pilgrimes were they alle *companionship*
That toward Caunterbury wolden> ryde. *wished to*
The chambres> and the stables weren wyde, *bedrooms*
And wel we weren esėd attė beste.°
And shortly, whan the sonnė was to reste,
So hadde I spoken with hem everichon> *every one*
That I was of hir felawship> anon,> *company / at once*
And madė forward> erly for to ryse, *agreement*

Aprille the traditional Spring opening. Zephirus, Nature, and the zodiacal dating are part of the stock of the medieval poet.
veyne vein (of plants), sap vessel; thus, "And bathed every vein in such a liquid, by the power of which the flower is begotten"
Zephirus the West wind
yonge sonne young, because just passed out of the first zodiacal sign (Fig. 37) of the solar year, Aries, the Ram, which in Chaucer's time was thought to govern March 12 to April 11
open iye i.e. do not sleep at all in Spring
palmeres originally, pilgrims who carried a palm leaf to show that they had been to the Holy Land; later applied to all pilgrims
To ferne . . . londes to far-off shrines, famous ones, in various countries
Caunterbury the most popular medieval place of pilgrimage in England because of the tomb there of St. Thomas Becket, murdered in the Cathedral in 1170 and canonized 1174
Southwerk Southwark, then a suburb of London on the south bank of the Thames, stood at the beginning of the road to Dover and Canterbury. The Tabard, now destroyed, was a famous inn. Its sign would have shown the short, sleeveless surcoat worn by knights and heralds, called a tabard.
And wel . . . beste and we were made comfortable in the best manner

To take oure wey theras> I yow devyse.> *where / tell*
But natheles,> whil I have tyme and space,° *nevertheless*
Er> that I ferther in this talė pace>, *before / pass*
Me thynketh it acordaunt to resoùn°
To tellė yow al the condicioùn°
Of ech of hem,> so as it semėd me, *them*
And whiche> they weren, and of what degree,> *who / status*
And eek in what array° that they were inne;
And at a knyght then wol I first biginne.

KNYGHT

A knyght ther was, and that a worthy> man, *distinguished*
That fro the tymė that he first bigan
To riden out, he lovėd chivalrie,
Trouthe and honoùr, fredom and curteisie.°
Ful worthy> was he in his lordės werre,> *brave / war*
And therto hadde he riden, no man ferre,> *further*
As wel in Cristendom as in hethenesse,> *pagan lands*
And evere honoured for his worthynesse.
At Alisaundre° he was whan it was wonne.
Ful oftė tyme he hadde the bord bigonne°
Aboven allė nacions in Pruce;
In Lettow hadde he reysėd,> and in Ruce, *campaigned*
No Cristen man so ofte of his degree.
In Gernade at the seege eek hadde he be
Of Algezir, and riden in Belmarye.
At Lyeys was he, and at Satalye,
Whan they were wonne; and in the Gretė See°
At many a noble armee> hadde he be. *invading force*
At mortal batailles° hadde he been fiftene,
And foughten for oure feith at Tramissene°
In lystės° thriės, and ay> slayn his foo.> *always / enemy*
This ilkė> worthy knyght hadde been also *same*
Somtymė> with the lord of Palatye *formerly*
Agayn> another hethen in Turkye. *against*

tyme and space an oral formula; the words carry less than their full value: "while I can"
resoùn perhaps French *raison*, right; or Latin *ratio*, rhetorical order; or reason
condicioùn whole state of being, inner and outer
array dress or order
Trouthe . . . curteisie knightly virtues; see Chaucer's *balade*, "Truth," below. *Trouthe* here is integrity; *fredom* is liberality, material and spiritual; *curteisie* is well-bred behavior.
Alisaundre The Knight had fought against all three of the great enemies of 14th-century Christendom: the Saracens in the Middle East (Christians captured Alexandria in Egypt, 1365 (Fig. 36); Attalia (Sattalye) in Turkey, 1361; Ayas (Lyes in Armenia, 1367); sometimes in alliance with the pagan "Lord of Palatye," the Turkish sultan, against other infidels—a not infrequent Christian-heathen alliance; the Moors in Spain and North Africa (Granada, Algeciras, Ben-Marin, 1344 and after); the barbarians of Lithuania (Lettow; to 1385), and the Tartars of Russia.
bord bigonne taken the head of the table at a banquet; perhaps of the Teutonic Order of Knights in (East) Prussia
Gretė See Mediterranean
batailles tournaments between champions fought to the death, for a decision between armies
Tramissene Tlemçen, Algeria, then a Berber stronghold
lystes space enclosed by barriers for tournaments or jousts (Fig. 48)

And everemore> he hadde a sovereyn prys,> *always / reputation*
And though that he were worthy, he was wys,> *prudent*
And of his port> as meeke as is a mayde. *behavior*
He nevere yet no vilainye ne sayde
In al his lyf unto no maner wight.°
He was a verray,> parfit,> gentil knyght. *true / perfect*
But for to tellen yow of his array,> *equipage*
His hors° were godė, but he was nat gay.> *gaudy*
Of fustian he werėd a gypoun°
Al bismoterėd> with his habergeoun, *rust-stained*
For he was late> ycome from his viage,> *just / expedition*
And wentė for to doon his pilgrimage.

SQUIER°

With hym ther was his sone, a young squièr,
A lovyere, and a lusty> bachelèr, *lively*
With lokkės crulle,> as they were layd in presse.> *curled / crimped*
Of twenty yeer of age he was, I gesse.
Of his statùre he was of evene> lengthe, *moderate*
And wonderly deliver,> and greet of strengthe. *agile*
And he hadde been somtyme in chyvachie°
In Flaundres, in Artoys, and Picardye,
And born hym> weel, as of so litel space,° *carried himself*
In hope to stonden> in his lady grace. *stand well*
Embrouded> was he, as it were a mede> *embroidered / meadow*
Al ful of fresshė flowrės, whyte and reede.°
Syngyng he was, or floytinge° al the day.
He was as fressh as is the month of May.
Short was his gowne, with slevės longe and wyde.
Wel coude he sitte on hors and fairė ryde.
He coudė songės make, and wel endite,> *write poetry*
Juste> and eek daunce, and weel portraye> and write. *joust / draw*
So hoote he lovėde, that by nightertale
He slepte namore than dooth a nightingale.
Curteis he was, lowly, and servysable,
And carf biforn his fader at the table.°

He nevere . . . wight Middle English uses an accumulation of negatives to strengthen, not cancel each other out; thus, "He never yet, in all his life, said anything base to anyone of any kind."
hors horses; an uninflected plural
gypoun jupon, the close-fitting tunic worn under a coat of mail (*habergeoun*). His was of a thick, coarse cloth (*fustian*).
squier properly speaking not yet a knight but one who served a knight. Later he is called *bacheler*, a young knight who has not yet set up his own banner and is still in the service of a senior knight.
chyvachie cavalry campaigns, perhaps the single one of 1383 during the Hundred Years' War between England and France
as of . . . space considering the short time he had campaigned
whyte and reede stock phrase: "of all colors"
floytinge whistling or playing the flute or pipe
So hoote . . . table (ll. 97–100) "So hotly did he love, that at night-time he slept no more than a nightingale. He was courtly of behavior, modest and ready to serve; and he carved in front of his father at the table." To carve the roast, so that his lord was fittingly served, was a frequently mentioned duty of a squire.

YEMAN°

A yeman hadde he, and servaùnts namo> *no more*
At that tyme, for him liste> ridė so; *it pleased*
And he was clad in cote and hood of grene.°
A sheef of pecok arwės, bright and kene,
Under his belt he bar> ful thriftily,> *carried / handily*
(Wel coude he dresse> his takel> yemanly: *see to / gear*
His arwes droupėd noght with fetherės lowe°)
And in his hand he baar> a myghty bowe.° *bore*
A not-heed° hadde he, with a brown visage.> *face*
Of wodėcraft> wel coude he al the usage. *woodmanship*
Upon his arm he bar a gay bracer,°
And by his syde, a swerd and a bokeler,°
And on that other syde, a gay daggere,
Harneisėd> wel, and sharp as point of spere; *mounted*
A Cristofre° on his brest, of silver shene;> *shining*
An horn he bar,> the bawdrik° was of grene. *bore*
A forster> was he soothly,> as I gesse. *forester / truly*

PRIORESSE°

Ther was also a nonne,> a prioresse, *nun*
That of hir smiling was ful simple and coy.°
Hire gretteste ooth> was but 'by Saint Loy.'° *greatest oath*
And she was clepėd> Madame Eglentyne.° *called*
Ful wel she song the service divine,
Entunėd> in hir nose ful semėly.> *intoned / becomingly*
And Frensh she spak ful faire and fetisly,> *prettily*
After the scole> of Stratford-attė-Bowe,° *style*
For Frensh of Paris was to hir unknowe.
At metė> wel ytaught was she withalle:> *meal-time / moreover*
She leet> no morsel from hir lippės falle, *let*
Ne wette hir fingrės in hir saucė depe;
Wel coude she carie a morsel, and wel kepe> *take care*
That no drope ne fille> upon hir brist.> *fell / breast*
In curteisie was set ful muchel hir list.°

Yeman a yeoman or free man, a commoner attending the knight as his only other servant. A knight was obliged to have a retinue, to uphold his dignity. This knight makes do with squire and yeoman.
he . . . grene The yeoman was dressed in the huntsman's Lincoln green, and had a sheaf of arrows with peacock feathers tucked into his belt.
lowe Peacock feathers tended to disturb the flight of the arrow, but the yeoman can counteract this.
bowe the long-bow was 6 feet tall
not-heed close-cropped head
bracer guard on the left forearm, to prevent friction from the bow-string
swerd . . . bokeler sword and small round shield
Cristofre medal of St. Christopher, patron of travelers
bawdrik baldric, strap worn round the waist or diagonally across the body
Prioresse mother superior of a nunnery
simple and coy sincere and demure; monastic rule enjoined that laughter should be controlled, unaffected, and silent. *Simple and coy* is a stock phrase in medieval literature when a lover is praising his mistress.
Loy St. Eligius (Eloi), patron of goldsmiths and carters
Eglentyne sweetbriar
Stratford-atte-Bowe anglicized French, learned at the Benedictine nunnery of St. Leonard's, Kent
In . . . list her pleasure was strongly fixed on polite behavior

Hir overlippė wypėd she so clene
That in hir coppe> ther was no ferthyng> sene *cup / morsel*
Of grecė,> whan she dronken hadde hir draughte. *grease*
Ful semėly after hir mete she raughte.°
And sikerly, she was of greet desport,°
And ful plesaùnt, and amyable of port,> *bearing*
And peyned hire to countrefetė cheere
Of court, and to been estatlich of manere,
And to ben holden digne of reverence.°
But for to speken of hire conscience,
She was so charitable and so pitous,> *full of pity*
She woldė wepe, if that she sawe a mous
Caught in a trappe, if it were deed> or bledde.> *dead / bleeding*
Of> smalė houndės hadde she that she fedde *some*
With rosted flesh,> or milk and wastel breed.° *meat*
But sore wepte she, if any of hem were deed,
Or if men smoot> it with a yerdė> smerte.> *struck / stick / hard*
And al was conscience> and tendre herte. *soft feelings*
Ful semėly hir wimpel pinchėd was,°
Hir nose tretys,> hir eyen greye as glas,° *well-made*
Hir mouth ful smal, and therto> softe and reed.> *also / red*
But sikerly> she hadde a fair forheed— *certainly*
It was almoost a spannė brood,° I trowe;> *believe*
For, hardily,> she was nat undergrowe. *assuredly*
Ful fetis> was hir cloke, as I was war.> *well-made / aware*
Of smal coral,° aboute hire arm she bar
A paire of bedės,° gauded al with grene,
And theron heng> a brooch of gold ful shene,> *hung / bright*
On which ther was first write a crownėd A,°
And after, *Amor vincit omnia.*°

NONNE AND III PREESTES

Another nonnė with hir haddė she
That was hir chapėleyne,> and preestės thre.° *chaplain*

Ful . . . raughte very politely she reached for her food
And . . . desport and certainly, she was of great charm
And . . . reverence (ll. 139–41) and took pains to imitate the behavior of court and to be dignified of manner and to be considered worthy of reverence
wastel breed cake-bread; French *gâteau;* superior quality white bread
Ful . . . was Her wimple was pleated very becomingly. The wimple was a nun's close linen head covering, which should have covered her forehead and the sides of her face.
greye as glas conventional phrase. Gray was the conventional color for a medieval beauty's eyes.
spanne distance from thumb to extended little finger
coral not only jewelry but then believed a preservative of health, physical and spiritual
paire of bedes Rosary. *Bedes* originally meant prayers, and each bead represented an *Ave Maria;* the *gaudes,* representing a *Pater Noster,* marked off each ten beads.
A Nuns were normally forbidden ornaments.
Amor . . . omnia Latin: "Love conquers all"
thre Only one Nun's Priest tells a tale. A nunnery might have more than one priest, to offer mass and to hear confessions, which a woman could not do.

MONK

A monk ther was, a fair> for the maistrie,° — *fine one*
An outridere,° that lovedė venerie,°
A manly man, to been an abbot able.
Ful many a deyntee> hors hadde he in stable, — *fine*
And whan he rood,> men myghte his brydel heere — *rode*
Gynglen> in a whistlynge wynd als cleere, — *jingle*
And eek> as loude, as dooth the chapel belle — *also*
Ther as> this lord was kepere° of the celle. — *where*
The reule> of Saint Maure° or of Saint Beneit, — *rule*
Bycause that it was old, and somdel streit>— — *somewhat strict*
This ilkė> monk leet oldė thyngės pace,° — *same*
And heeld after the newė world the space.> — *meanwhile*
He yaf nat of> that text a pullėd> hen — *gave not for / plucked*
That seith> that hunters beth> nat holy men,° — *says / are*
Ne that a monk, whan he is recchėlees,> — *negligent*
Is likned til> a fissh that is waterlees.° — *like to a*
This is to seyn,> a monk out of his cloystre— — *say*
But thilkė> text heeld he nat worth an oystre — *that very*
And I seyde his opinioùn was good.
What> sholde he studie, and make hymselven wood,> — *why / mad*
Upon a book in cloystre alwey to poure,°
Or swynken> with his handės, and laboùre, — *toil*
As Austyn° bit?> How shal the world be served? — *bids*
Lat Austyn have his swink to him reserved!°
Therfore, he was a pricasour> aright: — *hard rider*
Grehoundes> he hadde as swift as fowel> in flight; — *greyhounds / bird*
Of priking° and of hunting for the hare
Was al his lust;> for no cost wolde he spare. — *pleasure*
I seigh> his slevės purfiled> at the hond — *saw / trimmed*
With grys,> and that the fyneste of a lond. — *gray fur*
And for to festne> his hood under his chyn, — *fasten*
He hadde of gold wroght> a ful curious> pyn; — *made / elaborate*
A love-knotte° in the gretter> ende ther was. — *larger*
His heed was balled,> that shoon as any glas, — *bald*
And eek his face, as it hadde been anoint.
He was a lord ful fat, and in good poynt;°
Hise eyen stepe,> and rollynge in his heed, — *prominent*

for the maistrie surpassing all others
outridere a monk who rides out to supervise the monastery's property outside its immediate limits
venerie hunting, but also sexual pursuit
kepere supervisor of an outlying house or dependent community
Saint Maure (Maurus) credited with introducing the monastic *Rule* of St. Benedict (Beneit) to France
pace go their way
That . . . holy men St. Jerome (c. 342–420) and St. Augustine (354–430) condemn hunting.
waterlees Wyclif, Gower, and Langland use the comparison.
poure pore. The Benedictines were great supporters of study.
Austyn St. Augustine, on whose writings the Augustinian rule was based, believed in monastic labor.
Lat . . . reserved! Let Augustine have the toil (that he talks so much about) kept for himself alone!
priking literally, following the tracks of. *Prick* is the footprint or track of the hare; or the verb may simply here mean *riding*, as Spenser thought.
love-knotte strands of gold tied to signify the affection of lovers
in good poynt in good condition, plump

That stemėd as a forneys of a leed;°
His bootės souple,> his hors in greet estat.> *supple / array*
Now certeinly he was a fair prelat.°
He was nat pale, as a forpynėd goost.> *pined-away ghost*
A fat swan loved he best of any roost,
His palfrey> was as brown as is a berye. *saddle horse*

FRERE°

A frere ther was, a wantown° and a merye,
A limitour,° a ful solempnė> man. *imposing*
In alle the ordrės foure° is noon that can> *knows*
So muche of daliaùnce> and fair langàge. *flirtation*
He haddė maad ful many a mariàge
Of yongė wommen at his ownė cost.
Unto his ordre he was a noble post.> *support*
And wel biloved and famulier> was he *intimate*
With frankeleyns° overal> in his contree,> *throughout / district*
And with worthy wommen of the toun—
For he had power of confessioùn,
As seyde hymself, more than a curàt,> *parish priest*
For of> his ordre he was licenciat.° *by*
Ful swetėly herde he confessioùn,°
And plesaunt was his absolucioùn.
He was an esy> man to yeve> penaunce *indulgent / give*
Ther as> he wiste> to have a good pitaunce. *where / expected*
For unto a poure> ordre for to yive *poor*
Is signė that a man is wel yshrive;> *absolved*
For if he yaf,> he dorstė> make avaunt> *gave / dared / boast*
He wistė> that a man was repentaùnt; *knew*
For many a man so hard is of his herte,
He may nat wepe, althogh hym sorė smerte.°
Therfore, in stede of wepynge and preyères,> *prayers*
Men moot yeve silver to the pourė freres.
His tipet° was ay farsėd> ful of knyves *always stuffed*
And pynnės, for to yeven fairė wyves.> *women*
And certeinly, he hadde a mery note;

That . . . leed that glowed like a furnace under a cauldron
prelat a churchman of the upper ranks, who has received preferment
Frere Chaucer's portrait is composed of the regular accusations against the friars, the mendicant (begging) religious orders founded during the spiritual revival of the 13th century. Vowed to poverty and to preaching, they had multiplied and become rich by Chaucer's time.
wantown Ranges in meaning from "playful" to "lascivious."
limitour religious field-worker (begging, hearing confessions, burying, preaching) within the district (*limitatio*) assigned to his convent
ordres foure Dominicans, Franciscans, Carmelites, Augustinians
frankeleyns See l. 333.
licenciat licensed by the church to hear confessions
confessioùn The sinner who comes to confession must satisfy the confessor that he is contrite before being granted absolution. He must then perform an act of mortification imposed by the confessor, to express remorse and good intentions. This friar would impose a light penance on those able to give pious donations ("pitaunce") to his order: to be ready to part with money was to him a sure sign of repentance.
hym sore smerte he is greatly pained
tipet the long narrow piece of cloth, part of hood or sleeve, which could be used as pocket

Wel coude he singe, and pleyen on a rote;°
Of yeddinges he bar utterly the pris.°
His nekkė whit was as the flour-de-lys.°
Therto,˃ he strong was as a champioùn.° *moreover*
He knew the tavernes wel in every toun,
And everich˃ hostiler˃ and tappestere *every / innkeeper*
Bet than a lazar or a beggestere;°
For unto swich a worthy man as he
Acorded nat, as by his facultee,°
To have with sikė˃ lazars aqueyntaùnce. *sick*
It is nat honeste,˃ it may nat avaunce,˃ *good / get one anywhere*
For to deelen with no swich poraille,°
But al with riche, and sellers of vitaille.˃ *food and drink*
And overal ther as˃ profit sholde arise, *wherever*
Curteis˃ he was, and lowely˃ of servyse. *courteous / humble*
Ther nas no man nowher so vertuous.˃ *capable*
He was the bestė beggere in his hous;˃ *friary*
And yaf a certeyn fermė for the graunt°
Noon of his bretheren cam ther in his haunt.
For thogh a widwe˃ haddė noght a sho,˃ *widow / shoe*
So plesaunt was his *'In principio,'*°
Yet wolde he have a ferthyng˃ er he wente. *farthing*
His purchas was wel bettre than his rente.°
And rage he coude, as it were right a whelp.°
In lovė-dayes° ther coude he muchel˃ help, *much*
For ther he was nat lyk a cloisterer°
With a thredbare cope,˃ as is a poure scoler,˃ *cape / scholar*
But he was lyk a maister,° or a Pope.
Of double worsted° was his semicope,°
That rounded as a belle out of the presse.˃ *mould*
Somwhat he lipsėd,˃ for his wantownesse,˃ *lisped / affectation*
To make his English sweete upon his tonge;
And in his harping, whan that he hadde songe,˃ *sung*
Hise eyen twynkled in his heed aryght,˃ *truly*

rote stringed instrument
Of . . . pris for ballads, he took the prize entirely
flour-de-lys lily; more often used of a woman
champioùn literally, a knight specially chosen to fight in a tournament to the death
tappestere . . . beggestere tapster, better than a leper or a beggar. The ending *-ere* is normally feminine, but a tapster can be either male or female: barman or barmaid.
as . . . facultee in view of his profession
poraille poor people, whom a friar was bound by his vows to comfort and succor. The Franciscan rule was based on the Gospel injunction "Sell all thou hast and give to the poor."
And yaf . . . graunt He paid a certain sum for the monopoly of practicing in his district. This line and the next do not occur in all manuscripts and the accusation of "farming" is not supported by the historical facts.
'In principio' the opening words of St. John's gospel: "In the beginning [was the word . . .]"; constantly quoted by the friars to justify their preaching and also used by them as a salutation
purchas . . . rente His pickings on the side were better than the income he was authorized to collect.
And rage . . . whelp and he knew how to frolic like a puppy
love-dayes days set aside for amicable settlement of legal disputes by arbitration out of court. Clergy were forbidden to take part, except on behalf of the poor.
cloisterer a member of a religious order confined to the monastery
maister master, university graduate or teacher
double worsted expensive, heavy woolen cloth
semicope short (half-length) cloak

As doon> the sterrės> in the frosty nyght. *do / stars*
This worthy limitour was cleped> Huberd. *called*

MARCHANT

A marchant was ther, with a forkėd berd,> *beard*
In mottėlee,° and hye on horse he sat,
Upon his heed a Flaundrish> bevere hat,° *Flemish*
His bootės claspėd faire> and fetisly.> *neatly / elegantly*
His resòns> he spak ful solempnėly,> *sayings / pompously*
Souninge> alway th'encrees of his winning. *publishing*
He wolde the see were kept for any thyng°
Bitwixė Middelburgh° and Orėwelle.
Wel coude he in eschaungė° sheeldės° selle.
This worthy man ful wel his wit bisette:> *ingenuity employed*
Ther wistė> no wight that he was in dette, *knew*
So estatly> was he of his governaunce,> *impressive / conduct*
With his bargàynes,> and with his chevisaunce.> *bargaining / loans*
Forsothe,> he was a worthy man withalle; *In truth*
But sooth to seyn, I noot how men hym calle.°

CLERK° OF OXENFORD

A clerk ther was of Oxenford also,
That unto logik° haddė longe ygo.
As leenė was his hors as is a rake,
And he nas nat> right fat I undertake, *was not*
But lookėd holwe,> and therto sobrely.> *hollow / grave*
Ful thredbare was his overeste> courtepy,° *outermost*
For he hadde geten> hym yet no benefice,> *gotten / church living*
Ne was so worldly for to have office.°
For hym was lever> have at his beddes heed *more pleasing*
Twenty bookės, clad in blak or reed,
Of Aristotle° and his philosophie,
Than robės riche, or fithele,> or gay sautrie.° *fiddle*
But al be> that he was a philosòphre, *although*
Yet haddė he but litel gold° in cofre.> *coffer*
But al that he mighte of his freendės hente,> *get*

mottelee parti-colored cloth
bevere hat an expensive fur hat
He wolde . . . thyng he wished the sea policed, at all costs
Middelburgh Middelburg, in Holland, almost opposite Orwell, in Suffolk; both were important ports for the import and export of wool and cloth, the basis of English trade with Flanders at the time.
sheeldes *écus* (French coins). The Merchant was a successful illegal speculator in enemy currency.
But sooth . . . calle but, to tell the truth, I don't know what he was called
Clerk literally, cleric, advanced student (at Oxford). A clerk professed his intention of entering the priesthood before going to university. He might remain there in minor orders all his life, going no farther up the ladder in the church, and seeking no post outside. Many university scholars were clerks and the word gained the connotation of "learned man."
logik the art of reasoning and argument. The Clerk is long past the elementary stage of his education, and is an accomplished logician.
courtepy short jacket
office a secular, administrative post such as many clerics took to make their living
Aristotle The rediscovered Aristotle, in Latin translation, formed the basis of the university curriculum.
sautrie psaltery, a stringed instrument, played with the hand
But . . . gold "Philosophy" could also mean "alchemy"; so the Clerk did not have the philosopher's stone to turn base metal into gold.

On bookės and on lernynge he it spente,
And bisily gan for the soulės preye°
Of hem that yaf> hym wherwith to scoleye.> — *gave / study*
Of studie took he most cure> and most heede. — *care*
Noght o> word spak he morė than was neede, — *one*
And that was seyd in forme and reverence,°
And short, and quyk,> and ful of hy sentence.° — *lively*
Souninge in> moral vertu was his speche, — *tending towards*
And gladly wolde he lerne and gladly teche.

SERGEANT OF LAWE°

A sergeant of the lawė, war> and wys,> — *cautious / prudent*
That often haddė been at the Parvys°
Ther was also, ful riche of excellence.
Discreet he was, and of greet reverence°—
He semėd swich, his wordes weren so wise.
Justice he was ful often in assise°
By patente,° and by pleyn commissioùn.°
For his science,> and for his heigh renoun, — *knowledge*
Of fees and robės hadde he many oon.
So greet a purchasour> was nowher noon: — *property speculator*
Al was fee simple° to hym in effect;> — *virtually*
His purchasing mighte nat been infect.> — *proved invalid*
Nowher so bisy a man as he ther nas,> — *was not*
And yet he semėd bisier than he was.
In termės hadde he caas and doomės alle
That from the tyme of Kyng William° were yfalle.> — *had occurred*
Therto, he coude endite> and make a thing,> — *compose / deed*
Ther coudė no wight pinche> at his writyng; — *complain*
And every statut coude he pleyn> by rote. — *complete*
He rood but hoomly,> in a medlee> cote — *unpretentiously / parti-colored*
Girt with a ceint> of silk, with barrės> smale. — *belt / stripes*
Of his array telle I no lenger tale.

FRANKELEYN°

A frankėleyn was in his companye,
Whit was his beerd, as is the dayėsye.> — *daisy*
Of his complexioùn he was sangwyn.°

gan . . . preye prayed. The Middle English *gan* and *can* are often used to form a simple past tense.
reverence in due form, with decorum and respect
sentence Latin: *sententia* (moral) significance; weighty, memorable saying
Sergeant of Lawe a lawyer of high rank and competence, who could also act as judge
Parvys area in front of a church, where lawyers and their clients met
of greet reverence highly respected
assise judicial sessions held periodically throughout England
patente "open [letter]": the royal letter of appointment, to be displayed to all
pleyn commissioùn full commission, full authority to adjudicate
fee simple i.e. land owned outright, with no legal complications
termes . . . William Either he had memorized all the cases and decisions since the reign of William the Conqueror (1066–87) or he had the legal yearbooks from that time to his.
Frankeleyn originally "free (*franc*) man." Many rose to be wealthy landowners equivalent to the gentry, and important figures in their district.
sangwyn sanguine; his constitution or temperament (*complexioùn*) dominated by the humor of blood

Wel loved he by the morwe> a sop in wyn;° *in the morning*
To liven in delit° was evere his wone,> *habit*
For he was Epicurus° ownė sone,
That heeld opinioùn that pleyn> delit *full*
Was verraily> felicitee parfit. *truly*
An housholdere, and that a greet, was he;
Saint Julian° he was in his contree.> *district*
His breed, his ale, was alweys after oon;°
A bettre envynėd° man was nowher noon;
Withoutė bakė mete was never his hous
Of fish and flesh, and that so plentevous,> *plentiful*
It snewėd> in his hous of mete> and drynke, *snowed / food*
Of allė deyntees> that men coudė thynke. *dainties*
After> the sondry sesons of the yeer, *according to*
So chaunged he his mete and his soper.> *supper*
Ful many a fat partrich hadde he in muwe,> *coop*
And many a breem and many a luce in stewe.°
Wo was his cook but if> his saucė were *unless*
Poynaunt> and sharp, and redy al his geere. *piquant*
His table dormant in his halle° alway
Stood redy covered> al the longė day.° *set*
At sessioùns ther was he lord and sire;°
Ful oftė tyme he was knyght of the shire.°
An anlas,> and a gipser> al of silk *dagger / purse*
Heeng> at his girdel,> whit as mornė milk. *hung / belt*
A shirreve° hadde he been, and a countour.°
Was nowher swich a worthy vavasour.°

HABERDASSHERE,° CARPENTER, WEBBE, DYERE, TAPICER

An haberdasshere and a carpenter
A webbe,> a dyere and a tapycer,>— *weaver / tapestry-maker*
And they were clothed alle in o lyveree°
Of a solempne> and a greet fraternitee. *dignified*
Ful fresh and newe hir geere apikėd> was; *adorned*

sop in wyn piece of fine toasted bread, soaked in spiced wine
delit sensuous pleasure
Epicurus (342–270 B.C.) Greek philosopher, for whom absence of pain because of virtuous living was the supreme good. The popular form of his doctrine is that pleasure itself is the true end of life.
Saint Julian patron saint of hospitality
after oon of one standard
envyned stocked with wine
breem . . . stewe and many a carp and pike in his fishpond
halle the main living room
Stood . . . day Medieval tables were usually on trestles, set up as required and then taken down. The Franklin's was permanently established and permanently loaded.
At . . . sire He took the chair at the (quarterly) sessions of the justices of the peace.
knyght of the shire county member of parliament, not necessarily a dubbed knight; Chaucer was himself such a representative, for the county of Kent in 1386
shirreve sheriff; next to the lord-lieutenant, the most important administrative officer of the county, whose revenue he had to collect and take to the exchequer.
countour "auditor," "accountant"; also "special pleader"—a county official
vavasour a member of the landed gentry, below the aristocracy
Haberdasshere dealer in needles, tapes, buttons; or in hats. Chaucer never wrote tales for any of the characters listed here.
lyveree livery; the (uniform) clothes of their guild, a group of tradesmen with common commercial interests and social and religious observances

Hir knivės were ychaped> noght with bras — *mounted*
But al with silver; wroght ful clene and weel
Hire girdles and hir pouches everydeel.> — *in every part*
Wel semėd ech of hem a fair burgeys> — *burgher*
To sitten in a yeldhalle,> on a deÿs.> — *guildhall / dais*
Everich,> for the wisdom that he can, — *each*
Was shaply> for to been an alderman.° — *fit*
For catel> haddė they ynogh and rente,> — *property / income*
And eek hir wyvės wolde it wel assente;
And ellės certeyn werė they to blame.
It is ful fair to been yclept 'Madame',
And goon to vigiliės° al bifore,
And have a mantel royalliche ybore.

COOK

A cook they haddė with hem for the nones°
To boille the chikens with the marybones,> — *marrowbones*
And poudrė-marchant° tart, and galyngale.°
Wel coude he knowe> a draughte of Londoun ale. — *recognize*
He coude roste and sethe,> and broille and frye, — *boil*
Maken mortreux,> and wel bake a pye.> — *thick soups / meat-pie*
But greet harm was it, as it thoughtė> me, — *seemed to*
That on his shine> a mormal° haddė he. — *shin*
For blankmanger,° that made he with the beste.

SHIPMAN

A shipman was ther, wonynge> fer by> weste; — *living / in the*
For aught I woot,> he was of Dertėmouthe.° — *know*
He rood upon a rouncy,° as he couthe,> — *as best he could*
In a gowne of falding> to the knee. — *coarse wool*
A daggere hangynge on a laas> hadde he — *strap*
Aboute his nekke, under his arm adoun.
The hote somer hadde mad his hewe> al brown. — *color*
And certeinly he was a good felawe.
Ful many a draughte of wyn had he ydrawe°
Fro Burdeux-ward,° whil that the chapman sleep.> — *merchant slept*
Of nycė> conscience took he no keep.> — *fastidious / heed*
If that he faught, and hadde the hyer> hond, — *upper*
By water he sente hem hoom to every lond.°

alderman leading member of town council
vigilies vigils; eves of saints' days; ceremonies on the evenings before guild festivals, in which the aldermen's wives would take the head of the procession
for the nones oral formula, without much meaning: "then"
poudre-marchant sharp spicy flavoring in powder form
galyngale a preparation of sweet spices
mormal ulcer associated with dirty living (in all senses)
blankmanger chopped creamed chicken, flavored with sugar and spice
Dertemouthe Dartmouth; a port in Devon, on the southwest coast of England, still used as a naval base
rouncy a cob or short-legged horse
ydrawe drawn, i.e. dishonestly
Burdeux-ward from Bordeaux, the great wine-shipping port on the west coast of France
By water . . . lond i.e. he threw his captives overboard

But of his craft,˃ to rekene wel his tydes, — *calling*
His stremės,˃ and his daungers hym bisides,° — *currents*
His herberwe,˃ and his moone,° his lodemenage,° — *haven*
Ther nas noon swich from Hull° to Cartage.°
Hardy he was and wys to undertake.
With many a tempest hadde his berd been shake.
He knew wel alle the havenes,˃ as they were, — *harbors*
Fro Gootlond to the Cape of Fynystere,°
And every cryke˃ in Britaigne° and in Spayne. — *inlet*
His barge yclepėd was the Maudelayne.°

DOCTOUR OF PHISIK

With us ther was a doctour of phisik.˃ — *medicine*
In al this world ne was ther noon hym lik,
To speke of phisik and of surgerye.
For he was grounded in astronomye,°
He kepte˃ his paciėnt a ful greet deel — *treated*
In hourės,° by his magyk natureel.°
Wel coude he fortunen the ascendent°
Of hise ymagės for his paciėnt.
He knew the cause of everich maladye,
Were it of hoot, or coold, or moyste, or drye,
And where they engendred, and of what humour.°
He was a verray, parfit° practisour.˃ — *practitioner*
The cause yknowe,˃ and of his harm the roote, — *known*
Anon he yaf the sikė man his boote.˃ — *remedy*
Ful redy hadde he hise apothecaries
To sende hym droggės˃ and his letuaries,° — *drugs*

hym bisides all around him
moone i.e. phases of the moon
lodemenage navigation, pilotage
Hull port in Yorkshire, on the northeast coast of England
Cartage Cartagena, on the Mediterranean coast of Spain
Gootlond . . . Fynystere Gotland (island in the Baltic Sea) to Cape Finisterre, the westernmost point of Spain
Britaigne Brittany. The piling up of these names marks out the regular English sea-trade area: their cumulative meaning is "everywhere on the sea."
Maudelayne Magdalene, a popular name for a ship
astronomye astrology (see Glossary and Fig. 37); the movements of the planets insofar as they were thought to affect the constitutions of men
houres the astrologically favorable or unfavorable planetary (not clock) times for treatment of disease, governed by the conjunctions of the planets in zodiacal or other houses
natureel "Natural" magic was the harnessing of the natural and supernatural forces of created things to produce a desired result; as opposed to "black" magic, which involved the invocation of evil spirits.
fortunen the ascendent The ascendant was any one of the 360° of the zodiac rising above the horizon at a given moment. The doctor knew how to calculate the best time to make the talismanic images concentrating the forces which would help his patient recover. A degree of the zodiac favorable to a given disease in given circumstances and governing a given part of the body had to be ascendant and the planetary conjunctions in it also auspicious.
hoot . . . humour. All matter was held to contain the four primary contrasting qualities, hot and cold, moist and dry, in varying proportions, and the physician's aim was to keep them in harmonious and healthy balance in the patient's body. Man's constitution was composed of the four humors or vital fluids (the doctrine goes back to ancient Greek medicine): blood (hot and moist); phlegm (cold and moist); black bile (melancholy: cold and dry); yellow bile (choler: hot and dry). Their proportions, determined by the planetary conjunctions at a man's birth, in turn determined his temperament. Disturbance of their proportions caused disease: an excess of one humor or one quality had to be reduced by a medicine which would apply its contrary.
verray, parfit true and consummate
letuaries electuaries; medicinal pastes or preserves

For ech of hem made other for to wynne°—
Hir frendshipe nas nat newė to bigynne.
Wel knew he the olde Esculapius,°
And Deïscorides, and eek Rufus,
Olde Ypocras, Haly, and Galien,
Serapion, Razis, and Avicen,
Averrois, Damascien, and Constantyn,
Bernard, and Gatesden, and Gilbertyn.
Of his dietė mesurable> was he, *moderate*
For it was of no superfluitee,
But of greet norissing,> and digestible. *nourishment*
His studie was but litel on the Bible.
In sangwin and in pers° he clad was al,
Lynėd with taffata and with sendal;> *silk*
And yet he was but esy of dispence;> *expenditure*
He keptė that he wan> in pestilence. *gained*
For> gold in phisik is a cordial,° *because*
Therfore he lovėde gold in special.

THE WYF OF BATHE

A good-wyf° was ther, of bisidė° Bathe,
But she was somdel> deef and that was scathe.> *somewhat / a pity*
Of clooth-makyng she haddė swich an haunt,> *practice*
She passed> hem of Ypres and of Gaunt.° *surpassed*
In al the parisshe wif ne was ther noon
That to the offring bifore hire sholdė goon;°
And if ther dide, certeyn so wrooth> was she *angry*
That she was out of allė charitee.
Hir coverchiefs> ful fynė were of ground;> *head-drapery / in texture*
I dorstė> swere they weyeden° ten pound *dare / weighed*

made other . . . wynne gave the other an opportunity of profit
Esculapius This catalogue of medical authorities, perhaps drawn from a medieval encyclopedia, is not chronological. Aesculapius, the mythical founder of medicine, had treatises attributed to him in the Middle Ages, but is probably here only for the authority of his name. He was supposedly the son of Apollo, god of healing, and was already worshiped in Greece in the 6th century B.C. Dioscorides and Rufus of Ephesus were Greeks who flourished in the 1st and 2nd century A.D. and wrote on pharmacy and on anatomy respectively. Ypocras is the Greek, Hippocrates of Cos, 5th century B.C., the first scientific writer on medicine; Haly may be either of two famous 10th-century Arab doctors who played a large part in transmitting Greek medicine to the West. Galen, most influential of all, was court physician under Marcus Aurelius (2nd century A.D.) and wrote in Greek on many other topics besides medicine. Serapion is a name owned by a Greek (2nd century B.C.), a Damascus Christian (9th century), and an Arab (11th or 12th). Rhazes, also alchemist and philosopher, lived in Baghdad (9th to 10th century) and wrote a medical encyclopedia. Avicenna, the 11th-century Arab, and Averroes, the 12th-century Spanish Arab, were both famous philosophers who wrote on medicine. John of Damascus is a shadowy figure, perhaps of the 9th century. Constantine the African brought Arabic medicine to Salerno, a famous Italian medical school, in the 11th century. Bernard Gordon and John of Gaddesden were 14th-century authorities; Gilbertus Anglicus, 13th.
sangwin . . . pers scarlet and in Persian blue (a bluish gray)
cordial Potable (drinking) gold was sometimes used in medicine—perhaps for the heart (cordial)—but the joke here is at the doctor's expense.
good-wyf woman of some means and standing
biside just outside; the center of Bath's textile industry was the parish of St. Michael's without the North Gate
Ypres . . . Gaunt Flemish towns, famous for fine cloth; or *hem of* may refer to natives of these towns working in England.
to the offring . . . goon should make her offering in church before her

That on a Sonday were upon hir heed.
Hir hosen weren of fyn scarlet reed,
Ful streite yteyd,> and shoes ful moiste> and newe. *tightly laced / soft*
Bold was hir face, and fair and reed of hewe.
She was a worthy womman al hir lyve.
Housbondes at chirchė dore she haddė fyve,°
Withouten other companye in youthe—
But therof nedeth nat to speke as nowthe.> *just now*
And thriės> hadde she been at Jerusalem;° *three times*
She haddė passed many a straungė> strem; *foreign*
At Rome she haddė been, and at Boloigne,
In Galice at Seint Jame, and at Coloigne;°
She coudė> much of wandrynge° by the weye— *knew*
Gat-tothėd° was she, soothly> for to seye. *truly*
Upon an amblere° esily° she sat,
Ywimpled° wel, and on hir heed an hat
As brood as is a bokėler or a targe;°
A foot-mantel> aboute hir hipės large, *riding-skirt*
And on hir feet a paire of sporės> sharpe. *spurs*
In felawschip wel coude she laughe and carpe.> *talk*
Of> remedies° of love she knew per chaunce, *about*
For she coude of that art the oldė daunce.°

PERSOUN OF A TOUN

A good man was ther of religioùn,
And was a pourė persoun> of a toun, *parson*
But riche he was of holy thoght and werk.
He was also a lernėd man, a clerk,°
That Cristės gospel trewėly> wolde preche; *faithfully*
Hise parisshens> devoutly wolde he teche. *parishioners*
Benigne he was, and wonder> diligent, *marvelously*
And in adversitee ful paciėnt.
And swich> he was yprevėd> oftė sithes.> *such / proved / times*
Ful looth were hym to cursen for hise tithes,°
But rather wolde he yeven,> out of doute,° *give*
Unto his pourė parisshens aboute

Housbondes . . . fyve See John 4:18 and the Wife's Prologue below; *at church dore* refers to the fact that medieval marriages were performed outside the church door; nuptial mass was then celebrated within.
Jerusalem The greatest of all pilgrimages would take a full year.
Rome . . . Coloigne These are the chief European centers of pilgrimage: Rome; Galicia, in northwest Spain, which has the shrine of St. James the Greater at Compostela; Cologne, which has the tomb of the Three Kings; and Boulogne with its famous image of the Virgin.
She . . . wandrynge She left no pilgrimage undone, but she also strayed from the path of virtue
Gat-tothed Teeth set wide apart, according to medieval physiognomics, betokened a traveling woman—in both senses.
amblere comfortable horse, pacing, not trotting
esily comfortably, perhaps astride
Ywimpled The wimple covered head, sides of face and neck: it was by this time rather old-fashioned for a laywoman; see l. 151.
bokeler . . . targe small round shields
remedies an allusion to Ovid, the Roman poet (1st century A.D.), writer of *The Remedies of Love* and other lovers' manuals of the Middle Ages; but probably also meaning that she was expert in love potions
the olde daunce a literal translation of the French phrase; so, "All the old routine"
clerk learned man. See l. 287.
looth . . . tithes He was unwilling to excommunicate (*cursen*) anyone for non-payment of tithes.
out of doute without doubt, surely

Of his offring,° and eek of his substaunce.> *property*
He coude in litel thyng have suffisaunce.> *enough*
Wyd was his parisshe, and houses fer asonder,
But he ne leftė> nat, for reyn ne thonder, *neglected*
In siknesse nor in meschief,> to visìte *misfortune*
The ferreste> in his parisshe, muche and lite,° *farthest*
Upon his feet, and in his hand a staf.
This noble ensample> to his sheep° he yaf, *example*
That first he wroghte,> and afterward he taughte. *did*
Out of the gospel° he tho> wordės caughte,> *those / took*
And this figùre he added eek therto,
That if gold rustė, what shal iren do?
For if a preest be foul, on whom we truste,
No wonder is a lewėd> man to ruste. *simple*
And shame it is, if a preest take keep,> *heed*
A shiten> shepherde and a clenė sheep. *filthy*
Wel oghte a preest ensample for to yive,
By his clennesse, how that his sheep sholde live.
He settė nat his benefice to hyre°
And leet> his sheep encombred in the myre *left*
And ran to Londoun, unto Saint Poules,°
To seken hym a chaunterie° for soules,
Or with a bretherhed° to been withholde;> *supported*
But dwelte at hoom, and keptė wel his folde,
So that the wolf ne made it nat miscarie.
He was a shepherde, and no mercenarie.
And though he holy were, and vertuous,
He was to synful men nat despitous,> *contemptuous*
Ne of his specħė daungerous> ne digne,> *disdainful / superior*
But in his teching discreet and benygne.
To drawen folk to hevene by fairnesse,
By good ensample, was his bisynesse:
But> it were> any persone obstinat, *if / there were*
What so he were, of heigh or lowe estat,
Hym wolde he snybben> sharply for the nonys.> *rebuke / at any time*
A bettre preest I trowe> that nowher noon ys. *believe*
He waited> after no pompe and reverence,> *looked for / deference*
Ne makėd hym a spicėd conscience,°
But Cristės loore> and hise apostles twelve° *teaching*
He taughte, but first he folwed it himselve.

offring Whatever the people gave at mass was the property of the parish priest.
muche and lite great and small
sheep See John 10:1–14 for the parable of the Good Shepherd.
gospel Matthew 5:19(?)
benefice to hyre It was common practice to hire a substitute priest at a small wage and, pocketing the difference, take other employment as well.
Saint Poules St. Paul's Cathedral, London
chaunterie endowment providing for perpetual masses for the soul of the donor and his nominees
bretherhed Guilds (see l. 366) often had their own chaplain.
Ne . . . conscience either "did not cultivate a too-scrupulous conscience" or "did not pretend to a heightened sense of right and wrong"
apostles twelve [the teaching of] his twelve apostles [also]

PLOWMAN

With hym ther was a plowman, was his brother,
That hadde ylad˃ of dong˃ ful many a fother.˃ *carried / dung / load*
A trewė swinker˃ and a good was he, *toiler*
Lyvynge in pees˃ and parfit charitee. *peace*
God loved he best with al his holė˃ herte *whole*
At allė tymės, thogh hym gamed or smerte,°
And thanne his neighėbore right as himselve.°
He woldė thresshe, and therto dyke˃ and delve, *dig ditches*
For Cristės sake, for every pourė wight,
Withouten hire,˃ if it lay in his might.˃ *wages / power*
Hise tithės payėd he ful faire and wel,
Bothe of his propre˃ swink˃ and his catel.˃ *own / work / possessions*
In a tabard˃ he rood upon a mere.° *smock*

Ther was also a reve and a millere,
A somnour, and a pardoner also,
A maunciple,˃ and myself—ther were namo.˃ *steward / no more*

MILLER

The miller was a stout carl° for the nones.
Ful big he was of brawn,˃ and eek of bones. *muscle*
That provėd wel,˃ for overal˃ ther he cam, *was clear / wherever*
At wrastling he wolde have alwey the ram.°
He was short-sholdred,˃ brood,˃ a thikkė knarre.° *stocky / broad*
Ther was no dore that he ne wolde heve of˃ harre,˃ *lift off / hinges*
Or breke it at a renning˃ with his heed.˃ *running / head*
His berd as any sowe or fox was reed,°
And therto brood, as though it were a spade.
Upon the cop° right of his nose he hade
A werte,˃ and theron stood a tuft of herys,˃ *wart / hairs*
Reed as the bristlės of a sowės erys.˃ *ears*
Hise nosėthirlės˃ blakė were and wyde. *nostrils*
A swerd and a bokeler bar˃ he by his syde. *bore*
His mouth as greet was as a greet forneys.˃ *oven*
He was a janglere,˃ and a goliardeys,° *noisy babbler*
And that was moost of sinne and harlotries.°
Wel coude he stelen corn, and tollen thries;°

thogh . . . smerte whether it made him happy or afflicted him
God . . . himselve (ll. 535–37) See Matthew 22:37–39: "Thou shalt love the lord thy God . . . Thou shalt love thy neighbor as thyself."
mere mare: a lower-class mount
carl fellow, usually of the lower class
ram the usual prize at a wrestling match
knarre a knot in wood: so a tough, knotty man; physiognomically, an angry lecherous bully
reed A red beard or head was not to be trusted, according to physiognomic theory. Judas, the arch-traitor, was said to have had red hair; see also Reynard the Fox.
cop bridge, top, or tip
goliardeys from *goliards,* the student and clerical authors of satirical Latin verse in the 12th and 13th centuries, who called their leader and patron, a mythical figure, Golias. Their writings were often scurrilous, and *goliardeys* here has come to mean a teller of dirty jokes.
harlotries i.e. obscenities. Harlot was not applied only to women in the Middle Ages.
tollen . . . thries take his toll three times, instead of once. The Miller's payment was a percentage of what he ground.

And yet he hadde a thombe of gold,° pardee.> *by heaven*
A whit cote and a blew hood werėd> he. *wore*
A baggėpipe wel coude he blowe and sowne,> *sound*
And therwithal> he broghte us out of towne. *therewith*

MAUNCIPLE

A gentil maunciple° was ther of a Temple,°
Of which achatours> mightė take exemple *buyers*
For to be wise> in bying of vitaille;> *thrifty / victuals*
For whether that he payde, or took by taille,°
Algate> he wayted> so in his achat> *always / watched / buying*
That he was ay biforn,> and in good staat.> *ahead / financial position*
Now is nat that of God a ful fair grace
That swich a lewėd> mannės wit shal pace> *unlearned / surpass*
The wisdom of an heep of lernėd men?
Of maistrės> hadde he mo than thriės ten *masters*
That weren of lawe expert and curious,> *subtle*
Of whiche ther weren a doseyne> in that hous *dozen*
Worthy to been stiwardes of rente> and lond *income*
Of any lord that is in Engėlond,
To make hym lyvė by his propre good;°
In honour dettėlees, but> he were wood,> *unless / mad*
Or lyve as scarsly> as hym list> desire; *frugally / it pleases*
And able for to helpen al a shire
In any cas> that mightė falle or happe; *event*
And yet this manciple sette hir aller cappe.°

REVE°

The reve was a sclendrė> colerik° man. *slim*
His berd was shave as ny> as ever he can; *close*
His heer> was by his erės> round yshorn; *hair / ears*
His top was dokkėd° lyk a preest biforn.
Ful longė were his leggės, and ful lene,
Ylyk> a staf, ther was no calf ysene.> *like / visible*
Wel coude he kepe a gerner> and a bynne; *granary*
Ther was noon auditour coude of hym wynne.> *get the better of*
Wel wiste> he by the droghte and by the reyn> *knew in advance / rain*
The yeldynge of his seed and of his greyn.> *grain*

thombe of gold See the proverb: "An honest miller has a golden thumb" ; i.e. there are no honest millers.
maunciple steward at one of the Inns of Court (societies of lawyers in London) or at a college
Temple an Inn of Court, perhaps specifically the Middle or Inner Temple, whose quarters in London had formerly been occupied by the Knights Templars
by taille by tally, on credit. Credit was recorded by cutting (Fr. *tailler*) notches on a stick.
To . . . good keep him from bankruptcy by making him live without borrowing
sette . . . cappe made fools of them all
Reve Usually a man of lowly origin, elected by his fellow peasants for a term as a foreman on the manor. He looked after fields and woods, saw that work was done, collected dues, and gave annual account of all. On larger estates he would be subordinate to a bailiff, who in turn was subordinate to a steward.
colerik having an excess of the humor choler (see l. 422) making him suspicious, prone to anger. Physiognomically, he is avaricious and lustful.
dokked cropped; a sign of low social status in a layman. Clergy wore their hair cut short or tonsured as a token of humility.

His lordės sheep, his neet,> his dayerye,> *cattle / dairy*
His swyn, his hors, his stoor,> and his pultrye *produce*
Was hoolly> in this revės governyng, *wholly*
And by his covenant yaf the rekenyng,°
Sin> that his lord was twenty yeer of age. *since*
Ther coude no man bringe hym in arrerage.°
Ther nas baillif, ne herde,° nor other hyne,°
That he ne knew his sleighte and his covyne.°
They were adrad> of hym as of the deeth.° *afraid*
His wonyng> was ful faire upon an heeth;> *house / common*
With grenė treës shadwed was his place.
He coudė bettre than his lord purchace:> *buy*
Ful riche he was astorėd prively.> *stocked stealthily*
His lord wel coude he plesen subtilly,
To yeve and lene> hym of his ownė good,> *lend / property*
And have a thank, and yet a cote° and hood.
In youthe he haddė lerned a good mister:> *trade*
He was a wel good wrighte,> a carpenter. *craftsman*
This revė sat upon a ful good stot,°
That was al pomely> grey, and hightė> Scot. *dapple / was named*
A long surcote of pers upon he hade,°
And by his syde he bar> a rusty blade. *bore*
Of Northfolk° was this reve of which I telle,
Biside a toun men clepen Baldėswelle.> *Bawdswell*
Tukkėd> he was, as is a frere, aboute. *hitched up*
And ever he rood the hindreste> of oure route.> *hindmost / group*

SOMNOUR°

A somnour was ther with us in that place,
That hadde a fyr-reed> cherubinnės° face, *fiery red*
For sawcėfleem> he was, with eyėn narwe. *pimply*
As hoot he was, and lecherous as a sparwe,°
With scallėd> browės blake and pilėd° berd *scabby*
Of his visagė children were aferd.> *afraid*
Ther nas quiksilver, litarge, ne brimstoon,
Boras, ceruce, ne oille of tartre noon,°

And by . . . rekenyng according to his covenant [he] gave his account
arrerage find him in arrears, short on his accounts
herde herd, shepherd
hyne hind, farm laborer
sleighte . . . covyne cunning, quickness and guile, fraud
the deeth most frequently the plague, the most feared of epidemics. The Black Death (1348–49, 1360, 1379) was strong in men's memories.
cote Clothing was sometimes given as part of wages, sometimes as a bonus.
stot a favorite Norfolk breed of horse
A . . . hade He had on a long overcoat of Persian blue.
Northfolk Norfolk
Somnour A summoner bore the citation to a person, clergy or lay, required to appear in an ecclesiastical court, for offenses against canon law and morals; and had to make sure that he obeyed. By Chaucer's time, summoner was a byword for corruption.
cherubinnes Cherubim were fiery red (Ezekiel 1:13); physiognomically, the summoner is a drunken lecher.
As hoot . . . sparwe As hot and lecherous as a sparrow. This bird was a byword for those qualities; see Skelton, *Philip Sparrow* below.
piled straggling or falling out in patches
quiksilver . . . noon The medieval name for the summoner's skin disease was *alopecia*, thought to be sexual in origin; the remedies—mercury, peroxide of lead, sulphur, borax, white-lead ointment, oil of tartar—suggest that he may have been syphilitic.

Ne oynėment that woldė clense and byte,
That hym myghte helpen of his whelkės> white, *pimples*
Nor of the knobbės sittinge on his chekes.
Wel loved he garleek, oynons, and eek lekes,°
And for to drinken strong wyn, reed as blood.
Thanne wolde he speke and crie as he were wood.> *mad*
And whan that he wel dronken hadde the wyn,
Than wolde he spekė no word but Latyn.
A fewė termės hadde he, two or three,
That he had lernėd out of som decree—
No wonder is, he herde it al the day;
And eek ye knowen wel how that a jay> *jackdaw*
Can clepen> 'Watte'° as wel as kan the Pope. *say*
But whoso coude in other thyng hym grope,> *question*
Thanne hadde he spent al his philosophìe;> *learning*
Ay> '*Questio quid iuris,*'° wolde he crie. *always*
He was a gentil harlot° and a kinde;
A bettre felawe sholdė men noght fynde:
He woldė suffre> for a quart of wyn *permit*
A good felawe to have his concubyn
A twelf monthe, and excuse hym attė fulle.°
Ful privėly a fynch eek coude he pulle.°
And if he fond owher> a good felawe, *found anywhere*
He woldė techen hym to have noon awe,> *fear*
In swich> cas, of the erchėdekenės curs,° *such*
But if> a mannės soule were in his purs; *unless*
For in his purs he sholde ypunisshed be.
'Purs is the erchėdekenės Helle,'° seyde he.
But wel I woot he lyėd right indede;
Of cursing> oghte ech gilty man him drede, *excommunication*
For curs wol slee> right as assoilling> saveth, *kill / absolution*
And also war hym of a *Significavit.*°
In daunger> hadde he at his owene gise> *in his power / at will*
The yongė girlės° of the diocise,
And knew hir conseil,> and was al hir reed.> *secrets / advisor*
A gerland hadde he set upon his heed
As greet as it were for an alė-stake.°
A bokėleer hadde he maad hym of a cake.> *loaf of bread*

garleek . . . lekes pimple-inducing foods, with bad moral connotations (Numbers 11:5)
Watte common name for tame, "talking" jackdaw
'*Questio . . . iuris*' "I ask, what is the law [on this matter]": a legal catchphrase, common in the ecclesiastical courts
harlot rascal. See l. 563.
atte fulle i.e. completely. Sexual offenses were dealt with by the ecclesiastical courts, and the Summoner had no authority to use his discretion.
fynche . . . pulle "pluck a pigeon": have sex with a woman
erchedekenes curs excommunication by the archdeacon
Purs . . . Helle i.e. a man is punished only in his purse
And also . . . Significavit And also beware of a writ for imprisonment. The church courts could not imprison: for this they had to call in the civil authorities. *Significavit* was the first word of the writ which did this.
girles perhaps in its other meaning of "young people" of both sexes
ale-stake a pole, with a "bush" of green leaves on it to symbolize refreshment, marked an alehouse (Fig. 39)

PARDONER°

With hym ther was a gentil pardoner
Of Rouncivale,° his freend and his compeer,> *companion*
That streight was comen fro the court of Rome.
Ful loude he song> 'Com hider, love, to me!'° *sang*
This somnour bar to hym a stif> burdoun;° *strong*
Was nevere tromp> of half so greet a soun. *trumpet*
This pardoner hadde heer as yelow as wex,
But smothe it heng, as dooth a strike of flex;> *hank of flax*
By ounces,> henge hise lokkės that he hadde, *thin strands*
And therwith he hise shuldres overspradde;> *overspread*
But thinne it lay, by colpons,> oon and oon. *in "rats'-tails"*
But hood, for jolitee, ywered> he noon, *wore*
For it was trussėd up in his walet.> *pack*
Hym thoughte he rood al of the newe jet;> *fashion*
Dischevelee,> save his cappe, he rood al bare. *with hair loose*
Swiche glaringe° eyen hadde he as an hare.
A vernicle° hadde he sowed upon his cappe.
His walet lay biforn hym in his lappe,
Bretful> of pardoun, come from Rome al hoot.> *brimful / hot*
A voys he hadde as smal as hath a goot.> *goat*
No berd hadde he, ne nevere sholdė have;
As smothe it was as it were late yshave.
I trowe he were a geldyng or a mare.
But of his craft, fro Berwyk into Ware,°
Ne was ther swich another pardoner.
For in his male> he hadde a pilwe-beer,> *pack / pillow-case*
Which that he seydė was Oure Lady veyl.
He seyde he hadde a gobet of the seyl> *piece / sail*
That Seïnt Peter hadde, whan that he wente
Upon the see, til Jesu Crist hym hente.°
He hadde a croys of latoun,° ful of stones,
And in a glas he haddė piggės bones.
But with thisė relikes, whan that he fond> *found*
A pourė persoun> dwellynge upon lond,> *parson / up country*
Upon a day he gat> hym more moneye *got*
Than that the persoun gat in monthės tweye.

Pardoner A seller of "pardons," indulgences, papal bulls allowing some remittance of penance in return for money. Later, such bulls came to be regarded as giving some exemption from Purgatory and, by the simple, as guaranteeing forgiveness of sins. Unscrupulous salesmen used them to gain money for the church, specific institutions in it—and themselves.
Rouncivale St. Mary Roncevall, near Charing Cross in London, an English branch of an important Spanish religious house
'Com . . . me!' presumably a popular song
burdoun either burden, i.e. refrain, or accompaniment
glaringe staring, bulging
vernicle Pilgrims to Rome bought a small replica of the handkerchief (in St. Peter's) with which St. Veronica was said to have wiped away the sweat from Christ's face on the road to Calvary, on which occasion the likeness of his features had been miraculously transferred to the handkerchief.
Berwyk . . . Ware the length of England (Berwick on Tweed in Northumberland to Ware in Hertfordshire, near London)
That . . . hente either before Christ took Peter as a disciple; or when he tried to walk on the waters (Matthew 14:28–31)
croys of latoun cross made of a brassy base metal, to be passed off as gold (as the pig's bones were to be passed off as saints' relics)

And thus, with feynėd> flatery and japes,> *false / tricks*
He made the persoun and the peple his apes.> *dupes*
But trewėly to tellen attė laste,
He was in chirche a noble ecclesiaste;
Wel coude he rede a lessoun or a storie,> *sacred narrative*
But alderbest> he song an offertorie; *best of all*
For wel he wistė, whan that song was songe,
He mostė> preche and wel affile> his tonge *must / sharpen*
To wynnė silver, as he ful wel coude;
Therfore he song so meriely and loude.

Now have I told you shortly>in a clause> *briefly / short space*
Th'estat, th'array, the nombre, and eek the cause
Why that assembled was this companye
In Southwerk, at this gentil hostelrye
That highte the Tabard, fastė> by the Belle.° *close*
But now is tymė to yow for to telle
How that we baren> us that ilkė> nyght, *behaved / same*
Whan we were in that hostelrie alight;
And after wol I telle of oure viage,> *journey*
And al the remenaunt> of oure pilgrimage. *remainder*
But first I pray yow, of youre curteisye,
That ye n'arette> it nat my vileinye,> *attribute / ill-breeding*
Thogh that I pleynly speke in this matere,
To tellė yow hir wordės and hir cheere,> *behavior*
Ne thogh I speke hir wordės proprely.> *exactly*
For this ye knowen also> wel as I, *as*
Whoso shal telle a tale after a man,
He moot reherce> as ny> as evere he kan *must repeat / near*
Everich a word, if it be in his charge,> *power*
Al> speke he never so rudėliche> or large,> *although / coarsely / broadly*
Or ellis> he moot> telle his tale untrewe, *else / must*
Or feynė> thyng, or fyndė wordės newe. *falsify*
He may nat spare, althogh he were his brother;
He moot as wel seye o word as another.
Crist spak hymself ful brode> in holy writ, *plainly*
And wel ye woot no vileynye is it.
Eek Plato seïth, whoso can hym rede,
'The wordės mote be cosin to the dede.'°
Also I prey yow to foryeve it me,
Al> have I nat set folk in hir degree *although*
Heere in this tale, as that they sholdė stonde.
My wit is short, ye may wel understonde.
Greet cherė made oure host° us everichon,
And to the soper sette he us anon.

Belle another pilgrim inn. See l. 20.
Plato . . . dede' in Plato's *Timaeus*, which Chaucer might have read in Latin translation, though he probably found it in Boethius
host Harry Bailly, the landlord of the Tabard

He servėd us with vitaille˃ at the beste. *victuals*
Strong was the wyn, and wel to drynke us leste.˃ *it pleased*

A semely man oure hostė was withalle
For to han been a marchal° in an halle.
A largė˃ man he was, with eyen stepe˃— *broad / prominent*
A fairer burgeys˃ was ther noon in Chepe°— *burgher*
Boold of his speche, and wys, and wel ytaught,
And of manhod hym lakkedė right naught.°
Eek therto he was right a mery˃ man, *pleasant*
And after soper pleyen˃ he bigan, *to jest*
And spak of mirthe, amongės othere thynges—
Whan that we haddė maad oure rekeninges°—
And seydė thus: 'Now, lordinges,˃ trewėly, *ladies and gentlemen*
Ye been to me right welcome, hertėly.˃ *sincerely*
For by my trouthe, if that I shal nat lye,
I saugh nat this yeer so mery a compaunye
At onės in this herberwe˃ as is now. *inn*
Fayn˃ wolde I doon yow mirthė, wiste˃ I how. *willingly / knew*
And of a mirthe I am right now bithoght,
To doon yow ese,˃ and it shal costė noght. *pleasure*
Ye goon to Caunterbury—God yow speede!
The blisful martir quitė˃ yow youre mede!˃ *pay / reward*
And wel I woot, as ye goon by the weye,
Ye shapen˃ yow to talen˃ and to pleye; *intend / tell tales*
For trewėly, confort ne myrthe is noon
To ridė by the weye doumb as the stoon.˃ *stone*
And therfore wol I maken yow disport,
As I seyde erst,˃ and doon yow som confort. *before*
And if yow liketh alle, by oon assent,
For to stonden at˃ my jugėment, *abide by*
And for to werken˃ as I shal yow seye, *do*
Tomorwe, whan ye riden by the weye,
Now, by my fader˃ soulė that is deed, *father's*
But if˃ ye be merye, I wol yeve yow myn heed.˃ *unless / head*
Hold up youre hond, withouten morė speche.'
Oure counseil was nat longė for to seche.˃ *seek*
Us thoughte it was noght worth to make it wys,°
And graunted hym, withouten moore avys,˃ *deliberation*
And bad hym seye his verdit as hym leste.
'Lordinges,' quod he, 'now herkneth for the beste;
But taak it nought, I prey yow, in desdeyn.˃ *disdain*
This is the poynt, to speken short and pleyn,
That ech of yow, to shortė˃ with oure weye *shorten*

marchal master of ceremonies in a [lord's] hall
Chepe Cheapside, in the City of London, the commercial center
naught unlike the Pardoner
Whan . . . rekeninges after we had paid our bills
Us . . . wys it seemed to us not worthwhile to make a business of it

In this viage, shal tellė talės tweye°
To Caunterbury-ward, I mene it so,
And homward, he shal tellen othere two,
Of aventures that whilom˃ han bifalle. *once upon a time*
And which of yow that bereth hym best of alle,
That is to seyn, that telleth in this cas
Tales of best sentènce˃ and moost solas,˃ *profit / delight*
Shal have a soper at oure aller cost°
Heere in this placė, sitting by this post,˃ *inn sign*
Whan that we come agayn fro Caunterbury.
And for to makė yow the morė mery,
I wol myselven goodly˃ with yow ryde, *willingly*
Right at myn owene cost, and be youre gyde.
And whoso wole my jugėment withseye˃ *contradict*
Shal paye al that we spenden by the weye.
And if ye vouchėsauf that it be so,
Tel me anon, withouten wordės mo,˃ *more*
And I wol erly shapė˃ me therfore.' *prepare*
  This thyng was graunted, and ourė othes swore
With ful glad herte, and preyden˃ hym also *begged*
That he wolde vouchėsauf for to do so,
And that he woldė been oure governour,
And of oure talės juge and reportour,˃ *bringer of verdict*
And sette a soper, at a certeyn pris,˃ *price*
And we wol˃ reulėd been at his devys *will*
In heigh and lowe;˃ and thus by oon assent *completely*
We been acorded to his jugėment.
And therupon the wyn was fet˃ anon; *fetched*
We dronken, and to restė wente echon˃ *everyone*
Withouten any lenger taryinge.˃ *delay*
  Amorwe,˃ whan that day gan° for to springe, *in the morning*
Up roos oure hoost and was oure aller cok,°
And gadrede˃ us togidre,˃ alle in a flok, *gathered / together*
And forth we riden,˃ a litel moore than pas,˃ *rode / walking pace*
Unto the Watering of Saint Thomas.°
And there oure hoost bigan his hors areste,˃ *stopped*
And seyde: 'Lordynges, herkneth, if yow leste!˃ *it please*
Ye woot youre forward, and I it yow recorde.°
If even-song and morwe-song accorde,˃ *morning-song agree*
Lat se now who shal tellė the firste tale.
As evere mote˃ I drynkė wyn or ale, *may*
Whoso be rebel to my jugėment
Shal paye for al that by the wey is spent.

ech . . . tweye Less than a quarter of this number of tales was written.
at . . . cost at the cost of us all
gan an auxiliary, to make simple past tense
oure aller cok the rooster who woke us all
Watering . . . Thomas watering-place for horses, two miles on the way
Ye . . . recorde you know your agreement, and I recall it to you

Now draweth cut,° er that we ferrer twinne;> *travel farther*
He which that hath the shorteste shal biginne.
Sire Knyght,' quod he, 'my mayster and my lord,
Now draweth cut, for that is myn accord.> *agreement*
Cometh neer,' quod he, 'my lady Prioresse.
And ye, sire Clerk, lat be youre shamefastnesse,> *modesty*
Ne studieth noght. Ley hond to, euery man.'
  Anon to drawen every wight bigan,
And shortly, for to tellen as it was,
Were it by aventure,> or sort,> or cas,> *luck / fate / chance*
The sothe> is this, the cut fil> to the knyght, *truth / fell*
Of which ful blithe and glad was every wyght,
And telle he moste> his tale, as was resoùn,> *must / right*
By forward and by composicioùn,> *compact*
As ye han herd. What nedeth wordės mo?
And whan this goode man saugh that it was so,
As he that wys was and obedient
To kepe his forward by his free assent,
He seyde, 'Syn I shal biginne the game,
What, welcome be the cut, a> Goddės name! *in*
Now lat us ryde, and herkneth what I seye.'
  And with that word we ryden forth oure weye,
And he bigan with right a mery cheere> *face*
His tale anon, and seyde in this manere.°
Here endeth the prolog of this book
c. 1385–1400   1478

The Miller's Prologue and Tale

Chaucer has skillfully planted in the General Prologue a notion of what sort of tale we can expect from the bag-piping Miller. His drunken thrusting forward of himself to tell the next tale as soon as the grave, sober Knight has done with his is another pointer. The Reeve, slender, choleric man that he is—timid and prone to ineffectual anger on account of his constitution and his advanced age—also senses what is up: this is going to be a tale of old age, youth, carpentry, and cuckoldry, and, as an elderly carpenter and perhaps a cuckold himself, he bursts into fury. But the great, thick Miller coarsely puts the poor man aside and begins.

What we get is one of Chaucer's several *fabliaux:* a dirty story told with wit and point. The *fabliau* developed in France in the thirteenth century—though such verse tales exist in both Latin and the vernacular from an earlier period—and was hardly used there after the early fourteenth. French *fabliaux* are realistic, short, plain in style, and rapid in narration, but they are a skillful and courtly and not a popular or folk literary form. Rather, they are an aristocratic mocking of the antics of the lower classes: amoral, not pornographic. Chaucer's are among the few written in English, another example of his ability to take a convention and work in it to masterly effect.

cut lot. Straws of different lengths would be used.
in this manere Some manuscripts read "as ye may heere"—which will remind us that Chaucer's poetry was intended for reading aloud.

This is the literary mode in which Chaucer is working in such tales as the Miller's, the Reeve's, and the Merchant's—and to some extent in the Wife of Bath's Prologue. What we have holds the two requirements of the *fabliau* genre perfectly in balance: the dirty story which we might expect from the Miller, and the aristocratically brutal and polished tone. Chaucer has woven together what were probably two disparate narratives (one German, the other Italian in origin); both arrive at their climax at the same moment in one of the great comic scenes of English literature.

Prologue

Here folwen the wordes bitwene the Host and the Millere

Whan that the Knight had thus his tale ytold,
In al the routė> nas ther yong ne old *group*
That he ne seyde it was a noble storie,
And worthy for to drawen> to memorie; *recall*
And namėly> the gentils° everichoon. *especially*
Our Hoste lough> and swoor, 'So moot I goon, *laughed*
This gooth aright; unbokeled is the male;°
Lat see now who shal telle another tale:
For trewėly, the game is wel bigonne.
Now telleth ye, sir Monk, if that ye conne,> *can*
Somwhat, to quytė> with the Knightės tale.' *requite*
The Miller, that fordronken° was al pale,
So that unnethe> upon his hors he sat, *with difficulty*
He nolde avalen> neither hood ne hat, *would not take off*
Ne abydė no man for his curteisie,
But in Pilàtės vois° he gan to crye,
And swoor by armės and by blood and bones,°
'I can> a noble talė for the nones, *know*
With which I wol now quyte the Knightės tale.'
   Our Hostė saugh> that he was dronke of ale, *saw*
And seyde: 'Abydė, Robin, my leve> brother, *dear*
Som bettrė man shal telle us first another:
Abyde, and lat us werken thriftily.'> *sensibly*
   'By Goddes soul,' quod he, 'that wol nat I;
For I wol speke, or ellės go my wey.'
Our Hoste answerde: 'Tel on, a devel wey!°
Thou art a fool, thy wit is overcome.'
   'Now herkneth,' quod the Miller, 'alle and some>! *one*

gentils the better born among the pilgrims, to whom a chivalrous tale would most appeal

'So moot . . . male' as I may walk (i.e. continue able to walk), this is going well; the pack is unstrapped

fordronken completely drunk; or, reading "for dronken": because of being drunk

Pilates vois a high, harsh voice, like that used for Pontius Pilate in the mystery plays

by armes . . . bones i.e. by Christ's arms, blood, and bones. See the Pardoner's Tale, l. 188.

devel wey i.e. in the Devil's name; originally a strengthening of "away," the parts divided as in "unto the gardinward," l. 464.

But first I make a protestacioùn°
That I am dronke, I knowe it by my soun;> *how I sound*
And therfore, if that I misspeke or seye,
Wyte> it the ale of Southwerk, I yow preye; *blame it on*
For I wol telle a legende° and a lyf
Bothe of a carpenter, and of his wyf,
How that a clerk hath set the wrightės cappe.'°
The Reve answerde and seydė, 'Stint> thy clappe,> *stop / babble*
Lat be thy lewėd> dronken harlotrye.° *ignorant*
It is·a sinne and eek> a greet folye *also*
To apeiren> any man, or him diffame, *injure*
And eek to bringen wyvės in swich fame.> *reputation*
Thou mayst ynogh of othere thingės seyn.'
This dronken Miller spak ful sone ageyn,
And seydė, 'Levė> brother Osėwold, *dear*
Who hath no wyf, he is no cokewold.°
But I sey nat therfore that thou art oon;
Ther been ful godė wyvės many oon,> *a one*
And ever a thousand gode ayeyns oon badde,
That knowestow wel thyself, but if> thou madde.> *unless / are mad*
Why artow angry with my talė now?
I have a wyf, pardee, as well as thou,
Yet nolde> I, for the oxen in my plough, *would not*
Taken upon me more than ynough,
As demen of myself that I were oon;°
I wol belevė wel that I am noon.
An housbond shal> nat been inquisitif *must*
Of Goddės privetee,> nor of his wyf. *secrets*
So> he may findė Goddės foyson> there, *provided / plenty*
Of the remenant nedeth nat enquere.>' *enquire*
What sholde I morė seyn, but this Millere
He nolde his wordės for no man forbere,
But tolde his cherlės> tale in his manere; *lout's*
M'athinketh that I shal reherce it here.°
And therfore every gentil wight I preye,
For Goddės love, demeth nat that I seye
Of evel entente, but that> I moot> reherce *because / must*
Hir talės allė, be they bettre or werse,
Or ellės falsen som of my matere.
And therfore, whoso list it nat yhere,> *to listen*
Turne over the leef, and chese> another tale; *choose*
For he shal finde ynowė,> grete and smale, *plenty*

protestacioun formal, public avowal
legende usually a holy story, a saint's life
clerk . . . cappe scholar made a fool of the workman
harlotrye obscenity, low conduct of all kinds
Who . . . cokewold Only the man who has no wife cannot be a cuckold.
As . . . oon to think that I myself were one, i.e. a cuckold
M'athinketh . . . here I regret that I must tell it here

Of storial° thing that toucheth gentillesse,
And eek moralitee and holinesse;
Blameth nat me if that ye chese amis.
The Miller is a cherl, ye knowe wel this;
So was the Reve, and otherė many mo,
And harlotrye they tolden bothė two.
Avyseth˃ yow and putte me out of blame; *consider*
And eek men shal nat make ernèst of game.°

Here endeth the prologe

Tale

Here biginneth the Millere his Tale

Whylom˃ ther was dwellinge at Oxenford *once*
A richė gnof,˃ that gestės heeld to bord,° *boor*
And of his craft he was a carpenter.
With him ther was dwellinge a poore scoler,
Had lernėd art, but al his fantasye°
Was turnėd for to lerne astrologye,
And coude a certeyn of conclusioùns°
To demen by interrogacioùns,
If that men axėd˃ him in certein houres, *asked*
Whan that men sholde have droghte or ellės shoures,
Or if men axėd him what sholde bifalle
Of every thing; I may nat rekene hem alle.
This clerk was clepėd˃ hendė° Nicholas. *called*
Of dernė love he coude and of solas;°
And therto he was sleigh˃ and ful privee,˃ *sly / secretive*
And lyk a mayden mekė for to see.
A chambre hadde he in that hostelrye
Allone, withouten any companye,
Ful fetisly ydight˃ with herbės swote;˃ *adorned / sweet*
And he himself as swete as is the rote˃ *root*
Of licorys, or any cetewale.°

storial literally, historical; thus, not a made-up story but something refined, moral, exemplary, based on what really happened, told for pleasure and instruction
And eek . . . game and also one must not make serious tales of jokes
bord literally, table. The carpenter took in boarders, some of them students.
fantasye originally the mental process of sense perception: so, all his intellectual effort, with overtones of disapproval. This poor scholar had passed through the trivium and gone on to the quadrivium (see Glossary).
coude . . . conclusiouns i.e. and knew a certain number of conclusions or propositions, the use of which would allow him to determine astrologically the answers to such questions as "At this or that time, shall we have drought or rain?"
hende agreeable, handsome
Of derne . . . solas He knew all about love-in-secret and what pleasure was. That is, he knew all the refinements of concealment, to protect the lady's reputation (and his own), and the whole range of meaning of solace (comfort from the lady in and out of bed).
cetewale setwall, zedoary, an aromatic Eastern root. Licorice root was proverbially sweet.

His *Almageste*° and bokės grete and smale,
His astrelabie,° longinge for˃ his art,˃ — *belonging to / craft*
His augrim stonės° layen faire apart,
On shelvės couchėd,˃ at his beddes heed: — *laid*
His presse ycovered with a falding reed.°
And al above ther lay a gay sautrye,°
On which he made a-nightės melodye
So swetėly that al the chambre rong;˃ — *rang*
And *Angelus ad virginem*° he song;
And after that he song the *Kingės Note;*°
Ful often blessėd was his mery throte.
And thus this swetė clerk his tymė spente
After his freendės finding and his rente.°
  This carpenter had wedded newe˃ a wyf — *recently*
Which that he lovede morė than his lyf;
Of eightėtenė yeer she was of age.
Jalous he was, and heeld hir narwe˃ in cage, — *closely*
For she was wilde and yong, and he was old,°
And demed himself ben lyk a cokėwold.°
He knew nat Catoun,° for his wit was rude,
That bad man sholdė wedde his sìmilitude.°
Men sholdė wedden after˃ hir estaat,˃ — *according to / condition*
For youthe and elde˃ is often at debaat. — *age*
But sith that he was fallen in the snare,
He moste endure, as other folk, his care.
  Fair was this yongė wyf, and therwithal
As any wesele hir body gent and smal.°
A ceynt she werede barrėd al of silk,°
A barmclooth˃ eek as whyt as mornė milk — *apron*
Upon hir lendės,˃ ful of many a gore.˃ — *loins / pleat*
Whyt was hir smok,˃ and brouded˃ al bifore — *undergarment / embroidered*
And eek bihinde, on hir coler˃ aboute, — *collar*
Of˃ col-blak silk, withinne and eek withoute. — *with*
The tapės˃ of hir whytė voluper˃ — *ribbons / cap*

Almageste the astronomical treatise of Claudius Ptolemy, the Greek astronomer and geographer; see the Wife of Bath's Prologue, l. 188

atrelabie astrolabe; an astronomical instrument for taking observations of the sun, moon, and planets, measuring heights and distances, determining latitudes and longitudes, and preparing horoscopes

augrim stones stones or counters for use on an abacus

his presse . . . reed his large, shelved, doorless cupboard curtained off with coarse woolen cloth ("falding") of red

sautrye psaltery; a stringed instrument played with the hand

Angelus ad virginem "The Angel to the Virgin," the first words of a famous hymn on the Annunciation

Kinges Note "The King's Tune" has not been identified. Nicholas could sing sacred or secular songs to order and be thanked for either—his gay voice ("throte") was often blessed by his listeners.

After . . . rente He lived on what his friends provided for him and his own income.

For . . . old See Chaucer's Merchant's Tale, his "courtly" treatment of the old husband-young wife theme.

And . . . cokėwold and thought himself likely to be a cuckold

Catoun Dionysius Cato, 4th-century author of verses of moral instruction, the *Distichs,* a popular medieval schoolbook

bad . . . similitude a bad man should marry someone like him. This particular proverb occurs in a supplement to the *Distichs.*

As . . . smal her body graceful and slim as a weasel's

A . . . silk She wore a belt, with cross-stripes, of silk.

Were of the samė suyte° of hir coler;
Hir filet brood> of silk, and set ful hye; *headband broad*
And sikerly> she hadde a likerous> yë. *certainly / wanton*
Ful smale ypullėd° were hir browės two,
And tho were bent, and blake as any sloo.
She was ful more blisful on to see
Than is the newė perėjonette° tree;
And softer than the wolle> is of a wether.° *wool*
And by hir girdel> heeng> a purs of lether *belt / hung*
Tasseld with silk, and perlėd with latoun.°
In al this world, to seken up and doun,
There nis no man so wys, that coudė thenche> *imagine*
So gay a popelote,> or swich> a wenche. *poppet / such*
Ful brighter was the shyning of hir hewe
Than in the Towr the noble° yforgėd newe.
But of hir song, it was as loude and yerne> *lively*
As any swalwė sittinge on a berne.> *barn*
Therto she coudė skippe and makė game,
As any kide or calf folwinge his dame.> *mother*
Hir mouth was swete as bragot or the meeth,°
Or hord of apples leyd in hay or heeth.> *heather*
Winsinge> she was, as is a joly> colt, *skittish / lively*
Long as a mast, and upright> as a bolt.> *straight / arrow*
A brooch she baar upon hir lowe coler,
As brood as is the bos> of a bocler.> *boss / round shield*
Hir shoes were lacėd on hir leggės hye;
She was a prymėrole,° a piggės-nye°
For any lord to leggen> in his bedde,° *lay*
Or yet for any good yeman to wedde.
Now sire, and eft> sire, so bifel the cas, *again*
That on a day this hendė Nicholas
Fil> with this yongė wyf to rage> and pleye, *happened / sport*
Whyl that hir housbond was at Osėneye,°
As clerkės ben ful subtile> and ful queynte;> *clever / inventive*
And privėly he caughte hir by the queynte,°
And seyde, 'Ywis,> but if> ich> have my wille, *surely / unless / I*
For dernė love of thee, lemman, I spille.'°
And heeld> hir hardė by the haunchė-bones, *held*

suyte literally, suit, following; i.e. the ribbons of her cap matched her collar
smale ypulled plucked to a narrow line
perejonette early-ripe pear, in bloom. Its fruit was also delicate and sweet.
wether strictly, a castrated ram; here used simply for sheep
perled . . . latoun spangled with brass. Latoun was a base brassy metal, imitation gold; see the General Prologue, l. 701.
Towr . . . noble The Tower of London held the principal mint of the kingdom at the time. The noble, also called an angel, was a gold coin worth two-thirds of a pound.
bragot . . . meeth Bragget, honey and ale fermented together; meeth is mead, also a fermented honey drink.
prymerole a primrose, a cowslip
pigges-nye pig's eye, a charming little eye; so, a doll
lord . . . wedde The lord need not marry her, but the yeoman would have to be honorable.
Oseneye Osney, now a suburb of Oxford, then some distance from the city, site of Osney abbey, for which the carpenter did work
queynte pudendum. See the Wife of Bath's Prologue, l. 338, and Fig. 39
For derne . . . spille for my hidden love of you, darling, I'm dying

And seydė, 'Lemman, love me al at ones,> *on the spot*
Or I wol dyen, also> God me save!> *so*
And she sprong as a colt doth in the trave,°
And with hir heed she wryėd> faste awey, *twisted*
And seyde, 'I wol nat kisse thee, by my fey,> *faith*
Why, lat be,' quod she, 'lat be, Nicholas,
Or I wol crye out "Harrow"° and "allas!"
Do wey your handės for your curteisye!'
This Nicholas gan mercy for to crye,
And spak so faire, and profred hir so faste,°
That she hir love him graunted attė laste,
And swoor hir ooth, by Seint Thomas° of Kent,
That she wol been at his comandėment,
Whan that she may hir leyser° wel espye.
'Myn housbond is so ful of jalousye,
That but ye waytė> wel and been privee,> *watch / discreet*
I woot right wel I nam> but deed,' quod she. *am not*
'Ye mostė been ful derne, as in this cas.'
'Nay therof care> thee noght,' quod Nicholas, *worry*
'A clerk had litherly biset his whyle,°
But if he coude a carpenter bigyle.'
And thus they been acorded and ysworn
To wayte> a tyme, as I have told biforn. *look for*
Whan Nicholas had doon thus everydeel,
And thakkėd> hir aboute the lendes> weel, *patted / loins*
He kist hir swete, and taketh his sautrye,
And pleyeth faste, and maketh melodye.
Than fil> it thus, that to the parish chirche, *happened*
Cristės ownė werkės for to wirche,> *do*
This godė wyf wente on an haliday;°
Hir forheed shoon as bright as any day,
So was it wasshen whan she leet> hir werk. *gave over*
Now was ther of that chirche a parish clerk,
The which that was yclepėd> Absolon.° *called*
Crul> was his heer, and as the gold it shoon, *curled*
And strouted as a fannė large and brode.°
Ful streight and even lay his joly shode,°
His rode> was reed, his eyen greye as goos;> *complexion / goose-feather*

sprong . . . trave shied as a colt does in the trave—i.e. in the frame used to keep restive horses still while being shod
'Harrow' French *haro:* a cry of distress; see ll. 404, 717.
profred . . . faste offered himself so often
Thomas St. Thomas Becket, the premier saint of England; see General Prologue, l. 16; and below, l. 353.
leyser time to spare, opportunity
A clerk . . . whyle A clerk would have made poor use of his time.
haliday holy day, saint's day or feast day
Absolon For the name and the emphasis on the beauty of the hair, see Chaucer's *balade,* "Hide Absolon," and, for the original Absalom, II Samuel 14:26: " . . . he weighed the hair of his head at two hundred shekels, after the king's weight." Absalom is a traditional type of masculine beauty.
And strouted . . . brode and spread out wide and broad like a winnowing fan; i.e. a flat shovel or wide-mouthed basket for separating grain from chaff by throwing it in the air
Ful . . . shode The beautiful parting of his hair was very straight and exact.

With Powlės window corven on his shoes,°
In hoses> rede he wentė fetisly.> *stockings / elegantly*
Yclad he was ful smal° and proprėly,
Al in a kirtel> of a light wachet;° *tunic*
Ful faire and thikkė been the poyntės° set.
And therupon he hadde a gay surplys°
As whyt as is the blosme upon the rys.> *bough*
A mery child he was, so God me save,
Wel coude he laten blood and clippe and shave,°
And make a chartre of lond or acquitaunce.°
In twenty manere> coude he trippe and daunce *ways*
After the scole of Oxenfordė tho,°
And with his leggės casten> to and fro, *fling*
And pleyen songės on a small rubìble;°
Therto he song somtyme a loud quinible;°
And as wel coude he pleye on his giterne.°
In al the toun nas brewhous ne taverne
That he ne visited with his solas,> *gaiety*
Ther any gaylard tappesterė° was.
But sooth to seyn, he was somdel squaymous> *squeamish*
Of farting, and of spechė daungerous.> *disdainful*
  This Absolon, that joly> was and gay, *frisky*
Gooth with a sencer> on the haliday, *censer*
Sensinge the wyvės of the parish faste;
And many a lovely look on hem he caste,
And namely> on this carpenterės wyf. *especially*
To loke on hir him thoughte a mery lyf,
She was so propre and swete and likerous.°
I dar wel seyn, if she had been a mous,
And he a cat, he wolde hir hente> anon. *pounce on*
  This parish clerk, this joly Absolon,
Hath in his hertė swich a love-longinge,°
That of no wyf ne took he noon offringe—
For curteisye, he seyde, he woldė> noon. *wished for*
The moone, whan it was night, ful brightė shoon,> *shone*
And Absolon his giterne hath ytake,
For paramours,° he thoghtė for to wake.> *revel*

With . . . shoos Windowed shoes were shoes with uppers cut and latticed so as to resemble windows. *Powles,* St. Paul's Cathedral in London, is Chaucer's invention in the context.
smal neatly, with close-fitting clothes
wachet a light blue, sky-color
poyntes tagged laces to fasten the tunic, hold up the hose, and otherwise perform the function of buttons
surplys overgarment, loose robe
Wel . . . shave He knew well how to let blood, cut hair and shave: i.e. he was a skillful barber-surgeon; this knowledge would be part of a learned man's equipment.
And . . . acquitaunce He was a good conveyancer also, who could draw up a title to land or a legal release.
After . . . tho It is not clear whether Oxford then, or at any time, had a great reputation for, or special style of, dancing.
rubìble a two-stringed musical instrument played with a bow; a kind of fiddle
quinible the highest pitch of the voice
giterne a kind of guitar
gaylard tappestere lively, gay barmaid. Tappestere, the ending suggests, is probably feminine here.
propre . . . likerous handsome and sweet and toothsome
love-longinge lovesickness, lover's melancholy
paramours being in love

And forth he gooth, jolif and amorous,
Til he cam to the carpenterės hous
A litel after cokkės hadde ycrowe;
And dressėd him up by a shot windòwe°
That was upon the carpenterės wal.
He singeth in his vois gentil and smal,°
'Now, derė lady, if thy willė be,
I preyė yow that ye wol rewe> on me,' *pity*
Ful wel acordaunt to his giterninge.°
This carpenter awook, and herde him singe,
And spak unto his wyf, and seyde anon,
'What! Alison! heerestow nat Absolon
That chaunteth thus under our bourės> wal?' *bedroom*
And she answerde hir housbond therwithal,
'Yis, God wot, John, I here it everydel.'> *all*
   This passeth forth: what wol ye bet than wel?°
Fro day to day this joly Absolon
So woweth> hir, that him is wo bigon. *woos*
He waketh> al the night and al the day; *stays awake*
He kembed> hise lokkės brode,> and mad him gay; *combed / spreading*
He woweth> hir by menės and brocage,° *woos*
And swoor he woldė been hir ownė page;> *servant*
He singeth, brokkinge> as a nightingale; *trilling*
He sente hir pimènt,° meeth, and spycėd ale,
And wafres,> pyping hote out of the glede;> *wafers / coals*
And for she was of towne,> he profrėd mede;> *townswoman / bribery*
For som folk wol ben wonnen for richesse,
And som for strokes,> and som for gentillesse. *blows*
   Somtyme, to shewe his lightnesse and maistrye,°
He pleyeth Heròdės on a scaffold hye.°
But what availleth him as in this cas?
She loveth so this hendė Nicholas,
That Absolon may blowe the bukkės horn;°
He ne hadde for his labour but a scorn;
And thus she maketh Absolon hir ape,°
And al his ernest turneth til a jape.> *joke*
Ful sooth is this provèrbe, it is no lye,
Men seyn right thus, 'Alwey the nyė slye
Maketh the ferrė levė to be looth.'°

And . . . windòwe He placed himself by a casement. A shot-window was a window opening on hinges, like a shutter.
smal fine and delicate
Ful . . . giterninge in excellent accord with his guitar-playing
what wol . . . wel would you have things go better than well?
menes and brocage intermediaries and go-betweens
pimènt wine sweetened with honey and mixed with spices
lightnesse . . . maistrye quickness and mastery, virtuosity
pleyeth . . . hye Takes the part of Herod in a nativity play, on a high platform stage; this would imply a change of character, for Herod is usually shown as a blustering bully.
blowe . . . horn blow the buck's horn, i.e. get nowhere
she . . . ape she makes light of, makes a fool of Absolon
'Alwey . . . looth' "Always the clever man who is close at hand makes the distant, dear one unloved."

For though that Absolon be wood˃ or wrooth,˃ *mad / enraged*
Bycausė that he fer was from hir sighte,
This nyė˃ Nicholas stood in his lighte. *nearby*
Now bere thee wel,° thou hendė Nicholas!
For Absolon may waille and singe 'Allas!'
And so bifel it on a Saterday,
This carpenter was goon til˃ Osėnay; *to*
And hendė Nicholas and Alisoun
Acordėd been to this conclusioun,
That Nicholas shal shapen˃ him a wyle˃ *fix up / trick*
This sely˃ jalous housbond to bigyle; *poor innocent*
And if so be the gamė wente aright,
She sholdė slepen in his arm al night;
For this was his desyr and hir˃ also. *hers*
And right anon, withouten wordės mo,
This Nicholas no lenger woldė tarie,
But doth ful softe unto his chambre carie
Bothe mete˃ and drinkė for a day or tweye; *food*
And to hir housbonde bad hir for to seye,
If that he axėd˃ after Nicholas, *asked*
She sholdė seye she nistė˃ where he was: *did not know*
Of al that day she saugh him nat with yë;
She trowėd˃ that he was in maladye, *believed*
For, for no cry, hir maydė coude him calle;
He nolde answère, for nothing that mighte falle.
This passeth forth al thilkė˃ Saterday, *that*
That Nicholas stille° in his chambre lay,
And eet˃ and sleep,˃ or didė what him leste,˃ *ate / slept / pleased*
Til Sonday, that the sonnė gooth to reste.
This sely carpenter hath greet mervayle
Of Nicholas, or what thing mighte him ayle,
And seyde, 'I am adrad,˃ by Saint Thomas, *afraid*
It stondeth nat aright with Nicholas.
God shildė˃ that he deydė˃ sodeynly! *avert / is dead*
This world is now ful tikel,˃ sikerly;˃ *unstable / certainly*
I saugh˃ today a cors˃ yborn to chirche *saw / corpse*
That now, on Monday last, I saugh him wirche.˃ *at work*
Go up,' quod he unto his knave˃ anoon, *boy*
'Clepe˃ at his dore, or knokkė with a stoon,˃ *call / stone*
Loke how it is, and tel me boldėly.'
This knavė gooth him up ful sturdily,
And at the chambre dore, whyl that he stood,
He cryde and knokkėd as that he were wood:˃ *mad*
'What how! what do ye, maister Nicholay?
How may ye slepen al the longė day?'
But al for noght, he herdė nat a word;

bere thee wel conduct yourself well

stille all the time

An hole he fond, ful lowe upon a bord,
Ther as the cat was wont in for to crepe;
And at that hole he lookėd in ful depe,
And at the laste he hadde of him a sighte.
This Nicholas sat gaping ever uprighte,
As he had kykėd° on the newė mone.°
Adown he gooth, and tolde his maister sone˃ — *at once*
In what array˃ he saugh this ilkė˃ man. — *condition / same*
  This carpenter to blessen him˃ bigan, — *cross himself*
And seyde, 'Help us, Sainte Fridėswyde!°
A man woot litel what him shal bityde.
This man is fallė, with his astromye,°
In som woodnesse˃ or in som agonye; — *insanity*
I thoghte ay wel how that it sholdė be!°
Men sholde˃ nat knowe of Goddės privetee.˃ — *must / secrets*
Ye,˃ blessėd be alwey a lewėd˃ man, — *yes / ignorant*
That noght but oonly his bilevė can!˃ — *creed knows*
So ferde˃ another clerk with astromye; — *fared*
He walkėd in the feeldės for to prye˃ — *look*
Upon the sterrės,˃ what ther sholde bifalle, — *stars*
Til he was in a marlė-pit° yfalle;
He saugh nat that. But yet, by Saint Thomas,
Me reweth sore˃ of hendė Nicholas. — *I greatly pity*
He shal be rated of˃ his studying, — *scolded for*
If that I may, by Jesus, hevenė king!
  Get me a staf, that I may underspore,°
Whyl that thou, Robin, hevest˃ up the dore. — *lift*
He shal˃ out of his studying, as I gesse.' — *must*
And to the chambre dore he gan him dresse.˃ — *address himself*
His knavė was a strong carl˃ for the nones,° — *tough*
And by the haspe he haf˃ it up atones;˃ — *heaved / at once*
Into the floor the dorė fil anon.
This Nicholas sat ay as stille as stoon,°
And ever gaped upward into the air.
This carpentèr wende˃ he were in despair,° — *thought*
And hente˃ him by the sholdres mightily, — *seized*
And shook him harde, and crydė spitously,˃ — *vehemently*

kyked Scots "keeked," i.e. looked, peeped. Many of Chaucer's words stay in use longer in the North of England and in Scotland than in the South.
newe mone i.e. as if he had gone mad
Frideswyde St. Frideswide, an Anglo-Saxon saint, *d.* 735, patron saint of the city and University of Oxford
astromye Like Nowelis for Noah's, this mispronunciation is meant to emphasize the carpenter's lack of education; see l. 349.
I thoghte . . . be I knew all along that it would be like this
marle-pit pit from which marl, a clayey soil used as a fertilizer, is dug. The story of the astronomer Thales, to whom this accident happened, first occurs in Plato, and there are medieval versions.
underspore pry up; they are going to lift the door off its hinges
for the nones oral formula, with little meaning here
stille as stoon silent and still. "Still" keeps some of its older meaning in this proverbial comparison.
despair the condition of the sinner who falls into inactive melancholy because he believes that his sins are too great for God's mercy to forgive

'What! Nicholay! what, how! what! loke adown!
Awake, and thenk on Cristės passioùn;
I crouchė thee from elvės and fro wightes!'°
Therwith the night-spel seyde he anon rightes°
On fourė halvės> of the hous aboute, *sides*
And on the threshfold> of the dore withoute: *threshold*
'Jesu Crist, and seynt Benedight,°
Blesse this hous from every wikkėd wight,
For nightės verye,° the white Pater-noster!°
Where wentėstow,> Seynte Petres soster?'° *did you go*
And attė laste this hendė Nicholas
Gan for to sykė> sore, and seyde, 'Allas! *sigh*
Shal al the world be lost eftsonės> now?' *again*
This carpenter answerdė, 'What seystow?
What! thenk on God, as we don, men that swinke.'> *toil*
This Nicholas answerdė, 'Fecche me drinke;
And after wol I speke in privetee
Of certeyn thing that toucheth me and thee;
I wol telle it non other man, certeyn.'
This carpenter goth doun, and comth ageyn,
And broghte of mighty ale a largė quart;
And whan that ech of hem had dronke his part,
This Nicholas his dorė fastė shette,> *shut*
And doun the carpenter by him he sette.
He seydė, 'John, myn hostė lief> and dere, *beloved*
Thou shalt upon thy trouthė> swere me here, *oath*
That to no wight thou shalt this conseil wreye;> *secret betray*
For it is Cristės conseil that I seye,
And if thou telle it man,> thou are forlore;> *anyone / lost*
For this vengaùnce thou shalt han> therfore, *have*
That if thou wreyė me, thou shalt be wood!'°
'Nay, Crist forbede it, for His holy blood!'
Quod tho this sely man, 'I nam no labbe,
Ne, though I seye, I nam nat lief to gabbe.°
Sey what thou wolt, I shal it never telle
To child ne wyf, by Him that harwed Helle!'°

I crouche . . . wightes I cross you; i.e. defend you (with the sign of the cross) from supernatural beings and wicked creatures of all kinds. Elves are not necessarily small in Chaucer's English.
Therwith . . . rightes Then he said the night-charm at once. This was a formula to protect the house from evil influence while the occupants were asleep. Children's blessings, such as: "Mathew, Mark, Luke, and John / Bless the bed that I lie on," belong to this family.
Benedight St. Benedict, founder of Western monasticism
For . . . verye This may mean: against the evil spirits of night. The reading, *nerye* for *verye* can be made to give the sense: save [us] from the [perils of the] night.
white Pater-noster the white Lord's Prayer, most likely the prayer said against the powers of darkness on going to bed
Seynte Petres soster uncertain significance
if . . . wood if you betray me, you will go mad
Ne . . . gabbe I am no blabberer nor, though I say it myself, do I like to gossip.
by . . . Helle through Christ who harrowed Hell. The harrowing of Hell (Fig. 7), the descent of Christ to bring the just out of Limbo, got its English name from the outcry (harrow, see l. 178 above) of the devils as their doors were beaten down and they were defeated. It was an episode in several cycles of mystery plays.

'Now John,' quod Nicholas, 'I wol nat lye;
I have yfounde in myn astrologye,
As I have lokėd in the moonė bright,°
That now, a Monday next, at quarter-night,°
Shal falle a rayn and that so wilde and wood,> *fierce*
That half so greet was never Noës° flood.
This world,' he seyde, 'in lasse> than in an hour *less*
Shal al be dreynt,> so hidous is the shour; *drowned*
Thus shal mankyndė drenche> and lese> hir lyf.' *drown / lose*
This carpenter answerde, 'Allas, my wyf!
And shal she drenche? Allas! myn Alisoun!'
For sorwe of this he fil almòst adoun,°
And seyde, 'Is ther no remedie in this cas?'
'Why, yis, for> Gode,' quod hendė Nicholas, *before*
'If thou wolt werken after lore and reed;°
Thou mayst nat werken after thyn owene heed.> *head*
For thus seith Salomon, that was ful trewe,> *wise*
"Werk al by conseil, and thou shalt nat rewe."°
And if thou werken wolt by good conseil,
I undertake, withouten mast and seyl,> *sail*
Yet shal I saven hir and thee and me.
Hastow nat herd how savėd was Noë,
Whan that our Lord had warned him biforn
That al the world with water sholde be lorn?'> *lost*
'Yis,' quod this carpenter, 'ful yore> ago.' *long*
'Hastow nat herd,' quod Nicholas, 'also
The sorwe> of Noë with his felawshipe,> *difficulty / company*
Er that he mightė gete his wyf to shipe?°
Him had be lever,> I dar wel undertake, *rather*
At thilkė tyme, than alle hise wetherės blake,°
That she hadde had a ship hirself allone.
And therfore, wostou> what is best to done? *do you know*
This asketh> haste, and of an hastif> thing *requires / urgent*
Men may nat preche or maken tarying.
Anon go gete us faste into this in> *lodging*
A kneding trogh, or elles a kimelin,°
For ech of us, but loke that they be large,> *broad-bottomed*
In which we mowė> swimme> as in a barge, *may float*
And han therinne vitaillė suffisànt> *provisions sufficient*

moone bright On the importance of the moon in prognostication, see Franklin's Tale, l. 421.
quarter-night If this is the end of the first quarter of the night, i.e. about 9 p.m., the time-scheme of the story would be wrong; perhaps therefore, at the beginning of the last quarter, about 3 a.m.
Noës Noah's; *Noë* is the usual Latin form.
For sorwe . . . adoun for sorrow at this he almost fell down
If . . . reed if you will act according to learning and counsel
"Werk . . . rewe" do nothing without advice; and when thou hast once done, repent not (Ecclesiasticus 32:19, then attributed to Solomon)
Er . . . shipe Noah's difficulties in getting his wife on to the Ark provided the comic relief in the mystery plays on the Flood.
wetheres blake black rams (or wethers; see above, l. 141); i.e. his most highly prized sheep
A kneding trogh . . . kimelin a dough-trough or else a brewing vat

But for a day; fy on the remenant!°
The water shal aslake> and goon away *diminish*
Aboutė pryme° upon the nextė day.
But Robin may nat wite> of this, thy knave, *know*
Ne eek thy maydė Gille I may nat save;
Axė nat why, for though thou askė me,
I wol nat tellen Goddės privetee.
Suffiseth thee, but if> thy wittės madde,> *unless / are crazy*
To han> as greet a grace> as Noë hadde. *have / favor*
Thy wyf shal I wel saven, out of doute.
Go now thy wey, and speed thee heeraboute.
  'But whan thou hast, for hir and thee and me,
Ygeten us thise kneding-tubbės three,
Than shaltow hange hem in the roof ful hye,
That no man of our purveyaùncė° spye.
And whan thou thus hast doon as I have seyd,
And hast our vitaille faire in hem ylayd,
And eek an ax, to smyte the corde atwo> *in two*
When that the water comth, that we may go,
And broke an hole an heigh,> upon the gable, *up high*
Unto the gardinward,° over the stable,
That we may frely passen forth our way
Whan that the gretė showr is goon away
Than shaltow swimme as myrie,> I undertake, *carefree*
As doth the whytė doke> after hir drake. *duck*
Than wol I clepe,> "How! Alison! how! John! *call*
Be myrie, for the flood wol passe anon."> *soon*
And thou wolt seyn, "Hayl, maister Nicholay!
Good morwe, I se thee wel, for it is day."
And than shul we be lordės al our lyf
Of al the world, as Noë and his wyf.
  But of o thyng I warnė thee ful right,
Be wel avysėd,> on that ilkė night *careful*
That we ben entred into shippės bord,
That noon of us ne spekė nat a word,
Ne clepe, ne crye, but been in his prayere;
For it is Goddės ownė hestė dere.> *commandment precious*
  Thy wyf and thou mote hangė fer atwinne,> *far apart*
For that bitwixė yow shal be no sinne°
No more in looking than ther shal in dede;
This ordinance is seyd, go, God thee spede!
Tomorwe at night, whan men ben alle aslepe,
Into our kneding-tubbės wol we crepe,
And sitten ther, abyding Goddės grace.

fy . . . remenant no bother about the rest
Aboute pryme First thing in the morning; prime was the first of the canonical divisions of the day, 6 a.m. to 9 a.m.
purveyaùnce advance preparations

Unto the gardinward looking toward the garden
For . . . sinne at this second flood you must be as entirely pure as Noah, without even a venial sin on your conscience

Go now thy wey, I have no lenger space> *time*
To make of this no lenger sermoning.
Men seyn thus, "Send the wyse, and sey nothing";°
Thou art so wys, it nedeth thee nat teche;
Go, save our lyf, and that I thee biseche.'
  This sely carpenter goth forth his wey.
Ful ofte he seith 'Allas' and 'Weylawey,'
And to his wyf he tolde his privėtee;
And she was war,> and knew it bet> than he, *forewarned / better*
What al this queyntė cast> was for to seye. > *subtle plan / meant*
But nathėlees she ferde> as she wolde deye, *acted*
And seyde, 'Allas! go forth thy wey anon,
Help us to scape,> or we ben lost echon;> *escape / each one*
I am thy trewė verray> wedded wyf; *faithful true*
Go, derė spouse, and help to save our lyf.'
  Lo! which a greet thyng is affecciòun!°
Men may dye of imaginaciòun,
So depė> may impressiòun be take. *deeply*
This sely carpenter biginneth quake;
Him thinketh verraily> that he may see *truly*
Noës flood come walwing> as the see *rolling*
To drenchen> Alisoun, his hony dere. *drown*
He wepeth, weyleth, maketh sory chere,
He syketh> with ful many a sory swogh.> *sighs / groan*
He gooth and geteth him a kneding-trogh,
And after that a tubbe and a kimelin,
And privėly he sente hem to his in,> *house*
And heng> hem in the roof in privetee. *hung*
His ownė hand he madė laddres three,
To climben by the rongės> and the stalkes> *rungs / uprights*
Unto the tubbės hanginge in the balkes,> *rafters*
And hem vitailled,> bothė trogh and tubbe, *victualed*
With breed and chese, and good ale in a jubbe,> *jug*
Suffysinge right ynogh> as for a day. *in plenty*
But er that he had maad al this array,> *arrangement*
He sente his knave, and eek his wenche> also, *maidservant*
Upon his nede° to London for to go.
And on the Monday, whan it drow to> night, *approached*
He shette> his dore withoutė candel-light, *shut*
And dressėd> al thing as it sholdė be. *arranged*
And shortly, up they clomben> allė three; *climbed*
They sitten stillė wel a furlong-way.°
  'Now, Pater-noster, clom!'° seyde Nicholay,
And 'Clom,' quod John, and 'Clom,' seyde Alisoun.

"Send . . . nothing" proverbial: a word to the wise is enough
affeccioun the faculty of the soul concerned with emotion, desire, will; here emotional excitement or disturbance
Upon his nede for something he wanted; on an errand
furlong-way a short time—the time it takes to walk a furlong (1/8 mile)
Pater . . . clom Our Father, hush!

This carpenter seyde his devocioùn,
And stille he sit,˃ and biddeth˃ his preyere, *sits / prays*
Awaytinge on the reyn, if he it here.˃ *might hear*
  The dedė sleep, for wery bisinesse,
Fil˃ on this carpenter right, as I gesse, *descended*
Aboutė corfew tyme,° or litel more;
For travail˃ of his goost˃ he groneth sore, *affliction / spirit*
And eft˃ he routeth,˃ for his heed mislay.° *then / snores*
Doun of the laddrė stalketh˃ Nicholay, *climbs stealthily*
And Alisoun, ful softe adoun she spedde;
Withouten wordės mo, they goon to bedde
Theras˃ the carpenter is wont to lye. *where*
Ther was the revel and the melodye;
And thus lyth˃ Alison and Nicholas, *lie*
In bisinesse of mirthe and of solas,˃ *pleasure*
Til that the belle of Laudės° gan to ringe,
And frerės in the chauncel˃ gonnė singe. *chancel*
  This parish clerk, this amorous Absolon,
That is for love alwey so wo bigon,
Upon the Monday was at Osėneye
With companye, him to disporte and pleye,
And axėd upon cas˃ a cloisterer° *by chance*
Ful privėly after John the carpenter;
And he drough˃ him apart out of the chirche, *drew*
And seyde, 'I noot,˃ I saugh him here nat wirche˃ *don't know / work*
Sin Saterday; I trow that he be went
For timber, ther our abbot hath him sent;
For he is wont for timber for to go,
And dwellen at the grange° a day or two;
Or ellės he is at his hous, certeyn;
Wher that he be, I can nat sothly˃ seyn.' *truly*
  This Absolon ful joly˃ was and light,˃ *frisky / gay*
And thoghtė, 'Now is tymė wake˃ al night; *to wake*
For sikirly I saugh him nat stiringe
Aboute his dore sin day bigan to springe.
So moot˃ I thryve, I shal, at cokkės crowe,° *may*
Ful privėly knokken at his windowe
That stant˃ ful lowe upon his bourės˃ wal. *stands / bedroom*
To Alison now wol I tellen al
My love-longing, for yet I shal nat misse
That at the lestė wey˃ I shal hir kisse. *at least*

corfew tyme about dusk, when the town gates would be shut; perhaps 8 p.m.
his heed mislay his head lay awry
Laudes lauds; the first office (church service) of the day, usually between 3 and 4 a.m., before day actually broke
cloisterer a member of a religious order living in a convent or monastery; here an Augustinian canon of Osney Abbey
grange barn or granary; but here an outlying farm belonging to the Abbey
at cokkes crowe a vague indication of time. First cockcrow was not long after midnight; second about 3 a.m., about the time of lauds. So the time scheme works—just about lauds, when Nicholas and Alison were finishing their bouts, Absolon arrives.

Som maner confort shal I have, parfay,> *in faith*
My mouth hath icchėd° al this longė day;
That is a signe of kissing attė leste.
Al night me mette> eek, I was at a feste. *dreamed*
Therfor I wol gon slepe an houre or tweye,
And al the night than wol I wake and pleye.'
  Whan that the firstė cok hath crowe, anon
Up rist> this joly lover Absolon, *rises*
And him arrayeth gay, at point devys.°
But first he cheweth greyn° and lycorys,
To smellen swete, er he had kembed> his heer. *combed*
Under his tonge a trewė love° he beer,> *bore*
For therby wende he to ben gracïoùs.
He rometh> to the carpenterės hous, *walks*
And stille he stant under the shot windowe;
Unto his brest it raughte,> it was so lowe; *reached*
And softe he cogheth with a semisoun>— *low voice*
'What do ye, hony-comb, swete Alisoun?
My fairė brid,° my swetė cinamome,
Awaketh, lemman> myn, and speketh to me! *darling*
Wel litel thenken ye upon my wo,
That for your love I swetė> ther> I go. *sweat / wherever*
No wonder is thogh that I swelte> and swete; *swelter*
I moorne> as doth a lamb after the tete.> *long / teat*
Ywis,> lemman, I have swich love-longinge, *indeed*
That lyk a turtel° trewe is my moorninge;
I may nat ete na morė than a mayde.'
  'Go fro the window, Jakkė fool,' she sayde,
'As help me God, it wol nat be "Com ba> me," *kiss*
I love another, and elles I were to blame,
Wel bet> than thee, by Jesu, Absolon! *better*
Go forth thy wey, or I wol caste a ston,
And lat me slepe, a twenty devel wey!'°
  'Allas,' quod Absolon, 'and weylawey!
That trewė love was ever so yvel biset!> *hardly used*
Than kissė me, sin it may be no bet,
For Jesus love and for the love of me.'
  'Wiltow> than go thy wey therwith?' quod she. *will you*
  'Ye, certės, lemman,' quod this Absolon.
  'Thanne make thee redy,' quod she, 'I come anon.'
And unto Nicholas she seydė stille,> *quietly*
'Now hust,> and thou shalt laughen al thy fille.' *hush*
  This Absolon doun sette him on his knees,

My . . . icched Divination from involuntary movements was widely practiced in ancient times and in the Middle Ages.
at point devys very neatly and elegantly; to perfection
greyn grain of Paris or Paradise, a seed used as spice; like licorice, a sweetener of the breath
trewe love probably a four-leafed sprig of herb-paris, with a flower or berry in the middle, and looking like a true-love knot
brid bird, most likely; or perhaps bride
turtel turtledove, proverbially true to its mate, and pining away at its absence or death
a . . . wey for twenty devils' sake

And seyde, 'I am a lord at alle degrees;°
For after this I hope ther cometh more!
Lemman, thy grace, and swetė brid,> thyn ore>!' *bird / favor*
 The window she undoth, and that in haste,
'Have do,' quod she, 'com of, and speed thee faste,
Lest that our neighėborės thee espye.'
 This Absolon gan wype his mouth ful drye;
Derk was the night as pich, or as the cole,
And at the window out she putte hir hole,
And Absolon, him fil no bet ne wers,°
But with his mouth he kiste hir naked ers> *ass*
Ful savourly,> er he was war of this. *with great relish*
 Abak he sterte,> and thoghte it was amis, *jumped*
For wel he wiste a womman hath no berd;> *beard*
He felte a thing al rough and long yherd,> *haired*
And seydė, 'Fy! allas! what have I do?'
 'Teehee!' quod she, and clapte the window to;
And Absolon goth forth a sory pas.°
 'A berd, a berd!' quod hendė Nicholas,
'By Goddės corpus,> this goth faire and weel!' *body*
 This sely> Absolon herde every deel, *poor*
And on his lippe he gan for anger byte;
And to himself he seyde, 'I shal thee quyte>!' *pay back*
 Who rubbeth now, who froteth> now his lippes *scrubs*
With dust, with sond,> with straw, with clooth, with chippes, *sand*
But Absolon, that seith ful ofte, 'Allas!
My soule bitake I unto Sathanas,
But me wer lever than al this town,' quod he,
'Of this despyt awroken for to be!°
Allas!' quod he, 'allas! I ne hadde ybleynt!'> *turned away*
His hotė> love was cold and al yqueynt;> *hot / quenched*
For fro that tyme that he had kiste hir ers,
Of paramours he settė nat a kers,°
For he was helėd of his maladye;
Ful oftė paramours he gan deffye,> *give up*
And weep> as dooth a child that is ybete. *wept*
A softė paas° he wente over> the strete *across*
Until> a smith men clepėd Daun Gerveys,° *to*
That in his forgė smithėd plough harneys;> *equipment*
He sharpeth shaar° and culter bisily.
This Absolon knokketh al esily,> *quietly*

at alle degrees in all ways, completely
him . . . wers it happened to him neither better nor worse: i.e. it happened just like this
sory pas at a sad pace; walking dejectedly
My soule . . . be (ll. 642–44) I would give my soul to Satan. That is, I'll be damned, if I wouldn't rather have my revenge than be the owner of this whole town.
Of . . . kers On love of women he set no value at all; *kers* is cress, a worthless piece of vegetation.
softe paas quiet walk, quietly
Daun Gerveys Master Gervase (*Daun* is short for *dominus*, master). It is still before daybreak, but many would already be at work; and smiths were notorious early workers.
shaar plowshare, the blade that turns the turf over on its side; *culter*, coulter, the tip on the share which cuts the turf vertically

And seyde, 'Undo, Gerveys, and that anon.'
'What, who artow?' 'It am I, Absolon.'
'What, Absolon! for Cristės swetė tree,˃ *cross*
Why rysė ye so rathe,˃ ey, Benedicite!˃ *early / bless me*
What ayleth yow? som gay gerl, God it woot,
Hath broght yow thus upon the viritoot;°
By Seÿnt Note,° ye woot wel what I mene.'
This Absolon ne roghtė˃ nat a bene˃ *cared / bean*
Of al his pley, no word agayn he yaf;˃ *returned*
He haddė morė tow on his distȧf°
Than Gerveys knew, and seydė, 'Freend so dere,
That hotė culter in the chimenee˃ here, *fireplace*
As lene° it me, I have therwith to done,
And I wol bringe it thee agayn ful sone.'
Gerveys answerde, 'Certės, were it gold,
Or in a pokė nobles alle untold,°
Thou sholdest have, as I am trewė smith;
Ey, Cristės foo!° what wol ye do therwith?'
'Therof,' quod Absolon, 'be as be may;
I shal wel telle it thee tomorwe day'—
And caughte the culter by the coldė stele.˃ *handle*
Ful softe out at the dore he gan to stele,
And wente unto the carpenterės wal.
He cogheth first, and knokketh therwithal
Upon the windowe, right as he dide er.˃ *before*
This Alison answerde, 'Who is ther
That knokketh so? I warante° it a theef.'
'Why, nay,' quod he, 'God woot, my swetė leef,˃ *dear*
I am thyn Absolon, my derėling!
Of gold,' quod he, 'I have thee broght a ring;
My moder˃ yaf it me, so God me save, *mother*
Ful fyn it is, and therto wel ygrave;˃ *engraved*
This wol I gevė˃ thee, if thou me kisse!' *give*
This Nicholas was risen for to pisse,
And thoghte he wolde amenden˃ al the jape,˃ *better / jest*
He sholdė kisse his ers er that he scape.
And up the windowe dide˃ he hastily, *put*
And out his ers he putteth privėly
Over the buttok, to the haunchė-bon;
And therwith spak this clerk, this Absolon,
'Spek, swetė brid,˃ I noot˃ nat wher thou art.' *bird / don't know*
This Nicholas anon leet flee˃ a fart, *let fly*
As greet as it had been a thonder-dent,˃ *thunder-clap*

viritoot meaning unknown; perhaps, on the prowl
Seynt Note Neot, a 9th-century Saxon saint
He . . . distaf proverbial phrase: he had more flax to spin into linen thread; i.e. he had plenty of other things to think of
As lene please lend
Or . . . untold or gold coins all uncounted in a bag; for *nobles*, see l. 148
Cristes foo by Christ's foe, i.e. the Devil; or short for "by Christ's foot"; cf. l. 17
warante guarantee or wager

That with the strook he was almost yblent;> *blinded*
And he was redy with his iren hoot,> *hot*
And Nicholas amidde> the ers he smoot.> *in the middle of / smote*
  Of gooth the skin an handė-brede> aboute, *hand's breadth*
The hotė culter brendė so his toute,> *rump*
And for the smert he wendė for> to dye. *expected*
As he were wood,> for wo he gan to crye: *crazy*
'Help! water! water! help, for Goddės herte!'
  This carpenter out of his slomber sterte,
And herde oon cryen 'Water' as he were wood,
And thoghte, 'Allas! now comth Nowelis° flood!'
He sit him up withouten wordes mo,
And with his ax he smoot the corde atwo,
And down goth al; he fond neither to selle,
Ne breed ne ale, til he cam to the celle
Upon the floor;° and ther aswowne> he lay. *unconscious*
  Up sterte> hir Alison, and Nicholay, *jumped*
And cryden 'Out' and 'Harrow' in the strete.
The neighėborės, bothė smale and grete,
In ronnen,> for to gauren> on this man, *ran / gape*
That yet aswowne he lay, bothe pale and wan;
For with the fal he brosten> hadde his arm; *broken*
But stonde he moste> unto his owne harm. *must*
For whan he spak, he was anon bore doun> *overcome*
With> hendė Nicholas and Alisoun. *by*
They tolden every man that he was wood,
He was agast so of 'Nowelis flood'
Thurgh fantasye,> that of his vanitee> *imagination / folly*
He hadde yboght him kneding-tubbės three,
And hadde hem hangėd in the roof above;
And that he preyėd hem, for Goddės love,
To sitten in the roof, par companye.°
  The folk gan laughen at his fantasye;
Into the roof they kyken> and they gape, *peer*
And turnėd al his harm unto a jape.
For what so that this carpenter answerde,
It was for noght, no man his reson> herde; *argument*
With othės grete he was so sworn adoun,> *sworn under*
That he was holden> wood in al the toun; *held*
For every clerk anon right> heeld> with other. *at once / sided*
They seyde, 'The man is wood, my leve brother';
And every wight gan laughen of this stryf.> *fuss*

Nowelis Noah's; like astromye, l. 343, this is a mispronunciation of the carpenter's, confusing Noah with Nowel, Christmas

he . . . floor He found no opportunity to sell bread or ale until he reached the floorboards; i.e. he went down with a great rush. "Celle" and "floor" seem to mean the same thing; or "celle" is the floor, and "floor" the ground beneath it. Perhaps "celle" means the house's main room, above which the carpenter had been suspended.

par companye for company's sake; to keep him company

Thus swyvéd˃ was the carpenterés wyf, *screwed*
For al his keping˃ and his jalousye; *guarding*
And Absolon hath kist hir nether yë;˃ *lower eye*
And Nicholas is scalded in the toute.
This tale is doon, and God save al the route!˃ *company*

Here endeth the Millere his tale.

The Nun's Priest's Prologue and Tale

The Nun's Priest is one of the characters in the *Tales* of whom we know least: in the General Prologue he is one of three priests, given a bare mention after the Prioress. But only one Nun's Priest tells a tale; and our only description of him comes from the Host, who calls him brawny and a "tread-fowl" (Fig. 28).

His tale, which may have been written at any time after 1381 (there is a reference in it to the Peasants' Revolt of that year), is based on an animal fable which Chaucer probably found in one of the popular collections of stories concerning Reynard the Fox and his tricks which had begun to be built into beast epics in the twelfth century. The idea of presenting a story in which beasts act as human beings—and so giving some sort of moral lesson from a world thus turned upside down—goes back as far as Greek literature, and is associated with the name of Aesop, in the sixth century B.C. In these fables the fox is always the embodiment of deceit.

Preachers naturally found such stories useful in sermons. These would open with a text from the Bible or other sacred work, out of which flowed the *exordium,* the arresting beginning, and next the illustrative *exemplum.* Then came the application of its story (the *moralitee*) to the moral lives of the audience, and finally the *peroration,* the finale, with its exhortation to a better life. This is the classic model for an oration and the rhetorical principle on which a medieval sermon was built. The Nun's Priest's Tale is, in the mouth of its teller, such a sermon, in perfectly conventional form, with the lesson firmly stated at the end: don't trust flatterers.

The Nun's Priest's Tale is, however, far more than sermon or moral lesson: it is yet another illustration of that quality which makes Chaucer one of the greatest poets in the language: his ability to work within a convention and transform it. Here he has taken two conventions—the theory and practice of rhetoric and the beast fable—and put this superbly witty and lively comedy into the mouth of a nobody, an ordinary priest. Moreover, he seems to have intended it to follow immediately upon the tale told by a somebody: the sleek, huntsman Monk, whose pedestrian, lifeless series of "tragedies" make a dramatic contrast with the lively, witty, erudite tale of the Nun's Priest.

The Nun's Priest's Tale too is peopled with its great men—but they are barnyard animals. Chaunticleer displays vast learning on dreams—at least that is what he would wish us to think—claiming for himself, noblest of birds, the privilege of visions that, in the technical language of dream classification at the time, are truly prophetic. These are not the foolish, invalid dreams that come from physical causes such as his wife, with her lesser nature, thinks that his dream of the fox has been. They do not, he claims, result from something he has eaten or because of some excess of one or other humor (or bodily fluid): that sort of dream is for lesser mortals. But Chaunticleer is not quite on top of his subject: the joke is, in fact, that he has not perceived the true relation between what happens of necessity and what happens through free will. Someone so noble cannot quite be bound by his dream: he flies down and is lost.

The comedy of knowledge is seen also in Pertelote, but her learning though correct and full according to the medical theory of the day, is practical and down-to-earth. She is the complete feminine materialist, downright and doubly annoying to a masculine mind such as Chaunticleer's, which thinks it sees more deeply into the true nature of things.

Chaunticleer's vainglorious learning and Pertelote's sympathetic wisdom are subtly deployed to keep the story slow and even-paced in its first part; all the bustle and action are at the end. This skillful rhetorical design in Chaucer's hands contrasts with the continuous parody of rhetorical inflation that goes on throughout the poem, especially in Chaunticleer's speeches and finally in the stream of *exempla* which flows from the climactic moment of the poem. Constantly, as the poem goes on, the simplest matters are treated in a highly ornamental manner. Long illustrative stories are introduced. *Sententiae* are bandied about. Chaucer's parody of rhetoric is presented with the maximum rhetorical sophistication and force, in the first true mock-heroic masterpiece in English.

The question has often been asked whether there is not a great deal more to this story of a cock and a hen than meets the eye. The Nun's Priest's words, "Saint Paul saith that al that writen is / To oure doctrine it is ywrit, ywis," state one of the most consistently held notions about literature during the entire Middle Ages. Should we then see in the poem an indirect meaning or application other than the warning against flatterers issued by the teller of the tale? It has been read as a much more sophisticated allegory of the friars (the fox), the secular clergy, i.e. parish priests, and other ecclesiastics not bound by a rule (Chaunticleer), and the Church (the widow); or as the Christian (Chaunticleer) carried off by the Devil or seduced by the heretic (the fox), as in the *Bestiary*. The first of these readings develops from the application of methods of interpreting the Bible that were not widely used in England in Chaucer's day, and suffers from inconsistencies. The second, simpler explanation has more to recommend it—but everyone must make up his own mind about these explanations and the view of medieval literature that they imply.

Two other Reynard and Chaunticleer stories are added here. The selections from the *Bestiary* show another mode of moralizing the animal kingdom, which is a great deal more literal and crude than Chaucer's. The selection from Caxton shows how far the notion of the fox as a deceitful animal was turned to the specific purposes of satire against the clergy (Fig. 34).

The Prologue

The prologue of the Nonne Preestes Tale

'Ho!' quod the Knight, 'good sir, namore of this,
That ye han seyd is right ynough, ywis,
And mochel˃ more; for litel hevinesse˃ — *much / sadness*
Is right ynough to mochel˃ folk, I gesse. — *many*

I seye for me, it is a greet disese˃ — *distress*
Wheras men han ben in greet welthe and ese,˃ — *comfort*
To heren of hir sodeyn˃ fall, allas! — *sudden*
And the contrarie is joie and greet solas,˃ — *relief*
As whan a man hath been in poore estaat,°
And clymbeth up, and wexeth˃ fortunat, — *grows*
And ther abydeth in prosperitee,
Swich thing is gladsom, as it thinketh me,
And of swich thing were goodly for to telle.'
'Ye,' quod our hoste, 'by Seint Poulės° belle,
Ye seye right sooth; this monk, he clappeth˃ loude, — *prattles*
He spak how 'Fortune covered with a cloude'
I noot˃ never what, and als˃ of a 'Tragedie' — *know not / also*
Right now ye herde, and pardė!° no remedie
It is for to biwaillė,˃ ne compleyne — *bewail*
That that is doon; and als it is a peyne,
As ye han seyd,˃ to here˃ of hevinesse. — *said / hear*
Sir Monk, namore of this, so God yow blesse!
Your tale anoyeth˃ al this companye; — *displeases*
Swich talking is nat worth a boterflye;
For therin is ther no desport˃ ne game.˃ — *recreation / pleasure*
Wherfor, sir Monk, or Dan° Piers by your name,
I preye yow hertėly, telle us somwhat elles,˃ — *else*
For sikerly,˃ nere° clinking of your belles, — *certainly*
That on your brydel hange on every syde,
By heven˃ king, that for us allė dyde,˃ — *Heaven's / died*
I sholde er this han fallen doun for slepe,
Although the slough˃ had never been so depe; — *mire*
Than had your talė al be told in vayn.
For certeinly, as that thisė clerkės˃ seyn, — *learned men*
'Wheras˃ a man may have noon audience, — *when*
Noght helpeth it to tellen his sentence.'˃ — *matter, wisdom*
And wel I woot the substance is in me,°
If any thing shal wel reported be.
Sir, sey˃ somwhat of hunting, I yow preye.' — *say*
'Nay,' quod this monk, 'I have no lust˃ to pleye;˃ — *pleasure / jest*
Now let another telle, as I have told.'
Than spak our host, with rudė speche and bold,
And seyde unto the Nonnės Preest anon,˃ — *at once*
'Com neer,˃ thou preest, com hider,˃ thou Sir John,° — *closer / hither*
Tel us swich thing as may our hertės glade,˃ — *gladden*
Be blythė, though thou ryde upon a jade.˃ — *wretched horse*

estaat state, status. The image does not necessarily involve Fortune's wheel (see below and Fig. 41) but may do so.
Seint Poules St. Paul's Cathedral, the chief church of London
parde i.e. *par dieu*, by God
Dan Dan = *dominus*, master; a title of respect, especially for a religious and/or learned man
nere were it not for
wel . . . me i.e. and I know very well I have the capacity to understand; or: I know very well I understand the meat of the matter
Sir John the regular nickname for a priest

What though thyn hors be bothė foule> and lene,> *dirty / lean*
If he wol serve thee, rekkė> nat a bene;> *care / bean*
Look that thyn herte be mery evermo.'
'Yis, sir,' quod he, 'yis, host, so mote I go,
But> I be mery, ywis,> I wol be blamed.' *unless / indeed*
And right anon his tale he hath attamed,> *broached*
And thus he seyde unto us everichon,
This swetė preest, this goodly man, Sir John.

Explicit°

The Tale

Here biginneth the Nonne Preestes Tale of the Cok and Hen, Chauntėcleer and Pertėlote.

A povre> widwe, somdel stape> in age, *poor / advanced*
Was whylom> dwelling in a narwe> cotage, *formerly / little*
Bisyde a grovė, stonding in a dale.> *valley*
This widwe, of which I telle yow my tale,
Sin thilkė> day that she was last a wyf, *since the same*
In paciènce ladde> a ful simple lyf, *led*
For litel was hir catel° and hir rente;> *income*
By housbondrye,> of such as God hir sente, *economy*
She fond° hirself, and eek> hir doghtren> two. *also / daughters*
Three largė sowės hadde she, and namo,> *no more*
Three kyn,> and eek a sheep that hightė> Malle. *cows / was called*
Ful sooty was hir bour, and eek hir halle,°
In which she eet> ful many a sclendre> meel. *ate / frugal*
Of poynaunt sauce hir neded never a deel.°
No deyntee morsel passėd thurgh hir throte;
Hir dyete was accordant> to hir cote.> *according / cottage*
Replecciòun> ne made hir never syk;> *over-eating / sick*
Attempree> dyete was al hir phisyk,> *temperate / medicine*
And exercyse, and hertės suffisaunce.> *heart's contentment*
The goutė lette> hir nothing for to daunce, *hindered*
Napoplexye shentė> nat hir heed; *injured*
No wyn> ne drank she, neither whyt ne reed; *wine*
Hir bord> was servėd most with whyt and blak, *table*
Milk and brown breed,> in which she fond no lak,> *bread / defect*

Explicit Literally, it is finished.
catel chattels, property
fond found, provided for: see Miller's Tale, l. 112
bour . . . halle The widow's house probably had only one room serving as living room and bedroom for the widow, her daughters, and assorted livestock. Chaucer describes the little cottage in terms of a grand house, in which the hall was the large room where household and guests assembled for food and entertainment; the bower, originally the private apartments, by Chaucer's time was a usual term for bedroom.
Of poynaunt . . . deel she did not need even a touch of piquant sauce to provoke an appetite

Seynd° bacoun, and somtyme an ey> or tweye, *egg*
For she was, as it were, a maner deye.°
  A yerd> she hadde, enclosėd al aboute *yard*
With stikkės, and a dryė dich> withoute, *ditch*
In which she hadde a cok,> hight> Chauntėcleer,° *rooster / called*
In al the land, of crowing, nas> his peer.> *was not / equal*
His vois was merier> than the mery orgon> *gayer / organ*
On messė-dayes> that in the chirchė gon;° *mass-days*
Wel sikerer> was his crowing in his logge,> *surer / lodge*
Than is a clokke, or an abbèy orlogge.°
By nature knew he ech ascencioùn
Of equinoxial° in thilkė toun;
For whan degrees fiftenė were ascended,
Thanne crew he, that it mighte nat ben amended.> *bettered*
His comb was redder than the fyn coral,
And batailed,> as it were a castel wal. *battlemented*
His bile> was blak, and as the jeet> it shoon; *bill / jet*
Lyk asur° were his leggės, and his toon;> *toes*
His naylės> whytter than the lilie flour, *claws*
And lyk the burnėd> gold was his coloùr. *burnished*
This gentil> cok hadde in his governaùnce *noble*
Sevene hennės, for to doon al his plesaùnce,> *pleasure*
Whiche were his sustres> and his paramoùrs, *sisters*
And wonder lyk> to him, as of coloùrs. *amazingly like*
Of whiche the faireste hewėd> on hir throte> *colored / throat*
Was cleped> faire damoyselė° Pertėlote. *called*
Curteis° she was, discreet, and debonaire,
And compaignable, and bar> hirself so faire, *bore*
Sin thilkė day that she was seven night old,
That trewėly> she hath the herte in hold> *firmly / keeping*
Of Chauntėcleer, loken> in every lith;> *locked / limb*
He loved hir so, that wel was him therwith.°
But such a joye was it to here> hem singe, *hear*
Whan that the brightė sonnė gan to springe,> *rise*
In swete accord, 'My lief is faren in londe.'°
For thilkė tyme, as I have understonde,> *heard*
Bestės and briddės> coudė speke and singe. *birds*
  And so befel,> that in a dawėninge,> *it happened / dawn*

Seynd singed, i.e. broiled; or perhaps fat, as in French *saindoux*, lard
maner deye a kind of dairywoman
Chauntecleer the usual name for the cock in the Reynard story, from his clear singing voice
gon The verb is plural, because "orgon" was frequently plural, on the analogy of Latin *organa*, literally a set of pipes.
orlogge the great public clock, often giving astronomical information as well as time
equinoxial The equinoxial circle or celestial equator, thought to make a complete rotation round the earth every natural (24-hour) day, at the rate of 15° per hour. So Chaunticleer crowed every hour, on the hour.
asur lapis lazuli; bright blue
damoysele Literally, young (unmarried) woman, especially of good family. The word signals Chaucer's description of the hen-heroine, called Pinte in other Reynard stories, in terms of the lady in a poem of courtly love.
Curteis full of courtly qualities, refined in manners
wel . . . therwith all was well with him for it; he was perfectly happy
'My . . . londe' My dear one has gone away; a popular song of the time. See below, p. 417.

As Chauntėcleer among his wyvės alle
Sat on his perchė, that was in the halle,
And next him sat this fairė Pertėlote,
This Chauntėcleer gan gronen> in his throte, *(did) groan*
As man that in his dreem is drecchėd> sore. *afflicted*
And whan that Pertėlote thus herde him rore,> *roar*
She was agast,> and seyde, 'O hertė dere, *afraid*
What eyleth> yow, to grone in this manere? *ails*
Ye been a verray> sleper, fy for shame!' *fine*
And he answerde and seydė thus, 'Madame,
I pray yow, that ye take it nat agrief: °
By God, me mette> I was in swich meschief> *I dreamed / trouble*
Right now, that yet myn herte is sore afright.> *frightened*
Now God,' quod he, 'my swevene recche aright, °
And keep my body out of foul prisoun!
Me mette,> how that I romėd> up and down *dreamed / walked*
Withinne our yerde, wheras> I sawe a beste, *where*
Was lyk an hound, and wolde han maad areste
Upon my body, and wolde han had me deed. °
His colour was bitwixe yellow and reed;
And tippėd was his tail, and bothe his eres,> *ears*
With blak, unlyk the remnant> of his heres;> *rest / hairs*
His snowtė smal,> with glowinge eyen tweye.> *narrow / two*
Yet of his look for fere almost I deye;> *die*
This causėd me my groning, doutėles.'
'Avoy!'> quod she, 'fy on yow, hertėles!> *fie / coward*
Allas!' quod she, 'for, by that God above,
Now han ye lost myn herte and al my love;
I can nat love a coward, by my faith.
For certės,> what so any womman seith, *indeed*
We alle desyren, if it mightė be,
To han housbondės° hardy,> wyse, and free,> *brave / generous*
And secree,> and no nigard, ne no fool, *discreet*
Ne him that is agast> of every tool,> *afraid / weapon*
Ne noon avauntour, ° by that God above!
How dorste> ye seyn> for shame unto your love, *dare / say*
That any thing mightė make yow aferd?> *afraid*
Have ye no mannės herte, and han a berd?> *beard*
Allas! and conne> ye been agast of swevenis?> *can / dreams*
Nothing, God wot, but vanitee,> in sweven is. *emptiness*
Swevenes° engendren> of replecciouns,> *grow / over-eating*

take . . . agrief don't take my groaning amiss
my . . . aright interpret my dream well, i.e. make it be a dream that presages good fortune
wolde . . . deed (ll. 134–35) wanted (i.e. tried) to make seizure of my body and kill me. There is a tinge of legal process about "areste."
housbondes Pertelote describes the sort of husband she approves of in terms of the male ideal of courtly love.
avauntour either a boaster in general, or merely one who boasts of success in love, a crime against the code
Swevenes Learned argument now ensues about the nature, cause, and meaning of Chaunticleer's dream. Pertelote, down-to-earth, wise in practical things, attributes it to indigestion or to a possibly consequent overplus of one of the humors: Chaunticleer has been on the wrong

And ofte of fume,° and of complecciou̇ns,°
Whan humours been to habundant° in a wight.
Certės this dreem, which ye han met tonight,› *dreamed last night*
Cometh of the gretė superfluitee
Of yourė redė colera,° pardee,
Which causeth folk to dreden in here dremes
Of arwes,› and of fyr with redė lemes,› *arrows / flames*
Of gretė bestės, that they wol hem byte,
Of contek,› and of whelpės grete and lyte;° *strife*
Right as the humour of malèncolye°
Causeth ful many a man, in sleep, to crye,
For fere of blakė beres,› or bolės› blake, *bears / bulls*
Or ellės, blakė develės wole hem take.
Of othere humours coude I telle also,
That warken many a man in sleep ful wo;
But I wol passe as lightly› as I can. *rapidly*
  Lo Catoun,° which that was so wys a man,
Seyde he nat thus, ne do no fors° of dremes?
Now, sire,' quod she, 'whan we flee› fro the bemes,› *fly / rafters*
For Goddės love, as tak som laxatyf;
Up› peril of my soule, and of my lyf, *upon*
I counseille yow the beste, I wol nat lye,
That bothe of colere and of malèncolye
Ye purgė yow; and for› ye shul nat tarie, *so that*
Though in this toun is noon apothecarie,
I shal myself to herbės techen› yow, *direct*
That shul ben for your hele,› and for your prow;› *health / advantage*
And in our yerd tho› herbes shal I finde, *these*
The whiche han of hir propretee, by kinde,› *nature*
To purgen yow binethe, and eek above.°
Forget not this, for Goddės owene love!

---

diet. He needs only digestives followed by laxatives. There is danger, but to health only, not to life, and not from some exterior disaster. The dream is a natural dream, rising from his bodily state, not a dream sent from above, or below, to prophesy or deceive; not even a dream rising from a disturbance of the mind or emotions. "Peck it up, there's nothing wrong with you," the verse runs rapidly on. Pertelote's rhetoric is plain and to the point: she is for experience, not authority.

fume exhalation: either the vapor rising to the mind from the decoction or digestion of food and drink in the stomach, hastening the process begun by fermentation in wine or beer; or stomach gas, indigestion; or the vapor rising from one of the four humors, not counteracted by its opposite humors and so disturbing the psychosomatic balance

complecciou̇ns i.e. the individual combinations of bodily fluids or humors (General Prologue, l. 423), of which behavior, temperament, and outward appearance were both the signs and the result

habundant a learned spelling; it was wrongly thought that the word abundant was connected with Latin *habere,* to have

superfluitee . . . colera An excess of the humor of red choler, bile (hot and dry) mixed with blood (hot and moist). Medieval medical authorities such as Arnold of Villanova (13th century) agree with Pertelote's categories of things appearing in the dreams of men so afflicted (see the Wife of Bath's Prologue, l. 587). Choler was the humor of anger, hence the dreams of strife and aggression.

whelpes . . . lyte dogs, big and little

malencolye melancholy, black bile, thought to be secreted in the liver, causing a man to dream fearfully of black, sad, and menacing things

Catoun Dionysius Cato; cf. the Miller's Tale, l. 119

ne . . . fors Attach no importance, take no notice. "Cato's" advice is a Stoic philosopher's. Pertelote quotes only this single elementary authority by name.

To purgen . . . above purging both downward (laxative, aperient) and upward (emetic or snuff-like) to bring your humors into balance; or merely, to clear your stomach and your head

Ye been ful colerik of complecciou̇n.
Waré˃ the sonne in his ascencioùn — *beware lest*
Ne fynde yow nat repleet˃ of humours hote;° — *over-full*
And if it do, I dar wel leye˃ a grote,° — *wager*
That ye shul have a fevere terciane,°
Or an agù,˃ that may be youre bane.˃ — *ague / death*
A day or two ye shul have digestyves °
Of wormės, er ye take your laxatyves,°
Of lauriol, centaure, and fumėtere,
Or ellės of ellebor, that groweth there,
Of catapuce, or of gaytrės beryis,
Of erbe yvė, growing in our yerd, ther mery is;°
Pekke hem up right as they growe, and ete hem in.
Be mery, housbond, for your fader kin!˃ — *father's lineage*
Dredeth no dreem; I can say yow namore.'
'Madame,' quod he, 'graunt mercy˃ of your lore.˃ — *thank you / teaching*
But nathėlees, as touching daun Catoun,°
That hath of wisdom such a greet renoun,
Though that he bad no dremės for to drede,
By God, men may in oldė bokės rede
Of many a man, more of auctoritee
Than ever Catoun was, so mote I thee,˃ — *thrive*
That al the rėvers seyn of his sentence,˃ — *opinion*
And han wel founden by experience,
That dremės ben significacioùns,
As wel of joye as tribulacioùns
That folk enduren in this lyf present.
Ther nedeth make of this noon argument;
The verray˃ prevė˃ sheweth it in dede. — *actual / experience*
Oon of the gretteste auctour° that men rede
Seith thus, that whylom˃ two felawės wente — *formerly*
On pilgrimage, in a ful good entente;
And happėd so, thay come into a toun,
Wheras ther was swich congregacioun
Of peple, and eek so streit of herbergage,°
That they ne founde as muche as o cotage,

humours hote Hot humors (choler and blood) would be super-heated by the sun, especially when it was high in the heavens, so that further imbalance would be caused in a man in whom they were already in dangerous disproportion.
grote an English silver coin, worth only a small sum
terciane a tertian ague or fever, in which the paroxysm recurred on alternate days. Pertelote's diagnosis is medically impeccable.
digestyves Gentler in action than harsh laxatives, they absorb or dissipate bile, whether red or black. In the Middle Ages worms were used in human medicine.
laxatyves Pertelote offers a depth-charge rather than a purge, acting both upward and downward. Laureole causes vomiting, centaury purges the bowels, fumitory the urine; hellebore purges choler downward, catapuce is a general cathartic, and so are gaiter-berries and bitter herb-ivy.
ther mery is where it is agreeable, pleasant
Catoun Chaunticleer despises Pertelote and Master Cato, her one elementary authority, and his rhetoric is grave and stately.
Oon . . . auctour Either the greatest author, or one of the greatest; probably Cicero, one of the great ancient authorities on such matters, who tells the story which follows in his *Of Divination*. Valerius Maximus (see the Wife of Bath's Prologue, l. 648) also has it; Chaucer may have got it from another medieval source.
So . . . herbergage such a shortage of lodgings

In which they bothė mighte yloggėd> be. *lodged*
Wherfor thay mosten,> of necessitee, *must*
As for that night, departen> compaignye; *part*
And ech of hem goth to his hostelrye,
And took his logging as it woldė falle.> *happen*
That oon of hem was loggėd in a stalle,
Fer> in a yerd, with oxen of the plough; *isolated*
That other man was loggėd wel ynough,
As was his aventure,> or his fortune, *luck*
That us governeth alle as in commune.°
And so bifel, that, longe er it were day,
This man mette> in his bed, theras he lay, *dreamed*
How that his felawe gan upon him calle,
And seyde, "Allas! for in an oxės stalle
This night I shal be mordred> ther I lye. *murdered*
Now help me, derė brother, er I dye;
In allė hastė com to me," he sayde.
This man out of his sleep for fere abrayde;> *leapt*
But whan that he was waknėd of his sleep,
He turnėd him, and took of this no keep;> *notice*
Him thoughte his dreem nas but a vanitee.
Thus twyës in his sleping dremėd he.
And attė thriddė tyme yet his felawe
Cam, as him thoughte, and seide, "I am now slawe;> *slain*
Bihold my blody woundės, depe and wyde!
Arys> up erly in the morwė tyde,> *rise / morning*
And at the west gate of the toun," quod he,
"A cartė ful of donge> ther shaltow see, *dung*
In which my body is hid ful privėly;
Do> thilkė carte aresten> boldėly. *have / stopped*
My gold causėd my mordre, sooth to sayn";
And tolde him every poynt how he was slayn,
With a ful pitous> facė, pale of hewe. *pitiful*
And trustė wel, his dreem he fond> ful trewe; *found*
For on the morwe,> as sone as it was day, *morning*
To his felawės in> he took the way; *lodging*
And whan that he cam to this oxės stalle,
After his felawe he bigan to calle.
The hostiler> answerėd him anon, *innkeeper*
And seydė, "Sire, your felawe is agon,> *gone*
As sone as day he wente out of the toun."
This man gan fallen in suspecioùn,
Remembring on his dremės that he mette,> *dreamed*
And forth he goth, no lenger wolde he lette,> *stay*
Unto the west gate of the toun, and fond
A dong carte, as it were to dongė> lond, *manure*

That . . . commune that has power over each and every one of us

That was arrayėd> in the samė wyse — *ordered*
As he han herd the dedė> man devyse;> — *dead / describe*
And with an hardy herte he gan to crye
Vengeaunce and justice of this felonye:—
"My felawe mordrėd is this same night,
And in this carte he lyth> gapinge upright.> — *lies / on his back*
I crye out on the ministres,>" quod he, — *governors*
"That sholden kepe and reulen this citee;
Harrow!> allas! her lyth> my felawe slayn!" — *help / lies*
What sholde I more unto this talė sayn?
The peple out sterte,> and caste the cart to grounde, — *rushed out*
And in the middel of the dong they founde
The dedė man, that mordred was al newe.> — *recently*
  O blisful> God, that art so just and trewe! — *blessed*
Lo, how that thou biwreyest> mordre alway! — *uncover*
Mordre wol out, that see we day by day.
Mordre is so wlatsom> and abhominable° — *loathsome*
To God, that is so just and resonable,
That he ne wol nat suffre it helėd> be; — *hidden*
Though it abyde a yeer, or two, or three,
Mordre wol out, this my conclusioun.
And right anoon, ministrės of that toun
Han hent> the carter, and so sore him pyned,> — *taken / tortured*
And eek the hostiler so sore engyned,> — *racked*
That thay biknewe> hir wikkednesse anoon, — *confessed*
And were anhangėd> by the nekkė-boon. — *hanged*
  Here may men seen that dremės been to drede.> — *be feared*
And certės, in the samė book° I rede,> — *read*
Right in the nexte chapìtre after this,
(I gabbė> nat, so have I joye or blis,) — *babble*
Two men that wolde han passėd over see,
For certeyn cause, into a fer> contree, — *far*
If that the wind ne hadde been contrarie,
That made hem in a citee for to tarie,
That stood ful mery> upon an haven> syde. — *pleasant / harbor*
But on a day, agayn> the eventyde, — *toward*
The wind gan chaunge, and blew right as hem leste.°
Jolif> and glad they wente unto hir reste, — *in good spirits*
And casten> hem ful erly for to saille; — *intended*
But to that oo> man fil> a greet mervaille. — *one / happened*
That oon of hem, in sleping as he lay,
Him mette a wonder dreem, agayn the day;°
Him thoughte a man stood by his beddės syde,

abhominable The spelling is due to the belief that the word meant inhuman (Latin *ab:* non + *homo:* a man).
same book See l. 218: Cicero, and the other authorities; all have this story, but not in the next chapter.
The . . . leste the wind did change and blew just as they wanted
Him . . . day he dreamed a very strange dream, just before day. Such waking dreams were often thought of as having special importance as prophecies.

And him comaunded, that he sholde abyde,> *stay*
And seyde him thus, "If thou to-morwe wende,> *go*
Thou shalt be dreynt;> my tale is at an ende." *drowned*
He wook, and tolde his felawe what he mette,> *dreamed*
And preydė him his viage> for to lette;> *voyage / stop*
As for that day, he preyde him to abyde.
His felawė, that lay by his beddės syde,
Gan for to laughe, and scornėd him ful faste.
"No dreem," quod he, "may so myn herte agaste,> *frighten*
That I wol lettė> for to do my thinges.> *delay / business*
I settė not a straw by thy dreminges,
For swevenes been but vanitees and japes.
Men dreme alday> of owlės or of apes,° *constantly*
And eke of many a masė> therwithal; *bewilderment*
Men dreme of thing that nevere was ne shal.> *shall be*
But sith I see that thou wolt heer abyde,
And thus forsleuthen wilfully thy tyde,°
God wot it reweth me;> and have good day." *makes me sorry*
And thus he took his leve, and wente his way.
But er that he hadde halfe his cours ysayled,
Noot I nat why, ne what mischaunce it ayled,
But casuelly the shippės botmė rente,°
And ship and man under the water wente
In sighte of otherė shippės it byside,
That with hem saylėd at the samė tyde.
And therfor, fairė Pertėlote so dere,
By swiche ensamples° oldė maistow> lere,> *may you / learn*
That no man sholdė been to recchėlees> *regardless*
Of dremės, for I sey thee, doutėlees,
That many a dreem ful sore is for to drede.
 Lo, in the lyf of Saint Kenelm,° I rede,
That was Kenulphus sone, the noble king
Of Mercenrike,> how Kenelm mette a thing; *Mercia*
A lyte> er he was mordrėd, on a day, *little*
His mordrė in his avisioùn> he say.> *dream / saw*
His norice> him expounėd every del> *nurse / part*
His sweven, and bad him for to kepe him> wel *himself*
For> traisoun; but he nas but seven yeer old, *for fear of*
And therfore litel talė hath he told°

owles . . . apes foolish, absurd things
And thus . . . tyde either: And thus you deliberately miss your chance (or: the tide) for pure idleness; or: And thus you deliberately and idly waste your time
Noot I . . . rente I do not know why, nor what misfortune befell it, but by some accident the ship's bottom split
ensamples *exempla,* examples; the more ancient, the more effective as illustrations
Kenelm The last two dreams that Chaunticleer has told from Cicero are not fully prophetic, nor of the best and most trustworthy sort. He therefore gives examples of true visions, experienced by men who are more his equals. St. Kenelm became king of Mercia at the age of 7, in 821. His high-born innocence was allowed a dream of himself sitting high in a splendid tree, which one of his best friends cut down, whereupon his soul flew to heaven in the form of a bird. This was a true prophecy of his murder on the orders of his aunt.
litel . . . told he took little account

Of any dreem, so holy was his herte.
By God, I haddė lever than my sherte
That ye had rad his legende, as have I.°
Dame Pertėlote, I sey yow trewėly,
Macrobeus, that writ the *Avisioùn*°
In Affrike of the worthy Cipioùn,
Affermeth> dremes, and seïth that they been *confirms*
Warning of thingės that men after seen.
  And forthermore, I pray yow loketh wel
In the Olde Testament, of Danièl,°
If he held> dremės any vanitee. *considered*
Reed eek of Joseph,° and ther shul ye see
Wher> dremės ben somtyme> (I sey nat alle) *whether / sometimes*
Warning of thingės that shul after falle.
Loke of Egipt the king, daun> Pharäo,° *Lord*
His bakere and his botėler> also, *butler*
Wher they ne feltė noon effect in dremes.
Whoso wol seken actes of sondry remes,> *realms*
May rede of dremės many a wonder thing.
  Lo Cresus,° which that was of Lydė king,
Mette he nat that he sat upon a tree,
Which signified he sholde anhangėd> be? *hanged*
Lo heer Andromacha,° Ectorės wyf,
That day that Ector sholdė lese> his lyf, *lose*
She dremėd on the samė night biforn,
How that the lyf of Ector sholde be lorn,> *lost*
If thilkė day he wente into bataille;
She warnėd him, but it mighte nat availle;
He wentė for to fightė nathelees,

I . . . have I I had rather than my shirt; i.e. I'd give my shirt if you had read his life (legend: a saint's life), as I have

Avisioun The *Somnium Scipionis*, the *Dream of Scipio*, or *Avisioun of Cipioun* forms part of Cicero's *On the State* (*De Republica*), which was unknown to the Middle Ages. What they had was the long commentary on the *Dream* (*avisioun* or *visio* was the technical term for a true, prophetic vision experienced by a notable historical person), by Macrobius, written about 400, which was the source of much of the information available to the Middle Ages on the nature of dreams. The story is told of how Scipio Africanus Minor, in Africa, was taken, in his dream, by his grandfather Scipio, the conqueror of Hannibal, up to heaven through the spheres of the universe, and shown a vision of his future as final conqueror of Carthage, as well as how insignificant is worldly glory when compared with strictly virtuous conduct, mortal with immortal. (Cf. the *envoi* to Chaucer's *Troilus and Criseyde*, below.) Macrobius discusses the nature of dreams and, at greater length, the nature of virtue: medieval science and literature used the discussion of dreams a great deal; medieval moral theology used the discussion of the virtues at least as much.

Daniel The Bible, more authoritative still, is now added to the authority of the classics, with a general reference to the prophetic visions described in Daniel 5 ff.

Joseph Genesis 37:5ff.: Joseph's dream of his brothers' sheaves bowing down to him, signifying his future exaltation

Pharäo Genesis 40–41: Joseph's exposition of the dreams of Pharaoh's imprisoned butler and baker, signifying that the first would be restored to favor and the second executed; and of Pharaoh's dream of the seven fat and the seven lean cows, signifying years of plenty and of famine in Egypt.

Cresus Croesus, king of Lydia. Chaucer's version differs from others current: he refers to it more than once.

Andromacha Andromache, Hector's wife; her dream is not in Homer or any ancient "authority" for the Trojan War: it occurs in Dares the Phrygian, a late Latin author whom the Middle Ages believed to be more reliable than Homer in Trojan matters and on whom the medieval Troy romances which Chaucer knew are partly based. Andromache's dream also occurs in these romances.

But he was slayn anoon> of Achilles. — *at once*
But thilkė tale is al too long to telle,
And eek it is ny day, I may nat dwelle.
Shortly I seye, as for conclusioùn,
That I shal han of this avisioùn°
Adversitee; and I seye forthermore,
That I ne telle of laxatyves no store,°
For they ben venimous,> I woot it wel; — *poisonous*
I hem defye, I love hem never a del.> — *bit*
   Now let us speke of mirthe, and stinte> al this; — *cease*
Madàmė Pertėlote, so have I blis,°
Of o thing God hath sent me largė grace;
For whan I see the beautee of your face,
Ye ben so scarlet reed> about your yën,> — *red / eyes*
It maketh al my dredė for to dyen;> — *die (down)*
For, also siker as In principio,
Mulier est hominis confusio;°
Madàme, the sentence> of this Latin is— — *meaning*
Womman is mannės joye and al his blis.
For wan I fele anight your softė syde,
Albeit that I may nat on you ryde,
For that our perche is maad so narwe, alas!
I am so ful of joye and of solas> — *delight*
That I defye bothė sweven and dreem.'°
And with that word he fley> down fro the beem, — *flew*
For it was day, and eek his hennės alle;
And with a 'Chuk' he gan hem for to calle,
For he had founde a corn, lay> in the yerd. — *that lay*
Royal he was, he was namore aferd;> — *afraid*
He fethered Pertėlote twenty tyme,
And trad as oftė, er that it was pryme.°
He loketh as it were a grim leoùn;
And on his toos he rometh up and doun,
Him deynėd> not to sette his foot to grounde. — *he deigned*
He chukketh, whan he hath a corn yfounde,
And to him rennen> thanne his wyvės alle. — *run*
Thus royal, as a prince is in his halle,
Leve I this Chauntėcleer in his pastùre;
And after wol I tell his adventùre.
   Whan that the month in which the world bigan,

Shortly . . . avisioun Chaunticleer insists again that his was a truly prophetic dream: Briefly I say, in conclusion, that I shall have ill-fortune from this divinely-inspired vision.
ne . . . store I set no store whatever by laxatives. The several negatives intensify.
so . . . blis as I hope to go to heaven
For also . . . confusio For, as sure as "In the beginning," woman is the ruination of man. *In principio,* the first words of St. John's Gospel, were thought to possess a special truth. See General Prologue, l. 256.
sweven and dreem A distinction between true visions and mere insignificant dreams may be intended, but Chaucer's usage is not consistent or definite enough to be sure.
He fethered . . . pryme He embraced Pertelote twenty times and screwed her as often, before prime. Prime is the time—see the Miller's Tale, l. 446 above—between 6 a.m. and 9 a.m.

That hightė March, whan God first makėd man,°
Was complet, and ypassed were also,
Sin March bigan, thritty dayes and two,°
Bifel that Chauntėcleer, in al his pryde,
His seven wyvės walking by his syde,
Caste up his eyen to the brightė sonne,
That in the signe of Taurus hadde yronne
Twenty degrees and oon, and somwhat more;
And knew by kynde,> and by noon other lore, *nature*
That it was pryme, and crew with blisful stevene.> *voice*
'The sonne,' he sayde 'is clomben> up on hevene *has climbed*
Fourty degrees and oon, and more, ywis.> *indeed*
Madamė Pertėlote, my worldės blis,
Herkneth thise blisful briddės> how they singe, *birds*
And see the fresshė flourės how they springe;
Ful is myn herte of revel and solas.'
But sodeinly him fil> a sorweful cas;> *befell / chance*
For ever the latter ende of joye is wo.
God woot that worldly joye is sone ago;
And if a rethor° coudė faire endyte,> *write*
He in a cronique saufly> mighte it wryte, *chronicle safely*
As for a sovereyn notabilitee.°
Now every wys man, lat him herkne me;
This storie is also> trewe, I undertake, *as*
As is the book of Launcelot de Lake,°
That wommen holde in ful gret reverence.
Now wol I torne agayn to my sentence.> *purport*
  A col-fox,° ful of sly iniquitee,
That in the grove hadde wonėd> yerės three, *lived*
By heigh imaginacioùn forncast,°
The samė night thurghout the heggės brast> *hedges burst*
Into the yerd, ther Chauntėcleer the faire
Was wont, and eek his wyvės, to repaire;
And in a bed of wortės> stille he lay, *vegetables*

whan . . . man The common opinion was that the Creation took place at the spring equinox.
thritty . . . two This may be elaborate rhetorical parody. It is not certain whether we are intended to read April 3 or May 3. May 3 would be appropriate, since it is an unlucky "Egyptian" day (two or three days each month were marked as "evil" or "Egyptian" because of God's plagues on Egypt)—see the Franklin's Tale, l. 198. Chaucer also uses this day in his Knight's Tale, and in *Troilus and Criseyde*. On that day the sun would have passed through about 20° of Taurus, the Bull, the second zodiacal sign. It would be 40° high in the sky, from the horizon, at about 9 a.m.
rethor Rhetorician, i.e. polished writer; Chaucer (or the Nun's Priest) is making a tacit and insincere apology for lack of polish in writing; reinforcing, perhaps, the effect of the elaborate dating and timing just past.
sovereyn notabilitee something worthy of the most careful note—an important *sententia*
Launcelot de Lake The false lover of Queen Guinevere in the popular Arthurian romances (Dante put him into *Inferno*). The Nun's Priest is bringing home his little lesson to the ladies, for whose reading the stories of Lancelot were intended; to them these romances seemed true as well as beautiful. The Priest is also having a little private joke at the ladies' expense.
col-fox a fox with much black fur, or with black markings
forncast Predestined by divine planning. The Nun's Priest shifts to an attempt to reach a more exalted plane: he feels it necessary to argue the matter of whether Chaunticleer's fate was predestined or not; and he becomes the counterweight to Chaunticleer's valuation of his dream.

Til it was passėd undern° of the day,
Wayting˃ his tyme˃ on Chauntėcleer to falle, *watching / opportunity*
As gladly doon thise homicydes alle,
That in awayt liggen to mordre men.°
O false mordrer, lurking in thy den!
O newė Scariot,° newė Genilon!°
False dissimilour,˃ O Greek Sinon,° *dissembler*
That broghtest Troye al outrely˃ to sorwe! *completely*
O Chauntėcleer, acursėd be that morwe,
That thou into that yerd flough˃ fro the bemes! *flew*
Thou were ful wel ywarnėd by thy dremes,
That thilkė day was perilous to thee.
But what that God forwoot mot˃ nedes be, *foreknows must*
After˃ the opinioùn of certeyn clerkis.° *according to*
Witnesse on him, that any perfit˃ clerk is, *perfect*
That in scole is gret altercacioùn
In this matere, and greet disputisoùn,°
And hath ben of an hundred thousand men.
But I ne can not bulte˃ it to the bren,˃ *sift / bran*
As can the holy doctour Augustyn,
Or Boece, or the bishop Bradwardyn,
Whether that Goddės worthy forwiting˃ *noble foreknowledge*
Streyneth˃ me nedely˃ for to doon a thing, *constrains / necessarily*
('Nedely' clepe I simple necessitee);
Or ellės, if free choys be graunted me
To do that samė thing, or do it noght,
Though God forwoot˃ it, er that it was wroght; *foreknew*
Or if his witing˃ streyneth nevere a del *knowledge*
But by necessitee condicionel.°
I wol not han to do of swich matere;

undern literally, the intervening or middle period, of morning or afternoon; here mid-morning
As gladly . . . men as all such murderers usually (or: willingly) do, that lie in ambush to murder men
Scariot The Nun's Priest shifts into top preaching gear, and Chaucer into another mock-heroic mode, with a list of traitors and deceivers, beginning with the worst, Judas Iscariot, betrayer of Christ.
Genilon Ganelon, the traitor who caused the defeat of Charlemagne and the death of Roland in the medieval French epic *The Song of Roland*
Sinon the Greek decoy, who persuaded the Trojans to drag the Wooden Horse into Troy
After . . . clerkis The matter of free-will and predestination, of how much freedom of choice a man can have, given an all-knowing Creator, had been much discussed by Christian philosophers, especially by St. Augustine in his early 5th-century controversy with Pelagius. Augustine takes the side of predestination. Boethius (Boece) the early 6th-century Roman philosopher, whose *Consolation of Philosophy* Chaucer translated, evolved a solution (see below). Thomas Bradwardine, Archbishop of Canterbury, *d.* 1349, came in on the side of Augustine in his *On the Cause of God,* during a renewal of the controversy in the 14th century. The Nun's Priest says modestly that he cannot completely sift out the flour from the husks (bran) and decide who is right and who wrong.
Witnesse . . . disputisoùn (ll. 466–68). Any fully educated man can bear witness that in the schools (i.e. philosophical faculties of the universities) there is great argument and dispute on the matter.
condicionel Boethius's solution to the question was to divide necessity, predestination, and God's foreknowledge into two categories, simple and conditional. Strictly speaking, God foreknows everything, so that man has no full and true freedom of choice, but only a limited degree. Men are mortal and must die, by simple necessity. Man has no voice in the matter. But he is not constrained by necessity to walk, though if he does so, he does so necessarily. His necessary walking is conditional on his free choice whether to walk or stay still. See Boethius, *On the Consolation of Philosophy,* Bk. 5.

My tale is of a cok, as ye may here,
That took his counseil of his wyf, with sorwe,°
To walken in the yerd upon that morwe
That he had met˃ the dreem, that I yow tolde. *dreamed*
Wommennės counseils˃ been ful oftė colde;° *advice*
Wommennės counseil broghte us first to wo,
And made Adam fro Paradys to go,
Ther as he was ful mery,˃ and wel at ese. *content*
But for I noot,˃ to whom it mighte displese, *know not*
If I counseil of wommen woldė blame,
Passe over, for I seyde it in my game.˃ *jest*
Rede auctours, wher they trete of swich matere,
And what thay seyn of wommen ye may here.
Thise been the cokkės wordės, and nat myne;
I can noon harm of no womman divyne.˃ *discover*
  Faire in the sond,˃ to bathe hir merily, *dust*
Lyth Pertelote, and alle hir sustrės by,
Agayn˃ the sonne; and Chauntėcleer so free˃ *in / noble*
Song merier than the mermayde in the see;
For *Phisiologus*° seith sikerly,˃ *certainly*
How that they singen wel and merily.
And so bifel that, as he caste his yë,
Among the wortės, on a boterflye,˃ *butterfly*
He was war of this fox that lay ful lowe.
Nothing ne liste him thannė for to crowe,°
But cryde anon, 'Cok, cok,' and up he sterte,˃ *leapt*
As man that was affrayėd˃ in his herte. *frightened*
For naturelly a beest desyreth flee
Fro his contrarie,° if he may it see,
Though he never erst˃ had seyn it with his yë. *before*
  This Chauntėcleer, whan he gan him espye,
He wolde han fled, but that the fox anon
Seyde, 'Gentil sire, allas! wher wol ye gon?
Be ye affrayed of me that am your freend?
Now certės, I were worsė than a feend,
If I to yow wold˃ harm or vileinye. *intended*
I am nat come your counseil˃ for t'espye; *secrets*
But trewėly, the cause of my cominge
Was only for to herkne how that ye singe.
For trewėly ye have as mery a stevene˃ *voice*
As any aungel hath, that is in hevene;

with sorwe sad to say
colde chilly, comfortless
Phisiologus A book, not a man: the *Bestiary*. First written in Greek in Alexandria, 2nd century A.D., it was translated into Latin in the 4th or 5th, and attributed to one Theobaldus. Later, it was translated into the medieval European languages. It consisted of descriptions of real and fabulous creatures, with moralizations (see below). The Mermaids or Sirens, who lure sailors to destruction with the sweetness of their song, represented destructive worldly and fleshly delights.
Nothing . . . crowe he had no desire at all to crow, then
contrarie opposite, natural enemy; every creature was supposed to have an opposite to whom it felt antipathy by nature

Therwith ye han in musik more felinge
Than hadde Boece,° or any that can singe.
My lord your fader (God his soulė blesse!)
And eek your moder, of hir gentilesse,˃ *courtesy*
Han in myn hous ybeen, to my gret ese;
And certės, sire, ful fayn˃ wolde I yow plese. *gladly*
But for men speke of singing, I wol saye,
So mote I broukė wel° myn eyen tweye,
Save yow, I herdė never man so singe,
As dide your fader in the morweninge;
Certes, it was of˃ herte, al that he song.˃ *from the / sang*
And for to make his voys the morė strong,
He wolde so peyne him, that with bothe his yën
He moste winke,° so loudė he wolde cryen,
And stonden on his tiptoon therwithal,
And strecchė forth his nekkė long and smal.
And eek he was of swich discrecioùn,
That ther nas no man in no regioùn
That him in song or wisdom mightė passe.
I have wel rad in *Daun Burnel the Asse,*°
Among his vers, how that ther was a cok,
For that a preestės sone yaf him a knok
Upon his leg, whyl he was yong and nyce,˃ *foolish*
He made him for to lese˃ his benefyce.° *lose*
But certeyn, ther nis no comparisoùn
Bitwix the wisdom and discrecioùn
Of yourė fader, and of his subtiltee.
Now singeth, sire, for seïnte˃ charitee, *sainted*
Let see, conne˃ ye your fader countrefete˃?' *can / imitate*
This Chauntėcleer his wingės gan to bete,
As man that coude his tresoun˃ nat espye, *deceit*
So was he ravisshed with his flaterye.
  Allas! ye lordės, many a fals flatour˃ *flatterer*
Is in your courtes, and many a losengeour,˃ *fawner*
That plesen yow wel morė, by my feith,
Than he that soothfastnesse˃ unto yow seith. *truth*
Redeth Ecclesiaste° of flaterye;
Beth war, ye lordės, of hir trecherye.
  This Chauntėcleer stood hye upon his toos,
Strecching his nekke, and heeld his eyen cloos,

Therwith . . . Boece Boethius's *On Music* was a standard medieval textbook.
So . . . brouke wel as I may properly enjoy the use of
He wolde . . . winke he would take such pains that he had to close both his eyes
Daun . . . Asse Master Burnellus, the hero of *The Mirror of Fools,* a satirical poem by Nigel Wireker (12th century); a donkey dissatisfied with the length of his tail, he roamed the world looking for a longer one
For that . . . benefyce (ll. 548–50) Because a priest's son gave him a blow on his leg, when he was young and foolish, the cock caused him to lose his benefice by refusing to crow at the proper time and wake the young man on the morning he was to be ordained, so that he was late and missed his chance.
Ecclesiaste Ecclesiasticus 12:10–11, 16: Never trust thine enemy . . . take good heed and beware of him . . .

And gan to crowė loudė for the nones;°
And Daun Russel° the fox sterte up at ones,
And by the gargat hentė> Chauntėcleer, *throat grabbed*
And on his bak toward the wode him beer,> *bore*
For yet ne was ther no man that him sewed.> *pursued*
O destinee, that mayst nat been eschewed!> *escaped*
Allas, that Chauntėcleer fleigh> fro the bemes! *flew*
Allas, his wyf ne roghtė nat° of dremes!
And on a Friday° fil al this meschaunce.
O Venus, that art goddesse of plesaunce,
Sin that thy servant was this Chauntėcleer,
And in thy service dide al his powèr,
More for delyt, than world to multiplye,°
Why woldestow suffre him on thy day° to dye?
O Gaufred,° dere mayster soverayn,
That, whan thy worthy King Richard was slayn
With shot,° compleynedest his deth so sore,
Why ne hadde I now thy sentence> and thy lore,> *wisdom / learning*
The Friday for to chide, as diden ye?
(For on a Friday soothly slayn was he.)
Than wolde I shewe yow how that I coude pleyne> *lament*
For Chauntėclerės drede, and for his peyne.
Certes, swich cry ne lamentacioùn
Was never of ladies maad, whan Ilioùn> *Troy*
Was wonne, and Pirrus with his streitė swerd,°
Whan he hadde hent King Priam by the berd,
And slayn him (as saith us *Eneydos*),°
As maden alle the hennės in the clos,> *enclosure*
Whan they had seyn> of Chauntėcleer the sighte. *seen*
But sovereynly> Dame Pertėlotė shrighte,> *royally / shrieked*
Ful louder than dide Hasdrubalės° wyf,
Whan that hir housbond haddė lost his lyf,
And that the Romayns haddė brend> Cartage; *burned*
She was so ful of torment and of rage,> *violent grief*
That wilfully into the fyr she sterte,
And brende hirselven with a stedfast herte.

for the nones on this occasion
Daun Russel Master Red
roghte nat cared not for, took no account of
Friday traditionally an unlucky day of the week —and an "Egyptian" day (May 3) as well; see l. 424
More . . . multiplye more for the pleasure than to increase the population
thy day Friday is the day of the planet and goddess Venus; French *vendredi,* Italian *venerdi.*
Gaufred Geoffrey of Vinsauf, a 12th-century rhetorician, whose treatise on Latin poetics, *Poetria Nova,* published soon after the death of Richard I, Coeur-de-Lion, contained, as a model of a lament, verses on the death of that king. Friday is a day of mischance, especially because Richard was killed on it, and its very existence is lamented and scolded. Chaucer, and the Nun's Priest, are again professing weakness as rhetoricians.
shot a missile, actually an arrow
Pirrus . . . swerd Pyrrhus, with his naked (Latin: *stricta*) sword. Pyrrhus was the Greek who killed King Priam of Troy when the Greeks sacked the city.
as . . . Eneydos As Virgil's *Aeneid* tells us (II.550–53). Chaucer may have taken his references to Troy, Carthage, and Rome from Geoffrey's treatise cited above.
Hasdrubales See the Franklin's Tale, ll. 691 ff; this Hasdrubal was not Hannibal's brother, but the King of Carthage who committed suicide when his city was burned by the Romans in 146 B.C.

O woful hennės, right so cryden ye,
As, whan that Nero° brendė the citee
Of Romė, cryden senatourės wyves,
For that hir housbondes losten alle hir lyves;
Withouten gilt this Nero hath hem slayn.
Now wol I tornė to my tale agayn.
  This sely> widwe, and eek hir doghtres two, *poor*
Herden thise hennės crye and maken wo,
And out at dorės sterten> they anoon, *rushed*
And syen> the fox toward the grovė goon, *saw*
And bar upon his bak the cok away;
And cryden, 'Out! Harrow!> and weylaway! *help*
Ha, ha, the fox!' and after him they ran,
And eek with stavės many another man;
Ran Colle° our dogge, and Talbot, and Gerland,°
And Malkin,° with a distaf in hir hand;
Ran cow and calf, and eek the verray hogges
So were they fered> for berking of the dogges *afraid*
And shouting of the men and wimmen eke,
They ronnė> so, hem thoughte hir hertė breke.> *ran / would burst*
They yellėden as feendės> doon in helle; *devils*
The dokės> cryden as men wolde hem quelle;> *ducks / kill*
The gees for ferė flowen> over the trees; *flew*
Out of the hyvė cam the swarm of bees;
So hidous was the noyse, a! Benedicitė!
Certės,> he Jakkė Straw,° and his meynee,> *surely / company*
Ne madė never shoutės half so shrille,
Whan that they wolden any Fleming kille,
As thilkė day was maad upon the fox.
Of bras thay broghten bemės,> and of box,> *trumpets / boxwood*
Of horn, of boon,> in whiche they blewe and pouped,> *bone / tooted*
And therwithal thay shrykėd> and they houped;> *shrieked / whooped*
It semėd as that heven sholdė falle.
Now, godė men, I pray yow herkneth alle!
  Lo, how fortune turneth> sodeinly *overturns*
The hope and pryde eek of hir enemy!
This cok, that lay upon the foxes bak,
In al his drede, unto the fox he spak,
And seydė, 'Sire, if that I were as ye,

Nero Nero, wishing to re-enact the burning of Troy, set fire to Rome in 64 A.D. and enjoyed the laments that he heard from the dying and the survivors of all classes. He had previously put to death many innocent patricians.
Colle a common dog's name
Talbot, and Gerland two other dogs, or perhaps two men
Malkin traditional name for a maidservant
Jakke Straw One of the leaders of the Peasants' Revolt of 1381. Foreigners working and trading in London were commonly held to be doing native Englishmen out of their jobs and were therefore attacked. The Flemings were mainly cloth-workers (see the General Prologue, l. 450), and many were killed "with the usual row"—as a contemporary chronicler puts it. "Meynee" often has the sense of rabble. The Nun's Priest is bringing the noise and strife of his story close home to his hearers.

Yet sholde I seyn (as wis God helpė me°):
"Turneth agayn, ye proudė cherlės alle!
A verray pestilence upon yow falle!
Now am I come unto this wodės syde,
Maugree your heed,° the cok shal heer abyde;
I wol him ete, in feith, and that anon." '
The fox answerde, 'In feith, it shal be don;'
And as he spak that word, al sodeinly
This cok brak from his mouth deliverly,˃ *nimbly*
And heighe upon a tree he fleigh anon.
And whan the fox saugh that he was ygon,
'Allas!' quod he, 'O Chauntėcleer, allas!
I have to yow,' quod he, 'ydoon trespas,
Inasmuche as I makėd yow aferd,
Whan I yow hente, and broghte out of the yerd;
But, sire, I dide it in no wikke˃ entente; *evil*
Com doun, and I shal telle yow what I mente.
I shal seye sooth to yow, God help me so.'
'Nay than,' quod he, 'I shrewe˃ us bothė two, *curse*
And first I shrewe myself, bothe blood and bones,
If thou bigylė me ofter than ones.
Thou shalt namore, thurgh thy flaterye,
Do˃ me to singe and winkė with myn yë. *cause*
For he that winketh, whan he sholdė see,
Al wilfully, God lat him never thee˃!' *thrive*
'Nay,' quod the fox, 'but God yeve him meschaunce,
That is so undiscreet of governaunce,˃ *self-control*
That jangleth˃ whan he sholdė holde his pees.' *babbles*
Lo, swich it is for to be recchėlees,˃ *reckless*
And necligent, and truste on flaterye.
But ye that holden this tale a folye,
As of a fox, or of a cok and hen,
Taketh the moralitee,° good men.
For Saint Paul° seith, that al that writen is,
To our doctryne it is ywrite, ywis.
Taketh the fruyt, and lat the chaf be stille.
Now, godė God, if that it be thy wille,
As seith my Lord,° so make us alle good men;
And bringe us to his heighė blisse. Amen.

Here is ended the Nonne Preestes Tale.

as wis . . . me as surely as God may help me.
Maugree your heed in spite of your head; for anything you can do about it
moralitee Morality, lesson. The Nun's Priest winds up in a little confusion, but makes his point: this tale has a lesson for us all.
Saint Paul Romans 15:4: "For whatsoever things were written aforetime were written for our learning that we through patience and comfort of the scriptures might have hope." The Nun's Priest stops to drive home the moral lesson, turning his story into a sermon.
Lord i.e. Christ

Two Cock-and-Fox Stories

Here are two stories, one heavily moralizing the habits of the cock and the fox, one telling the story of Chaunticleer and Reynard as part of a long series of the fox's tricks and adventures.

The first, from the *Bestiary* (*Physiologus,* see l. 505n above), paints the kind of *moralitee* that the Nun's Priest would expect his hearers to have at the back of their minds. Such *exempla,* illustrative stories, were much used by preachers. Our text is a free modern version of a fifteenth-century Latin translation.

The second is from Caxton's translation from the Dutch in his *Reynard the Fox,* printed in 1481, which goes back ultimately to the French *Roman de Renart* (late twelfth century). There are more than forty such tales in Caxton's book. Caxton still moralizes the story, but he gives it none of Chaucer's wit and spirit; his public wanted stories and stories alone. The fox as a sham cleric was a regular feature of Reynard literature.

The text, based on the edition of 1481, is modernized in spelling and punctuation.

From The Bestiary—

Of the Fox

The nature or characteristic of the fox is as follows. The fox is an animal with a heart full of tricks and deceptions; for when it wishes to catch rooks and crows it stretches itself out on the ground and closes its eyes as if it had been lying dead for many days. The rooks and crows, greedy to dine off the corpse, come and begin to tear at it. Then the fox, quickly jumping up, seizes them and gobbles them up.

Morality In the fox we see the Devil, full of guile, who deceives sinners as the fox deceives birds like rooks and crows. The Devil cannot deceive good, honest, and holy men because they are clothed in the righteousness of virtue. . . .

Of the Cock

The nature or characteristic of the cock is that the more the night approaches, the louder it crows; and when day approaches, it sings more often.

Morality We should imitate its character, and the nearer the night approaches with its perils and doubts and with the Devil at hand, we should sing loudly and devoutly, asking the aid of God to defend us from all perils; and when the dawn is near, we should pray to God as often as we can. . . .

Another characteristic of the cock is that when it wishes to crow, it strikes itself with its wings three times beforehand.

Morality This shows that a man ought to beat himself on the breast for the blame of his sins and offenses before praying, so that he can sing better and more righteously his praises of God. . . .

From William Caxton's The History of Reynard the Fox

How the Cock Complained on Reynard

Chanticleer came forth and smote piteously his hands and his feathers; and on each side of the bier went twain sorrowful hens. That one was called Cantart and that other good hen, Crayant; they were two the fairest hens that were between

Holland[1] and Ardennes. These hens bare each of them a burning taper which was long and strait.[2] These two hens were Coppen's sisters, and they cried so piteously, 'Alas and weleaway!'[3] for the death of their dear sister Coppen. Two young hens bare the bier, which cackled so heavily[4] and wept so loud for the death of Coppen their mother, that it was far heard. Thus came they together before the King.

And Chanticleer then said, 'Merciful lord, my lord the King, please it you to hear our complaint and abhor the great scathe[5] that Reynard hath done to me and my children that here stand. It was so that in the beginning of April, when the weather is fair, as that I was hardy[6] and proud because of the great lineage that I am come of, and also had.[7] For I had eight fair sons and seven fair daughters which my wife had hatched, and they were all strong and fat and went in a yard which was walled round about, in which was a shed wherein were six great dogs which had totore[8] and plucked many a beast's skin in such wise as my children were not afraid. On whom Reynard the Thief had great envy because they were so secure that he could none get of them. How well ofttimes hath this fell[9] thief gone round about this wall and hath laid for us in such wise that the dogs have been set on him and have hunted him away. And once they leapt on him upon the bank, and that cost him somewhat for his theft. I saw that his skin smoked.[10] Nevertheless, he went his way.[11] God amend it![12]

'Thus were we quit of Reynard a long while. At last came he in likeness of an hermit,[13] and brought to me a letter for to read, sealed with the King's seal, in which stood written that the King had made peace over all in his realm, and that all manner beasts and fowls should do none harm nor scathe to one another. Yet said he to me more, that he was a cloisterer or a closed recluse[14] become, and that he would receive great penance for his sins. He showed me his slavin and pilch and an hair shirt thereunder;[15] and then said he, "Sir Chanticleer, after this time be no more afraid of me nor take no heed, for I

1. The northern coastal country, not the United Netherlands now called Holland, and the Ardennes, in the southern Netherlands; thus, from north to south, anywhere.
2. Slender.
3. Happiness is gone, alas!
4. Sorrowfully.
5. Harm.
6. Bold.
7. The great lineage that I am sprung from and that is sprung from me.
8. Torn to pieces.
9. Fierce.
10. I saw the dust rise from his skin.
11. He got away.
12. God see that things go better next time.
13. In the guise of a hermit.
14. Both words mean a member of a monastic order, prevented by religious vows from leaving the monastery or receiving visitors, except by special dispensation.
15. A slavin was a pilgrim's mantle; a pilch, originally an outer garment of dressed skin with the hair still on it, but later merely of leather or coarse wool. The hair shirt, which was woven of animal hair, was worn next to the skin by penitents and religious to mortify the flesh. There is a sort of joke here at Chanticleer's gullibility: Reynard's innermost shirt would naturally be of hair.

now will eat no more flesh.[16] I am forthon so old that I would fain remember my soul.[17] I will now go forth, for I have yet to say my sext, none, and mine evensong.[18] To God, I betake[19] you." Then went Reynard thence, saying his Credo;[20] and laid him under an hawthorn.

'Then I was glad and merry, and also took no heed, and went to my children and clucked them together, and went without the wall for to walk, whereof is much harm come to us. For Reynard lay under a bush and came creeping between us and the gate, so that he caught one of my children and laid him in his male.[21] Whereof we have great harm; for since he hath tasted of him there might never hunter nor hound save nor keep him from us. He hath waited by night and day in such wise that he hath stolen so many of my children that of fifteen I have but four; in such wise hath this thief forslongen[22] them. And yet yesterday was Coppen my daughter, that here lieth upon the bier, with the hounds rescued. This complain I to you, gracious King; have pity on my great and unreasonable damage and loss of my fair children!'

1481

The Wife of Bath's Prologue and Tale

The Wife of Bath's horoscope, as she herself states it in her Prologue, gives astrological clues to her character that would have been recognized by Chaucer's contemporaries. Her zodiacal sign is Taurus, one of the "mansions" of the planet Venus, the love star. Taurus was just rising above the horizon when the Wife was born but, most unfortunately, Mars, the warlike planet, was in conjunction with Venus at the same time. The sign just rising above the eastern horizon, the ascendant, was held to govern a nativity; and if only Venus had been alone in Taurus, the Wife would have been everything that was gentle, playful, loving, slim, and beautiful. But the effect of Mars turned gentleness to fierceness, play to aggression, love to insatiability, and slim, blonde beauty to heavier, fleshier, darker charms. The Wife is thus still an attractive woman, but more of a handful (Fig. 29).

All this we should have been led to expect, too, from her description in the General Prologue—her proud behavior, her confident skill in her trade, her roving eye—all add to and help to round out the picture into what has always been rightly thought one of Chaucer's most lifelike characters. But she also, like the Prioress, has a literary prototype in the *Roman de la Rose:* the Duenna, protectress, imparter of the secrets of catching men, and ironic commentator.

16. That is, I will make the religious observance of fasting by eating no meat.
17. Moreover, so old that I wish to be mindful of my soul.
18. The meeting must have taken place in the forenoon, since the canonical hours mentioned begin at noon. The recitation of the Divine Office, as contained in the Breviary, was (and is) obligatory for anyone in major orders in the Catholic Church. The office of sext was recited at the sixth hour (noon) after prime (the first hour, 6 a.m.); nones at the ninth (3 p.m.) and evensong (vespers) shortly before sunset.
19. Commend.
20. Creed, from the opening words *Credo in unum Deum* ("I believe in God"), the confession of faith; part of the mass. Reynard repeats it as an act of pretended devotion.
21. Bag.
22. Swallowed down.

It is characteristic of the Wife that, when her turn comes to tell a tale, she prefaces it with a great comic account of her life and marryings, dealing first with the question of whether her own successive experiences of marriage can be justified from Scripture —and in the eyes of the church and of society. Her experience falls foul of the authority of St. Jerome (c. 342–420), the most famous and influential representative of the tradition which, beginning in the unquestioning acceptance of male superiority in pre-classical societies, passes into Greek and Roman thought as explicit anti-feminism. *The Golden Book of Marriage* is attributed to Theophrastus (c. 372–287 B.C.), the pupil of Aristotle, but we know of it only from its use by later Christian writers, who drew on it for ammunition. They also drew—and so perhaps did Chaucer—on the savage sixth satire of the Roman poet Juvenal (c. 60–140 A.D.) directed against women. But it was the Fathers of the Christian Church, especially St. Jerome, who saw in the biblical account of Eden and its loss the first example of man brought to destruction by woman. Justification of their attitude was found in the pagan philosophy in which they had been educated, and the dispraise of women became the subject of works designed to encourage male and female chastity. The Fathers' great Christian weapon was St. Paul's First Epistle to the Corinthians, chapter 7, which figures largely in the Wife's Prologue. St. Jerome's tract, *Adversus Jovinianum* (Against Jovinian), written about A.D. 400, is the most comprehensive and influential statement of the anti-feminist case. Jovinian, a monk, had ventured to suggest that fasting and chastity were not necessarily higher states than reasonable indulgence in food, drink, and sex. Jerome refuted him with authorities, eloquence, and abuse. Jerome's tract was, however, only the beginning of a long tradition of Christian anti-feminist literature which Chaucer uses in the Wife's Prologue.

In presenting all this, Chaucer is operating in his accustomed mode of transformation. The Wife, we feel, has made out her case for successive remarriages with the brand of defiance that is conscious of running counter to social and religious pressures, hinting that part of her excuse must be that she is Venerian by temperament. Then, as the anti-feminist stories begin to flow and she warms to the description of her fifth husband, Jankin, and his little ways, her stature as Chaucer's character grows. Our sympathy for her as a representative of slandered womanhood increases. In the end, she stands unharmed by the whole tide of it. She is life itself, ready for another husband, or whatever the future has in store.

The tale that Chaucer gives her to tell is a version of the ancient and widely diffused folk-tale of the Loathly Lady: the repulsive hag, whom a vow or an obligation forces a young man to accept as his wife. The lady has received her ill-favored shape by enchantment and must keep it until true courtesy frees her from it; in some versions she has assumed it as a matter of choice. In each case, the true perceptions and the courtesy of the man who has somehow, wittingly or unwittingly, put himself in her power are tested. He has to show either that he is not led astray by outward unattractiveness, or that his obligation of noble behavior toward women is fulfilled, before the happy ending to the tale can ensue.

At least one other version of the story was current in Chaucer's day. This was the tale of Florent in the first book of John Gower's *Confessio Amantis* (Lover's Confession). It is also probable that more versions of it were available, such as those in the ballad *The Marriage of Sir Gawain* and the poem *The Wedding of Sir Gawain and Dame Ragnell*. The versions involving Sir Gawain turn on his knightly perfection. In accepting the loathly bride, he demonstrates his true nobility, holding to the obligation that courtesy has conferred on him. "He wolde algate his trowthe holde"—he wanted in all ways to keep faith—as the ballad puts it.

None of these versions, including Chaucer's, is derived from the other, yet all are clearly interrelated, in spite of minor differences. Chaucer's tale, in the Wife's mouth, becomes an *exemplum* of her view of what the marital situation should be, and what it is unlikely to be in male-dominated society without active intervention by women themselves. As the Wife tells it, the story illustrates the validity of the admission she has exhorted from her husband in her Prologue: "Myn owene trewe wyf, / Do as thee lust the terme of al thy lyf." The hero of the story, instead of being King Arthur, or Gawain, the flower of courtesy, is a rogue, who has to solve a riddle in order to exculpate himself from a rape. Having put himself into the Loathly Lady's power, in order to answer the Queen's riddle, he must acknowledge the superiority of the woman. To the Wife this is all quite plain and as it should be; there is no suggestion, as there is in the Gawain poems, that sovereignty is yielded out of *gentilesse,* in accordance with the subtler modes of another female retort to male domination· the code of courtly love (see Glossary). The terms of the choice offered the knight have been slanted by Chaucer to fit the Wife's character; they emphasize the nature of the submission that any man—even in an illustrative fiction—must make if he comes within her orbit. This knight is not offered the plain choice between beauty and ugliness: he must choose rather between a mate who is ugly but faithful and one who is beautiful and unfaithful. Things turn out fairly well for him in the end: he yields his authority to her, but his wife is both beautiful and obedient. She is the correlative of the discussion of *gentilesse.* In the overriding fiction of the *Tales,* however, the Wife has the last word, in her final prayer for young, vigorous husbands—and for mastery over them. Her Prologue and this final prayer for men apt to be mastered bracket her tale and give it its predominant tinge, so well suited to the teller, of feminine militancy in the face of male provocation. The final prayer lowers the level on which the nature of nobility is so high-mindedly discussed in the tale—but this does not mean that Chaucer does not intend the discussion to be taken seriously.

At the end of the Wife of Bath's Tale, there is added, by the editor, an example of another use than Chaucer's of one of the Wife's fifth husband's favorite stories (Prologue, ll. 763–70). It is a modern English translation of a fifteenth-century story from the *Gesta Romanorum* (Deeds of the Romans), with its moralization given in a summary form. The *Gesta Romanorum* is a collection of tales, perhaps composed in Franciscan circles, for use by preachers and others. It may be of English origin and was probably first put together about 1300.

This particular short tale is chosen as an illustration of how, given the firm intention of moralizing in a certain direction, any story can be turned into an allegory. The corollary of this is that we cannot say of any allegorical interpretation that it is impossible: someone, at some time, may have used it. Medieval allegory did not, of course, always function in such a crude and *ad hoc* fashion: it drew on a long and rich tradition of the allegorization of Scripture. But if we wish to see allegorical meanings in the *Tales,* we must carefully distinguish between the possible and the likely and bear in mind the complication of the fictional mode of the *Tales,* placed as they are in the mouths of so many different tellers.

Prologue

The Prologe of the Wyves Tale of Bathe

Experience, though noon auctoritee°
Were in this world, is right ynough for me
To speke of wo that is in mariàge;
For, lordinges,˃ sith I twelve yeer was of age, *ladies and gentlemen*
Thonkėd be God that is eterne on lyve,˃ *alive*
Housbondes at chirchėdore° I have had fyve;
(For I so oftė have ywedded be);
And alle were worthy men in hir degree.˃ *rank*
But me was told certeyn, nat longe agon˃ is, *ago*
That sith˃ that Crist ne wente nevèr but onis˃ *since / once*
To wedding, in the Cane° of Galilee,
That by the same ensample˃ taughte he me *example*
That I ne sholdė wedded be but ones.
Herkne eek,˃ lo! which˃ a sharp word for the nones° *also / what*
Besyde a welle˃ Jesus, God and man, *well*
Spak in repreve˃ of the Samaritan:° *reproof*
'Thou hast yhad fyve housbondės,' quod he,
'And thilkė˃ man, the which that hath now thee, *the same*
Is noght thyn housbond;' thus seyde he certeyn.
What that he mente therby, I can nat seyn;
But that I axe,˃ why that the fifthė man *ask*
Was noon housbond to the Samaritan?
How manye mighte she have in mariàge?
Yet herde I never tellen in myn age
Upon this nombre diffinicioùn;°
Men may devyne˃ and glosen˃ up and doun. *guess / interpret*
But wel I woot expres,˃ withoutė lye, *know expressly*
God bad us for to wexe° and multiplye;
That gentil˃ text can I wel understonde. *noble*
Eek wel I woot he seÿde, myn housbonde
Sholde lete˃ fader and moder, and take me;° *leave*
But of no nombre mencion made he,
Of bigamye or of octogamye;°

Experience . . . auctoritee The Wife begins by making her position clear. A good plain woman, she sets herself against contemporary respect for learning. She will use no book-learning, no citations of authorities, to make her case. In the event she quotes much of it, though she finally answers it by an act of violence.
chirchedore See the General Prologue, l. 460; the wedding ceremony was performed outside the church door, in public, after which nuptial mass was celebrated within the church.
Cane Cana, in Galilee, where the miracle of water into wine was performed (John 2:1ff.). The question of whether a woman could marry more than once was much discussed.
for the nones for the nonce, on the occasion, to the purpose—but a conventional formula, with little meaning
Samaritan John 4:16 ff. Jesus's retort to the Samaritan woman at the well was that she had had five husbands, but that her sixth man was not her husband. The passage was often cited in such discussions. The Wife adapts it slightly to her own case: she has had five husbands—but not yet six.
diffinicioun definition, but also carrying the sense of finite number, limit; neither five nor any other number has been laid down
wexe increase; Genesis 1:28: "Be fruitful and multiply and replenish the earth."
Sholde . . . take me Matthew 19:5
octogamye Chaucer took the word from St. Jerome. Here, bigamy and octogamy mean two and eight successive, not simultaneous, marriages.

Why sholdė men speke of it vileinye?> *evil*
  Lo, here the wysė king, dan° Salomon;
I trowe he haddė wyvės mo than oon.
As woldė God it leveful were to me
To be refresshėd half so ofte as he!°
Which yifte° of God hadde he for alle his wyvis!
No man hath swich,> that in this world alyve is. *such*
God woot, this noble king, as to my wit,> *knowledge*
The firstė night had many a mery fit> *bout*
With ech of hem, so wel was him on lyve!°
Blessed be God that I have wedded fyve
Of whiche I havė pykėd out the beste,°
Both of here nether> purs and of here cheste.> *lower / coffer*
Diversė scolės maken parfyt clerkes:> *perfect learned men*
And diverse practyk° in many sondry werkes
Maketh the werkman parfit sikerly;> *surely*
Of five husbondės scoleying> am I. *schooling*
Welcome the sixte, whan that ever he shal.°
Forsothe,> I wol nat kepe me chaste in al; *in truth*
Whan myn housbond is fro the world ygon,
Som Cristen man shal weddė me anon;
For thanne, th'Apostle° seith, that I am free
To wedde, a Goddes half, wher it lyketh> me. *it pleases*
He seith that to be wedded is no sinne;
Bet> is to be wedded than to brinne.> *better / burn*
What rekketh me,> thogh folk seye vileinye *do I care*
Of shrewėd> Lamech° and his bigamye? *cursed*
I woot> wel Abraham was an holy man, *know*
And Jacob eek, as ferforth as I can;°
And ech of hem hadde wyvės mo than two;
And many another holy man also.
  When saugh> ye ever, in any maner age, *saw*
That hyė God defended> marïage *forbade*
By expres word? I pray you, telleth me;
Or wher comanded he virginitee?
I woot as wel as ye, it is no drede,> *doubt*

dan Latin, *dominus,* master: Lord Solomon; he had 700 wives, besides 300 concubines (I Kings 11:3)
As wolde . . . he (ll. 37–38) Would to God it were permitted to me to take recreation half as often as he!
Which yifte what a gift
so wel . . . lyve such a happy life he led
beste I have picked out the best both in their balls and their bank balance; or perhaps: I have drawn out all their substance from either of these places
practyk practice, practical work
whan . . . shal whenever he shall turn up
th'Apostle St. Paul: I Corinthians 7:39 ("The wife is bound by the law as long as her husband liveth; but if her husband be dead, she is at liberty to be married to whom she will; only in the Lord"); *Bet is . . . brinne* I Corinthians 7:8–9 ("I say therefore to the unmarried and widows . . . if they cannot contain, let them marry: for it is better to marry than to burn").
Lamech Genesis 4:19–24; great-great-grandson of Cain. Lamech was a murderer and the first man to divide one flesh between two wives. The Wife is careful of the example of this villain; she prefers to invoke the example of the virtuous patriarchs Abraham and Jacob, both polygamists, but not—at least—murderers.
ferforth . . . can as far as I know

Th'Apostel,° whan he speketh of maydenhede;> *virginity*
He seyde, that precept therof hadde he noon.
Men may conseille a womman to been oon,> *single*
But conseilling is no comandėment;
He putte it in our owene jugėment.
For haddė God comanded maydenhede,
Thanne hadde he dampnėd> wedding with the dede;° *condemned*
And certės,> if ther were no seed ysowe,° *certainly*
Virginitee, wherof than sholde it growe?
Paul dorstė nat comanden attė> leste *at the*
A thing of which his maister yaf> noon heste.> *gave / command*
The dart° is set up for virginitee;
Cacche who so may, who renneth> best lat see. *runs*
But this word is nat take of° every wight,
But ther> as God list> give it of his might. *where / it pleases*
I woot wel, that th'Apostel was a mayde;> *virgin*
But natheless, thogh that he wroot and sayde,°
He wolde> that every wight were swich> as he,° *wished / such*
Al nis but conseil to virginitee;
And for to been a wyf, he yaf me leve
Of indulgence;° so it is no repreve> *reproof*
To weddė me,° if that my makė> dye— *mate*
Withoute excepcioùn of bigamye°—
Al were it good no womman for to touche°
(He mente as in his bed or in his couche,
For peril is bothe fyr> and tow> t'assemble— *fire / flax*
Ye knowe what this ensample may resemble°).
This is al and som,° he heeld virginitee
More parfit than wedding in frelėtee.°
Freletee clepe> I, but if> that he and she *call (it) / unless*
Wolde leden al hir lyf in chastitee.
I graunte it wel, I havė noon envye,
Thogh maydenhedė prėferre bigamye;> *surpass remarriage*
Hem lyketh> to be clene in body and goost,> *pleases / spirit*
Of myn estaat> I nil nat make no boost. *condition*

th'Apostel St. Paul: I Corinthians 7:25 ("Now concerning virgins, I have no commandment of the Lord"). The recommendation of virginity and the institution of monasticism rest on the tradition of the church, not on Scripture—but the church holds that its tradition is of equal authority.
with . . . dede when he did (the other); at the same time
if ther . . . ysowe if no seed were sown; the argument is used by St. Jerome
dart spear, apparently as a prize in a race, perhaps "set up" for the winner to take (*cacche*) at the finish line. Chaucer is translating St. Jerome, and perhaps making a sexual pun.
take of received, understood by
wroot and sayde wrotė and said. This sort of meaningless doublet, perhaps the survival of an oral formula, is a favorite with Chaucer's successors.
He . . . he I Corinthians 7:7 ("For I would that all men were even as myself [i.e. chaste]")
indulgence I Corinthians 7:6 ("I speak this by [your] permission [indulgence], not of commandment")
wedde me marry me. The verb is still reflexive; I Corinthians 7:39 again.
Withoute . . . bigamye so that no exception can be taken to my second marriage
touche I Corinthians 7:1
Ye . . . resemble you know what this figure means
al and som the sum total of it
in freletee for the frailty of our humanity

For wel ye knowe, a lord in his houshold,
He hath nat every vessel al of gold;
Somme been of tree,> and doon hir lord servyse. *wood*
God clepeth> folk to him in sondry wyse, *calls*
And everich hath of God a propre yifte,°
Som> this, som that—as him lyketh shifte.> *one / command*
Virginitee is greet perfecciòun,
And continence eek with devociòun.
But Crist, that of perfecciòun is welle,> *fountain-head*
Bad nat every wight he sholde go selle
All that he hadde, and give it to the pore,
And in swich wyse folwe him and his fore.°
He spak to hem that wolde live parfitly;> *perfectly*
And lordinges, by your leve, that am nat I.
I wol bistowe the flour of al myn age
In the actės and in fruit of marïage.
Telle me also, to what conclusioùn> *end*
Were membres maad> of generacioùn, *made*
And of so parfit wis a wright ywroght?°
Trusteth right wel, they wer nat maad for noght.
Glose> whoso wole, and seye bothe up and doun, *comment*
That they were makėd for purgacioùn> *purging*
Of urine, and our bothė thingės smale> *narrow*
Were eek to knowe a femele from a male,
And for noon other causė: sey ye no?
The experience woot wel it is noght so.
So that the clerkės be nat with me wrothe,
I sey this, that they makėd been for bothe,
This is to seye, for office,° and for ese
Of engendrure, ther> we nat God displese. *procreation where*
Why sholde men ellės in hir bokės sette,
That man shal yeldė> to his wyf hir dette? *pay*
Now wherwith sholde he make his payėment,
If he ne used his sely° instrument?
Than were they maad, upon> a creätùre, *in*
To purge uryne, and eek for engendrùre.
But I seye noght that every wight is holde,> *bound*
That hath swich harneys> as I to yow tolde, *tackle*
To goon and usen hem in engendrùre;
Than sholde men take of chastitee no cure.> *care*
Crist was a mayde,> and shapen as a man, *virgin*
And many a saint, sith that the world bigan:
Yet lived they ever in parfit chastitee.

propre yifte a gift of his own; his individual bent: I Corinthians 7:7
fore track, footsteps. Matthew 19:21 is the source for ll. 114–16.
And of . . . ywroght One reading would give here: And for what purpose was a creature made. The sense of the reading adopted—and so perfectly wise a Maker made—translates St. Jerome.
office might mean urinating, but more frequently means excretion; the sense here is more general: for natural functions
sely little, innocent

I nil envyė no virginitee;
Lat hem be breed> of purėd> whetė seed, *bread / refined*
And lat us wyvės hoten> barly breed; *be called*
And yet with barly breed, Mark° tellė can,
Our Lord Jesu refresshėd many a man.
In swich estaat as God hath clepėd° us
I wol persèvere, I nam nat precious.> *choosy*
In wyfhode> I wol use myn instrument *wifehood*
As frely> as my Maker hath it sent. *liberally*
If I be daungerous,° God yeve> me sorwe! *give*
Myn housbond shal it have bothe eve and morwe,> *morning*
Whan that him list> com forth and paye his dette. *it pleases him*
An housbonde I wol have, I nil nat° lette,
Which shal be bothe my dettour> and my thral,> *debtor / slave*
And have his tribulatioùn withal°
Upon his flessh, whyl that I am his wyf.
I have the power duringe al my lyf
Upon his propre> body, and noght he.° *own*
Right thus the Apostel tolde° it unto me;
And bad our housbondes for to love us weel.
Al this sentence> me lyketh every deel.> *matter / every part*
Up sterte> the Pardoner, and that anon,> *started / at once*
'Now dame,' quod> he, 'by God and by Saint John, *said*
Ye been a noble prechour in this cas!
I was aboute to wedde a wyf; allas!
What> sholde I bye it on my flesh so dere? *why*
Yet hadde I lever> wedde no wyf to-yere!'° *rather*
'Abyde!' quod she, 'my tale is nat bigonne;
Nay, thou shalt drinken of another tonne> *barrel*
Er that I go, shal savoure> wors than ale. *taste*
And whan that I have told thee forth my tale
Of tribulacioùn in marïage,
Of which I am expert in al myn age,
This to seyn, myself have been the whippe;
Than maystow chese> whether thou wolt sippe *choose*
Of thilkė tonne> that I shal abroche.> *barrel / broach*
Bewar of it, er thou too ny> approache; *near*
For I shal telle ensamples mo than ten.
Whoso that nil> be war by otherė men, *will not*
By him shul otherė men corrected be.
The samė wordės wryteth Ptholomee;°

Mark miracle of the loaves and fishes, when about 5000 were fed with five loaves. Mark (8:5) does not say that they were barley-loaves; John (6:9) does.
cleped called; see I Corinthians 7:20
daungerous careful, difficult of access
nil nat will not; double negative, intensifying
withal moreover; see I Corinthians 7:28
I have . . . he I Corinthians 7:4
tolde Ephesians 5:25
to-yere literally, this year, but meaning next year, sometime, never
Ptholomee Claudius Ptolemy, the most influential ancient astronomer, an Alexandrian Greek of the 2nd century A.D. whose chief work is the *Almagest*. This proverb does not appear in it, but is included in a collection of sayings attributed to him in the Middle Ages.

Rede in his *Almageste,* and take it there.'
'Dame, I wolde praye yow, if your wil it were,'
Seyde this Pardoner, 'as ye bigan,
Telle forth your talė, spareth for no man,
And teche us yongė men of your praktike.'> *practice*
'Gladly,' quod she, 'sith it may yow lyke.> *please*
But yet I praye to al this companye,
If that I speke after my fantasye,°
As taketh not agrief> of that I seye; *offense*
For myn ententė nis but for to pleye.> *divert*
Now sires, now wol I tellė forth my tale.
As ever mote I drinken wyn or ale,
I shal seye sooth, tho> housbondes that I hadde, *those*
As three of hem were gode> and two were badde. *good*
The threė men were gode, and riche, and olde;
Unnethė> mightė they the statut> holde *scarcely / covenant*
In which that they were bounden unto me.
Ye woot> wel what I mene of this, pardee! *know*
As help me God, I laughė whan I thinke
How pitously anight I made hem swinke;> *toil*
And by my fey,> I tolde of it no stoor.° *faith*
They had me yeven hir> gold and hir tresoor; *given their*
Me neded nat do lenger> diligence *longer*
To winne hir love, or doon hem reverence.
They lovėd me so wel by God above,
That I ne tolde no dayntee of hir love!°
A wys womman wol sette hir ever in oon:°
To gete hir lovė, theras> she hath noon. *where*
But sith I hadde hem hoolly> in myn hond, *completely*
And sith they hadde me yeven> all hir lond, *given*
What> sholde I taken heed hem for to plese, *why*
But it were for my profit and myn ese?
I sette hem so a-werkė,> by my fey, *to work*
That many a night they songen> weilawey!> *sang / alas*
The bacoun was nat fet> for hem, I trowe, *fetched*
That som men han in Essex at Dunmowe.°
I governed hem so wel, after> my lawe, *according to*
That ech of hem ful blisful> was and fawe> *happy / glad*
To bringė me gaye thingės fro the fayre.
They were ful glad whan I spak to hem fayre;
For God it woot, I chidde> hem spitously.> *chided / unmercifully*
Now herkneth, how I bar me° proprely,

fantasye strictly, a specific faculty of the mind, imagination; thus, "as I feel like"
I . . . stoor I did not take much account of it; or perhaps: I gained no money by it (since I'd already got it from them)
That I . . . love i.e. I needed to take no special pains to get their love
A wys . . . in oon a sensible woman will set herself one object
Dunmowe At this town and elsewhere a flitch or side of bacon was offered to any couple who could prove they had not quarreled or regretted their marriage during the year just past.
bar me behaved myself

Ye wysė wyvės, that can understonde.
Thus shulde ye speke and bere hem wrong on honde;°
For half so boldėly can ther no man
Swere and lyen> as a womman can. *lie*
I sey nat this by> wyves that ben wyse,> *about / careful*
But if> it be whan they hem misavyse.> *unless / go wrong*
A wys wyf, if that she can hir good,°
Shal beren him on hond the cow is wood,°
And takė witnesse of hir owene mayde
Of hir assent;° but herkneth how I sayde.
"Sir olde kaynard,> is this thyn array?> *dotard*
Why is my neighėborės wyf so gay?
She is honoùred over al ther> she goth;> *wherever / goes*
I sitte at hoom, I have no thrifty cloth.> *good clothes*
What dostow> at my neighėborės hous? *do you*
Is she so fair? artow so amorous?
What rowne> ye with our mayde? Benedicitė!° *whisper*
Sir oldė lechour, lat thy japes> be! *tricks*
And if I have a gossib> or a freend, *confidant*
Withouten gilt, thou chydest as a feend,> *fiend*
If that I walke or pleye unto his hous!
Thou comest hoom as dronken as a mous,
And prechest on thy bench, with yvel preef!°
Thou seist to me, it is a greet meschief> *misfortune*
To wedde a poorė womman, for costage;> *because of expense*
And if that she be riche, of heigh parage,> *descent*
Than seistow> that it is a tormentrye *you say*
To suffre hir pryde and hir malėncolye.°
And if that she be fair, thou verray knave,
Thou seyst that every holour> wol hir have; *adulterer*
She may no whyle in chastitee abyde,
That is assaillėd upon ech a side.
Thou seyst, som folk desyre us for richesse,
Somme for our shap, and somme for our fairnesse;
And som, for she can outher> singe or daunce, *either*
And som, for gentillesse> and daliaunce;> *kindness / favor*
Som, for hir handės and hir armės smale;> *slender*
Thus goth al to the devel by> thy tale. *according to*
Thou seyst, men may nat kepe> a castel wal; *hold*
It may so longe assailled been overal.> *everywhere*
And if that she be foul, thou seïst that she

bere . . . on honde pretend that they have insulted you
wys . . . good clever wife, if she knows what's good for her
Shal . . . wood Shall make him believe the chough is mad. Cf. Chaucer's Manciple's Tale: an anti-feminist *exemplum*. The chough or jackdaw, a talking bird, tells a husband that his wife has been unfaithful. She has been, but she persuades him that the bird is crazy and he wrings its neck.
And take . . . assent and she will call her own maid, who sides with her, to witness
array way of going on
Benedicite bless me
yvel preef bad luck to you
malencolye melancholy, excess of black bile; thus, indifference

Coveiteth> every man that she may se; *longs for*
For as a spaynel> she wol on him lepe, *spaniel*
Til that she findė som man hir to chepe;> *buy*
Ne noon so grey goos goth ther in the lake,
As, seïstow, that wol been withoute make.> *mate*
And seÿst, it is an hard thing for to welde> *control*
A thing that no man wol, his thankės,> helde.> *willingly / hold*
Thus seïstow, lorel,> whan thow goost to bedde; *wretch*
And that no wys> man nedeth for to wedde, *prudent*
Ne no man that entendeth> unto hevene. *hopes for*
With wildė thonder-dint> and firy levene> *thunderbolt / lightning*
Mote thy welkėd nekkė be to-broke! °
  Thow seÿst that dropping> houses, and eek smoke, *leaking*
And chyding wyves, maken men to flee
Out of hir owene hous; a! Benedicitė!
What eyleth> swich an old man for to chyde? *ails*
  Thow seyst, we wyvės wol our vyces hyde
Til we be fast,° and than we wol hem shewe;
Wel may that be a proverbe of a shrewe!> *scoundrel*
  Thou seïst, that oxen, asses, hors,° and houndes,
They been assayėd at diversė stoundes;> *times*
Bacins, lavours,> er that men hem bye, *washbasins*
Sponės and stoles,> and al swich housbondrye,> *stools / household goods*
And so been> pottės, clothės, and array;> *are / ornaments*
But folk of wyvės maken noon assay
Til they be wedded; oldė dotard shrewe!
And than, seïstow, we wol oure vices shewe.
  Thou seïst also, that it displeseth me
But if that thou wolt preysė my beautee.
And but thou poure alwey> upon my face, *gaze*
And clepė> me 'Faire dame' in every place; *call*
And but thou make a feste> on thilkė> day *feast / the same*
That I was born, and make me fresh and gay,
And but thou do to my norìce> honoùr, *nurse*
And to my chamberere> withinne my bour,> *chambermaid / room*
And to my fadres> folk and his allyes;> *father's / relatives*
Thus seïstow, olde barel ful of lyes!
  And yet of our apprentice Janekyn,
For his crisp heer,> shyninge as gold so fyn, *curly hair*
And for he squiereth me bothe up and doun,
Yet hastow caught a fals suspecioun;
I wol> hym noght, thogh thou were deed> tomorwe. *want / dead*

Mote . . . to-broke may your withered neck be broken; to- intensifies
fast firmly tied, married
hors Horses. The complaint that one can have a good look at a horse one is buying, but not at a prospective wife, goes back as far as the Roman poet Horace (65–8 B.C.). Sir Thomas More's solution may be found in *Utopia*, Bk. ii. Chaucer here, as he has done earlier, and as he goes on doing, is borrowing from Theophrastus, *The Golden Book of Marriage*, quoted by St. Jerome, perhaps, through a French reworking —in this case Eustache Deschamps' *Mirror of Marriage*.

But tel me this, why hydėstow, with sorwe,°
The keyės of thy cheste awey fro me?
It is my good˃ as wel as thyn, pardee. *property*
What wenestow˃ make an idiot of our dame? *think you to*
Now by that lord, that called is Saint Jame,°
Thou shalt not bothė, thogh that thou were wood,˃ *angry*
Be maister of my body and of my good;
That oon thou shalt forgo, maugree thyne yën;°
What nedeth thee of me to enquere˃ or spyën? *enquire*
I trowė, thou woldst loke˃ me in thy chiste!˃ *lock / money-chest*
Thou sholdest seye, 'Wyf, go wher thee liste,˃ *it pleases*
Tak your disport, I wol nat leve˃ no talis; *believe*
I knowe yow for a trewė wyf, dame Alis.'
We love no man that taketh keep˃ or charge˃ *heed / notice*
Wher that we goon, we wol˃ ben at our large.˃ *want / liberty*
Of allė men yblessed moot he be,
The wyse astrologien° Dan Ptholome,
That seith this proverbe in his *Almageste*,
'Of allė men his wisdom is the hyeste,
That rekketh˃ never who hath the world in honde.' *cares*
By this proverbė thou shalt understonde,
Have thou ynogh,° what thar˃ thee recche˃ or care *need / trouble*
How merily˃ that othere folkės fare? *happily*
For certeyn, oldė dotard, by your leve,
Ye shul have queyntė° right ynough˃ at eve. *plenty*
He is to greet a nigard that wol werne˃ *refuse*
A man to lighte his candle at his lanterne;
He shal have never the lassė˃ light, pardee; *less*
Have thou ynough, thee thar nat pleynė thee.
Thou seÿst also, that if we make us gay
With clothing and with precïous array,
That it is peril of our chastitee;
And yet, with sorwe, thou most enforcė˃ thee, *reinforce*
And seye thise wordės in the Apostle's name,
'In habit,˃ maad with chastitee and shame, *clothes*
Ye wommen shul˃ apparaille yow,' quod he,° *must*
'And noght in tressėd heer and gay perree,
As perlės, ne with gold, ne clothės riche;'
After thy text, ne after thy rubriche°

with sorwe literally, with sorrow; thus, damn it
Jame St. James (the Great), patron saint of Spain; see the General Prologue, l. 468. The Wife had made the pilgrimage to Santiago de Compostela.
maugree . . . yën despite (Fr. malgré) your eyes; i.e. damn your eyes
astrologien The line between astrologers and astronomers is hard to draw in the Middle Ages, but Ptolemy was by all counts an astronomer. For his aphorism, see l. 188n above; its sense is: he is the wisest of men who does not care if others have much wealth.
Have . . . ynogh if you have enough
queynte pudendum. It would not be in the Wife's nature to use a polite expression, but the form she uses may be a kind of genteelism, a variant spelling of *cuinte;* see her use of *quoniam, bele chose, chambre of Venus* below.
he I Timothy 2:9 ("modest apparel, with shamefastness and sobriety; not with braided hair or gold or pearls, or costly array"); "perree" (Fr. *pierrerie*) is jewelry
rubriche the opening words or headings in a manuscript, written in red to give the reader an orientation; thus, direction

I wol nat wirche as muchel> as a gnat.° *much*
Thou seydest this, that I was lyk a cat;°
For whoso woldė senge> a cattės skin, *singe*
Thanne wolde the cat wel dwellen in his in;> *house*
And if the cattės skin be slyk and gay,
She wol nat dwelle in housė half a day,
But forth she wole, er> any day be dawed,> *before / dawned*
To shewe hir skin, and goon a-caterwawed;> *caterwauling*
This is to seye, if I be gay, sir shrewe,
I wol renne> out, my borel> for to shewe. *run / clothes*
  Sire oldė fool, what eyleth> thee to spyën? *ails*
Thogh thou preye Argus,° with his hundred yën,
To be my wardė-cors,> as he can> best, *bodyguard / knows how*
In feith, he shal nat kepe me but me lest;> *unless it pleases me*
Yet coude I make his berd,° so moot I thee.> *thrive*
  Thou seydest eek, that ther ben thingės three,
The whichė thingės troublen al this erthe,
And that no wight ne may endure the ferthe;> *fourth*
O leve> sir shrewė, Jesu shorte> thy lyf! *dear / shorten*
Yet prechestow, and seyst, an hateful wyf
Yrekenėd> is for oon of thise meschances.> *reckoned / misfortunes*
Been ther none othere maner resemblances
That ye may lyknė your paràbles to,°
But if a sely wyf be oon> of tho>? *one / them*
  Thou lykenest eek wommanes love to helle,
To bareyne> land, ther> water may not dwelle. *barren / where*
Thou lyknest it also to wildė fyr;°
The more it brenneth,> the more it hath desyr *burns*
To consume every thing that brent> wol be. *burned*
Thou seyst, that right> as wormės° shende> a tree, *just / destroy*
Right so a wyf destroyeth hir housbonde;
This knowė they that been to wyvės bonde."> *bound*
  Lordinges, right thus, as ye have understonde,
Bar I stifly myne olde housbondes on honde,°
That thus they seyden in hir dronkenesse;
And al was fals, but that I took witnesse
On Janekin and on my nece also.
O Lord, the peyne I dide hem and the wo,
Ful giltėlees,> by Goddės swetė pyne!> *innocent / sufferings*
For as an hors I coudė byte and whyne.°

I . . . gnat i.e. I don't care a fly for them
cat a singed cat dwells at home (a proverb)
Argus Argus, unsleeping because of his hundred eyes, was set by Juno to watch Io, whom Jupiter was currently involved with; but Mercury charmed him asleep and killed him. Do what you like in the way of watching, says the Wife, it will do you no good.
make his berd outwit him
Been . . . to i.e. are there no other similarities you can apply your moral tales to rather than to a poor, innocent woman?
wilde fyr Wild fire was a naphtha preparation that was especially fierce and difficult to put out.
wormes grubs, crawling creatures of all kinds
Bar . . . honde I pressed my pretense on my old husbands
byte and whyne bite when in a bad temper and whinny when in a good

I coudė pleyne,> thogh I were in the gilt,> *complain / wrong*
Or ellės oftentyme hadde I ben spilt.> *ruined*
Whoso that first to millė comth, first grint;> *grinds*
I pleynėd first, so was our werre ystint.> *ceased*
They were ful glad to excusen hem ful blyve> *quickly*
Of thing of which they never agilte hir lyve.°
Of wenches wolde I beren him on honde,
Whan that for syk unnethės> mighte he stonde. *sickness scarcely*
Yet tikled it his hertė, for that he
Wende> that I hadde of him so greet chiertee.> *thought / love*
I swoor that al my walkinge out by nighte
Was for to espyė wenches that he dighte;> *laid*
Under that colour> hadde I many a mirthe. *pretense*
For al swich wit is yeven> us in our birthe; *given*
Deceitė, weping, spinning God hath yive
To wommen kindėly,> whyl> they may live. *by nature / as long as*
And thus of o thing I avauntė me,> *boast*
Atte ende I hadde the bettre in ech degree,
By sleighte,> or force, or by som maner thing, *cleverness*
As by continuel murmur> or grucching;> *complaint / grumbling*
Namely> abeddė hadden they meschaunce, *especially*
Ther wolde I chyde and do hem no plesaunce;> *pleasure*
I wolde no lenger in the bed abyde,
If that I felte his arm over my syde,
Til he had maad his raunson> unto me; *payment*
Than wolde I suffre him do his nycetee.> *folly*
And therfore every man this tale I telle,
Winne whoso> may, for al is for to selle. *whoever*
With empty hand men may none hawkės lure;
For winning> wolde I al his lust endure, *profit*
And make me a feynėd appetyt;
And yet in bacon° hadde I never delyt;
That made me that ever I wolde hem chyde.
For thogh the Pope had seten> hem biside, *sat*
I wolde nat spare hem at hir owene bord.> *table*
For by my trouthe, I quitte> hem word for word. *requited*
As help me verray God omnipotent,
Thogh I right now sholde make my testament,
I ne owe hem nat a word that it nis quit.
I broghte it so aboutė by my wit,
That they moste yeve it up, as for the beste;°
Or ellės hadde we never been in reste.
For thogh he lokėd as a wood leoùn,> *raging lion*
Yet sholde he faille of his conclusioùn.> *purpose*

Of thing . . . lyve of something of which they were never guilty in their lives
bacon old, dried, tough, pig's meat; cf. Lechery in *Dr. Faustus*, scene VI, ll. 151–52: "I am she who likes an inch of raw mutton better than an ell of dried stockfish."
as . . . beste and make the best of it

Thanne wolde I seyė, "Godė lief,> tak keep> *dear one / note*
How mekely loketh Wilkin ourė sheep;°
Com neer, my spouse, lat me ba> thy cheke! *kiss*
Ye sholdė been al pacïent and meke,
And han a swetė spycėd> conscience, *delicate*
Sith ye so preche of Jobės pacience.
Suffreth alwey, sin ye so wel can preche;
And but> ye do, certein we shal yow teche *unless*
That it is fair> to have a wyf in pees. *good*
Oon of us two moste bowen, doutėless;
And sith a man is more resonable°
Than womman is, ye moste been suffrable.> *long-suffering*
What ayleth yow to grucchė> thus and grone? *grumble*
Is it for ye wolde have my queynte allone?
Why taak it al, lo, have it everydeel;> *all*
Peter!° I shrewe> yow but> ye love it weel! *curse / unless*
For if I woldė selle my belė chose,> *fair thing*
I coudė walke as fresh> as is a rose; *sweet*
But I wol kepe it for your owene tooth.> *enjoyment*
Ye be to blame, by God, I sey yow sooth."
Swiche maner wordės haddė we on honde.°
Now wol I speken of my fourthe housbonde.
My fourthė housbonde was a revelour,
This is to seyn, he hadde a paramour;> *mistress*
And I was yong and ful of ragerye,> *passion*
Stiborn> and strong, and joly as a pye.> *vigorous / magpie*
Wel coude I dauncė to an harpe smale,°
And singe, ywis,> as any nightingale, *indeed*
Whan I had dronke a draughte of swetė wyn.
Metellius,° the foulė cherl, the swyn,
That with a staf birafte> his wyf hir lyf, *bereft*
For> she drank wyn, thogh> I hadde been his wyf, *because / if*
He sholdė nat han daunted me fro drinke;
And, after wyn, on Venus moste> I thinke: *most*
For al so siker> as cold engendreth hayl, *sure*
A likerous mouth moste han a likerous tayl.°
In womman vinolent° is no defence:
This knowen lechours by experience.
But, Lord Crist! whan that it remembreth° me

How . . . sheep i.e. you, old lamb, how patient you look
And . . . resonable Men were held to be more rational, more capable of intellectual operations, than women.
Peter by St. Peter
Swiche . . . honde this was the kind of words we dealt in
smale perhaps, gracefully; or an adjective going with "harp," in reference to its thin, elegant, graceful sound
Metellius For this anti-husband story, the Wife reaches into another bin of *exempla* much used in the Middle Ages—the handbook, by Valerius Maximus (1st century A.D.), of Greek and Roman history.
A likerous . . . tayl A gluttonous mouth means a lecherous tail. Gluttony and lechery go together in the moral treatises of the time, and sin in Eden is often shown as a combination of the two in 14th-century art.
vinolent full of wine
whan . . . me impersonal construction: when I look back and recollect it all

Upon my youthe, and on my jolitee,
It tikleth me aboute myn hertė rote.>   *heart's root*
Unto this day it dooth myn hertė bote>   *good*
That I have had my world as in my tyme.
But age, allas! that al wol envenyme,>   *poison*
Hath me biraft> my beautee and my pith;>   *deprived / strength*
Lat go, farewel, the Devil go therwith!
The flour is goon, ther is namore to telle,
The bren,> as I best can,° now moste I selle;   *bran*
But yet to be right mery wol I fonde.>   *try*
Now wol I tellen of my fourthe housbonde.
  I seye, I hadde in hertė greet despyt>   *contempt*
That he of any other had delyt.
But he was quit,> by God and by Saint Joce!°   *repaid*
I made him of the samė wode a croce;°
Nat of my body in no foul manere,
But certeinly, I madė folk swich chere,
That in his owene grece> I made him frye   *fat*
For angre, and for verray jalousye.
By God, in erthe I was his purgatorie,°
For which I hope his soulė be in glorie.
For God it woot, he sat ful ofte and song>   *sang*
Whan that his shoo ful bitterly him wrong.°
Ther was no wight, save God and he, that wiste,>   *knew*
In many wysė, how sorė I him twiste.>   *wrung*
He deyde> whan I cam fro Jerusalem,   *died*
And lyth ygrave> under the rode-beem,°   *buried*
Al> is his tombė noght so curious>   *although / splendid*
As was the sepulcre of him, Darius,°
Which that Appellės wroghtė subtilly;>   *skillfully*
It nis but waste to burie him preciously.>   *expensively*
Lat him fare wel,> God yevė> his soule reste,   *go in peace / give*
He is now in the grave and in his cheste.>   *coffin*
  Now of my fifthė housbond wol I telle.
God lete his soulė never come in helle!
And yet was he to me the mostė shrewe;>   *vicious*
That fele I on my ribbės al by rewe,°
And ever shal, unto myn ending day.

can as best I can—but still with a hint of the old meaning of "can": I know best how it is done
Joce a Breton saint; Chaucer found a knight with the same name in the French of Jean de Meun (d. 1305)
I . . . croce I made him a staff (crutch, not cross) of the same wood [to beat him with]; cf. l. 493: I made him fry in his own fat
I . . . purgatorie Matrimony as purgatory on earth was a frequent concept in medieval literature; the consolation for its pains was that, unlike heaven and hell, it did not retain people forever.
Whan . . . wrong when his shoe pinched him most painfully; the figure, in relation to marriage, goes back to St. Jerome, at least
rode-beem a beam across a church at the chancel-area, separating nave from choir, with the crucifix (rood) mounted on its middle
Darius king of the Persians (d. 330 B.C.), defeated by Alexander the Great, whose court painter was Apelles. Medieval versions of the story of Alexander make him magnanimously order from Apelles splendid tombs of marble, gold, and silver for Darius and his queen.
by rewe in a row, each one

But in our bed he was so fresh> and gay, *lively*
And therwithal so wel coude he me glose,> *flatter*
Whan that he wolde han> my belė chose, *have*
That thogh he hadde me bet> on every boon,> *beaten / bone*
He coudė winnen agayn my love anoon.> *at once*
I trowe I loved him bestė, for that he
Was of his lovė daungerous> to me. *sparing*
We wommen han, if that I shal nat lye,
In this matere a queyntė fantasye;> *fancy*
Wayte what° thing we may nat lightly have,
Therafter wol we crye al day and crave.
Forbede us thing, and that desyren we;
Prees> on us faste,> and thannė wol we flee. *press / hard*
With daunger° outė> we al our chaffàre;> *display / wares*
Greet prees> at market maketh derė ware,> *crowd / goods*
And too greet cheep> is holde at litel prys;> *bargain / value*
This knoweth every womman that is wys.
  My fifthė housbonde, God his soule blesse!
Which that I took for love and no richesse,
He somtyme> was a clerk° of Oxenford, *formerly*
And had left scole, and wente at hoom to bord> *as boarder*
With my gossib,° dwellinge in oure toun,
God have hir soule! hir name was Alisoun.
She knew myn herte and eek my privetee> *secrets*
Bet> than our parisshe preest, so moot I thee!> *better / thrive*
To hir biwreyėd> I my conseil> al. *disclosed / secrets*
For had myn housbonde pissėd on a wall,
Or doon a thing that sholde han cost his lyf,
To hir, and to another worthy wyf,
And to my nece,° which that I lovėd weel,
I wolde han told his conseil every deel.> *part*
And so I dide ful often, God it woot,> *knows*
That made his face ful often reed> and hoot> *red / hot*
For verray shame, and blamed himself for he
Had told to me so greet a privetee.
  And so bifel that onės, in a Lente,> *Lent*
(So often tymes I to my gossib wente,
For ever yet I lovede to be gay,
And for to walke, in March, Averille, and May,
Fro hous to hous, to herė sondry talės),
That Jankin clerk, and my gossib Dame Alis,
And I myself, into the feldės wente.
Myn housbond was at London al that Lente;
I hadde the bettre leyser> for to pleye,° *opportunity*

Wayte what whatever
daunger care, parsimony; caution
clerk See the General Prologue, l. 287.
gossib literally, God-relation: God-child, God-parent: thus, anyone to whom one is especially close
nece niece or cousin
pleye She should have passed Lent in religious observances.

And for to see, and eek for to be seye> — *seen*
Of lusty> folk; what wiste I wher my grace — *lively*
Was shapen for to be, or in what place?°
Therefore I made my visitacioùns,
To vigilies° and to processioùns,
To preching eek and to thise pilgrimàges,
To pleyes of miracles° and mariàges,
And wered upon my gayė scarlet gytes.°
Thise wormės, ne thise mothės, ne thise mites,
Upon my peril,° frete> hem never a deel;> — *ate / part*
And wostow> why? for they were used weel.> — *know you / much*
Now wol I tellen forth what happėd me.
I seye, that in the feeldės walked we,
Til trewėly we hadde swich daliànce,> — *pleasure*
This clerk and I, that of my purveyànce°
I spak to him, and seyde him, how that he,
If I were widwe, sholdė weddė me.
For certeinly, I sey for no bobance,> — *without boasting*
Yet was I never withouten purveyànce> — *prospect*
Of mariage, nof> otherė thingės eek. — *nor of*
I holde a mouses herte> nat worth a leek,° — *life*
That hath but oon hol for to stertė> to, — *escape*
And if that faillė, thanne is al ydo.°
I bar him on honde,> he hadde enchanted> me; — *pretended / bewitched*
My damė> taughtė me that soutiltee.> — *mother / trick*
And eek I seyde, I mette> of him al night; — *dreamed*
He wolde han slayn me as I lay up-right,> — *on my back*
And al my bed was ful of verray> blood, — *real*
But yet I hope that he shal do me good;
For blood bitokeneth gold,° as me was taught.
And al was fals, I dremed of it right naught,> — *nothing*
But as I folwėd ay> my damės lore,> — *always / teaching*
As wel of this as of other thingės more.
But now sir, lat me see, what I shal seyn?
Aha! by God, I have my tale ageyn.
Whan that my fourthė housbond was on bere,> — *bier*
I weep algate,> and madė sory chere,> — *anyway / behavior*
As wyvės moten,> for it is usàge,> — *must / custom*
And with my coverchief covered my visàge;

what . . . place I didn't know where my good luck was ordained to be; or: how could I know where my favor was destined to be bestowed
vigilies feasts or festivals on the eves of saints' days
miracles plays based on the historical books of the Bible and on legends of the saints
And . . . gytes and wore upon [me] my bright scarlet gowns
peril an oath: upon peril of my soul; damn me!
purveyance providing for my future (so that I wouldn't ever be without a husband—but you can't sleep with me until I'm a widow and we can be married)
leek The accumulation of little worthless things is meant to emphasize her own provident vigor, with a probable pun on *hole*. The mouse with only one place to go was proverbial.
thanne . . . al ydo then it is all up
blood . . . gold This was regular doctrine in the medieval books on the interpretation of dreams: one red thing (blood) betokens another (red gold); cf. the Nun's Priest's Tale.

But for that I was purveyed of˃ a make,˃ *provided with / mate*
I weep˃ but smal, and that I undertake. *wept*
To chirchė was myn housbond born amorwe˃ *carried in the morning*
With˃ neighėbores, that for him maden sorwe; *by*
And Jankin, ourė clerk, was oon of tho.
As help me God, whan that I saugh˃ him go *saw*
After the bere, me thoughte he hadde a paire
Of leggės and of feet so clene˃ and faire,˃ *neat / handsome*
That al myn herte I yaf unto˃ his hold.˃ *into / keeping*
He was, I trowe, a twenty winter old,
And I was fourty, if I shal seye sooth;
But yet I hadde alwey a coltės tooth.°
Gat-tothed° I was, and that bicam˃ me weel; *suited*
I hadde the prente˃ of Seÿnt Venus' seel.˃ *imprint / seal*
As help me God, I was a lusty˃ oon, *good-looking*
And faire and riche, and yong, and wel bigoon;˃ *fortunate*
And trewėly, as myne housbondes tolde me,
I had the bestė quoniam° mighte be.
For certės, I am al Venerien
In felinge,˃ and myn herte is Marcien.° *feelings*
Venus me yaf my lust, my likerousnesse,˃ *lecherousness*
And Mars yaf me my sturdy hardinesse.˃ *boldness*
Myn ascendent was Taur,° and Mars therinne.
Allas! allas! that ever love was sinne!
I folwed ay myn inclinacioùn˃ *bent*
By vertu of my constellacioùn;
That madė me I coudė noght withdrawe
My chambre of Venus from a good felawe.
Yet have I Martės mark upon my face,°
And also in another privee˃ place. *secret*
For, God so wis˃ be my savacioùn,˃ *surely / salvation*
I ne loved never by no discrecioùn,
But ever folwedė myn appetyt;
Al were he short or long, or blak or whyt,
I took no kepe,˃ so that he lyked˃ me, *heed / pleased*

coltes tooth a young appetite
Gat-tothed See the General Prologue, l. 470.
quoniam Latin: whereas, whatever; another of the Wife's coy words for pudendum
Venerien . . . Marcien influenced by the planets Venus and Mars; thus, lustful and bold
Taur The Wife's ascendant (the sign of the zodiac just rising in the east at her birth) was Taurus, the Bull: therefore, she would be industrious, energetic, prudent, a money-maker, one who usually comes out on top; florid, bold-eyed, wide-mouthed, short-legged, big-buttocked; gossipy, given to love affairs. Venus in her mansion of Taurus makes people cheerful, with good figures, attractive, lovable, passionate and voluptuous, lovers of fine clothes: there is, essentially, no evil in them. Mars, masculine, baleful, and angry, in conjunction (*constellacioùn*) with Venus in Taurus counteracts these good influences and has made the Wife into the holy terror that she is. She cannot keep her chamber of Venus from a good man. Between them, then, Taurus and Mars take away or change for the worse her most agreeable characteristics.
Yet . . . face Every person was thought to have placed on him, at conception or birth, a (birth) mark representing the ascendant sign and dominant star of the moment, by which his fortunes were ruled. They would appear on that part of the body ruled by a particular sign or planet. The Wife's sign, as she was born in Taurus, should be on the neck; she has also the "print of Saint Venus's seal," l. 610, a red mark, probably, on the thigh; and Mars's mark, a scar on the face and on the thigh or groin ("another privee place").

How pore> he was, ne eek of what degree. *poor*
What sholde I seye, but, at the monthės ende,
This joly> clerk Jankin, that was so hende,> *handsome / pleasant*
Hath weddėd me with greet solempnitee,> *ceremony*
And to him yaf I al the lond> and fee> *property / money*
That ever was me yeven therbifore;
But afterward repented me ful sore.
He noldė suffre> nothing of my list.> *allow / pleasure*
By God, he smoot me onės> on the list,° *once*
For that I rente> out of his book a leef, *tore*
That of the strook myn erė wex> al deef.> *became / deaf*
Stiborn> I was as is a leonesse, *fierce*
And of my tonge a verray jangleresse,> *babbler*
And walke I wolde, as I had doon biforn,> *before*
From hous to hous, although he had it sworn.> *forbidden*
For which he oftentymės woldė preche,
And me of oldė Romayn gestės° teche,
How he, Simplicius Gallus,° lefte his wyf,
And hir forsook for terme> of al his lyf, *duration*
Noght but for open-heeded> he hir say> *hatless / saw*
Lokinge out at his dore> upon a day.> *door / one day*
Another Romayn° tolde he me by name,
That, for> his wyf was at a somerės> game *because / summer's*
Withoute his witing,> he forsook hir eke. *knowledge*
And than wolde he upon> his Bible seke> *in / seek*
That ilkė> proverbe of Ecclesiaste,° *same*
Wher he comandeth and forbedeth faste,> *absolutely*
Man shal nat suffre> his wyf go roule> aboute; *allow / gad*
Than wolde he seye right thus, withouten doute,
"Whoso that buildeth his hous al of salwes,> *willow-twigs*
And priketh> his blindė hors over the falwes,> *rides / plowed ground*
And suffreth his wyf to go seken halwės,> *shrines*
Is worthy to been hangėd on the galwės>!" *gallows*
But al for noght, I settė noght an hawe°
Of his proverbės nor> his oldė sawe,> *nor of / sayings*
Ne I wolde nat of him corrected be.
I hate him that my vices telleth me,
And so do mo,> God woot! of us than I. *more*
This made him with me wood> al outrely;> *furious / completely*
I noldė noght forbere> him in no cas. *endure*

list i.e. cheek. To rhyme two words that look the same but have different meanings was thought good, as in French *rime riche.*
gestes Latin: (*res*) *gestae,* things done; the regular medieval word for stories of feats of arms
Gallus This story is from Valerius Maximus; see l. 466 above.
Romayn P. Sempronius Sophus, from the same chapter in Valerius
Ecclesiaste Ecclesiasticus 25:25: "Give . . . neither a wicked woman liberty to gad abroad." The clerk is threatening the Wife with authorities from the two most powerful sources known to the Middle Ages—the classics and the Bible. They are not just moral tales: all carry the specific threat of divorce.
I . . . hawe I give not a hawthorn berry

Now wol I seye yow sooth, by Seint Thomas,°
Why that I rente out of his book a leef,
For which he smoot me so that I was deef.
He hadde a book that gladly, night and day,
For his desport˃ he woldė rede alway.˃ *recreation / always*
He clepėd˃ it Valerie° and Theofraste,° *called*
At whichė book he lough˃ alwey ful faste.˃ *laughed / much*
And eek ther was somtyme˃ a clerk˃ at Rome, *once / scholar*
A cardinal, that hightė˃ Saint Jerome, *was called*
That made a book agayn˃ Jovinian;° *against*
In whichė book eek ther was Tertulan,°
Crisippus,° Trotula,° and Helowys,°
That was abbessė nat fer˃ fro Parys; *far*
And eek the Parables of Salomon,°
Ovydes Art,° and bokės many on,
And allė thise wer bounden in o volume.
And every night and day was his custume,˃ *custom*
Whan he had leyser˃ and vacacioùn˃ *lesiure / free time*
From other worldly occupacioùn,
To reden on this book of wikked wyves.˃ *women*
He knew of hem mo legendės and lyves
Than been of godė wyvės in the Bible.
For trusteth wel, it is an impossible˃ *impossibility*
That any clerk wol spekė good of wyves,
But if˃ it be of holy seintės lyves, *unless*
Ne of noon other womman never the mo.°
Who peyntedė the leoun, tel me who?°
By God, if wommen haddė writen stories,
As clerkės han withinne hir oratories,˃ *cells*
They wolde han writen of men more wikkednesse

Seint Thomas St. Thomas Becket of Canterbury, the premier saint of England; see General Prologue, l. 16
Valerie The clerk had a manuscript, perhaps specially written for him, containing a number of related texts teaching him the ways and wiles of women. Valerie is not Valerius Maximus, but the *Letter of Valerius to Rufinus About Not Marrying* by Walter Map (12th century).
Theofraste Theophrastus' work *On Marriage,* mentioned and used by St. Jerome; see l. 291n
Jovinian For the Jovinian-Jerome controversy see the Headnote. The Wife uses St. Jerome freely, against his sense, for her defense of herself; and, in his sense, for her and Jankin's examples of unchastity. Cf. Dorigen, in the Franklin's Tale, ll. 659 ff.
Tertulan Tertullian (*c.* 160–*c.* 220), Father of the Church, who wrote *An Exhortation to Chastity, On Having Only One Husband,* and *On Modesty*
Crisippus perhaps the Stoic philosopher
Trotula probably never existed; she was thought to have been the author of books on gynecology and pediatrics, as well as on cosmetics, and to have been active in the famous medical center Salerno, in southern Italy, during the 11th century
Helowys Héloïse (d. 1164), the secret wife of Peter Abélard, the great Parisian philosopher who was castrated by Héloïse's uncle, Fulbert, for seducing her. She became a nun, and was later prioress of Argenteuil, near Paris. The correspondence of Héloïse and Abélard has been preserved: it was famous in the Middle Ages.
Parables of Salomon the Proverbs of Solomon—not merely the biblical book Proverbs, but a compendium from all those biblical books of which Solomon was, or was thought to be, the author, including Ecclesiasticus and Wisdom
Ovydes Art the *Ars Amatoria* (Art of Love) by the Roman poet Ovid (43 B.C.–*c.*18 A.D.), the lover's textbook, for his time, the Middle Ages, and the Renaissance
Ne . . . mo a heavy negative line: and nothing at all of any other woman
Who . . . who In one of the Aesopic fables a lion, seeing a picture of a lion being killed by a man, points out that all depends on the point of view; a lion would paint a man being killed by a lion.

Than all the mark of Adam° may redresse.
The children of Mercurie and of Venus°
Been in hir wirking> ful contrarious;> *occupations / opposed*
Mercurie loveth wisdom and science,> *knowledge*
And Venus loveth ryot> and dispence.> *debauchery / expenditure*
And, for hir diverse disposicioùn,
Ech falleth in otherės exaltacioùn;°
And thus, God woot! Mercury is desolat
In Pisces, wher Venus is exaltat;
And Venus falleth ther Mercurie is reysed;> *exalted*
Therfore no womman of no clerk is preysed.
The clerk, whan he is old, and may noght do
Of Venus werkės worth his oldė sho,°
Than sit> he doun, and writ> in his dotàge *sits / writes*
That wommen can nat kepe hir mariàge!> *marriage-vows*
  But now to purpos,> why I toldė thee *point*
That I was beten for a book, pardee.
Upon a night Jankin, that was our syre,> *lord*
Redde on his book, as he sat by the fyre,
Of Eva° first, that, for hir wikkednesse,
Was al mankindė broght to wrecchednesse,> *destruction*
For which that Jesu Crist himself was slayn,
That boghte> us with his hertės blood agayn. *redeemed*
Lo, here expres> of womman may ye finde, *made clear*
That womman was the los> of al mankinde. *destruction*
  Tho> redde he me how Sampson° loste his heres,> *then / hair*
Slepinge, his lemman kitte> hem with hir sheres; *lover cut*
Thurgh whichė tresoun> loste he bothe his yën.> *betrayal / eyes*
  Tho> redde he me, if that I shal nat lyen, *then*
Of Hercules and of his Dianyre,°
That causėd him to sette himself afyre.
  Nothing forgat he the penaùnce and wo
That Socrates had with hise wyvės two;°

mark of Adam the image of Adam: men; cf. the Franklin's Tale, l. 172
The children . . . Venus I.e. those born under the influence of each. It is not clear whether Chaucer means that the operations of the planets are different or that the occupations of those born under them differ. Mercury was the planetary god of knowledge and eloquence; his children are scholars, painters, sculptors, skilled metalworkers and so on. Venus was the planetary goddess of love and lovers; her children are courtiers, weavers, and dyers. But Chaucer may simply mean clerks (Mercury) and women (Venus).
exaltacioun The zodiacal sign in which a planet's influence is greatest: it is at the same time the dejection of another planet whose nature is contrary. Venus (female: pleasure) is in exaltation *(exaltat)* in Pisces, the fishes; Mercury (male: wisdom) is therefore in dejection (*desolat*) in the same sign.
of . . . sho a clerk is not worth his own old shoe in the occupations of Venus
Eva the primal female sinner. This spelling of her name is frequently used because, backward, it spells *Ave*, the salutation to Mary at the Annunciation, the beginning of our salvation. Most of the examples which follow are common knowledge, or come from St. Jerome's *Against Jovinian*, Walter Map (l. 677n), or the *Romance of the Rose*.
Sampson the story of Samson and Delilah, Judges 16
Dianyre Deianeira caused the death of her unfaithful husband Hercules, by giving him the shirt of the centaur Nessus, previously killed by Hercules for trying to rape her. The shirt had been poisoned by Nessus' blood and gave Hercules such burning pain that he preferred to build a funeral pyre and die in its flames.
wo . . . two The Athenian philosopher was famous for his patience and had, according to Jerome and others, two wives, of whom Xantippe, the second, tormented him continually.

How Xantippe caste pisse upon his heed;> *head*
This sely> man sat stille, as he were deed; *poor*
He wyped his heed, namore dorste> he seyn *dared*
But 'Er that thonder stinte,> comth of a reyn.'> *ceases / rain*
Of Phasipha,° that was the quene of Crete—
For shrewėdnesse,> him thoughte the talė swete— *nastiness*
Fy! spek> namore—it is a grisly thing— *speak*
Of hir horrìble lust and hir lyking.> *pleasure*
Of Clitėmistra,° for hir lecherye,
That falsly made hir housbond for to dye,
He redde it with ful good devocioùn.
He tolde me eek for what occasioùn
Amphiorax° at Thebės loste his lyf;
Myn housbond hadde a legende of his wyf,
Eriphilem, that for an ouche of gold
Hath prively> unto the Grekės told *secretly*
Wher that hir housbonde hidde him in a place,
For which he hadde at Thebės sory grace.> *sad treatment*
Of Livia° tolde he me, and of Lucye,°
They bothė made hir housbondes for to dye;
That oon for love, that other was for hate;
Livia hir housbond, on an even> late, *evening*
Empoysoned hath, for that she was his fo.
Lucya, likerous,> loved hir housbond so, *lecherous*
That, for> he sholde alwey upon hir thinke, *so*
She yaf him swich a maner lovė drinke,
That he was deed,> er it were by the morwe;> *dead / morning*
And thus algatės> housbondės han sorwe. *all ways*
Than tolde he me, how oon Latumius°
Compleynėd to his felawe> Arrius, *companion*
That in his gardin growėd swich> a tree, *such*
On which, he seyde, how that his wyvės three
Hangėd hemself for hertė despitoùs.°
"O leve> brother," quod> this Arrius, *dear / said*
"Yif me a plante> of thilkė blissed tree, *cutting*
And in my gardin planted shal it be!"
Of latter date, of wyvės hath he red,
That somme han slayn hir housbondes in hir bed,
And lete> hir lechour dighte> hir al the night *let / lay*

Phasipha Pasiphaë, queen of Minos of Crete, fell in love with a bull and bore by him the Minotaur, half-man, half-bull.
Clitemistra Clytemnestra, Agamemnon's queen; she and her lover, Aegisthus, killed her husband on his return to Greece after the Trojan War.
Amphiorax Amphiareus, in hiding so as not to go to the siege of Thebes, was betrayed by his wife, Eriphyle, for a necklace (*ouche*) of gold and diamonds, and had to go on the expedition, where he knew himself fated to die. He was swallowed up in an earthquake at Thebes.
Livia Wife of Drusus, son of the Roman Emperor Tiberius. She poisoned her husband at the prompting of her lover Sejanus (23 A.D.).
Lucye Lucilia, wife of the Roman poet Lucretius (1st century B.C.), gave her husband a love-potion to keep him true to her. It killed him quickly: see Tennyson's *Lucretius*.
Latumius The story is told by Walter Map (l. 677n), who gives the name as Pacuvius; and it is in the *Gesta Romanorum* (see below) with a moralization. It comes, ultimately, from Cicero's *De Oratore*.
for . . . despitoùs for the malice of their hearts

Whyl that the corps> lay in the floor upright.> *corpse / on its back*
And somme han drivė> naylės° in hir brayn *driven*
Whyl that they slepte, and thus they han hem slayn.
Somme han hem yevė> poysoun in hir drinke. *given*
He spak more harm than hertė may bithinke.> *imagine*
And therwithal, he knew of mo> proverbes *more*
Than in this world ther growen gras or herbes.
"Bet> is," quod he, "thyn habitacioùn *better*
Be with a leoun or a foul dragoùn,°
Than with a womman usinge> for to chyde. *accustomed*
Bet is," quod he, "hye> in the roof abyde° *high*
Than with an angry wyf doun in the hous;
They been so wikkėd and contrarious;> *contrary*
They haten> that hir housbondes loveth ay." *hate*
He seyde, "A womman cast> hir shame away, *casts*
Whan she cast of> hir smok";° and forthermo, *off*
"A fair womman, but> she be chaast also, *unless*
Is lyk a gold ring in a sowės nose."°
Who woldė wenen,> or who wolde suppose *imagine*
The wo that in myn hertė was, and pyne>? *torment*
And whan I saugh> he woldė never fyne> *saw / finish*
To reden on this cursėd book al night,
Al sodeynly three levės have I plight> *plucked*
Out of his book, right as he radde,> and eke, *read*
I with my fist so took him on the cheke,
That in our fyr he fil> bakward adoun.> *fell / down*
And he up stirte> as dooth a wood> leoùn, *jumped / raging*
And with his fist he smoot> me on the heed,> *struck / head*
That in the floor I lay as I were deed.
And when he saugh how stillė that I lay,
He was agast,> and wolde han fled his way, *afraid*
Til attė laste out of my swogh> I breyde:> *swoon / burst*
"O! hastow slayn me, falsė theef?" I seyde,
"And for my land thus hastow mordred> me? *murdered*
Er I be deed, yet wol I kissė thee."
And neer> he cam, and knelėd faire adoun, *closer*
And seydė, "Derė suster° Alisoun,
As help me God, I shal thee never smyte;
That I have doon, it is thyself to wyte.> *blame*
Foryeve it me, and that I thee biseke."> *beg*
And yet eftsones> I hit him on the cheke, *again*
And seydė, "Theef, thus muchel> am I wreke;> *much / revenged*
Now wol I dye, I may no lenger> speke." *longer*

nayles Joel killed the tyrant Sisera thus (Judges 4:21).
Bet . . . dragoùn Ecclesiasticus 25:16
Bet . . . abyde Proverbs 21:9
A . . . smok from *Against Jovinian;* Jerome took it from the Greek historian Herodotus (died *c.* 425 B.C.)
A fair . . . nose See Proverbs 11:22: "As a jewel of gold in a swine's snout, so is a fair woman who is without discretion."
suster term of affection

But attė laste, with muchel care> and wo, — *trouble*
We fille acorded,> by us selven two. — *fell agreed*
He yaf me al the brydel> in myn hond — *bridle*
To han the governance of hous and lond,
And of his tonge> and of his hond also; — *tongue*
And made him brenne his book anon right tho.°
And whan that I hadde geten> unto me, — *gotten*
By maistrie,> al the soveraynėtee,> — *mastering / sovereignty*
And that he seyde, "Myn owene trewė wyf,
Do as thee lust> the terme> of al thy lyf, — *pleases / duration*
Keep thyn honour, and keep eek myn estaat">— — *possessions*
After that day we hadden never debaat.
God help me so, I was to him as kinde
As any wyf from Denmark unto Inde,> — *India*
And also trewe, and so was he to me.
I prey to God that sit> in magestee, — *sits*
So blesse his soulė, for His mercy dere!
Now wol I seye my tale, if ye wol here.'> — *hear*

Biholde the wordes bitween the Somonour and the Frere

The Frerė lough,> whan he hadde herd al this, — *laughed*
'Now, dame,' quod he, 'so have I joye or blis,
This is a long preamble of a tale!'
And whan the Somnour herde the Frerė gale,> — *exclaim*
'Lo!' quod the Somnour, 'Goddės armės two!
A frere wol entremette him evermo.°
Lo, godė men, a flye and eek a frere
Wol falle in every dish and eek matere.°
What spekestow of preambulacioùn?
What! amble, or trotte, or pees,° or go sit doun;
Thou lettest> our disport> in this manere.' — *hinderest / enjoyment*
'Ye, woltow so, sir Somnour?' quod the Frere,
'Now, by my feith, I shal, er that I go,
Telle of a Somnour swich a tale or two,
That alle the folk shal laughen in this place.'
'Now ellės,° Frerė, I bishrewe> thy face,' — *curse*
Quod this Somnoùr, 'and I bishrewė me,
But if I tellė talės two or thre
Of frerės er I come to Sidingborne,°
That I shal make thyn hertė for to morne;
For wel I woot thy pacience is goon.'
Our Hostė crydė 'Pees! and that anoon!'
And seydė, 'Lat the womman telle hir tale

And made . . . tho and I made him burn his book on the spot
A frere . . . evermo a friar will always be meddling
a flye . . . matere a proverb
pees be still; some prefer the reading "pisse"

Now elles now otherwise; i.e. now unless
Sidingborne Sittingbourne, in Kent, about 40 miles from London, more than two-thirds of the way to Canterbury. The pilgrim-journey to Canterbury usually took three days and part of a fourth.

Ye fare as folk that dronken been of ale.
Do, dame, tel forth your tale, and that is best.'
'Al redy, sir,' quod she, 'right as yow lest,›   *it pleases*
If I have licence of this worthy Frere.'
'Yis, dame,' quod he, 'tel forth, and I wol here.'

Here endeth the Wyf of Bathe hir Prologe.

Tale

Here biginneth the Tale of the Wyf of Bathe

In tholdė dayės of the king Arthoùr,
Of which that Britons› speken greet honoùr,   *Bretons*
All was this land fulfild of fayërye.°
The elf-queen, with hir joly companye,
Douncėd ful ofte in many a grenė mede;›   *meadow*
This was the olde opinion, as I rede.
I speke of manye hundred yeres ago;
But now can no man see none elvės mo.
For now the gretė charitee and prayeres
Of limitours° and othere holy freres,
As thikke as motės in the sonnė-beem,
That serchen every lond and every streem,
Blessinge hallės, chambres, kichenes, boures,
Citees, burghės,° castels, hyė toures,
Thropės, bernės, shipnės, dayëryes,°
This maketh that ther been no fayëryes.
For ther as wont to walken was an elf,
Ther walketh now the limitour himself
In undermelės° and in morweninges,›   *mornings*
And seÿth his matins and his holy thinges
As he goth in his limitacioùn.°
Wommen may go saufly› up and doun,   *safely*
In every bush, or under every tree;
Ther is noon other incubus but he,
And he ne wol doon hem but dishonoùr.°
And so bifel it, that this King Arthoùr
Hadde in his hous a lusty bacheler,

All . . . fayerye i.e. this land was teeming with supernatural creatures
limitours friars licensed to beg and hear confessions within a certain district; cf. the General Prologue, l. 209
burghes literally, boroughs; i.e. towns
Thropes . . . dayeryes thorps (i.e. villages), barns, stables, dairies
undermeles The word could mean mid-mornings or mid-afternoons: here it seems to be the latter.
And . . . limitacioùn And says his morning prayers and his holy office as he goes about his district. All clergy were bound to repeat the office at the required hours; friars were allowed to do so as they walked or rode.
Ther . . . dishonour There is no other incubus now but the friar—and he only dishonors them (without making them conceive). An incubus was an evil spirit (or fallen angel) who got children on women.

That on a day cam rydinge fro river;°
And happėd> that, allone as she was born, *it chanced*
He saugh a maydė walkinge him biforn,
Of whichė mayde anon, maugree hir heed,°
By verray force he rafte> hir maydenheed; *took*
For which oppressioùn> was swich clamoùr *rape*
And swich pursute> unto the King Arthoùr, *appeal*
That dampnėd was this knight for to be deed°
By cours of lawe, and sholde han lost his heed
Paraventure,> swich was the statut> tho; *perhaps / law*
But that the quene and othere ladies mo
So longė preyėden the king of grace,
Til he his lyf him graunted in the place,
And yaf him to the quene al at hir wille,
To chesė,> whether she wolde him save or spille.° *choose*
The quene thanketh the king with al hir might,
And after this thus spak she to the knight,
Whan that she saugh hir tyme,> upon a day: *opportunity*
'Thou standest yet,' quod she, 'in swich array,> *state*
That of thy lyf yet hastow no suretee.> *certainty*
I grante thee lyf, if thou canst tellen me
What thing is it that wommen most desyren?
Be war, and keep thy nekkė-boon> from yren.> *neck-bone / iron*
And if thou canst nat tellen it anon,
Yet wol I yeve> thee levė for to gon *give*
A twelf-month and a day, to seche> and lere> *seek / learn*
An answere suffisànt in this matere.
And suretee> wol I han, er that thou pace,> *pledge / go*
Thy body for to yelden in this place.'
Wo was this knight and sorwefully he syketh;> *sighs*
But what! he may nat do al as him lyketh.
And at the laste, he chees> him for to wende, *chose*
And come agayn, right at the yerės ende,
With swich answere as God wolde him purveye;> *provide*
And taketh his leve, and wendeth forth his weye.
He seketh every hous and every place,
Wheras he hopeth for to findė grace,
To lernė, what thing wommen loven most;
But he ne coude arryven in no cost,> *region*
Wheras he mightė finde in this matere
Two creätùrės àccordinge in fere.°
Somme seydė,> wommen loven best richesse, *said*
Somme seydė, honour, somme seyde, jolynesse;°
Somme, riche array, somme seyden, lust> abedde, *pleasure*

fro river i.e. from hawking for wild-fowl by the river-side
maugree hir heed literally, in spite of her head; thus, despite anything she could do
That . . . deed that this knight was condemned to death
save or spille spare or put to death
accordinge in fere agreeing together
jolynesse good looks, happiness

And oftė tyme to be widwe and wedde.
  Somme seydė, that our hertės been most esed,
Whan that we been yflatered and yplesed.
He gooth ful ny the sothe,> I wol nat lye; — *truth*
A man shal winne us best with flaterye;
And with attendance, and with bisinesse,> — *assiduity*
Been we ylymėd,> bothė more and lesse. — *ensnared*
  And sommė seyn, how that we loven best
For to be free, and do right as us lest,> — *it pleases*
And that no man repreve> us of our vyce, — *reprove*
But seye that we be wyse, and no thing nyce.> — *silly*
For trewėly, ther is noon of us alle,
If any wight wol clawe us on the galle,> — *sore place*
That we nil kikė,> for> he seith us sooth; — *kick / since*
Assay, and he shal finde it that so dooth.
For be we never so vicioùs withinne,
We wol> been holden> wyse, and clene of sinne. — *want / thought*
  And sommė seyn, that greet delyt han we
For to ben holden stable and eek secree,°
And in o purpos stedefastly to dwelle,
And nat biwreyė> thing that men us telle. — *disclose*
But that tale is nat worth a rakė-stele;> — *rake-handle*
Pardee, we wommen connė nothing hele;> — *hide*
Witnesse on Myda;° wol ye here the tale?
  Ovyde, amongės otherė thingės smale,
Seyde, Myda hadde, under his longė heres,
Growinge upon his heed two asses eres,
The which vycė> he hidde, as he best mighte, — *defect*
Ful subtilly> from every mannės sighte, — *cleverly*
That, save his wyf, ther wiste of it namo.> — *no more*
He loved hir most, and trusted hir also;
He preyėde hir, that to no creätùre
She sholdė tellen of his disfigùre.> — *disfigurement*
  She swoor him 'nay, for al this world to winne,
She noldė do that vileinye or sinne,
To make hir housbond han so foul a name;
She nolde nat telle it for hir owene shame.'
But nathėlees, hir thoughtė> that she dyde,> — *it seemed / was dying*
That she so longė sholde a conseil> hyde; — *secret*
Hir thoughte it swal> so sore aboute hir herte, — *swelled*
That nedėly som word hir moste asterte;°
And sith she dorste telle it to no man,
Doun to a mareys fastė> by she ran; — *marsh close*
Til she came there, hir hertė was afyre,

For . . . secree to be thought stable and discreet
Myda See Ovid, *Metamorphoses* XI. 174–93. Midas, King of Phrygia, had been given asses' ears by Apollo because he thought the music of Pan's pipes superior to that of the god's lyre. In Ovid's story, he was actually betrayed by his barber.
nedely . . . asterte necessarily some word must escape her

And, as a bitore bombleth in the myre,°
She leyde hir mouth unto the water doun:
'Biwreye> me nat, thou water, with thy soun,'> *betray / sound*
Quod she, 'to thee I telle it, and namo;> *no other*
Myn housbond hath longe asses erės two!
Now is myn herte all hool,> now is it oute; *whole*
I mighte no lenger kepe it, out of doute.'
Heer may ye se, thogh we a tyme abyde,
Yet out it moot,> we can no conseil hyde; *must*
The remenant of the tale if ye wol here,
Redeth Ovyde, and ther ye may it lere.> *learn*
  This knight, of which my tale is specially,
Whan that he saugh> he mighte nat come therby, *saw*
This is to seye, what wommen loven moost,
Withinne his brest ful sorweful was the goost;> *spirit*
But hoom he gooth, he mightė nat sojourne.> *stay*
The day was come, that hoomward moste> he tourne, *must*
And in his wey it happėd him to ryde,
In al this care, under> a forest syde, *by*
Wheras he saugh upon a daunce go
Of ladies foure and twenty, and yet mo;
Toward the whichė daunce he drow ful yerne,°
In hopė that som wisdom sholde he lerne.
But certeinly, er he came fully there,
Vanisshed was this daunce, he nistė> where. *knew not*
No creatùrė saugh he that bar> lyf, *bore*
Save on the grene he saugh sittinge a wyf;> *woman*
A fouler wight> ther may no man devyse.> *creature / imagine*
Agayn> the knight this oldė wyf gan ryse, *before*
And seyde, 'Sir knight, heer-forth ne lyth> no wey.> *lies / road*
Tel me, what that ye seken, by your fey?> *faith*
Paraventure it may the bettre be;
Thise oldė folk can muchel> thing,' quod she. *know much*
  'My levė mooder,'> quod this knight, certeyn, *dear mother*
'I nam> but deed, but if that I can seyn *am*
What thing it is that wommen most desyre;
Coude ye me wisse, I wolde wel quyte your hyre.'°
  'Plighte me thy trouthe, heer in myn hand,' quod she,
'The nextė thing that I requerė> thee, *ask*
Thou shalt it do, if it lye in thy might;
And I wol telle it yow er it be night.'
'Have heer my trouthė,' quod the knight, 'I grante.'
  'Thannė,' quod she, 'I dar me wel avante,> *boast*
Thy lyf is sauf,> for I wol stonde therby, *safe*

bitore . . . myre A bittern makes a booming sound in the mud. The bittern, a kind of small heron, was thought to make its characteristic bellowing cry by plunging its beak into the mud.

drow . . . yerne approached very eagerly

Coude . . . hyre if you could make me know, I would pay you a good reward for it

Upon my lyf, the queen wol seye as I.
Lat see which is the proudeste of hem alle,
That wereth on a coverchief or a calle,°
That dar seye nay, of that I shal thee teche;
Lat us go forth withouten lenger speche.'
Tho rounėd she a pistel in his ere,°
And bad him to be glad, and have no fere.
   When they be comen to the court, this knight
Seyde, 'He had holde his day, as he hadde hight,˃ *promised*
And redy was his answere,' as he sayde.
Ful many a noble wyf, and many a mayde,
And many a widwe, for that they ben wyse,
The quene hirself sittinge as a justỳse,
Assembled been, his answere for to here;
And afterward this knight was bode˃ appere. *bidden*
   To every wight commanded was silènce,
And that the knight sholde telle in audience,°
What thing that worldly wommen loven best.
This knight ne stood nat stille˃ as doth a best,˃ *silent / beast*
But to his questioùn anon answerde
With manly voys, that al the court it herde:
   'My ligė˃ lady, generally,' quod he, *liege*
'Wommen desyren to have sovereyntee˃ *dominion*
As wel over hir housbond as hir love,
And for to been in maistrie him above;
This is your moste desyr, thogh ye me kille,
Doth as yow list, I am heer at your wille.'°
   In al the court ne was ther wyf ne mayde,
Ne widwe, that contraried˃ that he sayde, *contradicted*
But seyden, 'He was worthy han˃ his lyf.' *to keep*
   And with that word up stirte˃ the oldė wyf, *started*
Which that the knight saugh sittinge in the grene:
'Mercy,' quod she, 'my sovereyn lady quene!
Er that your court departė, do me right.
I taughtė this answère unto the knight;
For which he plightė me his trouthė there,
The firstė thing I wolde of him requere,
He wolde it do, if it lay in his might.
Bifore the court than preye I thee, sir knight,'
Quod she, 'that thou me take unto thy wyf;
For wel thou wost˃ that I have kept˃ thy lyf. *knowest / saved*
If I sey fals, sey nay, upon thy fey!'
   This knight answerde, 'Allas! and weylawey!

That . . . calle that wears upon her head-covering or caul; the caul was a close-fitting netted cap or headdress
Tho rouned . . . ere then she whispered a short lesson (epistle) in his ear
in audience in formal hearing
thogh . . . wille even if you kill me (for saying it), do as pleases you, I am at your disposal here

I woot right wel that swich was my biheste.> *promise*
For Goddės love, as chees> a newe requeste; *choose*
Tak al my good, and lat my body go.'
 'Nay than,' quod she, 'I shrewe> us bothė two! *curse*
For thogh that I be foul, and old, and pore,
I nolde for al the metal, ne for ore,
That under erthe is grave,> or lyth> above, *buried / lies*
But if thy wyf I were, and eek thy love.'
 'My love?' quod he; 'nay, my dampnacioùn!> *damnation*
Allas! that any of my nacioùn°
Sholde ever so foulė disparàgėd> be!' *disgraced*
But al for noght, the ende is this, that he
Constreynėd> was, he nedės moste hir wedde; *forced*
And taketh his olde wyf, and gooth to bedde.
 Now wolden som men seye, paraventùre,
That, for my necligence, I do no cure°
To tellen yow the joye and al th'array°
That at the festė was that ilkė day.
To whichė thing shortly answere I shal;
I seye, ther nas no joye ne feste at al,
Ther nas but hevinesse and muchė sorwe;
For privėly he wedded hir on a morwe,> *morning*
And al day after hidde him as an oule;
So wo was him, his wyf lookėd so foule.
 Greet was the wo the knight hadde in his thoght,
Whan he was with his wyf abedde ybroght;
He walweth,> and he turneth to and fro. *tosses*
His oldė wyf lay smylinge evermo,
And seyde, 'O derė housbond, Benedicitė!> *bless me*
Fareth> every knight thus with his wyf as ye? *behaves*
Is this the lawe of King Arthùrės hous?
Is every knight of his so dangerous?> *unapproachable*
I am your owenė love and eek your wyf;
I am she, which that savėd hath your lyf;
And certės, yet dide I yow never unright;
Why fare ye thus with me this firstė night?
Ye faren lyk a man had lost his wit;
What is my gilt? for Goddes love, tel me it,
And it shal been amended, if I may.'
 'Amended?' quod this knight, 'allas! nay, nay!
It wol nat been amended never mo!
Thou art so loothly,> and so old also, *hateful*
And therto comen of so lowe a kinde,> *nature*
That litel wonder is, thogh I walwe and winde.> *toss and turn*
So woldė God myn hertė woldė breste!'> *break*

nacioùn birth; i.e. family
for . . . cure because of my negligence, I do not take the trouble
th'array the arrangements, special preparations

'Is this,' quod she, 'the cause of your unreste?'
'Ye, certainly,' quod he, 'no wonder is.'
'Now, sire,' quod she, 'I coude amende al this,
If that me liste, er it were dayės three,
So wel ye mightė bere yow° unto me.
But for ye speken of swich gentillesse°
As is descended out of old richesse,
That therfore sholden ye be gentil men,
Swich arrogàncė is nat worth an hen.
Loke who that is most vertuous alway,
Privee and apert,° and most entendeth ay°
To do the gentil dedės that he can,
And tak him for the grettest> gentil man. *greatest*
Crist wol,> we clayme of him our gentillesse, *wishes that*
Nat of our eldrės for hir old richesse.°
For thogh they yeve us al hir heritage,
For which we clayme to been of heigh parage,> *descent*
Yet may they nat biquethė, for nothing,
To noon of us hir vertuous living,
That made hem gentil men ycallėd be;
And bad us folwen hem in swich degree.°
  Wel can the wysė poete of Florènce,
That hightė> Dant,° speken in this sentènce;> *is called / wisdom*
Lo in swich maner rym is Dantės tale:
"Ful selde> up ryseth by his branches smale *seldom*
Prowesse> of man, for God, of his goodnesse, *excellence*
Wol that of him we clayme our gentillesse";
For of our eldrės may we nothing clayme
But temporel thing, that man may hurte and mayme.
  Eek every wight wot this as wel as I,
If gentillesse were planted naturelly
Unto a certeyn linage, doun the lyne,
Privee ne apert, than wolde they never fyne> *cease*
To doon of gentillesse the faire offyce;> *function*
They mightė do no vileinye or vyce.°
  Tak fyr,> and ber> it in the derkeste hous *fire / bear*
Bitwix this and the mount of Caucasus,°
And lat men shette> the dorės and go thenne;> *shut / thence*
Yet wol the fyr as fairė lye° and brenne,> *burn*
As twenty thousand men mighte it biholde;

bere yow behave
gentillesse gentleness, noble kindness; see Chaucer's poem below
Privee and apert in private and in public
entendeth ay always sets himself
Nat . . . richesse not from our ancestors, because of their ancient wealth
And . . . degree and they commanded us to follow them to that state
Dant Dante. The quotation is from his *Purgatorio* VII.121 ff. and emphasizes that gentilesse is not the inevitable result of noble blood and "old richesse."
If gentillesse . . . vyce (ll. 1140–44) If gentilesse were naturally implanted in a family and merely transmitted from father to son, then none of that family could ever do evil.
Caucasus i.e. to the furthest, coldest, and darkest of places
lye blaze; i.e. it is the nature of fire to be bright and warm, whether we are looking at it or not

His office naturel° ay wol it holde,
Up˃ peril of my lyf, til that it dye. *upon*
  Heer may ye see wel, how that genterye°
Is nat annexėd˃ to possessioùn,° *tied*
Sith folk ne doon hir operacioùn
Alwey, as dooth the fyr, lo! in his kinde.˃ *nature*
For, God it woot, men may wel often finde
A lordės sone˃ do shame and vileinye; *son*
And he that wol han prys of his gentrye°
For he was boren˃ of a gentil hous, *born*
And hadde hise eldrės noble and vertuous,
And nil himselven do no gentil dedis,
Ne folwe his gentil auncestre that deed˃ is, *dead*
He nis nat gentil, be he duk or erl;
For vileyns sinful dedės make a cherl.
For gentillessė nis but renomee˃ *renown*
Of thyne auncestres, for hir heigh bountee,°
Which is a strangė˃ thing to thy persone. *foreign*
Thy gentillessė cometh fro God allone;
Than comth our verray gentillesse of grace,
It was nothing biquethe us with our place.
  Thenketh how noble, as seith Valerius,°
Was thilkė Tullius Hostilius,°
That out of povert˃ roos to heigh noblesse. *poverty*
Redeth Senek,° and redeth eek Boëce,°
Ther shul ye seen expres that it no drede˃ is, *doubt*
That he is gentil that doth gentil dedis;
And therfore, leve˃ housbònd, I thus conclude, *dear*
Al˃ were it that myne auncestres were rude,˃ *although / lowly*
Yet may the hyė God, and so hope I,
Grantė me grace to liven vertuously.
Thanne am I gentil, whan that I biginne
To liven vertuously and weyvė˃ sinne. *leave off*
  And theras ye of povert me repreve,
The hyė God, on whom that we bileve,
In wilful˃ povert chees˃ to live his lyf. *voluntary / chose*
And certės every man, mayden, or wyf,
May understonde that Jesus, Hevenė king,
Ne wolde nat chese a vicioùs living.
Glad povert is an honest˃ thing, certèyn; *honorable*
This wol Senek and otherė clerkės seyn.

office naturel the function which belongs to it by nature
genterye noble conduct, gentilesse
possessioun worldly riches, hereditary wealth
he . . . gentrye he that wants to have reputation on account of gentle birth
For . . . bountee what you claim as your nobility is only due to your ancestors, because of their great goodness
Valerius Valerius Maximus, 1st century A.D. Roman author of a book of *exempla* for rhetoricians
Tullius Hostilius Tullus Hostilius, the third king of Rome, 673–642 B.C., who began life as a shepherd, according to the story, and is used by Valerius as an example of rags-to-riches
Senek Lucius Annaeus Seneca, *c.*5 B.C.–65 A.D., Roman Stoic philosopher and dramatist; see his *Moral Epistles* 44
Boëce Boethius

Whoso that halt him payd of° his poverte,
I holde him riche, al hadde he nat a sherte.> *shirt*
He that coveyteth is a povrė wight,°
For he wolde han that is nat in his might.
But he that noght hath, ne covèyteth have,
Is riche, although ye holde him but a knave.
Verray> povert, it singeth proprely;> *true / appropriately*
Juvenal seith of povert merily:
"The povrė man, whan he goth by the weye,
Bifore the thevės he may singe and pleye."°
Povert is hateful good, and, as I gesse,
A ful greet bringer out of bisiness;°
A greet amender eek of sapience> *wisdom*
To him that taketh it in pacience.
Povert is this, although it seme elenge:> *hard to bear*
Possessioùn, that no wight wol chalenge.> *claim*
Povert ful oftė, whan a man is lowe,
Maketh° his God and eek himself to knowe.
Povert a spectacle> is, as thinketh me, *eyeglass*
Thurgh which he may his verray frendės see.
And therfore, sire, sin that I noght> yow greve, *ought not*
Of my povert namore ye me repreve.> *reproach*
Now, sire, of eldė> ye reprevė me; *old age*
And certės, sire, thogh noon auctoritee
Were in no book, ye gentils of honour
Seyn that men sholde an old wight doon favour,
And clepe him fader,> for your gentillesse; *father*
And auctours> shal I finden, as I gesse. *authorities*
Now ther ye seye, that I am foul and old,
Than drede you noght to been a cokėwold;> *cuckold*
For filthe and eldė, also moot I thee,°
Been gretė wardeyns> upon chastitee. *guardians*
But nathelees, sin I knowe your delyt,
I shal fulfille your worldly appetyt.
Chese now,' quod she, 'oon of thise thingės tweye,
To han me foul and old til that I deye,
And be to yow a trewė humble wyf,
And never yow displese in al my lyf,
Or ellės ye wol han me yong and fair,
And take your aventure> of the repair° *chance*
That shal be to your hous, bycause of me,
Or in som other placė, may wel be.
Now chese yourselven, whether> that yow lyketh.' *which*

Whoso . . . of whoever is contented with
He . . . wight he that covets more money is a poor person, i.e. the true pauper
Juvenal . . . pleye Juvenal, *Satire* X. 22
bisinesse Preoccupations. Most of these definitions are taken ultimately from the favorite medieval moral text, *Hadrian and Epictetus,* an apocryphal dialogue between the Emperor and the Philosopher. Chaucer probably got them from the 13th-century encyclopedist Vincent of Beauvais.
Maketh makes him
also . . . thee as I may thrive
repair frequenting, resort

This knight avyseth him> and sorė syketh,> *considers / sighs*
But attė laste he seyde in this manere,
'My lady and my love, and wyf so dere,
I put me in your wysė governance;
Cheseth> yourself, which may be most plesance,> *choose / pleasure*
And most honour to yow and me also.
I do no fors the whether° of the two;
For as yow lyketh,> it suffiseth> me.' *it pleases / satisfies*
'Thanne have I gete> of yow maistrye,' quod she, *got*
'Sin I may chese, and governe as me lest?'> *pleases*
'Ye, certės, wyf,' quod he, 'I holde it best.'
'Kis me,' quod she, 'we be no lenger wrothe;
For, by my trouthe, I wol be to yow bothe,
This is to seyn, ye, bothė fair and good.
I prey to God that I mot sterven wood,°
But> I to yow be also> good and trewe *unless / as*
As ever was wyf, sin that the world was newe.
And, but I be to morn> as fair to sene *tomorrow morning*
As any lady, emperyce, or quene,
That is bitwixe the est and eke the west,
Doth with my lyf and deeth right as yow lest.
Cast up the curtin, loke how that it is.'
And whan the knight saugh verraily al this,
That she so fair was, and so yong therto,
For joye he hente> hir in his armės two, *took*
His hertė bathėd in a bath of blisse;
A thousand tyme arewe> he gan hir kisse. *in succession*
And she obeyėd him in every thing
That mightė doon him plesance> or lyking.> *happiness / pleasure*
And thus they live, unto hir lyvės ende,
In parfit> joye; and Jesu Crist us sende *perfect*
Housbondes mekė, yonge, and fresshe abedde,
And grace t'overbyde> hem that we wedde. *outlast*
And eek I preyė Jesu shorte> hir lyves *shorten*
That wol nat be govėrnėd by hir wyves;
And olde and angry nigardes of dispence,> *paying*
God sende hem sonė> verray> pestilence. *at once / true*

Here endeth the Wyves Tale of Bathe

From Gesta Romanorum

Of Hanging

Valerius tells us that a man named Paletinus one day burst into a flood of tears; and, calling his son and his neighbours around him, said, 'Alas! alas! I have now growing in my garden a fatal tree, on which my first poor wife hung herself, then my second, and after that my third. Have I not therefore cause

I . . . whether I do not care which   **mot . . . wood** may die crazy

for the wretchedness I exhibit?' 'Truly,' said one who was called Arrius, 'I marvel that you should weep at such an unusual instance of good fortune! Give me, I pray you, two or three sprigs of that gentle tree, which I will divide with my neighbours, and thereby afford every man an opportunity of indulging the laudable wishes of his spouse.' Paletinus complied with his friend's request; and ever after found this remarkable tree the most productive part of his estate.

Application

My beloved, the tree is the cross of Christ. The man's three wives are, pride, lusts of the heart, and lusts of the eyes, which ought to be thus suspended and destroyed. He who solicited a part of the tree is any good Christian.

The Franklin's Prologue and Tale

The Franklin's Tale is about *gentilesse,* true nobility and virtue (see Chaucer's short poem of that title). It explores the relation between *trouthe,* or integrity, the central notion of the short "balade of good counsel" and the keeping of an oath, which is part of *gentilesse;* and demonstrates how *fredom,* or generosity, if exercised by all those involved in a situation, will bring it to good issue. Perhaps Chaucer means to suggest, in the Franklin's preoccupation with the idea, a sense of the social position he occupies as a member of the rising country gentry, aspiring to the aristocracy.

According to the Franklin, his tale is an old "Breton lay," a literary genre first popularized in twelfth-century France as a short narrative romance in verse, usually on a theme of love, promises, and magical occurrences. Though many of the motifs of the tale occur in extant lays, the exact source of Chaucer's tale has not been discovered—and even the exact placing of the scene in a locality in Brittany paradoxically tells against it. There are extant fourteenth-century English poems of the "lay" type, but the form was at that date somewhat old-fashioned. Chaucer may be giving us some suggestion of the kind of man the Franklin was by putting into his mouth an out-of-date form set in the long ago.

The plot of the tale is probably taken either from Boccaccio's *Il Filocolo* or from his *Decameron* (it appears in both works); but the germ of the story goes back very much farther in time and can be found in a widely diffused Eastern folk-tale in which a woman's unconsidered promise to a second lover puts her in the same embarrassing position as Dorigen. Her first lover advises her to keep her promise, and her second then releases her from it. The question is asked, as it is in Boccaccio, which of the three showed the greatest generosity.

Chaucer's treatment of the story, with the mass of astrological and magical detail laid onto, but never obscuring, the delicate articulation of its central moral content, is not the statement of a question about love (*questione d'amore*). It is an exploration of the basis of marriage, refining some of the questions that have already been raised by the Wife of Bath, the Clerk, and the Merchant. Dorigen, opting for love in marriage of the most idealistic kind, is brought to realize that virtue is not single and cannot be exercised in isolation, so that virtues may come into conflict with each other as well as with vices.

Prologue

The Prologe of the Frankeleyns Tale

Thise oldė gentil Britons in hir dayes
Of diverse adventùrės maden layes,
Rymeyėd in hir firstė Briton tonge;°
Which layės with hir instruments they songe,
Or ellės redden˃ hem for hir pleasunce;˃ — *read / pleasure*
And oon of hem have I in remembraùnce,
Which I shal seyn with good wil as I can.
  But, sirės, bycause I am a burel˃ man, — *plain*
At my biginning first I yow biseche
Have me excusėd of my rudė speche;°
I lernėd never rethoryk, certeyn;
Thing that I speke, it moot˃ be bare and pleyn. — *must*
I sleep never on the mount of Pernaso,°
Ne lernėd Marcus Tullius Cithero.°
Coloùrs ne knowe I none, withouten drede,°
But swiche˃ coloùrs as growen in the mede˃, — *such / meadow*
Or ellės swiche as men dye or peynte.
Coloùrs of rethoryk ben me to queynte;˃ — *ingenious*
My spirit feeleth noght of swich matere
But if yow list,˃ my talė shul ye here. — *it pleases*

Thise . . . tonge (ll. 1–3) These noble old Bretons, in their own day, made lays about various happenings, written in rhyme in their earliest Breton language.
rude speche This is the conventional Chaucerian disclaimer, in an age where ornateness and enrichment of the language was highly thought of, whether the poet speaks in his own person or through the mouth of one of his characters. The Franklin speaks as a good plain man, who never knew rhetoric. As so often in Chaucer, the character is here made to protest his unfitness as an orator by using the exact form in which a skilled orator would do the same thing: *diminution* of oneself, to begin; then varying of the theme (ll. 10–19); with elegant circumlocution in the oblique references to poetry; and a play on the word *color* (ornament of style / natural color / artificial color), a figure of speech known as *adnomination*. The Franklin uses a slightly stiff and elaborate rhetoric for his higher-flown moments, but in general his narrative is direct.
Pernaso Parnassus, the double-peaked mountain in Phocis, Greece; sacred to Apollo, god of music and poetry; to his servants the nine Muses, daughters of Memory and guardians of poetry, music, dance, and learning; and to Dionysus (Bacchus), god of wine and song. Chaucer took the bit about sleeping on Parnassus (and the exact form of the word) from the Roman satirist Persius (34–62 A.D.): it was a very popular quotation.
Cithero Marcus Tullius Cicero (106–43 B.C.), the Roman statesman and writer, the best-known and most used of all classical rhetoricians in the Middle Ages. So, says the Franklin, I am eloquent in neither poetry nor prose.
withouten drede conventional oral formula: "without fear," hence, "certainly"

Tale

Here biginneth the Frankeleyns Tale

In Armorik,° that callėd is Britayne,
Ther was a knight that loved and dide his payne°
To serve a lady in his bestė wyse;˃ *manner*
And many a labour, many a greet empryse˃ *enterprise*
He for his lady wroghte,˃ er she were wonne. *did*
For she was oon the faireste° under sonne,
And eek˃ therto come of so heigh kinrede,˃ *also / ancestry*
That wel unnethės dorste˃ this knight, for drede, *hardly dared*
Telle hir his wo, his peyne, and his distresse.
But attė laste, she, for his worthinesse,
And namely˃ for his meke obeÿsaùnce,˃ *especially / obedience*
Hath swich a pitee caught of his penaùnce,
That privėly˃ she fil of his accord *secretly*
To take him for hir housbonde and hir lord,
Of swich lordshipe as men han over hir wyves.
And for to lede the more in blisse hir lyves,
Of his free will he swoor hir as a knight,
That never in al his lyf he, day ne night,
Ne sholde upon him takė no maistrye°
Agayn hir wil, ne kythe˃ hir jalousye, *show*
But hir obeye, and folwe hir will in all
As any lovere to his lady shall;
Save that the name of soveraynėtee,
That wolde he have for shame of his degree.°
She thankėd him, and with ful greet humblesse˃ *meekness*
She seyde: 'Sire, sith˃ of your gentillesse° *since*
Ye profre˃ me to have so large˃ a reyne, *offer / loose*
Ne woldė never God bitwixe us tweyne,
As in my gilt,˃ were outher˃ werre or stryf. *responsibility / either*
Sir, I wol be your humble trewė wyf,
Have heer my trouthe, til that myn hertė breste.'˃ *break*
Thus been they bothe in quiete and in reste.
For o thing, sirės, saufly˃ dar I seye,˃ *confidently / say*
That frendės everich˃ other moot˃ obeye, *each / must*
If they wol longė holden˃ companye. *keep*
Love wol nat ben constreynėd by maistrye;

Armorik Armorica (*Ar vor,* land by the sea) was the old name for Brittany, before, so the legend goes, it was named Little Britain "beyond the sea," to emphasize its links with Greater Britain. Chaucer uses this bit of recondite, ancient information to enhance the "once upon a time" atmosphere of the Franklin's romance of magic and true nobility.
payne The hero's pains, service, and undertakings for the lady; the woe, pain and distress he suffers in silence because he loves her; and his entire submission, mark him as the courtly lover.
oon the faireste either "one of the most beautiful" or "the most beautiful"
no maistrye i.e. his love would tame his natural masculine desire for domination, mastery
Save . . . degree only that he wished to have the title of ruler, so as not to bring shame on his status (as a husband); love might make them equal, but the ordinary and courtly appearances must be kept up
gentillesse magnanimous behavior becoming a man of true nobility in birth and feeling; it is self, not birth, that is important

Whan maistrie comth, the god of love anon
Beteth> hise winges, and farewel! he is gon! *beats*
Love is a thing as any spirit free;
Wommen of kinde> desiren libertee, *nature*
And nat to ben constreynėd as a thral;> *slave*
And so don men, if I soth> seyen shal.> *truth / must*
Loke who that is most pacient in love,
He is at his avantage al above.
Pacience is an heigh vertù, certeyn,
For it venquisseth, as thise clerkės seyn,°
Thingės that rigour sholdė never atteyne.
For every word men may nat chyde or pleyne.
Lerneth to suffre, or elles, so moot I goon,
Ye shul it lerne, wherso ye wole or noon.°
For in this world, certein, ther no wight is,
That he ne dooth or seith somtyme amis.
Irė, siknesse, or constellacioùn,°
Wyn,> wo, or chaunginge of complexioùn> *wine / constitution*
Causeth ful ofte to doon amis or speken.
On every wrong a man may nat be wreken.> *revenged*
After> the tymė,> moste be temperaunce *according to / occasion*
To every wight that can on> governaunce. *is wise in*
And therfore hath this wysė worthy knight,
To live in esė, suffrance> hir bihight,> *permission / promised*
And she to him ful wisly> gan to> swere *firmly / did*
That never sholde ther be defaute° in here.> *her*
 Heer may men seen an humble wys accord;
Thus hath she take hir servant and hir lord,°
Servant in love, and lord in mariàge;
Than was he bothe in lordship and servage;
Servage? nay, but in lordshipe above,
Sith he hath bothe his lady and his love;
His lady, certės,> and his wyf also, *indeed*
The which that> lawe of love acordeth> to. *who / agrees*
And whan he was in this prosperitee,> *happiness*
Hoom with his wyf he gooth to his contree,
Nat fer fro Penmark,° ther his dwelling was,
Wheras he liveth in blisse and in solas.> *comfort*
 Who coudė telle, but> he had wedded be, *unless*

Pacience . . . seyn a glance at the Clerk's Tale of the patient Griselda, with overtones from the Bible (Proverbs 16:32; James 1:4), and at such collections of moral precepts for schools as the *Distichs of Cato* (see the Miller's Tale, l. 119)
Lerneth . . . noon learn to bear things, or else, as true as I walk, you will have to learn it, whether you want to or not
constellacioun the combination of the planets, at any given time, was thought to influence every aspect of earthly life
defaute anything lacking
servant . . . lord The knight's love is better than love within the courtly conventions, for he has the best of both worlds, his mistress also being his wife.
Penmark Penmarc'h just south of Brest, in Brittany; its headland, like much of the coast of Brittany, has a rocky shore, with a chain of granite rocks out to sea. Chaucer may have seen the place or heard it described, since the rocks of Brittany were proverbial, and lay on a much-used trade route.

The joye, the ese, and the prosperitee
That is bitwixe an housbonde and his wyf?
A yeer and more lasted his blisful lyf,
Til that the knight of which I speke of thus,
That of Kayrrud° was cleped> Arveragus,° — *called*
Shoop> him to goon, and dwelle a yeer or tweyne> — *arranged / two*
In Engėlond, that cleped was eek> Briteyne,° — *also*
To seeke in armės worship and honour;
For al his lust> he sette in swich labour; — *pleasure*
And dwellėd ther two yeer, the book seith thus.
  Now wol I stinte> of this Arveragus, — *cease*
And speken I wole of Dorigene° his wyf,
That loveth hir housbonde as hir hertės lyf.
For his absence wepeth she and syketh,> — *sighs*
As doon thise noble wyvės° whan hem lyketh.> — *it pleases*
She moorneth,> waketh, waileth, fasteth, pleyneth;> — *mourns / complains*
Desyr of his presènce hir so distreyneth,> — *constrains*
That al this wydė world she sette> at noght. — *valued*
Hir frendės, whiche that knewe hir hevy thoght,
Conforten hir in al that ever they may;
They prechen hir, they telle hir night and day,
That causėlees she sleeth> hirself, allas! — *is killing*
And every confort possible in this cas
They doon to hir with al hir bisinesse,> — *diligence*
Al for to make hir leve hir hevinesse.
  By proces,> as ye knowen everichoon,> — *gradually / everyone*
Men may so longė graven> in a stoon,° — *engrave*
Til som figùre therinne emprented> be. — *imprinted*
So longe han they confòrted hir, til she
Receyvėd hath, by hope and by resoùn,> — *reason*
The emprenting of hir consolacioùn,
Thurgh which hir gretė sorwe gan aswage;> — *diminish*
She may nat alwey duren> in swich rage.> — *endure / great grief*
  And eek Arveragus, in al this care,> — *sorrow*
Hath sent hir lettres hoom of his welfare,
And that he wol come hastily> agayn; — *soon*
Or ellės hadde this sorwe hir hertė slayn.
  Hir freendės sawe hir sorwe gan to slake,> — *slacken*
And preyėde hir on knees, for Goddės sake,

Kayrrud A Celtic name, *kaer* is a fortified place; *rud* may mean red. The name does not occur near Penmarc'h.
Arveragus Latinized form of a Celtic name; Chaucer may have taken it from Geoffrey of Monmouth's 12th-century chronicle (*Historia Regum Britanniae*), where the name of Aurelius also occurs. Some scholars have suggested that Chaucer found the idea for this tale in the chronicle, but the evidence is inconclusive.
Briteyne See l. 21.
Dorigene a Breton name
For . . . wyves The Squire had already told a story involving a wife's grief at separation, reinforcing some remarks in the tale of his father, the Knight.
graven . . . stoon Chaucer refines the image which he probably found in Boccaccio. Constant dripping wears away a stone, as Boccaccio says, but in this courtly context the patience and delicacy needed by the gem-engraver are paralleled by the same qualities in Dorigen's friends when they try to console her. This is the atmosphere of the poem.

To come and romen˃ hir in companye, *go about*
Awey to dryve hir derkė fantasye.˃ *gloomy imaginings*
And finally, she graunted that requeste;
For wel she saugh˃ that it was for the beste. *saw*
  Now stood hir castel fastė by the see,
And often with hir freendės walketh she
Hir to disporte upon the bank on heigh,
Wheras she many a ship and bargė seigh.˃ *saw*
Seilinge˃ hir cours, wheras hem listė˃ go; *sailing / it pleased*
But than was that a parcel˃ of hir wo. *part*
For to hirself ful ofte 'Allas!' seith she,
'Is ther no ship, of so manye as I see,
Wol bringen hom my lord? than were myn herte
Al warisshed˃ of his bittre peynės smerte.˃' *cured / sharp*
  Another tyme ther wolde she sitte and thinke,
And caste hir eyen dounward fro the brinke.
But whan she saugh the grisly rokkės blake,°
For verray fere so wolde hir hertė quake,
That on hir feet she mighte hir noght sustene.˃ *sustain*
Than wolde she sitte adoun upon the grene,
And pitously˃ into the see biholde, *pitifully*
And seyn˃ right thus, with sorweful sykės˃ colde: *say / sighs*
  'Eternė God, that thurgh thy purveyaùnce˃ *foreknowledge*
Ledest the world by certein governaùnce,
In ydel,˃ as men seyn, ye nothing make; *vain*
But, Lord, thise grisly feendly˃ rokkės blake, *hostile*
That semen rather a foul confusioùn
Of werk than any fair creacioùn
Of swich a parfit wys God and a stable,˃ *sure*
Why han ye wroght this werk unresonable?
For by this werk, south, north, ne west, ne eest,
Ther nis yfostrėd˃ man, ne brid,˃ ne beest; *helped / bird*
It dooth no good, to my wit,˃ but anoyeth.˃ *knowledge / harms*
See ye nat, Lord, how mankinde it destroyeth?
An hundred thousand bodies of mankinde
Han rokkės slayn, al be they nat in minde,˃ *remembered*
Which mankinde is so fair part of thy werk
That thou it madest lyk to thyn owene merk.°
Than semėd it ye hadde a greet chiertee˃ *love*
Toward mankinde; but how than may it be
That ye swiche menės˃ make, it to destroyen, *means*

rokkes blake Black rocks; Dorigen's meditation, in her sorrow at being parted from Arveragus, with its accumulation of evil and hellishness as she looks at the rocks, is on the theme of how a good Creator could bring himself to create sorrow, evil, and misshapenness. He must have known what He was about, since He has "purveyaunce" (l. 157): foreknowledge, providence. Boethius (born *c.*480 A.D.) explains this in *The Consolation of Philosophy.* The godhead, perfect and single, is outside all His creation, though it is He who keeps all creation in being. Everything, even the causes of things, have true existence only within God's mind and as far as they are part of the plan of the universe which is in His mind and is called Providence. See Romans 8:28ff.

merk Likeness, image (Genesis 1:27: "So God created man in his own image"). *Merk* originally meant the image or likeness on a coin.

Which menės do no good, but ever anoyen?> *hurt*
I woot wel clerkes wol seÿn, as hem leste,> *it pleases*
By arguments,° that al is for the beste,
Though I ne can the causes nat yknowe.
But thilkė God, that madė wind to blowe,
As kepe my lord!° this my conclusioùn;
To clerkės lete> I al disputisoùn.> *leave / dispute*
But woldė God that alle thise rokkės blake
Were sonken> into Hellė for his sake! *sunken*
Thise rokkės sleen myn hertė for the fere.>' *fear*
Thus wolde she seyn, with many a pitous tere.
 Hir freendės sawe that it was no disport> *pleasure*
To romen> by the see, but disconfòrt; *walk*
And shopen> for to pleyen> somwher elles. *arranged / amuse themselves*
They leden hir by riverės and by welles,> *pools*
And eek in otherė places delitables;> *pleasant*
They dauncen, and they pleyen at ches and tables.°
 So on a> day, right in the morwė> tyde, *one / morning*
Unto a gardin that was ther bisyde,
In which that they had maad hir ordinaùnce> *orders*
Of vitaille> and of other purveyaùnce,> *food / prearrangements*
They goon and pleye hem al the longė day.
And this was on the sixtė morwe of May,°
Which May had peynted with his softė shoures
This gardin° ful of levės and of floures;
And craft of mannės hand so curiously> *ingeniously*
Arrayėd> hadde this gardin, trewėly, *laid out*
That never was ther gardin of swich prys,> *excellence*
But if> it were the verray Paradys. *unless*
The odour of flourės and the fresshė sighte
Wolde han maad any hertė for to lighte> *lighten*
That ever was born, but if too gret siknesse,
Or too gret sorwe helde it in distresse;
So ful it was of beautee with plesaunce.
At after diner gonnė> they to daunce, *began*
And singe also, save Dorigen allone,
Which made alwey hir còmpleint and hir mone;> *moan*

arguments Arguments, causes, conclusions are all terms in Scholastic logic: a mild bit of sarcasm by Dorigen on "explainers."
But . . . lord but may that same God as made winds blow, preserve my master
ches . . . tables chess and backgammon; the latter a board game, played by two opponents with dice and "men"
sixte . . . May The sixth morning of May. Two or three days in each month were marked as "evil" or "Egyptian" (because of God's plagues on Egypt) days in medieval calendars. May 6 is sometimes one. On such a day it was thought especially dangerous to fall ill or begin anything in which one hoped to be successful. See Nun's Priest's Tale, l. 424.
gardin The garden setting is meant to recall, with a hint of coming disaster, the exemplar of all gardens, the Garden of Eden, where Adam and Eve, our first parents, were said to have spent only one brief hour, before the first sin and their expulsion (Fig. 56). Medieval literature teems with descriptions of such lovely spots *(loci amoeni)*, especially in a love context: they give solace for pain physical, mental, and spiritual. Chaucer's description may have been borrowed from the French of Guillaume de Machaut (*c.* 1300–1377); it balances the description of the rocks, above.

For she ne saugh him on the dauncė go,
That was hir housbonde and hir love also.
But nathėlees she moste a tyme abyde,
And with good hopė lete hir sorwe slyde.
  Upon this daunce, amongės othere men,
Dauncėd a squyer° biforen Dorigen,
That fressher> was and jolyer of array, *handsomer*
As to my doom,> than is the monthe of May.° *judgment*
He singeth, daunceth, passinge> any man *surpassing*
That is, or was, sith> that the world bigan. *since*
Therwith he was, if men sholde him discryve,> *describe*
Oon of the bestė faringe> man on lyve; *most handsome*
Yong, strong, right vertuous,> and riche and wys, *accomplished*
And wel biloved, and holden in gret prys.> *esteem*
And shortly, if the sothe> I tellen shal, *truth*
Unwiting> of this Dorigen at al, *unknown*
This lusty squyer, servant to Venus,°
Which that yclepėd> was Aurelius, *called*
Had loved hir best of any creatùre
Two yeer and more, as was his aventùre,> *fortune*
But never dorste he telle hir his grevaùnce;> *distress*
Withouten coppe he drank al his penaùnce.°
He was despeyrėd, nothing dorste he seye,
Save in his songės somwhat wolde he wreye> *dissemble*
His wo, as in a general compleyning;
He seyde he loved, and was biloved nothing.
Of swich materė made he manye layes,
Songės, compleintės, roundels, virėlayes,°
How that he dorstė nat his sorwe telle,
But languissheth, as a Furie° dooth in Helle;
And die he moste, he seyde, as dide Ekko°
For Narcisus, that dorste nat telle hir wo.
In other manere than ye here> me seye, *hear*
Ne dorste he nat to hir his wo biwreye;> *reveal*
Save that, paràventure,> somtyme at daunces, *by chance*
Ther yongė folk kepen hir observaùnces,

squyer The squire has a Romano-British name (Aurelius) to suggest the long ago; and may be intended to recall Chaucer's Squire.
That fressher . . . May conventional description of a young man; in medieval calendars May is sometimes shown as a brightly dressed squire on horseback
Venus goddess of love
Withouten . . . penaunce perhaps "without measure he took his medicine" (*coppe*-cup); or "under difficulties"; or "he drank his penance eagerly"; i.e. scooping it up with his hands instead of using a cup—a reference to the contraries of love
layes . . . virelayes All these are varieties of the short lyrical love-song, of which the complaint could also deal with religious love. Lays and songs are general terms, meaning the same thing in this context: "lay" is not used in the technical sense of l. 2. The complaint bewails lack of success in love; see Chaucer's satirical *Complaint to His Purse* below. It was a French genre, like the roundel (rondeau) and virelay (see Glossary).
Furie The three Furies were daughters of Pluto, king of the underworld, who pursued evil-doers: always in pain themselves (*languissheth*), because in hell; see Skelton, *Philip Sparrow,* l. 74, below.
Ekko The nymph Echo loved Narcissus, who preferred his own reflected self to her. She took to the woods and pined away for grief, until there was nothing left of her but her voice (Fig. 54).

It may wel be he lokėd on hir face
In swich a wyse, as man that asketh grace;
But nothing wistė> she of his entente. — *knew*
Nathėlees, it happėd, er> they thennės wente, — *before*
Bycausė that he was hir neighėbour,
And was a man of worship and honour,
And hadde yknowen him of tymė yore,°
They fille in> speche; and forth more and more — *fell into*
Unto his purpose drough> Aurelius, — *moved*
And whan he saugh his tyme, he seydė thus:
'Madame,' quod he, 'by God that this world made,
So> that I wiste it mighte your hertė glade,> — *if / delight*
I wolde, that day that your Arveragus
Wente over the see, that I, Aurelius,
Had went ther> never I sholde have come agayn; — *gone where*
For wel I woot> my service is in vayn. — *know*
My guerdon> is but bresting> of myn herte; — *reward / breaking*
Madame, reweth> upon my peynės smerte;> — *have pity / sharp*
For with a word ye may me sleen> or save, — *slay*
Heer at your feet God wolde that I were grave!> — *buried*
I ne have as now no leyser> more to seye; — *leisure*
Have mercy, swete, or ye wol do> me deye>!' — *make / die*
She gan to loke upon Aurelius:
'Is this your wil,' quod she, 'and sey ye thus?
Never erst,'> quod she, 'ne wiste I what ye mente. — *before*
But now, Aurelie, I knowe your entente,
By thilkė God that yaf> me soule and lyf, — *gave*
Ne shal I never been untrewė wyf
In word ne werk,> as far as I have wit: — *deed*
I wol ben his to whom that I am knit;
Tak this for fynal answer as of me.'
But after that in pley> thus seydė she: — *jest*
'Aurelie,' quod she, 'by heighė God above,
Yet wolde I grauntė yow to been your love,
Sin I yow see so pitously complayne;
Loke what day that, endėlong> Britayne, — *all along*
Ye remove alle the rokkės, stoon by stoon,°
That they ne lettė> ship ne boot> to goon: — *hinder / boat*
I seye, whan ye han maad the coost> so clene — *coast*
Of rokkės, that ther nis no stoon ysene,
Than wol I love yow best of any man,
Have heer my trouthe,> in al that ever I can.' — *word*
'Is ther non other grace in yow?' quod he.
'No, by that Lord,' quod she, 'that makėd me!

And hadde . . . yore and she had known him for some time past
stoon by stoon Every one. Dorigen's condition is an extravagant parody (to emphasize her love for Arveragus) of the tasks that heroines of the romance would lay on their lovers; but with the connotation "sooner shall you move these rocks than me."

For wel I woot that it shal never bitydeˆ. — *happen*
Lat swiche foliės out of your hertė slyde.
What deynteeˆ sholde a man han in his lyf — *pleasure*
For to go love another mannės wyf,
That hath hir body whan so that him lyketh?'
  Aurelius ful oftė sorė sykethˆ; — *sighs*
Wo was Aureliė, whan that he this herde,
And with a sorweful herte he thus answerde:
  'Madame,' quod he, 'this were an inpossìbleˆ! — *impossibility*
Than moot I dye of sodeinˆ deth horrìble.' — *sudden*
And with that word he turnėd him anoonˆ. — *at once*
Tho come hir othere freendės many oon,
And in the aleyes romedenˆ up and doun, — *paths walked*
And nothing wiste of this conclusioùn,
But sodeinly bigonnė revelˆ newe — *began diversion*
Til that the brightė sonnė loste his heweˆ; — *color*
For th'orisonteˆ hath reftˆ the sonne his light; — *the horizon / taken*
(This is as muche to seye as it was night).
And hoom they goon in joye and in solas,
Save only wrecche Aurelius, allas!
He to his hous is goon with sorweful herte;
He seeth he may nat fro his deeth asterteˆ. — *escape*
Him semėd that he felte his hertė colde;
Up to the hevene his handės he gan holde,
And on his knowėsˆ bare he setteˆ him doun, — *knees / put*
And in his ravingˆ seyde his orisoùnˆ. — *delirium / prayer*
For verray wo out of his witˆ he breydeˆ. — *mind / went*
He nistėˆ what he spak, but thus he seyde; — *knew not*
With pitousˆ herte his pleynt hath he bigonne — *sad*
Unto the goddes, and first unto the sonne:
  He seyde, 'Appollo,° god and governour
Of every plauntė, herbė, tree and flour,
That yevestˆ, after thy declinacioùn,° — *gives*
To ech of hem his tyme and his sesoùn,
As thyn herberwėˆ chaungeth lowe or hye; — *position*
Lord Phebus, cast thy merciableˆ yë — *merciful*
On wrecche Aurelie, which that am but lornˆ. — *lost*
Lo, lord! my lady hath my deeth ysworn
Withoutė gilt,° but thy benignitee
Upon my dedlyˆ herte have som pitee! — *doomed*
For wel I wootˆ, lord Phebus, if yow lest, — *know*
Ye may me helpen, save my lady, best.°
Now voucheth saufˆ that I may yow devyseˆ — *grant / show*
How that I may been holpeˆ and in what wyse. — *helped*

Appollo Apollo (Phoebus), god of light, the sun
after thy declinacioùn according to your celestial latitude or seasonal position in the sky; *herberwe* (l. 327) is literally lodging

Withoute gilt i.e. when I am innocent
Ye may . . . best you can be my best helper of anyone, except my lady

Your blisful suster, Lucina° the shene,˃ — *shining*
That of the see is chief goddesse and quene,
Though Neptunus° have deitee in the see,
Yet emperesse aboven him is she:
Ye knowen wel, lord, that right as hir desyr
Is to be quiked˃ and lightned of your fyr,˃ — *enlivened / fire*
For which she folweth yow ful bisily,˃ — *assiduously*
Right so the see desyreth naturelly
To folwen hir, as she that is goddesse
Bothe in the see and riveres more and lesse.
Wherfore, lord Phebus, this is my requeste—
Do this miracle, or do myn hertė breste—
That now, next at this opposicioùn,°
Which in the signe shal be of the Leoùn,°
As preyeth hir so greet a flood to bringe,
That fyve fadme˃ at the leeste it overspringe˃ — *fathoms / rise above*
The hyeste rokke in Armorik Briteyne;
And lat this flood endurė yerės tweyne;
Than certės to my lady may I seye:
"Holdeth˃ your heste,˃ the rokkės been aweye." — *keep / promise*
Lord Phebus, dooth this miracle for me;
Preye hir she go no faster cours than ye;°
I seye, preyeth your suster that she go
No faster cours than ye thise yerės two.
Than shal she been evene attė fulle alway,
And spring-flood˃ lastė bothė night and day. — *spring-tide*
And, but˃ she vouchėsauf˃ in swiche manere — *unless / grant*
To grauntė me my sovereyn lady dere,
Prey hir to sinken every rok adoun
Into hir owene derkė regioùn
Under the ground, ther Pluto° dwelleth inne,
Or nevermo shal I my lady winne.
Thy temple in Delphos° wol I barefoot seke;
Lord Phebus, see the terės on my cheke,
And of my peyne have som compassioùn.'
And with that word in swowne˃ he fil adoun, — *swoon*

Lucina I.e. the triple goddess of the universe, manifesting herself as Luna (the moon) in the skies; Diana on earth; Proserpina (Hecate) in the underworld. He means the moon, who governs the tides of the sea and depends upon the sun for her light. The sun is to use his influence with the moon to bring a lasting spring tide, and cover the rocks. Lucina was that manifestation of the goddess who presided over childbirth.
Neptunus Neptune, god of the sea
opposicioun i.e. 180° apart, at full moon, when the influence of sun and moon reinforce each other to bring about the spring tides, and the water is higher than normal at both rise and ebb
Leoun The sun's power is greatest when it is in the zodiacal sign of Leo, the Lion, because that is its own mansion or house. But the sun was, on May 6, in Taurus, the Bull; and Aurelius is ready to wait until July for his miracle, which will be most effective because the sun will be in Leo and the moon in opposition in Aquarius, the Water-carrier, an appropriate sign for a flood.
Lord . . . ye The sun is being asked to slow the moon's pace (28-day orbit) to his own (1-year orbit) for two years, so that their oppositions will continue and the tide remain at flood all that time.
Pluto god of the underworld, husband of Proserpina-Luna
Delphos Delphi, in a valley of Mt. Parnassus, the chief shrine of Apollo and the seat of the most famous ancient oracle; Aurelius vows to make a barefoot pilgrimage there.

And longė tyme he lay forth> in a traunce. *continually*
His brother, which that knew of his penaunce,> *pain*
Up caughte him and to bedde he hath him broght.
Dispeyrèd> in this torment and this thoght *despairing*
Lete> I this woful creätùrė lye; *let*
Chese he, for me, whether he wol live or dye.°
Arveragus, with hele> and greet honour, *prosperity*
As he that was of chivalrye the flour,
Is comen hoom, and othere worthy men.
O blisful artow> now, thou Dorigen, *art thou*
That hast thy lusty housbonde in thyne armes,
The fresshė knight, the worthy man of armes,
That loveth thee, as his owene hertẹs lyf.
Nothing list him to been imaginatyf> *suspicious*
If any wight had spoke, whyl he was oute,> *abroad*
To hire of love; he hadde of it no doute.
He noght entendeth> to no swich matere, *attends*
But daunceth, justeth,> maketh hir good chere; *jousts*
And thus in joye and blisse I lete hem dwelle,
And of the syke> Aurelius wol I telle. *sick*
In langour and in torment furious
Two yeer and more lay wrecche Aurelius,
Er any foot he mighte on erthė goon;
Ne confort in this tymė hadde he noon,
Save of his brother, which that was a clerk;> *learned man*
He knew of al this wo and al this werk.
For to non other creätùre certeyn
Of this matère he dorstė no word seyn.
Under his brest he bar it more secree> *secret*
Than ever dide Pamphilus° for Galathee.
His brest was hool,> withoutė for to sene, *whole*
But in his herte ay> was the arwe> kene. *ever / arrow*
And wel ye knowe that of a sursanure°
In surgerye is perilous the cure,
But> men mighte touche the arwe, or come therby. *unless*
His brother weep and waylėd privėly,
Til attė laste him fil in remembraunce,
That whyl he was at Orliens° in Fraunce,
As yongė clerkės, that been likerous> *eager*

Chese . . . dye let him choose, as far I am concerned, whether he live or die
Pamphilus One of the catalogue of famous and unfortunate lovers. The name is a corruption of Polyphemus, the Sicilian Cyclops who loved and was rejected by the nymph Galatea. Pamphilus himself is the timid hero of the medieval Latin comic poem *Pamphilus de Amore,* who cannot make his girl without personal instruction from Venus and the help of a madam.
sursanure a wound healed only on the outside, with the cause of the wound (arrow) sealed inside and causing suppuration. Chaucer has enlarged a hint from *Pamphilus de Amore.*
Orliens The schools of Orleans, in France, had been famous since perhaps the 6th century; the University was founded in the early 13th century. Its reputation for learning, especially in the law, fostered the legend that some had acquired magical knowledge by deep study there. The equation, learned men/philosophers = magicians/alchemists, was easily made in the Middle Ages and later—see l. 853. With Orleans and its magicians, compare Oxford and Roger ("Friar") Bacon, or Wittenberg and Dr. Faustus.

To reden artės that been curious,°
Seken in every halke and every herne
Particuler sciènces for to lerne,°
He him remembred that, upon a day,
At Orliens in studie a book he say> — *saw*
Of magik naturel,° which his felawe,> — *companion*
That was that tyme a bacheler of lawe,
Al> were he ther to lerne another craft,> — *although / profession*
Had privėly° upon his desk ylaft;
Which book spak muchel> of the operacioùns,° — *much*
Touchinge the eighte and twenty mansioùns
That longen to the mone, and swich folye,
As in our dayės is nat worth a flye;
For holy chirchės° feith in our bileve> — *belief*
Ne suffreth noon illusion us to greve.> — *harm*
And whan this book was in his remembraùnce,
Anon for joye his hertė gan to daunce,
And to himself he seydė privėly:> — *privately*
'My brother shal be warisshed> hastily; — *cured*
For I am siker> that ther be sciènces, — *sure*
By whichė men make diverse apparènces
Swiche as thise subtile tregetourės° pleye.
For ofte at festės have I wel herd seye,
That tregetours, withinne an hallė large,
Have maad come in a water and a barge,
And in the hallė rowen up and doun.
Somtyme hath semėd come a grim leoùn;> — *lion*
And somtyme flourės springe as in a mede;
Somtyme a vyne, and grapės whyte and rede;
Somtyme a castel, al of lym and stoon;
And whan hem lykėd, voyded> it anoon. — *emptied*
Thus semėd it to every mannės sighte.
   Now than conclude I thus, that if I mighte
At Orliens som old felawe yfinde,> — *find*
That hadde this monės mansiòns in minde,
Or other magik naturel above,> — *in addition*
He sholde wel make my brother han his love.

artes . . . curious books of instruction that are recondite, or: arts that are occult
Seken . . . lerne seek, in every hiding-place and corner to learn out-of-the-way knowledge
magik naturel See General Prologue, l. 418.
prively i.e. he had left it hidden, so that he would not be known to have it
operacioùns Magical workings concerning the 28 mansions of the moon, one for each day of the lunar month (see Astrology in the Glossary). Moreover, as the nearest planet to earth the moon is the most powerful planetary influence to be manipulated; as possessing the shortest orbit it is the trickiest to manipulate; as the planet of darkness the most obvious for magic. The position of the moon was vital for any astrological purpose.
chirches The church naturally condemned any attempt to alter the course of a nature pre-ordained and created by God, who was the only truth. The truth of astrology could never be more than apparent. Magical operations were permitted, as long as they were natural and not black, but they could only be rational, scientific demonstrations of God's wonders and purposes, not imitations or disturbances of them.
tregetoures Conjurors, illusionists; also used for jugglers, sleight-of-hand entertainers. The brother is unknowingly insulting the noble craft of true magicians, who claim to work on a larger scale.

For with an apparènce a clerk may make
To mannės sighte, that alle the rokkės blake
Of Britaigne weren yvoyded˃ everichon, *swept away*
And shippės by the brinkė comen and gon,
And in swich forme endure a day or two;
Than were my brother warisshed˃ of his wo. *cured*
Than moste she nedės holden hir biheste,
Or ellės he shal shame hir atte leste.'
  What˃ sholde I make a lenger tale of this? *why*
Unto his brotherės bed he comen is,
And swich confort he yaf him for to gon
To Orliens, that he up stirte˃ anon, *jumped*
And on his wey forthward thanne is he fare,˃ *gone*
In hope for to ben lissėd˃ of his care. *cured*
  Whan they were come almost to that citee,
But if˃ it were a two furlong° or three, *all but*
A yong clerk rominge by himself they mette,
Which that in Latin thriftily˃ hem grette, *well*
And after that he seyde a wonder thing:
'I knowe,' quod he, 'the cause of your coming';
And er they ferther any fotė˃ wente, *foot*
He tolde hem al that was in hir entente.
  This Briton˃ clerk him askėd of felawes *Breton*
The whiche that he had knowe in oldė dawes;˃ *days*
And he answerde him that they dede were,
For which he weep ful oftė many a tere.
  Doun of his hors Aurelius lighte˃ anon, *alighted*
And forth with this magicien is he gon
Hoom to his hous, and made hem wel at ese.
Hem lakkėd no vitaìlle that mighte hem plese;
So wel arrayėd hous as there was oon
Aurelius in his lyf saugh never nòon.°
  He shewed him, er he wentė to sopeer,˃ *supper*
Forestės, parkės ful of wildė deer;
Ther saugh he hertės˃ with hir hornės hye, *harts*
The gretteste that ever werė seyn with yë.
He saugh of hem an hondred slayn with houndes,
And somme with arwes blede of bittre woundes.°
He saugh, whan voided˃ were thise wildė deer, *gone*
Thise fauconers˃ upon a fair river,˃ *falconers / river bank*
That with hir hawkės han the heron slayn.
  Tho saugh he knightės jousting in a playn;
And after this, he dide him swich plesaunce,
That he him shewed his lady on a daunce
On which himself he dauncėd, as him thoughte.˃ *it seemed*

furlong one-eighth mile
never noon intensifying double negative: Aurelius never saw such a well-ordered (or: well-supplied) house in his life as that one

He sough . . . woundes he saw a hundred of them killed (after hunting) with dogs; and some bleeding with painful arrow-wounds

And whan this maister, that this magik wroughte,> *did*
Saugh it was tyme, he clapte his handės two,
And farewel! al our revel° was ago.> *gone*
And yet remoeved they never out of the hous,
Whyl they saugh al this sightė merveillous,
But in his studie, theras his bookės be,
They seten stille, and no wight but they three.
  To him this maister callėd his squyèr,
And seyde him thus: 'Is redy our sopèr?
Almost an houre it is, I undertake,> *swear*
Sith I yow bad our soper for to make,
Whan that thise worthy men wenten with me
Into my studie, theras my bookės be.'
  'Sire,' quod this squyer, 'whan it lyketh> yow, *pleases*
It is al redy, though ye wol> right now.' *want it*
'Go we than soupe,' quod he, 'as for the beste;°
This amorous folk somtyme mote> han reste.' *must*
  At after-soper fille they in tretee,> *discussion*
What sommė sholde this maistres guerdon> be, *master's reward*
To remoeven alle the rokkės of Britayne,
And eek from Gerounde° to the mouth of Sayne.
  He made it straunge,> and swoor, so God him save, *difficult*
Lasse than a thousand pound he wolde nat have,
Ne gladly for that somme he wolde nat goon.
  Aurelius, with blisful herte anoon,
Answerdė thus, 'Fy on a thousand pound!
This wydė world, which that men seye is round,°
I wolde it yeve, if I were lord of it.
This bargayn is ful drive,> for we ben knit. *complete*
Ye shal be payėd trewely, by my trouthe!> *word of honor*
But loketh now, for no necligence or slouthe,> *laziness*
Ye tarie> us heer no lenger than to-morwe.' *delay*
'Nay,' quod this clerk, 'have heer my feith to borwe.> *as pledge*
  To bedde is goon Aurelius whan him leste,
And wel ny al that night he hadde his reste;
What for his labour and his hope of blisse,
His woful herte of penaunce hadde a lisse.> *relief*
  Upon the morwe, whan that it was day,
To Britaigne tokė they the rightė> way, *direct*
Aurelius, and this magicien bisyde,
And been descended ther> they wolde abyde; *where*
And this was, as the bokės me remembre,> *tell*
The coldė frosty seson of Decembre.

revel See Prospero, in *The Tempest* IV.i; overall, Chaucer and Shakespeare often say much the same thing about the ennobling power of love.
Go . . . beste let us go sup, said he, it is the best thing

Gerounde the river Gironde, as far south of Penmarc'h as the river Seine is north
world . . . round See *Rosemounde* below and see Fig. 55.

Phebus wex old, and hewėd lyk latoùn,
That in his hotė declinatioùn
Shoon as the burnėd gold with stremės brighte;°
But now in Capricorn adoun he lighte,> *alighted*
Wheras he shoon ful pale, I dar wel seyn.> *say*
The bittre frostės, with the sleet and reyn,
Destroyėd hath the grene in every yerd.> *yard*
Janus sit by the fyr, with double berd,°
And drinketh of his bugle-horn the wyn.
Biforn him stant brawn° of the tuskėd swyn,
And 'Nowel'° cryeth every lusty> man. *jocund*
Aurelius, in al that ever he can,
Doth to his maister chere> and reverence,> *entertainment / respect*
And preyeth him to doon his diligence
To bringen him out of his peynės smerte,
Or with a swerd that he wolde slitte his herte.
This subtil> clerk swich routhe> had of this man, *skilled / pity*
That night and day he spedde> him that> he can, *hastened / as much as*
To wayte> a tyme> of his conclusioùn;° *watch / opportunity*
This is to seye, to make illusioùn,
By swich an apparènce of jogelrye>— *conjuring*
I ne can> no termės of astrologye— *know*
That she and every wight sholde wene> and seye,> *think / say*
That of Britaigne the rokkės were aweye,
Or ellės they were sonken under grounde.
So attė laste he hath his tyme yfounde
To maken his japės and his wrecchednesse°
Of swich a supersticious cursednesse.
His tables Toletanės° forth he broght,

Phebus . . . brighte (ll. 537–39) The sun grew old and latten-colored, he who in his hot position shone, with bright beams, like burnished gold. (For latten, and the same base metal-gold comparison, see the General Prologue, l. 701.) The sun has declined from its highest latitude in Cancer (summer solstice) to its lowest in Capricorn (Figs. 43, 45, winter solstice—December 12 in the 14th century). So Aurelius has had to wait even longer for the miracle he wanted (l. 350).
Janus . . . berd Janus sits by the fire, with his double face (literally, "beard"). Janus, the Roman god of comings-in and goings-out, had two faces, one looking forward, the other back. He gave his name to the month of January and represents the turn of the year.
brawn boar's flesh; a boar was a traditional, prized Christmas dish
'Nowel' A greeting for Christmas, the great feast, lasting from Christmas Day to Twelfth Night. "Nowel" = Latin: *natalis,* birthday. The cry ends this gay, homely little interlude and we return to serious, high-flown magical endeavor.
conclusioun object and end of his "operation"
japes . . . wrecchednesse tricks and wickednesses, so diabolically cursed
Toletanes I.e. of Toledo, in Spain; astronomical tables, for calculating the positions of the heavenly bodies; also called Alfonsine tables, having been made by order of Alfonso X of Castile about 1272. The magician was up-to-date: these were the most accurate available. The pile-up of technical terms reinforces the impression of competence and we are expected to be bullied into respect by its mysteries. *Collect* years show the amount of a planet's motion over more than 20 years; *expans* years over a period of anything less than that. *Rotes* are tables for making astrological propositions; *geres* are paraphernalia; *centre* is part of an astrolabe; *argument* is an astronomical mathematical quantity from which another may be deduced. *Proportioneels convenients* are fitting proportionals, to find planetary movements during part of a year. The eighth sphere was the sphere of the fixed stars. The magician allows for its slow rotation. *Alnath* was in the eighth sphere, at the beginning of the constellation Aries, below the stable Aries in the ninth sphere—the sign of the zodiac—so that the two were out of kilter. The mass of astrological terms goes on—Alnath was also the first mansion of the moon; *face* and *terme* (l. 580) seem to be divisions of the zodiacal sign.

Ful wel corrected, ne ther lakkėd noght,
Neither his collect ne his expans yeres,
Ne his rotės, ne his othere geres,
As been his centres and his arguments,
And his proporcionels convenients
For his equaciòns in every thing.
And, by his eightė spere in his wirking,
He knew ful wel how fer Alnath was shove
Fro the heed of thilkė fixe Aries above
That in the ninthė speere considered is;
Ful subtilly> he calculėd> al this. *skillfully / calculated*
When he had founde his firstė mansioùn,
He knew the remenant> by proporcioùn;> *rest / adjustment*
And knew the arysing of his monė> weel, *moon*
And in whos face, and terme, and every deel;
And knew ful weel the monės mansioùn
Acordaunt> to his operacioùn, *answering*
And knew also his othere observaùnces> *rites*
For swiche illusiouns and swiche meschaunces> *evil doings*
As hethen folk usėd in thilkė dayes;
For which no lenger> makėd he delayes, *longer*
But thurgh his magik, for a wyke or tweye,
It semed that alle the rokkės were aweye.
Aurelius, which that yet despeirėd> is *desperate*
Wher> he shal han his love or fare amis, *whether*
Awaiteth night and day on this miracle;
And whan he knew that ther was noon obstàcle,
That voided were thise rokkės everichon,
Doun to his maistres feet he fil anon,
And seyde, 'I woful wrecche, Aurelius,
Thankė yow, lord, and lady myn Venus,
That me han holpen> fro my carės colde': *helped*
And to the temple his wey forth hath he holde,> *taken*
Wheras he knew he sholde his lady see.
And whan he saugh his tyme, anon right> he, *at once*
With dredful> herte and with ful humble chere,> *fearful / appearance*
Salewėd> hath his sovereyn lady dere: *saluted*
'My rightė lady,' quod this woful man,
'Whom I most drede and love as I best can,
And lothest> were of al this world displese, *most reluctant*
Nere it° that I for yow have swich disese,> *pain*
That I moste dyen> heer at your foot anon, *die*
Noght wolde I telle how me is wo bigon;
But certės outher> moste I dye or pleyne; *either*
Ye slee me giltėlees for verray peyne.
But of my deeth, thogh that ye have no routhe,> *pity*

Nere it were it not

Avyseth˃ yow, er that ye breke your trouthe. — *consider*
Repenteth yow, for thilkė God above,
Er ye me sleen˃ bycause that I yow love. — *slay*
For, madame, wel ye woot˃ what ye han hight;˃ — *know / promised*
Nat that I chalange˃ any thing of right — *claim*
Of yow my sovereyn lady, but your grace;
But in a gardin yond, at swich a place,
Ye woot right wel what ye bihighten˃ me; — *promised*
And in myn hand your trouthė plighten˃ ye — *word gave*
To love me best. God woot, ye seydė so,
Al be that I unworthy be therto.
Madame, I speke it for the honour of yow,
More than to save myn hertės lyf right now:
I have do so as ye comanded me;
And if ye vouchėsauf,˃ ye may go see. — *grant*
Doth as yow list, have your biheste˃ in minde, — *promise*
For quik˃ or deed, right ther ye shul me finde; — *living*
In yow lyth al, to do˃ me live or deye— — *make*
But wel I woot the rokkės been aweye!'
He taketh his leve, and she astonied˃ stood, — *stunned*
In al hir facė nas a drope of blood;
She wendė˃ never han come in swich a trappe: — *expected*
'Allas!' quod she, 'that ever this sholde happe!˃ — *chance*
For wende I never, by possibilitee,
That swich a monstre° or merveille mighte be!
It is agayns the process of natùre':
And hoom she gooth a sorweful creäture.
For verray fere unnethė˃ may she go, — *scarcely*
She wepeth, wailleth, all a day or two,
And swowneth,˃ that it routhė˃ was to see; — *swoons / pity*
But why it was, to no wight toldė she;
For out of toune was goon Arveragus.
But to hirself she spak, and seydė thus,
With facė pale and with ful sorweful chere,
In hir compleynt,° as ye shul after here.
'Allas,' quod she, 'on thee, Fortune,° I pleyne,
That unwar˃ wrappėd hast me in thy cheyne; — *unawares*
Fro which, t'escape, woot I no socoùr˃ — *help*
Save only deeth or ellės dishonoùr;
Oon of thise two bihoveth˃ me to chese.˃ — *it is necessary / choose*
But nathėlees, yet have I lever˃ to lese˃ — *rather / lose*
My lyf than of my body have a shame,
Or knowe myselven fals,˃ or lese my name,˃ — *false / reputation*
And with my deth I may be quit,˃ ywis. — *freed*

monstre unnatural thing
compleynt see l. 239 above
Fortune The Roman goddess, taken over by the Middle Ages to help explain the existence of wrong and injustice in the world; blind and capricious, she offers and takes away her gifts of exterior goods and is not to be trusted (Fig. 41).

Hath ther nat many a noble wyf, er this,
And many a mayde yslayn hirself, allas!
Rather than with hir body doon trespas?
  Yis, certės, lo, thise stories° beren witnesse;
Whan thretty tyraunts,° ful of cursednesse,
Had slayn Phidoun in Athenes, attė feste,> — *at the feast*
They comanded his doghtrės for t'areste,
And bringen hem biforn hem in despyt> — *contempt*
Al naked, to fulfille hir foul delyt,> — *pleasure*
And in hir fadrės> blood they made hem daunce — *fathers'*
Upon the pavement. God yeve hem mischaunce!
For which thise woful maydens, ful of drede,
Rather than they wolde lese hir maydenhede,
They privėly> ben stirt> into a welle, — *stealthily / leaped*
And dreynte> hemselven, as the bokės telle. — *drowned*
  They of Messenė° lete enquere> and seke — *caused to enquire*
Of Lacedomie fifty maydens eke,
On whiche they wolden doon hir lecherye;
But was ther noon of al that companye
That she nas slayn, and with a good entente
Chees> rather for to dyė than assente — *chose*
To be oppressėd> of hir maydenhede. — *raped*
Why sholde I thanne to dyė been in drede?
  Lo, eek, the tiraunt Aristoclides
That loved a mayden, heet> Stimphalides, — *called*
Whan that hir fader slayn was on a night,
Unto Dianės temple goth she right,> — *straight*
And hente> the image in hir handės two, — *took*
Fro which imagė wolde she never go.
No wight ne mighte hir handes of it arace,> — *tear*
Til she was slayn right in the selvė> place. — *same*
Now sith that maydens hadden swich despyt> — *scorn*

stories All these *exempla* of maids, wives, and widows come from the most famous anti-feminist work of the Middle Ages, St. Jerome's late 4th-century treatise *Against Jovinian* (see the Wife of Bath's Prologue, l. 679). Chaucer makes the Franklin use this text as a counterblast to the Wife, who tears from it anything that will support her case for generation; Dorigen is more scrupulous and uses only Jerome's own stories in praise of womanly virtue. Chaucer follows Jerome very closely, but Jerome's versions are often garbled.

tyraunts The Thirty Tyrants began a reign of of terror in Athens when they seized power at the end of the Peloponnesian War (404 B.C.). Pheidon was one of them. The long list that now follows isolates, as *exempla* do, a single trait or incident; these are not intended to be a comment on the character of Aurelius or to cast him in the role of a monster who combines the worst features of all these would-be rapists. It is a list of women who had kept faith.

Messene The men of Messene attempted to rape fifty Spartan virgins; Aristoclides killed Stymphalis for refusing to sleep with him; Hasdrubal's wife (see the Nun's Priest's Tale, l. 597) joined her husband in death when Carthage was taken; Lucretia killed herself after her rape by Tarquinius Sextus; Miletus was sacked by the Gauls; Abradates' wife Panthea killed herself on his corpse; Demotion's daughter died rather than marry another after her fiancé's death; Scedasus' two daughters killed themselves after being raped by two Spartans—and so on, through Nicanor, Nicerates, Alcibiades: Alcestis, who accepted death in place of her husband; Penelope, the wife of Odysseus, who kept herself by tricks from the suitors who laid siege to her in her husband's absence; Laodameia, who joined her husband Protesilaus in the shades when he was killed by Hector at Troy; Portia, wife of Brutus, the conspirator; Artemisia, who built the mausoleum at Halicarnassus for her husband and was honored throughout barbarian lands for it; Teuta, queen of Illyria; Bilia, who was a martyr for her husband; Rhodogone and Valeria, who both refused a second marriage.

To been defouled with mannės foul delyt,
Wel oghte a wyf rather hirselven slee> *slay*
Than be defoulėd, as it thinketh> me. *seems*
What shal I seyn of Hasdrubalės wyf,
That at Cartage birafte> hirself hir lyf> *took*
For whan she saugh that Romayns wan> the toun, *won*
She took hir children alle, and skipte> adoun *jumped*
Into the fyr, and chees rather to dye
Than any Romayn dide hir vileinye.
Hath nat Lucresse yslayn hirself, allas!
At Romė, whannė she oppressėd was
Of Tarquin, for hir thoughte it was a shame
To liven whan she haddė lost hir name?
The sevene maydens of Milesie also
Han slayn hemself, for verray drede and wo,
Rather than folk of Gaule hem sholde oppresse.
Mo than a thousand stories, as I gesse,
Coude I now telle as touchinge this matere.
Whan Habradate was slayn, his wyf so dere
Hirselven slow,> and leet hir blood to glyde> *slew / flow*
In Habradatės woundės depe and wyde,
And seyde, "My body, at the leestė way,
Ther shal no wight defoulen, if I may."> *can help it*
What sholde I mo ensamples heerof sayn,
Sith that so manye han hemselven slayn
Wel rather than they wolde defoulėd be?
I wol conclude, that it is bet> for me *better*
To sleen myself, than been defoulėd thus.
I wol be trewe unto Arveragus,
Or rather sleen myself in som manere,
As dide Democionės doghter dere,> *dear*
Bycause that she wolde nat defoulėd be.
O Cedasus! it is ful greet pitee,
To reden how thy doghtren deyde,> allas! *daughters died*
That slowe hemselven for swich maner cas.> *happening*
As greet a pitee was it, or wel more,
The Theban mayden, that for Nichanore
Hirselven slow,> right for swich maner wo. *slew*
Another Theban mayden dide right so;
For oon of Macedoine hadde hir oppressed,
She with hir deeth hir maydenhede redressed.
What shal I seye of Niceratės wyf,
That for swich cas birafte hirself hir lyf?
How trewe eek was to Alcebiades
His love, that rather for to dyen chees> *chose*
Than for to suffre his body unburied be!
Lo which> a wyf was Alcestė,' quod she. *what*
'What seith Omer of gode> Penalopee? *good*

Al Grecė knoweth of hir chastitee.
Pardee, of Laodomya is writen thus,
That whan at Troye was slayn Protheselaus,
No lenger wolde she live after his day.
The same of noble Porcia telle I may;
Withoutė Brutus coudė she nat live,
To whom she hadde al hool˃ hir hertė yive. *completely*
The parfit˃ wyfhod of Arthemesye *perfect*
Honourėd is thurgh al the Barbarye.
O Teuta, queen! thy wyfly chastitee
To allė wyvės may a mirour be.
The samė thing I seye of Bilia,
Of Rodogone, and eek Valeria.'
Thus pleynėd Dorigene a day or tweye,
Purposinge˃ ever that she woldė deye. *intending*
But nathėlees, upon the thriddė˃ night, *third*
Hom˃ cam Arveragus, this worthy knight, *home*
And askėd hir, why that she weep so sore?
And she gan wepen ever lenger the more.°
'Allas!' quod she, 'that ever was I born!
Thus have I seyd,' quod she, 'thus have I sworn'—
And told him al as ye han herd bifore;
It nedeth nat reherce˃ it yow namore. *tell*
This housbond with glad chere,˃ in freendly wyse, *look*
Answerde and seyde as I shal yow devyse.˃ *tell*
'Is ther oght ellės,˃ Dorigen, but this?' *else*
'Nay, nay,' quod she 'God help me so, as wys
This is to muche, and it were Goddės wille.'°
'Ye, wyf,' quod he, 'lat slepen that is stille;
It may be wel, paràventure,˃ yet to-day. *perhaps*
Ye shul your trouthė holden, by my fay!˃ *faith*
For God so wisly have mercy on me,°
I hadde wel lever ystikėd˃ for to be, *rather stabbed*
For verray love which that I to yow have,
But if ye sholde your trouthė kepe and save.
Trouthe is the hyeste˃ thing that man may kepe.' *highest*
But with that word he brast˃ anon to wepe, *burst*
And seyde, 'I yow forbede, up˃ peyne of deeth,˃ *on / death*
That never, whyl thee lasteth lyf ne breeth,
To no wight tel thou of this aventùre˃— *happening*
As I may best, I wol my wo endure—
Ne make no contenance˃ of hevinesse,˃ *appearance / sadness*
That folk of yow may demen harm˃ or gesse.' *suspect evil*
And forth he cleped˃ a squyer and a mayde: *called*

And she . . . more and she wept more and more, the longer she went on
God help . . . wille God help me, this is too much, even if it is God's will
For God . . . me as surely as God will have mercy on me

'Goth forth anon with Dorigen,' he sayde,
'And bringeth hir to swich a place anon.'
They take hir leve, and on hir wey they gon;
But they ne wistė why she thider wente.
He noldė no wight tellen his entente.
  Paràventure an heep> of yow, ywis,> *lot / indeed*
Wold holden him a lewėd> man in this, *stupid*
That he wol putte his wyf in jupartye;> *jeopardy*
Herkneth the tale, er ye upon hir crye.
She may have bettre fortune than yow semeth;
And whan that ye han herd the talė, demeth.> *judge*
  This squyer, which that highte Aurelius,
On Dorigen that was so amorous,> *in love*
Of aventùrė> happėd hir to mete *chance*
Amidde the toun, right in the quikkest> strete, *busiest*
As she was boun> to goon the wey forthright> *ready / direct*
Toward the gardin theras she had hight.> *promised*
And he was to the gardinward° also;
For wel he spyed, whan she woldė go
Out of hir hous to any maner> place. *kind of*
But thus they mette, of aventure or grace;°
And he saleweth> hir with glad entente,> *salutes / mind*
And askėd of hir whiderward> she wente? *whither*
  And she answerde, half as she were mad,
'Unto the gardin, as myn housbond bad,
My trouthe for to holde, allas! allas!'
  Aurelius gan wondren on this cas,> *chance*
And in his herte had greet compassioùn
Of hir and of hir lamentacioùn,
And of Arveragus, the worthy knight,
That bad hir holden al that she had hight,
So looth> him was his wyf sholde breke hir trouthe; *hateful to*
And in his herte he caughte of this greet routhe,> *compassion*
Consideringe the beste on every syde,
That fro his lust yet were him lever abyde> *rather abstain*
Than doon so heigh a cherlish> wrecchednesse *mean*
Agayns franchyse> and allė gentillesse;> *generosity / courtesy*
For which in fewė wordės seyde he thus:
  'Madame, seyth> to your lord Arveragus, *say*
That sith I see his gretė gentillesse
To yow, and eek I see wel your distresse,
That him were lever han shame (and that were routhe)
Than ye to me sholde brekė thus your trouthe,
I have wel lever ever to suffre wo°

gardinward toward the garden
of . . . grace by chance or (God's) grace—a favorite conventional formula, meaning: however it happened

I have . . . wo I had much rather suffer unhappiness forever

Than I departe> the love bitwix yow two. *part*
I yow relessė,> madame, into your hond *release*
Quit,> every surement> and every bond,° *paid / security*
That ye han maad to me as heerbiforn,> *heretofore*
Sith thilkė tymė which that ye were born.
My trouthe I plighte, I shal yow never repreve> *reproach*
Of no biheste.> And here I take my leve, *promise*
As of the treweste and the bestė wyf
That ever yet I knew in al my lyf.
But every wyf be war of hir biheste,
On Dorigene remembreth attė leste.
Thus can a squyer doon a gentil> dede, *noble*
As well as can a knight, withouten drede.'
  She thonketh him upon hir knees al bare,
And hoom unto hir housbond is she fare,> *gone*
And tolde him al as ye han herd me sayd.> *say*
And be ye siker,> he was so weel apayd, *sure*
That it were inpossìble me to wryte.
  What sholde I lenger> of this cas endyte?> *longer / write*
Arveragus and Dorigene his wyf
In sovereyn> blissė leden forth hir lyf. *supreme*
Never eft ne was ther angre hem bitwene;
He cherisseth hir as though she were a quene;
And she was to him trewe for evermore.
Of thise two folk ye gete of me namore.
  Aurelius, that his cost hath al forlorn,> *lost*
Curseth the tyme that ever he was born:
'Allas,' quod he, 'allas! that I bihighte> *promised*
Of purėd> gold a thousand pound of wighte> *refined / weight*
Unto this philosòphre°! how shal I do?
I see namore but that I am fordo.> *undone*
Myn heritagė moot> I nedės selle, *must*
And been a begger. Heer may I nat dwelle,
And shamen al my kinrede in this place,
But> I of him may getė bettre grace. *unless*
But nathėlees, I wol of him assaye,> *attempt*
At certeyn dayės, yeer by yeer, to paye,
And thankė him of his grete curteisye;
My trouthė wol I kepe, I wol nat lye.'
  With hertė soor> he gooth unto his cofre,> *sore / coffer*
And broghtė gold unto this philosòphre,
The value of fyve hundred pound, I gesse,
And him bisecheth,> of his gentillesse, *begs*
To graunte him dayės of the remenaunt,°

I yow . . . bond legal language: a solemn, formal renunciation, in contractual terms; with puns on the meanings of the words in the terminology of courtly love

philosòphre wise man; often a magician/alchemist (see l. 410)

dayes . . . remenaunt time to pay the rest

And seydė, 'Maister, I dar wel make avaunt,> *boast*
I faillėd never of my trouthe as yit;> *so far*
For sikerly> my dettė shal be quit> *certainly / paid*
Towardės yow, however that I fare
To goon abeggėd> in my kirtle> bare. *begging / tunic*
But woldė ye vouchesauf, upon seurtee,> *surety*
Two yeer or three for to respyten> me, *give respite*
Than were I wel. For ellės moot I selle
Myn heritage; ther is namore to telle.'
  This philosòphre sobrely> answerde, *gravely*
And seyde thus, whan he thisė wordės herde:
'Have I nat holden covenant unto thee?'
'Yes, certės, wel and trewėly,' quod he.
'Hastow nat had thy lady as thee lyketh?'
'No, no,' quod he, and sorwefully he syketh.> *sighs*
'What was the causė? tel me if thou can.'
Aurelius his tale anon bigan,
And tolde him al, as ye han herd bifore;
It nedeth nat to yow reherce> it more. *tell*
  He seide, 'Arveragus, of gentillesse,
Had lever dye in sorwe and in distresse
Than that his wyf were of hir trouthė fals.'
The sorwe of Dorigen he tolde him als,> *also*
How looth hir was to been a wikked wyf,
And that she lever had lost that day hir lyf,
And that hir trouthe she swoor,> thurgh innocence. *swore*
'She never erst herde speke of apparènce;°
That made me han> of hir so greet pitee. *have*
And right as frely> as he sente hir me, *generously*
As frely sente I hir to him ageyn.
This al and som,° ther is namore to seyn.'
  This philosòphre answerde, 'Levė brother,
Everich of yow dide gentilly til> other. *nobly to*
Thou art a squyer, and he is a knight;
But God forbedė, for his blisful might,
But if a clerk coude doon a gentil dede
As wel as any of yow, it is no drede!°
  Sire, I relessė thee thy thousand pound,
As thou right now were cropen out of the ground,°
Ne never er> now ne haddest knowen me. *before*
For sire, I wol nat take a peny of thee
For al my craft,> ne noght for my travaille.> *work / trouble*
Thou hast ypayėd wel for my vitaille.
It is ynogh, and farewel, have good day.'

'She . . . apparence she never before had heard so much as talk of illusions (such as Aurelius had had conjured up)
al and som i.e. everything
But God . . . drede (ll. 902–4) but God forbid, in his blessed power, that a learned man can't do a courteous deed—there's no doubt (he can)
As thou . . . ground as if you'd just come out of a hole in the ground

And took his hors, and forth he gooth his way.
  Lordinges, this question wolde I aske now,
Which was the mostė free,˃ as thinketh yow° *generous*
Now telleth me, er that ye ferther wende.
I can˃ namore, my tale is at an ende. *can say*

Here is ended the Frankeleyns Tale

The Pardoner's Prologue and Tale

Chaucer's portrait of the Pardoner in the General Prologue has prepared us for his Tale, but not fully for either the open cynicism of his behavior or the dark power of his story. His Prologue here, with its direct self-revelation—a technique that Chaucer does not often employ in the *Tales*—is followed by the long, indirect comment of his tale, an impressive demonstration of his abilities to preach upon his favorite theme: "Love of money is the root of evil." In the Epilogue the virtuoso feels that he ought to improve the occasion by attempting to do a little business.

From the General Prologue it is clear that this ecclesiastical fund-raiser is a rogue and a cheat, with his fake relics and pious threats, though Chaucer concedes his ability as a performer in church—an ability to be borne out by his tale. We need no more than Chaucer's description to let us know this; in the General Prologue, he seems to have reserved his most direct picture of villainy for the last, his portrait of the Pardoner. The Pardoner is a born eunuch, whom medieval character psychology made out much worse than a man who had merely been castrated. Eunuchs were, according to the doctrine, always evil-natured, foolish, lustful, and presumptuous, but those who had been born so were much worse; they could be recognized from their lack of beard, long scrawny necks and thin bodies, high voices, and prominent, rolling, lecherous eyes—physical defects indicating defects of character. Inclined to lechery, but unable to fulfill their desires, they are reduced, like the Pardoner in his Prologue, to boasting of them; he openly confesses he is a "ful vicious man" (Fig. 31).

The audience would have been familiar with the activities of this man, both from literature (the figure of Hypocrisy in the *Roman de la Rose* is strongly similar) and from life. Pardoners were already a source of some embarrassment to the Church, which licensed them to sell "pardons" to raise money for church purposes. Unscrupulous pardoners claimed more for their wares than they were authorized to do, and ordinary people believed them. What they were licensed to sell was partial remission of penance for sin, granted by papal authority through a "bull" or written proclamation—that is to say, a man could show his remorse for sin by a charitable contribution instead of by performing some act commanded by his confessor. Gradually, the notion grew up—encouraged by such corrupt practitioners as Chaucer's Pardoner—that exemption from purgatory (the place or state of expiation before admission to heaven) could be so purchased. A pardon was never intended by the Church to grant forgiveness of sins, but ignorant people could be made to believe that it did.

A pardoner was officially appointed and could operate only with the permission of the bishop, who could also license him to preach—a source of much dispute with the friars, who earned part of their livelihood from the same source. In practice, he would often display and sell relics—bodily parts of Christ or the saints or objects associated with them—which were venerated and thought by the simple to give the entree to heaven.

The Pardoner's demonstration of his powers as a preacher is one of the most economical and powerful of *The Canterbury Tales.* It is cast in the form of a set sermon on the desire for money as the root of all evil, opening with a denunciation of the sins of the tavern—drunkenness, gluttony, lechery, blasphemy, and gambling, with the implication that one sin leads to another, that all are related—but reserving his main theme, or *exemplum,* until the audience has been thoroughly drawn into the story (Fig. 38).

The story itself, like many tales that found their way to Europe in the Middle Ages, is Eastern in origin and known in many versions, medieval and modern: it is used by Kipling in his *The King's Ankus.* The irony of it is centered on the fact that three hardened sinners, who have never given a Christian thought to Death, set out in anger and drunkenness to find this murdering creature and kill him. Their ignorance of what they do and what they seek is continually played on; they cannot realize that they are attempting the thing that only Christ and belief in Christ can do, give victory over death and the grave.

The wordes of the Host to the Phisicien and the Pardoner

Oure Hostė gan to swere˃ as he were wood;˃ — *did swear / mad*
'Harrow!°' quod he, 'by naylės and by blood!°
This was a fals cherl and a fals justise.°
As shamful deeth as hertė may devyse
Come to thise juges and hir advocats!
Algate˃ this sely° mayde is slayn, allas! — *anyway*
Allas! to derė boghtė she beautee!
Wherfore I seye al day,˃ as men may see — *always*
That yiftės of Fortùne or of Natùre°
Ben cause of deeth to many a creätùre.
Hire beautee was hire deth, I dar wel sayn.
Allas! so pitously as she was slayn!
Of bothė yiftės that I speke˃ of now — *spoke*
Men han ful oftė morė harm than prow.˃ — *profit*
But trewėly, myn owene maister dere,
This is a pitous talė for to heere.
But nathėlees, passe over, is no fors.˃ — *it is no matter*

Harrow help!; here an expression only of astonishment; see the Miller's Tale, l. 178, and the Nun's Priest's Tale, l. 614
by nayles . . . blood By the nails that held Christ on the cross, and by His blood; or, by God's fingernails; but see l. 365. The Pardoner's Tale will later reprove such oaths.
This . . . justise The Host is referring to the Physician's Tale, which has just been told, of Appius and Virginia. Appius Claudius, the Roman magistrate, wanted the beautiful maiden Virginia as his mistress, and, in a trumped-up law-suit, adjudged her to be the slave of an unscrupulous dependent of his (*cherl:* plebeian, low-born man). Virginia's father killed her on the spot, to preserve her chastity.
sely defenseless, innocent
yiftes . . . Natùre the gifts of Nature are usually youth, beauty, and so on; the gifts of Fortune are wealth and high rank. The distinction is a frequent topos in medieval and Renaissance literature.

I pray to God, so save thy gentil cors,> *body*
And eek thyne urinals and thy jordanes,°
Thyn ypocras,° and eek thy galianes,°
And every boist> ful of thy letuarie;° *box*
God blesse hem, and oure lady Seïnte Marie!
So mot I theen,> thou art a propre man, *as I may thrive*
And lyk a prelat,° by Saïnt Ronyan!°
Seyde I nat wel? I can nat speke in terme;> *technically*
But wel I woot> thou doost> myn herte to erme,° *know / make*
That I almost have caught a cardinacle.°
By corpus bonės!° but> I have triacle,° *unless*
Or elles a draughte of moiste and corny° ale,
Or but I here anon> a mery tale, *quickly*
Myn herte is lost for pitee of this mayde.
Thou bel amy,° thou Pardoner,' he seyde,
'Telle us som myrthe or japės° right anon.'
'It shal be doon,' quod he, 'by Saint Ronyon!
But first,' quod he, 'heere at this alėstake°
I wol bothe drinke, and eten of a cake.'
But right anon thise gentils gonne to crye,
'Nay, lat hym telle us of no ribaudye!> *ribaldry*
Telle us som moral thing, that we may lere> *learn*
Som wit,° and thannė wol we gladly here.'
'I graunte, ywis,'> quod he, 'but I mot thinke *certainly*
Upon som honest> thing while that I drinke.' *a respectable*

urinals . . . jordanes Urinals are glass phials used for collecting urine; jordans are here probably round-bellied glass vessels used when urine was to be diagnosed. Or, jordan may here mean chamber-pot: the Host, in his pride at being able to "speak good," may be either mixing up his terms a bit, or he may be mocking the Physician as a looker into urine-pots.
ypocras corruption of the name of Hippocrates, the founder of Greek medicine. It was red wine mixed with spices and sugar, strained through a cloth, and taken as a pleasant drink after food and as a kind of tonic.
galianes either "medicines" or, perhaps, Galen's works; possibly a blunder of the Host's, but certainly connected with the great Greco-Roman doctor Galen (2nd century A.D.), whose name was usually spelled Galien in the Middle Ages
letuarie electuary: medicine in the form of conserve or paste, to be mixed with syrup or other liquid
prelat church dignitary
Ronyan either St. Ronan or St. Ninian; or there may be a pun on runnion (sexual organ)
erme grieve
cardinacle a confusion between cardiacle (the reading of some manuscripts), i.e. cardiac spasm or pain, and cardinal
By . . . bones a blasphemous oath, an illiterate conflation of God's bones! and Corpus Dei! (God's body!)
triacle the best restorative medicine: *theriakon* was originally a remedy for snake-bite and other poisons, and contained the flesh of the snake that had bit one
moiste and corny fresh, new, and malty
bel amy fair friend
som . . . japes something diverting or some jokes
alestake the pole sticking out at an angle from an alehouse wall, with a green bush or garland on it as a sign that refreshment is available (Fig. 39); *cake:* piece of bread
wit knowledge; something that will improve us mentally and morally

Here folweth The Prologe of the Pardoners Tale

Radix malorum est Cupiditas: Ad Thimotheum, sexto.°

'Lordings,'˃ quod he, 'in chirchės˃ whan I preche,
ladies and gentlemen / churches
I peynė me˃ to han an hauteyn° speche, *take pains*
And ringe it out as round as gooth a belle,
For I can al by rotė˃ that I telle. *know all by heart*
My theme° is alwey oon,˃ and ever was— *one*
Radix malorum est Cupiditas.
First I pronouncė whennės˃ that I come, *whence*
And than my bullės° shewe I, alle and somme.˃ *one and all*
Our ligė lordės seel° on my patente,°
That shewe I first, my body to warente,°
That no man be so bold, ne preest ne clerk,°
Me to destourbe˃ of Cristės holy werk; *hinder*
And after that than telle I forth my tales:°
Bullės of popės and of cardinales,
Of patriarkes, and bishoppės I shewe;
And in Latẏn I speke a wordės fewe,
To saffron˃ with my predicacioùn,˃ *color / preaching*
And for to stire˃ men to devocioùn. *incite*
Than shewe I forth my longė cristal stones,°
Ycrammėd ful of cloutės˃ and of bones; *rags*
Reliks° been they, as wenen˃ they, echoon.˃ *think / each one*
Than have I in latoùn° a sholder-boon
Which that was of an holy Jewės° shepe.
"Good men," seye I, "Tak of my wordės kepe;˃ *heed*
If that this boon˃ be wasshe in any welle,° *bone*
If cow, or calf, or sheep, or oxė swelle
That any worm hath ete, or worm ystonge,°

Radix . . . sexto "The love of money is the root of evil" (I Timothy 6:10)
hauteyn loud; the word has overtones of exaltation, pride
theme Text. The medieval preacher regularly announced his text, made a sort of introduction (pro-theme), then an exposition or dilatation; followed by an *exemplum* or story which would illustrate the theme; next came an application or peroration, in which the lesson was drawn; and then a closing formula. Not all sermons were arranged to such an exact scheme, and these parts tend to run into each other, but most are built around theme, exposition, *exemplum*, and application. The Pardoner's Tale is more directly a sermon than the Nun's Priest's, but both are in the genre.
bulles papal mandates, permitting the sale of indulgences and setting out their benefits; and perhaps also his bishop's confirmations, which he would carry as his credentials
lordes seel i.e. the pope's or bishop's seal on his official license
patente document open for inspection by anyone
warente warrant; to protect against violence from other clergy or their hirelings who might try to stop him by violence
preest ne clerk no member of the clergy whatever
And . . . tales and after that I carry on with my stories
stones glass jars or encasings
Reliks Trade in false relics was both frequent and a regular object of satire.
latoun Base brassy metal; see the General Prologue, l. 701. The sheep's shoulder-blade was mounted in this imitation gold.
Jewes one of the Old Testament patriarchs, who were pastoralists
welle well, pool, or spring
That . . . ystonge That has eaten any worm or any snake has bitten. Diseases of cattle were thought to come from eating worms; see Milton's *Lycidas*, l. 46. Worm in the second half of the clause probably has its older meaning of serpent.

Tak water of that welle, and wash his tonge,
And it is hool anon;> and forthermore, *sound at once*
Of pokkės> and of scabbe, and every sore *pox*
Shal every sheep be hool, that of this welle
Drinketh a draughte. Tak kepe eek> what I telle, *notice also*
If that the good-man,° that the bestės oweth,> *beasts owns*
Wol every wike,> er that the cok him croweth,° *week*
Fastinge, drinken of this welle a draughte,
As thilkė> holy Jewe our eldrės taughte, *the same*
His bestės and his stoor° shal multiplye.
And, sirs, also it heleth> jalousye; *heals*
For, though a man be falle in jalous rage,
Let maken with this water his potage,> *soup*
And never shal he more his wyf mistriste,> *mistrust*
Though he the sooth> of hir defautė wiste;> *truth / infidelity know*
Al had she> taken preestės two or three. *even though she had*
  Heer is a miteyn° eek,> that ye may see. *also*
He that his hond wol> putte in this miteyn, *will*
He shal have multiplying of his greyn,> *grain*
Whan he hath sowen, be it whete> or otes,> *wheat / oats*
So that> he offrė pens, or ellės grotes.° *as long as*
  Good men and wommen, o> thing warne I yow, *one*
If any wight> be in this chirchė now, *person*
That hath doon sinnė horrible, that he
Dar nat,> for shame, of it yshriven be,° *dare not*
Or any womman, be she yong or old,
That hath ymaad hir housbond cokėwold,> *cuckold*
Swich folk shul have no powėr ne no grace
To offren° to my reliks in this place.
And whoso findeth him out of swich> blame, *such*
He wol com up and offre in Goddes name,
And I assoille> him by the auctoritee> *absolve / authority*
Which that by bulle ygraunted was to me."
  By this gaude> have I wonnė, yeer by yeer, *trick*
An hundred mark° sith> I was Pardoner. *since*
I stondė lyk a clerk in my pulpet,
And whan the lewėd peple is doun yset,°
I prechė, so as ye han herd bifore,
And telle an hundred falsė japės> more. *deceptions*
Than peyne I me> to strecchė forth the nekke, *take pains*

good-man worthy man, man of substance
er . . . croweth before cock-crow
stoor property, produce, what he has stored in his barns
miteyn a sower's glove
pens . . . grotes pennies or else groats, i.e. silver coins worth four pennies
yshriven be confess it, be shriven of it
Swich . . . offren such people shall not have the power nor the favor to make offerings in reverence to my relics; unconfessed persons cannot receive the sacraments, or worship at my shrine
mark The mark was worth 13s. 4d., two-thirds of a pound; 100 marks was a large sum, about five times Chaucer's salary from the king; and ten times a schoolmaster's salary.
whan . . . yset when the congregation has sat down; *lewėd:* simple, lay, uneducated. *Yset* may imply that medieval churches had seats for the congregation; but they may well have either brought their own or sat on the floor.

And est and west upon the peple I bekke,> *nod my head*
As doth a dowvė> sitting on a berne.> *dove / barn*
Myn hondės and my tongė goon so yerne.> *eagerly*
That it is joye to see my bisinesse.> *activity*
Of avaryce and of swich cursednesse
Is al my preching, for to make hem free> *open-handed*
To yeve her pens,> and namely> unto me. *money / especially*
For my entente is nat but> for to winne,> *only / gain*
And nothing for correccioùn of sinne.
I rekkė> never, whan that they ben beried,> *care / buried*
Though that her soulės goon a blakėberied!°
For certės, many a predicacioùn
Comth oftetyme of yvel entencioùn;°
Som for plesaunce> of folk and flaterye, *pleasure*
To been avauncėd> by ipocrisye, *promoted*
And som for veyne glorìe,> and som for hate. *vainglory*
For, whan I dar non otherweyes debate,°
Than wol I stinge him with my tongė smerte> *sharply*
In preching, so that he shal nat asterte> *escape*
To been defamėd falsly, if that he
Hath trespased° to my brethren or to me.
For, though I tellė noght his propre> name, *actual*
Men shal wel knowė that it is the same
By signės and by othere circumstances.
Thus quyte> I folk that doon us displesànces;> *repay / annoyances*
Thus spitte I out my venim under hewe> *color*
Of holynesse, to semė holy and trewe.
  But shortly myn entente I wol devyse;> *describe*
I preche of nothing but for coveityse.°
Therfor my theme is yet, and ever was—
  Radix malorum est cupiditas.
Thus can I preche agayn that samė vyce
Which that I use, and that is avaryce.
But, though myself be gilty in that sinne,
Yet can I maken other folk to twinne> *separate*
From avaryce, and sorė to repente.
But that is nat my principal entente.
I prechė nothing> but for coveityse; *not at all*
Of this matere it oughte ynogh suffyse.°
  Than telle I hem ensamples° many oon
Of oldė stories, longė tyme agoon:
For lewėd> peple loven talės olde; *simple*

goon a-blakeberied go blackberrying, wander anywhere, to Hell, for all I care
many . . . entencioùn good preaching often comes from bad intention; i.e. even my badness can be turned to good by Christ; see ll. 173–74
whan . . . debate when I dare attack in no other way
trespased sinned against, injured
I . . . coveityse I preach about nothing except for covetousness
Of . . . suffyse that's enough of that
ensamples *exempla*

Swich thingės can they wel reporte> and holde.> *repeat / remember*
What> trowė> ye, the whylės I may preche, *believe*
And winnė gold and silver for> I teche, *because*
That I wol live in povert wilfully?°
Nay, nay, I thoghte> it never trewėly! *intended*
For I wol preche and begge in sondry londes;
I wol not do no labour with myn hondes,
Ne makė baskettes,° and live therby,
Because I wol nat beggen ydelly.°
I wol non of the apostles counterfete;°
I wol have money, wollė,> chese,> and whete,> *wool / cheese / wheat*
Al were it yeven of the povrest page,°
Or of the povrest widwe in a village,
Al sholde hir children stervė° for famyne.
Nay! I wol drinke licour of the vyne,
And have a joly wenche in every toun.
But herkneth,> lordings, in conclusioùn; *listen*
Your lyking> is that I shal telle a tale. *pleasure*
Now have I dronke a draughte of corny ale;
By God, I hope I shal yow telle a thing
That shal, by resoun, been at> your lyking. *to*
For, though myself be a ful vicious man,
A moral talė° yet I yow telle can,
Which I am wont to prechė, for to winne.> *gain*
Now holde your pees, my tale I wol beginne.'

The Tale

In Flaundres whylom> was a companye *once upon a time*
Of yongė folk, that haunteden> folye, *practiced*
As ryot, hasard, stewės,° and tavernes,
Wheras, with harpės, lutės, and giternes,°
They daunce and pleye at dees> bothe day and night, *dice*
And ete also and drinken over hir might,> *capacity*
Thurgh which they doon the devel sacrifyse
Within that develes temple, in cursed wyse
By superfluitee> abhominàble;° *overindulgence*

wilfully gladly, voluntarily. Glad Poverty, to be content with what one has, is the reply to Fortune.
make baskettes St. Paul the Hermit is said to have made his living thus.
Because . . . ydelly I will not be a beggar in idleness, or without making money—a hit, like the preceding few lines, at the friars, the preaching orders who were his rivals in supporting themselves by charitable contributions
counterfete imitate; i.e. by giving up all to follow Christ, which was the precept on which the Franciscan Order was founded
Al . . . page although it were given by the poorest servant-lad
Al . . . sterve even though her children should die (of famine)
For . . . tale See ll. 121–22.
ryot . . . stewes riotous living, gambling, brothels
giternes kind of guitar
abhominable thus spelled because supposed to mean inhuman

Hir othės> been so grete and so dampnàble,> *oaths / damnable*
That it is grisly for to here hem swere;
Our blissed Lordės body they to-tere,°
Hem thoughtė Jewės rente> him noght ynough; *tore*
And ech of hem at otherės sinnė lough.> *laughed*
And right anon than comen tombesterės°
Fetys> and smale,> and yongė fruytesterės, *well-made / slim*
Singers with harpės, baudės, wafererės,
Whiche been the verray> develės officerės *true*
To kindle and blowe the fyr of lecherye,
That is annexėd unto glotonye;°
The Holy Writ° take I to my witnesse,
That luxurie> is in wyn and dronkenesse. *lechery*
Lo, how that dronken Loth,° unkindely,> *unnaturally*
Lay by his doghtrės two, unwitingly;
So dronke he was, he nistė> what he wroghte. *did not know*
Heròdės, whoso wel the stories soghte,°
Whan he of wyn was replet at his feste,> *feast*
Right at his owenė table he yaf> his heste> *gave / command*
To sleen> the Baptist John ful giltėlees.> *slay / innocent*
Senek° seith eek> a good word doutėlees; *also*
He seith, he can no differencė finde
Bitwix a man that is out of his minde
And a man which that is dronkėlewe,> *drunk*
But that woodnesse, yfallen in a shrewe,°
Persevereth lenger than doth dronkenesse.
O glotonyė, ful of cursednesse,> *evil*
O causė first° of our confusioùn,> *downfall*
O original of our dampnacioùn,> *damnation*
Til Crist had boght> us with his blood agayn! *redeemed*
Lo, how derė,> shortly for to sayn, *dearly*
Aboght> was thilkė> cursed vileinye; *paid for / same*
Corrupt> was al this world for glotonye! *corrupted*
Adam our fader,> and his wyf also, *father*
Fro Paradys to labour and to wo
Were driven for that vyce, it is no drede;> *doubt*
For whyl that Adam fasted, as I rede,°
He was in Paradys; and whan that he

to-tere tear to pieces, by oaths referring to God or Christ's body and limbs (Fig. 40).
tombesteres Dancing girls; *fruytesteres,* fruit sellers; and *wafereres,* cake vendors. But the *tombesteres* may be male tumblers and the *wafereres* male pastry cooks, confectioners; the *baudes*—prostitutes—too can be male or female.
annexed . . . glotonye That is a near neighbor to gluttony. From the first sin in Eden, which combined them, lechery and gluttony are close cousins, not to be separated, as Chaucer says in the Parson's Tale. (See Fig. 39.)
Holy Writ Ephesians 5:18
Loth Lot, who slept with his daughters while drunk (Genesis 19:32 ff.)
Heròdes . . . soghte Herod, whoever looks up the stories properly (see Mark 6:17–29 and Matthew 14:1–11)
Senek Lucius Annaeus Seneca (*c.*4 B.C.–*c.*65 A.D.), Roman Stoic philosopher and dramatist, in his *Moral Letters,* 83:18
But . . . shrewe except that madness, come upon a wicked man
cause first i.e. by Eve's eating the forbidden fruit and giving it to Adam
rede in St. Jerome's *Against Jovinian,* for which see the Wife of Bath's Prologue, l. 681

Eet˃ of the fruyt defended˃ on the tree, — *ate / forbidden*
Anon° he was outcast to wo and peyne.
O glotonye, on thee wel oghte us pleyne!˃ — *cry out*
O, wiste a man˃ how many maladyes — *if only one knew*
Folwen of èxcesse and of glotonyes,
He woldė been the morė mesuràble˃ — *moderate*
Of his dietė, sittinge at his table.
Allas! the shortė throte, the tendrė mouth,°
Maketh that, Est and West, and North and South,
In erthe, in eir,˃ in water men to swinke˃ — *air / toil*
To gete a glotoun deyntee˃ mete and drinke! — *delicious*
Of this matere, o Paul,° wel canstow trete,˃ — *can you write*
'Mete unto wombe, and wombe eek unto mete,
Shal God destroyen bothe,' as Paulus seith.
Allas! a foul thing is it, by my feith,
To seye˃ this word, and fouler is the dede, — *say*
Whan man so drinketh of the whyte and rede,°
That of his throte he maketh his privee,˃ — *privy*
Thurgh thilkė cursėd superfluitee.˃ — *excess*
The apostel° weping seith ful pitously,˃ — *sadly*
'Ther walken many of whiche yow told have I,
I seye it now weping with pitous voys,
That they been enemys of Cristės croys,
Of whiche the ende is deeth, wombe˃ is her god.' — *stomach*
O wombe! O bely! O stinking cod,°
Fulfild˃ of donge˃ and of corrupcioùn! — *filled full / dung*
At either ende of thee foul is the soun.˃ — *sound*
How greet labour and cost is thee to finde!˃ — *provide for*
Thise cokės,° how they stampe,˃ and streyne, and grinde, — *pound*
And turnen substaunce into accident,°
To fulfille al thy likerous° talent!
Out of the hardė bonės knokkė they
The mary,˃ for they castė noght awey — *marrow*
That may go thurgh the golet˃ softe and swote;˃ — *gullet / sweetly*

Anon It was a frequent opinion that Adam and Eve spent only one hour together in Paradise.
shorte . . . mouth little throat and soft mouth; or: the brief pleasure of swallowing—a paraphrase of a passage in St. Jerome's *Against Jovinian*
Paul I Corinthians 6:13 ("Meats for the belly and the belly for meats; but God shall destroy them both")
whyte and rede both kinds of wine
apostel St. Paul, Philippians 3:18 ("For many walk, of whom I have told you often, and now tell you even weeping, that they are the enemies of the cross of Christ: whose end is destruction, whose God is their belly")
cod Bag; more frequently used of the scrotum. The discourse on gluttony is from Pope Innocent III's (1160–1216) *De Contemptu Mundi* (On Despising the World), a tract against earthly pleasures.
cokes The passage on the cooks is a close paraphrase of Innocent III.
substaunce . . . accident This philosophic pun is also in Innocent III. In Aristotelian (and so in Scholastic) philosophy, substance is the permanent, inherent, and essential; accident is the changeable and outward, which can be changed without affecting the substance. In ordinary usage, substance is material; in this case, food. So the cooks change substance (the meat, etc.) into its attributes of flavor, taste, smell, etc., the essential into the non-essential. Chaucer may be glancing at the controversies of his day between the opposing philosophic schools of Realists and Nominalists; or at the alchemists, whose aim was to find a way of changing substance.
likerous greedy, fond of choice food; *talent* [evil] inclination, desire, appetite

Of spicerye,> of leef, and bark, and rote> *spices / root*
Shal been his sauce ymakėd, by delyt> *through pleasure*
To make him yet a newer appetyt.
But certės, he that haunteth swich delyces> *pleasures*
Is deed,> whyl that he liveth in tho> vyces.° *dead / those*
A lecherous thing is wyn, and dronkėnesse°
Is ful of stryving> and of wrecchednesse.> *quarreling / evil*
O dronkė man, disfigured is thy face,
Sour is thy breeth, foul artow> to embrace, *are you*
And thurgh thy dronkė nose semeth the soun> *sound*
As though thou seydest ay> 'Sampsoun, Sampsoun'; *always*
And yet, God wot,> Sampsoun drank never no wyn.° *knows*
Thou fallest, as it were a stikėd swyn;> *stuck pig*
Thy tonge is lost, and al thyn honest cure;°
For dronkenesse is verray sepulture> *true burial*
Of mannės wit and his discrecioùn.
In whom that drinke hath dominacioùn,
He can no conseil° kepe, it is no drede.> *doubt*
Now kepe yow fro the whyte and fro the rede,
And namely> fro the whytė wyn of Lepe,° *especially*
That is to selle> in Fish-strete or in Chepe.° *for sale*
This wyn of Spaynė crepeth subtilly°
In otherė wynės, growing fastė> by, *close*
Of which ther ryseth swich fumositee,°
That whan a man hath dronken draughtės three,
And weneth> that he be at hoom in Chepe, *believes*
He is in Spaynė, right at the toune of Lepe,
Nat at the Rochel, ne at Burdeux toun;
And thannė wol he seye, 'Sampsoun, Sampsoun.'
But herkneth, lordings, o word, I yow praye,
That alle the sovereyn actės,> dar I seye, *supreme deeds*
Of victories in the Oldė Testament,
Thurgh verray God, that is omnipotent,
Were doon in abstinence and in preyère;
Loketh> the Bible, and ther ye may it lere.> *look at / learn*
Loke, Attila,° the gretė conquerour,
Deyde in his sleep, with shame and dishonoùr,

But . . . vyces I Timothy 5:6 ("But she that liveth in pleasure is dead while she liveth"). Quotations from St. Paul, often also used by St. Jerome and Innocent III, are continually interwoven.
dronkenesse Proverbs 20:1 ("Wine is a mocker, strong drink is raging")
Sampsoun . . . wyn Judges 13:4,7; Samson's mother is commanded to drink no wine, and told that her son will be a Nazarite, a sect denying itself wine and strong drink.
cure care for decent behavior, self-respect
conseil secrets, discretion
Lepe a town near Cadiz, Spain, famous for strong wines
Chepe Fish Street and either Eastcheap, near it, or Cheapside; all streets in the City of London, the commercial center
This . . . subtilly a joke about either the mixing of stronger, cheaper Spanish wines with the finer French wines exported from Bordeaux and La Rochelle; or simply selling Spanish wines as French
fumositee See the Nun's Priest's Tale, l. 158.
Attila leader of the Huns—invaders of Italy in the 5th century—who died drunk, of a burst blood vessel, on the last of his many wedding nights

Bledinge ay> at his nose in dronkėnesse; *continually*
A capitayn shoulde live in sobrenesse.
And over> al this, avyseth> yow right wel *above / consider*
What was comaunded unto Lamuel°—
Nat Samuel, but Lamuel, seye I—
Redeth the Bible, and finde it expresly
Of wyn-yeving> to hem that han justyse.° *wine-serving*
Namore of this, for it may wel suffyse.
  And now that I have spoke of glotonye,
Now wol I yow defenden hasardrye.> *forbid gambling*
Hasard is verray moder> of lesinges,> *mother / lies*
And of deceite, and cursed forsweringes,°
Blasphemė of Crist, manslaughtre, and wast> also *waste*
Of catel° and of tyme; and forthermo,
It is repreve> and contrarie of honoùr *reproach*
For to ben holde a commune hasardoùr.> *gambler*
And ever the hyër he is of estaat,> *status*
The more is he holden desolaat.> *abandoned*
If that a prince useth hasardrye,
In allė governaunce and policye
He is, as by commune opinioùn,
Yholde> the lasse in reputacioùn. *considered*
  Stilbon,° that was a wys> embassadoùr, *prudent*
Was sent to Corinthe, in ful greet honoùr,
Fro Lacidomie,> to make hir alliaùnce. *Sparta*
And whan he cam, him happedė, par chaunce,°
That alle the grettest that were of that lond,
Pleyinge attė hasard° he hem fond.
For which, as sone as it mightė be,
He stal him> hoom agayn to his contree, *stole away*
And seyde, 'Ther wol I nat lesė> my name; *lose*
Ne I wol nat take on me so greet defame,> *dishonor*
Yow for to allye unto none hasardoùrs.
Sendeth otherė wyse embassadoùrs;
For, by my trouthe, me were lever> dye, *I had rather*
Than I yow sholde to hasardoùrs allye.
For ye that been so glorious in honoùrs
Shul nat allyen yow with hasardoùrs
As by my will, ne as by my tretee.'> *treaty*
This wyse philosòphre thus seyde he.
  Loke eek> that, to the king Demetrius° *also*

Lamuel Proverbs 31:4–5; Lemuel's mother told him: "It is not for kings to drink wine . . . nor for princes strong drink."
han justyse have judicial power
forsweringes Perjury; the passage is imitated from the Latin *Policraticus*, a mirror for princes by John of Salisbury (*c.*1115–80).
catel chattels, possessions, material wealth
Stilbon This story is also in John of Salisbury, where the ambassador's name is Chilon. Stilbon was a name for the planet Mercury.
him . . . chaunce it happened to him, by chance
hasard here, dice
Demetrius Probably Demetrius Nicator, king of the Parthians, an Ásian people; his story is also in the *Policraticus*. Chaucer may have confused him with another Demetrius, and got the name Stilbon above, from a passage in Seneca, where the two are mentioned together.

The king of Parthės, as the book seith us,
Sente him a paire of dees> of gold in scorn, — *dice*
For he hadde usėd hasard therbiforn;
For which he heeld his glorie or his renoùn
At no value or reputacioùn.
Lordės may finden other maner pley> — *kind of pastime*
Honeste ynough to dryve the day awey.> — *pass the time*
  Now wol I speke of othės> false and grete — *oaths*
A word or two, as oldė bokės trete.
Gret swering is a thing abhominàble,
And false swering is yet more reprevàble.> — *reprehensible*
The heighė God forbad swering at al,
Witnesse on Mathew;° but in special
Of swering seith the holy Jeremye,°
'Thou shalt seye sooth thyn othės, and nat lye,
And swere in dome, and eek in rightwisnesse';
But ydel swering is a cursėdnesse.
Bihold and see, that in the firstė table°
Of heighė Goddės hestės> honurable, — *commandments*
How that the seconde heste of Him is this—
'Tak nat my name in ydel or amis.'
Lo, rather> he forbedeth swich swering — *sooner*
Than homicyde or many a cursed thing;
I seye that, as by ordre, thus it stondeth;
This knoweth that His hestės understondeth,°
How that the second° heste of God is that.
And forther-over,> I wol thee telle al plat,> — *moreover / flat*
That vengeance shal nat parten> from his hous, — *depart*
That of his othes> is too outrageous.° — *oaths*
'By Goddės precious herte, and by his nayles,°
And by the blode of Crist that is in Hayles,°
Seven is my chaunce,> and thyn is cink> and treye;> — *throw / five / three*
By Goddės armės, if thou falsly pleye,
This dagger shal thurghout thyn herte go'—
This fruyt cometh of the bicchėd bonės° two,
Forswering,> irė, falsnesse, homicyde. — *perjury*
Now, for the love of Crist that for us dyde,
Leveth your othės, bothė grete and smale;
But, sirs, now wol I tellė forth my tale.
  Thise ryotourės> three, of whiche I telle, — *revelers*

Mathew Matthew 5:34 ("But I say unto you, swear not at all")
Jeremye Jeremiah 4:2 ("And thou shalt swear: [As] the Lord liveth, in truth, in judgment (*dome*) and in righteousness")
table of the Law, the Ten Commandments, written on two tablets of stone; the first tablet contained the first four, concerning duty toward God
This . . . understondeth this he knows who understandeth his (God's) commandments
second according to the Vulgate; in the English Bible, the third Commandment
outrageous See Ecclesiaticus 23:12.
nayles See above, l. 2; nails of the Cross, often shown with Christ's pierced heart.
Hayles Hailes, an abbey in Gloucestershire, supposed to possess a phial of Christ's blood
bicched bones bitched, or damned, dice

Longe erst er> prymė° rong of any belle, *before*
Were set hem in a taverne for to drinke;
And as they satte, they herde a bellė clinke
Biforn a cors,> was caried to his grave; *corpse*
That oon of hem gan callen° to his knave,> *servant*
'Go bet,'° quod he, 'and axė redily,> *ask promptly*
What cors is this that passeth heer forby;> *nearby*
And look> that thou reporte his namė wel.' *be sure*
'Sir,' quod this boy, 'it nedeth never-a-del.°
It was me told, er ye cam heer, two houres;
He was, pardee,° an old felawe> of youres; *companion*
And sodeynly he was yslayn tonight,> *last night*
For-dronkė,° as he sat on his bench upright;
Ther cam a privee> theef, men clepeth> Deeth, *secret / call*
That in this contree al the peple sleeth,> *slays*
And with his spere° he smoot his herte atwo,> *in two*
And wente his wey withouten wordės mo.
He hath a thousand slayn this pestilence:> *during this plague*
And, maister, er ye come in his presence,
Me thinketh that it werė necessarie
For to be war> of swich an adversarie: *be careful*
Beth redy for to meete him evermore.
Thus taughtė me my dame,> I sey namore.' *mother*
'By saintė Marie,' seyde this taverner,> *innkeeper*
'The child seith sooth, for he hath slayn this yeer,
Henne> over a myle, within a greet village, *hence*
Both man and womman, child and hyne,> and page *farm-laborer*
I trowe> his habitacioùn be there; *believe*
To been avysėd> greet wisdom it were, *forewarned*
Er that he dide a man a dishonoùr.'
'Ye, Goddės armės,' quod this ryotoùr,
'Is it swich peril with him for to meete?
I shal him seke by wey and eek by streete,°
I make avow to Goddės dignė> bones! *worshipful*
Herkneth, felawes, we three been al ones;> *of one mind*
Lat ech of us holde up his hond til> other, *to the*
And ech of us bicomen otherės brother,
And we wol sleen> this falsė traytour Deeth; *slay*
He shal be slayn, which that so many sleeth,
By Goddės dignitee,> er it be night.' *reverence*
Togidres han thise three her trouthės plight,°

pryme some time between 6 a.m. and 9 a.m.; or just after sunrise; see the Miller's Tale, l. 446, and the Nun's Priest's Tale, ll. 412, 431
gan callen did call
bet better, i.e. as fast as you can
it . . . never-a-del it isn't the least bit necessary
pardee indeed (literally, *par Dieu*, by God)
For-dronke blind drunk
spere Death's dart
by wey . . . streete by path and paved road; by highway and byway; everywhere
her . . . plight pledged their words, swearing to be as brothers by blood

To live and dyen ech of hem for other,
As though he were his owene yboren˃ brother. *born*
And up they sterte˃ al dronken, in this rage, *leapt*
And forth they goon towardės that village,
Of which the taverner had spoke biforn,
And many a grisly˃ ooth than han they sworn, *terrible*
And Cristės blessėd body° they to-rente˃— *tore apart*
'Deeth shal be deed,˃ if that they may him hente.'˃ *dead / catch*
  Whan they han goon nat fully half a myle,
Right as they wolde han troden˃ over a style, *stepped*
An old man° and a povrė˃ with hem mette. *poor*
This oldė man ful mekėly hem grette,˃ *greeted*
And seydė thus, 'Now, lordės, God yow see!'˃ *protect*
  The proudest of thise ryotourės three
Answerde agayn, 'What! carl,˃ with sory grace,° *churl*
Why artow˃ al forwrappėd˃ save thy face˃ *are you / completely swathed*
Why livestow so longe in so greet age?'
  This oldė man gan loke in his visàge,
And seydė thus, 'For˃ I ne can nat finde *because*
A man, though that I walkėd into Inde,°
Neither in citee nor in no village,
That woldė chaunge his youthė for myn age;
And therfore moot˃ I han myn agė stille,˃ *must / always*
As longė time as it is Goddės wille.
  Ne deeth, allas! ne wol nat han my lyf;
Thus walke I, lyk a restėlees caityf,˃ *captive*
And on the ground, which is my modrės˃ gate, *mother's*
I knokkė with my staf, bothe erly and late,
And seyė, "Levė˃ moder, leet me in! *dear*
Lo, how I vanish, flesh, and blood, and skin!
Allas! whan shul my bonės been at reste?
Moder, with yow woldė I chaunge˃ my cheste, *exchange*
That in my chambre longė tymė hath be,
Ye! for an heyrė clowt to wrappė me!"°
But yet to me she wol nat do that grace,
For which ful pale and welkėd˃ is my face. *withered*
  But, sirs, to yow it is no curteisye
To speken to an old man vileinye,˃ *roughness*
But˃ he trespasse in worde, or elles in dede. *unless*
In Holy Writ ye may yourself wel rede,°

body See Fig. 40.
old man seemingly Chaucer's invention. In the Italian version there is a hermit, fleeing from Death as the riotors go to meet him.
with . . . grace with wretched looks, or, an imprecation: Devil take it
Inde India, an image of remoteness, the Far East. Chaucer makes his old man a version of the legendary Wandering Jew, Ahasuerus, who was condemned to walk the earth eternally for having refused a resting place to Christ on the road to Calvary. To find death would be for him a release.
Moder . . . me (ll. 448–50) Mother, I should like to exchange with you my chest [earthly possessions], which has long been in my bedroom, even for a hair-cloth to wrap myself in; i.e. he asks Earth to take him, in a common shroud
rede Leviticus 19:32: "Thou shalt rise up before the hoary head."

"Agayns˃ an old man, hoor˃ upon his heed, — *before / white*
Ye sholde aryse"; wherfor I yeve˃ yow reed,˃ — *give / advice*
Ne dooth unto an old man noon harm now,
Namorė than ye wolde men dide to yow
In agė, if that ye so longe abyde;
And God be with yow, wher ye go or ryde.°
I moot go thider as I have to˃ go.' — *where I must*
'Nay, oldė cherl, by God, thou shalt nat so,'
Seydė this other hasardour anon;
'Thou partest nat so lightly,˃ by Saint John! — *easily*
Thou spak right now of thilkė traitour Deeth,
That in this contree alle our frendės sleeth.
Have heer my trouthe,˃ as thou art his aspye,˃ — *word / spy*
Tel wher he is, or thou shalt it abye,˃ — *pay for it*
By God, and by the holy sacrament!°
For soothly thou art oon of his assent,°
To sleen us yongė folk, thou falsė theef!'
'Now, sirs,' quod he, 'if that yow be so leef˃ — *wishful*
To findė Deeth, turne up this crookėd wey,
For in that grove I laft˃ him, by my fey,˃ — *left / faith*
Under a tree, and ther he wol abyde;
Nat for your boost˃ he wol him nothing hyde. — *boasting*
See ye that ook?˃ Right ther ye shul him finde. — *oak*
God savė yow, that boghte agayn˃ mankinde, — *redeemed*
And yow amende!'° Thus seyde this oldė man.
And everich˃ of thise ryotourės ran, — *each*
Til he cam to that tree, and ther they founde
Of florins° fyne of golde ycoynėd rounde
Wel ny an eightė busshels, as hem thoughte.
No lenger thanne after Deeth they soughte,
But ech of hem so glad was of that sighte,
For that the florins been so faire and brighte,
That doun they sette hem by this precious hord.
The worste of hem he spake the firstė word.
'Brethren,' quod he, 'tak kepė what I seye;
My wit is greet, though that I bourde˃ and pleye. — *jest*
This tresor hath Fortune unto us yiven,˃ — *given*
In mirthe and jolitee our lyf to liven,
And lightly˃ as it comth, so wol we spende. — *easily*
Ey! Goddės precious dignitee!˃ who wende˃ — *reverence / expected*
To-day, that we sholde han so fair a grace?
But mighte this gold be cariėd fro this place
Hoom to myn hous, or ellės unto youres—
For wel ye woot that al this gold is oures—

wher . . . ryde whether you walk or ride; an oral formula: whatever you do
sacrament Eucharist
oon . . . assent one of those who accept him; one of his following

And . . . amende bring you to better state
florins originally coined in Florence. In Chaucer's time the English florin, worth 6s. 8d. (one-third of a pound), was relatively new.

Than werė we in heigh felicitee.
But trewėly, by daye it may nat be;
Men woldė seyn that we were thevės stronge,> *violent*
And for our owenė tresor doon us honge.> *have us hanged*
This tresor moste ycariėd be by nighte
As wysly> and as slyly as it mighte. *carefully*
Wherfore I rede> that cut° among us alle *advise*
Be drawe, and lat se wher the cut wol falle;
And he that hath the cut with hertė blythe
Shal rennė> to the toune, and that ful swythe,> *run / quickly*
And bringe us breed and wyn ful privėly.> *secretly*
And two of us shul kepen> subtilly *guard*
This tresor wel; and, if he wol nat tarie,
Whan it is night, we wol this tresor carie
By oon assent,> wheras us thinketh best.' *agreement*
That oon of hem the cut broughte in his fest,> *closed fist*
And bad hem drawe, and loke wher it wol falle;
And it fil> on the yongeste of hem alle; *fell*
And forth toward the toun he wente anon.
And also> sone as that he was gon, *as*
That oon of hem spak thus unto that other,
'Thou knowest wel thou art my swornė brother,
Thy profit wol I tellė thee anon.
Thou woost wel that our felawe is agon;> *gone*
And heer is gold, and that ful greet plentee,
That shal departed> been among us three. *divided*
But nathėles, if I can shape> it so *arrange*
That it departed were among us two,
Hadde I nat doon a freendės torn> to thee?' *turn*
  That other answerde, 'I noot> how that may be; *do not know*
He woot how that the gold is with us tweye,
What shal we doon, what shal we to him seye?'
  'Shal it be conseil?'> seyde the firstė shrewe,> *secret / villain*
'And I shal tellen thee, in wordės fewe,
What we shal doon, and bringe it wel aboute.'
  'I grauntė,' quod that other, 'out of doute,
That, by my trouthe, I wol thee nat biwreye.'> *expose*
  'Now,' quod the firste, 'thou woost wel we be tweye,> *two*
And two of us shul strenger> be than oon. *must stronger*
Look whan that he is set,> and right anoon *seated*
Arys,> as though thou woldest with him pleye; *get up*
And I shal ryve> him thurgh the sydes tweye *pierce*
Whyl that thou strogelest with him as in game,
And with thy dagger look thou do the same;
And than shal al this gold departed be,
My derė freend, bitwixen me and thee;

cut lot; see the General Prologue, l. 837. They draw lots to see who will go to town.

Than may we bothe our lustės> al fulfille, — *desires*
And pleye at dees> right at our owene wille.' — *dice*
And thus acorded> been thise shrewės tweye — *agreed*
To sleen> the thridde, as ye han herd me seye. — *slay*
  This yongest, which that wente unto the toun,
Ful ofte in herte he rolleth up and doun
The beautee of thise florins newe and brighte.
'O Lord!' quod he, 'if so were that I mighte
Have al this tresor to myself allone,
Ther is no man that liveth under the trone> — *throne*
Of God, that sholdė live so mery as I!'
And attė laste the Feend,> our enemy, — *devil*
Putte in his thought that he shold poyson beye,> — *buy*
With which he mightė sleen his felawes tweye;
For why the Feend fond him in swich lyvinge,°
That he had levė> him to sorwe bringe, — *leave*
For this was outrėly> his fulle entente — *utterly*
To sleen hem bothe, and never to repente.
And forth he gooth, no lenger wolde he tarie,
Into the toun, unto a pothecarie,> — *apothecary*
And preyėd him, that he him woldė selle
Som poyson, that he mighte his rattės quelle;> — *kill*
And eek ther was a polcat> in his hawe,> — *polecat / yard*
That, as he seyde, his capouns hadde yslawe,> — *slain*
And fayn> he woldė wreke> him, if he mighte, — *gladly / revenge*
On vermin,° that destroyėd> him by nighte. — *ruined*
  The pothecarie answerde, 'And thou shalt have
A thing that, also> God my soulė save, — *as*
In al this world ther nis no creätùre,
That ete or dronke hath of this confitùre> — *mixture*
Noght but the mountance> of a corn> of whete, — *amount / grain*
That he ne shal his lyf anon forlete;> — *lose*
Ye, sterve> he shal, and that in lassė whyle — *die*
Than thou wolt goon a paas> nat but a myle; — *at walking pace*
This poyson is so strong and violent.'
  This cursed man hath in his hond yhent> — *taken*
This poyson in a box, and sith> he ran — *then*
Into the nextė strete, unto a man,
And borwed of him largė botels three;
And in the two his poyson pourėd he;
The thridde he keptė clenė for his drinke.
For al the night he shoop> him for to swinke> — *intended / toil*
In caryinge of the gold out of that place.
And whan this ryotour, with sory grace,
Had filled with wyn his gretė botels three,

For why . . . lyvinge because the Devil found him in such a state of life that he had leave to bring him to grief. Since God foreordains all, the Devil can only act with His permission.
vermin any reptile or marauding animal

To his felawes agayn repaireth he.
What nedeth it to sermone of it more?
For right as they had cast> his deeth bifore, — *plotted*
Right so they han him slayn, and that anon.
And whan that this was doon, thus spak that oon,
'Now lat us sitte and drinke, and make us merie,
And afterward we wol his body berie.'> — *bury*
And with that word it happėd him, par cas,> — *by chance*
To take the botel ther> the poyson was, — *where*
And drank, and yaf his felawe drinke also,
For which anon they storven> bothė two. — *died*
But, certės, I suppose that Avicen°
Wroot never in no canon, ne in no fen,
Mo wonder signės° of empoisoning
Than hadde thise wrecchės two, er> hir ending. — *before*
Thus ended been thise homicydės two,
And eek the false empoysoner also.

O cursed sinnė,° ful of cursednesse!
O traytours homicyde, o wikkednesse!
O glotonye, luxurie,> and hasardrye! — *lechery*
Thou blasphemoùr of Crist with vileinye
And othės> grete, of usage> and of pryde! — *oaths / habit*
Allas! mankinde, how may it bityde,> — *happen*
That to thy creatoùr which that thee wroghte,> — *made*
And with his precious hertė-blood thee boghte,> — *redeemed*
Thou art so fals and so unkinde,> allas!° — *unnatural*
Now, goode men, God forgeve yow your trespas,
And ware> yow fro the sinne of avaryce. — *guard*
Myn holy pardoun may yow alle waryce,> — *preserve*
So that ye offre nobles° or sterlinges,°
Or ellės silver brochės, sponės, ringes.
Boweth your heed> under this holy bulle! — *head*
Cometh up, ye wyves, offreth of your wolle!> — *wool*
Your name I entre heer in my rolle anon;
Into the blisse of hevene shul ye gon;
I yow assoilė,> by myn heigh power, — *absolve*
Yow that wol offre, as clene and eek as cleer
As ye were born and, lo, sirs, thus I preche.
And Jesu Crist, that is our soulės leche,> — *physician*

Avicen Avicenna (d. 1037), the Arab philosopher and physician, whose *Canon of Medicine,* divided into fens or sections, was a standard textbook and included a section on poisons. Cf. the General Prologue, l. 434.
wonder signes extraordinary symptoms
sinne The Pardoner turns to the application of his *exemplum* and to his *peroration:* exclamation upon the horror of sin, followed by invitation to repent—on the Pardoner's terms.
Allas! mankinde . . . allas (ll. 614–17) an imitation of the Reproach of Christ, part of the Office for the fourth Sunday in Lent and often made into English lyric verse; Christ addresses man from the Cross: "Man, full dearly I have thee bought / How is it that thou lov'st me not? . . ."
nobles gold, valuable coins; see the Miller's Tale, l. 148
sterlinges silver pennies, less valuable, 80 to the noble

So grauntė yow his pardon to receyve;
For that is best; I wol yow nat deceyve.
But sirs, o word forgat I in my tale,
I have relikes and pardon in my male,> *bag*
As faire as any man in Engėlond,
Whiche were me yeven by the popės hond.
If any of yow wol, of devocioùn,
Offren, and han myn absolucioùn,
Cometh forth anon, and kneleth heer adoun,
And mekėly receyveth my pardoùn:
Or ellės, taketh pardon as ye wende,> *go*
Al newe and fresh, at every tounės ende,
So that ye offren alwey newe and newe> *again and again*
Nobles and pens, which that be gode and trewe.°
It is an honour> to everich that is heer, *good thing*
That ye mowe have a suffisant> pardoneer *competent*
T'assoillė yow, in contree as ye ryde,
For aventurės> which that may bityde. *chances*
Peràventure> ther may falle oon or two *perhaps*
Doun of his hors, and breke his nekke atwo.
Look which a seuretee> is it to yow alle *safeguard*
That I am in your felaweship yfalle,
That may assoille yow, bothė more and lasse,°
Whan that the soule shal fro the body passe.
I redė> that our hoste heer shal biginne, *counsel*
For he is most envolupėd> in sinne. *wrapped*
Com forth, sir Hoste, and offre first anon,
And thou shalt kisse the reliks everichon,
Ye, for a grote! unbokel> anon thy purs.' *unbuckle*

'Nay, nay,' quod he, 'than have> I Cristės curs! *would have*
Lat be,' quod he, 'it shal nat be, so theech!> *may I thrive*
Thou woldest make me kissė thyn old breech,> *breeches*
And swere it were a relik of a saint,
Thogh it were with thy fundement depeint!> *stained*
But by the croys which that Saint Eleynė° fond,
I wolde I hadde thy coillons> in myn hond *testicles*
In stede of relikes or of seintuarie;> *reliquary*
Lat cutte hem of, I wol thee helpe hem carie;
Thay shul be shrynėd in an hoggės tord.'> *turd*
This pardoner answerdė nat a word;
So wrooth he was, no word ne wolde he seye.
'Now,' quod our Host, 'I wol no lenger pleye
With thee, ne with noon other angry man.'

Nobles . . . trewe Nobles and pennies, good and not forgeries. The debasement of currency, by forgery and otherwise, was a continual problem.

more and lasse great and small; everybody

Eleyne St. Helena, mother of the Emperor Constantine the Great, and said to have discovered the true Cross

But right anon the worthy Knight bigan,
Whan that he saugh that al the peple lough, *laughed*
'Namore of this, for it is right ynough;
Sir Pardoner, be glad and mery of chere;
And ye, sir Host, that been to me so dere,
I prey yow that ye kisse the Pardoner.°
And Pardoner, I prey thee, drawe thee neer,
And, as we diden, lat us laughe and pleye.'
Anon they kiste, and riden forth hir weye.

Here is ended the Pardoners Tale

Retraction

Heere taketh the makere of this book his leve

Now preye I to hem alle that herkne[1] this litel tretys[2] or rede, that if ther be any thyng in it that liketh[3] hem, that therof they thanken oure Lord Jhesu Crist, of whom procedeth al wit[4] and al goodnesse. And if ther be any thyng that displese hem, I preye hem also that they arrette it to the defaute of myn unkonnynge,[5] and nat to my wyl, that wolde ful fayn have seyd bettre if I hadde had konnynge. For oure book[6] seith, 'Al that is writen is writen for oure doctrine,'[7] and that is myn entente. Wherfore I biseke[8] yow mekely, for the mercy of God, that ye preye for me that Crist have mercy on me and foryeve me my giltes; and namely[9] of my translacions and enditynges[10] of worldly vanitees, the whiche I revoke in my retracciouns: as is the book of Troilus;[11] the book also of Fame;[12] the book of the xxv. Ladies;[13] the book of the Duchesse; the book of Seint Valentynes day of the Parlement of Briddes;[14] the tales of Caunterbury, thilke that sownen into[15] synne; the book of the Leoun;[16] and many another book, if they were in my remembrance, and many

kisse the Pardoner Kissing between men, especially as a sign of peace-making, was normal. The Knight and the Host use the familiar "thou" when addressing the Pardoner, but the more formal "you" with each other.

1. Hear, listen to.
2. Treatise.
3. Pleases.
4. Knowledge.
5. Ascribe it to my defect of lack of skill.
6. The Bible.
7. Romans 15:4; see the Nun's Priest's Tale, l. 675.
8. Beseech.
9. Especially.
10. Verses.
11. *Troilus and Criseyde.*
12. *The House of Fame.*
13. *The Legend of Good Women.*
14. Birds, i.e. *The Parliament of Fowls.*
15. Tend toward.
16. This has not survived and we do not know what it was.

a song and many a leccherous lay; that Crist for his grete mercy foryeve me the synne. But of the translacion of Boece de Consolacione,[17] and othere bookes of legendes of saintes, and omelies,[18] and moralitee, and devocioun, that thanke I oure Lord Jhesu Crist and his blisful[19] Mooder, and alle the saintes of hevene, bisekynge hem that they from hennes forth[20] unto my lyves ende sende me grace to biwayle my giltes, and to studie to the salvacioun of my soule, and graunte me grace of verray penitence, confessioun and satisfaccioun to doon in this present lyf, thurgh the benigne grace of hym that is kyng of kynges and preest over alle preestes, that boghte[21] us with the precious blood of his herte; so that I may been oon of hem at the day of doom[22] that shulle be saved. *Qui cum patre et Spiritu Sancto vivit et regnat Deus per omnia secula.*[23] *Amen.*

Heere is ended the book of the tales of Caunterbury, compiled by Geffrey Chaucer, of whos soule Jhesu Crist have mercy. Amen.

c. 1400

Shorter Poems

In many ways the handful of short poems that Chaucer wrote are the best introduction to his genius and to some of the basic concepts of his world of thought. The metric and the verse forms of all of the short poems are borrowed from French, the concepts that they play with are ultimately French; yet each is individually Chaucerian, with his characteristic witty turn. The first two here given, "Gentilesse" and "Truth," are *balades* on the French model, rhyming stanzas with refrain, seriously exploring the moral virtues of their titles. The roundel from *The Parliament of Fowls* is a "straight" performance, and so is Troilus's song, translated from a sonnet by Petrarch into the French *rime royal* of the long poem from which it is taken. The *balade* from *The Legend of Good Women* is a serious, rhetorical amassing of examples of true ladies, but "To Rosemounde" is a parody of the courtly love lyric, and "The Complaint to His Purse" a turning upside-down of all the values of the courtly code of love, expressed in the strictest and most exact form of the love complaint. "To Adam" is a biting comment on the fallibility of scribes, written as if it were one of those rhyming tags by which manuscript copyists congratulate themselves on the completion of their task.

17. Boethius, *De Consolatione Philosophiae* (Of the Consolation of Philosophy).
18. Homilies.
19. Blessed.
20. Henceforth.
21. Bought, redeemed.
22. Judgment.
23. "Who, with the Father and the Holy Ghost, lives and reigns, God in all eternity"; a doxology, or praise to God, at completion of a prayer or intercession.

Gentilesse°

The firstė stok,° fader˃ of gentilesse— *father*
What man that claymeth gentil for to be
Must followe his trace, and alle his wittės° dresse
Vertu to sewe,˃ and vyces for to flee. *follow*
For unto vertu longeth dignitėe,˃ *belongs rank*
And noght the revers, saufly dar˃ I deme,˃ *safely dare / judge*
Al were he mytre, croune, or diademe.°

This firstė stok was ful of rightwisnesse,˃ *righteousness*
Trewe of his word, sobre, pitous,˃ and free,˃ *merciful / generous*
Clene of his gost,˃ and lovėd besinesse,˃ *pure in spirit / industry*
Ageinst the vyce of slouthe,˃ in honestee;˃ *sloth / righteousness*
And, but˃ his heir love vertu, as dide he, *unless*
He is noght gentil, thogh he richė seme,°
Al were he mytre, croune, or diademe.

Vyce may wel be heir to old richesse;
But ther may no man, as men may wel see,
Bequethe his heir his vertuous noblesse
That is appropred˃ unto no degree, *assigned solely*
But to the firstė fader in magestee,
That maketh him his heyre that can him queme,˃ *please*
Al were he mytre, croune, or diademe.
c. 1385

Truth

Flee fro the prees˃ and dwell with soothfastnesse;˃ *throng / truth*
  Suffice unto thy good, though it be smal;
For hord˃ hath hate, and climbing tikelnesse,˃ *hoarding / insecurity*
  Prees hath envye, and welė blent overal;°
  Savour no more than thee behovė shal.°
    Wirche˃ wel thyself, that other folk canst rede;˃ *act / advise*
    And Trouthė shal delivere, it is no drede.°

Tempest thee not al crokėd to redresse,°
  In trust of hir that turneth as a bal°—

Gentilesse Four important discussions of the sources and nature of *gentilesse* are Boethius, *De Consolatione Philosophiae* III, prose 6 and meter 6; Dante, *Convivio,* tract. 4; the *Roman de la Rose,* ll. 18607–896; and Chaucer's Wife of Bath's Tale, ll. 1109–64.
stok Literally, trunk, stem (of a tree); thus, founder of a family or line of descent. The reference is probably to Christ, the perfection of humanity and the New Adam, i.e. the repairer of the perfect condition of humanity possessed by Adam before the Fall.
Must . . . wittes he must follow in his footsteps and dispose all his wits, i.e. the five senses of sight, hearing, smell, taste, touch
Al . . . diademe even if he should wear miter, crown, or diadem—i.e. should be a prince of the church, a king, or a nobleman
thogh . . . seme though he is outwardly rich
Prees . . . overal the crowd is full of striving, and prosperity blinds one completely
Savour . . . shal taste no more than you ought
And . . . drede And truth shall make you free, there is no fear; see the words of Christ to his disciples, John 8:32: "And ye shall know the truth and the truth shall make you free."
Tempest . . . redresse do not harass yourself to set right all that is not straight
hir . . . bal Fortune, unstable and continually turning. She is sometimes, a little later, shown as sitting on a ball which is balanced on a knife edge.

For grete rest stant˃ in litel bisinesse;˃ *stands / agitation*
And eek be ware to sporne ayen an al;°
Strive not as doth the crokkė with the wal.°
Dauntė˃ thyself, that dauntest otheres dede;˃ *govern / deed*
And Trouthė shal delivere, it is no drede.

That thee is sent, receive in buxumnesse;˃ *with good grace*
The wrestling for this worlde asketh˃ a fal: *asks for*
Here is none home, here nis but wildernesse:
Forth, pilgrim,° forth! Forth, beest,° out of thy stal!˃ *stall*
Know thy countree,˃ look up,° thank God of˃ al. *(heavenly) homeland / for*
Hold the high way and let thy gost˃ thee lede; *spirit*
And Trouthė shal delivere, it is no drede.

Envoy

Therfore, thou Vache,° leve thyn olde wrecchednesse˃ *evil condition*
Unto the world; leve˃ now to be thrall.˃ *cease / slave*
Crye Him mercy° that of His heigh goodnesse
Made thee of nought, and in especial
Draw unto him, and praye in general,
For thee and eek for othere, hevenlich meede.˃ *reward*
And Trouthė shal delivere, it is no drede.
c. 1390

Roundel° *from* The Parliament of Fowls

Now welcome, somer, with thy sunnė softe,˃ *warm*
That hast this wintres wedres overshake˃ *storms shaken off*
And driven away the longė nightės blake!

Saint Valentin,° that art ful hy on-lofte,˃ *aloft*
Thus singen smalė fowlės˃ for thy sake: *birds*
'Now welcome, somer, with thy sunnė softe,
That hast this wintres wedres overshake!'

Wel han they causė for to gladden ofte,°
Sith˃ ech of hem recovered hath his make;˃ *since / mate*
Ful blissful mowe˃ they singė when they wake: *may*
'Now welcome, somer, with thy sunnė softe,

al awl; i.e. be careful not to kick against the pricks (Acts 9:5)
Strive . . . wal Do not contend, or you will be broken, like an earthenware pot against a wall. See the Aesopic fable of the metal and earthen pots.
pilgrim Life as a pilgrimage was an especially popular image in the Middle Ages.
beest Animals, not having reason, could not be expected to behave reasonably, i.e. virtuously. A man who does not behave reasonably reduces himself to the condition of an animal. Chaucer now begins to play with this notion.
look up A quadruped's head hung down, which was held to be a sign of its lack of rationality. If it were rational, it would look up.
Vache you cow (Fr. *vache*), i.e. beast; probably with a pun on the name of Sir Philip de la Vache
Crye . . . mercy Beg mercy of Him; or: thank Him, who fashioned you from nothing
Roundel a short poem, also called a triolet—developed in France—in which the first lines recur as a refrain; see the Franklin's Tale, l. 240
Saint Valentin The traditional association of St. Valentine with courtship has no foundation except that his day, February 14, was a Roman fertility festival at the beginning of spring.
Wel . . . ofte they have good reason to rejoice often

That hast this wintres wedres overshake
And driven away the longė nightės blake!'
1382–83

From Troilus and Criseyde

Book I

CANTUS TROILI°

'If no love is,> O God, what fele I so? *there is*
And if love is, what thing and whiche is he?
If love be good, from whennes> comth my wo? *whence*
If it be wikke,> a wonder thinketh me,° *bad*
When every torment and adversitee
That cometh of him, may to me savory> thinke; *pleasant*
For ay> thurst I, the more that I it drinke. *ever*

And if that at myn owene lust> I brenne,> *pleasure / burn*
Fro whennes cometh my wailing and my pleynte?> *complaint*
If harme agree me,° wher-to pleyne I thenne?
I noot,> ne why unwery that I faynte. *do not know*
O quikė> deeth, o swetė harm° so queynte,> *living / curious*
How may of thee in me swich quantitee,°
But if that I consentė that it be?

And if that I consentė, I wrongfully
Compleyne, y-wis;> thus possėd° to and fro, *certainly*
Al sterėlees° withinne a boot am I
Amid the see,> bytwixen> windės two, *sea / between*
That in contrarie stonden> evermo. *opposition stand*
Allas! what is this wonder> maladye? *strange*
For hete> of cold, for cold of hete, I dye.' *heat*
c. 1385

Cantus Troili the song of Troilus, now fallen in love with Criseyde, a translation from the Italian of Petrarch's Sonnet LXXXVIII to Laura, "S'amor non è," "amplified" to three *Troilus*-stanzas. It is the first English work based on any of Petrarch's Italian poetry, complete with mistranslations.
a wonder . . . me it seems to me very strange (a marvel)
If . . . me if hurt gives me pleasure
quike . . . harm rhetorical use of contradictory terms (oxymoron), especially common in Petrarch and in ancient, medieval, and Renaissance love poetry
How may . . . quantitee How can there be such a quantity of you [the contrasts of love] in me, unless I consent to it?
possed pushed; thus, tossed
sterelees i.e. completely rudderless in a boat. The image of the sea-tossed lover is a favorite one in classical and Petrarchan poetry.

Balade *from* The Legend of Good Women°

Hide, Absolon,° thy giltė˃ tresses clere;˃ — *golden / shining*
Ester, lay thou thy meekness al adoun;°
Hide, Jonathas,° al thy frendly manère;
Penalopee° and Marcia Catoùn,°
Make of your wifhood no comparisoùn;
Hide ye your beautés, Isoude° and Eleyne:°
My lady comth, that al this may disteine.˃ — *outshine*

Thy fairė body let it not appere,
Lavine;° and thou, Lucresse° of Romė toun,
And Polixene,° that boughten˃ love so dere,˃ — *bought / dearly*
And Cleopatre,° with al thy passioùn,
Hide ye your trouthe˃ of love and your renoùn; — *fidelity*
And thou, Tisbé,° that hast˃ for love swich˃ peine: — *had / such*
My lady comth, that al this may disteine.

Hero,° Dido,° Laodamia,° alle y-fere,˃ — *together*
And Phillis,° hanging for thy Demophoun,°
And Canacee,° espiėd˃ by thy chere,˃ — *found out / appearance*
Ysiphilee,° betraisėd with˃ Jasoùn, — *betrayed by*
Make of your trouthė˃ neither bost˃ ne soun;˃ — *fidelity / boast / vaunt*
Nor Ypermestre° or Adriane,° ye tweine:˃ — *two*
My lady comth, that al this may disteine.
c. 1385

The Legend . . . Women For a discussion of this poem, see the Headnote to Chaucer. Though *The Legend* is the first English poem in heroic couplets, this lyric in *balade* form occurs in it.
Absolon Absalom, famed for the beauty of his hair; see the Miller's Tale, l. 128
Ester . . . adoun Esther, resign your title to graciousness. Esther was the beautiful Jewish maiden whom King Ahasuerus chose as his queen instead of Queen Vashti.
Jonathas Jonathan, David's friend, the pattern of "friendliness"
Penalopee Penelope, the patient and loyal wife of Ulysses
Marcia Catoun daughter of Cato of Utica, who refused to remarry
Isoude Isolde, who gave up husband and life for love of Tristram
Eleyne Helen, wife of Menelaus, who ran off with Paris and provoked the Trojan War
Lavine Lavinia, wife of Aeneas
Lucresse Lucretia, who killed herself after her rape by Tarquin
Polixene Polyxena, who stayed with her father Priam and was killed with him
Cleopatre Cleopatra, mistress of Julius Caesar and Mark Antony, who killed herself at Antony's death
Tisbé Thisbe, who killed herself because she thought her lover Pyramus dead
Hero Hero of Sestos, loved by Leander
Dido Dido of Carthage, lover of Aeneas
Laodamia Laodameia, wife of Protesilaus, who accompanied him to the shades
Phillis Phyllis, who hanged herself when her lover Demophon abandoned her
Canacee committed suicide when her incest with her brother Macaraeus was discovered
Ysiphilee Hypsipyle, pregnant and abandoned by Jason, leader of the Argonauts
Ypermestre Hypermnestra, who refused to murder her husband
Adriane Ariadne, abandoned wife of Theseus. Both she and Hypermnestra had abandoned their fathers for love.

To Rosemounde°

Madame, ye ben of al beautè shryne
As fer as cercled is the mappėmounde,°
For as the cristal° glorious ye shyne,
And likė ruby ben your chekės rounde.
Therwith ye ben so mery and so jocoùnde°
That at a revel whan that I see you daunce,
It is an oynėment> unto my wounde, *ointment*
Thogh ye to me ne do no daliaùnce.°

For thogh I wepe of terės> ful a tyne,> *tears / vat*
Yet may that wo myn hertė nat confounde;
Your semy voys, that ye so smal out-twyne,°
Maketh my thoght in joy and blis habounde.°
So curteisly° I go, with lovė bounde,
That to myself I sey, in my penaùnce,°
'Suffyseth me to love you, Rosemounde,
Thogh ye to me ne do no daliaùnce.'

Nas never pyk walwed in galauntyne°
As I in love am walwed and ywounde,> *wound about*
For which ful ofte I of myself divyne> *discover*
That I am trewė Tristam° the secoùnde.
My love may not refreydė nor affounde;°
I brenne> ay in an amorous plesaùnce.> *burn / pleasure*
Do what you lyst,> I wil your thral> be founde, (*it*) *pleases you / slave*
Thogh ye to me ne do no daliaùnce.

c. 1385?

The Complaint° of Chaucer to His Purse

To you, my purse, and to noon other wight> *creature*
Compleyne I, for ye be my lady dere!
I am so sory,> now that ye be light, *sad*

To Rosemounde This *balade* is a virtuoso parody of the love lyric in which the lady is the subject of extravagant comparisons. The movement of the verse is perfectly under control, and rhyme and rhetoric are also handled masterfully, so that absurdity is allowed to creep in only at intervals: the vat of tears and the fish swimming in sauce.

mappemounde map of the world, see Fig. 55; you are the shrine of all the beauty that is within the circle of the whole world

cristal Jewel imagery is usual in such contexts and is much used by Chaucer's imitators.

jocounde gay and elegant

ye . . . daliaunce you do not give me any kindness; *daliaunce:* consenting, encouraging behavior from the lady to the lover

Your . . . out-twyne your little voice, which you so delicately spin out

habounde to be abundant; the word was thought to be connected with Latin *habere,* to have

curteisly courteously, like a true lover

penaunce sad state, because my love is not returned

pyk . . . galauntyne pike, smothered in galantine. It was usual to serve pike covered with this pickle sauce made of bread, vinegar, and cinnamon.

Tristam Tristram, the lover of Isolde, type of the true and constant in love

refreyde . . . affounde be cooled again and chilled

Complaint In conventional three-stanza *balade* form, with an envoi addressing it to a royal or noble patron, in the hope of reward; see the Franklin's Tale, l. 240. Chaucer's witty request is imitated from the French. It was successful, since a few days after his accession in 1399 Henry IV renewed and augmented the pension granted to the poet by Richard II in 1394.

That certės,> but> ye make me hevy chere, *certainly / unless*
Me were as leef be leyd upon my bere;°
For which unto your mercy thus I crye:
Beth hevy again, or ellės mot> I dye! *must*

Now voucheth> sauf this day, or> it be night, *grant / before*
That I of yow the blisful soun> may here, *blessed sound*
Or see your colour, lik the sonnė bright,
That of yelownesse hadde never pere.> *equal*
Ye be my lif, ye be myn hertės stere,> *steersman*
Quene of comfòrt and of good companye:
Beeth hevy ageyne, or ellės mot I dye!

Now purse, that been to me my livės lyght
And saviour, as doun in this world here,
Out of this tounė helpe me thurgh your might,
Syn> that ye wol nat ben my tresorere;> *since / treasurer*
For I am shave> as nye> as any frere.° *shaven / close*
But yet I pray unto your curtesie:
Beth hevy agen,> or ellės mot I dye! *again*

Envoy [*to Henry IV*]

O conquerour of Brutės Albyon,°
Which that by line> and free eleccioùn> *lineage / choice*
Been verray> king, this song to you I sende; *true*
And ye, that mowėn> alle oure harmes amende, *may*
Have minde> upon my supplicacioùn! *remember*
1399

To Adam, His Scribe

Adam scrivein,> if ever it thee bifalle *scribe*
Boèce° or *Troilus*° for to writen newe,
Under thy long lokkes thou most> have the scalle> *may you / scab*
But after my making thou write more trewe!°
So ofte a-daye> I mot> thy werk renewe, *each day / must*
It to correcte and eek> to rubbe and scrape; *also*
And al is through thy negligence and rape.> *haste*
c. 1390

Me . . . bere I'd just as soon be dead
For . . . frere A friar's head was tonsured, i.e. shaven.
O . . . Albyon The legend was that Brutus, great-grandson of Aeneas, founder of Rome, brought Trojans to Britain (Albion) and founded New Troy (London) as his capital.

Boèce Chaucer's translation of Boethius, *De Consolatione Philosophiae*
Troilus *Troilus and Criseyde*
But . . . trewe unless you copy accurately [according to] what I have composed

SIR GAWAIN AND THE GREEN KNIGHT

c. 1380–1400

Of the author of *Sir Gawain and the Green Knight,* the finest of medieval English romances, nothing is known for certain. From this poem we can tell that he was a great literary artist working in a provincial center located in the northwest Midland area, perhaps in Lancashire, Staffordshire, or Cheshire, at least 150 miles distant from London. We can also say that he wrote toward the end of the century, so that he was more or less Chaucer's contemporary.

His poem exists in one manuscript (Fig. 42); it was not printed until 1839. The manuscript contains two other poems in the same unrhymed alliterative meter, though not divided into stanzas like *Sir Gawain.* They are: *Patience,* the Biblical story of Jonah, to illustrate the virtue of patience, and *Purity,* the stories of the Flood, of Sodom and Gomorrah, and of Belshazzar, to illustrate God's vengeance on impurity. It also contains a third poem, *Pearl,* a dream allegory which is an elegy for the poet's two-year-old daughter culminating in a vision of the Heavenly Jerusalem. This poem also uses the alliterative technique, but subordinates it to a pattern of four-stressed rhyming lines in twelve-line stanzas, elaborately linked together. All these poems, as well as a fifth, the legend of St. Erkenwald, Bishop of London, known from another manuscript, are probably by the same poet. It is not easy to be sure of this, however. Though all the poems are in the same dialect and are often remarkably like one another, the techniques of alliterative poetry, with its firm conventions of phrase, rhythm, and set piece, make it difficult to distinguish between imitation of one poet by another and variations by the same. If the author of *Sir Gawain* wrote all five, he was a great poet in range, power, subtlety, invention, and individuality. If he wrote *Sir Gawain* alone he was, with Chaucer and Langland, still one of the three finest English poets of his century.

Langland and the *Gawain* poet were products of a provincial, not a London culture of which little is known beyond the poems produced there by these authors. Their alliterative meter was unfashionable in London by the time they were writing, though perhaps the stanzaic arrangement of *Sir Gawain,* varying the long lines with the rhyming "bob and wheel" (see Glossary), might have been regarded as less monotonous than Langland's poetic. Also, the directness and sting of Langland's satire may not have been acceptable to the court and the wider reading public of the metropolis. Although the numerous manuscripts show that Langland was widely read, the fact that most of them were made in the area of his presumed origin is significant. Of the *Gawain* poet, we possess one manuscript only, in a provincial dialect that would have seemed difficult, barbarous, and nearly unintelligible to a London reader.

Whatever contemporary metropolitan London thought of *Sir Gawain* and whatever its difficulties, and ours, with the language, there can be no doubt of its stature. Its basic structure is taut and simple, its narrative subtle, its vocabulary rich. A knight, challenged by a supernatural adversary, is required first to show courage in the face of such a being, further courage in accepting his challenge; and then honor, constancy, and "truth" in the fulfillment of that obligation, meeting on his way to do so temptations of all kinds. This plot the poet may have found in a French romance or a Celtic story, which has not survived. Elements of the plot may go back much farther: the beheading of the Green Knight is often said to be a rationalization of a primitive fertility rite, the winter sacrifice to assure the return of spring. It is a very long way from this to the poem as we have it, and the beheading game is to be found in Irish sources of some centuries earlier than *Sir Gawain* as well as in French Arthurian romances, where fulfillment of the obligation sometimes leads to the lifting of an enchantment. There may be an echo of this last in the reference to Morgan le Fay at the end of the poem.

None of these echoes will account for the unique poem of *Sir Gawain and the Green Knight.* The close-knit and economically told story is ornamented with blazing set pieces, such as the description of Arthur's Christmas feast, of Sir Gawain's arming for his journey, the account of the castle, miraculously appearing in the wilderness when Sir Gawain three times crosses himself, and the full treatment of the hunts. Yet each of these digressions is carefully placed and has its function in the story: Arthur's Christmas court is soon contrasted with the dreariness of the next winter, when the knight must set out. (It is characteristic of romance that narrative time tends to be compressed into a rapid series of significant events, the intervening long spaces being passed over in a few lines.) The splendid arming of Sir Gawain, stressing the physical danger of his quest, is meant to make us aware that less tangible dangers are lurking for him. The castle, appearing at his prayer, is to be his first moral testing ground. The three hunts, of two noble, dangerous animals and a base one, elaborately balanced against Gawain's temptations and the return he must make to the lord of the castle, are still in the mind as Sir Gawain stands his three blows.

Despite the supernatural Green Knight, the miraculous appearance of the castle, and the reference to the sorceress Morgan le Fay, the *Gawain* poet has reduced the element of the marvelous in his romance. We are already on the way to Malory with the strong sense of reality and the actual that takes over as soon as the Green Knight has galloped out of the hall at Arthur's court with his head in his hand. The poet has been careful to set his poem in the long-ago, but once the action gets under way we perceive that this is the story of a man whose power of moral recognition and right action is put to the test. It is a man of the greatest virtue who is being tested—the best knight of Arthur's court, itself the mirror of all virtue. (The poet takes the older view, since by his time it was generally Sir Lancelot who set the pattern.) He is being tried in a way that all of us can recognize and apply to ourselves.

As in Chaucer's Franklin's Tale, or as in his Clerk's Tale of the patient Griselda, the audience is being invited to consider the rival claims of two powerful obligations. In the Franklin's Tale, the dilemma is whether to keep the marriage vow of fidelity or the conditional promise; in the Clerk's it is how far one must honor the oath of obedience in marriage. The *Gawain* poet's exploration is no less noble than Chaucer's. Once out of Arthur's court, Gawain becomes a man like ourselves. Meeting his obligation will not be pleasant for him, but he must set off, through the cold of winter, from the Christmas warmth of Arthur's Camelot to the bleak cold of North Wales in December: a real place, not the shadowy country of the earlier romances. Coming to the castle, he is flattered by the warmth and the welcome he finds there, lulled after the chilly journey, reassured that he is near his goal. Once there, he is tested once more, before he is fully prepared, and fails the final test not only by accepting, but also by concealing his acceptance of, the magic girdle which is to save his life. His trials come in layers, too. When the castle's lady presses herself on him, he must decide among courtesy toward her, his obligation as a knight, and courtesy toward his host, equally his obligation. Morality is always a matter of choice between overlaps, not opposites.

Whether the poet intended us to see in Sir Gawain's deceitful conduct the beginning of self-knowledge is not clear. The poem is probably less a conscious attempt to cut the Arthurian heroes down to size than it is a Christian exploration, in the form of a romance, of "the cycle of social living, alienation, self-discovery, desolation, recovery and restoration" (J. A. Burrow). Its exemplary value, the questions constantly before the reader: how to recognize temptation and how to steer the right moral course, must have given the poem its power over medieval audiences and is still its attraction. Arm, protect himself as he will, among his fellows at court, with the pentangle, with "powerful," talismanic gems, with the magic belt, Gawain has still to face the cycle of experience. He does not come home to journey's end and rest, but back to society, wearing the badge that will remind him of his condition, and seeing others wear it too, in token that humility, true penitence, and trust in God's grace are man's only possible rejoinder to his sinful condition.

The translation, which attempts to keep the meter and alliteration of the original, is by Brian Stone, published in 1959 and fully revised in 1972. It is based on the text of Sir Israel Gollancz (1940), with readings adopted from that of J. R. R. Tolkien and E. V. Gordon (2nd ed., 1967). Annotation is by the present editor.

Sir Gawain and the Green Knight°

Fitt° *1*

I

The siege and the assault being ceased at Troy,°
The battlements broken down and burnt to brands and ashes,
The treacherous trickster° whose treasons there flourished
Was famed for his falsehood, the foulest on earth.
Aeneas the noble and his knightly kin
Then conquered kingdoms, and kept in their hand
Wellnigh all the wealth of the western lands.
Royal Romulus° to Rome first turned,
Set up the city in splendid pomp,
Then named her with his own name, which now she still has:
Ticius° founded Tuscany, townships raising,
Longbeard° in Lombardy lifted up homes,

Sir . . . Knight The manuscript of the poem is untitled. The numbering of parts and stanzas is also modern.
Fitt the Old and Middle English word for a section or canto of a poem
Troy Medieval belief was that western European civilization began after the destruction of Troy by the Greeks, after which the Trojan Aeneas eventually reached Italy. The descendants of Aeneas made themselves masters of the rest of the European continent.
trickster Probably Aeneas himself, or perhaps Antenor. Both, according to medieval tradition, were traitors who plotted to hand over Troy to the Greeks if they could not get away by other means. Antenor, the legendary founder of Padua, is the less likely candidate, since he is not necessary for the little genealogy by which we are here being taken to the founder of Britain. The "treachery" of both is meant to set off the "truth" of Gawain.
Romulus the legendary founder of Rome, therefore given Trojan ancestry
Ticius perhaps Tuscus, legendary founder of Tuscany; or Tirius, his father
Longbeard *Langaberde:* Langobardus, legendary ancestor of the Lombards, and allegedly Aeneas's descendant

And far over the French flood Felix Brutus°
On many spacious slopes set Britain with joy
And grace;
Where war and feud and wonder
Have ruled the realm a space,
And after, bliss and blunder
By turns have run their race.

II

And when this Britain was built by this brave noble,
Here bold men bred, in battle exulting,
Stirrers of trouble in turbulent times.
Here many a marvel, more than in other lands,
Has befallen by fortune since that far time.
But of all who abode here of Britain's kings,
Arthur° was highest in honour, as I have heard;
So I intend to tell you of a true wonder,
Which many folk mention as a manifest marvel,
A happening eminent among Arthur's adventures.
Listen to my lay but a little while.
Straightway shall I speak it, in city as I heard it,°
With tongue;
As scribes have set it duly
In the lore of the land so long,
With letters linking° truly
In story bold and strong.

III

This king lay at Camelot° one Christmastide°
With many mighty lords, manly liegemen,
Members rightly reckoned of the Round Table,°
In splendid celebration, seemly and carefree.
There tussling in tournament time and again
Jousted in jollity these gentle knights,
Then in court carnival sang catches and danced;°
For fifteen days the feasting there was full in like measure

Felix Brutus grandson or great-grandson of Aeneas, and founder of Britain. *Felix* ("happy") may reflect the *sele* ("fortunate"), used of him in other sources—and *felix* was a conventional adjective for founders.
Arthur a Welsh form of the Latin Artorius; in contrast to most names in Middle English Arthurian romance, which reach it through Old French (see Fig. 46)
heard it an appeal to an older, probably non-existent authority, a regular medieval way of placing author and reader on the same footing
letters linking i.e. by the alliterative technique; but the meaning may also be "embodied in truthful words"
Camelot King Arthur's capital, identified by Malory as Winchester, but placed by others in Wales or in the southwestern (Celtic) parts of England
Christmastide One of the great religious feasts and occasions for chivalric gatherings: festivities lasted until Twelfth Night, the eve of Epiphany (January 6). Arthur was said to hold court and wear his crown five times a year: at Easter, Ascension Day, Pentecost, All Saints, and Christmas (see Malory, *Morte Darthur,* below).
Round Table part of Queen Guinevere's dowry to King Arthur, made for King Uther by the wonder-worker Merlin; a "holy table" for 150 knights, preventing dispute about whose was the more honorable place (see Fig. 47)
sang . . . danced performed "caroles," or dances accompanied by song

With all the meat and merry-making men could devise,
Gladly ringing glee, glorious to hear,
A noble din by day, dancing at night!
All was happiness in the height in halls and chambers
For lords and their ladies, delectable joy.
With all delights on earth they housed there together,
Saving Christ's self, the most celebrated knights,
The loveliest ladies to live in all time,
And the comeliest king ever to keep court.
For this fine fellowship was in its fair prime
Far famed,
Stood well in heaven's will,
Its high-souled king acclaimed:
So hardy a host on hill
Could not with ease be named.

IV

The year being so young that yester-even saw its birth,
That day double on the dais were the diners served.
Mass sung and service ended, straight from the chapel
The King and his company came into hall.
Called on with cries from clergy and laity,
Noël° was newly announced, named time and again.
Then lords and ladies leaped forth, largesse distributing,
Offered New Year gifts° in high voices, handed them out,
Bustling and bantering about these offerings.
Ladies laughed full loudly, though losing their wealth,
And he that won was not woeful, you may well believe.
All this merriment they made until meal time.
Then in progress to their places they passed after washing,
In authorized order, the high-ranking first;°
With glorious Guinevere,° gay in the midst,
On the princely platform with its precious hangings
Of splendid silk at the sides, a state° over her
Of rich tapestry of Toulouse° and Turkestan°
Brilliantly embroidered with the best gems
Of warranted worth that wealth at any time
Could buy.
Fairest of form was this queen,
Glinting and grey° of eye;
No man could say he had seen
A lovelier, but with a lie.

Noël Latin *natalis*, birthday
New Year gifts the regular medieval custom
first at the kind of table the poet knew, at which guests were seated in order of rank, not the Round Table (see Figs. 43, 47)
Guinevere Arthur's queen
state canopy
Toulouse *tolouse*, a rich fabric, perhaps from Toulouse in France
Turkestan *tars*, rich and costly Eastern stuff
grey the regular color for a medieval heroine's eyes

V

But Arthur would not eat until all were served.
He was charming and cheerful, child-like and gay,
And loving active life, little did he favour
Lying down for long or lolling on a seat,
So robust his young blood and his beating brain.
Still, he was stirred now by something else:
His noble announcement that he never would eat
On such a fair feast-day till informed in full
Of some unusual adventure,° as yet untold,
Of some momentous marvel that he might believe,
About ancestors, or arms, or other high theme;
Or till a stranger should seek out a strong knight of his,
To join with him in jousting, in jeopardy to lay
Life against life, each allowing the other
The favour of Fortune, the fairer lot.
Such was the King's custom when he kept court,
At every fine feast among his free° retinue
        In hall.
    So he throve amid the throng,
    A ruler royal and tall,
    Still standing staunch and strong,
    And young like the year withal.

VI

Erect stood the strong king, stately of mien,
Trifling time with talk before the topmost table.°
Good Gawain° was placed at Guinevere's side,
And Agravain° of the Hard Hand sat on the other side,
Both the King's sister's sons, staunchest of knights.
Above, Bishop Baldwin began the board,°
And Ywain, Urien's son,° ate next to him.
These were disposed on the dais and with dignity served,
And many mighty men next, marshalled at side tables.
Then the first course came in with such cracking of trumpets,
(Whence bright bedecked blazons° in banners hung)
Such din of drumming and a deal of fine piping,
Such wild warbles whelming and echoing

adventure a custom of Arthur's often mentioned in French romances. The adventure (chance encounter, French *aventure*) might happen to one of the company then and there, or merely be reported by someone present.
free *fre*, noble
topmost table Arthur would face down the hall, from the middle of the long side of the high table on the dais, the most honored guests to either side of him. The side tables (l. 115) were on the floor of the hall, along the walls, at right angles to the high table. The guests sat on benches or forms.
Gawain Gawain is usually presented, in early Arthurian romance, as the greatest of Arthur's knights for his courtesy and war-like prowess. Later, his status is reduced. He was Arthur's nephew and his estates were in Scotland.
Agravain Gawain's brother
Baldwin . . . board The bishop, Arthur's adviser, sat in the place of honor at his right hand.
Ywain, . . . son. Ywain and Urien may have been historical Welsh kings. Ywain was also Arthur's nephew and one of his best knights.
blazons coats of arms

That hearts were uplifted high at the strains.
Then delicacies and dainties were delivered to the guests,
Fresh food in foison,° such freight of full dishes
That space was scarce at the social tables
For the several soups set before them in silver
On the cloth.
Each feaster made free with the fare,
Took lightly and nothing loth;
Twelve plates were for every pair,
Good beer and bright wine both.

VII

Of their meal I shall mention no more just now,
For it is evident to all that ample was served;
Now another noise,° quite new, neared suddenly,
Likely to allow the liege lord to eat;
For barely had the blast of trump abated one minute
And the first course in the court been courteously served,
When there heaved in at the hall door an awesome fellow
Who in height outstripped all earthly men.
From throat to thigh he was so thickset and square,
His loins and limbs were so long and so great,
That he was half a giant on earth, I believe;
Yet mainly and most of all a man he seemed,
And the handsomest of horsemen, though huge, at that;
For though at back and at breast his body was broad,
His hips and haunches were elegant and small,
And perfectly proportioned were all parts of the man,
As seen.
Men gaped at the hue of him
Ingrained in garb and mien,
A fellow fiercely grim,
And all a glittering green.

VIII

And garments of green girt the fellow about—
A two-third-length tunic, tight at the waist,
A comely cloak on top, accomplished with lining
Of the finest fur to be found, made of one piece,
Marvellous fur-trimmed material, with matching hood
Lying back from his locks and laid on his shoulders;
Fitly held-up hose, in hue the same green,
That was caught at the calf, with clinking spurs beneath
Of bright gold on bases of embroidered silk,
But no iron shoe armoured that horseman's feet.

foison plenty
noise The "adventure" was arriving which had to take place before Arthur would consent to eat.

And verily his vesture was all vivid green,
So were the bars on his belt and the brilliants set
In ravishing array on the rich accoutrements
About himself and his saddle on silken work.
It would be tedious to tell a tithe of the trifles
Embossed and embroidered, such as birds and flies,°
In gay green gauds,° with gold everywhere.
The breast-hangings of the horse, its haughty crupper,°
The enamelled knobs and nails on its bridle,
And the stirrups that he stood on, were all stained with the same;
So were the splendid saddle-skirts and bows
That ever glimmered and glinted with their green stones.
The steed that he spurred on was similar in hue
        To the sight,
    Green and huge of grain,
    Mettlesome in might
    And brusque with bit and rein—
    A steed to serve that knight!

IX

Yes, garbed all in green was the gallant rider,
And the hair of his head was the same hue as his horse,
And floated finely like a fan round his shoulders;
And a great bushy beard on his breast flowing down,
With the heavy hair hanging from his head,
Was shorn below the shoulder, sheared right round,
So that half his arms were under the encircling hair,
Covered as by a king's cape, that closes at the neck.
The mane of that mighty horse, much like the beard,
Well crisped and combed, was copiously plaited
With twists of twining gold, twinkling in the green,
First a green gossamer, a golden one next.
His flowing tail and forelock followed suit,
And both were bound with bands of bright green,
Ornamented to the end with exquisite stones,
While a thong running through them threaded on high
Many bright golden bells, burnished and ringing.
Such a horse, such a horseman, in the whole wide world
Was never seen or observed by those assembled before,
        Not one.
    Lightning-like he seemed
    And swift to strike and stun.
    His dreadful blows, men deemed,
    Once dealt, meant death was done.

flies butterflies
gauds ornaments
crupper harness strap passing under the horse's tail, or saddle skirts. The harness and trappings of a knight's horse were often very elaborate.

X

Yet hauberk° and helmet had he none,
Nor plastron° nor plate-armour proper to combat,
Nor shield for shoving, nor sharp spear for lunging;
But he held a holly° cluster in one hand, holly
That is greenest when groves are gaunt and bare,
And an axe in his other hand, huge and monstrous,
A hideous helmet-smasher for anyone to tell of;
The head of that axe was an ell-rod long.
Of green hammered gold and steel was the socket,
And the blade was burnished bright, with a broad edge,
Acutely honed for cutting, as keenest razors are.
The grim man gripped it by its great strong handle,
Which was wound with iron all the way to the end,
And graven in green with graceful designs.
A cord curved round it, was caught at the head,
Then hitched to the haft at intervals in loops,
With costly tassels attached thereto in plenty
On bosses of bright green embroidered richly.
In he rode, and up the hall, this man,
Driving towards the high dais, dreading no danger.
He gave no one a greeting, but glared over all.
His opening utterance was, 'Who and where
Is the governor of this gathering? Gladly would I
Behold him with my eyes and have speech with him.'
He frowned;
Took note of every knight
As he ramped and rode around;
Then stopped to study who might
Be the noble most renowned.

XI

The assembled folk stared, long scanning the fellow,
For all men marvelled what it might mean
That a horseman and his horse should have such a colour
As to grow green as grass, and greener yet, it seemed,
More gaudily° glowing than green enamel on gold.
Those standing studied him and sidled towards him
With all the world's wonder as to what he would do.
For astonishing sights they had seen, but such a one never;
Therefore a phantom from Fairyland the folk there deemed him.
So even the doughty were daunted and dared not reply,
All sitting stock-still, astounded by his voice.

hauberk coat of chain-mail armor
plastron armor for upper breast and neck
holly evergreen cluster from that shrub, perhaps to signify the knight's immortality, or merely to match his color. Holly is the symbol of Christmas and of the immortal Christ, the red berry symbolizing his blood.
gaudily beautifully

Throughout the high hall was a hush like death;
Suddenly as if all had slipped into sleep, their voices were
At rest;
Hushed not wholly for fear,
But some at honour's behest;
But let him whom all revere
Greet that gruesome guest.

XII

For Arthur sensed an exploit before the high dais,
And accorded him courteous greeting, no craven he,
Saying to him, 'Sir knight, you are certainly welcome.
I am head of this house: Arthur is my name.
Please deign to dismount and dwell with us
Till you impart your purpose, at a proper time.'
'May He that sits in heaven help me,' said the knight,
'But my intention was not to tarry in this turreted hall.
But as your reputation, royal sir, is raised up so high,
And your castle and cavaliers are accounted the best,
The mightiest of mail-clad men in mounted fighting,
The most warlike, the worthiest the world has bred,
Most valiant to vie with in virile contests,
And as chivalry is shown here, so I am assured,
At this time, I tell you, that has attracted me here.
By this branch that I bear, you may be certain
That I proceed in peace, no peril seeking;
For had I fared forth in fighting gear,
My hauberk and helmet, both at home now,
My shield and sharp spear, all shining bright,
And other weapons to wield, I would have brought;
However, as I wish for no war here, I wear soft clothes.
But if you are as bold as brave men affirm,
You will gladly grant me the good sport I demand
By right.'
Then Arthur answer gave:
'If you, most noble knight,
Unarmoured combat crave,
We'll fail you not in fight.'

XIII

'No, it is not combat I crave, for come to that,
On this bench only beardless boys are sitting.
If I were hasped in armour on a high steed,
No man among you could match me, your might being meagre.
So I crave in this court a Christmas game,
For it is Yuletide and New Year, and young men abound here.
If any in this household is so hardy in spirit,

Of such mettlesome mind and so madly rash
As to strike a strong blow in return for another,
I shall offer to him this fine axe freely;
This axe, which is heavy enough, to handle as he please.
And I shall bide the first blow, as bare as I sit here.
If some intrepid man is tempted to try what I suggest,
Let him leap towards me and lay hold of this weapon,
Acquiring clear possession of it, no claim from me ensuing.
Then shall I stand up to his stroke, quite still on this floor—
So long as I shall have leave to launch a return blow
Unchecked.
Yet he shall have a year
And a day's reprieve,° I direct.
Now hasten and let me hear
Who answers, to what effect.'

XIV

If he had astonished them at the start, yet stiller now
Were the henchmen in hall, both high and low.
The rider wrenched himself round in his saddle
And rolled his red eyes about roughly and strangely,
Bending° his brows, bristling and bright, on all,
His beard swaying as he strained to see who would rise.
When none came to accord with him, he coughed aloud,
Then pulled himself up proudly, and spoke as follows:
'What, is this Arthur's house, the honour of which
Is bruited abroad so abundantly?
Has your pride disappeared? Your prowess gone?
Your victories, your valour, your vaunts, where are they?
The revel and renown of the Round Table
Is now overwhelmed by a word from one man's voice,
For all flinch for fear from a fight not begun!'
Upon this, he laughed so loudly that the lord grieved.
His fair features filled with blood
For shame.
He raged as roaring gale;
His followers felt the same.
The King, not one to quail,
To that cavalier then came.

XV

'By heaven,' then said Arthur, 'What you ask is foolish,
But as you firmly seek folly, find it you shall.
No good man here is aghast at your great words.
Hand me your axe now, for heaven's sake,
And I shall bestow the boon you bid us give.'

year . . . reprieve the usual term for a legal contract **Bending** directing

He sprang towards him swiftly, seized it from his hand,
And fiercely the other fellow footed the floor.°
Now Arthur had his axe, and holding it by the haft
Swung it about sternly, as if to strike with it.
The strong man stood before him, stretched to his full height,
Higher than any in the hall by a head and more.
Stern of face he stood there, stroking his beard,
Turning down his tunic in a tranquil manner,
Less unmanned and dismayed by the mighty strokes
Than if a banqueter at the bench° had brought him a drink
        Of wine.
    Then Gawain at Guinevere's side
    Bowed and spoke his design:
    'Before all, King, confide
    This fight to me. May it be mine.'

XVI

'If you would, worthy lord,' said Gawain to the king,
'Bid me stir from this seat and stand beside you,
Allowing me without lèse-majesty° to leave the table,
And if my liege lady were not displeased thereby,
I should come there to counsel you before this court of nobles.
For it appears unmeet to me, as manners go,
When your hall hears uttered such a haughty request,
Though you gladly agree, for you to grant it yourself,
When on the benches about you many such bold men sit,
Under heaven, I hold, the highest-mettled,
There being no braver knights when battle is joined.
I am the weakest, the most wanting in wisdom, I know,
And my life, if lost, would be least missed, truly.
Only through your being my uncle, am I to be valued;
No bounty but your blood in my body do I know.°
And since this affair is too foolish to fall to you,
And I first asked it of you, make it over to me;
And if I fail to speak fittingly, let this full court judge
        Without blame.'
    Then wisely they whispered of it,
    And after, all said the same:
    That the crowned king should be quit,°
    And Gawain given the game.

XVII

Then the King commanded the courtly knight to rise.
He directly uprose, approached courteously,

footed the floor jumped off his horse
banqueter . . . bench a man at his seat
lèse-majesty French *lèse-majesté,* offense against the dignity of a ruler, severe discourtesy
No bounty . . . know i.e. the only good in my body comes from your blood
quit excused from the contest

Knelt low to his liege lord, laid hold of the weapon;
And he graciously let him have it, lifted up his hand
And gave him God's blessing, gladly urging him
To be strong in spirit and stout of sinew.
'Cousin, take care,' said the King, 'To chop once,°
And if you strike with success, certainly I think
You will take the return blow without trouble in time.'
Gripping the great axe, Gawain goes to the man
Who awaits him unwavering, not quailing at all.
Then said to Sir Gawain the stout knight in green,
'Let us affirm our pact freshly, before going farther.
I beg you, bold sir, to be so good
As to tell me your true name, as I trust you to.'
'In good faith,' said the good knight, 'Gawain is my name,
And whatever happens after, I offer you this blow,
And in twelve months' time I shall take the return blow
With whatever weapon you wish, and with no one else
Shall I strive.'
The other with pledge replied,
'I'm the merriest man alive
It's a blow from you I must bide,
Sir Gawain, so may I thrive.'

XVIII

'By God,' said the Green Knight, 'Sir Gawain, I rejoice
That I shall have from your hand what I have asked for here.
And you have gladly gone over, in good discourse,
The covenant I requested of the King in full,
Except that you shall assent, swearing in truth,
To seek me yourself, in such place as you think
To find me under the firmament, and fetch your payment
For what you deal me today before this dignified gathering.'
'How shall I hunt for you? How find your home?'
Said Gawain, 'By God that made me, I go in ignorance;
Nor, knight, do I know your name or your court.
But instruct me truly thereof, and tell me your name,
And I shall wear out my wits to find my way there;
Here is my oath on it, in absolute honour!'
'That is enough this New Year,° no more is needed,'
Said the gallant in green to Gawain the courteous,
'To tell you the truth, when I have taken the blow
After you have duly dealt it, I shall directly inform you
About my house and my home and my own name.
Then you may keep your covenant, and call on me,
And if I waft you no words, then well may you prosper,

take . . . once take care that you give one stroke only

New Year a time associated with friendship and piety

Stay long in your own land and look for no further
Trial.
Now grip your weapon grim;
Let us see your fighting style.'
'Gladly,' said Gawain to him,
Stroking the steel the while.

XIX

On the ground the Green Knight graciously stood,
With head slightly slanting to expose the flesh.
His long and lovely locks he laid over his crown,
Baring the naked neck for the business now due.
Gawain gripped his axe and gathered it on high,
Advanced the left foot before him on the ground,
And slashed swiftly down on the exposed part,
So that the sharp blade sheared through, shattering the bones,
Sank deep in the sleek flesh, split it in two,
And the scintillating steel struck the ground.
The fair head fell from the neck, struck the floor,
And people spurned it as it rolled around.
Blood spurted from the body, bright against the green.
Yet the fellow did not fall, nor falter one whit,
But stoutly sprang forward on legs still sturdy,
Roughly reached out among the ranks of nobles,
Seized his splendid head and straightway lifted it.
Then he strode to his steed, snatched the bridle,
Stepped into the stirrup and swung aloft,
Holding his head in his hand by the hair.
He settled himself in the saddle as steadily
As if nothing had happened to him, though he had
No head.
He twisted his trunk about,
That gruesome body that bled;
He caused much dread and doubt
By the time his say was said.

XX

For he held the head in his hand upright,
Pointed the face at the fairest in fame° on the dais;
And it lifted its eyelids and looked glaringly,
And menacingly said with its mouth as you may now hear:
'Be prepared to perform what you promised, Gawain;
Seek faithfully till you find me, my fine fellow,
According to your oath in this hall in these knights' hearing.
Go to the Green Chapel without gainsaying to get
Such a stroke as you have struck. Strictly you deserve

fairest in fame noblest; those at the high table

That due redemption on the day of New Year.
As the Knight of the Green Chapel I am known to many;
Therefore if you ask for me, I shall be found.
So come, or else be called coward accordingly!'
Then he savagely swerved, sawing at the reins,
Rushed out at the hall door, his head in his hand,
And the flint-struck fire flew up from the hooves.
What place he departed to no person there knew,
Nor could any account be given of the country he had come from.
        What then?
    At the Green Knight Gawain and King
    Grinned and laughed again;
    But plainly approved the thing
    As a marvel in the world of men.

XXI

Though honoured King Arthur was at heart astounded,
He let no sign of it be seen, but said clearly
To the comely queen in courtly speech,
'Do not be dismayed, dear lady, today:
Such cleverness° comes well at Christmastide,
Like the playing of interludes,° laughter and song,
As lords and ladies delight in courtly carols.
However, I am now able to eat the repast,
Having seen, I must say, a sight to wonder at.'
He glanced at Sir Gawain, and gracefully said,
'Now sir, hang up your axe: you have hewn enough.'
And on the backcloth above the dais it was boldly hung
Where all men might mark it and marvel at it
And with truthful testimony tell the wonder of it.
Then to the table the two went together,
The King and the constant knight, and keen° men served them
Double portions of each dainty with all due dignity,
All manner of meat,° and minstrelsy too.
Daylong they delighted till darkness came
        To their shores.
    Now Gawain give a thought,
    Lest peril make you pause
    In seeking out the sport
    That you have claimed as yours.

cleverness or: curious deeds
interludes pageants, short humorous plays, at entertainments or between the acts of sacred dramas
keen quick
meat food

Fitt 2

XXII

Such earnest° of noble action° had Arthur at New Year,
For he was avid to hear exploits vaunted.
Though starved of such speeches when seated at first,
Now had they high matter indeed, their hands full° of it.
Gawain was glad to begin the games in hall,
But though the end be heavy, have no wonder,
For if men are spritely in spirit after strong drink,
Soon the year slides past, never the same twice;
There is no foretelling its fulfilment from the start.
Yes, this Yuletide passed and the year following;
Season after season in succession went by.
After Christmas comes the crabbed Lenten time,
Which forces on the flesh fish and food yet plainer.
Then weather° more vernal wars with the wintry world,
The cold ebbs and declines, the clouds lift,
In shining flowers the rain sheds warmth
And falls upon the fair plain, where flowers appear;
The grassy lawns and groves alike are garbed in green;
Birds prepare to build, and brightly sing
The solace of the ensuing summer that soothes hill
And dell.
By hedgerows rank and rich
The blossoms bloom and swell,
And sounds of sweetest pitch
From lovely woodlands well.

XXIII

Then comes the season of summer with soft winds,
When Zephyrus° himself breathes on seeds and herbs.
In paradise is the plant that springs in the open
When the dripping dew drops from its leaves,
And it bears the blissful gleam of the bright sun.
Then Harvest comes hurrying, urging it on,
Warning it because of winter to wax ripe soon;
He drives the dust to rise with the drought he brings,
Forcing it to fly up from the face of the earth.
Wrathful winds in raging skies wrestle with the sun;
Leaves are lashed loose from the trees and lie on the ground
And the grass becomes grey which was green before.
What rose from root at first now ripens and rots;

earnest pledge
action MS. "adventures," meaning chance encounters
Now . . . full literally: Now they were fully provided with stern deeds (to talk of), whole fistfuls of them
weather famous passage of welcome to spring, preparing for change in the action of the poem and echoing Gawain's lack of care—as yet—for the debt he will have to pay when the year sinks again
Zephyrus the west wind

So the year in passing yields its many yesterdays,
And winter returns, as the way of the world is,
I swear;
So came the Michaelmas° moon,
With winter threatening there,
And Gawain considered soon
The fell way he must fare.

XXIV

Yet he stayed in hall with Arthur till All Saints Day,°
When Arthur provided plentifully, especially for Gawain,
A rich feast and high revelry at the Round Table.
The gallant lords and gay ladies grieved for Gawain,
Anxious on his account; but all the same
They mentioned only matters of mirthful import,
Joylessly joking for that gentle knight's sake.
For after dinner with drooping heart he addressed his uncle
And spoke plainly of his departure, putting it thus:
'Now, liege lord of my life, I beg my leave of you.
You know the kind of covenant it is: I care little
To tell over the trials of it, trifling as they are,
But I am bound to bear the blow and must be gone tomorrow
To seek the gallant in green, as God sees fit to guide me.'
Then the most courtly in that company came together,
Ywain and Eric and others in troops,
Sir Dodinal the Fierce, the Duke of Clarence,
Lancelot and Lionel and Lucan the Good,
Sir Bors and Sir Bedivere, both strong men,
And many admired knights, with Mador of the Gate.°
All the company of the court came near to the King
With carking° care in their hearts, to counsel the knight.
Much searing sorrow was suffered in the hall
That such a gallant man as Gawain should go in quest
To suffer a savage blow, and his sword no more
Should bear.
Said Gawain, gay of cheer,
'Whether fate be foul or fair,
Why falter I or fear?
What should man do but dare?'

Michaelmas Feast of St. Michael, September 29
All Saints Day November 1, one of the great religious festivals. See l. 37n above.
Eric . . . Gate (ll. 551–55) i.e. the flower of the court. Eric was famous in French romances; Sir Dodinal was a great hunter in the wild; the Duke of Clarence, one of whose adventures parallels Gawain's, was Arthur's nephew; Lancelot was, in the later Arthurian tradition, one of Arthur's greatest knights and Queen Guinevere's lover; Lionel was Lancelot's cousin; Lucan was the royal butler, an important official (see Malory, *Morte Darthur,* below) and one of the last survivors of the knights at Arthur's death; Bors was probably Lionel's brother; Bedivere was one of the earliest of Arthur's knights, and in Malory is Arthur's last companion; Mador was the keeper of the castle gate.
carking oppressive

XXV

He dwelt there all that day, and at dawn on the morrow
Asked for his armour. Every item was brought.
First a crimson carpet was cast over the floor
And the great pile of gilded war-gear glittered upon it.
The strong man stepped on it, took the steel in hand.
The doublet he dressed in was dear Turkestan stuff.
Then came the courtly cape, cut with skill,
Finely lined with fur, and fastened close.
Then they set the steel shoes on the strong man's feet,
Lapped his legs in steel with lovely greaves,°
Complete with knee-pieces, polished bright
And connecting at the knee with gold-knobbed hinges.
Then came the cuisses,° which cunningly enclosed
His thighs thick of thew,° and which thongs secured.
Next the hauberk, interlinked with argent° steel rings
Which rested on rich material, wrapped the warrior round.
He had polished armour on arms and elbows,
Glinting and gay, and gloves of metal,
And all the goodly gear to give help whatever
          Betide;
    With surcoat richly wrought,
    Gold spurs attached in pride,
    A silken sword-belt athwart,
    And steadfast blade at his side.

XXVI

When he was hasped in armour his harness° was noble;
The least lace or loop was lustrous with gold.
So, harnessed as he was, he heard his mass
As it was offered at the high altar in worship.
Then he came to the King and his court-fellows,
Took leave with loving courtesy of lord and lady,
Who commended him to Christ and kissed him farewell.
By now Gringolet° had been got ready, and girt with a saddle
That gleamed most gaily with many golden fringes,
Everywhere nailed newly for this noble occasion.
The bridle was embossed and bound with bright gold;
So were the furnishings° of the fore-harness° and the fine skirts.
The crupper and the caparison° accorded with the saddle-bows,
And all was arrayed on red with nails of richest gold,
Which glittered and glanced like gleams of the sun.

greaves armor for the leg, from ankle to knee
cuisses armor for the thigh
thew muscle
argent silvery
harness man's armor
Gringolet the name of Gawain's horse, most likely via 12th-century French, but possibly Welsh in origin, meaning "white-hard"
furnishings ornaments
fore-harness armor for the horse's fore-parts
caparison rich ornamental cloth covering for a horse

Then his casque,° equipped with clasps of great strength
And padded inside, he seized and swiftly kissed;
It towered high on his head and was hasped at the back,
With a brilliant silk band over the burnished neck-guard,
Embroidered and bossed° with the best gems
On broad silken borders, with birds about the seams,
Such as parrots painted with periwinkles° between,
And turtles° and true-love-knots° traced as thickly
As if many beauties in a bower° had been busy seven winters
        Thereabout.
    The circlet on his head
    Was prized more precious no doubt,
    And perfectly diamonded,
    Threw a gleaming lustre out.

XXVII

Then they showed him the shield of shining gules,°
With the Pentangle° in pure gold depicted thereon.
He brandished it by the baldric,° and about his neck
He slung it in a seemly way, and it suited him well.
And I intend to tell you, though I tarry therefore,
Why the Pentangle is proper to this prince of knights.
It is a symbol which Solomon conceived once
To betoken holy truth, by its intrinsic right,
For it is a figure which has five points,
And each line overlaps and is locked with another;
And it is endless everywhere, and the English call it,
In all the land, I hear, the Endless Knot.°
Therefore it goes with Sir Gawain and his gleaming armour,
For, ever faithful in five things, each in fivefold manner,°
Gawain was reputed good and, like gold well refined,
He was devoid of all villainy, every virtue displaying
        In the field.
    Thus this Pentangle new

casque helmet
bossed studded
parrots . . . periwinkles The silk would have something of the appearance of border decoration in contemporary manuscripts.
turtles turtledoves—emphasizing Gawain's true and faithful courtesy and knighthood in love as in war
true-love-knots two bands with a knot in the center to symbolize union
bower ladies' quarters
gules the heraldic name for red; Gawain's arms are usually green and gold
Pentangle Not elsewhere part of Gawain's coat of arms, it was a five-pointed star, which could be drawn without taking pen from paper, symbol of safety and perfection, and came to be known as Solomon's sign. It is related to the similar hexagram of two interlocking triangles, the "Star of David." The pentangle/pentagram was also used as a magic sign, to give power over spirits; it is sometimes associated with the five letters of the name of Jesus or with his five wounds.
baldric a belt, often richly embroidered, worn diagonally across the body to support sword, bugle, or other such article
Endless Knot i.e. because its interlacing lines are joined and continuous
five . . . manner These five times five are each a side of the pentangle: the five wits, i.e. senses—sight, hearing, touch, taste, smell; the five fingers; the five wounds of Christ on the cross—two hands, two feet, and side; the five joys of the Virgin, the joyful mysteries of the rosary—Annunciation, Nativity, Resurrection, Ascension, and Assumption; and the five social virtues. The five wits and especially the five wounds and five joys were frequently the subject of religious meditation and religious lyrics.

He carried on coat and shield,
As a man of troth most true
And knightly name annealed.

XXVIII

First he was found faultless in his five wits.
Next, his five fingers never failed the knight,
And all his trust on earth was in the five wounds
Which came to Christ on the Cross, as the Creed tells.
And whenever the bold man was busy on the battlefield,
Through all other things he thought on this,
That his prowess all depended on the five pure Joys
That the holy Queen of Heaven had of her Child.
Accordingly the courteous knight had that queen's image°
Etched on the inside of his armoured shield,
So that when he beheld her, his heart did not fail.
The fifth five I find the famous man practised
Were—Liberality and Lovingkindness leading the rest;
Then his Continence and Courtesy,° which were never corrupted;
And Piety, the surpassing virtue. These pure five
Were more firmly fixed on that fine man
Than on any other, and every multiple,
Each interlocking° with another, had no end,
Being fixed to five points which never failed,°
Never assembling on one side, nor sundering either,
With no end at any angle; nor can I find
Where the design started or proceeded to its end.
Thus on his shining shield this knot was shaped
Royally in red gold upon red gules.
That is the pure Pentangle, so people who are wise
are taught.
Now Gawain was ready and gay;
His spear he promptly caught
And gave them all good day
For ever, as he thought.

XXIX

He struck the steed with his spurs and sprang on his way
So forcefully that the fire flew up from the flinty stones.
All who saw that seemly sight were sick at heart,
And all said to each other softly, in the same breath,

image Arthur was said to have had the Virgin's picture on his armor and shield, and to draw strength from the sight. Gawain's spotless piety and courage are emphasized by the transfer of the image.

Liberality . . . Courtesy Gawain's knightly virtues do not here include the one that he displays most in the poem: truth to one's word. Liberality and loving-kindness—beneficence and brotherly love—are courtly virtues; so is continence, or sinlessness; all together go to make up courtesy, truly chivalrous behavior.

interlocking i.e. as in the pentangle; each virtue reinforcing and feeding into the others

five points . . . failed Five was thought the first perfect number, the union of male three and female two.

In care for that comely knight, 'By Christ, it is evil
That yon lord should be lost, who lives so nobly!
To find his fellow on earth, in faith, is not easy.
It would have been wiser to have worked more warily,
And to have dubbed the dear man a duke of the realm.
A magnificent master of men he might have been,
And so had a happier fate than to be utterly destroyed,
Beheaded by an unearthly being out of arrogance.
Who supposed the Prince would approve such counsel
As is giddily given in Christmas games by knights?'
Many were the watery tears that whelmed from weeping eyes,
When on quest that worthy knight went from the court
That day.
He faltered not nor feared,
But quickly went his way;
His road was rough and weird,
Or so the stories say.

XXX

Now the gallant Sir Gawain in God's name goes
Riding through the realm of Britain,° no rapture in his mind.
Often the long night he lay alone and companionless,
And did not find in front of him food of his choice;
He had no comrade but his courser in the country woods and hills,
No traveller to talk to on the track but God,
Till he was nearly nigh to Northern Wales.°
The isles of Anglesey he kept always on his left,
And fared across the fords by the foreshore
Over at Holy Head to the other side
Into the wilderness of Wirral,° where few dwelled
To whom God or good-hearted man gave his love.
And always as he went, he asked whomever he met
If they knew or had knowledge of a knight in green,
Or could guide him to the ground where a green chapel stood.
And there was none but said him nay, for never in their lives
Had they set eyes on someone of such a hue
As green.
His way was wild and strange
By dreary hill and dean.°
His mood would many times change
Before that fane° was seen.

Britain MS. *Logres,* Arthur's kingdom; England south of the Humber
Northern Wales Gawain came from Camelot in southern England north through Logres almost up to the north coast of Wales, and then cut east, keeping Anglesey on his left. The poet seems to expect that people will know the route, which probably then led across the River Dee between Chester and the estuary. The modern Holyhead in Anglesey cannot be the Holyhead of the poem.
Wirral the Wilderness of Wirral in Cheshire, a forested area, noted in the 14th century for criminals and outlaws
dean valley
fane church

XXXI

He rode far from his friends, a forsaken man,
Scaling many cliffs in country unknown.
At every bank or beach where the brave man crossed water,
He found a foe in front of him, except by a freak of chance,
And so foul and fierce a one that he was forced to fight.
So many marvels° did the man meet in the mountains,
It would be too tedious to tell a tenth of them.
He had death-struggles with dragons, did battle with wolves,
Warred with wild men who dwelt among the crags,
Battled with bulls and bears and boars at other times,
And ogres that panted after him on the high fells.
Had he not been doughty in endurance and dutiful to God,
Doubtless he would have been done to death time and again.
Yet the warring little worried him; worse was the winter,
When the cold clear water cascaded from the clouds
And froze before it could fall to the fallow° earth.
Half-slain by the sleet, he slept in his armour
Night after night among the naked rocks,
Where the cold streams splashed from the steep crests
Or hung high over his head in hard icicles.
So in peril and pain, in parlous plight,
This knight covered the country till Christmas Eve
Alone;
And he that eventide
To Mary made his moan,
And begged her be his guide
Till some shelter should be shown.

XXXII

Merrily in the morning by a mountain he rode
Into a wondrously wild wooded cleft,
With high hills on each side overpeering a forest
Of huge hoary oaks, a hundred together.
The hazel and the hawthorn were intertwined
With rough ragged moss trailing everywhere,
And on the bleak branches birds in misery
Piteously piped away, pinched with cold.
The gallant knight on Gringolet galloped under them
Through many a swamp and marsh, a man all alone,
Fearing lest he should fail, through adverse fortune,
To see the service of him who that same night
Was born of a bright maiden to banish our strife.
And so sighing he said, 'I beseech thee, Lord
And thee Mary, mildest mother so dear,

marvels like any hero of romance, riding out in search of adventure

fallow dun-colored, untilled

That in some haven with due honour I may hear Mass
And Matins tomorrow morning: meekly I ask it,
And promptly thereto I pray my Pater and Ave
And Creed.'°
He crossed himself and cried
For his sins, and said, 'Christ speed
My cause, his cross my guide!'°
So prayed he, spurring his steed.

XXXIII

Thrice the sign of the Saviour° on himself he had made,
When in the wood he was aware of a dwelling with a moat
On a promontory above a plateau, penned in by the boughs
And tremendous trunks of trees, and trenched° about;
The comeliest castle that ever a knight owned,
It was pitched on a plain, with a park all round,
Impregnably palisaded with pointed stakes,
And containing many trees in its two-mile circumference.
The courteous knight contemplated the castle from one side
As it shimmered and shone through the shining oaks.
Then humbly he took off his helmet and offered thanks
To Jesus and Saint Julian,° gentle patrons both,
Who had given him grace and gratified his wish.
'Now grant it be good lodging!' the gallant knight said.
Then he goaded Gringolet with his golden heels,
And mostly by chance emerged on the main highway,
Which brought the brave man to the bridge's end
With one cast.
The drawbridge vertical,
The gates shut firm and fast,
The well-provided wall—
It blenched at never a blast.

XXXIV

The knight, still on his steed, stayed on the bank
Of the deep double ditch that drove round the place.°
The wall went into the water wonderfully deep,
And then to a huge height upwards it reared
In hard hewn stone, up to the cornice;
Built under the battlements in the best style, courses jutted°
And turrets protruded between,° constructed
With loopholes in plenty with locking shutters.

Pater . . . Creed the Lord's Prayer, the Hail Mary, and the Creed
Christ . . . guide common formula of prayer
sign of the Saviour i.e., he crossed himself
trenched moated
Saint Julian patron saint of travelers
place a castle of the elaborate, pinnacled, chimneyed, later 14th-century type, on the way to being more a place to live in than a stronghold (Fig. 44)
jutted continuous horizontal bands of stone projected from the wall below the battlements, to discourage scalers
between at intervals

No better barbican° had ever been beheld by that knight.
And inside he could see a splendid high hall
With towers and turrets on top, all tipped with crenellations,°
And pretty pinnacles placed along its length,
With carved copes,° cunningly worked.
Many chalk-white chimneys the chevalier saw
On the tops of towers twinkling whitely,
So many painted pinnacles sprinkled everywhere,
Congregated in clusters among the crenellations,
That it appeared like a prospect of paper patterning.
To the gallant knight on Gringolet it seemed good enough
If he could ever gain entrance to the inner court,
And harbour in that house while Holy Day lasted,
Well cheered.
He hailed, and at a height
A civil porter appeared,
Who welcomed the wandering knight,
And his inquiry heard.

XXXV

'Good sir,' said Gawain, 'will you give my message
To the high lord of this house, that I ask for lodging?'
'Yes, by Saint Peter,'° replied the porter, 'and I think
You may lodge here as long as you like, sir knight.'
Then away he went eagerly, and swiftly returned
With a host of well-wishers to welcome the knight.
They let down the drawbridge and in a dignified way
Came out and did honour to him, kneeling
Courteously on the cold ground to accord him worthy welcome.
They prayed him to pass the portcullis, now pulled up high,
And he readily bid them rise and rode over the bridge.
Servants held his saddle while he stepped down,
And his steed was stabled by sturdy men in plenty.
Strong knights and squires descended then
To bring the bold warrior blithely into hall.
When he took off his helmet, many hurried forward
To receive it and to serve this stately man,
And his bright sword and buckler° were both taken as well.
Then graciously he greeted each gallant knight,
And many proud men pressed forward to pay their respects.
Garbed in his fine garments, he was guided to the hall,
Where a fine fire was burning fiercely on the hearth.
Then the prince of those people appeared from his chamber
To meet in mannerly style the man in his hall.
'You are welcome to dwell here as you wish,' he said,

barbican outer fortification of a castle
crenellations battlements
copes ornamental tops
Saint Peter One porter swears by another, the castle porter by the porter of heaven.
buckler shield

'Treat everything as your own, and have what you please
In this place.'
'I yield my best thanks yet:
May Christ make good your grace!'
Said Gawain and, gladly met,
They clasped in close embrace.

XXXVI

Gawain gazed at the gallant who had greeted him well
And it seemed to him the stronghold possessed a brave lord,
A powerful man in his prime, of stupendous size.
Broad and bright was his beard, all beaver-hued;
Strong and sturdy he stood on his stalwart legs;
His face was fierce as fire, free° was his speech,
And he seemed in good sooth a suitable man
To be prince of a people with companions of mettle.
This prince led him to an apartment and expressly commanded
That a man be commissioned to minister to Gawain;
And at his bidding a band of men bent to serve
Brought him to a beautiful room where the bedding was noble.
The bed-curtains, of brilliant silk with bright gold hems,
Had skilfully-sewn coverlets with comely facings,
And the fairest fur on the fringes was worked.
With ruddy gold rings on the cords ran the curtains;
Toulouse and Turkestan tapestries on the wall
And fine carpets underfoot, on the floor, were fittingly matched.
There amid merry talk the man was disrobed,
And stripped of his battle-sark° and his splendid clothes.
Retainers readily brought him rich robes
Of the choicest kind to choose from and change into.
In a trice when he took one, and was attired in it,
And it sat on him in style, with spreading skirts,
It certainly seemed to those assembled as if spring
In all its hues were evident before them;
His lithe limbs below the garment were gleaming with beauty.
Jesus never made, so men judged, more gentle and handsome
A knight:
From wherever in the world he were,
At sight it seemed he might
Be a prince without a peer
In field where fell men fight.

XXXVII

At the chimneyed hearth where charcoal burned, a chair was placed
For Sir Gawain in gracious style, gorgeously decked
With cushions on quilted work, both cunningly wrought;

free noble

battle-sark shirt of mail

SCOTLAND
Danish and Norse occupied territory north of this line.
NORTHUMBRIA
N
IRELAND
ISLE OF MAN
KINGDOM OF YORK
York
WIRRAL
Lincoln
Chester
WALES
ENGLISH MERCIA
EAST ANGLIA
Coventry
Cambridge
MALVERN HILLS
Maldon
Oxford
London
KENT
Canterbury
Winchester
WESSEX
Southampton
Hastings
ISLE OF WIGHT
Miles
0
50
100
A. Karl

1. Medieval England.

2. The Geography of Beowulf. After F. Klaeber, *Beowulf*.

3. The Site of the Battle of Maldon. From E. V. Gordon, ed., *The Battle of Maldon*.

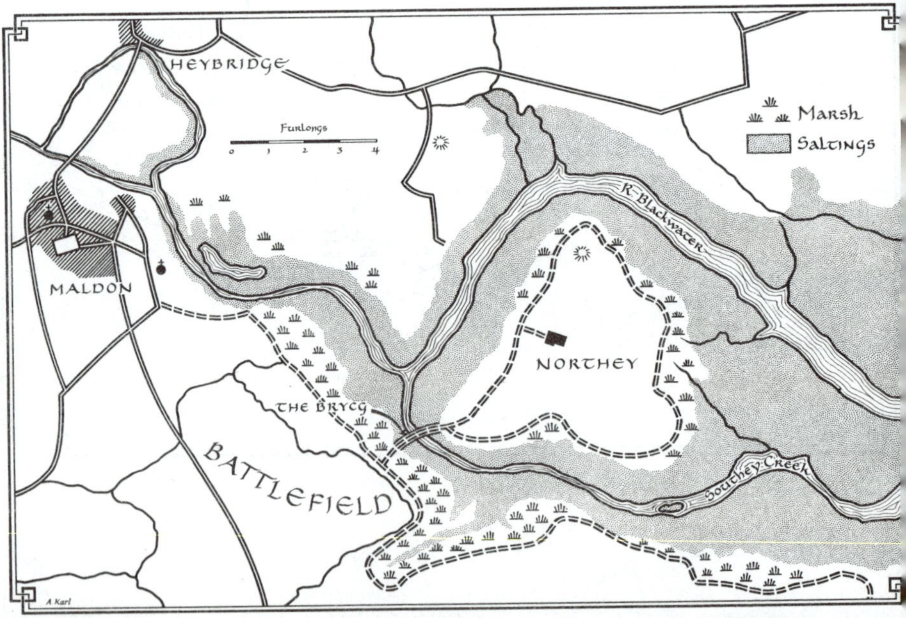

[...]ra dyde mægen hreð manna na

min ne þearft hafalan hydan ac hi[...]

me habban wile d[r]eore fahne gif mec

deað nimeð· byreð blodig wæl byrg[...]

þenceð eteð angenga unmurnlice

mearcað mor hopu no ðu ymb mine[...]

ne þearft lices feorme leng sorgi[...]

an· Onsend higelace gif mec hild

nime beadu scruda betst þ mine breos[...]

wereð hrægla selest þ is hrædlan laf

welandes geweorc gæð a wyrd swa hio scel·

·VII·

Hroðgar maþelode helm scyldinga

fere fyhtum þu wine min beowulf 7

for arstafum usic sohtest gesloh

þin fæder fæhðe mæste· wearþ he

heaþolafe to hand bonan mid wilfingu[...]

ða hine gara cyn for here brogan

habban ne mihte· þanon he gesohte

suð dena folc ofer yða gewealc ar

4. *Beowulf*, ll. 444-64, the manuscript, c. 1000. *British Museum*, MS Cotton Vitellius A. XV, fol. 140r.

5. Cruciform Carpet-page, with interlace ornament, from Lindisfarne Gospels. Northumbria, c. 700. *British Museum,* MS Cotton Nero D. IV, fol. 26v.

6. The Annunciation, from the Benedictional of St. Æthelwold, Bishop of Winchester 975-80. Winchester, c. 975. *British Museum*, MS Add. 49598, fol. 5v.

7. The Harrowing of Hell, from an English Psalter. First quarter of twelfth century. Hildesheim, *St. Godehard*, p. 49.

8. Goliath threatening David, from a Winchester Psalter. English, c. 1050. *British Museum,* MS Cotton Tiberius C. VI, fol. 9r.

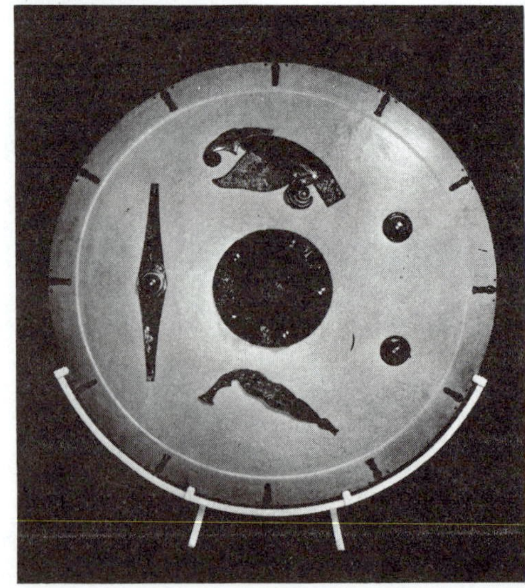

9. Sutton Hoo: Shield (front view, reconstruction). ?First half of the seventh century. *British Museum.*

10. David as Musician, from a Canterbury Psalter. English, c. 750. *British Museum,* MS Cotton Vespasian A. I, fol. 30v.

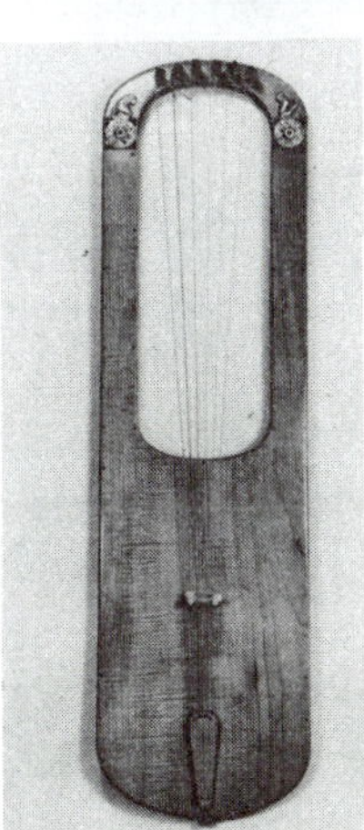

11. Sutton Hoo: the Harp as at present reconstructed. ?First half of seventh century. *British Museum.*

12. The Oseberg Ship. Viking luxury ship, not a warship. From a barrow in Norway, c. 800. Oslo, *Universitetets Oldsaksamling.*

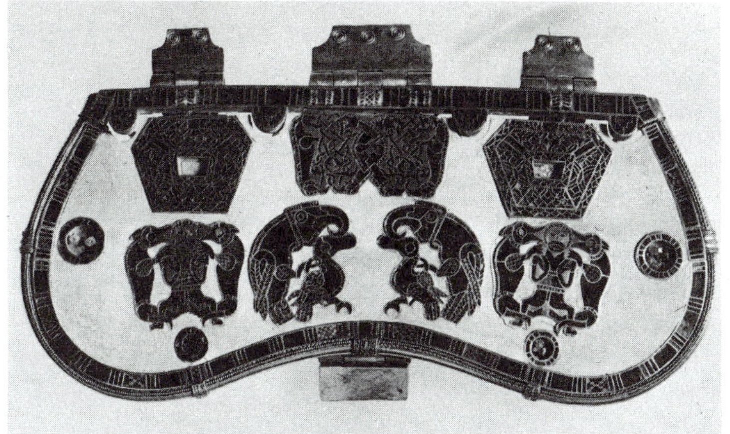

13. Sutton Hoo: Purse-lid of gold, enamel, glass, and garnet. ?English, first half of seventh century, *British Museum*.

14. Sutton Hoo: the great gold Belt Buckle, with ornament of interlaced snakes and animals. English, first half of seventh century. *British Museum*.

15. Sutton Hoo: Shoulder Clasps, one of a pair, of gold, garnet, and enamel. ?English, first half of seventh century. *British Museum*.

16. Sutton Hoo: large and small Drinking Horns. ?Early seventh century. There were seven in all: two large ones, of aurochs horn, had a capacity of six imperial quarts, a greatest diameter of 7.2″, and circumference of 41½″ along the outer curve; the small horns were cow horns. *British Museum.*

17. Sutton Hoo: Stag, height about 4″ from the head of the Scepter. ?First half of seventh century. *British Museum.*

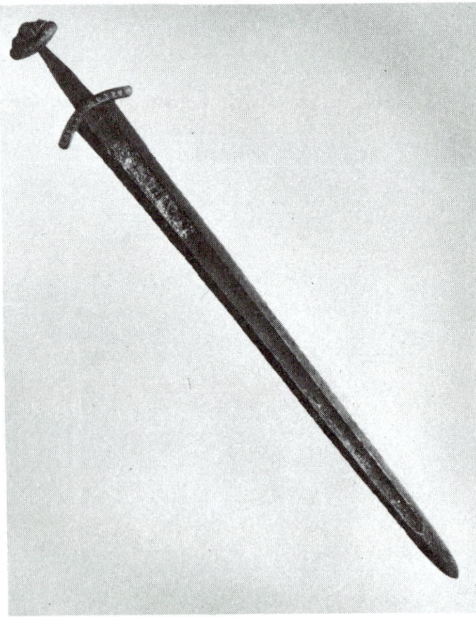

18. Sword with inlaid decoration. English, ninth or tenth century. *British Museum.*

19. Sutton Hoo: the Helmet. Swedish work, early sixth century. *British Museum.*

20. Boar Crest, from Benty Grange Helmet. English, seventh century. Sheffield, *City Museum.*

21. The Fetter Lane Sword Pommel, with snake design. English, ninth century. *British Museum.*

22. The Franks Casket (front) of whalebone ivory, is carved in relief. Northumbrian workmanship, early eighth century. *Left:* a scene from the story of Weland; *Right:* the Adoration of the Magi; both surrounded by a runic inscription in the Northumbrian dialect of Old English. *British Museum.*

23. Christ and Mary Magdalene, stone relief from the Ruthwell Cross, Ruthwell, Dumfriesshire. (The runes of the *Dream of the Rood* are not shown.) Northumbrian, ?early eighth century.

24. Chaucer reading his poem *Troilus and Criseyde* at court. English, c. 1410. Cambridge, *Corpus Christi College,* MS 61, fol. lv.

IN OYLE
THIS WAS PAINTED BEFORE IN

25. Richard II, with Saints Edmund, Edward the Confessor, and John the Baptist, adoring the Virgin and Child (Wilton Diptych). English, c. 1395-1405. London, *The National Gallery*.

26. *Upper left:* Geoffrey Chaucer, from the Ellesmere MS of the *Canterbury Tales.* English c. 1410. His clothes and the pen case hung around his neck identify him as a man of letters. San Marino, California, *Henry E. Huntington Library,* MS 26. c.9, fol. 159v. 27. *Upper right:* The Miller, fol. 34v. 28. *Lower left:* The Nun's Priest, fol. 185. 29. *Lower right:* The Wife of Bath, fol. 72.

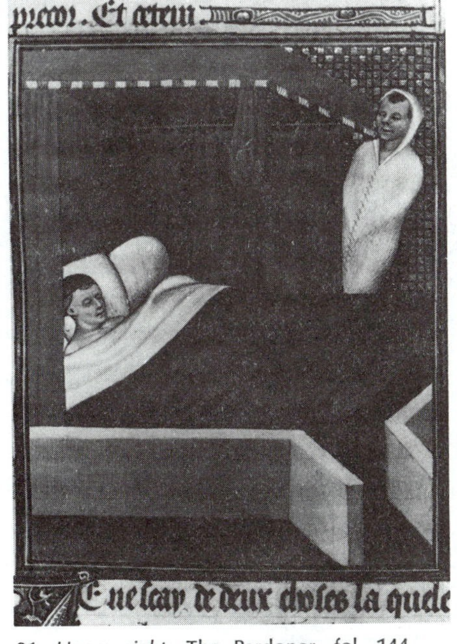

30. *Upper left:* The Franklin, fol. 129v. 31. *Upper right:* The Pardoner, fol. 144. 32. *Lower left:* Friar confessing a nun, from Luttrell Psalter. English, c. 1340. *British Museum*, MS Add. 42130, fol. 74. 33. *Lower right:* The Drowned Man warns Simonides in a dream not to sail, from Boccaccio, *De casibus virorum illustrium*. French, 1409-14. Paris, *Bibliothèque de l'Arsenal*, MS 5193, fol. 76v.

34. Reynard as a bishop, preaching to the birds; and Reynard escaping with a goose, chased by the farmer's wife, from the Smithfield Decretals. English, c. 1340. *British Museum,* MS Royal 10.E.IV, fol. 49v.

35. St. Thomas Becket taking ship from England (*above*) and his martyrdom in Canterbury Cathedral (*below*), on a Limoges enamel *châsse* (case for relics, etc.). French, thirteenth century. *British Museum.*

36. The Capture of Alexandria, in which the Knight took part. French, fourteenth century. Paris, *Bibliotheque Nationale,* MS franç. 1584, fol. 309.

37. Zodiac Man and Vein Man, with the Qualities. By the Brothers Limbourg; from the *Très Riches Heures du duc de Berry*. Franco-Flemish, before 1416. Chantilly, *Musée Condé,* MS 65 (1284), fol. 14v. *Photo Giraudon.*

An important part of the physician's skill was to know the correct time of year, month, or day in which treatment, especially by bloodletting, would be feasible and effective by virtue of a favorable relation between macrocosm and microcosm: planets, zodiacal signs, qualities, humors, sex, and parts of the body. The zodiacal sign of the Ram governs the head, so that a time when the sun was in the Ram would be favorable for treating that part. Taurus governed the neck, Gemini the shoulders and arms, and so on. In this miniature, the "qualities," hot, cold, moist, and dry, which are combined in the "humors," blood, phlegm, choler, and melancholy, are associated with zodiacal signs and with male and female sexes in the corners, which are the cardinal points of the compass.

38. The Buying of the Poison and the Deaths of the "Rioters," from Chaucer's Pardoner's Tale. English wood-relief, c. 1400. London, private collection.

39. Lechery. English, mid-fourteenth century. The man's gesture (which is also that of Nicholas of Chaucer's Miller's Tale) is obviously associated with lechery, as is the tavern before which the couple stand, with its ale-bush. *British Museum,* Taymouth Hours, fol. 177.

40. Swearing and Gambling: "rioters" tear Christ's body apart. Broughton, Bucks., wall-painting in St. Lawrence Church. English c. 1430. *Royal Commission on Historical Monuments, Crown Copyright.*

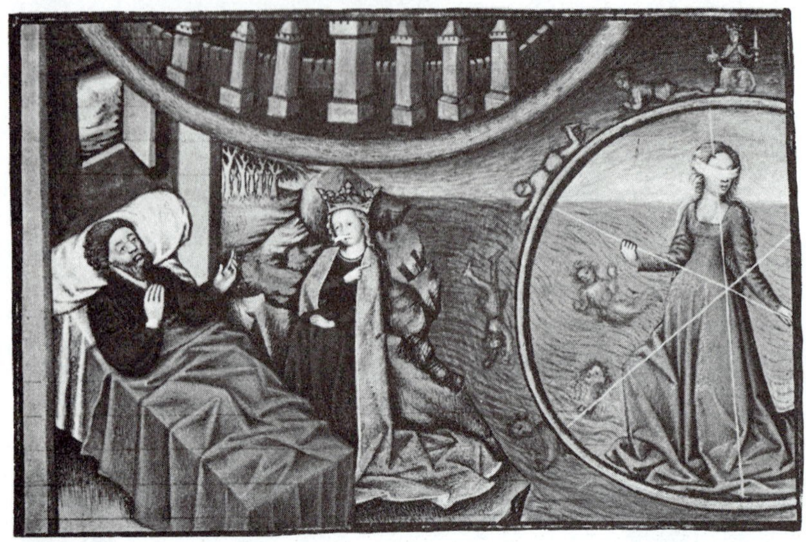

41. Philosophy and Blind Fortune with her Wheel, from Boethius, *De Consolatione Philosophiae* (trans. Jean de Meun). French, c. 1450-60. *British Museum,* MS Add. 10341, fol. 31v.

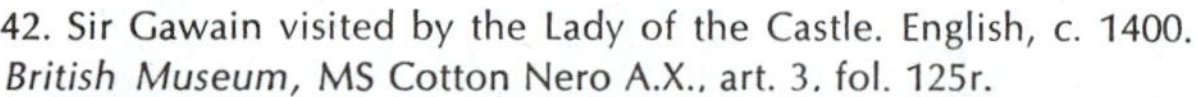

42. Sir Gawain visited by the Lady of the Castle. English, c. 1400. *British Museum,* MS Cotton Nero A.X., art. 3. fol. 125r.

43. A New Year feast in the court of Jean duc de Berry, with the sun in his chariot in the zodiacal signs of Capricorn and Aquarius (January), and a tournament in the background. By the Brothers Limbourg; from the *Très Riches Heures du duc de Berry,* Chantilly, *Musée Condé,* MS 65 (1284), fol. 1v. *Giraudon.*

44. A Castle, with the vintage being gathered, and the sun in the signs of Virgo and Libra (September). Begun by the Brothers Limbourg before 1416, and completed by Jean Colombe c. 1485; from the *Très Riches Heures du duc de Berry*, Chantilly, *Musée Condé*, MS 65 (1284), fol. 9v. *Giraudon*.

45. A Boar Hunt, with the sun in Sagittarius and Capricorn (December). By the Brothers Limbourg; from the *Très Riches Heures du duc de Berry*, Chantilly, *Musée Condé*, MS 65 (1284), fol. 12v. *Giraudon*.

46. King Arthur, from the Berry tapestry of the Nine Worthies. French, late fourteenth century. *New York, the Cloisters, Metropolitan Museum of Art.*

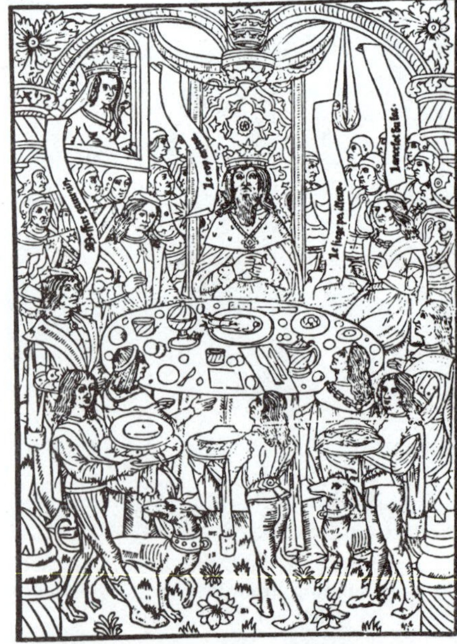

47. The Round Table. From *Lancelot,* Rouen, Dupré, 1488.

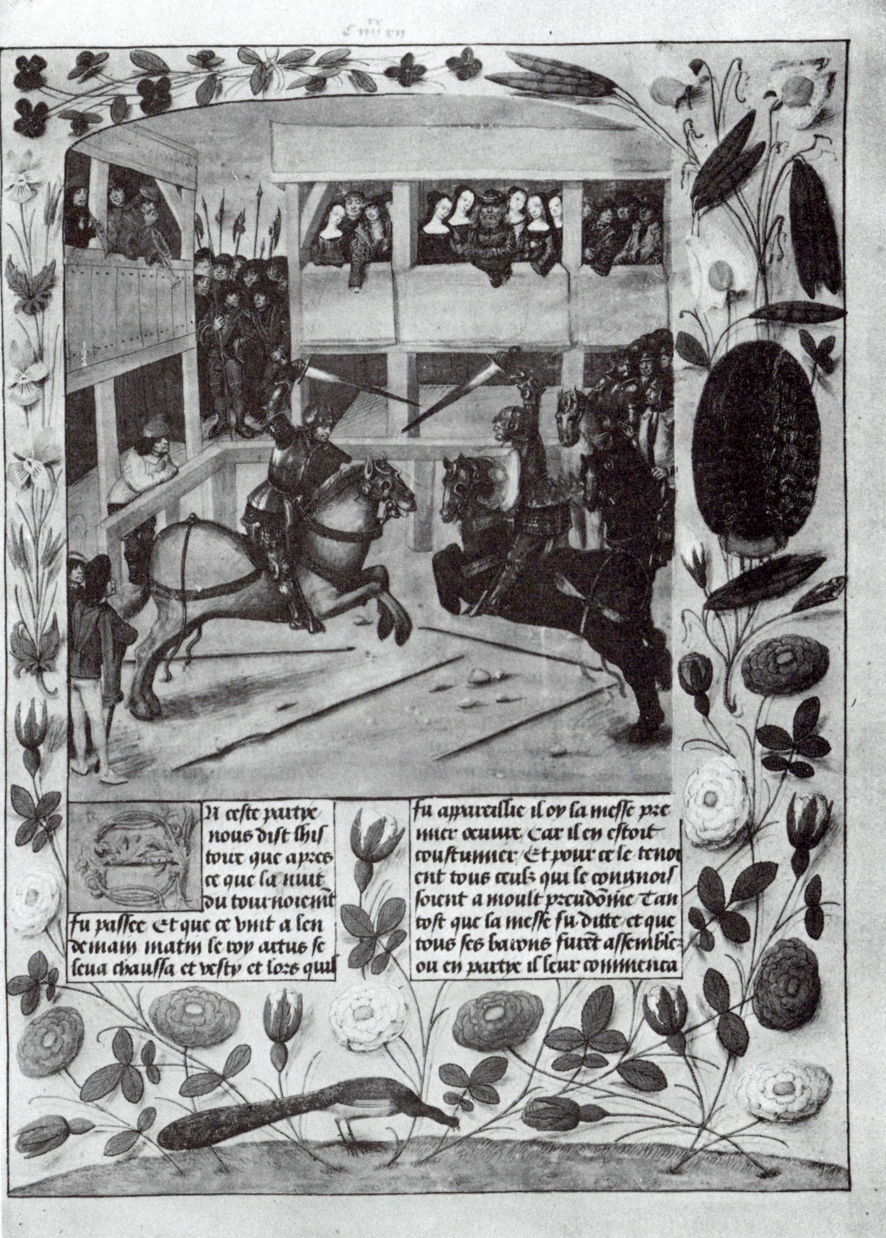

48. A Joust before King Arthur. By the so-called Master of Edward IV, from a Flemish manuscript of (?) Hélie de Borron, *Guiron le courtois*, c. 1480-1500. Oxford, *Bodleian Library*, MS Douce 383, fol. 16r.

49. The Annunciation to the Shepherds. By the Brothers Limbourg. *Très Riches Heures du duc de Berry,* Chantilly, *Musée Condé,* MS 65 (1284), fol. 48r. *Giraudon.*

50. The Last Judgment. By the Brothers Limbourg; from *Très Riches Heures du duc de Berry,* Chantilly, *Musée Condé,* MS 65 (1284), fol. 34r. *Giraudon.*

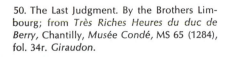

51. Everyman seeking Profit. By Peter Bruegel the Elder (1525/30–1569), Flemish, about 1558. Later than the play of *Everyman* and illustrating a Flemish proverb, this nevertheless depicts what the play warns against.

52. Death in True Piety, from *Ars Moriendi,* Netherlandish block-book, 1466. The soul of the penitent received into Heaven by the mediation of Christ, with Mary, John, and Mary Magdalene below the Cross. The confessor places a candle in the dying man's hand, while the frustrated devils exclaim in fury and despair.

53. The Miracles of the Cherry Tree and the Cornfield. See "Cherry-Tree Carol." The cornfield below is a reference to a miracle that enabled Joseph, Mary, and the Christ Child to escape their pursuers on the Flight into Egypt. By Jean Colombe c. 1485; from the Très Riches Heures *du duc de Berry*, Chantilly, *Musée Condé*, MS 65 (1284), fol. 57r. *Giraudon.*

54. The Garden of the *Romance of the Rose*. French, 15th century. The Dreamer asleep (*below*) and the Lover admitted by Idleness into the Garden (*above*); Covetousness, Avarice, Envy, Sorrow, on the walls; Danger (Stand-offishness) with a club inside; Narcissus at the fountain in the center. *British Museum*, MS Egerton 1069, fol. 1r.

55. *Mappa mundi* (mappemonde), from Jean Mansel, *La Fleur des histoires*. Flemish, c. 1455. Brussels, *Bibliothèque Royale,* MS 9231, fol. 281v.

Other maps are much more detailed. This is more schematic and decorative than utilitarian: it shows earth surrounded by the other elements (water, air, and fire) in concentric circles, and the starry heaven outside them. As usual, the East is at the top with the phoenix in the woods of Paradise, Noah's Ark on Mt. Ararat, and the sons of Noah (from whom post-diluvial man is sprung) on the three then-known continents: Sem on Asia, Ham (Cham) on Africa, and Japhet on Europe.

56. Paradise. By the Brothers Limbourg; from the *Très Riches Heures du duc de Berry,* Chantilly, *Musée Condé,* MS 65 (1284), fol. 25v. *Giraudon.*

Paradise, high in the mountains, walled with the Fountain of Life at the center; Eve tempted by the Serpent "with a lady visage"; Eve tempting Adam; Adam pointing to Eve as the source of the trouble as God rebukes them; the Expulsion by the fiery angel.

And then on that man a magnificent mantle was thrown,
A gleaming garment gorgeously embroidered,
Fairly lined with fur, the finest skins
Of ermine on earth, and his hood of the same.
In that splendid seat he sat in dignity,
And warmth came to him at once, bringing well-being.
In a trice on fine trestles a table was put up,°
Then covered with a cloth shining clean and white,
And set with silver spoons, salt-cellars and overlays.
The worthy knight washed willingly, and went to his meat.
In seemly enough style servants brought him
Several fine soups, seasoned lavishly,
Twice-fold, as is fitting, and fish of all kinds—
Some baked in bread, some browned on coals,
Some seethed,° some stewed and savoured with spice,
But always subtly sauced, and so the man liked it.
The gentle knight generously judged it a feast,
And often said so, while the servers spurred him on thus
As he ate:
'This present penance° do:
It soon shall be offset.'
The knight rejoiced anew,
For the wine his spirits whet.

XXXVIII

Then in seemly style they searchingly inquired,
Putting to the prince private questions,
So that he courteously conceded he came of that court
Where high-souled Arthur held sway alone,
Ruler most royal of the Round Table;
And that Sir Gawain himself now sat in the house,
Having come that Christmas, by course of fortune.
Loudly laughed the lord when he learned what knight
He had in his house; such happiness it brought
That all the men within the moat made merry,
And promptly appeared in the presence of Gawain,
To whose person are proper all prowess and worth,
And pure and perfect manners, and praises unceasing.
His reputation rates first in the ranks of men.
Each knight neared his neighbour and softly said,
'Now we shall see displayed the seemliest manners
And the faultless figures of virtuous discourse.
Without asking we may hear how to hold conversation
Since we have seized upon this scion of good breeding.

In . . . up Tables were put up and taken down as required in the Middle Ages. See Chaucer, the General Prologue, l. 355.
seethed boiled
penance On the eve of Christmas, Gawain is technically abstaining—i.e. eating no meat—but he is being given a feast of fish. Still, they tell him, he will do better on Christmas Day.

God has given us of his grace good measure,
In granting us such a guest as Gawain is,
When, contented at Christ's birth, the courtiers shall sit
And sing.
This noble knight will prove
What manners the mighty bring;
His converse of courtly love
Shall spur our studying.'

XXXIX

When the fine man had finished his food and risen,
It was nigh and near to the night's mid-hour.
Priests to their prayers paced their way
And rang the bells royally, as rightly they should,
To honour that high feast with evensong.
The lord inclines to prayer, the lady too;
Into her private pew she prettily walks;
Gawain advances gaily and goes there quickly,
But the lord gripped his gown and guided him to his seat,
Acknowledged him by name and benevolently said
In the whole world he was the most welcome of men.
Gawain spoke his gratitude, they gravely embraced,
And sat in serious mood the whole service through.
Then the lady had a longing to look on the knight;
With her bevy of beauties she abandoned her pew.
Most beautiful of body and bright of complexion,
Most winsome in ways of all women alive,
She seemed to Sir Gawain, excelling Guinevere.
To squire that splendid dame, he strode through the chancel.
Another lady led her by the left hand,
A matron, much older, past middle age,
Who was highly honoured by an escort of squires.
Most unlike to look on those ladies were,
For if the one was winsome, then withered was the other.
Hues rich and rubious° were arrayed on the one,
Rough wrinkles on the other rutted the cheeks.
Kerchiefed with clear pearls clustering was the one,
Her breast and bright throat bare to the sight,
Shining like sheen of snow shed on the hills;
The other was swathed with a wimple° wound to the throat
And choking her swarthy chin in chalk-white veils.
On her forehead were folded enveloping silks,
Trellised about with trefoils and tiny rings.
Nothing was bare on that beldame but the black brows,
The two eyes, protruding nose and stark lips,
And those were a sorry sight and exceedingly bleary:

rubious ruby-red

wimple cloth covering the neck, sides of the head, and forehead

A grand lady, God knows, of greatness in the world
Well tried!
Her body was stumpy and squat,
Her buttocks bulging and wide;
More pleasure a man could plot
With the sweet one at her side.

XL

When Gawain had gazed on that gracious-looking creature
He gained leave of the lord to go along with the ladies.
He saluted the senior, sweeping a low bow,
But briefly embraced the beautiful one,
Kissing her in courtly style and complimenting her.
They craved his acquaintance and he quickly requested
To be their faithful follower, if they would so favour him.
They took him between them, and talking, they led him
To a high room. By the hearth they asked first
For spices, which unstintingly men sped to bring,
And always with heart-warming, heady wine.
In lovingkindness the lord leaped up repeatedly
And many times reminded them that mirth should flow;
Elaborately lifted up his hood, looped it on a spear,
And offered it as a mark of honour to whoever should prove able
To make the most mirth that merry Yuletide.
'And I shall essay, I swear, to strive with the best
Before this garment goes from me, by my good friends' help.'
So with his mirth the mighty lord made things merry
To gladden Sir Gawain with games in hall
That night;
Until, the time being spent,
The lord demanded light.
Gawain took his leave and went
To rest in rare delight.

XLI

On that morning when men call to mind the birth
Of our dear Lord born to die for our destiny,
Joy waxes in dwellings the world over for His sake:
And so it befell there on the feast day with fine fare.
Both at main meals and minor repasts strong men served
Rare dishes with fine dressings to the dais company.
Highest, in the place of honour, the ancient crone sat,
And the lord, so I believe, politely next.
Together sat Gawain and the gay lady
In mid-table, where the meal was mannerly served first;
And after throughout the hall, as was held best,
Each gallant by degree was graciously served.
There was meat and merry-making and much delight,

To such an extent that it would try me to tell of it,
Even if perhaps I made the effort to describe it.
But yet I know the knight and the nobly pretty one
Found such solace and satisfaction seated together,
In the discreet confidences of their courtly dalliance,
Their irreproachably pure and polished repartee,
That with princes' sport their play of wit surpassingly
Compares.
Pipes and side-drums sound,
Trumpets entune their airs;
Each soul its solace found,
And the two were enthralled with theirs.

XLII

That day they made much merriment, and on the morrow again,
And thickly the joys thronged on the third day after;
But gentle was the jubilation on St. John's Day,°
The final one for feasting, so the folk there thought.
As there were guests geared to go in the grey dawn
They watched the night out with wine in wonderful style,
Leaping night-long in their lordly dances.
At last when it was late those who lived far off,
Each one, bid farewell before wending their ways.
Gawain also said good-bye, but the good host grasped him,
Led him to the hearth of his own chamber,
And held him back hard, heartily thanking him
For the fine favour he had manifested to him
In honouring his house that high feast-tide,
Brightening his abode with his brilliant company:
'As long as I live, sir, I believe I shall thrive
Now Gawain has been my guest at God's own feast.'
'Great thanks, sir,' said Gawain, 'In good faith, yours,
All yours is the honour, may the High King requite it!
I stand at your service, knight, to satisfy your will
As good use engages me, in great things and small,
By right.'
The lord then bid his best
Longer to delay the knight,
But Gawain, replying, pressed
His departure in all despite.

XLIII

Then with courteous inquiry the castellan° asked
What fierce exploit had sent him forth, at that festive season,
From the King's court at Camelot, so quickly and alone,
Before the holy time was over in the homes of men.

St. John's Day feast of John the Evangelist, December 27

castellan keeper of the castle

'You may in truth well demand,' admitted the knight.
'A high and urgent errand hastened me from thence,
For I myself am summoned to seek out a place
To find which I know not where in the world to look.
For all the land in Logres°—may our Lord help me!
I would not fail to find it on the feast of New Year.
So this is my suit, sir, which I beseech of you here,
That you tell me in truth if tale ever reached you
Of the Green Chapel, or what ground or glebe° it stands on,
Or of the knight who holds it, whose hue is green.
For at that place I am pledged, by the pact between us,
To meet that man, if I remain alive.
From now until the New Year is not a great time,
And if God will grant it me, more gladly would I see him
Than gain any good possession, by God's son!
I must wend my way, with your good will, therefore;
I am reduced to three days in which to do my business,
And I think it fitter to fall dead than fail in my errand.'
Then the lord said laughingly, 'You may linger a while,
For I shall tell you where your tryst is by your term's end.
Give yourself no more grief for the Green Chapel's whereabouts,
For you may lie back in your bed, brave man, at ease
Till full morning on the First, and then fare forth
To the meeting-place at mid-morning to manage how you may
Out there.
Leave not till New Year's Day,
Then get up and go with cheer;
You shall be shown the way;
It is hardly two miles from here.'

XLIV

Then Gawain was glad and gleefully exclaimed,
'Now above all, most heartily do I offer you thanks!
For my goal is now gained, and by grace of yours
I shall dwell here and do what you deem good for me.'
So the lord seized Sir Gawain, seated him beside himself,
And to enliven their delight, he had the ladies fetched,
And much gentle merriment they long made together.
The lord, as one like to take leave of his senses
And not aware of what he was doing, spoke warmly and merrily.
Then he spoke to Sir Gawain, saying out loud,
'You have determined to do the deed I ask:
Will you hold to your undertaking here and now?'
'Yes, sir, in good sooth,' said the true knight,
'While I stay in your stronghold, I shall stand at your command.'
'Since you have spurred,' the lord said, 'from afar,

Logres Britain south of the Humber **glebe** field

Then watched awake° with me, you are not well supplied
With either sustenance or sleep, for certain, I know;
So you shall lie long in your room, late and at ease
Tomorrow till the time of mass, and then take your meal
When you will, with my wife beside you
To comfort you with her company till I come back to court.
You stay,
And I shall get up at dawn.
I will to the hunt away.'
When Gawain's agreement was sworn
He bowed, as brave knights may.

XLV

'Moreover,' said the man, 'Let us make a bargain
That whatever I win in the woods be yours,
And any achievement you chance on here, you exchange for it.
Sweet sir, truly swear to such a bartering,
Whether fair fortune or foul befall from it.'
'By God,' said the good Gawain, 'I agree to that,
And I am happy that you have an eye to sport.'
Then the prince of that people said, 'What pledge of wine
Is brought to seal the bargain?' And they burst out laughing.
They took drink and toyed in trifling talk,
These lords and ladies, as long as they liked,
And then with French refinement and many fair words
They stood, softly speaking, to say good-night,
Kissing as they parted company in courtly style.
With lithe liege servants in plenty and lambent torches,
Each brave man was brought to his bed at last,
Full soft.
Before they fared to bed
They rehearsed their bargain oft.
That people's prince, men said,
Could fly his wit aloft.

Fitt 3

XLVI

In the faint light before dawn folk were stirring;
Guests who had to go gave orders to their grooms,
Who busied themselves briskly with the beasts, saddling,
Trimming their tackle and tying on their luggage.
Arrayed for riding in the richest style,
Guests leaped on their mounts lightly, laid hold of their bridles,
And each rider rode out on his own chosen way.
The beloved lord of the land was not the last up,

watched awake reveled

Being arrayed for riding with his retinue in force.
He ate a sop° hastily when he had heard mass,
And hurried with horn to the hunting field;
Before the sun's first rays fell on the earth,
On their high steeds were he and his knights.
Then these cunning hunters came to couple° their hounds,
Cast open the kennel° doors and called them out,
And blew on their bugles three bold notes.°
The hounds broke out barking, baying fiercely,
And when they went chasing, they were whipped back.
There were a hundred choice huntsmen there, whose fame
        Resounds.
    To their stations keepers strode;
    Huntsmen unleashed hounds:
    The forest overflowed
    With the strident bugle sounds.

XLVII

At the first cry wild creatures quivered with dread.
The deer in distraction darted down to the dales
Or up to the high ground, but eagerly they were
Driven back by the beaters, who bellowed lustily.
They let the harts with high-branching heads have their freedom,
And the brave bucks, too, with their broad antlers,
For the noble prince had expressly prohibited
Meddling with male deer in the months of close season.°
But the hinds were held back with a 'Hey' and a 'Whoa!'
And does driven with much din to the deep valleys.
Lo! the arrows' slanting flight as they were loosed!
A shaft flew forth at every forest turning,
The broad head biting on the brown flank.
They screamed as the blood streamed out, sank dead on the sward,
Always harried by hounds hard on their heels,
And the hurrying hunters' high horn notes.
Like the rending of ramped° hills roared the din.
If one of the wild beasts slipped away from the archers
It was dragged down and met death at the dog-bases
After being hunted from the high ground and harried to the water,
So skilled were the hunt-servants at stations lower down,
So gigantic the greyhounds that grabbed them in a flash,
Seizing them savagely, as swift, I swear,
        As sight.

sop bread dipped in spiced wine; see Chaucer, the General Prologue, l. 336
couple put leashes on
kennel The hounds would have been in one large kennel.
notes The hunting horn had only one note, so that differentiation was by long and short. The names of the calls were mote, trut, trororout, trorororout.
close season Winter, September to June, was the closed season for male deer; only females were hunted during winter.
ramped sloping

The lord, in humour high
Would spur, then stop and alight.
In bliss the day went by
Till dark drew on, and night.

XLVIII

Thus by the forest borders the brave lord sported,
And the good man Gawain, on his gay bed lying,
Lay hidden till the light of day gleamed on the walls.
Covered with fair canopy, the curtains closed,
And as in slumber he slept on, there slipped into his mind
A slight, suspicious sound, and the door stealthily opened.
He raised up his head out of the bedclothes,
Caught up the corner of the curtain a little
And watched warily towards it, to see what it was.
It was the lady, loveliest to look upon,
Who secretly and silently secured the door,
Then bore towards his bed: the brave knight, embarrassed,
Lay flat with fine adroitness and feigned sleep.
Silently she stepped on, stole to his bed,
Caught up the curtain, crept within,
And seated herself softly on the side of the bed.
There she watched a long while, waiting for him to wake.
Slyly close this long while lay the knight,
Considering in his soul this circumstance,
Its sense and likely sequel, for it seemed marvellous.
'Still, it would be more circumspect,' he said to himself,
'To speak and discover her desire in due course.'
So he stirred and stretched himself, twisting towards her,
Opened his eyes and acted as if astounded;
And, to seem the safer by such service, crossed himself
In dread.
With chin and cheek so fair,
White ranged with rosy red,
With laughing lips, and air
Of love, she lightly said:

XLIX

'Good morning, Sir Gawain,' the gay one murmured,
'How unsafely you sleep, that one may slip in here!
Now you are taken in a trice. Unless a truce come between us,
I shall bind you to your bed—of that be sure.'
The lady uttered laughingly those playful words.
'Good morning, gay lady,' Gawain blithely greeted her.
'Do with me as you will: that well pleases me.
For I surrender speedily and sue for grace,
Which, to my mind, since I must, is much the best course.'
And thus he repaid her with repartee and ready laughter.
'But if, lovely lady, your leave were forthcoming,

And you were pleased to free your prisoner and pray him to rise,
I would abandon my bed for a better habiliment,
And have more happiness in our honey talk.'
'Nay, verily, fine sir,' urged the voice of that sweet one,
'You shall not budge from your bed. I have a better idea.
I shall hold you fast here on this other side as well
And so chat on with the chevalier my chains have caught.
For I know well, my knight, that your name is Sir Gawain,
Whom all the world worships, wherever he ride;
For lords and their ladies, and all living folk,
Hold your honour in high esteem, and your courtesy.
And now—here you are truly, and we are utterly alone;
My lord and his liege man are a long way off;
Others still bide in their beds, my bower-maidens too;
Shut fast and firmly with a fine hasp is the door;
And since I have in this house him who pleases all,
As long as my time lasts I shall lingering in talk take
My fill.
My young body is yours,
Do with it what you will;
My strong necessities force
Me to be your servant still.'°

L

'In good truth,' said Gawain, 'that is a gain indeed,
Though I am hardly the hero of whom you speak.
To be held in such honour as you here suggest,
I am altogether unworthy, I own it freely.
By God, I should be glad if you granted it right,
For me to essay by speech or some other service,
To pleasure such a perfect lady—pure joy it would be.'
'In good truth, Sir Gawain,' the gay lady replied,
'If I slighted or set at naught your spotless fame
And your all-pleasing prowess, it would show poor breeding.
But there is no lack of ladies who would love, noble one,
To hold you in their arms, as I have you here,
And linger in the luxury of your delightful discourse,
Which would perfectly pleasure them and appease their woes,—
Rather than have riches or the red gold they own.
But as I love that Lord, the Celestial Ruler,
I have wholly in my hand what all desire
Through his grace.'
Not loth was she to allure,
This lady fair of face;
But the knight with speeches pure
Answered in each case.

My young . . . still (ll. 1237–40) This seems like a direct assault for the first temptation of Gawain, engineered at least—see below—by a sorceress.

LI

'Madam,' said the merry man, 'May Mary requite you!
For in good faith I have found in you free-hearted generosity.
Certain men for their deeds receive esteem from others,
But for myself, I do not deserve the respect they show me;
Your honourable mind makes you utter only what is good.'
'Now by Mary,' said the noble lady, 'Not so it seems to me,
For were I worth the whole of womankind,
And all the wealth in the world were in my hand,
And if bargaining I were to bid to bring myself a lord,
With your noble qualities, knight, made known to me now,
Your good looks, gracious manner, and great courtesy,
All of which I had heard of before, but here prove true,
No lord that is living could be allowed to excel you.'
'Indeed, dear lady, you did better,' said the knight,
'But I am proud of the precious price you put on me,
And solemnly as your servant say you are my sovereign.
May Christ requite it you: I have become your knight.'
Then of many matters they talked till mid-morning and after,
And all the time she behaved as if she adored him;
But Sir Gawain was on guard in a gracious manner.
Though she was the winsomest woman the warrior had known,
He was less love-laden because of the loss he must
Now face—
His destruction by the stroke,
For come it must was the case.
The lady of leaving then spoke;
He assented with speedy grace.

LII

Then she gave him good-bye, glinting with laughter,
And standing up, astounded him with these strong words:
'May He who prospers every speech for this pleasure reward you!
I cannot bring myself to believe that you could be Gawain.'
'How so?' said the knight, speaking urgently,
For he feared he had failed to observe the forms of courtesy.
But the beauteous one blessed him and brought out this argument:
'Such a great man as Gawain is granted to be,
The very vessel of virtue and fine courtesy,
Could scarcely have stayed such a sojourn with a lady
Without craving a kiss out of courtesy,
Touched by some trifling hint at the tail-end of a speech.'
'So be it, as you say,' then said Gawain,
'I shall kiss at your command, as becomes a knight
Who fears to offend you; no further plea is needed.'
Whereupon she approached him, and penned him in her arms,
Leaned over him lovingly and gave the lord a kiss.
Then they commended each other to Christ in comely style,

And without more words she went out by the door.
He made ready to rise with rapid haste,
Summoned his servant, selected his garb,
And walked down, when he was dressed, debonairly° to mass.
Then he went to the well-served meal which awaited him.
And made merry sport till the moon rose
At night.
Never was baron bold
So taken by ladies bright,
The young one and the old:
They throve all three in delight.

LIII

And still at his sport spurred the castellan,
Hunting the barren hinds in holt° and on heath.
So many had he slain, by the setting of the sun,
Of does and other deer, that it was downright wonderful.
Then at the finish the folk flocked in eagerly,
And quickly collected the killed deer in a heap.
Those highest in rank came up with hosts of attendants,
Picked out what appeared to be the plumpest beasts
And, according to custom, had them cut open with finesse.
Some who ceremoniously assessed° them there
Found two fingers' breadth of fat on the worst.
Then they slit open the slot, seized the first stomach,°
Scraped it with a keen knife and tied up the tripes.
Next they hacked off all the legs, the hide was stripped,
The belly broken open and the bowels removed
Carefully, lest they loosen the ligature of the knot.
Then they gripped the gullet, disengaged deftly
The wezand° from the windpipe and whipped out the guts.
Then their sharp knives shore through the shoulder-bones,
Which they slid out of a small hole, leaving the sides° intact.
Then they cleft the chest clean through, cutting it in two.
Then again at the gullet a man began to work
And straight away rived it, right to the fork,
Flicked out the shoulder-fillets, and faithfully then
He rapidly ripped free the rib-fillets.
Similarly, as is seemly, the spine was cleared
All the way to the haunch, which hung from it;
And they heaved up the whole haunch and hewed it off;
And that is called, according to its kind, the numbles,°
I find.

debonairly elegantly
holt wood
assessed i.e. to see how good and thick the flesh was. The chief of the hunt cut a slit down the breast, or brisket. Hunting was a highly formalized, aristocratic pastime, with an elaborate language and etiquette.
slit . . . stomach slit open the hollow at the base of the throat; and seized the gullet
wezand esophagus
sides skin of the sides
numbles offal from back and loins

At the thigh-forks then they strain
And free the folds behind,
Hurrying to hack all in twain,
The backbone to unbind.

LIV

Then they hewed off the head and also the neck,
And after sundered the sides swiftly from the chine,
And into the foliage they flung the fee of the raven.°
Then each fellow, for his fee,° as it fell to him to have,
Skewered through the stout flanks beside the ribs,
And then by the hocks of the haunches they hung up their booty.
On one of the finest fells° they fed their hounds,
And let them have the lights,° the liver and the tripes,
With bread well imbrued with blood mixed with them.
Boldly they blew the kill amid the baying of hounds.
Then off they went homewards, holding their meat,
Stalwartly sounding many stout horn-calls.
As dark was descending, they were drawing near
To the comely castle where quietly our knight stayed.
Fires roared,
And blithely hearts were beating
As into hall came the lord.
When Gawain gave him greeting,
Joy abounded at the board.

LV

Then the master commanded everyone to meet in the hall,
Called the ladies to come down with their company of maidens.
Before all the folk on the floor, he bid men
Fetch the venison and place it before him.
Then gaily and in good humour to Gawain he called,
Told over the tally of the sturdy beasts,
And showed him the fine fat flesh flayed from the ribs.
'How does the sport please you? Do you praise me for it?
Am I thoroughly thanked for thriving as a huntsman?'
'Certainly,' said the other, 'Such splendid spoils
Have I not seen for seven years in the season of winter.'
'And I give you all, Gawain,' said the good man then,
'For according to our covenant you may claim it as your own.'
'Certes, that is so, and I say the same to you,'
Said Gawain, 'For my true gains in this great house,
I am not loth to allow, must belong to you.'

fee . . . raven bit of gristle flung into a tree for the crows and ravens gathered around the hunt
fellow . . . fee The portions of the carcasses were assigned to members of the hunt in strict order.
fells skins
lights lungs

And he put his arms round his handsome neck, hugging him,
And kissed him in the comeliest way he could think of.
'Accept my takings, sir, for I received no more;
Gladly would I grant them, however great they were.'
'And therefore I thank you,' the thane said, 'Good!
Yours may be the better gift, if you would break° it to me
Where your wisdom won you wealth of that kind.'
'No such clause in our contract! Request nothing else!'
Said the other, 'You have your due: ask more,
None should.'
They laughed in blithe assent
With worthy words and good;
Then to supper they swiftly went,
To fresh delicious food.

LVI

And sitting afterwards by the hearth of an audience chamber,
Where retainers repeatedly brought them rare wines,
In their jolly jesting they jointly agreed
On a settlement similar to the preceding one;
To exchange the chance achievements of the morrow,
No matter how novel they were, at night when they met.
They accorded on this compact, the whole court observing,
And the bumper was brought forth in banter to seal it.
And at last they lovingly took leave of each other,
Each man hastening thereafter to his bed.
The cock having crowed and called only thrice,°
The lord leaped from bed, and his liege men too,
So that mass and a meal were meetly dealt with,
And by first light the folk to the forest were bound
For the chase.
Proudly the hunt with horns
Soon drove through a desert place:
Uncoupled through the thorns°
The great hounds pressed apace.

LVII

By a quagmire they quickly scented quarry and gave tongue,
And the chief huntsman urged on the first hounds up,
Spurring them on with a splendid spate of words.°
The hounds, hearing it, hurried there at once,
Fell on the trail furiously, forty together,
And made such echoing uproar, all howling at once,
That the rocky banks round about rang with the din.

break disclose
cock . . . thrice Third cock-crow was just before dawn.
thorns looking for boars, which lurk in such difficult places
spate . . . words Hounds needed more encouragement to tackle boars. See Fig. 45.

Hunters inspirited them with sound of speech and horn.
Then together in a group, across the ground they surged
At speed between a pool and a spiteful crag.
On a stony knoll by a steep cliff at the side of a bog,
Where rugged rocks had roughly tumbled down,
They careered on the quest, the cry following;
They surrounded the crag and the rocky knoll as well,
Certain their prey skulked inside their ring,
For the baying of the bloodhounds meant the beast was there.
Then they beat upon the bushes and bade him come out,
And he swung out savagely aslant the line of men,
A baneful boar of unbelievable size,
A solitary long since sundered from the herd,
Being old and brawny, the biggest of them all,
And grim and ghastly when he grunted: great was the grief
When he thrust through the hounds, hurling three to earth,
And sped on scot-free, swift and unscathed.
They hallooed, yelled, 'Look out!' cried 'Hey, we have him!'
And blew horns boldly, to bring the bloodhounds together;
Many were the merry cries from men and dogs
As they hurried clamouring after their quarry to kill him on
The track.
Many times he turns at bay
And tears the dogs which attack.
He hurts the hounds, and they
Moan in a piteous pack.

LVIII

Then men shoved forward, shaped to shoot at him,
Loosed arrows at him, hitting him often,
But the points, for all their power, could not pierce his flanks,
Nor would the barbs bite on his bristling brow.°
Though the smooth-shaven shaft shattered in pieces,
Wherever it hit, the head rebounded.
But when the boar was battered by blows unceasing,
Goaded and driven demented, he dashed at the men,
Striking them savagely as he assailed them in rushes,
So that some lacking stomach stood back in fear.
But the lord on a lithe horse lunged after him,
Blew on his bugle like a bold knight in battle,
Rallied the hounds as he rode through the rank thickets,
Pursuing this savage boar till the sun set.
And so they disported themselves this day
While our lovable lord lay in his bed.
At home the gracious Gawain in gorgeous clothes
Reclined:

brow The bristles grow thicker here on a boar in winter.

The gay one did not forget
To come with welcome kind,
And early him beset
To make him change his mind.

LIX

She came to the curtain and cast her eye
On Sir Gawain, who at once gave her gracious welcome,
And she answered him eagerly, with ardent words,
Sat at his side softly, and with a spurt of laughter
And a loving look, delivered these words:
'It seems to me strange, if, sir, you are Gawain,
A person so powerfully disposed to good,
Yet nevertheless know nothing of noble conventions,
And when made aware of them, wave them away!
Quickly you have cast off what I schooled you in yesterday
By the truest of all tokens of talk I know of.'
'What?' said the wondering knight, 'I am not aware of one.
But if it be true what you tell, I am entirely to blame.'
'I counselled you then about kissing,' the comely one said;
'When a favour is conferred, it must be forthwith accepted:
That is becoming for a courtly knight who keeps the rules.'
'Sweet one, unsay that speech,' said the brave man,
'For I dared not do that lest I be denied.
If I were forward and were refused, the fault would be mine.'
'But none,' said the noblewoman, 'could deny you, by my faith!
You are strong enough to constrain with your strength if you wish,
If any were so ill-bred as to offer you resistance.'
'Yes, good guidance you give me, by God,' replied Gawain,
'But threateners are ill thought of and do not thrive in my country,
Nor do gifts thrive when given without good will.
I am here at your behest, to offer a kiss to when you like;
You may do it whenever you deem fit, or desist,
In this place.'
The beautiful lady bent
And fairly kissed his face;
Much speech the two then spent
On love, its grief and grace.

LX

'I would know of you, knight,' the noble lady said,
'If it did not anger you, what argument you use,
Being so hale and hearty as you are at this time,
So generous a gentleman as you are justly famed to be;
Since the choicest thing in chivalry, the chief thing praised,
Is the loyal sport of love, the very lore of arms?°

lore of arms the "learning" of the knightly profession

For the tale of the contentions of true knights
Is told by the title and text of their feats,
How lords for their true loves put their lives at hazard,
Endured dreadful trials for their dear loves' sakes,
And with valour avenged and made void their woes,
Bringing home abundant bliss by their virtues.
You are the gentlest and most just of your generation;
Everywhere your honour and high fame are known;
Yet I have sat at your side two separate times here
Without hearing you utter in any way
A single syllable of the saga of love.
Being so polished and punctilious a pledge-fulfiller,°
You ought to be eager to lay open to a young thing
Your discoveries in the craft of courtly love.
What! Are you ignorant, with all your renown?
Or do you deem me too dull to drink in your dalliance?
        For shame!
    I sit here unchaperoned, and stay
    To acquire some courtly game;
    So while my lord is away,
    Teach me your true wit's fame.'

LXI

'In good faith,' said Gawain, 'may God requite you!
It gives me great happiness, and is good sport to me,
That so fine a fair one as you should find her way here
And take pains with so poor a man, make pastime with her knight,
With any kind of clemency—it comforts me greatly.
But for me to take on the travail of interpreting true love
And construing the subjects of the stories of arms
To you who, I hold, have more skill
In that art, by half, than a hundred of such
As I am or ever shall be on the earth I inhabit,
Would in faith be a manifold folly, noble lady.
To please you I would press with all the power in my soul,
For I am highly beholden to you, and evermore shall be
True servant to your bounteous self, so save me God!'
So that stately lady tempted him and tried him with questions
To win him to wickedness, whatever else she thought.°
But he defended himself so firmly that no fault appeared,
Nor was there any evil apparent on either side,
        But bliss;
    For long they laughed and played
    Till she gave him a gracious kiss.

pledge-fulfiller The chief virtue that Gawain displays throughout the poem. The lady's exposition of a knight's social obligations takes in almost all the qualities he would be expected to display.

whatever . . . thought There was some ulterior motive in the temptations, beyond simple gratification of desire.

A fond farewell she bade,
And went her way on this.

LXII

Sir Gawain bestirred himself and went to mass:
Then dinner was dressed and with due honour served.
All day long the lord and the ladies disported,
But the castellan coursed across the country time and again,
Hunted his hapless boar as it hurtled over the hills,
Then bit the backs of his best hounds asunder
Standing at bay, till the bowmen obliged him to break free
Out into the open for all he could do,
So fast the arrows flew when the folk there concentrated.
Even the strongest he sometimes made start back,
But in time he became so tired he could tear away no more,
And with the speed he still possessed, he spurted to a hole
On a rise by a rock with a running stream beside.
He got the bank at his back, and began to abrade the ground.
The froth was foaming foully at his mouth,
And he whetted his white tusks; a weary time it was
For the bold men about, who were bound to harass him
From a distance, for none dared to draw near him
For dread.
He had hurt so many men
That it entered no one's head
To be torn by his tusks again,
And he raging and seeing red.

LXIII

Till the castellan came himself, encouraging his horse,
And saw the boar at bay with his band of men around.
He alighted in lively fashion, left his coursers,
Drew and brandished his bright sword and boldly strode forward,
Striding at speed through the stream to where the savage beast was.
The wild thing was aware of the weapon and its wielder,
And so bridled° with its bristles in a burst of fierce snorts
That all were anxious for the lord, lest he have the worst of it.
Straight away the savage brute sprang at the man,
And baron and boar were both in a heap
In the swirling water: the worst went to the beast,
For the man had marked him well at the moment of impact,
Had put the point precisely at the pit° of his chest,
And drove it in to the hilt, so that the heart was shattered,
And the spent beast sank snarling and was swept downstream,
Teeth bare.
A hundred hounds and more

bridled made his bristles stand on end

pit in the "slot"; see above, l. 1330

Attack and seize and tear;
Men tug him to the shore
And the dogs destroy him there.

LXIV

Bugles blew the triumph, horns blared loud.
There was hallooing in high pride by all present;
Braches° bayed at the beast, as bidden by their masters,
The chief huntsmen in charge of that chase so hard.
Then one who was wise in wood-crafts°
Started in style to slash open the boar.
First he hewed off the head° and hoisted it on high,
Then rent him roughly along the ridge of his back,
Brought out the bowels and broiled them on coals
For blending with bread as the braches' reward.°
Then he broke out the brawn° from the bright broad flanks,
Took out the offal,° as is fit,
Attached the two halves entirely together,
And on a strong stake stoutly hung them.
Then home they hurried with the huge beast,
With the boar's head borne before the baron himself,
Who had destroyed him in the stream by the strength of his arm,
Above all:
It seemed to him an age
Till he greeted Gawain in hall.
To reap his rightful wage
The latter came at his call.

LXV

The lord exclaimed loudly, laughing merrily
When he saw Sir Gawain, and spoke joyously.
The sweet ladies were sent for, and the servants assembled.
Then he showed them the shields, and surely described
The large size and length, and the malignity
Of the fierce boar's fighting when he fled in the woods;
So that Gawain congratulated him on his great deed,
Commended it as a merit he had manifested well.
For a beast with so much brawn, the bold man said,
A boar of such breadth, he had not before seen.
When they handled the huge head the upright man praised it,
Expressed horror thereat for the ear of the lord.
'Now Gawain,' said the good man, 'this game is your own
By our contracted treaty, in truth, you know.'
'It is so,' said the knight, 'and as certainly

Braches small hounds, rather like beagles
wood-crafts woodmanship, including all kinds of hunting
hewed . . . head Both to bleed the carcass as soon as possible, and in triumph; a boar was the traditional noble Christmas dish, and the head was carried into hall with ceremony.
reward the technical hunting term
brawn boar's flesh
offal edible entrails

I shall give you all my gains as guerdon,° in faith.'
He clasped the castellan's neck and kissed him kindly,
And then served him a second time in the same style.
'In all our transactions since I came to sojourn,' asserted Gawain,
'Up to tonight, as of now, there's nothing that
I owe.'
'By Saint Giles,'° the castellan quipped,
'You're the finest fellow I know:
Your wealth will have us whipped
If your trade continues so!'

LXVI

Then the trestles and tables were trimly set out,
Complete with cloths, and clearly flaming cressets°
And waxen torches were placed in the wall-brackets
By retainers, who then tended the entire hall-gathering.
Much gladness and glee then gushed forth there
By the fire on the floor: and in multifarious ways
They sang noble songs at supper and afterwards,
A concert of Christmas carols and new dance-songs,°
With the most mannerly mirth a man could tell of,
And our courteous knight kept constant company with the lady.
In a bewitchingly well-mannered way she made up to him,
Secretly soliciting the stalwart knight
So that he was astounded, and upset in himself.
But his upbringing forbade him to rebuff her utterly,
So he behaved towards her honourably, whatever aspersions might
Be cast.
They revelled in the hall
As long as their pleasure might last,
And then at the castellan's call
To the chamber hearth they passed.

LXVII

There they drank and discoursed and decided to enjoy
Similar solace and sport on New Year's Eve.
But the princely knight asked permission to depart in the morning,
For his appointed time was approaching, and perforce he must go.
But the lord would not let him and implored him to linger,
Saying, 'I swear to you, as a staunch true knight,
You shall gain the Green Chapel to give your dues,
My lord, in the light of New Year, long before sunrise.
Therefore remain in your room and rest in comfort,
While I fare hunting in the forest; in fulfilment of our oath

guerdon reward
Saint Giles a 7th-century hermit, whose only companion was a stag, which led a huntsman-king to the saint. The association makes St. Giles a fitting patron for the knight of the castle.
cressets torches
carols . . . songs literally, conducts and carols: Christmas part-songs and dance-songs

Exchanging what we achieve when the chase is over.
For twice I have tested you, and twice found you true.
Now "Third time, throw best!" Think of that tomorrow!
Let us make merry while we may, set our minds on joy,
For hard fate can hit man whenever it likes.'
This was graciously granted and Gawain stayed.
Blithely drink was brought, then to bed with lights
They pressed.
All night Sir Gawain sleeps
Softly and still at rest;
But the lord his custom keeps
And is early up and dressed.

LXVIII

After mass, he and his men made a small meal.[°]
Merry was the morning; he demanded his horse.
The men were ready mounted before the main gate,
A host of knightly horsemen to follow after him.
Wonderfully fair was the forest-land, for the frost remained,
And the rising sun shone ruddily on the ragged clouds,
In its beauty brushing their blackness off the heavens.
The huntsmen unleashed the hounds by a holt-side,[°]
And the rocks and surrounding bushes rang with their horn-calls.
Some found and followed the fox's[°] tracks,
And wove various ways in their wily fashion.
A small hound cried the scent, the senior huntsman called
His fellow foxhounds to him and, feverishly sniffing,
The rout of dogs rushed forward on the right path.
The fox hurried fast, for they found him soon
And, seeing him distinctly, pursued him at speed,
Unmistakably giving tongue with tumultuous din.
Deviously in difficult country he doubled on his tracks,
Swerved and wheeled away, often waited listening,
Till at last by a little ditch he leaped a quickset hedge,
And stole out stealthily at the side of a valley,
Considering his stratagem had given the slip to the hounds.
But he stumbled on a tracking-dogs' tryst-place unawares,
And there in a cleft three hounds threatened him at once,
All grey.
He swiftly started back
And, full of deep dismay,
He dashed on a different track;
To the woods he went away.

small meal a bite
holt-side wood-side
fox's Descriptions of medieval set fox-hunts are rare; Chaucer's Nun's Priest's Tale is an example in another genre.

LXIX

Then came the lively delight of listening to the hounds
When they had all met in a muster, mingling together,
For, catching sight of him, they cried such curses on him
That the clustering cliffs seemed to be crashing down.
Here he was hallooed when the hunters met him,
There savagely snarled at by intercepting hounds;
Then he was called thief and threatened often;
With the tracking dogs on his tail, no tarrying was possible.
When out in the open he was often run at,
So he often swerved in again, that artful Reynard.
Yes, he led the lord and his liegemen a dance
In this manner among the mountains till mid-afternoon,
While harmoniously at home the honoured knight slept
Between the comely curtains in the cold morning.
But the lady's longing to woo would not let her sleep,
Now would she impair the purpose pitched in her heart,
But rose up rapidly and ran to him
In a ravishing robe that reached to the ground,
Trimmed with finest fur from pure pelts,
Not coifed as to custom,° but with costly jewels
Strung in scores on her splendid hairnet.
Her fine-featured face and fair throat were unveiled,
Her breast was bare and her back as well.
She came in by the chamber door and closed it after her,
Cast open a casement and called on the knight,
And briskly thus rebuked him with bountiful words
Of good cheer.
'Ah sir! What, sound asleep?
The morning's crisp and clear.'
He had been drowsing deep,
But now he had to hear.

LXX

The noble sighed ceaselessly in unsettled slumber
As threatening thoughts thronged in the dawn light
About destiny, which the day after would deal him his fate
At the Green Chapel where Gawain was to greet his man,
And be bound to bear his buffet unresisting.
But having recovered consciousness in comely fashion,
He heaved himself out of dreams and answered hurriedly.
The lovely lady advanced, laughing adorably,
Swooped over his splendid face and sweetly kissed him.
He welcomed her worthily with noble cheer
And, gazing on her gay and glorious attire,

coifed . . . custom For this third, subtler, and more important temptation, she has prepared more fully and less modestly.

Her features so faultless and fine of complexion,
He felt a flush of rapture suffuse his heart.
Sweet and genial smiling slid them into joy
Till bliss burst forth between them, beaming gay
And bright;
With joy the two contended
In talk of true delight,
And peril would have impended
Had Mary not minded her knight.

LXXI

For that peerless princess pressed him so hotly,
So invited him to the very verge, that he felt forced
Either to allow her love or blackguardly rebuff her.
He was concerned for his courtesy, lest he be called caitiff,
But more especially for his evil plight if he should plunge into sin,
And dishonour the owner of the house treacherously.
'God shield me! That shall not happen, for sure,' said the knight.
So with laughing love-talk he deflected gently
The downright° declarations that dropped from her lips.
Said the beauty to the bold man, 'Blame will be yours
If you love not the living body lying close to you
More than all wooers in the world who are wounded in heart;
Unless you have a lover more beloved, who delights you more,
A maiden to whom you are committed, so immutably bound
That you do not seek to sever from her—which I see is so.
Tell me the truth of it, I entreat you now;
By all the loves there are, do not hide the truth
With guile.'
Then gently, 'By Saint John,'°
Said the knight with a smile,
'I owe my oath to none,
Nor wish to yet a while.'

LXXII

'Those words,' said the fair woman, 'are the worst there could be,
But I am truly answered, to my utter anguish.
Give me now a gracious kiss, and I shall go from here
As a maid that loves much, mourning on this earth.'
Then, sighing, she stooped, and seemlily kissed him,
And, severing herself from him, stood up and said,
'At this adieu, my dear one, do me this pleasure:
Give me something as gift, your glove° if no more,
To mitigate my mourning when I remember you.'
'Now certainly, for your sake,' said the knight,
'I wish I had here the handsomest thing I own,

downright literally, loving
Saint John the oath by the "beloved disciple," whose feast day was December 27—appropriate to the time, the situation, and the character of Gawain
glove a frequent love token

For you have deserved, forsooth, superabundantly
And rightfully, a richer reward than I could give.
But as tokens of true love, trifles mean little.
It is not to your honour to have at this time
A mere glove as Gawain's gift to treasure.
For I am here on an errand in unknown regions,
And have no bondsmen, no baggages with dear-bought things in them.
This afflicts me now, fair lady, for your sake.
Man must do as he must; neither lament it
Nor repine.'
'No, highly honoured one,'
Replied that lady fine,
'Though gift you give me none,
You must have something of mine.'

LXXIII

She proffered him a rich ring wrought in red gold,
With a sparkling stone set conspicuously in it,
Which beamed as brilliantly as the bright sun;
You may well believe its worth was wonderfully great.
But the courteous man declined it and quickly said,
'Before God, gracious lady, no giving just now!
Not having anything to offer, I shall accept nothing.'
She offered it him urgently and he refused again,
Fast affirming his refusal on his faith as a knight.
Put out by this repulse, she presently said,
'If you reject my ring as too rich in value,
Doubtless you would be less deeply indebted to me
If I gave you my girdle,° a less gainful gift.'
She swiftly slipped off the cincture° of her gown
Which went round her waist under the wonderful mantle,
A girdle of green silk with a golden hem,
Embroidered only at the edges, with hand-stitched ornament.
And she pleaded with the prince in a pleasant manner
To take it notwithstanding its trifling worth;
But he told her that he could touch no treasure at all,
Not gold nor any gift, till God gave him grace
To pursue to success the search he was bound on.
'And therefore I beg you not to be displeased:
Press no more your purpose, for I promise it never
Can be.
I owe you a hundredfold
For grace you have granted me;
And ever through hot and cold
I shall stay your devotee.'

girdle belt, which turns out to have magical properties (ll. 1851 ff.), as elsewhere in the romances

cincture French *ceinture*, belt

LXXIV

'Do you say "no" to this silk?' then said the beauty;
'Because it is simple in itself? And so it seems.
Lo! It is little indeed, and so less worth your esteem.
But one who was aware of the worth twined in it
Would appraise its properties as more precious perhaps,
For the man that binds his body with this belt of green,
As long as he laps it closely about him,
No hero under heaven can hack him to pieces,
For he cannot be killed by any cunning on earth.'
Then the prince pondered, and it appeared to him
A precious gem to protect him in the peril appointed him
When he gained the Green Chapel to be given checkmate:°
It would be a splendid stratagem to escape being slain.
Then he allowed her to solicit him and let her speak.
She pressed the belt upon him with potent words
And having got his agreement, she gave it him gladly,
Beseeching him for her sake to conceal it always,
And hide it from her husband with all diligence.
That never should another know of it, the noble swore
Outright.
Then often his thanks gave he
With all his heart and might,
And thrice by then had she
Kissed the constant knight.

LXXV

Then with a word of farewell she went away
For she could not force further satisfaction from him.
Directly she withdrew, Sir Gawain dressed himself,
Rose and arrayed himself in rich garments,
But laid aside the love-lace the lady had given him,
Secreted it carefully where he could discover it later.
Then he went his way at once to the chapel,
Privily° approached a priest and prayed him there
To listen to his life's sins and enlighten him
On how he might have salvation in the hereafter.
Then, confessing his faults, he fairly shrove himself,°
Begging mercy for both major and minor sins.
He asked the holy man for absolution
And was absolved with certainty and sent out so pure
That Doomsday° could have been declared the day after.
Then he made merrier among the noble ladies,
With comely carolling and all kinds of pleasure,

checkmate to get the final blow; see l. 2195
Privily secretly, discreetly
shrove himself But he keeps the belt; the poet seems not to regard this as major or minor sin, since Gawain confesses and receives absolution.
Doomsday the Day of General Judgment. Gawain has been made so clean of sin as to be ready for heaven tomorrow, should tomorrow be Judgment Day.

Than ever he had done, with ecstasy, till came
Dark night.
Such honour he did to all,
They said, 'Never has this knight
Since coming into hall
Expressed such pure delight.'

LXXVI

Now long may he linger there, love sheltering him!
The prince was still on the plain, pleasuring in the chase,
Having finished off the fox he had followed so far.
As he leaped over a hedge looking out for the quarry,
Where he heard the hounds that were harrying the fox,
Reynárd came running through a rough thicket
With the pack all pell-mell, panting at his heels.
The lord, aware of the wild beast, waited craftily,
Then drew his dazzling sword and drove at the fox.
The beast baulked at the blade to break° sideways,
But a dog bounded at him before he could,
And right in front of the horse's feet they fell on him,
All worrying their wily prey with a wild uproar.
The lord quickly alighted and lifted him up,
Wrenched him beyond reach of the ravening fangs,
Held him high over his head and hallooed lustily,
While the angry hounds in hordes bayed at him.
Thither hurried the huntsmen with horns in plenty,
Sounding the rally° splendidly till they saw their lord.
When the company of his court had come up to the kill,
All who bore bugles blew at once,
And the others without horns hallooed loudly.
The requiem that was raised for Reynard's soul
And the commotion made it the merriest meet ever,
Men said.
The hounds must have their fee:
They pat them on the head,
Then hold the fox; and he
Is reft of his skin of red.

LXXVII

Then they set off for home, it being almost night,
Blowing their big horns bravely as they went.
At last the lord alighted at his beloved castle
And found upon the floor a fire, and beside it
The good Sir Gawain in a glad humour
By reason of the rich friendship he had reaped from the ladies.
He wore a turquoise tunic° extending to the ground;

break turn away
rally recall

tunic robe. Blue was the color of fidelity.

His softly-furred surcoat suited him well,
And his hood of the same hue hung from his shoulder.
All trimmed with ermine were hood and surcoat.
Meeting the master in the middle of the floor,
Gawain went forward gladly and greeted him thus:
'Forthwith, I shall be the first to fulfil the contract
We settled so suitably without sparing the wine.'
Then he clasped the castellan and kissed him thrice
As sweetly and steadily as a strong knight could.
'By Christ!' quoth the other, 'You will carve yourself a fortune
By traffic in this trade when the terms suit you!'
'Do not chop logic about the exchange,' chipped in Gawain,
'As I have properly paid over the profit I made.'
'Marry,' said the other man, 'Mine is inferior,
For I have hunted all day and have only taken
This ill-favoured fox's skin,° may the Fiend take it!
And that is a poor price to pay for such precious things
As you have pressed upon me here, three pure kisses
So good.'
'Enough!' acknowledged Gawain,
'I thank you, by the Rood.'°
And how the fox was slain
The lord told him as they stood.

LXXVIII

With mirth and minstrelsy, and meals when they liked,
They made as merry then as ever men could;
With the laughter of ladies and delightful jesting,
Gawain and his good host were very gay together,
Save when excess or sottishness seemed likely.
Master and men made many a witty sally,
Until presently, at the appointed parting-time,
The brave men were bidden to bed at last.
Then of his host the hero humbly took leave,
The first to bid farewell, fairly thanking him:
'May the High King° requite you for your courtesy at this feast,
And the wonderful week of my dwelling here!
I would offer to be one of your own men if you liked,
But that I must move on tomorrow, as you know,
If you will give me the guide you granted me,
To show me the Green Chapel where my share of doom
Will be dealt on New Year's Day, as God deems for me.'
'With all my heart!' said the host, 'In good faith,
All that I ever promised you, I shall perform.'
He assigned him a servant to set him on his way,

fox's skin Even this, the worst gift on the third day, is also the nearest yet to a fair exchange.

Rood cross

High King Christ

And lead him in the hills without any delay,
Faring through forest and thicket by the most straightforward route
They might.
With every honour due
Gawain then thanked the knight,
And having bid him adieu,
Took leave of the ladies bright.

LXXIX

So he spoke to them sadly, sorrowing as he kissed,°
And urged on them heartily his endless thanks,
And they gave to Sir Gawain words of grace in return,
Commending him to Christ with cries of chill sadness.
Then from the whole household he honourably took his leave,
Making all the men that he met amends
For their several services and solicitous care,
For they had been busily attendant, bustling about him;
And every soul was as sad to say farewell
As if they had always had the hero in their house.
Then the lords led him with lights to his chamber,
And blithely brought him to bed to rest.
If he slept—I dare not assert it—less soundly than usual,
There was much on his mind for the morrow, if he meant to give
It thought.
Let him lie there still,
He almost has what he sought;
So tarry a while until
The process I report.

Fitt 4

LXXX

Now the New Year neared, the night passed,
Daylight fought darkness as the Deity ordained.
But wild was the weather the world awoke to;
Bitterly the clouds cast down cold on the earth,
Inflicting on the flesh flails from the north.
Bleakly the snow blustered, and beasts were frozen;
The whistling wind wailed from the heights,
Driving great drifts deep in the dales.
Keenly the lord listened as he lay in his bed;
Though his lids were closed, he was sleeping little.
Every cock that crew recalled to him his tryst.
Before the day had dawned, he had dressed himself,°

sorrowing . . . kissed Elaborate leavetaking would be thought necessary in courtesy.

dressed himself literally, risen from bed

For the light from a lamp illuminated his chamber.
He summoned his servant, who swiftly answered,
Commanded that his mail-coat and mount's saddle be brought.
The man fared forth and fetched him his armour,
And set Sir Gawain's array in splendid style.
First he clad him in his clothes to counter the cold,
Then in his other armour which had been well kept;
His breast- and belly-armour had been burnished bright,
And the rusty rings of his rich mail-coat rolled clean,°
And all being as fresh as at first, he was fain to give thanks
Indeed.
Each wiped and polished piece
He donned with due heed.
The gayest from here to Greece,
The strong man sent for his steed.

LXXXI

While he was putting on apparel of the most princely kind—
His surcoat, with its symbol of spotless deeds
Environed on velvet with virtuous° gems,
Was embellished° and bound with embroidered seams,
And finely fur-lined with the fairest skins—
He did not leave the lace belt, the lady's gift:
For his own good, Gawain did not forget that!
When he had strapped the sword on his swelling hips,
The knight lapped his loins with his love-token° twice,
Quickly wrapped it with relish round his waist.
The green silken girdle suited the gallant well,
Backed by the royal red cloth that richly showed.
But Gawain wore the girdle not for its great value,
Nor through pride in the pendants, in spite of their polish,
Nor for the gleaming gold which glinted on the ends,
But to save himself when of necessity he must
Stand an evil stroke, not resisting it with knife
Or sword.
When ready and robed aright,
Out came the comely lord;
To the men of name and might
His thanks in plenty poured.

LXXXII

Then was Gringolet got ready, that great huge horse.
Having been assiduously° stabled in seemly quarters,
The fiery steed was fit and fretting for a gallop.

rolled clean in sand
virtuous powerful. Gems were believed to possess protective, talismanic qualities.
embellished embroidered
love-token He wears it outside his surcoat, not expecting to see his host again.
assiduously literally, to his liking

Sir Gawain stepped to him and, inspecting his coat,
Said earnestly to himself, asserting with truth,
'Here in this castle is a company whose conduct is honourable.
The man who maintains them, may he have joy!
The delightful lady, love befall her while she lives!
Thus for charity they cherish a chance guest
Honourably and open-handedly; may He on high,
The King of Heaven, requite you and your company too!
And if I could live any longer in lands on earth,
Some rich recompense, if I could, I should readily give you.'
Then he stepped into the stirrup and swung aloft.
His man showed him° his shield; on his shoulder he put it,
And gave the spur to Gringolet with his gold-spiked heels.
The horse sprang forward from the paving, pausing no more
To prance.
His man was mounted and fit,
Laden with spear and lance.
'This castle to Christ I commit:
May He its fortune enhance!'

LXXXIII

The drawbridge was let down and the broad double gates
Were unbarred and borne open on both sides.
Passing over the planks, the prince blessed himself
And praised the kneeling porter, who proffered him 'Good day,'
Praying God to grant that Gawain would be saved.
And Gawain went on his way with the one man
To put him on the right path for that perilous place
Where the sad assault must be received by him.
By bluffs where boughs were bare they passed,
Climbed by cliffs where the cold clung:
Under the high clouds, ugly mists
Merged damply with the moors and melted on the mountains;
Each hill had a hat, a huge mantle of mist.
Brooks burst forth above them, boiling over their banks
And showering down sharply in shimmering cascades.
Wonderfully wild was their way through the woods;
Till soon the sun in the sway of that season
Brought day.
They were on a lofty hill
Where snow beside them lay,
When the servant stopped still
And told his master to stay.

LXXXIV

'For I have guided you to this ground, Sir Gawain, at this time,
And now you are not far from the noted place

His . . . him or: the guide produced

Which you have searched for and sought with such special zeal.
But I must say to you, forsooth, since I know you,
And you are a lord whom I love with no little regard,
Take my governance as guide, and it shall go better for you.
For the place is perilous that you are pressing towards.
In that wilderness dwells the worst man in the world,
For he is valiant and fierce and fond of fighting,
And mightier than any man that may be on earth,
And his body is bigger than the best four
In Arthur's house, or Hector,° or any other.
At the Green Chapel he gains his great adventures.
No man passes that place, however proud in arms,
Without being dealt a death-blow by his dreadful hand.
For he is an immoderate man, to mercy a stranger;
For whether churl or chaplain by the chapel rides,
Monk or mass-priest or man of other kind,
He thinks it as convenient to kill him as keep alive himself.°
Therefore I say, as certainly as you sit in your saddle,
If you come there you'll be killed, I caution you, knight,
Take my troth for it, though you had twenty lives
            And more.
        He has lived here since long ago
        And filled the field with gore.
        You cannot counter his blow,
        It strikes so sudden and sore.

LXXXV

'Therefore, good Sir Gawain, leave the grim man alone!
Ride by another route, to some region remote!
Go in the name of God, and Christ grace your fortune!
And I shall go home again and undertake
To swear solemnly by God and his saints as well
(By my halidom,° so help me God, and every other oath)
Stoutly to keep your secret, not saying to a soul
That ever you tried to turn tail from any man I knew.'
'Great thanks,' replied Gawain, somewhat galled, and said,
'It is worthy of you to wish for my well-being, man,
And I believe you would loyally lock it in your heart.
But however quiet you kept it, if I quit this place,
Fled from the fellow in the fashion you propose,
I should become a cowardly knight with no excuse whatever.
For I will go to the Green Chapel, to get what Fate sends,
And have whatever words I wish with that worthy,
Whether weal or woe is what Fate
            Demands.

Hector the Trojan hero, or Sir Ector, one of King Arthur's best knights
convenient . . . himself He is not bound by the laws of true chivalry, which would respect the clergy and disdain to kill a base-born churl.
halidom holy thing, e.g., a relic, on which an oath could be taken

Fierce though that fellow be,
Clutching his club° where he stands,
Our Lord can certainly see
That his own are in safe hands.'

LXXXVI

'By Mary!' said the other man, 'If you mean what you say,
You are determined to take all your trouble on yourself.
If you wish to lose your life, I'll no longer hinder you.
Here's your lance for your hand, your helmet for your head.
Ride down this rough track round yonder cliff
Till you arrive in a rugged ravine at the bottom,
Then look about on the flat, on your left hand,
And you will view there in the vale that very chapel,
And the grim gallant who guards it always.
Now, noble Gawain, good-bye in God's name.
For all the gold on God's earth I would not go with you,
Nor foot it an inch further through this forest as your fellow.'
Whereupon he wrenched at his reins, that rider in the woods,
Hit the horse with his heels as hard as he could,
Sent him leaping along, and left the knight there
Alone.
'By God!' said Gawain, 'I swear
I will not weep or groan:
Being given to God's good care,
My trust in Him shall be shown.'

LXXXVII

Then he gave the spur to Gringolet and galloped down the path,
Thrust through a thicket there by a bank,
And rode down the rough slope right into the ravine.
Then he searched about, but it seemed savage and wild,
And no sign did he see of any sort of building;
But on both sides banks, beetling and steep,
And great crooked crags, cruelly jagged;
The bristling barbs of rock seemed to brush the sky.
Then he held in his horse, halted there,
Scanned on every side in search of the chapel.
He saw no such thing anywhere, which seemed remarkable,
Save, hard by in the open, a hillock of sorts,
A smooth-surfaced barrow° on a slope beside a stream
Which flowed forth fast there in its course,
Foaming and frothing as if feverishly boiling.
The knight, urging his horse, pressed onwards to the mound,
Dismounted manfully and made fast to a lime-tree

club the sort of weapon one would expect from a giant in the wilderness. It has never been specified what weapon Gawain is to get his blow from. In l. 384 the Green Knight was offered a choice of weapons.
barrow artificial mound

The reins, hooking them round a rough branch;
Then he went to the barrow, which he walked round, inspecting,
Wondering what in the world it might be.
It had a hole in each end and on either side,
And was overgrown with grass in great patches.
All hollow it was within, only an old cavern
Or the crevice of an ancient crag: he could not explain it
Aright.
'O God, is the Chapel Green
This mound?' said the noble knight.
'At such might Satan be seen
Saying matins at midnight.'

LXXXVIII

'Now certainly the place is deserted,' said Gawain,
'It is a hideous oratory, all overgrown,
And well graced for the gallant garbed in green
To deal out his devotions in the Devil's fashion.
Now I feel in my five wits, it is the Fiend himself
That has tricked me into this tryst, to destroy me here.
This is a chapel of mischance—checkmate° to it!
It is the most evil holy place I ever entered.'
With his high helmet on his head, and holding his lance,
He roamed up to the roof of that rough dwelling.
Then from that height he heard, from a hard rock
On the bank beyond the brook, a barbarous noise.
What! It clattered amid the cliffs fit to cleave them apart,
As if a great scythe were being ground on a grindstone there.
What! It whirred and it whetted, like water in a mill.
What! It made a rushing, ringing din, rueful to hear.
'By God!' then said Gawain, 'that is going on,
I suppose, as a salute to myself, to greet me
Hard by.
God's will be warranted:
"Alas!" is a craven cry.
No din shall make me dread
Although today I die.'

LXXXIX

Then the courteous knight called out clamorously,
'Who holds sway here and has an assignation with me?
For the good knight Gawain is on the ground here.
If anyone there wants anything, wend your way hither fast,
And further your needs either now, or not at all.'
'Bide there!' said one on the bank above his head,
'And you shall swiftly receive what I once swore to give you.'

checkmate destruction; see l. 1857

Yet for a time he continued his tumult of scraping,
Turning away as he whetted, before he would descend.
Then he thrust himself round a thick crag through a hole,
Whirling round a wedge of rock with a frightful weapon,
A Danish axe° duly honed for dealing the blow,
With a broad biting edge, bow-bent along the handle,
Ground on a grindstone, a great four-foot blade—
No less, by that love-lace° gleaming so brightly!
And the gallant in green was garbed as at first,
His looks and limbs the same, his locks and beard;
Save that steadily on his feet he strode on the ground,
Setting the handle to the stony earth and stalking beside it.
He would not wade through the water when he came to it,
But vaulted over on his axe, then with huge strides
Advanced violently and fiercely along the field's width
        On the snow.
    Sir Gawain went to greet
    The knight, not bowing low.
    The man said, 'Sir so sweet,
    Your honour the trysts you owe.'°

XC

'Gawain,' said the Green Knight, 'may God guard you!
You are welcome to my dwelling, I warrant you,
And you have timed your travel here as a true man ought.
You know plainly the pact we pledged between us:
This time a twelvemonth ago you took your portion,
And now at this New Year I should nimbly requite you.
And we are on our own here in this valley
With no seconds to sunder us, spar as we will.
Take your helmet off your head, and have your payment here.
And offer no more argument or action than I did
When you whipped off my head with one stroke.'
'No,' said Gawain, 'by God who gave me a soul,
The grievous gash to come I grudge you not at all;
Strike but the one stroke and I shall stand still
And offer you no hindrance; you may act freely,
        I swear.'
    Head bent,° Sir Gawain bowed,
    And showed the bright flesh bare.
    He behaved as if uncowed,
    Being loth to display his care.

Danish axe the sort of ferocious, long-bladed axe originally used by the Viking pirates, without a spike on the back. At King Arthur's court the Green Knight had carried a *guisarme,* spiked and richly ornamented, a much more knightly weapon.

love-lace The original reads simply "thong."

trysts you owe The stress is on Gawain's keeping of his oath.

Head bent The words pick up the description of the Green Knight awaiting the stroke at Arthur's court.

XCI

Then the gallant in green quickly got ready,
Heaved his horrid weapon on high to hit Gawain,
With all the brute force in his body bearing it aloft,
Swinging savagely enough to strike him dead.
Had it driven down as direly as he aimed,
The daring dauntless man would have died from the blow.
But Gawain glanced up at the grim axe beside him
As it came shooting through the shivering air to shatter him,
And his shoulders shrank slightly from the sharp edge.
The other suddenly stayed the descending axe,
And then reproved the prince with many proud words:
'You are not Gawain,' said the gallant, 'whose greatness is such
That by hill or hollow no army ever frightened him;
For now you flinch for fear before you feel harm.
I never did know that knight to be a coward.
I neither flinched nor fled when you let fly your blow,
Nor offered any quibble in the house of King Arthur.
My head flew to my feet, but flee I did not.
Yet you quail cravenly though unscathed so far.
So I am bound to be called the better man
　　　　Therefore.'
　　Said Gawain, 'Not again
　　Shall I flinch as I did before;
　　But if my head pitch to the plain,
　　It's off for evermore.'

XCII

'But be brisk, man, by your faith, and bring me to the point;
Deal me my destiny and do it out of hand,
For I shall stand your stroke, not starting at all
Till your axe has hit me. Here is my oath on it.'
'Have at you then!' said the other, heaving up his axe,
Behaving as angrily as if he were mad.
He menaced him mightily, but made no contact,°
Smartly withholding his hand without hurting him.
Gawain waited unswerving, with not a wavering limb,
But stood still as a stone or the stump of a tree
Gripping the rocky ground with a hundred grappling roots.
Then again the Green Knight began to gird:°
'So now you have a whole heart I must hit you.
May the high knighthood which Arthur conferred
Preserve you and save your neck, if so it avail you!'
Then said Gawain, storming with sudden rage,
'Thrash on, you thrustful fellow, you threaten too much.

made . . . contact possible manuscript reading: *ryve*, i.e. "cleave"; thus, "did not cut through the man"; or: *ryne*, "touch"

gird mock

It seems your spirit is struck with self-dread.'
'Forsooth,' the other said, 'you speak so fiercely
I will no longer lengthen matters by delaying your business,
I vow.'
He stood astride to smite,
Lips pouting, puckered brow.
No wonder he lacked delight
Who expected no help now.

XCIII

Up went the axe at once and hurtled down straight
At the naked neck with its knife-like edge.
Though it swung down savagely, slight was the wound,
A mere snick on the side, so that the skin was broken.
Through the fair fat to the flesh fell the blade,
And over his shoulders the shimmering blood shot to the ground.
When Sir Gawain saw his gore glinting on the snow,
He leapt feet close together a spear's length away,
Hurriedly heaved his helmet on to his head,
And shrugging his shoulders, shot his shield to the front,
Swung out his bright sword and said fiercely,
(For never had the knight since being nursed by his mother
Been so buoyantly happy, so blithe in this world)
'Cease your blows, sir, strike me no more.
I have sustained a stroke here unresistingly,
And if you offer any more I shall earnestly reply,
Resisting, rest assured, with the most rancorous
Despite.
The single stroke is wrought
To which we pledged our plight
In high King Arthur's court:
Enough now, therefore, knight!'

XCIV

The bold man stood back and bent over his axe,
Putting the haft to earth, and leaning on the head.
He gazed at Sir Gawain on the ground before him,
Considering the spirited and stout way he stood,
Audacious in arms; his heart warmed to him.
Then he gave utterance gladly in his great voice,
With resounding speech saying to the knight,
'Bold man, do not be so bloodily resolute.
No one here has offered you evil discourteously,
Contrary to the covenant made at the King's court.
I promised a stroke, which you received: consider yourself paid.
I cancel all other obligations of whatever kind.
If I had been more active, perhaps I could
Have made you suffer by striking a savager stroke.

First in foolery I made a feint at striking,
Not rending you with a riving cut—and right I was,
On account of the first night's covenant we accorded;
For you truthfully kept your trust in troth with me,
Giving me your gains, as a good man should.
The further feinted blow was for the following day,
When you kissed my comely wife, and the kisses came to me:
For those two things, harmlessly I thrust twice at you
Feinted blows.
Truth for truth's the word;
No need for dread, God knows.
From your failure at the third
The tap you took arose.

XCV

'For that braided belt you wear belongs to me.
I am well aware that my own wife gave it you.
Your conduct and your kissings are completely known to me,
And the wooing by my wife—my work set it on.
I instructed her to try you, and you truly seem
To be the most perfect paladin ever to pace the earth.
As the pearl to the white pea in precious worth,
So in good faith is Gawain to other gay knights.
But here your faith failed you, you flagged somewhat, sir,
Yet it was not for a well-wrought thing, nor for wooing either,
But for love of your life, which is less blameworthy.'
The other strong man stood considering this a while,
So filled with fury that his flesh trembled,
And the blood from his breast burst forth in his face
As he shrank for shame at what the chevalier spoke of.
The first words the fair knight could frame were:
'Curses on both cowardice and covetousness!°
Their vice and villainy are virtue's undoing.'
Then he took the knot, with a twist twitched it loose,
And fiercely flung the fair girdle to the knight.
'Lo! There is the false thing, foul fortune befall it!
I was craven about our encounter, and cowardice taught me
To accord with covetousness and corrupt my nature
And the liberality and loyalty belonging to chivalry.
Now I am faulty and false and found fearful always.
In the train of treachery and untruth go woe
And shame.
I acknowledge, knight, how ill
I behaved, and take the blame.
Award what penance you will:
Henceforth I'll shun ill-fame.'

covetousness more than desire for wealth and possessions: entanglement in the values of this world

XCVI

Then the other lord laughed and politely said,
'In my view you have made amends for your misdemeanour;
You have confessed your faults fully with fair acknowledgement,
And plainly done penance at the point of my axe.
You are absolved of your sin and as stainless now
As if you had never fallen in fault since first you were born.
As for the gold-hemmed girdle, I give it you, sir,
Seeing it is as green as my gown. Sir Gawain, you may
Think about this trial when you throng in company
With paragons of princes, for it is a perfect token,
At knightly gatherings, of the great adventure at the Green Chapel.
You shall come back to my castle this cold New Year.
To revel away the rest of this rich feast
We shall go.
Thus urging him, the lord
Said, 'You and my wife, I know
We shall bring to clear accord,
Though she was your fierce foe.'

XCVII

'No, forsooth,' said the knight, seizing his helmet,
And doffing it with dignity as he delivered his thanks,
'My stay has sufficed me.° Still, luck go with you!
May He who bestows all good, honour you with it!
And commend me to the courteous lady, your comely wife;
Indeed, my due regards to both dear ladies,
Who with their wanton wiles have thus waylaid their knight.
But it is no marvel for a foolish man to be maddened thus
And saddled with sorrow by the sleights of women.°
For here on earth was Adam taken in by one,
And Solomon by many such, and Samson likewise;
Delilah dealt him his doom; and David, later still,
Was blinded by Bathsheba, and badly suffered for it.
Since these were troubled by their tricks, it would be true joy
To love them but not believe° them, if a lord could,
For these were the finest of former times, most favoured by fortune
Of all under the heavenly kingdom whose hearts were
Abused;
These four all fell to schemes
Of women whom they used.
If I am snared, it seems
I ought to be excused.°

My stay . . . me I have been long enough away from Arthur's court
sleights of women The stock anti-feminist *exempla* of the Old Testament: Adam and Eve (Genesis 3); Solomon and his 700 wives and 300 concubines (I Kings 11:3); Samson and Delilah (Judges 16); David and Bathsheba, wife of Uriah (II Samuel 11:2–4). See Chaucer's Wife of Bath's Prologue. They seem to come in oddly, but the point is merely that these were all women who had made men swerve from the path of (knightly) virtue.
believe i.e. put full trust in
If . . . excused Gawain seems now to be excusing himself on the ground that if such great men were deceived by women, it is no wonder if it happens to him.

XCVIII

'But your girdle,' said Gawain, 'God requite you for it!
Not for the glorious gold shall I gladly wear it,
Nor for the stuff nor the silk for the swaying pendants,
Nor for its worth, fine workmanship or wonderful honour;
But as a sign of my sin I shall see it often,
Remembering with remorse, when I am mounted in glory,
The fault and faintheartedness of the perverse flesh,
How it tends to attract tarnishing sin.
So when pride° shall prick me for my prowess in arms,
One look at this love-lace will make lowly my heart.
But one demand I make of you, may it not incommode you:
Since you are master of the demesne I have remained in a while,
Make known, by your knighthood—and now may He above,
Who sits on high and holds up heaven, requite you!—
How you pronounce your true name; and no more requests.'
'Truly,' the other told him, 'I shall tell you my title.
Bertilak of the High Desert° I am called here in this land.
Through the might of Morgan the Fay,° who remains in my house
Through the wiles of her witchcraft, a lore well learned,—
Many of the magical arts of Merlin° she acquired,
For she lavished fervent love long ago
On that susceptible sage: certainly your knights know
Of their fame.
So "Morgan the Goddess"
She accordingly became;
The proudest she can oppress
And to her purpose tame—

XCIX

'She sent me forth in this form to your famous hall
To put to the proof the great pride of the house,
The reputation for high renown of the Round Table;
She bewitched me in this weird way to bewilder your wits,
And to grieve Guinevere and goad her to death
With ghastly fear of that ghost's ghoulish speaking
With his head in his hand before the high table.
That is the aged beldame who is at home:
She is indeed your own aunt, Arthur's half-sister,
Daughter of the Duchess of Tintagel° who in due course,

pride mother of the deadly sins, which a knight, especially, must avoid
Bertilak The name Bertilak is Celtic. High Desert *(Haut-desert)* probably refers to his castle.
Morgan le Fay sorceress half-sister of King Arthur, who imprisoned his knights, first called "goddess" (l. 2452) by the 12th-century Gerald of Wales. She was said to have told Arthur of Lancelot's adultery with Guinevere; and Guinevere is said to have revealed her intrigue with another knight—hence their enmity (l. 2460).
Merlin the wizard of Arthur's court, who fell in love with Morgan and taught her his magic
Duchess of Tintagel See Malory, *Morte Darthur,* below. The story is first told by Geoffrey of Monmouth (12th century). Igraine, Duchess of Tintagel, conceived Arthur by King Uther Pendragon, who deceived her in the likeness of her husband; after her husband's death she married Uther.

By Uther, was mother of Arthur, who now holds sway.
Therefore I beg you, bold sir, come back to your aunt,
Make merry in my house, for my men love you,
And by my faith, brave sir, I bear you as much good will
As I grant any man under God, for your great honesty.'
But Gawain firmly refused with a final negative.
They clasped and kissed, commending each other
To the Prince of Paradise,° and parted on the cold ground
Right there.
Gawain on steed serene
Spurred to court with courage fair,
And the gallant garbed in green
To wherever he would elsewhere.

C

Now Gawain goes riding on Gringolet
In lonely lands, his life saved by grace.
Often he stayed at a house, and often in the open,
And often overcame hazards in the valleys,
Which at this time I do not intend to tell you about.
The hurt he had had in his neck was healed,
And the glittering girdle that girt him round
Obliquely, like a baldric, was bound by his side
And laced under the left arm with a lasting knot,
In token that he was taken in a tarnishing sin;
And so he came to court, quite unscathed.
When the great became aware of Gawain's arrival,
There was general jubilation at the joyful news.
The King kissed the knight, and the Queen likewise,
And so did many a staunch noble who sought to salute him.
They all asked him about his expedition,
And he truthfully told them of his tribulations—
What chanced at the chapel, the good cheer of the knight,
The lady's love-making, and lastly, the girdle.
He displayed the scar of the snick° on his neck
Where the bold man's blow had hit, his bad faith to
Proclaim;
He groaned at his disgrace,
Unfolding his ill-fame,
And blood suffused his face
When he showed his mark of shame.

CI

'Look, my lord,' said Gawain, the lace in his hand.
'This belt confirms the blame I bear on my neck,
My bane and debasement, the burden I bear

Prince of Paradise Christ

snick nick

For being caught by cowardice and covetousness.
This is the figure of the faithlessness found in me,
Which I must needs wear while I live.
For man can conceal sin but not dissever from it,
So when it is once fixed, it will never be worked loose.'
First the king, then all the court, comforted the knight,
And all the lords and ladies belonging to the Table
Laughed at it loudly, and concluded amiably
That each brave man of the brotherhood should bear a baldric,°
A band, obliquely about him, of bright green,
Of the same hue as Sir Gawain's and for his sake wear it.
So it ranked as renown to the Round Table,
And an everlasting honour to him who had it,
As is rendered in Romance's rarest book.
Thus in the days of Arthur this exploit was achieved,
To which the books of Brutus° bear witness;
After the bold baron, Brutus, came here,
The siege and the assault being ceased at Troy
        Before.
    Such exploits, I'll be sworn,
    Have happened here of yore.
    Now Christ with his crown of thorn
    Bring us his bliss evermore! AMEN.
      HONY SOYT QUI MAL PENCE

c. 1380–1400

THE VISION OF PIERS PLOWMAN

It is surprising how little we know about when, where, and by whom *The Vision of Will Concerning Piers Plowman* was written. The poem was widely known and read, for it exists in a large number of manuscripts of the fourteenth and fifteenth centuries, was printed several times in the sixteenth, and was used, known, and referred to by sixteenth-century poets such as Skelton, by the religious Reformers a little later, and by others. But the few clues that we have to the identity of its author amount to little. He names himself several times as Will; he seems to have come from the West of England and to have been brought up in the area of the Malvern Hills, in Worcestershire, the scene of his vision. Many of the manuscripts of his book were copied there and thereabouts, and the long alliterative line that he uses for his meter survived, or was revived, with more strength in the West than elsewhere during the fourteenth century. The poet certainly spent some time in London.

The name of William Langland, traditionally associated with the poem, must serve

baldric This has been thought to mean, in conjunction with the motto of the Order of the Garter—*Hony soyt qui mal pence*—placed at the end of the poem by the scribe, that the poem commemorates the founding of the Garter by Edward III about 1347. But the colors are wrong: the garter was dark blue. A later Gawain romance makes the lace white and sees in it the origin of the collar worn by Knights of the Bath. The association looks like an afterthought, not intended by the *Gawain* poet, despite his concern with chivalric values.

books of Brutus i.e. any chronicle or romance of the "matter of Britain" until scholarship finds a better. Even so, we are not much ahead, since we know nothing of William Langland either, and may be giving this name to at least two separate poets. *Piers Plowman* exists in three versions, called by scholars A, B, and C, all composed between about 1360 and about 1385. A, the earliest and shortest (about 2500 lines), opens with an allegorical vision of the corruption of society and the attempt to purify it through Piers the Plowman. Piers personifies the ordinary man, seeking goodness through humility, honest endeavor, and obedience to the law of God. This section is followed by another, much shorter: *The Vita de Dowel, Dobet and Dobest* (The Life of Do Well, Do Better, and Do Best), in which another vision is presented. In his quest for the good Christian life and for the rational and intellectual foundations of faith, the poet asks information from Thought (intellectual activity), Wit (rational understanding resulting from thought), Study (Wit's wife: formal, disciplined reading and thought), and others. The search is inconclusive.

The B text, of about fifteen years later, is a radical revision and expansion of A. Adding further books, or passus (Latin *passus,* a step or stage), this version almost trebles the length of the whole. The search for Do Well is expanded, leading to Do Better (the life of Christ) and then to Do Best (the life of the church), each of them embodied in Piers.

The C text is a revised version of B, about ten years later, of much the same length, with some major cuts and additions.

Scholars are divided as to whether these three versions are the work of one man, or more. Though many now believe that one man was the author, this is not certain and the situation is baffling. It is less easy to explain the correspondences between the versions if more than one poet had been at work than it is to explain the differences if we accept A, B, and C as the work of a single poet rewriting his poem, keeping his theme intact, developing parts of it, and cutting out others, in response to changes in opinion and interest, and to contemporary events and pressures. It is hard to imagine a reviser, C, entering so thoroughly into the highly individual, vivid, and complicated style and personality of the original poet, B, and rising, in his additions, to the power and intensity of the earlier version. Nevertheless, the poetic quality of C is sometimes weaker, so that it may be the work of a later reviser rather than the poet of the B text's final revision, made toward the end of his life.

"Langland," then, is a fiction, but a convenient one. His long dream-allegory poem describes those ingredients of the social and religious condition of England in his day which he wishes to see reformed. The form in which it is cast allows the poet to pass easily from one mode of existence to another, from the description and outspoken criticism of current religious and social practices to the introduction of allegorical personages such as Holy Church, Lady Meed, Conscience, Kind Wit, and the rest. As in a dream, the real fits perfectly well with the abstract or symbolic; and the dream may help us to see the essential truth behind the apparent, the spiritual implication of the actual. Neither cancels out the other: they are coordinates.

This is not to say that the poem always has the fourfold significance that in the medieval period was drawn out of the text of the Bible—that it can everywhere be read for its literal meaning, its allegorical significance, its application to Christ and the church, and its application to divine love. The poem always functions on at least two levels, however—literal and figural—and sometimes on more; and it transposes easily from one to another.

So, this first and most important principle underlying the procedures of *Piers*

Plowman—its allegorical nature—gives it its unity, which is thematic rather than narrative. Transitions are often bewilderingly rapid. The story line is constantly being interrupted, or apparently interrupted, so that the larger figural significance can be emphasized, and the position of a given event in the scheme of salvation pointed out. Langland's poem exists not as a story, but as an exploration of Christian truth and its implications for someone who wishes to follow it. It is, like the *Divine Comedy* of Dante, basically an account of how the soul might get to God, its final resting place, in spite of difficulties and detours.

In genre, *Piers Plowman* is difficult to characterize. It uses the techniques of the dream allegory, but for religious purposes, to examine the nature of heavenly love and virtue, not of earthly love between the sexes. Unlike some dream-allegory poems of its time, it nevertheless remains in the world: there is no journey up to heaven or to a *figura* of the Earthly Paradise. *Piers Plowman* is also frequently cast in the stock medieval form, descended from the classical, of debate or dialogue, in which the nature of a given thing is established by question and answer, or statement and counter-statement. It is a satire on, or a complaint against, the abuses of the world, especially against the love of money. It is often like a commentary on biblical texts and on the precepts of Christianity; or like a huge sermon or series of sermons, packed with *exempla* and exhortation.

This sounds like confusion—and it is true that the poem is difficult to read and to hold together. Yet it is strongly and carefully structured, beginning with an examination of the necessity to seek salvation, and the difficulties of the search, passing to the problems posed in attempting to act rightly, then to the vision of God's love and mercy and finally to the role of God's church in the salvation of the individual. *Piers Plowman* is learned, didactic, and above all a religious work, resembling no other of its time and place, using poetry rather than prayer as a means of seeking understanding, ceaselessly stalking this elusive subject. Its message is the message of God, not of art.

Characteristically, Langland chose not to use the fashionable rhyming verse which the Londoner Chaucer (his only superior as a poet in the century) employed. To the polish, precision, firm rapidity, and sophistication of this French technique Langland prefers the loose, long, easy-paced, swinging, older English alliterative line, based on the four-stress accentual measure, the meter of the *Gawain* poet also. But where the *Gawain* poet gives an effect of jeweled richness and ornament, reinforced by his elaborate digressions and descriptions, Langland is unique in the sheer size of his vision, in his expressive force and energy, the tautness he often achieves, the way in which he can use alliteration to establish and reinforce patterns of sense as well as patterns of sound.

Langland's vision of what the world might be did not leave room for much sympathy for the world as it was, corrupted by the love of money and by vice of all sorts pretending to be virtue, especially among the clergy. But his concern for the poor, the oppressed, and the wretched is passionate and tender. The figures of the simple, uninstructed Dreamer—a man like ourselves, or of Piers the Plowman—who also takes on the dimensions of Adam, Moses, Christ, St. Peter, the good Pope, and the true Christian—allow him the opportunity of pointing the contrast between true goodness and simplicity and the polluted values of all those whose professions are not matched by their practice. As the Plowman—who does not appear until well on in the poem—he is in the line of rustic social, and later religious, critics which stretches back to classical times and beyond.

Given this and given the passion and point of Langland's denunciations, it is not surprising that the first echoes of his influence come from the Peasants' Revolt of 1381, when phrases from *Piers Plowman* are found being used in a revolutionary context. The poem continued to be thought of as an armory of anti-clerical phrases and sentiments throughout the fifteenth century. Imitations of this dimension were written—and ascribed to Chaucer, whose satirical methods are much more controlled, refined, and oblique. The influence of Langland and of these imitations is still strong in the polemical literature of the English Reformation.

Langland himself would have been aghast at this. As his first printer put it in 1550, he had "godly, learnedly and wittily rebuked" all vice, but his vision of goodness was always a vision of what might come to pass within the Catholic Church and her institutions, not outside it. It was the passion and energy of his renunciation of abuses in society, of which the spiritual leaders ought to be the clergy, his contention that the corruption of the best is the worst kind of corruption, that laid him open to this use.

The text here used is a modernization, by the editor, of the B text as given in W. W. Skeat's edition (Oxford 1886; reprinted, with additional bibliography, 1954). An attempt has been made to keep the rhythm and alliteration of the original, and some archaic words have been retained where either sense or alliteration seemed to demand this.

The Vision of Piers Plowman

[In the Prologue and Passus I, Piers himself makes no appearance. In them, and as far as Passus VIII, the poet is concerned with St. Paul's "first man . . . of the earth, earthy," with the primary, major occupations in which men engage, by which ordinary society exists. The Dreamer's vision of the field full of folk going about its sinful, anarchic, money-making business without thought of the tower of Truth above or the dungeon of Error below, is a picture of the society which must be changed, church and state alike. The fable of the rats and mice, and of belling the cat, is a parody of the confusion and self-seeking of current politics.

The Prologue describes the state of society as it is. In Passus I, Langland goes on to show how it is that all this may be redeemed and brought to order, if only man will be conscious of Truth, i.e. if he will accept the law of God, which is the truth, and the law of love that are given to him. These laws he must obey faithfully, i.e. display his own truth, as all orders of society ought to do, in imitation of the angels. The church will be man's safeguard, and the means of mediating God's love to the people.]

From *The Prologue*

In a summer season, when soft was the sun°
I shaped me into shrouds as though I were a shepherd,
In habit like a hermit, unholy of works,°
Went wide in this world, wonders to hear.

In . . . sun the spring opening, conventional for dream allegory, preparing the readers for the type of fiction, peopled with personifications, that they will meet, the poet acting as "presenter," through the dream
I . . . works i.e. I put myself into rough (or: long) clothes, like a shepherd, as if I were a hermit, evil in my doings. Langland is severe on "feigned contemplatives," living as hermits to avoid working for a living. He may also be showing himself aware that his own life as a poet looks an idle one, bringing himself down, like Chaucer, to the reader with a mock-modest formula.

But on a May morning, on Malvern Hills,°
There befell me a ferly, of fairy methought.°
I was wearily wandered out, and went me to rest
Under a broad bank by a brook's side,
And as I lay and leaned> and looked into the waters, *reclined*
I slumbered> into sleep, it sounded so merry. *dozed*
  Then did I meet> a marvellous sweven,> *dream / dream*
That I was in a wilderness, wist> I never where; *knew*
As I looked into the east,° high into the sun,
I saw a tower on a toft,> triely> made; *hill / excellently*
A deep dale beneath, a dungeon° therein,
With deep ditches and dark and dreadful to see.
A fair field full of folk found I there between,
Of all manner of men, the mean> and the rich, *poor*
Working and wandering as the world demands.
Some put themselves to the plough and played full seldom:
In setting> and sowing sweated full hard *planting*
To win what wasters° with gluttony destroy.
And some put themselves in pride, apparelled themselves like that,
In countenance of clothing came disguised.°
  In prayers and in penance put themselves many,
All for love of Our Lord lived full strictly,
In hope for to have heaven-kingdom's bliss;
Like anchorites and hermits who hold to their cells°
And covet not in country to cairen> about, *wander*
For no lickerish> living their licham> to please. *fancy / body*
  And some chose chaffer; they achieved the better°—
Or so it seems to our sight, that such men thrive.
And some mirths to make, as minstrels know how,
And get gold with their glee>—guiltless, I believe— *singing*
But japers> and janglers,> Judas's children, *jokers / blabbers*
Feign them fantasies and make fools of themselves
And have their wit at will to work if they wished;°
What Paul° preaches of them, I will not prove it here:
Qui loquitur turpiloquium is Lucifer's hind.°
  Bidders> and beggars fast about went *beggars*
With their bellies and their bags of bread full crammed,
Faited° for their food, fought at the alehouse:
In gluttony, God knows, they go to bed,

Malvern Hills the poet's native spot, in Worcestershire, about 130 miles northwest of London. The area was noted for its religious houses, at one of which Langland may have gone to school.
a ferly . . . methought i.e. a marvel, which seemed to me supernatural
east i.e. in God's direction
dungeon literally, a keep or central stronghold-tower, i.e. prison
win . . . wasters i.e. provider and conspicuous consumer
In countenance . . . disguised i.e. came got up in pompous clothes
hold . . . cells i.e. they kept their vows—a crucial issue for Langland
some . . . better some chose trade and succeeded better
Feign . . . wished (ll. 36–37) pretend that they have visions and that they are feebleminded —and yet they have their wits at their command and could work if they wished
Paul See II Thessalonians 3:10: "If any would not work, neither should he eat."
Qui . . . hind The man who speaks slander is the servant of the Devil
Faited i.e. begged fraudulently

And rise with ribaldry, those robber knaves.
Sleep and sorry sloth pursue them always.
  Pilgrims and palmers° plighted them together
To seek St. James° and saints in Rome.
They went forth in their way with many wise tales—
And had leave to lie all their lives thereafter.
I saw some that said they had sought saints:
For every tale that they told, their tongues were tempered to lie
More than to say sooth, it seemed by their speech.
  Hermits in a heap, with hooked staves
Went to Walsingham° and their wenches after them:
Great lubbers and long that loth were to swink,> *toil*
Clothed themselves in copes to be known from the others,°
And shaped themselves hermits, their ease to have.
  I found there friars, all the four orders,°
Preaching to the people for profit of themselves,
Glossing° the Gospel as seemed good to them,
For covetousness of copes construing it as they wished.
Many of these Master Friars° may clothe themselves at pleasure,
For their money and their merchandise march together.°
For since Charity has been chapman and the chief to shrive lords,°
Many ferlies> have fallen in a few years. *marvels*
Unless Holy Church and they hold better together,
The most mischief on mould> is mounting well> fast. *earth / very*
  There preached a Pardoner° as if he were a priest,
Brought forth a bull,° with bishop's seals,
And said that himself might absolve them all,°
Of falsehood in fasting, of vows broken.
Simple men believed him well and liked his words,
Came up and kneeled to kiss his bulls.
He banged> them with his brevet° and blinded their eyes, *tapped*
And raked in with his ragman° rings and brooches.
Thus they give their gold to gluttons to keep,
And lend> it to losels> that lechery practice. *give / rogues*
Were the bishop blessed and worth both his ears,
His seal should not be sent to deceive the people.

palmers originally pilgrims who had been at Jerusalem; but by now pilgrims of any sort
St. James the shrine of St. James of Compostela, in Galicia, northwestern Spain
Walsingham the shrine of Our Lady of Walsingham, in Norfolk, next in prestige to Canterbury as a place of pilgrimage in England
Clothed . . . others i.e. put on religious clothing, to mark themselves out from other people
orders Dominicans, Franciscans, Augustinians, Carmelites
Glossing interpreting, a regular accusation against the friars
Master Friars those who have completed their religious training
money . . . together their avarice and their trade (in confessions) go hand in hand
Charity . . . lords Charity has bought and sold like a merchant and been confessor-in-chief to noblemen. The friars' ideal had been poverty and charity, but they had become wealthy. Most of the important men of the time had friars for confessors.
Pardoner See Chaucer, the General Prologue, ll. 671 ff.—also for satiric method. He could give, by papal permission, indulgences in exchange for money given to charity.
bull papal edict proclaiming the indulgence which the Pardoner was selling
absolve . . . all He claimed this falsely. All he was empowered to do was remit penance; he could not absolve men from sin.
brevet letter of authority
ragman roll of parchment

But it is not by the bishop that the boy preaches,°
For the parish priest and the pardoner part> the silver, *share*
Which the poor people of the parish ought to have, if it were not done.
Parsons and parish priests complained to the bishop
That their parishes were poor since the time of plague,°
So as to have a licence and a leave at London to live
And sing there for simony,° for silver is sweet.
  Bishops and bachelors, both masters and doctors°
That have cure° under Christ and, in token, tonsure,°
A sign that they should shrive> their parishioners, *confess*
Preach to them and pray for them, and feed the poor—
They lie in London, in Lent and else.°
Some serve the King and his silver tell,> *account for*
In Exchequer and Chancery, challenge his debts
From wards and wardmoots, waifs and strays.°
And some serve,° as servants, lords and ladies
And in the stead of stewards, sit and judge.
Their mass and their matins and many of their hours°
Are done undevoutly. Dread is, at the last,
Lest Christ in consistory° curse full many.
I perceived the power,° that Peter had, to keep
To bind and to unbind, as the book> tells *Bible*
How he placed it with love, as Our Lord commanded,
To four virtues, the best of all virtues
That cardinals be called, and closing the gates
To where Christ is in His Kingdom—to close and to shut,
And to open it to them and Heaven's bliss show.
But of the cardinals at court,° that caught that name,
And power presumed in themselves a Pope to make,
Who has that power that Peter had—impugn I wish not.
Since to love and learning the election belongs,
Therefore I can—but cannot—of Curia say more.°

by . . . preaches for the benefit of the bishop that the rogue preaches; i.e. the bishop does not receive the money to apply to charity, as he should
plague especially the Black Death of 1348–49 and the other outbreaks of the 1360's and 1370's, causing famine and depopulation in rural areas
licence . . . simony Be given leave to be an absentee rector and hold more than one office by acting as chantry or guild priest in London. A chantry was an endowment to pay for masses for the repose of specified souls. Simony is the buying and selling of spiritual things, so named from Simon Magus, who wished to buy spiritual power from the Apostles (Acts 8:18–24).
masters . . . doctors graduates (in theology)
cure care of souls
tonsure shaving of the head, to indicate religious profession
lie . . . else stay in London during Lent (when, especially, they should be in their parishes) and at other times
In . . . strays (ll. 93–94) In the courts of Exchequer and Chancery (two of the law-courts of the time, with specific jurisdiction) claim the debts owed the king from the wards (districts of the city) at the ward-meetings, and the waifs (property without an owner) and strayed cattle (which both became royal property); i.e. the priests acted as legal officials. Cf. Chaucer's commendation of the Clerk, General Prologue, l. 294.
some serve Serving priests, attached to a household, with secular functions, were often complained of.
hours A priest was obliged to say his office (from his breviary) at the canonical hours.
consistory church council or assembly of prelates—here, the Day of Judgment
power St. Peter gave the power of the keys (Matthew 16:19) to the four cardinal virtues—prudence, temperance, fortitude, and justice. The word "cardinal" is derived from the Latin *cardo*, a hinge. These virtues ought to be the spiritual hinges of Christendom: instead the hinges are the corrupt cardinals of the church.
court the Curia, the papal court at Rome
Since . . . more I have more to say about them, but cannot say it, out of reverence

Then came there a King,° Knights leading him,
Might of the Commons made him to reign:
And then came Kind Wit° and clerks he made
For to counsel the King and the Commons keep safe.
The King, and the Knights and clergy both,
Cast˃ that the Commons must needs find˃ their selves. *decreed / provide for*
The Commons contrived, by Kind Wit, crafts:
And for the profit of all people, ploughmen° ordained
To till and to travail, as true life demands.
The King and the Commons—Kind Wit made a third—
Shaped law and loyalty, each knew rights and duty.°

. . .

Then ran out a rout° of rats, all at once,
And little mice with them, more than a thousand,
And came to a council for their common profit.
For a cat from a court came when he pleased
And leaped on them lightly˃ and latched on them at will, *quickly*
And played with them perilously and pushed them about.
'For doubt of diverse dreads, we dare not look about.
And if we grudge˃ about his games, he'll give us all grief, *complain*
Scratch us and claw us and in his clutches hold
So that we loathe life before he lets us go.
Could we with any wit his will withstand
We might be lofty lords and live at our ease.'
A rat of renown, most reasonable˃ of tongue *eloquent*
Said as a sovereign˃ help, for his part: *most excellent*
'I have seen sirs˃,' said he, 'in the City of London° *men*
Bear bighes˃ full bright about their necks *necklaces*
And others collars° of crafty˃ work; uncoupled they go *skillful*
Both in warren and waste,° wherever they wish;
And at other times they are elsewhere, as I hear tell.
Were there a bell on their bighe, by Jesus, it seems to me,
Men could know where they went and run from them!
And right thus,' said the rat, 'reason counsels me

King Langland now begins an exposition of how a country ought to be governed, with the king, aided by his knights, depending for his power on the Commons, and all estates knit in a harmonious whole.
Kind Wit natural intelligence, understanding, by which learned men give the king advice and so preserve his subjects from oppression by him
ploughmen i.e. all rustic laborers
duty Langland here, in the short passage omitted, develops the theme of the King and his Commons and their roles in government.
rout Crowd. Langland now passes suddenly into a fable, in which the story of belling the cat is applied to the political situation of his time. The tale occurs in collections of animal stories from the 12th century onward. Langland may be making specific reference here to the Parliaments of 1376 and 1377, when the Commons were attempting to assert their rights. The cat would then be old Edward III, the kitten the young Richard II, who succeeded him at the age of ten in 1377. Richard's youth and his succession to a strong ruler like Edward III gave much concern to Parliament, and a council was established. The rats are the burgesses and important members of Parliament, the mice the lower order of such men. They are anxious to control the king, though without a king's authority they would live in anarchy. Langland's theme is always the interdependence of all orders under a ruler within a hierarchy (in church and state), every member conscientiously performing his allotted function.
City of London the business and legal center
collars chains of office, worn round the neck
uncoupled . . . waste they go unimpeded wherever they wish; "warren" is literally an enclosed space for breeding game; "waste" is common, unused land

To buy a bell of brass or of bright silver,
And attach it to a collar, for our common profit,
And knot it on the cat's neck. Then may we hear
Whether he is riding or resting, or running to play.
And if it please him to play, then out we may peep
And appear in his presence, as long as he is so inclined;
And if he's feeling warlike, be wary and shun his way.'
All the rout of rats assented to this scheme.
But, though the bell was bought, and fastened to the bighe
There was no rat in all the rout, for all the realm of France,
That dared bind the bell about the cat's neck,
Nor hang it about the cat's halse,> to win all England; *neck*
And they held themselves unhardy> and their counsel feeble *cowardly*
And felt all their labour lost and all their long planning.
A mouse,° that knew much good counsel, as it seemed,
Stepped out boldly and stood before them all,
And to the rout of rats rehearsed> these words: *spoke*
'Though we killed the cat, there would come another,
To scratch us and all our kind, even if we crept under benches.
Therefore I counsel all the commons to let the cat be;
And let us be not so bold as to show him the bell.
For I heard my sire say, seven years past,
"Where the cat is a kitten, the court is unwell."°
That Holy Writ witnesses, whoever wishes to read it:
Ve terre ubi puer rex est etc.°
For no rank may have rest there, for rats by night.
While he is catching coneys> he covets not our corpses, *rabbits*
But is full fed with "venison":° let us not defame him.
For better is a little loss than a long sorrow:
Confusion among us all, though we lose a shrew.°
For many men's malt we mice could destroy—
And also the rout of rats could rend men's clothes—
Were it not for the cat in the court, who can jump on you:
For if you rats had your way, you could not rule yourselves.
'I say for my part,' said the mouse, 'I see so much consequence,
The cat or the kitten shall never, by my counsel, be grieved;
(No carping about the collar: it cost me nothing—
But even if it had cost me chattels, confess it I would not°);
But suffer them as they wish to do—as they please—
Coupled or uncoupled, to catch what they can.
Therefore every wise wight> I warn; wit well your own!'° *creature*

mouse perhaps one Peter de la Mare, who in 1377 proposed a council to advise the young King Richard II
Where . . . unwell i.e. be careful, because a new, young king may not know how to handle things and control his nobles, who will oppress the Commons
Ve . . . etc. Woe to the land where the king is a child (adaptation of Ecclesiastes 10:16)
venison rabbit meat
better . . . shrew we would do better to lose one or two of ourselves, perhaps a worthless one of us, than mourn a great slaughter by provoking him
No . . . not I don't want to talk about the collar—I didn't contribute to the cost and even if I had I wouldn't tell you
wit . . . own know your own; i.e. look to your own affairs

What this meteles> means, you men that are merry *dream*
Devine, for I dare not, by dear God in Heaven!
Yet hove> there a hundred in hoves° of silk *waited*
Serjeants° they seemed that served at the bar
Pleaded for pence and impounded the law°
And not for love of Our Lord unloosed their lips once.
You might better measure mist on Malvern Hills
Than get a mumble from their mouths, unless money were showed.
Barons and burgesses and bondmen also
I saw in this assembly as you shall hear afterwards.
Bakers and brewers and butchers many,
Wool-websters° and weavers of linen,
Tailors and tinkers, and tollers° in markets,
Masons and miners and many other crafts,
Of all kinds of living labourers leaped forth some,
Such as ditchers and delvers> that do their deeds ill, *diggers*
And drive on the long day with 'Dieu vous save, Dame Emme!'°
Cooks and their knaves> cried 'Hot pies, hot! *kitchen-boys*
Good gris° and geese! Go dine, go!'
Taverners to them told the same story:
'White wine of Alsace and red wine of Gascony,
Of the Rhine and of La Rochelle, the roast to digest.'
All this saw I asleep and seven sithes> more. *times*

Passus I

What this mountain means, and the murky dale
And the field full of folk, I shall you fairly show.
A lady lovely of lere,> in linen clothed *face*
Came down from a castle and called me fair,
Said, 'Son, do you sleep? Do you see these people
How busy they are about the maze?
The most part of these people that pass on this earth,
Have they worship in this world,° they wish for no better,
Of another heaven than here they hold no account.'
I was afraid of her face, though she was fair,
And said 'Mercy, Madam, what is the meaning of this?'
'The tower on the toft,' said she, 'Truth is therein.
And would have you work as His word teaches;
For He is the Father of Faith and formed you all
With both fell> and face and gave you five wits,° *skin*
To worship Him with them while you are here.
And for this He hight> the earth to help you, each one *ordered*

hoves lawyers' hoods
Serjeants sergeants-at-law, eminent pleaders; see Chaucer, General Prologue, ll. 311 ff.
Pleaded . . . law made pleas in court for money and made the law their property
Wool-websters wool-weavers (women); cf. Chaucer's *webbe,* weaver, General Prologue, l. 364
tollers collectors of tolls or dues from stall-holders
Dieu . . . Emme "God save you, Dame Emma!", either a line from a song or a greeting in hope of a tip
gris little (sucking) pigs
worship . . . world earthly honor and success
five wits five senses—sight, smell, hearing, touch, taste

Of wool, of linen, of livelihood at need
In measurable> manner to make yourself at ease. *temperate*
And commanded, of His courtesy, in common three things°
None are needed but they, and name them I will—
And reckon them by reason>—repeat you them after me? *in order*
The first is clothing, to save you from chill
And meat at meal-time, for misease> of yourself *against discomfort*
And drink when you are dry—but take nothing beyond reason
Lest you worth> the worse when you must work. *become*
For Lot° while he lived through his liking of drink,
Did with his daughters what pleased the Devil
Delighted in drink as the Devil wanted—
And Lechery latched> him and he lay by them both. *caught*
And all he wited> wine that wicked deed. *accused*
Inebriamus eum vino, dormiamus cum eo,
Ut servare possemus de Patre nostro semen.°
Through wine and through women there Lot was encumbered
And there begot in gluttony girls that were churls.°
Therefore dread delectable drink and you shall do the better.
Measure> is medicine, though you much yearn— *moderation*
It is not all good to the ghost> that the gut asks *spirit*
Nor a living for your licham> that lief> is to your soul. *body / dear*
Believe not your licham, for a liar teaches him
Which is the wretched world that wishes to betray you.
For the Fiend and your flesh° pursue you together:
This and that pursue your soul; and say this in your heart,°
And so that you shall be wary, I wiss> you the best.' *tell*
'Madam, merci,'> I said, 'Your words please me well. *thank you*
But the wealth of this world,° that men hold so fast
Tell me to whom, Madam, that treasure belongs?'
'Go to the Gospel,' said she, 'see what God said Himself
Though the people apposed Him of a penny in the Temple:°
Whether they should with it honour King Caesar.
And God asked of them of whom spoke the lettering
And the image, too, that stood thereon.
"Caesar's," they said; "Each of us sees well."
"*Reddite Caesari,*" said God, "that *Caesari* belongs,

three things i.e. those necessary to sustain life; cf. Ecclesiasticus 29:31: "The chief thing for life is water and bread and clothing and an house to cover shame"

Lot Lot and Noah were the two great biblical *exempla* of drunkenness, and Lot also of the closely related sin of lechery, on account of his incest. He is regularly used in sermon literature as a caution against drunkenness and its consequences; cf. Chaucer's Pardoner's Tale, l. 199. Lot's story is told in Genesis 19:30–38.

Inebriamus . . . semen Genesis 19:32: "Come, let us make our father drink wine and we will lie with him, that we may preserve seed of our father"—the text of Langland's "sermon"

girls . . . churls i.e. children that were baseborn. *Girl* at this time can mean male or female; here it refers to Lot's two sons, Moab and Ammon.

world . . . flesh The World, the Flesh, and the Devil are the enemies of the soul.

say . . . heart perhaps: suggest evil to your heart

wealth . . . world The rest of this *passus* examines the theme of the right use of worldly wealth and goods.

apposed . . . Temple When the people questioned him about a penny in the temple; see Matthew 22:16–22. Christ the Teacher is placed in direct opposition to the world, the liar who is the teacher of the *licham* (l. 37).

Et quae sunt Dei, Deo;° or else you do ill."
For rightfully Reason° ought to rule you completely,
And Kind Wit° be warden your wealth to ward,> *guard*
And tutor> of your treasure, and take> it you at need, *custodian / bring*
For husbandry° and he hold together.'
Then I frained> her fairly, by Him that her made, *asked*
'That dungeon in the dale, that dreadful is of sight,
What may it be meaning, Madam, I beseech you?'
'That is the Castle of Care, whoever comes into it
May ban> that he born was in body or in soul. *curse*
There wons> a wight> that Wrong is called, *lives / creature*
Father of Falsehood—and founded it himself.
Adam and Eve he egged on° to ill
Counselled Cain° to kill his brother;
Judas he japed with Jewish silver°
Who after on an alder° hanged himself then.
He is letter of love,° and he lies to them all,
Those who trust in his treasure, he soonest betrays.'
Then had I wonder in my wit what woman she was
That such wise words of Holy Writ showed
And asked her by the High Name,° ere she thence went
What she was witterly> that wissed> me so fair? *in fact / instructed*
'Holy Church° I am,' said she, 'You ought to know me.
I undertook> you first and taught you faith *received*
And you brought me borrows,> my bidding to fulfill *pledges*
And to love me loyally while your life endures.'
Then I kneeled on my knees and cried to her for grace
And prayed her pitifully to pray for my sins;
And also ken me kindly° in Christ to believe
That I might work his will that wrought> me a man. *made*
'Teach> me to no treasure, but tell me this ilk> *direct / same*
How I may save my soul,° you that sacred are held.'
'When all treasures are tried,' said she, 'Truth° is the best;
I do it on *Deus caritas* to deem the sooth.°
It is as dear-worth> a drury> as dear God himself. *valuable / love gift*

Reddite . . . Deo Again the theme of the discourse is emphasized by being quoted verbatim in Latin: "Render therefore unto Caesar the things which are Caesar's and unto God the things which are God's" (Matthew 22:21).
Reason the mind's reflective faculty
Kind Wit natural wisdom or intelligence, the gift of God, with a natural tendency toward good
husbandry i.e. wise use of worldy goods
Adam . . . on Wrong, the Devil, was the Serpent in Eden that tempted Adam & Eve (Genesis 3:1 ff.) to sin the first sin of all, which embraces all the others.
Cain the first murderer (Genesis 4:8)
Jewish silver the thirty pieces of silver for which Judas betrayed Christ (Matthew 26:15)—the prime example of wrong use of money
alder Judas was supposed to have hanged himself on an alder tree.
letter of love hinderer of love; i.e. hostile to Christ
High Name the name of God
Holy Church Christ's representative on earth, who received the Dreamer at baptism, when he promised by proxy to keep her commandments
ken . . . kindly teach me naturally, instinctively
save . . . soul i.e. store up treasure in heaven, not on earth
Truth i.e. the law of God and the Christian's obedience to that law
I . . . sooth I base myself on "God is love" (i.e. on the text from I John 4:8), so that I may judge truly; again the announcement of the text that will govern the proposition to be explored—God is Truth and God is Love

Whoever is true in his tongue and tells nothing else°
And does the works that go with it and wills no-one ill,
He is a god by the Gospel, aground and aloft
And alike to Our Lord, by St. Luke's words.°
The clerks that know this should ken it about°
For Christian and unchristian claim truth each of them.
Kings and knights should keep it by reason°
Ride and rap> down in realms about> *strike / around*
And take> transgressors and tie them fast, *capture*
Till Truth has determined their trespass to the end.°
And that is the profession apertly that appends to knights,°
Not to fast only one Friday in five-score> winters; *a hundred*
But to hold> with him and with her that wish for all truth *stay*
And never leave them, for love nor for latching> on silver. *seizing*
For David in his day dubbed knights°
And made them swear on their swords to serve Truth ever:
And whoever passes that point is apostate to the order.°
But Christ, King of Kings, knighted ten:°
Cherubin and seraphim, seven such and one other,
And gave them might in his majesty—the merrier they seemed—
And over his mean meyny,° made them archangels
Taught them by the Trinity, truth to know,
And to be buxom> at his bidding: he bade them nought else. *obedient*
Lucifer° with legions, learned it in heaven
But because he broke buxomness, his bliss did he tine> *lose*
And fell from that fellowship, in a fiend's likeness
Into a deep, dark hell, to dwell there forever;
And more thousands with him, than man knows to number
Leaped out with Lucifer, in loathly form,
For they believed on him that lied in this manner:
Ponam pedem in aquilone, et similis ero altissimo.°

And all that hoped it might be so, no heaven might hold them
But they fell out in fiends' likeness, nine days° together,

nothing else i.e. speaks only truth
St. Luke's words The texts Langland is alluding to are probably Luke 16:10, the parable of the steward, and Luke 8:21: "My mother and my brethren are these which hear the word of God and do it."
clerks . . . about learned men that know this should make it widely known
by reason according to reason
determined . . . end made a full and final examination of their sin
profession . . . knights and that is clearly the vow (and its execution) that belongs to knights
David . . . knights The knights that David made may be the Levites, whom he appointed to keep the Ark of the Covenant (I Chronicles 15).
whoever . . . order He who transgresses that canon has become a deserter from the order. Langland has been talking about the evil of the neglect of spiritual duties by earthly knights—but those described in the next lines are much worse, because they were once the best and fell from pride.
knighted ten i.e. the ten orders of angels, as they were before Lucifer and his angels fell; cherubim, seraphim, and thrones (the three highest); dominions, virtues, powers; and principalities, archangels, and angels. Lucifer's angels, the tenth order, are the representatives of the first act of disobedience, prior to and worse than man's, irredeemable.
mean meyny lower orders
Lucifer The only injunction laid upon angels and men is obedience to God's commands. This is what Lucifer breaks.
Ponam . . . altissimo "I will set my foot in the north and I will be like the most high" (cf. Isaiah 14:13–14). Lucifer usually is placed in the north—by Milton among others—and Hell in Germanic mythology is placed in that region also.
nine days the usual interval; cf. Milton, *Paradise Lost* VI.871

Till God, of His goodness, did stop and stint˃ *pause*
And made heavens to stay firm and to stand still.˃ *silent*
When these wicked ones went, wonderwise they fell,
Some in air, some on earth,° and some in Hell-deep;
But Lucifer lowest lies of them all:
For pride that he put out,˃ his pain has no end *showed*
And all that work with wrong, wend˃ they must *go*
After their death-day and dwell with that shrew.˃ *wicked one*
But those that work well, as Holy Writ tells,
And end—as I ere˃ said—in Truth that is best, *before*
May be sure that their souls shall wend to Heaven,
Where Truth is in Trinity and enthrones them all.
Therefore I say, as I said before, by sight˃ of these texts, *witness*
When all treasures are tried, Truth is the best.
Learn˃ it to these lewd˃ men, for lettered men it know: *teach / simple*
That Truth is treasure, the triest˃ on earth.' *finest*
'Yet have I no kind knowledge,' said I; 'yet must you ken me better,°
By what craft in my corpse° it commences, and where.'
'You dotard daff˃,' said she, 'dull are your wits; *idiot*
Too little Latin you learned, lad, in your youth:
Heu michi, quod sterilem duxi vitam iuvenilem!°

It is kind knowledge,' said she, 'that kens in your heart
For to love your Lord liever˃ than yourself; *more dearly*
No deadly sin to do, die though you should;
This I trow˃ be truth. Who can teach you better, *believe*
Look you suffer him to say,° and sithen˃ learn it after. *then*
For thus witnesses His Word, work you thereafter;
For Truth tells that love is treacle° of Heaven
There may no sin be on him seen that uses that spice.˃ *medicine*
And all His works he wrought, with love as him list,˃ *it pleased*
And learned it Moses as the lievest thing° and most like heaven;
And also the plant of peace, most precious of virtues.
For Heaven might not hold it, it was so heavy in itself,
Till it had of the earth, eaten its fill.
And when it had of this fold,˃ flesh and blood taken, *earth*
There was never leaf upon linden° lighter thereafter

when . . . earth I.e. they became the evil spirits of earth and air as well as the devils of hell. This explanation lasts until at least the 17th century.
have I . . . better I have no natural way of knowing . . . you must teach me better. He cannot understand by his natural faculties and needs the teaching of the church to set him right.
craft . . . corpse power in my body; i.e. what is its origin in me
Heu . . . iuvenilem "Ah me, how useless a life I led when I was young." The source has not been identified.
suffer . . . say allow to speak
treacle the finest and most effective medicine, originally a remedy for snakebite, compounded from vipers' flesh
lievest thing dearest thing. Love is gradually modulating into the person of Christ in this section. The reference to Moses is to the Tables of the Law, the Ten Commandments, the first four concerned with the love of God and the second six with the love of one's neighbor, on which hang "all the Law and the Prophets."
leaf upon linden proverbial expression for lightness. Once Love has become incarnate in Christ upon earth (the sprig of the tree of Jesse) it becomes paradoxically light, where in heaven it had been too heavy to be held there. Love holds in itself the contraries of overwhelming weight and force, so that none can resist it, and unbelievable quickness and fineness, so that it can creep in anywhere.

And portative> and piercing as the point of a needle, *rapid*
So that no armour might let> it, and no high walls. *stop*
Therefore is love the leader, of the Lord's folk of Heaven,
And a mean;> as the Mayor is between the King and the Commons, *mediator*
Right so is Love a leader and the Law shapes.°
Upon man for his misdeeds, the amercement> he taxes.> *fine / exacts*
And for to know it kindly, it commences by might°
And in the heart is its head and its high source.
For from kind knowing in heart, there a might> begins.° *power*
And that falls> to the Father, that formed us all; *belongs*
Looked on us with love and let His Son die
Meekly for our misdeeds, to amend us all.
And yet wished He them no woe, that wrought> Him that torment, *made*
But meekly by mouth mercy he besought
To have pity on that people that pained> Him to death. *tortured*
Here might you see examples—in Himself one
That He was mightful and meek and mercy did grant
To them that hanged him on high and his heart holed.> *pierced*
Therefore I rede> you richly, have ruth> of the poor; *counsel / pity*
Though you be mighty to moot,° be meek in your works.
For by the same measures that you mete,> amiss or otherwise, *deal out*
You shall be weighed therewith, when you wend hence:
Eadem mensura qua mensi fueritis, remecietur vobis.°

For though you be true of your tongue and truly win,> *honestly gain*
And as chaste as a child, that in church weeps,
Unless you love loyally and lend> to the poor *give*
Such goods as God sends you goodly divide,
You have no more merit, in mass or in hours,°
Than Malkin from her maidenhead which no man desires.°
For James the Gentle judged in his books
That faith without the feat,° is right nothing worth
And as dead as a door-tree,° unless the deeds follow:
Fides sine operibus mortua est, etc.

Therefore chastity without charity will be chained in Hell:
It is as lewd> as a lamp that no light is in. *worthless*
Many chaplains are chaste, but charity is absent;
Are no men more avaricious than they, when they are advanced;°

love . . . shapes In the supernatural world Love dictates all that God does and softens his justice. To men on earth the love that he showed in the Incarnation does the same.
for . . . might Love can be recognized naturally (by instinct), for it begins as a strong impulse.
for . . . begins for from natural understanding in the heart, there begins this impulse
mighty . . . moot powerful in the law courts
Eadem . . . vobis Cf. Luke 6:38; "With the same measure that ye mete withal, it shall be measured to you again." Cf. Matthew 7:2.
hours the canonical hours
Than . . . desires Than Maudie from her maidenhead, which nobody wants to take; i.e. you can be as good as you like, but unless you are active in good works, in charity, it will help you nothing. Malkin is sometimes used of a whore; here she seems to be an unattractive old thing, but chaste.
faith . . . feat See James 2:26: "Faith without works is dead." The Latin is quoted two lines on.
door-tree door-post. Some manuscripts read door-nail.
when . . . advanced when given preferment, promoted in the church

Unkind to their kin and to all Christians,
Chew up their charity and chide for more.°
Such chastity without charity will be chained in Hell!
   Many curates> keep themselves clean in their flesh: *priests*
They are encumbered with covetousness, they cannot put it from them,
So hard has avarice hasped> them together. *clamped*
And that is no truth of the Trinity, but treachery of Hell,
And a lesson to lewd men, the later to dole out.°
   Therefore these words be written in the Gospel:
Date et dabitur vobis:° for I dole> you all. *give to*
And that is the lack of love and lets out my grace,
To comfort the care-full, encumbered with sin.
   Love is leech> of life, and next Our Lord's self; *healer*
And also the graith gate> that goes to Heaven. *narrow way*
Therefore I say, as I said ere through the texts:
When all treasures be tried, Truth is the best.
   Now I have told you what truth is, than which no treasure is better,
I may no longer linger with you: now Our Lord look to you.'
c. 1377

DRAMA

MYSTERY PLAYS (MIRACLES)

When a medieval author speaks of a comedy or tragedy he does not mean a play: he usually means a poem intended to edify and instruct, which ends happily or unhappily. The poem may be a sophisticated presentation of character and motive, often through dialogue (like Chaucer's *Troilus and Criseyde*); or it may be cast in the form of dialogue or debate (*The Owl and the Nightingale*).

The Middle Ages knew nothing of Greek drama. Medieval authors treated the Roman tragedies of Seneca as storehouses of useful knowledge, moral and philological; and though the tenth-century German nun Hrotsvitha wrote Christian Latin comedies in purified imitation of Terence, Roman writers of comedy were thought of in the same way as Seneca. A different kind of Latin text was the starting point for medieval drama: the Latin of the mass, with its daily re-enactment of the Passion of Christ, essentially dramatic in its performance and designed to keep remembrance of the Passion, its antecedents and its implications, before the eyes and minds of the people. Other services of the church also played their part, but the decisive factor was the elaborate ceremonies developed for the great festivals, such as Easter and Christmas. The dramatic element is present in the mass not only as spoken dialogue and ceremonial interchange between celebrant and acolytes, but as sung dialogue. In antiphonal singing, two halves of the choir deliver alternate versicles and responsories. One of the texts (or "tropes") of these antiphons for the Easter mass is an adaptation of the exchange between the three Marys and the angel at the empty tomb of the risen

Chew . . . more get through what they are given and scream for more
a lesson . . . out an indication to wicked men that they should be slow in giving
Date . . . vobis Luke 6:38: "Give and it shall be given unto you."

Christ (Matthew 28:1–7 and Mark 16:1–7), known (from its opening phrase) as the *Quem quaeritis* ("Whom do you seek?").

One voice, or set of voices, representing the angel, sang: "Whom seek ye in the sepulchre, ye followers of Christ?" and was answered: "Jesus of Nazareth, the crucified, O heavenly ones." The angelic voices then sang: "He is not here; He is risen as He foretold; go and tell how He is risen from the tomb."

Many of the steps by which this reverent rudimentary form of dramatic representation within the church, with its sung dialogue in Latin, developed into the vernacular spoken play performed in the city, on non-consecrated ground, are still not clear. Secular forms of popular and courtly entertainment—dancing, games, festivals, and perhaps folk ritual, with the "acts" of professional minstrels, dancers, jugglers and acrobats, singly or in roving bands—must have made their contribution, but we cannot say exactly how they did so or what that contribution was. The purpose of medieval drama, however, always remained sacred: drama was the "quick [i.e. living] book" in which the ordinary Christian might read the mysteries of his faith (hence the name "mystery" by which the plays came to be known). They reinforce the message of sermons and other forms of religious instruction by presenting in dramatic form the biblical story of mankind, from Creation and Fall to Redemption and Judgment.

Though in England their performance was generally the prerogative of associations of pious laymen, the plays were devised and probably written by clergy. The clergy retained at least a guiding hand on the cycles. The English vernacular play, in nine- or ten-line stanzes, loose in rhythm and in a prosody sometimes reminiscent of such poems as *Sir Gawain and the Green Knight,* is a relatively late development. There was already vernacular drama in France in the twelfth century, but the earliest extant English plays date from the fourteenth century, and the texts we possess usually belong to the fifteenth or sixteenth. During the lifetime of the biblical drama cycles in England, between the fourteenth and the seventeenth centuries, more than a hundred towns performed single plays or consecutive cycles of from five to forty-eight separate plays. While these towns were chiefly in the North of England—York and Wakefield are the most famous—or the Midlands (Coventry, in Warwickshire), plays were performed in London, and there is a surviving late cycle in Cornish, a Celtic language spoken in the extreme South-West. The demise of the form was hastened by a policy of systematic suppression during the sixteenth century, especially during the reign of Elizabeth I.

Generally speaking, the actual performance of the plays was in the hands of the trade guilds, which came into prominence during the fourteenth century. These were associations of laymen who followed the same craft, often with a priest or priests attached to them as chaplains. They regulated trade and also performed the functions of religious confraternities—that is, brotherhoods associated with a particular church and under the patronage of a particular saint, meeting on religious festivals for liturgical celebration and social functions, and dispensing charity. Their members were often substantial citizens, the leaders of the new mercantile classes; and from their ranks civic officials were chosen. These guilds were responsible for the entire business of staging the plays, each guild choosing a play whose subject matter fitted with the craft it represented. Thus at Chester the Water-Drawers of the river Dee took the play of Noah. Parts were regularly taken in successive years by the same actors, sometimes especially imported from other towns.

The cycles were played from dawn to dusk, in the open, at set points in the city, on "pageants" (*paginae*), wagons that consisted of roofed platforms on wheels and were moved from point to point, so that the audience could see the successive stages of the cycle while remaining in one place—or on fixed stages. At York forty-eight pageants were presented at twelve points in the city. These "pageants" and stages must have been of fair size. Two levels were sometimes created by the use of a balcony or of the ground in front of the stage. Scenery was scanty and not very realistic, though the late property lists surviving are often quite long, and include such items as "Hell-Mouth." Some ingenuity was employed in staging—such as the special waist-high wall round "Paradise," to allow Adam and Eve to be seen and heard without showing their nakedness; yet much in the way of stage setting must have been supplied by the players' words themselves—as in *The Second Shepherds' Play*, where one of the shepherds remarks that he will "abide on a balk, or sit on a stone." Costumes, in the style of the time, were often elaborate, and stage wardrobes were maintained: wigs, robes, a close-fitting skin for the Serpent in Eden, and skin-tight white leather suits for the naked Adam and Eve were a few of the items.

The staging of these plays at the feast of Whitsun (Pentecost) was natural. Corpus Christi, a few days after Whitsun, was an even more favored day. It was the commemoration of the institution of the Eucharist at the Last Supper, and its observance as a high festival had recently been commanded by papal decree: from the early fourteenth century onward it was kept throughout England. Since it fell in early June, one could hope for good weather for the outdoor performances, for a sunny holy-day to watch the tidings of joy that the plays conveyed: the redemption of mankind from death and damnation, from the consequence of Adam's sin in Paradise (Fig. 57). The cycles of plays end triumphantly, showing the history of mankind as a progress toward salvation.

This is what even the short cycles present: the fulfillment of the Old Testament, its culmination in the New. They emphasize the typological dimension, in which Old Testament events are seen as fulfilled in those of the New. The sacrifice of Abraham, for example, is a prefiguration of the Crucifixion; while the brazen serpent set up by Moses to expel serpents, prefigures Christ hung on a cross to expel the serpents of sin.

The inclusiveness of the biblical drama of salvation allowed plenty of scope for its presentation. Incidents from outside the canonical books of the Bible, and from independent invention, were added to the plays. (The sheep-stealing scenes of *The Second Shepherds' Play* are an example of comic elaboration from outside the source texts.) The most important sources for these incidents were the apocryphal Gospels, written in perhaps the second or third century and for the Middle Ages having an authority as great as that of the genuine New Testament books. These were full of homely and miraculous detail about the lives of the Virgin and of Christ—the legend told in "The Cherry-tree Carol," for example, or the story of how Christ broke down the gates of Hell, in the Harrowing of Hell (Figs. 53 and 7).

Within such a large repertoire of play and incident, there was much room for improvisation. Conventions of acting and presentation grew up: a loud, high voice for Pontius Pilate; the portrayal of Herod as a cruel, ranting tyrant; the brutality of Christ's torturers and their carrying off by devils. The domestic difficulties of Noah and the drinking scene between his wife and her cronies in the Chester play are also variations on a well-used theme. All these examples of comic elaboration, often seemingly introduced for their own sake, and certainly serving as comic relief—contribute to the larger design of the plays and their dramatic culmination in the Redemption.

The author of *The Second Shepherds' Play* is anonymous. Usually referred to as the Wakefield Master, after the prosperous market town in Yorkshire where his plays were performed, and almost certainly a cleric, he seems to have written between 1400 and 1450. His pageants form a group in the Towneley manuscript, probably a "register" of the Wakefield plays, and so called after the family that formerly owned it.

The main comic incident by which the Angel's Annunciation to the Shepherds (Fig. 49) is fleshed out into the full-length Wakefield *Second Shepherds' Play* comes from an old folk-tale. Its skillful handling, by which the swaddled sheep is made the figure of the Christ Child in the manger, is the responsibility of the Wakefield Master. The rustic comedy, complete with the complaints of laboring men against the landlords and employers, wretched food and clothing, and troublesome wife and family, moves gently into the promise of spiritual plenty. In the same way, the swaddled sheep in the cradle, horned like the Devil, is balanced by the Christ Child of the touching and tender finale. Mak the sheep-stealer's deceitful wife Gill, grumbling at her lot and groaning in pretended post-natal anguish, is set against the apotheosis of motherhood, the Virgin Mary. The shepherds' song and the "song" of Gill, Mak, and the sheep are ironically described in the same technical terms as the Angel's glorious hymn. The shepherds' mercy to Mak finds its counterpart in the promised mercy of the Child to the Shepherds.

Mak is a comic character in his own right, the trickster of earlier folk-tradition, but also something more: a more rounded comic character than anything previously found in an English play. Not even his antics, all the same, can bring us—nor were they intended to bring the audience—to prefer them to the tenderness and sweetness of the journey to Bethlehem and the scene of adoration there.

MORALITY PLAYS

In the mystery plays, the divine and the human speak to each other quite naturally across a small stage, making clear the relevance of natural and supernatural, actual and historical, events to each other. The other medieval dramatic mode of bringing this lesson home to men was the morality play, which began to develop at about the same time and was sometimes also played under the auspices of the guilds. The morality, however, was a single play, not a cycle. It too, appears to begin in northern English cities. But where the mystery play dramatized biblical events in order to show their relevance to everyday life, the morality, in a more directly didactic way, dramatized the conflict between good and evil, the struggle between opposing qualities, between virtue and vice, which Christianity teaches is always in progress within the soul of the individual Christian. In the morality play this contest was presented through personification allegory, the virtues and vices contending for the soul of man. Such battles of personifications of virtues and vices appear for the first time in a Latin poem by Prudentius, about A.D. 400, the *Psychomachia,* where the conflict is shown in the form of a series of armed contests between a given virtue and its opposite vice (Patience vs. Anger, Pride vs. Humility). There the form is narrative, not dramatic.

By the later Middle Ages both personification allegory and the moral theology of vices and virtues had developed to a much more sophisticated state. In particular an elaborate series of subdivisions of virtues and vices had been evolved and carefully connected with the observances and customs of the church, especially with the theory and practice of penance—that is, with the formal recognition and confession of sin by the sinner, to the priest, followed by his absolution, on condition of his performing certain penances or undergoing discipline. One of the shaping themes of *Everyman,* for example, is the necessity of penitence for sin before death and the full participation in the church's observances concerning it.

Like the mystery play, the morality has much in common with didactic literature—the literature of moral instruction such as the sermon, the religious lyric and the book of devotion. The *Ars Moriendi* (Art of Dying Well) is one devotional work which has been shown to have a relation to *Everyman:* it too depicts a man, on the point of death, deserted by all the gifts of Fortune and Nature—wealth, friends, strength, senses—and with no support but his trust in the mercy of God and in the virtues of faith, hope, and charity. It is these which, by God's grace, will save his soul from damnation.

Not all the moralities are as somber and unrelieved as *Everyman,* which is perhaps the most famous of them. The morality *Mankind,* of about 1475, has some lighter elements, including comic characters such as Mischief, Naught, and New Guise; and a late example, John Skelton's *Magnificence,* of about 1515/16, is also satiric and comic as well as moral.

Everyman may be a translation of a Dutch play on the same theme, *Elckerlijk,* but some scholars maintain that the Dutch play is a translation of the English. It is certain that they are closely related. The English play seems to have been written about 1485, by an anonymous author, but was not published until 1528 or 1529. It is not entirely typical of the English morality—as we have seen—in its uniformly dark tone, with little humor and little satire. Nor is it a play about the battle for man's soul between opposites: it works by showing Everyman stripped of the worldly gifts on which he had thought himself able to rely, concentrating on the increasing isolation of a man on the point of death, until he descends alone into the grave, with only Good Deeds to stand between him and Judgment (see Fig. 52).

The central story, of a man forsaken by all his friends but one, who pleads for him before the king, is Eastern in origin and had found its way into Western collections of fables and moral tales by the twelfth century. The turn given it by the author of *Everyman* toward a moral allegory of preparation for death is typical of the later Middle Ages. He uses it for a dramatic exposition which is at the same time a statement of the universal human predicament and an exposition of the doctrine of the church. We do not know the hour when Death will summon us. We cannot deny the summons and must be always prepared, not relying on any worldly gifts, but on our good deeds, being penitent for the evil we have done. It is not that Everyman has been wholly evil: the message is not that the gifts of fortune which he has enjoyed are wrong in themselves, but that excessive attachment to such temporal gifts as wealth and friends is as wrong as excessive trust in gifts of nature such as strength and beauty. None of these will see Everyman through to salvation by themselves—wealth, friends, even family, if they are not recognized as transitory goods, will lead a man to damnation. Knowledge—i.e. self-knowledge through all the five senses, which leads to a clear vision of oneself as sinful and in need of God's mercy, and so to acknowledgment of sin and contrition—will be the first sign that he recognizes the true way to heaven, and Knowledge will ensure that Good Deeds will be able to stand bv him.

The Wakefield Second Shepherds' Play°

(Secunda Pastorum)

FIRST SHEPHERD (COLL)	GILL, *his wife*
SECOND SHEPHERD (GIB)	ANGEL
THIRD SHEPHERD (DAW)	MARY
MAK	CHRIST-CHILD

[*Enter* FIRST SHEPHERD]

FIRST SHEPHERD Lord! What these weathers are cold, and I am ill happed.°
I am near-hand˃ dold,° so long have I napped. *almost*
My legs they fold,˃ my fingers are chapped; *fail*
It is not as I would, for I am all lapped˃ *enfolded*
In sorrow.
In storms and tempest,
Now in the east, now in the west,
Woe is him has never rest
Midday nor morrow!˃ *morning*

But we sely husbands˃ that walk on the moor, *poor husbandmen*
In faith, we are near-hands out of the door;°
No wonder, as it stands, if we be poor,
For the tilth˃ of our lands lies fallow˃ as the floor, *arable / unseeded*
As ye ken.˃ *know*
We are so hammed,
For-taxed and rammed,
We are made hand-tamed
With these gentlery men.°

Thus they reave˃ us our rest. Our Lady them wary!˃ *rob of / curse*
These men that are lord-fast,° they cause the plough tarry.
That men say is for the best we find it contrary.
Thus are husbands oppressed, in point to miscarry,
On live.°
Thus hold they us under;
Thus they bring us in blunder.˃ *misfortune*
It were great wonder
And˃ ever should we thrive. *if*

What . . . happed How cold this weather is and I am poorly clad.
dold dulled; numb in body and brain
we . . . door we are nearly homeless
hammed . . . men crippled, over-taxed, and crushed, we are brought to submission by these gentry; the peasant's lot, as the landlords and the government become more exacting and powerful
lord-fast bound to a lord
in point . . . live in danger of destruction during our lives

This text is based on that of A. W. Pollard, *The Towneley Plays* (1897), but very freely treated. Spelling has been modernized and normalized, except where this would impair rhyme or meter, and modern punctuation has been used. The stage directions in the manuscript have been translated from the original Latin, and those added by the present editor have been placed within brackets.

For may he get a painted° sleeve, or a brooch, now-a-days,
Woe to him that him grieves,˃ or once gainsays; *complains*
Dare no man him repreve, what mastery he mays°
And yet may no man leve˃ one word that he says, *believe*
    No letter.
He can make purveyance,°
With boast and bragance;˃ *bragging*
And all is through maintenance°
    Of men that are greater.

There shall come a swain as proud as a po;°
He must borrow my wain,˃ my plough also. *wagon*
Then I am full fain˃ to grant ere he go. *glad*
Thus live we in pain, anger, and woe
    By night and day.
He must have if he langed,˃ *wished*
If I should forgang it;°
I were better be hanged
    Than once say him nay.

It does me good, as I walk thus by mine own,
Of this world for to talk in manner of moan.
To my sheep will I stalk and hearken anon;
There abide on a balk,° or sit on a stone,
    Full soon.
For I trow,˃ pardee,˃ *think / by God*
True men if they be,
We get more company
    Ere it be noon.

[*Enter* SECOND SHEPHERD]

SECOND SHEPHERD Bensté° and Dominus! What may this bemean?˃ *mean*
Why, fares this world thus? Oft have we not seen.°
Lord, these weathers are spitous,˃ and the winds full keen, *cruel*
And the frosts so hideous, they water mine een:˃ *eyes*
    No lie.
Now in dry, now in wet,
Now in snow, now in sleet,
When my shoon˃ freeze to my feet, *shoes*
    It is not all easy.

painted i.e. embroidered with a badge; like the brooch, a sign on the "maintained" man (l. 35) of the delegated authority of his lord. Mak later pretends to be such a man.
Dare . . . mays no man dare oppose him, such power has he
purveyance the preferential right of purchasing provisions and so forth at a price fixed by the buyer
maintenance keeping of retainers, "maintained" men

po Latin *pavo:* peacock
If . . . it even though I have to go without
balk strip of pasture dividing two ploughed parts of common land, where shepherds grazed sheep; or perhaps simply a ridge
Bensté *Benedicite:* Bless me; *Dominus:* Good Lord
Oft . . . seen We have not often seen the like of this.

But as far as I ken, or yet as I go,
We sely wedmen dree mickle woe;°
We have sorrow then and then;> it falls oft so. *always*
Silly Capell° our hen, both to and fro
She cackles;
But begin she to croak,
To groan or to cluck,
Woe is him our cock,°
For he is in the shackles.

These men that are wed have not all their will.
When they are full hard bestead,> they sigh full still.> *pressed / always*
God wot> they are led full hard and full ill; *knows*
In bower nor in bed they say naught theretill.> *thereto*
This tide> *time*
My part have I fun,> *found*
I know my lesson.
Woe is him that is bun,> *bound*
For he must abide.> *endure*

But now late in our lives—a marvel to me,
That I think my heart rives> such wonders to see, *breaks*
What that destiny drives, it should so be°—
Some men will have two wives, and some men three
In store.
Some are woe that has any;°
But so far can> I, *know*
Woe is him that has many,
For he feels sore.> *pain*

But, young men, of wooing, for God that you bought,> *redeemed*
Be well ware> of wedding, and think in your thought, *very wary*
'Had I wist'> is a thing that serves of naught. *known*
Mickle still> mourning has wedding home brought, *much constant*
And griefs,
With many a sharp shower;°
For thou mayst catch in an hour
That shall sow thee full sour°
As long as thou lives.

For, as ever read I 'pistle,° I have one to> my fere,> *as / mate*
Sharp as a thistle, as rough as a brere,> *briar*

But . . . woe But as far as I know or as far as I can go, we poor married men suffer much woe.
Capell regular name for a hen; capple: bird's crest
Woe . . . cock Bad luck for our rooster: the Shepherd is comparing the husband's lot in marriage to the rooster's bondage to the hen: conventional medieval antifeminism.
What . . . be Whatever Destiny sets in motion must happen.
Some are . . . any For some it is (enough) unhappiness to have one wife.
shower pain or fight
sow . . . sour pain you very sorely
as . . . 'pistle as I hope to go on reading the Epistle; i.e. he seems to imagine himself minor clergy

She is browed like a bristle, with a sour-loten cheer;°
Had she once wet her whistle, she could sing full clear
Her paternoster.
She is great as a whale;
She has a gallon of gall;
By Him that died for us all,
I would I had run to˃ I had lost her! *till*

FIRST SHEPHERD God, look over the raw!° Full deafly ye stand.
SECOND SHEPHERD Yea, the devil in thy maw—so tariand!°
Sawst thou awre˃ of Daw?° *anywhere*
FIRST SHEPHERD Yea, on a lea-land˃ *pasture*
Heard I him blaw.° He comes here at hand,
Not far. Stand still.
SECOND SHEPHERD Why?
FIRST SHEPHERD For he comes, hope˃ I. *expect*
SECOND SHEPHERD He will make˃ us both a lie *tell*
But if˃ we beware. *unless*

[*Enter* THIRD SHEPHERD]

THIRD SHEPHERD Christ's cross me speed,˃ and Saint Nicholas!° *prosper*
Thereof had I need; it is worse than it was.
Whoso could, take heed and let the world pass;
It is ever in dread˃ and brickle˃ as glass, *doubt / brittle*
And slithes.˃ *slips away*
This world fore˃ never so, *fared*
With marvels mo˃ and mo, *more*
Now in weal, now in woe,
And all things writhes.˃ *change*

Was never sin˃ Noah's flood° such floods seen, *since*
Winds and rains so rude,˃ and storms so keen; *rough*
Some stammered, some stood in doubt, as I ween.°
Now God turn all to good! I say as I mean,
For ponder:˃ *consider*
These floods so they drown,
Both in fields and in town,
And bear all down,
And that is a wonder.

She . . . cheer She has bristling brows, with a sour-looking face.
raw i.e. row, possibly meaning hedgerow (sense obscure)
Yea . . . tariand Yes, indeed; may the Devil be in your guts for dawdling so long.
Daw perhaps a diminutive of David; or, more likely, "stupid, foolish rustic"
blaw blow, i.e. sound his horn
Nicholas It is close to the first Christmas. St. Nicholas's feast day was December 6. He was also the patron of children, and is therefore invoked by the youngest shepherd.
Noah's flood A further reminder of Christmas since Noah was the Old Testament "type" of Christ. His deliverance from the flood was likened to our deliverance from sin.
Some . . . ween Some [men at Noah's Flood] staggered and were afraid, I understand.

We that walk in the nights our cattle to keep, *property*
We see sudden sights when other men sleep.
Yet methink my heart lights; I see shrews peep. *rogues looking*
Ye are two ill wights! I will give my sheep
    A turn.°
But full ill have I meant;°
As I walk on this bent *field*
I may lightly repent, *quickly*
    My toes if I spurn. *stub*

[*To the other two*]
Ah, sir, God you save, and master mine!
A drink fain would I have, and somewhat to dine.

FIRST SHEPHERD Christ's curse, my knave, thou art a lither hine!°

SECOND SHEPHERD What! the boy list rave! Abide unto syne° *likes to*
    We have made it.°
Ill thrift on thy pate!
Though the shrew came late,
Yet is he in state *ready*
    To dine—if he had it.

THIRD SHEPHERD Such servants as I, that sweats and swinks, *toil*
Eat our bread full dry, and that me forthinks. *displeases*
We are oft wet and weary when master men winks; *sleep*
Yet come full late both dinners and drinks.
    But nately *thoroughly*
Both our dame and our sire,
When we have run in the mire,
They can nip at our hire, *cut / wages*
    And pay us full lately.

But hear my troth, master, for the fare that ye make,
I shall do thereafter, work as I take
I shall do a little, sir, and among ever lake,°
For yet lay my supper never on my stomach
    In fields.
Whereto should I threap? *haggle*
With my staff can I leap; *escape*
And men say 'Light cheap
    Litherly foryields.'°

FIRST SHEPHERD Thou were an ill lad, to ride on wooing
With a man that had but little of spending.°

Ye are . . . turn You are two worthless creatures! I will go and look at my sheep.
But . . . meant I have done much evil. (These lines do not make easy sense.)
Christ's . . . hine Christ's curse on you, boy, you are a worthless farmhand.
Abide . . . syne wait until later
We . . . it i.e. we've already eaten dinner
But hear . . . lake (ll. 163–65) But listen to my pledge, master. In return for the food you give, I shall do according to that—work as I am paid. I shall work a bit, sir, and enjoy myself between times.
Litherly foryields proverbial: a cheap bargain gives a poor return
Thou . . . spending You would be a bad one to be taken wooing by a man who hadn't much to spend.

SECOND SHEPHERD Peace, boy! I bade; no more jangling,
Or I shall make thee full rad, by the Heaven's King,
With thy gawds.°
Where are our sheep, boy? We scorn.°
THIRD SHEPHERD Sir, this same day at morn
I them left in the corn,
When they rang lauds.°

They have pasture good; they cannot go wrong.
FIRST SHEPHERD That is right. By the rood,> these nights are long! *cross*
Yet I would, ere we yode> one gave us a song. *went*
SECOND SHEPHERD So I thought as I stood, to mirth us among.°
THIRD SHEPHERD I grant.
FIRST SHEPHERD Let me sing the tenory.
SECOND SHEPHERD And I the treble so high.
THIRD SHEPHERD Then the mean falls to me.°
Let see how ye chant.

Enter MAK, *with a cloak over his tunic.*°

MAK Now, Lord, for thy names seven, that made both moon and starns
Well more than I can neven, thy will, Lord, of me tharns.
I am all uneven; that moves oft my harns.°
Now would God I were in heaven, for there weep no barns> *children*
So still.> *continually*
FIRST SHEPHERD Who is that pipes so poor?°
MAK Would God ye wist> how I fore!> *knew / fared*
Lo, a man that walks on the moor,
And has not all his will!

SECOND SHEPHERD Mak, where hast thou gane?> Tell us tiding.> *gone / news*
THIRD SHEPHERD Is he come? Then ilkane> take heed to *everyone*
his thing.> *possessions*
[*Takes the cloak from him.*]
MAK What! Ich° be a yeoman, I tell you, of the king;
The self and the same, sond> from a great lording,> *messenger / lord*
And sich.> *suchlike*
Fie on you! Go thence!
Out of my presence!
I must have reverence.
Why, who be ich?

no . . . gawds perhaps: no more arguing, or I'll make you (stop) very quickly, by God, for all your tricks
We scorn sense obscure; perhaps: we scorn you
rang lauds i.e. rang the bells for the first church office of the day, before dawn
to . . . among to give us pleasure in the meantime
mean . . . me the middle part is mine. In medieval three-part harmony the tenor was the bass part, "holding" the melody.
Enter . . . tunic Mak is elaborately dressed and speaks with a superior, urban, southern English accent. He is playing the role of "maintained man" or yeoman, lording it over the rustics.
Lord . . . harns (ll. 190–93) Lord, for Thy seven names, Thou who madest both moon and stars (and) far more than I can name, Thy will is wanting in regard to me. I am all at sixes and sevens—and it often disturbs my mind. God's seven names are a Hebrew tradition.
pipes so poor i.e. cries so sadly
Ich the Southern form of I

FIRST SHEPHERD Why make ye it so quaint?° Mak, ye do wrang,˃ *wrong*
SECOND SHEPHERD But Mak, list ye saint? I trow for that you lang.°
THIRD SHEPHERD I trow the shrew˃ can paint!˃ The devil *rascal / deceive*
might him hang!
MAK Ich shall make complaint, and make you all to thwang,°
At a word,
And tell even˃ how ye doth.˃ *just / do*
FIRST SHEPHERD But, Mak, is that sooth?
Now take out that southern tooth,°
And set in a turd.°

SECOND SHEPHERD Mak, the devil in your ee!˃ A stroke *eye*
would I lene˃ you. *give*
THIRD SHEPHERD Mak, know ye not me? By God, I could teen˃ you. *hurt*
MAK God look˃ you all three! Methought I had seen you. *save*
Ye are a fair company.
FIRST SHEPHERD Can ye now mean you?°
SECOND SHEPHERD Shrew, peep!°
Thus late as thou goes,
What will men suppose?˃ *suspect*
And thou hast an ill noise˃ *reputation*
Of˃ stealing of sheep. *for*

MAK And I am true as steel, all men wate,˃ *know*
But a sickness I feel that holds me full hote;˃ *feverish*
My belly fares not well, it is out of estate.˃ *condition*
THIRD SHEPHERD Seldom lies the devil dead by the gate.°
MAK Therefore
Full sore am I and ill;
If I stand stone still,
I eat not a needle°
This month and more.

FIRST SHEPHERD How fares thy wife? By my hood, how fares sho?˃ *she*
MAK Lies waltering,˃ by the rood, by the fire, lo! *sprawling*
And a house full of brood.˃ She drinks well, too; *children*
Ill speed other good that she will do!°
But sho
Eats as fast as she can;
And ilk˃ year that comes to man *each*
She brings forth a lakan˃— *baby*
And some years two.

Why . . . quaint Why are you so high and mighty?
Mak . . . lang Mak, do you want to seem a saint? I think you do long for it.
make . . . thwang have you all flogged
take . . . tooth give up that southern accent
set . . . turd stop your mouth with shit; the insult enhances the rustic-urban contrast
Can . . . you Can you remember now?
Shrew, peep "Rogue, looking about!" or "Rogue, look out!"
Seldom . . . gate Seldom does the Devil lie dead by the road ("gate" is a northern form); i.e. the Devil is always prowling about.
If . . . needle May I be turned to stone if I ate the smallest bit.
Ill speed . . . do Bad luck to the other good that she can do; i.e. if that is the only good thing she can do, let her not do anything else like it.

But were I now more gracious> and richer by far, *wealthy*
I were eaten out of house and of harbar.> *home*
Yet is she a foul dowse° if ye come near;
There is none that trows> nor knows a war> *thinks of / worse*
Than ken> I. *know*
Now will ye see what I proffer?
To give all in my coffer
Tomorn at next to offer
Her head-masspenny.°

SECOND SHEPHERD I wot so forwaked° is none in this shire.
I would sleep, if I taked less to my hire.°
THIRD SHEPHERD I am cold and naked, and would have a fire.
FIRST SHEPHERD I am weary, forraked,° and run in the mire.
Wake, thou!
SECOND SHEPHERD Nay, I will lie down by,
For I must sleep, truly.
THIRD SHEPHERD As good a man's son was I
As any of you.

But, Mak, come hither! Between shalt thou lie down.
MAK Then might I let you, bedene, of that ye would rown,°
No dread.
From my top to my toe,
Manus tuas commendo,
Pontio Pilato,
Christ's cross me speed!°

Then he gets up, while the other shepherds are asleep, and says:

Now were time> for a man that lacks what he would *chance*
To stalk privily than> unto a fold, *then*
And neemly> to work than, and be not too bold, *nimbly*
For he might abuy> the bargain, if it were told, *purchase dearly*
At the ending.
Now were time for to reel,> *move quickly*
But he needs good counsel
That fain would fare weel,> *well*
And has but little spending.

But about you a circill> as round as a moon, *magic circle*
To> I have done that I will, till that it be noon, *till*
That ye lie stone still to that I have done,
And I shall say theretill> of good words a fone> *as well / few*
On height

dowse French *douce:* sweetheart
Tomorn . . . masspenny (to be able) to offer, tomorrow morning at the latest, a penny to the priest to sing mass for her departed soul
I . . . forwaked I know that so worn out with being awake
if . . . hire even if I were to get less wages
forraked worn out with walking
might . . . rown I might hinder you, certainly, from whispering together what you want.
Manus . . . speed Thy hands I commend to Pontius Pilate, Christ's cross prosper me: a blasphemous parody of Luke 23:46

Over your heads my hand I lift:
'Out go your eyen, fordo your sight!'°
But yet I must make better shift
    And it be right.°

Lord, what> they sleep hard! That may ye all hear. *how*
Was I never a shephard, but now will I lere> *learn*
If the flock be scared, yet shall I nip nere.°
How! Draw hitherward! Now mends our cheer
    From sorrow.
A fat sheep, I dare say;
A good fleece, dare I lay!> *bet*
Eft-whit> when I may, *pay back*
    But this will I borrow.

[MAK *carries the sheep to his house*]

How, Gill, art thou in? Get us some light.
WIFE Who makes such din this time of the night?
I am set> for to spin; I hope not I might *sitting*
Rise a penny to win.° I shrew> them on height! *curse*
    So fares
A housewife that has been
To be raised thus between;
Here may no note be seen,
    For such small chares.°
MAK Good wife, open the hek!> Seest thou not what I bring? *inner door*
WIFE I may thole> thee draw the snek.> Ah, come in, my sweeting! *let / latch*
MAK Yea, thou thar> not reck> of my long standing. *need / mind*
WIFE By thy naked neck art thou like for to hing.> *hang*
MAK Do way:> *get away*
I am worthy my meat,> *worth my keep*
For in a strait> can I get *tight spot*
More than they that swink> and sweat *toil*
    All the long day.

Thus it fell to my lot, Gill, I had such grace.
WIFE It were a foul blot to be hanged for the case.
MAK I have scaped,> Gillot, often as hard a glase.> *escaped / blow*
WIFE But so long goes the pot to the water, men say,
    At last
Comes it home broken.°

Out . . . sight Your power of sight is lost. Mak is the wicked black magician, a clear villain. He has just previously recited the "white" night spell (cf. Chaucer, the Miller's Tale, l. 379) to keep them all from harm.
But yet . . . right But still I must do better before it will come right.
nip nere probably: grab a sheep more closely, tightly
I hope . . . win I don't think I could get up, even to gain a penny.
So fares . . . chares (ll. 300–304) So does it fare with anyone who has been a housewife, to be got up thus all the time. There is no work to show here, because of such little chores.
But . . . broken Proverbial.

MAK Well know I the token,> *portent*
But let it never be spoken;
But come and help fast.

I would he were flain;> I lis> well eat. *skinned / want*
This twelvemonth was I not so fain of one sheep's meat.
WIFE Come they ere he be slain, and hear the sheep bleat—
MAK Then might I be ta'en! That were a cold sweat!
Go spar> *fasten*
The gate-door.> *outer door*
WIFE Yes, Mak,
For and> they come at thy back— *if*
MAK Then might I buy, for all the pack,
The devil of the war.°

WIFE A good bourd> have I spied, since thou can> none. *trick / know*
Here shall we him hide to that they be gone
In my cradle. Abide, let me alone,
And I shall lie beside in childbed, and groan.
MAK Thou red:> *get ready*
And I shall say thou was light> *delivered*
Of a knave> child this night. *boy*
WIFE Now well is day bright,
That ever I was bred.°

This is a good guise> and a fair cast;> *way / idea*
Yet a woman's advise helps at the last!
I wot> never who spies.> Again go thou fast. *know / is looking*
MAK But> I come ere they rise, else blows a cold blast! *unless*
I will go sleep.

[MAK *returns to the shepherds*]

Yet sleeps all this meney> *company*
And I shall go stalk privily,
As it never had been I
That carried their sheep.

FIRST SHEPHERD *Resurrex a mortruus!*° Have hold my hand.
Judas carnas dominus!° I may not well stand;
My foot sleeps, by Jesus; and I walter fastand.> *sprawl fasting*
I thought that we laid us full near England.
SECOND SHEPHERD Ah, yea.
Lord, what> I have slept weel.> *how / well*
As fresh as an eel,

Then might . . . war Perhaps: Then might I have, from the whole pack of them, the devil of the worse of it—i.e. the devil of a bad time.
Now . . . bred Now happy be the day that I was born.
Resurrex . . . mortruus The bad Latin: "I have risen from the dead"—i.e. I've been dead asleep—is also a blasphemous reference to Christ's resurrection.
Judas . . . dominus worse Latin, presumably meaning "Judas incarnate Lord"

As light I me feel
As leaf on a tree.

THIRD SHEPHERD Bensté° be herein! So my body quakes,
My heart is out of skin, whatso› it makes.› *whatever / causes*
Who makes all this din? So my brows blakes.°
To the door will I win. Hark, fellows,› wakes! *comrades*
We were four:
See ye awre of Mak now?°
FIRST SHEPHERD We were up ere thou.
SECOND SHEPHERD Man, I give God a vow,
Yet yede he nawre.°

THIRD SHEPHERD Methought he was lapped› in a wolf's skin. *wrapped*
FIRST SHEPHERD So are many happed now, namely, within.°
THIRD SHEPHERD When we had long napped, methought with a gin› *snare*
A fat sheep he trapped; but he made no din.
SECOND SHEPHERD Be still!
Thy dream makes thee wood.› *mad*
It is but phantom, by the rood.
FIRST SHEPHERD Now God turn all to good,
If it be his will!

SECOND SHEPHERD Rise, Mak! For shame! Thou liest right lang.
MAK Now Christ's holy name be us amang!
What is this? For Saint Jame, I may not well gang!› *walk*
I trow I be the same. Ah! my neck has lain wrang› *crooked*
Enough. [*They help* MAK *up*]
Mickle› thank! Since yester-even, *much*
Now, by Saint Stephen,
I was flayed with a sweven:
My heart out of slough.°

I thought Gill began to croak and travail› full sad,› *labor / hard*
Well night at the first cock, of a young lad
For to mend› our flock. Then be I never glad; *increase*
I have tow on my rock° more than ever I had.
Ah, my head!
A house full of young tharms!› *bellies*
The devil knock out their harns!› *brains*
Woe is him has many barns!› *children*
And thereto little bread!

I must go home, by your leave, to Gill, as I thought.› *intended*
I pray you look› my sleeve that I steal nought; *examine*

Bensté See l. 54n.
brows blakes brows darken; i.e. sight is dim, he is struggling to consciousness
See . . . now Can you see Mak anywhere now?
Yet . . . nawre He's gone nowhere yet.
So are many . . . within Many are wrapped so now, especially within; cf. Matthew 7:15: "inwardly they are ravening wolves."
flayed . . . slough Literally, I was skinned by a dream (so that) my heart was outside my skin; i.e. I was so terrified that my heart seemed exposed.
tow on my rock flax on my distaff; i.e. trouble enough already

I am loath you to grieve or from you take aught.

THIRD SHEPHERD Go forth; ill might thou chieve!> Now would I we sought,° — *prosper*

This morn,
That we had all our store.

FIRST SHEPHERD But I will go before;
Let us meet.

SECOND SHEPHERD Whore?> — *where*

THIRD SHEPHERD At the crooked thorn.

[MAK'*s house*]

MAK Undo this door! Who is here? How long shall I stand?

WIFE Who makes such a bere?> Now walk in the wenyand!° — *din*

MAK Ah, Gill, what cheer? It is I, Mak, your husband.

WIFE Then may we see here the devil in a band,°
Sir Guile!
Lo, he comes with a lote> — *noise*
As he were holden in> the throat. — *held by*
I may not sit at my note> — *work*
A hand-long> while. — *short*

MAK Will ye hear what fare> she makes to get her a glose?> — *fuss / excuse*
And does naught but lakes,> and claws her toes? — *play*

WIFE Why, who wanders? Who wakes? Who comes? Who goes?
Who brews? Who bakes? What makes me thus hose?> — *hoarse*
And than,
It is ruth> to behold, — *a pity*
Now in hot, now in cold,
Full woeful is the household
That wants> a woman. — *lacks*

But what end has thou made with the herds,> Mak? — *shepherds*

MAK The last word that they said, when I turned my back,
They would look that they had their sheep, all the pack.
I hope> they will not be well paid> when they their sheep lack, — *expect / pleased*
Pardie!> — *by God*
But how-so> the game goes, — *however*
To me they will suppose,> — *suspect*
And make a foul noise,
And cry out upon me.

But thou must do as thou hight.> — *promised*

WIFE I accord me theretill;°
I shall swaddle him right in my cradle.
If it were a greater sleight, yet could I help till.°
I will lie down straight.> Come, hap> me. — *at once / cover*

Now . . . sought now I want us to search
Now . . . wenyand May you go in the waning moon—a time of ill omen.
devil in a band the devil in a noose, bound
I . . . theretill I agree to that
If . . . till Even if the trick were more difficult, I could still help with it.

MAK I will.
WIFE Behind!
Come Coll and his marrow> *mate*
They will nip us full narrow.
MAK But I may cry 'Out, harrow!'> *help*
The sheep if they find.

WIFE Hearken ay when they call; they will come anon.
Come and make ready all, and sing by thine own;
Sing lullay° thou shall, for I must groan,
And cry out by the wall on Mary and John,°
For sore.> *pain*
Sing lullay on fast
When thou hears at the last;
And but> I play a false cast,> *unless / trick*
Trust me no more.

[*At the crooked hawthorn*]

THIRD SHEPHERD Ah, Coll, good morn! Why sleepst thou not?
FIRST SHEPHERD Alas, that ever was I born! We have a foul blot.
A fat wether> have we lorn.> *ram / lost*
THIRD SHEPHERD Marry, God's forbot!> *God forbid*
SECOND SHEPHERD Who should do us that scorn?> That were a foul spot.> *injury* *insult*
FIRST SHEPHERD Some shrew.
I have sought with my dogs
All Horbury shrogs,°
And of fifteen hogs
Found I but one ewe.°

THIRD SHEPHERD Now trow> me if ye will; by Saint Thomas of Kent,° *believe*
Either Mak or Gill was at that assent.> *conspiracy*
FIRST SHEPHERD Peace, man, be still!> I saw when he went. *silent*
Thou slanders him ill. Thou ought to repent,
Good speed.> *instantly*
SECOND SHEPHERD Now as ever might I thee,> *thrive*
If I should even here dee,> *die*
I would say it were he
That did that same deed.

THIRD SHEPHERD Go we thither, I rede,> and run on our feet. *advise*
I shall never eat bread the sooth to I weet.> *until I know*
FIRST SHEPHERD No drink in my head, with him till I meet.

lullay perhaps, lullaby, a foreshadowing of the Nativity
Mary and John the Virgin and St. John, Christ's beloved disciple—powerful helpers of man
Horbury shrogs Horbury thickets. Horbury is a town near Wakefield, where this play was performed.
of fifteen . . . ewe with fifteen young sheep I found only the ewe; i.e. the ram was gone
Saint . . . Kent St. Thomas (Becket) of Canterbury

SECOND SHEPHERD I will rest in no stead> till that I him greet, *place*
My brother!
One I will hight:°
Till I see him in sight
Shall I never sleep one night
There> I do another. *where*

[MAK'S *house.* GILL *groans and* MAK *sings a lullaby*]

THIRD SHEPHERD Will ye hear how they hack?° Our sire list> *wants to*
croon.
FIRST SHEPHERD Heard I never none crack> so clear out of tune! *sing*
Call on him.
SECOND SHEPHERD Mak! Undo your door soon.> *at once*
MAK Who is it that spake, as> it were noon, *as if*
On loft?> *aloud*
Who is that, I say?
THIRD SHEPHERD Good fellows, were it day°—
MAK As far as ye may,
Good,> speak soft *good men*

Over a sick woman's head, that is at malease;
I had liefer be dead ere she had any disease.°
WIFE Go to another stead! I may not well wheeze.> *breathe*
Each foot that ye tread goes thorough my nese,> *nose*
So high!> *loudly*
FIRST SHEPHERD Tell us, Mak, if ye may,
How fare ye, I say?
MAK But are ye in this town today?°
Now how fare ye?

Ye have run in the mire, and are wet yet.
I shall make you a fire, if ye will sit.
A nurse would I hire. Think ye on that.°
Well quit is my hire—my dream, this is it—
A season.°
I have barns,> if ye knew, *children*
Well mo> than enew.> *more / enough*
But we must drink as we brew,
And that is but reason.> *right*

I would ye dined ere ye yode.> Methinks that ye sweat. *went*
SECOND SHEPHERD Nay, neither mends our mood, drink nor meat.

One . . . hight One thing I'll promise.
hack sing contrapuntally
were it day if only it were day
Over . . . disease Standing over a sick woman who is not well; I had rather be dead than that she should suffer distress.
But . . . today i.e. fancy seeing you here. Townsman Mak is again in opposition to the rustics.
Think . . . that The reading is difficult and "that" is an emendation; perhaps: Think about it; or, reading "yet": Do you still remember (my dream)?
Well . . . season My wages are fully paid for the time being: this is my dream (of Gill having another child, ll. 348 ff.).

MAK Why, sir, ails you aught but good?
THIRD SHEPHERD Yea, our sheep that we get> *tend*
Are stolen as they yode. Our loss is great.
MAK Sirs, drink!
Had I been thore,> *there*
Some should have bought it> full sore. *paid for*
FIRST SHEPHERD Marry, some men trow> that ye wore;> *believe / were*
And that us forthinks.> *troubles*

SECOND SHEPHERD Mak, some men trows that it should be ye.
THIRD SHEPHERD Either ye or your spouse. So say we.
MAK Now, if ye have suspouse> to Gill or to me, *suspicion*
Come and rip> our house, and then ye may see *ransack*
Who had her;
If I any sheep fot,> *fetched*
Any cow or stott.> *heifer*
And Gill, my wife, rose not
Here since she laid her.

As I am true and leal,> to God here I pray *honest*
That this be the first meal that I shall eat this day.
FIRST SHEPHERD Mak, as have I sele, advise thee, I say:
He learned timely to steal that could not say nay.°
WIFE I swelt!> *am dying*
Out, thieves, from my wones!> *house*
Ye come to rob us, for the nones.°
MAK Hear ye not how she groans?
Your hearts should melt.

WIFE Out, thieves, from my barn!° Nigh> him not thore!> *come near / there*
MAK Wist ye how she had farn,> your hearts would be sore. *fared*
Ye do wrong, I you warn, that thus come before
To a woman that has farne.° But I say no more.
WIFE Ah, my middle!
I pray to God so mild,
If ever I you beguiled,
That I eat> this child *may eat*
That lies in this cradle.

MAK Peace, woman, for God's pain, and cry not so!
Thou spills> thy brain, and makes me full woe. *spoil, injure*
SECOND SHEPHERD I trow our sheep be slain. What find ye two?
THIRD SHEPHERD All work we in vain; as well may we go.
But, hatters,°
I can find no flesh,
Hard nor nesh,> *soft*

Mak . . . nay Now Mak, as I hope to be blessed, think it over, I say: he learned to steal young who could not say no.
Ye come . . . nones You come on purpose to rob us.
barn bairn, child
farne farrowed, pigged
hatters Obscure; perhaps "Damn it!"

Salt nor fresh,
But> two tome> platters. *only / empty*

Quick cattle but this, tame nor wild,
None, as have I bliss, as loud as he smiled.°
WIFE No, so God me bliss,> and give me joy of my child! *bless*
FIRST SHEPHERD We have marked> amiss; I hold us beguiled. *aimed*
SECOND SHEPHERD Sir, done.> *completely*
Sir, Our Lady him save!
Is your child a knave?> *boy*
MAK Any lord might him have,
This child to his son.

When he wakens he kips,° that joy is to see.
THIRD SHEPHERD In good time to his hips, and in sely.°
Who were his gossips,> so soon ready?° *godparents*
MAK So fair fall their lips!
FIRST SHEPHERD Hark now, a le!> *lie*
MAK So God them thank,
Parkin and Gibbon Waller, I say,
And gentle John Horn,° in good fay,> *faith*
He made all the garray> *commotion*
With his great shank.> *long legs*

SECOND SHEPHERD Mak, friends will we be, for we are all one.> *agreed*
MAK We! Now I hold for me,° for amends get I none.
Farewell, all three! All glad were ye gone!°
THIRD SHEPHERD Fair words may there be, but love there is none
This year.
[*Shepherds go out*]
FIRST SHEPHERD Gave ye the child anything?
SECOND SHEPHERD I trow, not one farthing!
THIRD SHEPHERD Fast again> will I fling; *back*
Abide ye me there.

[*Shepherds re-enter*]

Mak, take it to no grief,> if I come to thy barn. *amiss*
MAK Nay, thou does me great repreef;> and foul has thou farn.> *shame / done*
THIRD SHEPHERD The child will it not grief, that little day-starn.°
Mak, with your leef,> let me give your barn *leave*
But sixpence.
MAK Nay, do way! He sleeps.
THIRD SHEPHERD Methinks he peeps.

Quick . . . smiled No livestock, tame or wild, as I hope to be saved, smelled as high as this baby.
kips Obscure; perhaps kicks, or keeps, i.e. behaves
In good . . . sely May he have a good and happy future.
Who . . . ready A child was often baptized on the day it was born.
Parkin . . . Horn other shepherds
I . . . me I must look after myself.
All glad . . . gone Good luck to you as you go.
day-starn day-star, morning star, a preparation for Christ, the true day-star

MAK When he wakens he weeps;
I pray you go hence.

THIRD SHEPHERD Give me leave him to kiss, and lift up the clout.> *cloth*
What the devil is this? He has a long snout!
FIRST SHEPHERD He is marked amiss. We wate ill about.
SECOND SHEPHERD Ill-spun weft, ywis,> ay> comes foul out.° *indeed / always*
Aye, so!°
He is like to our sheep!
THIRD SHEPHERD How, Gib! May I peep?
FIRST SHEPHERD I trow, kind will creep
Where it may not go!°

SECOND SHEPHERD This was a quaint gawd and a fair cast!°
It was a high fraud!
THIRD SHEPHERD Yea, sirs, was't.
Let burn this bawd, and bind her fast.
Ah, false scaud,> hang at the last, *scold*
So shall thou.
Will ye see how they swaddle
His four feet in the middle?°
Saw I never in a cradle
A horned lad° ere now.

MAK Peace, bid I! What! Let be your fare!> *carrying-on*
I am he that him gat,> and yond woman him bare. *begot*
FIRST SHEPHERD What devil shall he hatt?> Mak? *be called*
Lo, God, Mak's heir!
SECOND SHEPHERD Let be all that. Now God give him care,
I say.
WIFE A pretty child is he
As sits on a woman's knee;
A dilly-downe,> pardie, *darling*
To gar> a man laugh. *make*

THIRD SHEPHERD I know him by the ear-mark; that is a good token.
MAK. I tell you, sirs, hark! His nose was broken;
Sithen> told me a clerk that he was forspoken.> *later / bewitched*
FIRST SHEPHERD This is a false wark; I would fain be wroken.> *revenged*
Get weapon!
WIFE He was taken with> an elf, *by*
I saw it myself;

He is . . . out He is misshapen. It is wrong of us to go on looking about. We are wasting our time. A badly spun thread makes a bad piece of cloth.
Aye, so! a double-take
kind . . . go Nature will creep in where it cannot walk: i.e. it will show itself in one way or another. Cf. *Everyman,* l. 316.
quaint . . . cast a clever dodge and a good trick
His . . . middle The sheep has been thoroughly swaddled.
horned lad i.e. this is no baby, it's a monster, the Devil

When the clock struck twelve
Was he forshapen.> *transformed*

SECOND SHEPHERD Ye two are well feft, same in a stead.°
THIRD SHEPHERD Sin they maintain their theft, let do them to dead!°
MAK If I trespass eft,> gird> off my head! *sin again / strike*
With you will I be left.°
FIRST SHEPHERD Sirs, do my rede:> *advice*
For this trespass
We will neither ban> nor flyte> *curse / scold*
Fight nor chide,
But have done as tite> *as soon as we can*
And cast> him in canvas. *toss*

[*They toss* MAK *in a blanket and go*]

FIRST SHEPHERD Lord, what> I am sore; in point for to brist> *how / burst*
In faith, I may no more; therefore will I rist.> *rest*
SECOND SHEPHERD As a sheep of seven score° he weighed in my fist.
For to sleep aywhore> methinks that I list.> *anywhere / please*
THIRD SHEPHERD Now I pray you,
Lie down on this green.
FIRST SHEPHERD On these thieves yet I mene.> *think*
THIRD SHEPHERD Whereto should ye teen> *be troubled*
So, as I say you? [*They sleep*]

An ANGEL *sings 'Gloria in excelsis'; then let him say:*°

ANGEL Rise, herd-men hend!> For now is he born *gentle*
That shall take from the fiend that Adam had lorn:°
That warlock° to shend> this night is he born; *destroy*
God is made your friend now at this morn,
He behests.> *promises*
At Bedlem> go see, *Bethlehem*
There> lies that free> *where / noble one*
In a crib full poorly
Between two beasts.

FIRST SHEPHERD This was a quaint steven° that ever yet I heard.
It is a marvel to neven,> thus to be scared. *tell*
SECOND SHEPHERD Of God's son of heaven he spake upward.> *on high*
All the wood in a levin> methought that he gard *lightning*
Appear.°

Ye two . . . stead You two are well provided, the two of you in one place; i.e. you're as fine a couple of rogues as ever shared a roof.
Sin . . . to dead Since they will not acknowledge their theft, let them be put to death.
With . . . left I will stand by your judgment.
seven score 140 pounds
An Angel . . . say an original stage direction for the Annunciation to the Shepherds, including the Angelic Hymn "Glory be to God on high"
that . . . lorn what Adam lost for us; i.e. he will repair our fallen nature and take us from the hands of the Devil
warlock a practitioner of black magic; here the Devil himself
quaint steven beautiful voice
All . . . Appear He seemed to me to make the whole wood as bright as day; literally: as if in a lightning flash.

THIRD SHEPHERD He spake of a barn> *child*
In Bedlem, I you warn.> *tell*
FIRST SHEPHERD That betokens yond starn.> *yonder star*
Let us seek him there.

SECOND SHEPHERD Say, what was his song? Heard ye not how he cracked it,
Three breves to a long?°
THIRD SHEPHERD Yea, marry, he hacked it;°
Was no crotchet wrong, nor nothing that lacked it.
FIRST SHEPHERD For to sing us among, right as he knacked° it,
I can.> *know how*
SECOND SHEPHERD Let see how ye croon.
Can ye bark at the moon?°
THIRD SHEPHERD Hold your tongues, have done!
FIRST SHEPHERD Hark after, than!

SECOND SHEPHERD To Bedlem he bade that we should gang;> *go*
I am ful rad> that we tarry too lang. *afraid*
THIRD SHEPHERD Be merry and not sad; of mirth is our sang;> *song*
Everlasting glad> to meed> may we fang> *joy / reward / get*
Without noise.
FIRST SHEPHERD Hie we thither forthy> *therefore*
If> we be wet and weary, *though*
To that child and that lady.
We have it not to lose.°

SECOND SHEPHERD We find by the prophecy—let be your din—
Of David and Isay—and mo then I min°—
They prophesied by clergy> that in a virgin *learning*
Should He light> and lie, to sloken> our sin *alight / slacken*
And slake> it, *relieve*
Our kind> from woe. *race*
For Isay° said so:
'Ecce virgo
Concipiet' a child that is naked.

THIRD SHEPHERD Full glad may we be, and> we abide that day *if*
That lovely to see, that all mights may.°
Lord, well were me, for once and for ay,
Might I kneel on my knee some word for to say
To that Child.
But the angel said,
In a crib was He laid;
He was poorly arrayed,
Both mean> and mild. *lowly*

cracked . . . long sang it loudly, three short notes to a long, in perfect rhythm
hacked it improvised a contrapuntal part
knacked sang skilfully
Can . . . moon In trying to imitate the Angel, you are like a dog barking at the moon.
We . . . lose We must not omit to do it.
Of David . . . min David and Isaiah and more than I remember; two of the prophets of Christ, a procession of whom comprises the cast in an early form of drama, the *Ordo prophetarum*
Isay Isaiah 7:14: "Behold a Virgin shall conceive and bear a child." This was regularly included in the Christmas tropes.
That . . . may to see that beautiful one who is almighty

FIRST SHEPHERD Patriarchs that has been, and prophets beforn,
They desired to have seen this Child that is born.
They are gone full clean;> that have they lorn.> *utterly / missed*
We shall see Him, I ween,> ere it be morn, *think*
To> token. *as*
When I see Him and feel,
Then wot> I full weel *know*
It is true as steel
That prophets have spoken:

To so poor as we are that He would appear,
First find, and declare by His messenger.°
SECOND SHEPHERD Go we now, let us fare; the place is us near.
THIRD SHEPHERD I am ready and yare;> go we in fere> *prepared / together*
To that bright.> *lovely one*
Lord, if thy will be—
We are lewd> all three— *simple*
Grant us some kind of glee> *happiness*
To comfort Thy wight.> *creatures*

[*They enter the stable*]

FIRST SHEPHERD Hail, comely and clean!> Hail, young Child! *pure*
Hail, Maker, as I mean, of> a maiden so mild! *come from*
Thou has waried, I ween, the warlock so wild;°
The false guiler of teen,° now goes he beguiled.
Lo, he merry is!
Lo, he laughs, my sweeting!
A well fair meeting!
I have holden> my heting.> *kept / promise*
Have a bob> of cherries!° *bunch*

SECOND SHEPHERD Hail, sovereign Saviour, for Thou has us sought!
Hail, freely food> and flower, that all things has wrought! *noble child*
Hail, full of favour, that made all of naught!
Hail! I kneel and I cower.> A bird have I brought *crouch*
To my barn.> *baby*
Hail, little tiny mop!> *doll*
Of our creed> Thou art crop.> *faith / head*
I would drink of Thy cop,°
Little day-starn.

THIRD SHEPHERD Hail, darling dear, full of Godhead!
I pray Thee be near when that I have need.
Hail! Sweet is Thy cheer!> My heart would bleed *face*
To see Thee sit here in so poor weed,> *clothes*
With no pennies.

First . . . messenger first to find us and then to make it known through this messenger
Thou . . . wild I believe that thou hast cursed the Devil so fierce.
false . . . teen the false, tormenting deceiver
cherries fruit not in season, to suggest the miracle of Christ's birth
cop cup; a rustic prophecy of the Eucharist

Hail! Put forth Thy dall!> *fist*
I bring Thee but a ball:
Have and play Thee withal,
    And go to the tennis.°

MARY The Father of Heaven, God omnipotent,
That set> all in seven> his Son has He sent. *created / seven days*
My name couthe He neven and light ere He went.
I conceived Him full even, through might, as He meant;°
    And now is He born.
He> keep you from woe! *may he*
I shall pray Him so.
Tell it forth as ye go,
    And min on> this morn. *remember*

FIRST SHEPHERD Farewell, Lady, so fair to behold,
With Thy child on Thy knee!
SECOND SHEPHERD But he lies full cold.
Lord, well is me. Now we go, thou behold.
THIRD SHEPHERD Forsooth, already it seems to be told
    Full oft.
FIRST SHEPHERD What grace we have fun!> *received*
SECOND SHEPHERD Come forth; now are we won!> *redeemed*
THIRD SHEPHERD To sing are we bun.> *bound*
    Let take on loft!°

c. 1400–1450

Everyman°

MESSENGER
GOD
DEATH
EVERYMAN
FELLOWSHIP
KINDRED
COUSIN
GOODS
GOOD DEEDS
KNOWLEDGE
CONFESSION
BEAUTY
STRENGTH
DISCRETION
FIVE WITS
ANGEL
DOCTOR

Here beginneth a treatise how the High Father of Heaven sendeth Death to summon every creature to come and give account of their lives in this world, and is in manner of a moral play.

tennis Royal tennis was already a popular game at the end of the 14th century.
My name . . . meant (ll. 739–40) My name did He name and He alighted in me before He went. I conceived Him through God's might, just as His purpose was.
Let . . . loft Let us strike up.

This text is based on the first printed version by John Skot, of about 1528–29, as edited by W. W. Greg (Louvain, 1904). There is no manuscript. The text has been very freely treated, spelling has been modernized, except where this would interfere with rhyme or meter, and modern punctuation has been used. Some stage directions have been added and are set off in brackets.

MESSENGER I pray you all give your audience,˃ *hearing*
And hear this matter with reverence,
By figure° a moral play:
The *Summoning of Everyman* called it is,
That of our lives and ending shows
How transitory we be all day.˃ *every day*
This matter is wondrous precious,
But the intent of it is more gracious,°
And sweet to bear away.
The story saith: Man, in the beginning,
Look well, and take good heed to the ending,°
Be you never so gay!
Ye think sin in the beginning full sweet,
Which in the end causeth the soul to weep,
When the body lieth in clay.
Here shall you see how Fellowship and Jollity,
Both Strength, Pleasure, and Beauty,°
Will fade from thee as flower in May.
For ye shall hear how our Heaven-King
Calleth Everyman to a general reckoning.
Give audience, and hear what he doth say. [*Exit*]

GOD° *speaketh:*

GOD I perceive, here in my majesty,
How that all creatures be to me unkind,°
Living without dread in worldly prosperity.
Of ghostly˃ sight the people be so blind,° *spiritual*
Drowned in sin, they know me not for their God;
In worldly riches is all their mind,˃ *intention*
They fear not of my righteousness the sharp rod;
My law° that I showed, when I for them died
They forget clean, and shedding of my blood red;
I hanged between two,° it cannot be denied;
To get them life I suffered˃ to be dead; *consented*
I healed their feet,° with thorns hurt was my head.
I could do no more than I did, truly;
And now I see the people do clean forsake me.
They use the seven deadly sins damnàble;

matter . . . figure Matter and form (figure) are Aristotelian principles taken over by medieval science and philosophy; form shapes and directs matter. The matter here is the story and the moral doctrine; figure, the shape in which it is presented, i.e. visually and dramatically.
the intent . . . gracious the purport, the comfort we can take from it, are more holy and good
take . . . ending proverbial saying; Ecclesiasticus 7:36: "Remember the end, and thou shalt never do amiss"
Strength . . . Beauty exterior, social gifts and goods, from Nature or Fortune, not constant and eternal
God the Trinity, especially the Son, probably speaking from a position raised above the stage, as in mystery plays
unkind unnatural and ungrateful
people . . . blind Compare Ephesians 4:18; the blindness of sin was a commonplace.
law i.e. the law of love, the Gospel
hanged . . . two I was crucified between two thieves
healed . . . feet an allusion to Christ's washing the disciples' feet, symbolizing his power to heal mankind in spirit

As pride, covetise,> wrath, and lechery,° *avarice*
Now in the world be made commendàble;
And thus they leave of angels the heavenly company.
Every man liveth so after his own pleasure,
And yet of their life they be nothing sure.°
I see the more that I them forbear
The worse they be from year to year;
And that liveth appaireth> fast. *degenerates*
Therefore I will, in all the haste,
Have a reckoning of every man's person;
For, and> I leave the people thus alone *if*
In their life and wicked tempests,> *turmoil*
Verily they will become much worse than beasts;
For now one would by envy another up eat;°
Charity° they all do clean forget.
I hoped well that every man
In my glory should make his mansion,
And thereto I had them all elect;> *chosen*
But now I see, like traitors deject,> *degraded*
They thank me not for the pleasure that I to them meant,> *intended*
Nor yet for their being that I them have lent.> *given*
I proffered the people great multitude of mercy,
And few there be that asketh it heartily;> *sincerely*
They be so cumbered with> worldly riches, *involved in*
That needs on them I must do justice,
On every man living, without fear.
Where art thou, Death, thou mighty messenger?

[*Enter* DEATH]

DEATH Almighty God, I am here at your will,
Your commandment to fulfil.
GOD Go thou to Everyman,°
And show him, in my name,
A pilgrimage° he must on him take,
Which he in no wise may escape;
And that he bring with him a sure reckoning
Without delay or any tarrying.
DEATH Lord, I will in the world go run overall,> *everywhere*
And cruelly out search both great and small. [*Exit* GOD]
Every man will I beset> that liveth beastly> *attack / bestially*
Out of God's laws, and dreadeth not folly.

pride . . . lechery Four of the seven deadly sins, the others being envy, gluttony, and sloth. They represent the World, the Flesh, and the Devil and often attend the personifications of these.
And . . . sure and yet they are in no way secure in their lives
envy . . . eat Envy is often represented as biting, but usually as eating her own entrails; see Galatians 5:15.
Charity love of God, love of one's neighbor, and love of oneself
Everyman mankind, personified here for the first time in the play. The Messenger has been talking, we feel, in general terms, but now the matter comes home to us more strongly.
pilgrimage Life as a pilgrimage is an especially common image in the later Middle Ages.

He that loveth riches I will strike with my dart,
His sight to blind, and from heaven to depart>— *separate*
Except that alms be his good friend°—
In hell for to dwell, world without end.
Lo, yonder I see Everyman walking;
Full little he thinketh on my coming;
His mind is on fleshly lusts and his treasure;°
And great pain it shall cause him to endure
Before the Lord, Heaven-King. [*Enter* EVERYMAN]
Everyman, stand still! Whither art thou going
Thus gaily? Hast thou thy Maker forgeet?> *forgotten*
EVERYMAN Why askest thou?
Wouldst thou weet?> *know*
DEATH Yea, sir; I will show you:
In great haste I am sent to thee
From God, out of his Majesty.
EVERYMAN What, sent to me?
DEATH Yea, certainly.
Though thou have forgot him here,
He thinketh on thee in the heavenly sphere,
As, ere we depart, thou shalt know.
EVERYMAN What desireth God of me?
DEATH That shall I show thee:
A reckoning he will needs have
Without any longer respite.
EVERYMAN To give a reckoning longer leisure I crave;
This blind> matter troubleth my wit.> *difficult / intellect*
DEATH On thee thou must take a long journey;
Therefore thy book of count> with thee thou bring; *accounts*
For turn again> thou cannot by no way. *return*
And look thou be sure of thy reckoning,
For before God thou shalt answer, and show
Thy many bad deeds, and good but a few,
How thou hast spent thy life, and in what wise,
Before the Chief Lord of Paradise.
Have ado that we were in that way,°
For weet> thou well, thou shalt make none attornay.° *know*
EVERYMAN Full unready I am such reckoning to give.
I know thee not. What messenger art thou?
DEATH I am Death, that no man dreadeth.°
For every man I 'rest,> and no man spareth; *arrest*
For it is God's commandment°

Except . . . friend unless the alms he has given in life stand him in good stead—the restricted meaning of charity
lusts . . . treasure pleasures of the flesh (lechery, gluttony, sloth) and the world (avarice); but Death will give Everyman some leisure to repent
Have . . . way let us set about making that journey
thou . . . attornay you can give no one power of attorney; i.e. send no substitute
that . . . dreadeth that fears no man. One of the regular properties of death in sermon literature: he neither spares nor fears rich or poor, he cares for no bribe, he gives no respite
God's commandment from Eden: Genesis 3:19

That all to me should be obedient.
EVERYMAN O Death! thou comest when I had thee least in mind!°
In thy power it lieth me to save,
Yet of my good> will I give thee, if thou will be kind. *goods*
Yea, a thousand pound shalt thou have,
And> defer this matter till another day. *if you*
DEATH Everyman, it may not be, by no way!
I set> not by gold, silver, nor riches, *set store*
Nor by pope, emperor, king, duke, nor princes.
For, and> I would receive> gifts great, *if / accept*
All the world I might get;
But my custom is clean contrary.
I give thee no respite. Come hence, and not tarry.
EVERYMAN Alas! shall I have no longer respite?
I may say Death giveth no warning.
To think on thee, it maketh my heart sick,
For all unready is my book of reckoning.
But twelve year and I might have abiding,
My counting-book I would make so clear,°
That my reckoning I should not need to fear.
Wherefore, Death, I pray thee, for God's mercy,
Spare me till I be provided of remedy.
DEATH Thee availeth not to cry, weep, and pray;
But haste thee lightly> that thou were gone that journay, *quickly*
And prove> thy friends if thou can. *test*
For weet thou well the tide abideth no man;°
And in the world each living creature
For Adam's sin must die of nature.°
EVERYMAN Death, if I should this pilgrimage take,
And my reckoning surely make,
Show me, for saint> charity, *holy*
Should I not come again shortly?
DEATH No, Everyman; and> thou be once there, *if*
Thou mayst never more come here,
Trust me verily.
EVERYMAN O gracious> God, in the high seat celestial, *merciful*
Have mercy on me in this most need!
Shall I have no company from this vale terrestrial
Of mine acquaintance that way me to lead?°
DEATH Yea, if any be so hardy,
That would go with thee and bear thee company.
Hie> thee that thou were gone to God's magnificence, *hasten*
Thy reckoning to give before his presence.

Death . . . mind See Matthew 24:50–51.
But . . . clear if I could have a deferment for only twelve years, I would make my account-book so clear of debt
tide . . . man time waits for no man: proverbial
of nature in the course of nature; St. Paul, Romans 5:12: "as by one man sin entered into the world, and death by sin; and so death passed upon all men"
Shall . . . lead May I have no one of my acquaintance as company to lead the way from this terrestrial valley? Now the solitariness of Death begins to be emphasized.

What! weenest˃ thou thy life is given thee, — *suppose*
And thy worldly goods also?
EVERYMAN I had weened so, verily.
DEATH Nay, nay; it was but lent thee;
For, as soon as thou art go˃ — *gone*
Another a while shall have it, and then go therefro˃ — *from it*
Even as thou hast done.
Everyman, thou art mad! Thou hast thy wits five,°
And here on earth will not amend thy life;
For suddenly I do come.
EVERYMAN O wretched caitiff!° whither shall I flee,
That I might 'scape this endless sorrow?
Now, gentle˃ Death, spare me till tomorrow, — *noble*
That I may amend me
With good advisement.˃ — *consideration*
DEATH Nay, thereto I will not consent,
Nor no man will I respite,
But to the heart suddenly I shall smite
Without any advisement.˃ — *warning*
And now out of thy sight I will me hie;
See thou make thee ready shortly,
For thou mayst say this is the day
That no man living may 'scape away. [*Exit* DEATH]
EVERYMAN [*alone*] Alas! I may well weep with sighs deep.
Now have I no manner of company
To help me in my journey and me to keep;˃ — *guard*
And also my writing˃ is full unready. — *account book*
How shall I do now for to excuse me?
I would to God I had never be gete!˃ — *been begotten*
To my soul a full great profit˃ it had be; — *benefit*
For now I fear pains huge and great.
The time passeth; Lord, help, that all wrought.˃ — *made*
For though I mourn, it availeth nought.
The day passeth, and is almost ago;˃ — *gone*
I wot˃ not well what for to do. — *know*
To whom were I best my complaint to make?
What and˃ I to Fellowship thereof spake, — *if*
And showed him of this sudden chance,
For in him is all mine affiance?˃ — *trust*
We have in the world so many a day
Been good friends in sport and play.
I see him yonder, certainly.
I trust that he will bear me company;
Therefore to him will I speak to ease my sorrow.
Well met, good Fellowship, and good morrow!

wits five Personified later on, they are the agents of perception: sight, smell, hearing, taste, and touch.

wretched caitiff captive wretch

FELLOWSHIP *speaketh:*

FELLOWSHIP Everyman, good morrow, by this day!°
Sir, why lookest thou so piteously?
If any thing be amiss, I pray thee me say,
That I may help to remedy.
EVERYMAN Yea, good Fellowship, yea,
I am in great jeopardy.
FELLOWSHIP My true friend, show to me your mind;
I will not forsake thee to thy life's end
In the way of good company.°
EVERYMAN That was well spoken, and lovingly.
FELLOWSHIP Sir, I must needs know your heaviness;˃ *sorrow*
I have pity to see you in any distress;
If any have you wronged, ye shall revenged be,
Though I on the ground be slain for thee,
Though that I know before that I should die.
EVERYMAN Verily, Fellowship, gramercy.˃ *thank you*
FELLOWSHIP Tush! by thy thanks I set not a stree˃ *straw*
Show me your grief,˃ and say no more. *trouble*
EVERYMAN If I my heart should to you break,˃ *disclose*
And then you to turn your mind from me,
And would not me comfort when ye hear me speak,
Then should I ten times sorrier be.
FELLOWSHIP Sir, I say as I will do indeed.
EVERYMAN Then be you a good friend at need;°
I have found you true herebefore.
FELLOWSHIP And so ye shall evermore;
For, in faith, and thou go to hell,
I will not forsake thee by the way!
EVERYMAN Ye speak like a good friend; I believe you well.
I shall deserve˃ it, and˃ I may. *repay / if*
FELLOWSHIP I speak of no deserving, by this day!
For he that will say and nothing do
Is not worthy with good company to go;
Therefore show me the grief of your mind,
As to your friend most loving and kind.
EVERYMAN I shall show you how it is:
Commanded I am to go a journay,
A long way, hard and dangerous,
And give a strait count˃ without delay, *strict account*
Before the high judge, Adonaì.°
Wherefore, I pray you, bear me company,
As ye have promised, in this journay.

good . . . day A hearty good day to you! This sets the tone of Fellowship's empty promises.
good company pleasure and diversion; but Everyman mistakes the sense of "good"

Then . . . need proverbial
Adonaì Master, Lord; Hebrew name for God, substitute for the unutterable name of Jehovah; in Christian liturgy, Christ

FELLOWSHIP That is matter indeed. Promise is duty;°
But, and I should take such a voyage on me,
I know it well, it should be to my pain.
Also it makes me afeard,> certain. *afraid*
But let us take counsel here as well as we can,
For your words would fear> a strong man. *frighten*
EVERYMAN Why, ye said if I had need,
Ye would me never forsake, quick ne> dead, *living nor*
Though it were to hell, truly.
FELLOWSHIP So I said, certainly,
But such pleasures> be set aside, the sooth> to say. *jokes / truth*
And also, if we took such a journey,
When should we come again?
EVERYMAN Nay, never again till the day of doom.> *Judgment*
FELLOWSHIP In faith, then will not I come there!
Who hath you these tidings brought?
EVERYMAN Indeed, Death was with me here.
FELLOWSHIP Now, by God that all hath bought,> *redeemed*
If Death were the messenger,
For no man that is living today
I will not go that loath> journay— *hateful*
Not for the father that begat me!
EVERYMAN Ye promised otherwise, pardie.> *by God*
FELLOWSHIP I wot well I said so, truly;
And yet if thou wilt eat, and drink, and make good cheer,
Or haunt to women the lusty company,°
I would not forsake you while the day is clear,
Trust me verily!
EVERYMAN Yea, thereto ye would be ready;
To go to mirth,> solace,> and play, *gaiety / pleasure*
Your mind will sooner apply> *attend*
Than to bear me company in my long journey.
FELLOWSHIP Now, in good faith, I will not that way.
But and thou wilt murder, or any man kill,
In that I will help thee with a good will.
EVERYMAN O, that is a simple> advice indeed! *stupid*
Gentle> fellow, help me in my necessity; *dear*
We have loved long, and now I need;> *am in need*
And now, gentle Fellowship, remember me.
FELLOWSHIP Whether ye have loved me or no,
By Saint John, I will not with thee go.
EVERYMAN Yet, I pray thee, take the labour, and do so much for me
To bring> me forward, for saint> charity, *escort / holy*
And comfort me till I come without the town.
FELLOWSHIP Nay, and thou would give me a new gown,°

Promise . . . duty proverbial; cf. l. 821
haunt . . . company frequent the pleasant company of women

and . . . gown Even if you give me a new gown. A man's salary often included a regular payment in kind.

I will not a foot with thee go;
But, and thou had tarried, I would not have left thee so.
And, as now, God speed thee in thy journey,
For from thee I will depart as fast as I may.

EVERYMAN Whither away, Fellowship? Will you forsake me?

FELLOWSHIP Yea, by my fay,> to God I betake> thee. *faith / commend*

EVERYMAN Farewell, good Fellowship! For thee my heart is sore;
Adieu for ever! I shall see thee no more.

FELLOWSHIP In faith, Everyman, farewell now at the end!
For you I will remember that parting is mourning.°

[*Exit* FELLOWSHIP]

EVERYMAN Alack! shall we thus depart> indeed *part*
(Ah, Lady, help!) without any more comfort?
Lo, Fellowship forsaketh me in my most need.
For help in this world whither shall I resort?
Fellowship herebefore with me would merry make,
And now little sorrow for me doth he take.
It is said, 'In prosperity men friends may find,
Which in adversity be full unkind.'°
Now whither for succour shall I flee,
Sith> that Fellowship hath forsaken me? *since*
To my kinsmen I will, truly,
Praying them to help me in my necessity;
I believe that they will do so,
For kind will creep where it may not go.°
I will go 'say,> for yonder I see them, *assay, try*
Where> be ye now my friends and kinsmen. *whether*

[*Enter* KINDRED *and* COUSIN]

KINDRED Here be we now, at your commandment.
Cousin, I pray you show us your intent
In any wise, and not spare.°

COUSIN Yea, Everyman, and to us declare
If ye be disposed to go anywhither,> *anywhere*
For, weet you well, we will live and die togither.

KINDRED In wealth and woe we will with you hold,> *stay*
For over his kin a man may be bold.°

EVERYMAN Gramercy,> my friends and kinsmen kind. *thank you*
Now shall I show you the grief of my mind.
I was commanded by a messenger
That is a high king's chief officer;
He bade me go a pilgrimage, to my pain,

parting . . . mourning proverbial
In . . . unkind again proverbial
kind . . . go Kinship will crawl where it cannot walk; i.e. relatives will always do what they can. Cf. *The Second Shepherds' Play*, ll. 280–81.
In . . . spare in every way, and don't hold back. The relatives are more ingratiating than Fellowship.
over . . . bold a man may ask much of his family

And I know well I shall never come again;
Also I must give a reckoning strait,> *strict*
For I have a great enemy that hath me in wait,°
Which intendeth me for to hinder.
KINDRED What account is that which ye must render?
That would I know.
EVERYMAN Of all my works I must show
How I have lived, and my days spent;
Also of ill deeds that I have used> *practiced*
In my time, sith life was me lent;
And of all virtues that I have refused.
Therefore I pray you go thither with me,
To help to make mine account, for saint charity.
COUSIN What, to go thither? Is that the matter?> *what's doing*
Nay, Everyman, I had liefer fast bread and water°
All this five year and more.
EVERYMAN Alas, that ever I was bore!> *born*
For now shall I never be merry
If that you forsake me.
KINDRED Ah, sir, what ye be a merry man!°
Take good heart to you, and make no moan.
But one thing I warn you, by Saint Anne,
As for me, ye shall go alone.
EVERYMAN My Cousin, will you not with me go?
COUSIN No, by our Lady! I have the cramp in my toe.
Trust not to me; for, so God me speed,> *prosper*
I will deceive> you in your most need. *fail*
KINDRED It availeth not us to 'tice.°
Ye shall have my maid with all my heart;
She loveth to go to feasts, there to be nice,> *gay*
And to dance, and abroad to start;°
I will give her leave to help you in that journey,
If that you and she may agree.
EVERYMAN Now show me the very effect> of your mind. *intention*
Will you go with me, or abide behind?
KINDRED Abide behind? Yea, that will I, and> I may! *if*
Therefore farewell till another day. [*Exit* KINDRED]
EVERYMAN How should I be merry or glad?
For fair promises men to me make,
But when I have most need, they me forsake.
I am deceived; that maketh me sad.
COUSIN Cousin Everyman, farewell now,
For verily I will not go with you;

I . . . wait I have a powerful enemy who is lying in wait for me; i.e. the Devil, who watches and tempts until the last moment, to see if he can get a man's soul.
I . . . water I had rather fast on bread and water
ye . . . man what a joker you are
It . . . 'tice There's no point in your trying to entice us.
start gad about

Also of mine own life an unready reckoning
I have to account; therefore I make tarrying.
Now God keep thee, for now I go. [*Exit* COUSIN]
EVERYMAN Ah, Jesus, is all come hereto?> *to this*
Lo, fair words maketh fools fain;°
They promise, and nothing will do, certain.> *certainly*
My kinsmen promised me faithfully
For to abide with me steadfastly,
And now fast away do they flee:
Even so Fellowship promised me.
What friend were best me of to provide?°
I lose my time here longer to abide.
Yet in my mind a thing there is:
All my life I have loved riches;
If that my Good> now help me might, *possessions*
He would make my heart full light.
I will speak to him in this distress.
Where art thou, my Goods and riches?
GOODS [*within*] Who calleth me? Everyman? What, hast thou haste?
I lie here in corners, trussed and piled so high,
And in chests I am locked so fast,
Also sacked in bags. Thou mayst see with thine eye.
I cannot stir; in packs low I lie.
What would ye have? Lightly> me say. *quickly*
EVERYMAN Come hither, Goods, in all the haste thou may.
For of counsel I must desire thee.°

[*Enter* GOODS]

GOODS Sir, and> ye in the world have sorrow or adversity, *if*
That can I help you to remedy shortly.
EVERYMAN It is another disease> that grieveth me; *distress*
In> this world it is not, I tell thee so. *of*
I am sent for, another way to go,
To give a strait count general°
Before the highest Jupiter° of all;
And all my life I have had joy and pleasure in thee;
Therefore I pray thee go with me,
For, peradventure, thou mayst before God Almighty
My reckoning help to clean and purify:
For it is said ever among,°
That money maketh all right that is wrong.
GOODS Nay, Everyman; I sing another song,
I follow no man in such voyages;
For, and I went with thee,

fair . . . fain fine words make fools glad (proverbial)
What . . . provide What friend it would be best to provide myself with?
For . . . thee For I must beg your advice.
count general general account, balance
highest Jupiter i.e. Almighty God
For . . . among for it is always said everywhere

Thou shouldst fare much the worse for me;
For because on me thou did set thy mind,
Thy reckoning I have made blotted and blind,> *illegible*
That thine account thou cannot make truly;> *correctly*
And that hast thou for the love of me.
EVERYMAN That would grieve me full sore,
When I should come to that fearful answer.°
Up, let us go thither together.
GOODS Nay, not so! I am too brittle, I may not endure;
I will follow no man one foot, be ye sure.
EVERYMAN Alas, I have thee loved, and had great pleasure
All my life-days in goods and treasure.
GOODS That is to thy damnation, without lesing!> *lie*
For my love is contrary to the love everlasting.
But if thou had me loved moderately during,> *meanwhile*
As> to the poor to give part of me, *so as*
Then shouldst thou not in this dolour> be, *distress*
Nor in this great sorrow and care.
EVERYMAN Lo, now was I deceived ere I was ware,> *aware*
And all I may wite> misspending of time. *blame*
GOODS What, weenest> thou that I am thine? *suppose*
EVERYMAN I had weened so.
GOODS Nay, Everyman, I say no.
As for a while I was lent thee,
A season> thou hast had me in prosperity. *time*
My condition> is man's soul to kill; *nature*
If I save one, a thousand I do spill;> *ruin*
Weenest thou that I will follow thee
From this world? Nay, verily.
EVERYMAN I had weened otherwise.
GOODS Therefore to thy soul Good is a thief;
For when thou art dead, this is my guise>— *practice*
Another to deceive in the same wise
As I have done thee, and all to his soul's reprief.> *harm*
EVERYMAN O false Good, cursed thou be!
Thou traitor to God, that hast deceived me
And caught me in thy snare.
GOODS Marry, thou brought thyself in care,> *sorrow*
Whereof I am glad.
I must needs laugh, I cannot be sad.
EVERYMAN Ah, Good, thou hast had long my heartly> love; *sincere*
I gave thee that which should be the Lord's above.°
But wilt thou not go with me indeed?
I pray thee truth to say.
GOODS No, so God me speed!
Therefore farewell, and have good day. [*Exit* GOODS]

When . . . answer when I must come to that terrible account; i.e. when I am judged by God

I gave . . . above the definition of deadly sin

EVERYMAN O, to whom shall I make my moan
For to go with me in that heavy˃ journay? *sad*
First Fellowship said he would with me gone;˃ *go*
His words were very pleasant and gay,
But afterward he left me alone.
Then spake I to my kinsmen, all in despair,°
And also they gave me words fair,
They lacked no fair speaking,
But all forsook me in the ending.
Then went I to my Goods, that I loved best,
In hope to have comfort, but there had I least;
For my Goods sharply did me tell
That he bringeth many into hell.
Then of myself I was ashamed,
And so I am worthy to be blamed;
Thus may I well myself hate.
Of whom shall I now counsel take?
I think that I shall never speed˃ *prosper*
Till that I go to my Good Deed.
But, alas, she is so weak
That she can neither go˃ nor speak. *walk*
Yet will I venture on her now.
My Good Deeds,° where be you?

[GOOD DEEDS *speaks from the ground*]

GOOD DEEDS Here I lie, cold in the ground.
Thy sins hath me sore bound,
That I cannot stere.˃ *stir*
EVERYMAN O Good Deeds! I stand in fear;
I must you pray of counsel,
For help now should come right well.°
GOOD DEEDS Everyman, I have understanding
That ye be summoned account to make
Before Messias, of Jerusalem King;°
And you do by me,° that journey with you will I take.
EVERYMAN Therefore I come to you my moan to make;
I pray you that ye will go with me.
GOOD DEEDS I would full fain,˃ but I cannot stand, verily. *gladly*
EVERYMAN Why, is there anything on you fall?˃ *fallen*
GOOD DEEDS Yea, sir, I may thank you of all;
If ye had perfectly cheered˃ me, *fully encouraged*
Your book of count full ready had be.
Look, the books of your works and deeds eke;˃ *also*
Ah, see how they lie under the feet,

despair the most dangerous spiritual condition, the sin against the Holy Ghost: lack of trust in God's promised and infinite mercy

Good Deeds Good Deeds lies helpless; Everyman's virtuous actions are nullified by his sins.

help . . . well help now would be very welcome

Messias . . . King Christ

And . . . me if you do as I advise

To your soul's heaviness.> *sorrow*
EVERYMAN Our Lord Jesus help me!
For one letter here I cannot see.
GOOD DEEDS There is a blind reckoning in time of distress!°
EVERYMAN Good Deeds, I pray you, help me in this need,
Or else I am for ever damned indeed;
Therefore help me to make reckoning
Before the Redeemer of all thing,
That King is, and was, and ever shall.
GOOD DEEDS Everyman, I am sorry of your fall,
And fain would I help you, and> I were able. *if*
EVERYMAN Good Deeds, your counsel I pray you give me.
GOOD DEEDS That shall I do verily;
Though that on my feet I may not go,
I have a sister that shall with you also,
Called Knowledge,° which shall with you abide,
To help you to make that dreadful reckoning.

[*Enter* KNOWLEDGE]

KNOWLEDGE Everyman, I will go with thee, and be thy guide
In thy most need to go by thy side.
EVERYMAN In good condition I am now in every thing,
And am wholly content with this good thing;
Thanked be God my Creator.
GOOD DEEDS And when she hath brought thee there,
Where thou shalt heal thee of thy smart,> *pain*
Then go you with your reckoning and your Good Deeds together
For to make you joyful at heart
Before the blessed Trinity.
EVERMAN My Good Deeds, gramercy!
I am well content, certainly,
With your words sweet.
KNOWLEDGE Now go we together lovingly
To Confession,° that cleansing river.
EVERYMAN For joy I weep; I would we were there!
But, I pray you, give me cognition> *knowledge*
Where dwelleth that holy man, Confession.
KNOWLEDGE In the house of salvation;°
We shall find him in that place,
That shall us comfort, by God's grace.

[KNOWLEDGE *conducts* EVERYMAN *to* CONFESSION]

Lo, this is Confession. Kneel down and ask mercy,
For he is in good conceit> with God almighty. *esteem*

There . . . distress There is an illegible account in the hour of need; i.e. the sinful man finds that he cannot see the accounts.
Knowledge acknowledgment of sin, the first step to contrition; the recognition that God is merciful as well as just
Confession i.e. the personification of auricular confession, Shrift (l. 552), second of the four parts of the sacrament of penance, the others being contrition, true sorrow for sin (l. 549), absolution (ll. 568 ff.), and satisfaction (l. 707)
house of salvation church

EVERYMAN [*Kneeling*] O glorious fountain,° that all uncleanness
doth clarify,> *purify*
Wash from me the spots of vice unclean,
That on me no sin may be seen.
I come, with Knowledge, for my redemption,
Redempt with hearty and full contrition;°
For I am commanded a pilgrimage to take,
And great accounts before God to make.
Now, I pray you, Shrift,> mother of salvation. *Confession*
Help my Good Deeds for my piteous exclamation.°
CONFESSION I know your sorrow° well, Everyman.
Because with Knowledge ye come to me,
I will you comfort as well as I can,
And a precious jewel I will give thee,
Called Penance, voider> of adversity; *expeller*
Therewith shall your body chastised be,
With abstinence, and perseverance in God's service.
Here shall you receive that scourge° of me.
Which is penance strong> that ye must endure *harsh*
To remember thy Saviour was scourged for thee
With sharp scourges, and suffered it patiently;
So must thou ere thou 'scape> that painful pilgrimage.° *end*
Knowledge, keep> him in this voyage, *look after*
And by that time Good Deeds will be with thee.
But in any wise be siker> of mercy, *sure*
For your time draweth fast. And ye will saved be,
Ask God mercy, and He will grant, truly.
When with the scourge of penance man doth him bind,> *himself beat*
The oil of forgiveness° then shall he find. [*Exit* CONFESSION]
EVERYMAN Thanked be God for his gracious work!
For now I will my penance begin;
This hath rejoiced and lighted my heart,°
Though the knots be painful and hard within.°
KNOWLEDGE Everyman, look your penance that ye fulfil,
What pain that ever it to you be;
And Knowledge shall give you counsel at will
How your account ye shall make clearly.

fountain See Zechariah 13:1.
Redempt . . . contrition redeemed with sincere and complete contrition, distinguished from attrition, insincere or incomplete sorrow for sin
for . . . exclamation in answer to my pathetic cry
sorrow sorrow for sin, but the actual words of absolution are not spoken: this is a stage performance
scourge Scourging or beating as satisfaction for sin might be performed by oneself or by the priest. It had become a more frequent form of satisfaction in the 14th century and remained common in the 15th and 16th.
So . . . pilgrimage Everyman has confessed his sins, with sincere contrition, and received absolution, so that God's mercy will save him from eternal punishment. But he has not yet made full satisfaction, i.e. suffered punishment on earth (the scourging prescribed is only partial satisfaction) or after death in the purifying but not eternal fire of Purgatory (l. 618). Only then will he attain the true end of life's pilgrimage, eternal bliss.
oil of forgiveness the holy oil of Extreme Unction, the sacrament administered to the dying
lighted my heart His heart is illumined by grace, and he can bear the scourge.
Though . . . within though the knots of the scourge be painful and hard to my soul within

[EVERYMAN *kneels*]

EVERYMAN O eternal God,° O heavenly figure,
O way of righteousness, O goodly vision,
Which descended down in> a Virgin pure *into*
Because he would every man redeem,
Which Adam forfeited by his disobedience.
O blessed Godhead, elect and high Divine,> *divinity*
Forgive me my grievous offence:
Here I cry thee mercy in this presence.°
O ghostly> Treasure, O Ransomer and Redeemer, *spiritual*
Of all the world Hope and Conduiter> *guide*
Mirror of joy, Foundator of mercy,
Which enlumineth> heaven and earth thereby, *lights up*
Hear my clamorous complaint,> though it late be. *lament*
Receive my prayers, of thy benignity.
Though I be a sinner most abhominable,
Yet let my name be written in Moses' table.°
O Mary, pray to the Maker of all thing,
Me for to help at my ending;
And save me from the power of my enemy,°
For Death assaileth me strongly.
And, Lady, that I may by means of thy prayer°
Of your Son's glory to be partner,
By the means of his Passion I it crave;
I beseech you, help my soul to save. [*He rises*]
Knowledge, give me the scourge of penance;
My flesh therewith shall give acquittance.°
I will now begin, if God give me grace.

KNOWLEDGE Everyman, God give you time and space.> *opportunity*
Thus I bequeath you in> the hands of our Saviour, *to*
Now may you make your reckoning sure.

EVERYMAN In the name of the Holy Trinity,
My body sore> punished shall be. [*Scourges himself*] *harshly*
Take this, body, for the sin of the flesh!
Also> thou delightest to go gay and fresh,° *because*
And in the way of damnation thou did me bring,
Therefore suffer now strokes of punishing.
Now of penance I will wade the water clear,
To save me from Purgatory,° that sharp fire.

O . . . God Everyman's exclamations resemble the prayers recommended to the dying.
presence in the presence of Knowledge and Confession
Moses' table The two tables of the Law were thought of by medieval theologians as prefiguring the sacraments of Baptism and Penance. Everyman, now a penitent, asks to escape damnation by having his name inscribed on the table of penance.
enemy the Devil
And . . . prayer He asks the Virgin for intercession: And Lady, I beg that, through your prayer, I may be partaker of your Son's glory, by His Passion.
acquittance satisfaction, requital
gay and fresh well clothed and scented
Purgatory Those dying in God's grace must be purified in the fire of Purgatory from their venial sins, and suffer punishment still due for forgiven mortal sins, before admission to the Beatific Vision.

[GOOD DEEDS *rises from the ground*]

GOOD DEEDS I thank God, now I can walk and go,°
And am delivered of my sickness and woe.
Therefore with Everyman I will go, and not spare;
His good works I will help him to declare.
KNOWLEDGE Now, Everyman, be merry and glad!
Your Good Deeds cometh now, ye may> not be sad. *must*
Now is your Good Deeds whole and sound,
Going> upright upon the ground. *walking*
EVERYMAN My heart is light, and shall be evermore.
Now will I smite faster than I did before.
GOOD DEEDS Everyman, pilgrim, my special friend,
Blessed be thou without end.
For thee is preparate> the eternal glory. *prepared*
Ye have me made whole and sound,
Therefore I will bide by thee in every stound.> *trouble*
EVERYMAN Welcome, my Good Deeds; now I hear thy voice,
I weep for very sweetness of love.
KNOWLEDGE Be no more sad, but ever rejoice;
God seeth thy living> in his throne above. *way of life*
Put on this garment° to thy behove> *advantage*
Which is wet with your tears,
Or else before God you may it miss,
When you to your journey's end come shall.
EVERYMAN Gentle Knowledge, what do ye it call?
KNOWLEDGE It is the garment of sorrow;
From pain it will you borrow;> *redeem*
Contrition it is
That getteth forgiveness;
It pleaseth God passing> well. *exceedingly*
GOOD DEEDS Everyman, will you wear it for your heal?°

[EVERYMAN *puts on the garment of contrition*]

EVERYMAN Now blessed be Jesu, Mary's Son,
For now have I on true contrition.
And let us go now without tarrying;
Good Deeds, have we clear our reckoning?
GOOD DEEDS Yea, indeed I have it here.
EVERYMAN Then I trust we need not fear.
Now, friends, let us not part in twain.
KNOWLEDGE Nay, Everyman, that will we not, certain.
GOOD DEEDS Yet must thou lead with thee
Three persons of great might.

now . . . go Good Deeds has been powerless up to now because, until mortal sins are confessed and absolved, good deeds have no merit.
garment the clothing of contrition; perhaps the white sheet worn by public penitents. It would either hide his gay clothes or cover his naked body; and would suggest the shroud he will shortly wear.
heal health, salvation

EVERYMAN Who should they be?

GOOD DEEDS Discretion and Strength they hight,> *are called*
And thy Beauty may not abide behind.

KNOWLEDGE Also ye must call to mind
Your Five Wits° as for your counsellors.

GOOD DEEDS You must have them ready at all hours.

EVERYMAN How shall I get them hither?

KNOWLEDGE You must call them all together,
And they will hear you incontinent.> *immediately*

EVERYMAN My friends, come hither and be present;
Discretion, Strength, my Five Wits, and Beauty.

[*Enter* DISCRETION, STRENGTH, FIVE WITS, *and* BEAUTY]

BEAUTY Here at your will we be all ready.
What will ye that we should do?

GOOD DEEDS That ye would with Everyman go,
And help him in his pilgrimage.
Advise you,> will ye with him or not in that voyage? *consider*

STRENGTH We will bring him all thither,
To his help and comfort, ye may believe me.

DISCRETION So will we go with him all together.

EVERYMAN Almighty God loved> may thou be! *praised*
I give thee laud> that I have hither brought *praise*
Strength, Discretion, Beauty, and Five Wits. Lack I nought;
And my Good Deeds, with Knowledge clear,
All be in company at my will here.°
I desire no more to> my business. *for*

STRENGTH And I, Strength, will by you stand in distress,
Though thou would in battle fight on the ground.

FIVE WITS And though it were through the world round,
We will not depart for sweet nor sour.°

BEAUTY No more will> I, unto> death's hour, *wish / until*
Whatsoever thereof befall.

DISCRETION Everyman, advise you first of all;
Go with a good advisement and deliberation.
We all give you virtuous monition> *powerful forewarning*
That all shall be well.

EVERYMAN My friends, hearken what I will tell:
I pray God reward you in his heavenly sphere.
Now hearken, all that be here,
For I will make my testament°
Here before you all present:
In alms half my good I will give with my hands twain

Five Wits The five senses and the gifts of Nature, along with Discretion, which allows him to use them as a rational creature, are now mobilized.
All . . . here are all together here at my command
for . . . sour in happiness nor adversity
testament disposal of spiritual and earthly possessions. A will always began with the disposal of the soul to God and made provision for charitable gifts as well as apportioning property to heirs.

In the way of charity, with good intent,
And the other half still˃ shall remain *which still*
In queath° to be returned there˃ it ought to be. *where*
This I do in despite˃ of the fiend of hell, *contempt*
To go quit out of his peril
Ever after and this day.°

KNOWLEDGE Everyman, hearken what I say;
Go to Priesthood,° I you advise,
And receive of him in any wise˃ *without fail*
The holy sacrament and ointment together;
Then shortly see ye turn again hither;
We will all abide you here.

FIVE WITS Yea, Everyman, hie˃ you that ye ready were. *hasten*
There is no emperor, king, duke, nor baron,
That of God hath commission°
As hath the least priest in the world being;˃ *alive*
For of the blessed sacraments pure and benign
He beareth the keys, and thereof hath the cure˃ *charge*
For man's redemption—it is ever sure—
Which God for our soul's medicine
Gave us out of his heart with great pine˃ *suffering*
Here in this transitory life, for thee and me.
The blessed sacraments seven° there be:
Baptism, confirmation, with priesthood good,
And the sacrament of God's precious flesh and blood,
Marriage, the holy extreme unction, and penance.
These seven be good to have in remembrance,
Gracious˃ sacraments of high divinity. *full of grace*

EVERYMAN Fain˃ would I receive that Holy Body˃ *gladly / Eucharist*
And meekly to my ghostly˃ father I will go. *spiritual*

FIVE WITS Everyman, that is the best that ye can do.
God will you to salvation bring,
For priesthood exceedeth all other thing;
To us Holy Scripture they do teach,
And converteth˃ man from sin, heaven to reach; *turn away*
God hath to them more power given,
Than to any angel that is in heaven.
With five words° he may consecrate
God's body in flesh and blood to make,
And handleth his Maker between his hands.

In queath as a bequest; strictly, the restitution of improperly acquired property
To . . . day to pass free out of his power to harm, today and forever
Priesthood i.e. someone who has received the sacrament of Holy Orders; a priest who alone can give the sinner Everyman, now in a state of grace, Communion and Extreme Unction (l. 709)
There . . . commission All civil authority was derived from God; but a priest's authority, being spiritual, not temporal, was held to be superior.
blessed . . . seven Catholic doctrine counts seven sacraments: Baptism, Confirmation, Eucharist, Penance, Extreme Unction (now called the Anointing of the Sick), Matrimony, and Holy Orders. In the text Holy Orders is placed third, to stress the importance of the priesthood.
five words the consecration of the host, as used by the priest at Mass: *"Corpus Domini nostri Jesu Christi"* (the body of our Lord Jesus Christ)

The priest bindeth and unbindeth all bands,°
Both in earth and in heaven.
Thou ministers> all the sacraments seven; *administer*
Though we kissed thy feet, thou were worthy;°
Thou art surgeon that cureth sin deadly:
No remedy we find under God
But all only priesthood.°
Everyman, God gave priests that dignity,
And setteth them in his stead among us to be;
Thus be they above angels in degree.> *rank*

[*Exit* EVERYMAN]

KNOWLEDGE If priests be good,° it is so, surely.
But when Jesus hanged on the cross with great smart,> *suffering*
There he gave out of his blessèd heart
The same sacrament in great torment:
He sold them not to us, that Lord omnipotent.
Therefore Saint Peter the Apostle doth say°
That Jesu's curse hath all they
Which God their Saviour do buy or sell,
Or they for any, money do take or tell.°
Sinful priests giveth the sinners example bad;
Their children sitteth by other men's fires,° I have heard;
And some haunteth women's company
With unclean life, as> lusts of lechery. *such as*
These be with sin made blind.
FIVE WITS I trust to God no such may we find.
Therefore let us priesthood honour,
And follow their doctrine for our souls' succour.
We be their sheep, and they shepherds be
By whom we all be kept in surety.
Peace,> for yonder I see Everyman come, *quiet*
Which hath made true satisfaction.
GOOD DEEDS Methink it is he indeed.

[*Re-enter* EVERYMAN]

EVERYMAN Now Jesu be your alder speed.°
I have received the sacrament for my redemption,
And then mine extreme unction:

bindeth . . . bands the power of binding and loosing, Matthew 16:19, 18:18; the priest, heir of the Apostles, can retain or remit sins
Though . . . worthy i.e. you would be worthy to have your feet kissed
But . . . priesthood except priesthood alone
If . . . good then they are above the angels. The attack on sinful priests is frequent in English literature from at least Chaucer onwards. This one may draw its doctrine of good priests' being above the angels from Thomas à Kempis, the presumed author of the 15th-century devotional work *The Imitation of Christ*.
Peter . . . say Acts 8:18–20. The reference is to the sin of simony, the buying and selling of spiritual things, so named from Simon Magus, who was cursed by St. Peter for wishing to buy the gifts of the Holy Ghost.
Or . . . tell or who, for any sacrament, accept or count out money
Their . . . fires i.e. they farm out their bastards upon their parishioners; or, they have committed adultery with their parishioners' wives
Jesu . . . speed Jesus prosper you all

Blessed be all they that counselled me to take it!
And now, friends, let us go without longer respite;
I thank God that ye have tarried so long.
Now set each of you on this rood° your hand,
And shortly> follow me. *quickly*
I go before, there> I would be; *where*
God be our guide.
STRENGTH Everyman, we will not from you go,
Till ye have done this voyage long.
DISCRETION I, Discretion, will bide by you also.
KNOWLEDGE And though this pilgrimage be never so strong,> *hard*
I will never part you fro.> *from*
STRENGTH Everyman, I will be as sure by thee
As ever I did by Judas Maccabee.°

[*They go together to the grave*]

EVERYMAN Alas! I am so faint I may not stand,
My limbs under me doth fold.
Friends, let us not turn again to this land,
Not for all the world's gold;
For into this cave must I creep,
And turn> to earth, and there to sleep. *return*
BEAUTY What, into this grave? Alas!°
EVERYMAN Yea, there shall you consume,> more and less.> *decay / utterly*
BEAUTY And what, should I smother here?
EVERYMAN Yea, by my faith, and never more appear.
In this world live no more we shall,
But in heaven before the highest Lord of all.
BEAUTY I cross out all this;° adieu, by Saint John!
I take my tap in my lap° and am gone.
EVERYMAN What, Beauty, whither will ye?
BEAUTY Peace! I am deaf. I look not behind me,
Not and> thou would give me all the gold in thy chest. [*Exit* BEAUTY] *if*
EVERYMAN Alas, whereto may I trust?
Beauty goeth fast away from me;
She promised with me to live and die.
STRENGTH Everyman, I will thee also forsake and deny.
Thy game liketh> me not at all. *pleases*
EVERYMAN Why then, ye will forsake me all!
Sweet Strength, tarry a little space!> *while*
STRENGTH Nay, sir, by the rood of grace!
I will hie me from thee fast,
Though thou weep till thy heart to-brast.> *break in pieces*

rood cross, i.e. as placed in the hands of the dying

Judas Maccabee Judas Maccabaeus, one of the Nine Worthies (see Glossary) and leader of the Jews in their revolt against Syria; see I Maccabees 3:4: "In his acts he was like a lion and like a lion's whelp roaring for his prey."

Alas The gifts of Nature, reason (Discretion), and the senses desert him now, in that order, and he goes alone to the grave, except for Good Works.

I . . . this I cancel all this

tap . . . lap Tape, i.e. I tuck my skirts up and secure them; or tap, the tow on a distaff; or one may read "cap." The reading is difficult, the sense plain: "I'm off!"

EVERYMAN Ye would ever bide by me, ye said.
STRENGTH Yea,> I have you far enough conveyed.> *true / escorted*
Ye be old enough, I understand,
Your pilgrimage to take on> hand. *in*
I repent me that I hither came.
EVERYMAN Strength, you to displease I am to blame;°
Yet promise is debt, this ye well wot.> *know*
STRENGTH In faith, I care not.
Thou art but a fool to complain;
You spend your speech and waste your brain.
Go, thrust thee into the ground. [*Exit* STRENGTH]
EVERYMAN I had weened> surer I should you have found. *expected*
He that trusteth in his Strength
She him deceiveth at the length.
Both Strength and Beauty forsaketh me;
Yet they promised me fair and lovingly.
DISCRETION Everyman, I will after Strength be gone;
As for me, I will leave you alone.
EVERYMAN Why, Discretion, will ye forsake me?
DISCRETION Yea, in faith, I will go from thee,
For when Strength goeth before
I follow after evermore.
EVERYMAN Yet, I pray thee, for the love of the Trinity,
Look in my grave once piteously.
DISCRETION Nay, so nigh will I not come.
Farewell, every one! [*Exit* DISCRETION]
EVERYMAN O all thing faileth, save God alone—
Beauty, Strength, and Discretion;
For when Death bloweth his blast,
They all run from me full fast.
FIVE WITS Everyman, my leave now of thee I take;
I will follow the other, for here I thee forsake.
EVERYMAN Alas, then may I wail and weep,
For I took you for my best friend.
FIVE WITS I will no longer thee keep;> *guard*
Now farewell, and there an end. [*Exit* FIVE WITS]
EVERYMAN O Jesu, help! All hath forsaken me!
GOOD DEEDS Nay, Everyman; I will bide with thee,
I will not forsake thee indeed;
Thou shalt find me a good friend at need.
EVERYMAN Gramercy, Good Deeds! Now may I true friends see.
They have forsaken me, every one;
I loved them better than my Good Deeds alone.
Knowledge, will ye forsake me also?
KNOWLEDGE Yea, Everyman, when ye to Death shall go;
But not yet, for no manner of danger.

Strength . . . blame Strength, I am to blame for displeasing you.

EVERYMAN Gramercy, Knowledge, with all my heart.
KNOWLEDGE Nay, yet I will not from hence depart
Till I see where ye shall become.°
EVERYMAN Methink, alas, that I must be gone
To make my reckoning and my debts pay,
For I see my time is nigh spent away.
Take example, all ye that this do hear or see,
How they that I loved best do forsake me,
Except my Good Deeds that bideth truly.
GOOD DEEDS All earthly things is but vanity:°
Beauty, Strength, and Discretion do man forsake,
Foolish friends and kinsmen, that fair spake—
All fleeth save Good Deeds, and that am I.
EVERYMAN Have mercy on me, God most mighty;
And stand by me, thou Mother and Maid, holy Mary.
GOOD DEEDS Fear not: I will speak for thee.
EVERYMAN Here I cry God mercy.
GOOD DEEDS Short our end, and minish our pain.°
Let us go and never come again.
EVERYMAN Into thy hands, Lord, my soul I commend.
Receive it, Lord, that it be not lost.
As thou me boughtest, so me defend,
And save me from the fiënd's boast,
That I may appear with that blessed host
That shall be saved at the day of doom.°
In manus tuas—of mights most
For ever—*commendo spiritum meum.*°

[EVERYMAN *and* GOOD DEEDS *descend into the grave*]

KNOWLEDGE Now hath he suffered that we all shall endure;
The Good Deeds shall make all sure.
Now hath he made ending.
Methinketh that I hear angels sing,
And make great joy and melody
Where Everyman's soul received shall be.
ANGEL [*within*] Come, excellent elect° spouse to Jesu!
Hereabove thou shalt go
Because of thy singular virtue.
Now the soul is taken the body fro,˃ *from*
Thy reckoning is crystal clear.
Now shalt thou into the heavenly sphere,°

where . . . become what shall become of you
All . . . vanity Ecclesiastes 12:8
Short . . . pain Shorten our time of dying and diminish our pain.
day of doom General Judgment. All men come twice to judgment, according to Catholic doctrine, once at death and once on Doomsday, at the end of the world (Fig. 50).
In manus . . . meum "Into thy hands, most mighty and everlasting One, I commend my spirit"; the words, spoken by Christ just before his death (Luke 23:46), are recommended for repetition by the dying in *Ars Moriendi* (The Art of Dying Well) (Fig. 52).
elect chosen; the soul as the bride of Christ is a common late-medieval image
heavenly sphere the highest of all the spheres, the changeless Empyrean

Unto the which all ye shall come
That liveth well before the day of doom.

[*Exit* KNOWLEDGE. *Enter* DOCTOR.°]

DOCTOR This memorial> men may have in mind; *reminder*
Ye hearers, take it of worth,° old and young,
And forsake Pride, for he deceiveth you in the end,
And remember Beauty, Five Wits, Strength, and Discretion,
They all at the last do Everyman forsake,
Save his Good Deeds there doth he take.
But beware, for and> they be small *if*
Before God, he hath no help at all.
None excuse may be there for Everyman.
Alas, how shall he do then?
For, after death, amends may no man make,
For then mercy and pity doth him forsake.
If his reckoning be not clear when he doth come,
God will say, *Ite, maledicti, in ignem aeternum.*°
And he that hath his account whole and sound,
High in heaven he shall be crowned;
Unto which place God bring us all thither,
That we may live body and soul together.
Thereto help the Trinity!
Amen, say ye, for saint charity.

THUS ENDETH THIS MORAL PLAY OF EVERYMAN.

c. 1485 1528–29

MIDDLE ENGLISH LYRICS

Anyone coming to Middle English lyric poetry with Ruskin's definition in his mind ("lyric poetry is the expression by the poet of his own feelings") will be disconcerted, for neither in the shorter religious verse which goes by that name, nor in the love poetry and other secular verse, is there any indication of an emotion which is other than widely felt and general. The imagery is not individual, but conventional; and the themes are conventional also. The poems have little metrical subtlety or range and many of them have little music of their own, though the secular lyrics were set to music very often, and the religious occasionally. For both types, musical settings were more common in the fifteenth century than earlier, while some early lyrics were set in the sixteenth century. One that we know was given music early is "Summer Is Ycumen In," perhaps the work of a monk of Reading Abbey about 1240, though the tune we have for it may be as late as 1310. In the manuscript, an alternative set of pious words is provided, in Latin—which may indicate that the church was not happy with the prevalence of secular song among its clergy. We know that a bishop of

Doctor A learned theologian provides the Epilogue, in a short sermon, pointing the moral.
take . . . worth take heed
Ite . . . aeternum "Depart, ye cursèd, into everlasting fire" (Matthew 25:41). Everyman has had his judgment at death, but this quotation emphasizes his function as Mankind by invoking the General Judgment.

Ossory, in the fourteenth century, collected about sixty Latin texts in the *Red Book of Ossory* to go with popular airs of the day—taking the Devil's best tunes from him. Among the secular airs so used was that of "The Maid of the Moor."

Many of the lyrics that we have are translations from French or Latin. Almost all are anonymous. If we except the lyric poems on French models of Chaucer and his followers, we can find few short poems of the thirteenth, fourteenth, and fifteenth centuries to which we can put an author's name.

They are also extremely difficult to date accurately. We can sometimes say that, in the form in which we have them, they are "early" or "late," but this is not very definite and we cannot tell how they looked and sounded in their original form. Often an early poem has been re-worked by a later poet or altered, perhaps inadvertently, by a later copyist.

The poems given here aim to provide a sample of variety, but by no means exhaust it. Of the secular lyrics, there are imitations of the French *reverdie* or spring song, and versions of the love complaint which are so simple and direct that they seem to come from another world than Chaucer's poems in the same genre. Their very lack of sophistication is the quality that appeals to us today. The two riddling poems are examples of a popular genre, which goes back to Anglo-Saxon and Latin poetry of the early Middle Ages, and here uses sexual puns and symbolism. "The Agincourt Carol" is a kind of parody of a solemn, religious thanksgiving, or of a sacred carol celebrating the victory of Christ's birth, the refrain being part of the Mass and associated especially with Christmas. The drinking song "Bring Us in Good Ale" is a hearty form that has something in common with Latin drinking poetry of the twelfth century. Precise relations are much more difficult to establish.

These poems are in the main a bare announcement of experience: they do not dwell on it or explore its nature. They are simple, but not sensuous and passionate, they do not individualize. Above all they do not seek for conceit or surprise and originality, and they have little self-regard. But they somehow convey the impression of freshness in the renewal of spring, or new love; or of gaiety and pleasure.

The religious lyrics, likewise, do not seek to startle with originality of emotion or description, or to particularize the character of the feelings they deal with. With some exceptions, they use the same genres and verse forms as the secular poetry of their day. (Until the fifteenth century the *balade* remained almost entirely a secular form in England, whereas it was used for religious subjects in France; the complaint, or *planctus,* originally sacred, was used for both sacred and secular lament.) Almost all the English religious lyrics, with the fifteenth century providing more exceptions than earlier times, are meditations, or didactic pieces based on meditations. Their themes are death and the last things, Christ's passion, centered on the figure of the crucified Savior, divine love, divine mercy, the Virgin and her joys and sorrows. Beside these things, the question of who wrote the poems is irrelevant: it is the common religious experience that counts to the medieval author and his audience. The medieval author in this instance seems very often to have been a friar, using the religious poem as a means of bringing home the central Christian truths. Such an author frequently uses conventions that are not immediately apparent to us. Chief among these is typology (see Glossary)—to which the mystery plays owe so much. The simile in "I Sing of a Maiden," for example, which likens Christ entering the womb of Mary to "dew in Aprill / That falleth on the grass," reads as charmingly naïve. One's first reaction would be that dew as a symbol for grace is striking and might well be ancient—which is correct. But the image has a more precise reference, being an adaptation of the typological interpretation of Gideon's fleece (Judges 6:37-40). For a sign that he would save Israel, God impregnated with dew the fleece that Gideon had laid out, and then, to confirm his promise, kept the fleece dry while the dew fell on the ground. So now, for a sign that he will save mankind, God impregnates the Virgin. Similarly, the gay little carol "Adam Lay Ybounden" is a statement of the doctrine of the fortunate fall: we must be grateful to Adam, for he has made it necessary for God to show us what true womanhood is, in the Virgin, mother of Christ.

The carols are a slightly different case, in that they all seem to have been composed for singing, rather than as meditations. They are more public celebrations than private and intimate poems, in a relatively simple but highly rhythmical form, often in quatrains, with a chorus. Like ballads, they give the sense of being compendious, of compressing much narrative into little space. They are associated with Christmas—cf. "The Cherry-tree Carol" in Popular Ballads below. The two last carols given here, however, are untypical in that neither is concerned with joy and with Christmas, one being cast in the form of a *chanson d'aventure,* a form of love poetry in which the poem is represented as overheard conversation. It has the macaronic refrain used by Dunbar in his "Lament for the Makers," taken from the Office of the Dead, and it is rather a hybrid, combining the love poem's form with sacred content, and also having something of the nature of a meditation on death (again like Dunbar's poem)—a kind of *ubi sunt* motif, lamenting the passing of all things earthly: Where are they now? The "Corpus Christi Carol" is one of those poems that appeals as a poem, however uncertain one is about its precise meaning and application. Clearly it has reference to the Eucharist, the body of Christ, the sacrament of the altar which is the remembrance of the Sacrifice. Its other resonances just as clearly have relations with the symbolism of legends of the Grail, but the poem remains mysterious.

The basis of most of the texts—and many of the titles—of the poems in this section is Celia and Kenneth Sisam (eds.), *The Oxford Book of Medieval English Verse.*

Spring

Lenten is come with love to towne,°
With blosmen> and with briddės> rowne,> *blossom / birds' voices*
  That al this blissė bringeth:
Dayėsėyės> in the dales, *daisies*
Notės swete of nightėgales—
  Ech fowl> song singeth. *bird*
The threstelcok him threteth o,°
Away is herė> winter wo,> *their / sorrow*
  When wodėrovė> springeth. *woodruff*
Thes fowlės singeth ferly fele,> *wonderfully many*

Lenten . . . towne Lent, i.e. Spring, has come joyously to the dwellings of men, i.e. to the world.

The threstelcok . . . o the cock-thrush trills (or: chides) continually

And wliteth on here winnė wele,°
  That al the wodė˃ ringeth. — *forest*

The rosė raileth˃ hirė rode,˃ — *displays / redness*
The levės on the lightė wode˃ — *bright wood*
  Waxen˃ al with wille.˃ — *grow / joyously*
The moonė mandeth hirė blee,°
The lilie is lofsom˃ to see, — *beautiful*
  The fenil˃ and the fille.˃ — *fennel / thyme*
Wowės˃ thesė wildė drakės; — *woo*
Milės murgeth herė makės,°
  As strem that striketh stille.°
Mody meneth, so doth mo—
Ich'ot ich am one of tho
  For love that likės ille.°

The moonė mandeth hirė light;
So doth the seemly˃ sunnė bright, — *beautiful*
  When briddės˃ singeth breme.˃ — *birds / gloriously*
Dewės donketh˃ the downes; — *moisten*
Deerės with here dernė rownes,
  Domės for to deme;°
Wormės woweth under cloude;˃ — *earth*
Wimmen waxeth wonder proude˃— — *excited*
  So wel it wil hem seme.°
If me shal wantė wille of on,
This winnė wele I wil forgon,
  And wight in wode be fleme.°
  c. 1330

Now Springs the Spray

Now springės the spray,°
  All for love ich am so seek˃ — *sick*
That slepen˃ I ne may.˃ — *sleep / can*

As I me rode this endrė day
  O my playinge,°

And . . . wele perhaps: and whistle of their wealth in joys
mandeth . . . blee casts her radiance
murgeth . . . makes gladden their mates; the meaning of "Miles" is unknown
strem . . . stille stream that flows softly
Mody . . . ille (ll. 22–24) The passionate man makes moan—and so do others. I know I am one of those that love has made unhappy (ill-pleased). *Mody* is Old English *mōdig:* proud, angry.
Deeres . . . deme (ll. 29–30) animals with their silent (secret) voices through which they speak to one another (literally, make statements)
So . . . seme It will seem to them so good.
If . . . fleme If I must go without my will of (i.e. not sleep with) one of them, I want to forego this joyous wealth (of spring) and at once become an outlaw (a creature exiled in the woods).
Now . . . spray Now that the twig is in leaf. This poem is an adaptation of a French *chanson d'aventure,* though the English version does not let the teller win the maiden, as the French does.
As . . . playinge as I was riding the other day, for my diversion

Seigh˃ ich where a litel may˃ — *saw / maid*
Bigan to singe:
'The clot him clinge!
Wai is him i love-longinge
Shal libben ay!'°
Now springės, *etc.*

Soon ich herde that mirie note
Thider I drough;
I fonde hire in an erber swote°
Under a bough,
With joy enough.˃ — *much*
Soon˃ I asked: 'Thou mirie˃ may, — *at once / happy*
Why singest thou ay?'˃ — *all the time*
Now springės, *etc.*

Then answèrde that maiden swote˃ — *sweet*
Mid˃ wordės few: — *with*
'My lemmàn me haves bihote
Of lovė trewe:°
He chaunges anew.
If I may, it shal him rew,°
By this day!'
Now springės, *etc.*
c. 1300

Sumer Is Ycumen In°

Sing, cuccu, nu! Sing, cuccu!
Sing, cuccu! Sing, cuccu, nu!
Sumer is ycumen˃ in, — *has come*
Ludė˃ sing, cuccu! — *loudly*
Groweth seed and bloweth med˃ — *blossoms meadow*
And springth the wodė nu.˃ — *wood now*

Sing, cuccu!
Awė˃ bleeteth after lamb, — *ewe*
Lowth after calvė cu,˃ — *calf cow*
Bulloc sterteth,˃ buckė verteth.° — *leaps*
Meriė sing, cuccu!
Cuccu, cuccu,

The clot . . . ay (ll. 8–10) May the clod (earth, grave) waste him away! Wretched is he who, in lovesickness, must live forever.
Soon . . . swote As soon as I heard that charming song, I went there; I found her in a delightful arbor
My . . . trewe My lover has vowed me his true love.
If . . . rew If I can (manage it), he shall be sorry.

Sumer . . . In A straightforward song of welcome to the new season, a *reverdie* or spring song, without a trace of moralization or of love-longing, it is in the form of a *rota* or round, in which the voices repeat one another in succession, pausing and beginning in turn.
verteth either "jumps, twists," from Latin *vertere,* to turn, or "breaks wind, farts"; probably the former

Wel singės thu,> cuccu; *thou*
Ne swink> thu never nu! *don't stop*
c. 1240

Alison

Betwenė> March and Avėril, *during*
When spray> biginneth to springe,> *twig / shoot*
The litel fowl> hath hirė wil> *bird / takes pleasure*
  On hirė lud> to singe. *in her language*
  Ich libbe> in love-longinge *I live*
  For semlokest> of allė thinge;> *loveliest / creatures*
  Heo may> me blissė bringe— *she can*
    Ich am in hire bandòun.> *power*
      An hendy hap ich habbe yhent;°
      Ich'ot> from hevene it is me sent; *I know*
      From allė> wimmen my love is lent,> *all other / departed*
        And light> on Alysoun. *fallen*

On hew hire her is fair ynough,°
  Hire browė> browne, hire eyė blake;> *eyebrows / dark*
With lofsom chere heo on me lough,°
  With middel smal and wel ymake.°
  Bute> heo me willė to hire take *unless*
For to been hire owėn make,> *mate*
  Longe to liven ich'ille> forsake, *I will*
    And feyė> fallen adown. *doomed to die*
      An hendy hap, *etc.*

Nightės when I wende and wake—
  Forthy myn wongės waxeth won:°
Levedy,> al for thinė sake *lady*
  Longing is ylent me on.> *come on me*
  In world n'is> non so witer mon> *is not / wise man*
  That al hire bounté tellė con:°
  Hire swire> is whiter than the swan, *neck*
    And fairest may> in town. *maid*
      An hendy hap, *etc.*

Ich am for wowing al forwake,°
  Wery so water in wore,
Lest any revė me my make
  Ich habbe yyernėd yore.

An . . . yhent a happy lot I have received
On . . . ynough in color her hair is entirely beautiful
With . . . lough with lovable looks she smiled on me
With . . . ymake with a slender and well-made waist
Nightes . . . won at nights I toss and am restless, so that my cheeks turn pale
That . . . con that he knows enough to describe all her worth
Ich . . . forwake through my wooing I am worn out from lying awake

Betere is tholiėn whilė sore
Than mournen evermore.°
Gainest under gore,°
Herknė to my roun.˃ — *words*
An hendy hap, *etc.*
c. 1330

Separated Lovers

My lefe˃ is faren˃ in londe;° — *dear / gone*
Allas! why is she so?
And I am so sore in bonde˃ — *cruelly confined*
I may not come her to.
She hath my hert in hold°
Wherever she ride or go,°
With trew love a thousandfold.

14th century

Western Wind

Westron wind,° when will thou blow?
The small° rain down can˃ rain: — *does*
Christ, if my love were in my arms
And I in my bed again!

early 16th century

He Is Far

Were it undo that is ydo,˃ — *done*
I wold be war.°

I loved a child˃ of this contree, — *young man*
And so I wende˃ he had do me; — *thought*
Now myself the soothe˃ I see, — *truth*
That he is far.

He saide to me he wolde be trewe
And chaunge me for no other newe;˃ — *new love*
Now I sike˃ and am pale of hewe,˃ — *sigh / colour*
For he is far.

Wery . . . evermore (ll. 32–36) As tired as water in a (?) turbulent pool. I have been long anxious lest anyone take my girl (mate) away from me. It is better to endure pain for a time than to mourn forever.
Gainest . . . gore most beautiful beneath clothing; i.e. alive
in londe up-country, away. This is presumably the song sung by Pertelote and Chauntecleer in Chaucer's Nun's Priest's Tale, l. 113; see above.
She . . . hold she holds my heart captive wherever she is
ride or go literally, ride or walk, but a formula, not to be translated at the full value of the words
Westron wind Zephyrus, the spring wind
small thin, biting
I . . . war I would be (more) careful

He saide his sawes> he wold fulfille; *promises*
Therfore I let him have al his wille.
Now I sike and mournė stille,°
For he is far.

14th century

I Have a Young Sister°

I have a yong suster> *sister*
Far beyonden see,> *over the sea*
Many be the drouries> *gifts*
That she sentė me.

She sentė me the cherrye
Withouten any stone;
And so she did the dove
Withouten any bone.

She sentė me the brere> *briar*
Withouten any rind;> *bark*
She bad me love my lemman> *lover*
Withoutė longing.°

How shuld any cherrye
Be withoutė stone?
And how shuld any dove
Be withoutė bone?

How shuld any brere
Been withoutė rind?
How shuld I love myn lemman
Withoutė longing?

When the cherrye was a flowr
Then had it no stone.
When the dovė was an ey> *egg*
Then had it no bone.

When the brerė was onbred> *unbred*
Then had it no rind.
When the maiden hath that> she loveth *what*
She is without longing.

15th century

Now . . . stille now I sigh and mourn always (or: in secret)

I Have . . . Sister This and the next poem are riddles, using sexual *doubles entendres* in a way popular in French and English 15th-century poetry (sometimes illustrated). The riddle-poem technique (cf. the ballad of "The Two Magicians" below) survives in nursery rhymes—as does this very poem.

longing love-sickness

The Maid of the Moor°

Maiden in the mor lay,> — *lived*
  In the mor lay,
Sevenightė fulle,> — *a week fully*
Sevenightė fulle,
Maiden in the mor lay,
  In the mor lay,
Sevenightė fulle and a day.

Well> was hirė mete;> — *good / food*
  What was hirė mete?
The primėrole> and the— — *primrose*
The primėrole and the—
Well was hirė mete;
  What was hirė mete?
The primėrole and the violete.

Well was hirė dring;> — *drink*
  What was hirė dring?
The cheldė> water of the— — *cold*
The cheldė water of the—
Well was hirė dring;
  What was hirė dring?
The cheldė water of the wellė-spring.> — *spring*

Well was hirė bowr;> — *chamber*
  What was hirė bowr?
The redė rose and the—
The redė rose and the—
Well was hirė bowr;
  What was hirė bowr?
The redė rose and the lilie-flowr.

14th century

The Maid . . . Moor Until quite recently, this little poem existed peacefully as a secular piece of popular origin and obscure meaning, riddling perhaps, but artless, of wide and immediate appeal. Then it was suggested that, beneath its secular surface, there lay a spiritual, allegorical meaning. The moor, for example, might symbolize the waste world before the coming of Christ, so that "welle-spring" could be the fountain of God's grace, and the maiden the Virgin Mary. The articulation of the poem, read in this sense, is far from perfect—and we have no evidence that it was ever so read, though a sacred interpretation or use of it, in whole or in part, might well have occurred to contemporary readers of a pious turn of mind or a religious profession. (Cf. the interpretation of the tale from the *Gesta Romanorum* following Chaucer's Wife of Bath's Tale above.) Those who wished to retain the secular interpretation pointed out that, in the *Red Book of Ossory*, pious Latin words had been provided to replace—as it seemed—the English, something that would hardly have been thought worthwhile if the poem had been regarded as religious in the first place. A new counter to this argument has now been provided. It seems as though what the bishop of Ossory was doing was not replacing secular words, but merely using secular tunes—among them that to which "The Maid of the Moor" was rendered—for sacred purposes, just as, at the end of the last century, the tune of "Clementine" was used for solemn songs. A case has now been made for explicating this lyric in terms of the medieval legend of the penitence of St. Mary Magdalene in the wilderness (moor)—though the Magdalene's maiden status is more than questionable. Those who prefer a secular interpretation have the tone of the poem in their favor: few, if any, short religious poems read like this one.

The Agincourt Carol°

Deo gracias, Anglia,
Redde pro victoria.°

Our King went forth to Normandy
With grace and might of chivalry;°
Ther> God for him wrought mervelusly;>   *where / wonderfully*
Wherfore England may call and cry
'Deo gracias.'

He sette a sege,> the sooth> for to say,   *laid siege / truth*
To Harfleur town with royal aray;
That town he won and made afray>   *attack*
That Fraunce shal rewe> til Domėsday:°   *regret*
Deo gracias.

Then went our King with alle his host
Thorough Fraunce, for all the Frenshė boast;
He spared no drede of lest ne most°
Til he come> to Agincourt coast:>   *came / district*
Deo gracias.

Then, forsooth, that knight comely
In Agincourt feeld he fought manly.>   *manfully*
Thorough grace of God most mighty
He had both the feeld and the victory:
Deo gracias.

There dukes and erles,> lord and baròne   *earls*
Were take and slain, and that wel sone;>   *very quickly*
And sume were ledde into Lundòne
With joy and merth and gret renone:>   *pomp*
Deo gracias.

Now gracious God He save our King,
His peple, and alle his wel-willing;>   *well-wishers*
Yef> him good life and good ending,   *give*
That we with merth mowe savely> sing   *may confidently*
'Deo gracias.'

1415

The Agincourt Carol Henry V's victory at Agincourt on October 25, 1415, must indeed have seemed something to be grateful to God for. After taking Harfleur he was in difficulties and the French could have starved him into submission. They chose to fight, with a force many times Henry's. Unusual quantities of rain had made the ground a morass: the French chose to use armored knights on horseback. The English archers, unarmored and on foot, shot and cut them down, losing only 100 killed plus 13 men-at-arms. The French lost 5000 nobles killed and 1000 taken prisoner. There is a legend that Henry, returning to England, was greeted by crowds who shouted his praises for the victory: he stopped them, saying that thanks for it were owed solely to God.

Deo . . . victoria England, give thanks to God for victory; see the Headnote and also "Adam Lay Ybounden" below

With . . . chivalry with God on his side and strength of knights

Domesday the Day of (general) Judgment, the end of the world (Fig. 50)

He . . . most he neither spared nor feared the least nor the greatest

Bring Us In Good Ale°

Bring us in good ale, and bring us in good ale!
For our blessed Lady's sake, bring us in good ale!

Bring us in no brown bread, for that is made of bran.°
Nor bring us in no white bread, for therein is no game,> *pleasure*
  But bring us in good ale!

Bring us in no beef, for there is many bones,
But bring us in good ale, for that goth down at ones,> *once*
  And bring us in good ale!

Bring us in no bacon, for that is passing> fat, *very*
But bring us in good ale, and give us enough of that,
  And bring us in good ale!

Bring us in no mutton, for that is often lean,
Nor bring us in no tripes, for they be seldom clean,
  But bring us in good ale!

Bring us in no eggs, for there are many shells,
But bring us in good ale, and give us nothing else,
  And bring us in good ale!

Bring us in no butter, for therein are many hores,> *hairs*
Nor bring us in no pigs' flesh, for that will make us boars,
  But bring us in good ale!

Bring us in no capons' flesh, for that is often dear,
Nor bring us in no ducks' flesh, for they slobber in the mere,
  But bring us in good ale!

15th century

I Have Set My Heart So High

I have set my hert so hye,
  Me liketh no love that lowere is;°
And alle the paines that I may drye,> *endure*
  Me think it do me good, ywis.°

For on that Lorde that loved us alle
  So hertėly> have I set my thought, *devotedly*
It is my joye on Him to calle:
  For love me hath in balės brought,°
  Me think it do me good, ywis.

c. 1380

Bring . . . Ale both a carol and a drinking song, defining by negatives
bran powdered wheat husk
Me . . . lowere is that no love inferior to this satisfies me
Me . . . ywis it seems to me that they do me good, indeed
For . . . brought since love has brought me to torments

All Too Late°

When mine eynen> misteth — *eyes*
And mine eren sisseth> — *ears sing*
And my nose coldeth
And my tunge foldeth> — *tongue fails*
And my rude> slaketh — *ruddiness*
And mine lippes blaketh°
And my mouth grenneth> — *gapes*
And my spotel renneth> — *spittle runs*
And myn her riseth> — *hair stands on end*
And myn herte griseth> — *heart quakes*
And mine handen bivieth> — *hands tremble*
And mine feet stivieth>— — *stiffen*
Al too late, al too late,
Whenne the bere> is at the gate! — *bier*
Thenne I shal flit> — *must go*
From bedde to flore,
From flore to here,°
From here to bere,
From bere to pit,> — *grave*
And the pit fordit.> — *will be closed*
Thenne lith myn hous uppe myn nese;
Of al this world ne give ich a pese!°
c. 1275

Divine Love°

Christ made to man a fair presènt,
His bloody body with love ybrent;> — *afire*
That blisful body His lif hath lent> — *given*
For love of man whom sinne hath blent.> — *blinded*
O love, love, what hast thou ment?
Me thinketh> that love to wrathe is went.> — *it seems / turned*
Thy lovėliche> handes love hath to-rent,> — *lovely / torn to pieces*
And thy lithe> armes wel streite ytent;° — *gentle*
Thy brest is bare, thy body is bent,
For wrong hath wonne and right is shent.> — *destroyed*

Thy mildė> bones love hath to-drawe,> — *gentle / dragged apart*
Thy nailes, thy feet been al to-gnawe.> — *consumed*

All Too Late Such catalogues of the signs of death are found in late classical and medieval Latin (one is ascribed to St. Jerome) and other European languages, including Old English. Cf. Falstaff's death, in Shakespeare's *Henry V*. Here the signs are turned into a little *contemptus mundi* poem.
my rude . . . blaketh my complexion fades and my lips grow pale
here shroud of hair-cloth; common and rough, with a hint of torment to come
Thenne . . . pese When my house (i.e. the grave) presses upon my face (literally, nose), I shall not give a pea for this world.
Divine Love This poem takes the form of a meditation on the Passion, the Five Wounds, and the Love of Christ.
wel . . . ytent very cruelly pulled apart

The Lord of love love hath now slawe°—
When love is strong, love hath no lawe.

His herte is rent, His body is bent,
  Upon the roodė-tree;> *cross-tree*
Wrong is went,> the Devil is shent,> *departed / destroyed*
  Christ, thorugh> the might of thee. *through*

For thee that herte is laid> to wedde. *pledged*
Swich was the love that herte us kedde,> *showed*
That hertė brast,> that hertė bledde, *burst*
That hertė-blood oure soulės fedde.

That herte He yaf> for treuthe° of love; *gave*
Therfore in Him one> is trewe love. *alone*
For love of thee that herte is yove;> *given*
Keep thou that herte, and thou art above.> *victorious*

Love, love, wher shalt thou wone?> *live*
Thy woning-sted is thee binome.°
For Christės herte, that was thyn home;
He is ded, now hast thou none.

Love, love, why dost thou so?
Love, thou brekest myn herte a-two.

Love hath shewed his gretė might,
For love hath made of day the night;
Love hath slawe the King of right,
And love hath ended the strongė fight.

So muchel love was nevere non;°
That witeth> ful wel Marìe and John,° *know*
And also witeth they everichon> *all those*
That love with Him hath made at on.> *brought together*

Love maketh, Christ, thyn hertė myn:> *mine*
So maketh love myn hertė thyn.
Thenne shal my love be trewe and fyn,
And love in love shal makė fyn.> *an end*

c. 1375

I Sing of a Maiden

I sing of a maiden
  That is makėles;> *matchless*
King of alle kingės

Lord . . . slawe love has now slain the King of Love
treuthe a pun on "truth"; faith, pledge, truth
Thy . . . binome Thy dwelling-place (i.e. Christ) is taken from thee.
So . . . non There was never such great love; John 15:13: "Greater love hath no man than this . . ."
Marie and John Christ's mother and (by tradition) the beloved disciple, to whom Christ entrusted his mother at the foot of the Cross (John 19:26) (Fig. 52).

To her son she ches.> *chose*
He cam also stille> *as silently*
Ther> His moder> was, *where / mother*
As dew in Aprille
That falleth on the gras.
He cam also stille
To His moderes bowr,°
As dew in Aprille
That falleth on the flowr.
He cam also stille
Ther His moder lay,
As dew in Aprille
That falleth on the spray.
Moder and maiden
Was never none but she;
Wel may swich> a lady *such*
Godės moder be.

15th century?

Adam Lay Ybounden°

Adam lay ybounden,> *bound*
Bounden in a bond;
Four thousand winter°
Thought> him not to long; *seemed to*
And al was for an appel,°
An appel that he took,
As clerkės> finden writen *learned men*
In her> book. *their*

Ne hadde the appel takė> been, *taken*
The appel takė been,
Ne hadde never our Lady
A> been hevenė-queen.° *have*
Blessėd be the time
That appel takė was!
Therfore we moun> singen *may*
'Deo Gracias!'°

15th century

bowr bower, room; thus, womb
Adam Lay Ybounden This famous carol on the Annunciation, in honor of the Virgin, carries the notion of Adam's fall (Fig. 56) as *felix culpa* ("happy fault") back one generation, from Christ, the Redeemer of the fault, to his Mother, who conceived him without sin and was crowned by him Queen of Heaven.
Four . . . winter Adam's bondage in Limbo, expiating his great sin by exclusion from the full beatific vision, was often so computed. Enduring without complaint for that time, he was liberated by Christ in the Harrowing of Hell. (Fig. 7)
appel The forbidden fruit was identified as an apple by the 4th century A.D., because of the useful pun *malum*/evil: *malum*/apple. The Vulgate has *pomum:* fruit.
hevene-queen Queen of Heaven. The coronation of the Virgin was becoming more and more popular at this time in literature and art.
Deo Gracias "Thanks be to God": liturgical formula used in the mass after the Epistle and the last Gospel, in which the good tidings of salvation are given to the people

Corpus Christi Carol°

Lully, lulley; lully, lulley;
The fawcon˃ hath born my mak˃ away. *falcon / mate*

He bare him up, he bare him down;
He bare him into an orchard brown.

In that orchard there was an hall,
That was hangėd with purpel and pall.°

And in that hall there was a bed;°
It was hangėd with gold so red.

And in that bed there lieth a knight,°
His woundės bleeding day and night.

By that bedes side there kneeleth a may,°
And she weepeth both night and day.

And by that bedes side there standeth a ston,°
'Corpus Christi'° writen theron.

15th century

POPULAR BALLADS

Ballads are short, anonymous, narrative poems, preserved by oral transmission and sung, often with accompaniment and dance, before gatherings of people. They exist in all nations. Some ballad themes and stories pass freely from one culture to another and from language to language over many centuries, their words and characters altered to fit the new context. Some are passed on with very little change. Their subject is usually tragic, death by accident or by treachery in love or in war, often with supernatural accompaniments, being the most frequent. Motif and incident may be taken from a folklore tradition stretching back many centuries, or from a comparatively recent historical occurrence. Since ballads were passed on by word of mouth, they exist in many versions even within one language and are sung to more than one tune. But since ballad meter is so simple, a single tune will do duty for many

Corpus Christi Carol There is much dispute over the interpretation of this carol. Some think it refers to the stealing away of Henry VIII's affections from his first wife, Catherine of Aragon, by his second, Anne Boleyn, whose badge was a white falcon—but then why should the falcon bear her Henry to the place where the abandoned first wife is weeping before the sacrament (ll. 11–12)? Others make it refer to the Grail, the paten of the Last Supper, said to have been brought by Joseph of Arimathea to Avalon, Isle of Apples (Glastonbury, in Somerset, ll. 3–4), so that the hall would be the Castle of the Keeper of the Grail, the wounded knight of l. 9. Or it may be that the poem is "about" the Eucharist, and the orchard is the church, the hall the aumbry or cupboard in which the body of Christ lies, and the "may" or maiden the Virgin Mary. The poem may be even more closely connected with the sacrifice of Christ in that the "hall" may be an Easter sepulcher, in which the Eucharist was laid on Good Friday to be raised again on Easter Day. Whatever the precise nature of the symbolic meaning, the poem succeeds superbly as poem and mystery. Cf. the ballad "The Three Ravens."

purpel and pall rich purple fabric

bed either the couch of the wounded Keeper of the Grail or the altar of the mass, on which the body of Christ is offered in re-enactment of his sacrifice

knight either the Keeper of the Grail, or Christ, present in the eucharist

may either the maid who serves the Grail, or the Virgin Mary

ston the stone may be the paten of the eucharist, a symbol of the stone at the entrance to Christ's sepulcher

Corpus Christi "Body of Christ"

ballads. (We have a more sophisticated parallel in the case of hymns, where the rhythm is also simple: the same words are sung to many tunes, and the same tune is used for many hymns.) Basically, ballad meter is the Western norm for the simple melodic phrase, four primary beats to the line. The lines are usually arranged in quatrains, i.e. groups of four lines.

The simplicity of ballad form implies a simplicity of language and of syntax, as well as an economy of expression. Few ballads are longer than a page or two of print, and those that exceed this limit are generally historical narratives with a simple story-line. Since they were intended to be understood by an audience that would hear them only once and since they were performed by a single singer, they could not make use of the sophisticated imagery and complicated sentence structure of the written lyric. The ballads operate with "and" clauses, not "though" or "if" clauses, with successive statements, not with statement followed by qualifications. Their imagery, even where it seems not fully articulate and is difficult to interpret fully, is simple and direct.

The popular ballad is essentially a primitive art form, composed and transmitted in a society such as that of the Scottish Border counties between the later Middle Ages and the early nineteenth century. These societies are made up of small, self-contained local units, relatively unmixed and homogeneous; their outlook is limited to their own locality and their own past; and they value ballad-makers both as story-tellers and as news-vendors. Naturally, the demands of this audience influenced ballad composers, and its criticisms of a performance influenced the singers. Earlier theories of the origin of the popular ballad gave the audience a much greater role than this and saw the ballads as the corporate poetic expression of the folk, the cooperative productions of a whole community, related to the chorus songs and dances which accompany primitive work and play. This idea is not now widely accepted: it originated in late eighteenth-century Germany at a time when the ballads were beginning to be collected, studied, and imitated.

Modern study has shown the importance of the bard, the singer of tales, in primitive societies and the privileged position he often occupies in them, even where he has some other trade or duty. Each performance that he gives of a ballad, old or new, is a unit in itself and may include variations. He is the chief, but not the only, hander-on of the ballads to other executants. The handing-on may be lateral, across a society or societies; or vertical and chronological, through successive generations in the same community or family. These considerations explain both the existence of many variants of a single ballad and the often surprising consistency in those variants. As in all orally transmitted literature, differences between variants may be the result of conscious manipulation to fit the ballad to new circumstances or a different audience—of children, perhaps, rather than adults (as in some of the versions of "Lord Randal"), or an audience drawn from another community on whom the allusions would be lost, or which is more sophisticated in its tastes. Or they may be accidental, the result of over- or under-sophistication in the transmitter, of failure of understanding or memory, or even of simple mishearing.

A good number of the ballads that we now possess were not written down until the eighteenth century or even later, and when they were recorded in this way, they were recorded in a composite of the forms in which they were then being recited. In consequence, it is not possible to decide, of many of them, what the original version would have looked liked, or when it was composed. All we can say is that most were composed at some time between 1200 and 1700, though some are later than that. The earliest references in other literature to ballads belong to the later fourteenth century: Langland, in *Piers Plowman,* has a slighting remark about the Robin Hood ballads. Of some, we have sixteenth-century versions; others, such as "The Carpenter's Wife" ("The Demon Lover") we know from mid-seventeenth-century printed broadsides; others again, like "The Three Ravens," are found in early seventeenth-century printed collections; yet others in manuscript poetical miscellanies of the same century. Of some, such as "Sir Patrick Spence," we have no version before the eighteenth century, or the mid-nineteenth ("The Unquiet Grave"), so that we cannot be quite sure that we are not dealing with a modern poem masquerading as an old ballad.

That we know them at all is due to eighteenth-century antiquarian scholarship, with its interest in origins and in the romantic past of one's own people. It is also due to the rise, during the eighteenth and nineteenth centuries, of the primitive and "natural" as a valued literary mode. Sir Philip Sidney, in the *Defence of Poesie* (1595), felt it necessary to apologize for his barbarousness in finding himself moved by the ballad of "Chevy Chase." Joseph Addison, in 1711, finds ballad verse despicably simple, but the sentiment moving because genuine and unaffected. As the eighteenth century goes on, the distinction between natural and artificial poetry is more and more used to favor the natural. The publication, in 1765, of Bishop Thomas Percy's *Reliques of Ancient English Poetry,* its texts largely drawn from a manuscript of about 1650, marks the beginning of modern ballad study and ballad collection. Percy's example inspired others, in Germany as well as in England (the communal theory of ballad composition mentioned above was developed by German scholars on the basis of their reading of Percy's collection). But the most important result of his publication was the new impetus it gave to ballad collecting in the North, notably to Sir Walter Scott, whose *Minstrelsy of the Scottish Border,* published in 1802–3, incorporated the results of ten years' work taking down ballads from the lips of the ballad singers themselves. Like all his contemporaries, Scott emended and improved these versions: his aim was to construct one coherent poem from the variants.

In this he was moved by practical considerations as well as by his interest in the ballads as records of older beliefs and superstitions and of past events—as can be seen from the use he made of their material and their prosody in his own poems. It was Scott who set the pattern for the nineteenth-century ballad of romantic chivalry and love.

By the time Scott published his *Minstrelsy* the ballad had already been accepted in England and Germany as a new literary model for the short poem of tragic love, of rustic life, of childhood, or of any combination of these, together with the poem of "faerie" and the supernatural. The simplicity of language and prosody could reflect the directness and purity of the emotions involved, whether war-like, loving, gentle or pathetic; or it could reflect the directness of the relationship between the natural and the supernatural worlds. The *Lyrical Ballads* of Wordsworth and Coleridge share an influence from this direction with the poems based on ballad meter written by such poets as Thomas Chatterton, William Blake, and Robert Burns. The literary ballad further evolved in the nineteenth century in the hands of writers as different as Thomas Moore, Dante Gabriel Rossetti, and Algernon Charles Swinburne. Later still, the ballad influences the poetry of Rudyard Kipling, A. E. Housman, and W. B. Yeats.

Most of the texts selected here are tragic in tone. Many give the feeling of suspension between natural and supernatural, and the sensation that one has been plunged, without preparation, into the middle of the action, which are hallmarks of the ballad. In many, the quality of dramatic performance that also goes with ballads is to be seen. (It has been said that reading a ballad is like going to the theater when the play has already reached its fifth act.) A tune is given for most, since the ballad can barely be said to exist without its tune, which shapes and controls it in important ways. The tune also enhances the impression of performance, of a single act performed with variations, which is essential to our understanding of this form of poetry. The same effect of performance, almost of rite, is aided, in many of the ballads, by the repeated refrain or burden. In some ballads this consists of nonsense, incantatory words or syllables.

The first ballad below, "The Cherry-tree Carol," has a biblical theme, handled with great tenderness and delicacy. It might equally well have been put among the religious lyrics above, but is included here because of its meter and as a specimen of the overtly sacred ballad. The next five are "faerie" ballads, involving supernatural beings and feats, forfeits, riddles, changings of shape, the returning dead, with overtones of tragic love. Only the first of them—and the ballad of Thomas the Rhymer, for which see The Other World section below—suggest that an encounter with the supernatural can breed anything but ill. The next two ("Lord Randal" and "The Three Ravens") are also grim in tone, with echoes of violence and perhaps of Border feuds. The single Robin Hood ballad gives an adequate impression of the not very high poetic quality, the simplicity, and low intensity of this large class. The final ballad, "Sir Patrick Spence," is possibly based on historical incidents.

The standard collection of ballads is still F. J. Child's monumental five-volume *The English and Scottish Ballads* (1882–98), now supplemented by B. H. Bronson's four volumes of *The Traditional Tunes of the Child Ballads* (1959–70). Child succeeded in assembling all the significant versions of each ballad then known: references to his numberings are given in the footnotes. The versions and tunes used here are, with modifications, those of *The Oxford Book of Ballads* (ed. J. Kinsley, 1969). Some spellings and capitalization have been normalized, but Northern forms have been retained where they occur.

The Cherry-tree Carol°

Joseph was an old man,
  And an old man was he,
When he wedded Mary
  In the land of Galilee.

Joseph and Mary walked
  Through an orchard good,
Where was cherries and berries
  So red as any blood.

Joseph and Mary walked
  Through an orchard green,
Where was berries and cherries
  As thick as might be seen.

O then bespoke˃ Mary *spoke*
  So meek and so mild:°
'Pluck me one cherry, Joseph,
  For I am with child.'

O then bespoke Joseph
  With words most unkind:
'Let him pluck thee a cherry
  That brought˃ thee with child.' *got*

O then bespoke the Babe
  Within his Mother's womb:
'Bow down then the tallest tree
  For my Mother to have some.'

Then bowed down the highest tree
  Unto his Mother's hand;
Then she cried, 'See, Joseph,
  I have cherries at command.'

O then bespake Joseph:
  'I have done Mary wrong;

The Cherry-tree Carol Child, no. 54. Air: William Sandys, *Christmas Carols . . .*, 1833. This carol in ballad meter, of uncertain date, is a version of one of the miracles (Fig. 53) told in the apocryphal *Gospel of Pseudo-Matthew*, chapter 20, perhaps 2nd or 3rd century A.D., which is chiefly concerned with the infancy of Christ. There were several such apocryphal Gospels, popularly believed during the Middle Ages to be as authentic and authoritative as the canonical ones. They have much influence on literature and art. In the mystery plays, Joseph's suspicions of Mary are treated as comedy, but in lyrics of that period they are not.
So . . . mild alliterative oral formula: Mary's usual attributes

But cheer up, my dearest,
  And be not cast down.'

Then Mary plucked a cherry
  As red as the blood,°
Then Mary went home
  With her heavy load.

Then Mary took her Babe°
  And sat him on her knee,
Saying, 'My dear Son, tell me
  What this world will be.'

'O I shall be as dead, Mother,
  As the stones in the wall;
O the stones in the streets, Mother,
  Shall mourn for me all.

Upon Easter-day, Mother,
  My uprising shall be;
O the sun and the moon,° Mother,
  Shall both rise with me.'

The Wee Wee Man°

As I was walking all alane
  Between a water and a wa';> *wall*
And there I spied a wee wee man
  And he was the least> that ere I saw. *smallest*

blood The mood changes. The blood-red cherry symbolizes the blood of Christ, the Passion for which he was born, and the Redemption.
Babe The ballad narrative compresses the time scheme, and the poem gathers speed as it approaches the climax of Christ's death and resurrection.
sun . . . moon Isaiah 30:26
The Wee Wee Man Child, no. 38. Air: J. Johnson, *The Scots Musical Museum* (1787 f.). A "faerie" ballad, first collected in the 18th century, with similarities to "Thomas the Rhymer" (see below).

His legs were scarce a shathmont's° length
And thick and thimber˃ was his thigh, — *heavy*
Between his brows there was a span°
And between his shoulders there was three.

He took up a meikle˃ stane — *big*
And he flang 't as far as I could see;
Tho I had been as Wallace wight°
I couldna liften˃ it to my knee. — *have lifted*

'O wee wee man but thou be strong,
O tell me whare thy dwelling be';
'My dwelling's down at yon bonny bower
O will you go with me and see?'

On we lap˃ and awa we rade˃ — *leapt / rode*
Till we came to yon bonny green;°
We lighted˃ down for to bait° our horse — *dismounted*
And out there came a lady fine;

Four and twenty at her back
And they were a'˃ clad out in green; — *all*
Tho the King of Scotland had been there
The warst o' them might hae˃ been his Queen. — *have*

On we lap and awa we rade
Till we cam to yon bonny ha'˃ — *hall*
Whare the roof was o' the beaten gold
And the floor was o' the cristal a'.˃ — *all*

When we came to the stair foot
Ladies were dancing jimp˃ and sma',˃ — *graceful / slender*
But in the twinkling of an eye
My wee wee man was clean awa'.

The Two Magicians°

The lady stands in her bower˃ door — *boudoir*
As straight as willow wand;˃ — *twig*
The blacksmith° stood a little foreby˃ — *aside*
Wi' hammer in his hand.

shathmont's a measurement, about 6 inches, from the tip of the outstretched thumb across the palm of the hand
span the extended hand, from outstretched thumb to outstretched little finger, about 9 inches
as Wallace wight as strong as Sir William Wallace (*c.* 1207–1305), the Scottish national hero, outlaw, and rebel against the English
green fairy place and fairy color
bait feed and rest a horse
The Two Magicians Child, no. 44. There are two texts, one Scottish, the version above, and one weaker English. The ballad exists in many other European languages, particularly French. This transformation contest is cousin to the riddling-contest ballad. Two opponents match transformations, or question and answer, in order to gain or avoid gaining a mate, who may also be the opponent in the contest. The changing of shape to win or avoid something has parallels in all mythologies.
blacksmith a trade renowned in folklore for lechery, potency, and lack of attractiveness

'Weel may ye dress ye, lady fair,
  Into your robes o' red;
Before the morn at this same time
  I'll gain your maidenhead.'

'Awa', awa', ye coal-black smith,
  Would ye do me the wrang
To think to gain my maidenhead
  That I hae˃ kept sae˃ lang?'   *have / so*

Then she has hadden˃ up her hand   *held*
  And she sware by the mold:˃   *earth*
'I wu'dna˃ be a blacksmith's wife   *would not*
  For the full˃ o' a chest o' gold.   *whole*

I'd rather I were dead and gone
  And my body laid in grave,
Ere a rusty stock° o' coal-black smith
  My maidenhead should have.'

But he has hadden up his hand
  And he sware by the mass;
'I'll cause ye be my light leman˃   *wanton lover*
  For the hauf˃ o' that and less.'   *half*

    'O bide,° lady, bide,
      And aye˃ he bade her bide: *always*
    The rusty smith your leman shall be
      For a'˃ your muckle˃ pride.'   *all / great*

Then she became a turtle dove
  To fly up in the air,
And he became another dove
  And they flew pair and pair.°
    'O bide, lady, bide, &c.'

She turned hersell˃ into an eel   *herself*
  To swim into yon burn,˃   *brook*
And he became a speckled trout
  To gie the eel a turn.
    'O bide, lady, bide, &c.'

Then she became a duck, a duck,
  To puddle in a peel,˃   *pool*
And he became a rose-kaim'd˃ drake   *red-combed*
  To gie the duck a dreel.˃   *doing over*
    'O bide, lady, bide, &c.'

rusty stock i.e. churlish, stupid oaf; or "rusty" may be literally rust-smeared

O bide . . . The burden, or refrain, appears every sixth stanza: "Stay, lady, stay."

pair and pair together, two by two

She turned hersell into a hare
  To rin˃ upon yon hill, *run*
And he became a gude˃ greyhound *good*
  And boldly he did fill.°
    'O bide, lady, bide, &c.'

Then she became a gay grey mare
  And stood in yonder slack,˃ *hollow*
And he became a gilt saddle
  And sat upon her back.
    Was she wae,° he held her sae,
      And still˃ he bade her bide: *always*
    The rusty smith her leman was
      For a' her muckle pride.

Then she became a het girdle˃ *hot griddle*
  And he became a cake,
And a' the ways she turned hersell
  The blacksmith was her make.°
    Was she wae, &c.

She turned hersell into a ship
  To sail out ower˃ the flood, *over*
He ca'd a nail intill her tail°
  And syne˃ the ship she stood. *then*
    Was she wae, &c.

Then she became a silken plaid˃ *coverlet*
  And stretched upon a bed,
And he became a green° covering
  And gained her maidenhead.
    Was she wae, &c.

fill fulfil, perform
Was she wae Woe was her; she was woeful. Holding fast, no matter what the transformations, was the way to win such a contest.

make mate or match; the pun is probably intended
He . . . tail he called (i.e. drove) a nail into her stern
green the color of nature and love

The Carpenter's Wife°
[The Demon Lover]

'O whare hae˃ ya been, my dearest dear, *where have*
These seven lang years and more?'
'O I am come to seek my former vows
That ye promised me before.'

'Awa wi'˃ your former vows,' she says, *away with*
'Or else ye will breed strife:
Awa wi' your former vows,' she says,
'For I'm become a wife.

I am married to a ship-carpenter,
A ship-carpenter he's bound;˃ *engaged*
I wadna° he kend˃ my mind this nicht˃ *knew / night*
For twice five hundred pound.'

'I have seven ships upon the sea
Laden with the finest gold,
And mariners to wait us upon;
All these you may behold.

And I have shoes for my love's feet
Beaten of the purest gold,
And lined wi' the velvet soft
To keep my love's feet from the cold.'

She has put her foot on gude˃ ship-board, *good*
And on shipboard she's gane,˃ *gone*
And the veil that hung oure˃ her face *over*
Was a' wi' gowd begane.˃ *gold overlaid*

'O how do you love the ship,' he said,
'Or how do you love the sea?
And how do you love the bold mariners
That wait upon thee and me?'

The Carpenter's Wife Child, no. 243. Air: William Motherwell, *Minstrelsy, Ancient and Modern* (1827). Also called "The House Carpenter." Over 145 versions have been collected. First known in English Restoration broadsides, one version is entitled: "A warning for married women, being an example of Mrs. Jane Reynolds (a West-country woman), born near Plymouth, who, having plighted her troth to a seaman, was afterwards married to a carpenter, and at last carried away by a spirit, the manner how shall presently be recited. To a West-country tune called 'The Fair Maid of Bristol,' 'Bateman' or 'John Tone'."
wadna would not wish

'O I do love the ship,' she said,
'And I do love the sea;
But woe be to the dim mariners
That nowhere I can see!'

She had na> sailed a league, a league, *not*
A league but barely twa,> *two*
Till she did mind on> the husband she left *remember*
And her wee young son alsua.> *also*

'O haud> your tongue, my dearest dear, *hold*
Let all your follies abee;> *abide*
I'll show whare> the white lilies grow *where*
On the banks of Italie.'°

She had na sailed a league, a league,
A league but barely three,
Till grim, grim grew his countenance
And gurly> grew the sea. *stormy*

'O haud your tongue, my dearest dear,
Let all your follies abee;
I'll show whare the white lilies grow
In the bottom of the sea.'

He's tane> her by the milk-white hand *taken*
And he's thrown her in the main;
And full five and twenty hundred ships
Perished all on the coast of Spain.

The Wife of Usher's Well°

There lived a wife> at Usher's Well *woman*
And a wealthy wife was she;
She had three stout and stalwart sons
And sent them o'er the sea.

They hadna> been a week from her, *had not*
A week but barely ane,> *one*

Italie i.e. a fair country, far away
The Wife . . . Well Child, no. 79; Air: Scott, *Minstrelsy;* a widespread ballad and tune in the modern Appalachians

When word came to the carline wife°
That her three sons were gane.˃ *lost*

They hadna been a week from her,
A week but barely three,
Whan word came to the carline wife
That her sons she'd never see.

'I wish the wind may never cease,
Nor fishes° in the flood,
Till my three sons come hame to me
In earthly flesh and blood.'

It fell about the Martinmas°
Whan nights are lang and mirk,˃ *dark*
The carline wife's three sons came hame
And their hats were of the birk.˃ *birch*

It neither grew in syke˃ nor ditch *stream*
Nor yet in ony sheugh,°
But at the gates o' Paradise
That birk grew fair eneugh.˃ *very*

'Blow up the fire, my maidens,
Bring water from the well;
For all my house shall feast this night
Since my three sons are well.'

And she has made to them a bed,
She's made it large and wide,
And she's ta'en her mantle her about,
Sat down at the bed-side.

Up then crew° the red, red cock
And up and crew the grey;
The eldest to the youngest said,
' 'Tis time we were away.'

The cock he hadna crawed but once
And clapp'd his wings at a'
Whan the youngest to the eldest said,
'Brother, we must awa'.

The cock doth craw, the day doth daw,˃ *dawn*
The channering worm doth chide;°
Gin˃ we be mist out of our place *if*
A sair pain we maun bide.°

carline wife old woman, witch
fishes perhaps a corrupt reading
Martinmas Feast of St. Martin, November 11, not long after All Hallows Eve; the beginning of winter, a dark, bloody time, when cattle and hogs were slaughtered for winter food
sheugh trench, ditch, or furrow; thus, ground
crew The dead could not be abroad after first cockcrow.
The . . . chide the grumbling worm chides us; i.e. calls us back to the grave
A . . . bide a harsh torture we must endure

Fare ye weel, my mother dear;
Fareweel to barn and byre,˃ *cow-barn*
And fare ye weel, the bonny lass
That kindles my mother's fire.'

The Unquiet Grave°

The wind doth blow today, my love,
And a few small drops of rain;
I never had but one true-love,
In cold grave she was lain.

I'll do as much for my true-love
As any young man may:
I'll sit and mourn all at her grave
For a twelvemonth and a day.

The twelvemonth and a day being up
The dead began to speak:
'Oh who sits weeping on my grave°
And will not let me sleep?'

''Tis I, my love, sits on your grave
And will not let you sleep;
For I crave one kiss of your clay-cold lips
And that is all I seek.'

'You crave one kiss of my clay-cold lips,
But my breath smells earthy strong;
If you have one kiss of my clay-cold lips
Your time will not be long.

'Tis down in yonder garden green,
Love, where we used to walk,
The finest flower that ere was seen
Is withered to a stalk.

The Unquiet Grave Child, no. 78. Air: C. J. Sharp, *English Folk-Songs* . . . (1907). First published, 1868. The lateness of this ballad may be suspicious: it was current in oral tradition in Sussex in the mid-19th century. Its first lines are similar to a 15th-century carol, to which it may be related; and it exists in well over 40 versions.

Oh . . . grave It is both an Oriental and a Western superstition that after a certain time mourning disturbs the dead, and brings them out to claim the disturber.

The stalk is withered dry, my love,
So will our hearts decay;
So make yourself content, my love,
Till God calls you away.'

Lord Randal°

'O where ha' you been, Lord Randal my son?
And where ha' you been, my handsome young man?'
'I ha' been at the greenwood; mother, make my bed soon,
For I'm wearied wi' hunting and fain wad° lie down.' *gladly would*

'An' wha° met ye there, Lord Randal my son? *who*
An' wha met you there, my handsome young man?'
'O I met wi' my true-love; mother, make my bed soon,
For I'm wearied wi' huntin' an' fain wad lie down.'

'And what did she give you, Lord Randal my son?
And what did she give you, my handsome young man?'
'Eels fried in a pan; mother, make my bed soon,
For I'm wearied wi' huntin' and fain wad lie down.'

'And wha gat your leavins,° Lord Randal my son? *leavings*
And wha gat your leavins, my handsome young man?'
'My hawks and my hounds; mother, make my bed soon,
For I'm wearied wi' hunting and fain wad lie down.'

'And what becam of them, Lord Randal my son?
And what becam of them, my handsome young man?'

Lord Randal Child, no. 12. Air: J. Johnson, *Scots Musical Museum* (1787 f.). This famous ballad has analogues in both Italian and German, which survive in forms older than the English. The young man is sometimes poisoned by his false true love and sometimes by his wicked step-mother, as in the popular fairy-tales. There may be a connection with Ranulf, Earl of Chester (d. 1232), whose heir's wife was supposed to have poisoned her husband. The English version cannot be traced back farther than the late 18th century; the Italian is at least a century older. The form of this ballad varies less than most in its various versions; each stanza is divided equally between question and answer, with the second line of the answer used as a refrain.

'They stretched their legs out an' died; mother, make my bed soon,
For I'm wearied wi' huntin' and fain wad lie down.'

'O I fear you are poisoned, Lord Randal my son,°
I fear you are poisoned, my handsome young man.'
'O yes, I am poisoned; mother, make my bed soon,
For I'm sick at the heart and fain wad lie down.'

'What d'ye leave to your mother, Lord Randal my son?
What d'ye leave to your mother, my handsome young man?'
'Four and twenty milk kye;˃ mother, make my bed soon, *cows*
For I'm sick at the heart and fain wad lie down.'

'What d'ye leave to your sister, Lord Randal my son?
What d'ye leave to your sister, my handsome young man?'
'My gold and my silver; mother, make my bed soon,
For I'm sick at the heart an' fain wad lie down.'

'What d'ye leave to your brother, Lord Randal my son?
What d'ye leave to your brother, my handsome young man?'
'My houses and my lands; mother, make my bed soon,
For I'm sick at the heart and fain wad lie down.'

'What d'ye leave to your true-love, Lord Randal my son?
What d'ye leave to your true-love, my handsome young man?'
'I leave her hell and fire; mother, make my bed soon,
For I'm sick at the heart and fain wad lie down.'

The Three Ravens°

There were three ravens sat on a tree,
  Down a downe, hay down, hay downe,
There were three ravens sat on a tree,
  With a downe;

I . . . son The poem, beginning its second half, darkens, and the refrain changes from an expression of listlessness to a fear of coming death. **The Three Ravens** Child, no. 26. Air: Thomas Ravenscroft, *Melismata* . . . (1611). In this form, or as the grimmer "Twa Carbies" (Two Crows), very well known and widespread. It is also one of the earliest ballads we have, and this version may be the elaboration of an early popular poem by the addition of material similar to the "Corpus Christi Carol" (see above). Rhythm and refrain also suggest a carol or dance song.

There were three ravens sat on a tree,
They were as blacke as they might be,
With a downe derrie, derrie, derrie, downe, downe.

The one of them said to his make,> *mate*
Where shall we our breakfast take?

Downe in yonder greenė field
There lies a knight slain under his shield.

His hounds they lie downe at his feete,
So well they can> their master keepe. *do*

His hawkes they flie so eagerly> *fiercely*
There's no fowle> dare him come nie.> *bird / near*

Downe there comes a fallow doe°
As great with yong> as she might goe. *young*

She lift up his bloody hed
And kist his wounds that were so red.

She got him up upon her back
And carried him to earthen lake.°

She buried him before the prime,°
She was dead her selfe ere even-song° time.

God send every gentleman
Such hawkes, such hounds, and such a leman.> *lover*

The Birth of Robin Hood°

O Willie's large o' limb and lith> *joint*
And come o'> high degree, *of*
And he is gane> to Earl Richard° *gone*
To serve for meat> and fee. *food*

Earl Richard had but ae> daughter *one*
Fair as a lily flower;

doe The fallow deer was yellowish-brown in color and smaller than the red deer. Like the white doe of other ballads and of folklore, perhaps this creature is the knight's lover changed into a doe. Or she may be the Christian soul come for Christ, her bridegroom; or the knight may be the wounded Keeper of the Grail, the Maimed King of the Grail legend. There is surely some allusion to the daily sacrifice of Christ in the Mass.
earthen lake pit, cavity in the earth; i.e. grave
prime the first liturgical hour (6 a.m.), or any time between that and 9 a.m. (great prime)
even-song vespers, the evening office (6 p.m.), or dusk
The Birth . . . Hood Text after Robert Jamieson, *Popular Ballads and Songs from Tradition* (1806). One of many Robin Hood ballads, some of them very long and the nearest approach in ballad form to the long, heroic, folk tale in verse produced by "singers of tales," composers of oral epics. The earliest mentions of Robin Hood are in the ballads: Sloth, in *Piers Plowman*, says he knows "rhymes of Robin Hood and Randolf, Earl of Chester." Others are certainly of the 15th century. The stories of his activities are a form of indirect complaint and social criticism.
Earl Richard Robin's birth, of a yeoman and a noblewoman, accounts for his possessing all the best qualities of each class.

And they made up their love-contract
  Like proper paramour.°

It fell upon a simmer's nicht˃ — *summer's night*
  Whan the leaves were fair and green,
That Willie met his gay ladie
  Intil˃ the wood alane.˃ — *within / alone*

'O narrow is my gown, Willie,
  That wont to be sae˃ wide; — *so*
And gane is a'˃ my fair colour — *all*
  That wont˃ to be my pride. — *used*

But gin˃ my father should get word — *if*
  What's past between us twa,˃ — *two*
Before that he should eat or drink
  He'd hang you o'er that wa'.˃ — *wall*

But ye'll come to my bower,˃ Willie, — *room*
  Just as the sun gaes down;
And keep me in your arms twa
  And latna˃ me fa'˃ down.' — *let not / fall*

O whan the sun was now gane down
  He's doen him˃ till her bower; — *taken himself*
And there by the lee˃ licht o' the moon — *pale*
  Her window she lookit o'er.

Intill a robe o' red scarlet
  She lap,˃ fearless o' harm; — *hurried*
And Willie was large o' lith and limb
  And keppit˃ her in his arm. — *held*

And they've gane to the gude˃ greenwood; — *good*
  And ere the night was deen˃ — *done*
She's born to him a bonny young son
  Amang the leaves sae green.

Whan night was gane and day was come
  And the sun began to peep,
Up and raise the Earl Richard
  Out o' his drowsy sleep.

He's ca'd˃ upon his merry young men — *called*
  By ane,˃ by twa, and by three: — *by ones*
'O what's come˃ o' my daughter dear, — *become*
  That she's nae come to me?

I dreamt a dreary˃ dream last night— — *terrible*
  God grant it come to gude—

Like . . . paramour in accord with the canons of true courteous love

I dreamt I saw my daughter dear
  Drown in the saut> sea flood. *salt*

But gin my daughter be dead or sick,
  Or yet be stown awa,> *stolen away*
I make a vow, and I'll keep it true,
  I'll hang ye ane and a'.'

They sought her back, they sought her fore,
  They sought her up and down;
They got her in the gude greenwood
  Nursing her bonny young son.

He took the bonny boy in his arms
  And kist him tenderlie;
Says, 'Though I would your father hang,
  Your mother's dear to me.'

He kist him o'er and o'er again:
  'My grandson I thee claim;
And Robin Hood in gude greenwood,
  And that shall be your name.'

And mony ane sings o' grass, o' grass,
  And mony ane sings o' corn,
And mony ane sings o' Robin Hood
  Kens> little whare he was born. *knows*

It wasna> in the ha',> the ha' *was not / hall*
  Nor in the painted bower,
But it was in the gude greenwood
  Amang the lily flower.

Sir Patrick Spence°

The king sits in Dunferline° toune,> *town*
  Drinking the blude-reid> wine: *blood-red*
'O quhar> will I get a guid> sailor, *where / good*
  To sail this schip of mine?'

Up and spak an eldern> knicht, *old*
  Sat at the king's richt> knee *right*
'Sir Patrick Spence is the best sailor,
  That sails upon the see.'

The king has written a braid° letter,
  And signed it wi' his hand;
And sent it to Sir Patrick Spence,
  Was walking on the sand.

The first line that Sir Patrick red,
  A loud lauch> lauched he: *laugh*
The next line that Sir Patrick red,
  The teir> blinded his e'e.> *tear / eye*

'O quha> is this has don this deid,> *who / deed*
  This ill deid don to me;
To send me out this time o' the yeir,> *year*
  To sail upon the see?

Mak haste, mak haste, my mirry men all,
  Our guid schip sails the morne.'
'O say na sae,> my master deir,> *not so / dear*
  For I feir> a deadlie storme. *fear*

Late, late yestreen> I saw the new moone *last evening*
  Wi' the auld> moone in hir arme;° *old*
And I feir, I feir, my deir master,
  That we will com to harme.'

Sir Patrick Spence Child, no. 58. Air: Child, 1882. This famous and popular ballad (cf. the first line of Coleridge, "Dejection: An Ode") may be an 18th-century fabrication. It is not known earlier than Bishop Thomas Percy's *Reliques* (1765). Possibly, a historical event lies somewhere in the background: either the drowning of many Scots nobles in 1281, on their return voyage from escorting the Scottish king's daughter, Margaret, and her new husband, Eric of Norway, to their new house; or the death at sea of Margaret's daughter, the Maid of Norway, when she was being fetched home to be married, a few years later. But no Sir Patrick Spence is connected with either voyage.

Dunferline Dunfermline, royal borough north of the Firth of Forth, on the west coast of Scotland. The kings of Scotland formerly lived there.

braid broad, open; patent, a commission for all to see

Late . . . arme the waning moon: an evil portent

O our Scots nobles wer richt laith> *loath*
To weet> their cork-heil'd schoone;° *wet*
Bot lang owre a'> the play wer played, *ere all*
Thair hats they swam aboone.°

O lang, lang may thair ladies sit
Wi' thair fans into their hand,
Or eir> they se Sir Patrick Spence *before*
Com sailing to the land.

O lang, lang may the ladies stand
Wi' thair gold kems> in their hair, *combs*
Waiting for thair ain> deir lords, *own*
For they'll se thame> na mair.> *them / more*

Half owre,> haf owre to Aberdour,° *half-way over*
It's fiftie fadom° deip:> *deep*
And thair lies guid Sir Patrick Spence,
Wi' the Scots lords at his feit.> *feet*

SIR THOMAS MALORY
c. 1410–1471

What we know of Sir Thomas Malory the man, we know in essentials from his book—or books: that he was a knight, that he finished the work that we call *Morte Darthur* in prison in the ninth year of the reign of Edward IV, i.e. between March 1469 and March 1470. The details—where he was born and when, why and for how long he was in prison, when he began his career as a writer, when he died—have all to be established from other documents. We must infer that these relate to Malory the author; we cannot be certain. They add up to a character which, it seems to many, does not fit the man who wrote the first—and only—English version of the Arthurian chivalric stories which is both comprehensive in scope and great as literature.

Assuming that the knight of the documents and the knight-author of the book are the same, we can say that he was born in the early years of the fifteenth century, had estates in Warwickshire, served with the Earl of Warwick, and was Member of Parliament for Warwickshire, all before 1445. In 1443 he fell foul of the law and from 1450 onward he was either in prison or on the run from the authorities for escaping from custody (by swimming a moat), ambush with intent to murder, breaking into a man's house and raping his wife (this may mean, as it may in the case of Chaucer, that he merely carried her off against her will), cattle raiding, extortion, breaking into an abbey, assaulting the abbot and stealing property, jail-breaking with violence. Malory pleaded not guilty to them all, but we cannot know the exact truth either of the charges or the plea. The royal pardon he received in 1456 is no guarantee

schoone shoes; elegant shoes, not clogs, but pantofles
aboone either: they were floating head downward; or: their hats were floating on the surface
Aberdour on the north shore of the Firth of Forth, below Dunfermline
fadom fathoms, 6 feet each

of his innocence, especially as he was shortly afterward imprisoned again, remaining in jail for most of the next five or six years. The interval between this and his next imprisonment he seems to have passed in campaigning, first for the Yorkists and then for the Lancastrians. Some of this pattern of violence, crime, and shifting loyalties is probably the effect of the disturbed times of the Wars of the Roses (see Glossary) in which he had to survive. Some of his exploits may be less serious than the formal accusations make them appear. Nevertheless, the impression remains of an adventurous and unscrupulous opportunist nobleman, rash and sudden, who may have owed his neck to his knighthood and to the fact that he never, as far as we know, murdered anyone. He may well have died still a prisoner.

In 1468 Malory had been excluded from the amnesties granted to the Lancastrians by the Yorkist King Edward IV. It seems likely that he wrote most of his over twelve hundred large pages (in the modern edition) in prison, for there is a reference to his being a prisoner quite early on in the manuscript, and this would mean that he either composed or translated quickly, to finish it in a little over two years at most, or that he had begun it earlier.

Malory's romance is a glorification of chivalric values and of King Arthur, the British king, at one and the same time. We do not know what he himself called his book. The only manuscript, discovered in 1934, lacks its beginning and its end and is not Malory's autograph. In 1485, William Caxton, using another manuscript, edited the text rather freely, cutting some passages, rewriting others in what he thought a more suitable style, and adding chapter headings. Caxton gave it no title—many fifteenth-century printed books lack a title at their beginning—but he gave it a preface and a colophon (inscription at the end) in which he called it "the book of King Arthur and of his noble knights of the Round Table" *and* "this noble and joyous book entitled Le Morte Darthur." *Morte Darthur* it has remained. There is at present much dispute as to how far the effect of Caxton's editing was to make one book out of what Malory intended to be several, and how far the aims of author and publisher diverged from each other in other respects. It may be that Malory intended that any one of his major episodes could be read singly, but this would not mean that he did not intend the reader to begin at the first and read his way through to the end. There are repetitions and there are confusing inconsistencies in the chronological scheme, so that we are often in doubt about the time-relation of one event or stage in the story to another, but the episodes are related, not independent. The narrative often advances in parallels and overlaps, but it advances.

It may also be true that Caxton saw the chivalry of the *Morte Darthur* as more of a moral force, inciting men to practice its virtue and expect honor for them, than Malory, for whom the example of Arthur and his knights was something more political and practical, an example of a firmly ordered, well-ruled commonwealth under a strong king.

This practical intention behind the work goes well with the way he handles his story. He was, in the main, translating and adapting from the immensely long French cycles of Arthurian romance, which were built around an elaborate religious and doctrinal framework, glorifying the Holy Grail as the object of the knightly quest. These "French books," as Malory calls them, had spiritualized the earlier Lancelot-Grail stories by opposing to the earthly chivalry of the Round Table the perfections of divine love, as symbolized in the Grail, and of contempt for the world. Malory drops the French theology. For him the Round Table is something good in itself, not something less good in contrast to a divine ideal. Its shortcomings are human. In the end, being of the mortal world, it fails: Arthur, the image of the good king and of order, is killed by the forces of evil and disorder. But Arthur, in his own person or that of a later English king, will come again. The knights fail in oath and loyalty one by one—as in Lancelot's adultery with Guinevere and in his too-late arrival to help Arthur in the final battle. The moral dimensions of Malory's story are those of Sir Kay's claiming the throne in the first selection below; or poor Sir Bedivere, in the second, torn between his love for King Arthur, the loyalty he owes him, and his wish to have Arthur's rich sword Excalibur for himself. All of these things are culpable, and all are, in the end, condemned by Malory, but with no suggestion that all such worldly failings merely show the worthlessness of the world.

He also frequently tones down the magical and supernatural elements: the Lady of the Lake, instead of walking on the water without getting her feet wet, very sensibly uses a boat. Malory's attitude, even in chivalric adventure, is down-to-earth: at one famous point he makes it clear that Queen Guinevere knew that the search for Lancelot would be a costly matter and sent the knights who were to find him their expenses in advance. Malory's knights are not like the knights of romance satirized in the seventeenth century by Samuel Butler in *Hudibras:*

> Unless they grazed, there's not one word
> Of their provision on record,
> Which made some confidently write,
> They had no stomachs but to fight.

One must not, all the same, assume that Malory did not mean them to be exemplary or that he was not fired by the notion of knight-errantry, originally developed in France in the twelfth century. His deliberate rejection of the fairy-tale element in the French romances of Arthur and his knights makes him give the tales a greater reality and importance as *exempla.* The courteous and gentle knight will, he says, find favor in every place. He must never fight for fighting's sake; simply to show his strength like this is to be a bully. Sir Lancelot is described as the pattern (in earlier versions it had been Sir Gawain). In Malory, Lancelot is the most courteous, the truest of friends and of lovers among sinful men, the kindest man who ever gave a blow with his sword, the handsomest, the humblest and gentlest in company with men and women, the fiercest to his deadly enemy. King Arthur, too, is the true embodiment of heroic knighthood, the conqueror, the ruler of the Roman Empire, the ideal ruler: strong, wise, prudent, humane, generous, courteous.

Malory is recommending the example of Arthur to the English king, as well as recommending the example of Arthur's knights to English nobility. It is even possible that he was at times comparing the deeds of Arthur to those of Henry V, establishing a succession of greatness and asserting by implication England's succession to the position of Rome and the leadership of the world. The claim is already present in earlier versions of the Arthurian story and was to be made explicitly by the Tudor monarchs.

The historical Arthur may have been a British king who resisted the Anglo-Saxon invasions of the sixth century. Tradition made of him the ruler of all Europe, the English equivalent of Charlemagne, to whom the sovereignty of the Roman Empire had been transferred. Geoffrey of Monmouth gathered up these traditions in his *History of the Kings of Britain* (c. 1136), adding some of his own, so that the picture of Arthur and his court as a model of knightly society (Figs. 46–48) together with the plot of the Arthurian romances, was established. Later Arthurian romances depend upon Geoffrey, but their refinement into courtly stories, exalting the love of man for woman to the plane of the spiritual and establishing the ideal of knighthood as the performance of great deeds for its sake, was the work of French authors, such as Chrétien de Troyes, under the influence of the Provençal poets. Malory did not use these earlier French versions for his adaptation-translation. By his time, the Arthurian legends had been embodied in long prose cycles, and he had also at his disposal an English alliterative poem called *Morte Arthure.*

His technique was always, it seems, to "reduce," and this is generally taken to mean that he selected and compressed as well as translated. He keeps the order of the French "novels," with occasional additions and variations, but often destroys, perhaps deliberately, the elaborate system of cross-links and interconnections in the story. He cuts down the minor characters and subtleties of motive, and puts his story into an English which Caxton must have approved, composed of "the common terms that be daily used," fluent and quick, with a touch of archaic quality about it, straightforward but sensitive, balanced but not artificial, simple but not bare and low, almost spoken English, but rising—as in the famous passage on the death of Arthur—to a rich movement which is assured, majestic, and masterly.

Morte Darthur

The selections given below are two of the best known in Malory's book: how Arthur became king by pulling out the sword from the stone and how he met his death. Both display Malory's superb narrative skill and the care and composure of his literary idiom.

His tale begins with the King of all England, Uther Pendragon, lusting after Igraine, the wife of his enemy the Duke of Cornwall, lord of the castle of Tintagel. Igraine refuses to sleep with the king, and she and her husband abruptly terminate the visit they have been making to Uther, whereupon he renews war with them. For love of Igraine, Uther falls sick and the magician Merlin is called in, to bring it about that Uther, taking the form of the Duke of Cornwall, shall gain entrance to the castle of Tintagel and to Igraine, just at the moment when her true husband is being killed. Shortly after, Igraine and Uther are married. The story of Uther and Igraine comes in the first place from the *History of the Kings of Britain* by Geoffrey of Monmouth (1100?–1154).

One of the ways in which Malory's story is affected by the times in which he lived is the tinge of reminiscence, perhaps unconscious, of the conditions and events of the Wars of the Roses. In the first selection, for example, there is a possible allusion to Henry VI at the first battle of St. Albans. Moreover, the way in which Malory constantly makes the North the enemy, apparently has a special weakness for Wales, and makes the king's strength center on London and its vicinity, may carry a suggestion of the Yorkists as the enemy and the Lancastrians as the party in the right.

As the title of his book indicates, Malory must have regarded the death of Arthur as the climactic moment of his story. He rises to the occasion in recounting, as Tennyson was to do four centuries later, the final passing of the British king into his long sleep, half Christian death, half fairy slumber, from which he may come again, if the need is great enough, to the salvation of his old kingdom: the "once and future king."

Arthur, laying siege to Sir Lancelot's castle, has made him yield up Arthur's queen, Guinevere, whose lover Lancelot has been; and Lancelot has left England for France. Sir Gawain, Arthur's nephew, who has quarreled with Lancelot, persuades Arthur that Lancelot has not been punished enough and Arthur raises an army to besiege Lancelot in France. During Arthur's absence his bastard son Sir Mordred seizes the kingdom, and Arthur, hearing the news, hastily brings his army back. As they land at Dover, Mordred attacks and Gawain is killed, repentant at having involved Arthur in his fruitless expedition, and calling on Lancelot to honor his oath of allegiance and come to the help of the king. He does not do so, and those who had supported him previously in England enlist with Mordred.

The final battle approaches and Arthur dreams (on Trinity Sunday) that he sits high on his throne, which is tied to a wheel (the Wheel of Fortune; Fig 41) above a turbulent black pool full of serpents and monsters, into which he is thrown as the wheel turns. In a second dream he sees Sir Gawain, and the ladies on behalf of whom he had fought. Gawain warns him that if, he gives battle next day, he will be killed. He must make a truce with Mordred for a month, so that Lancelot can reach him with help. Arthur agrees, and a tournament is arranged in which Arthur, Mordred, and fourteen knights from either side will participate. But Arthur has commanded that, if sword be drawn on either side, the tournament shall become a battle. When a knight, stung by an adder, draws his sword and kills it, battle commences, though Arthur fears his fate.

The first selection is modernized in spelling and punctuation after Caxton's printing of 1485, since the Winchester manuscript is defective at the beginning. It is from Bk. I, *Merlin,* Chaps. 3–6: "Of the birth of King Arthur and of his nurture, and of the death of King Uther Pendragon, and how Arthur was chosen king and of the wonders and marvels of a sword taken out of a stone by the said Arthur." The second selection is modernized in spelling and freely treated, after E. Vinaver's second edition of the Winchester manuscript, with some readings from Caxton's printing and some editorial expansions introduced. It is from Bk. XXI, *The Day of Destiny,* Chaps. 4–7.

From Morte Darthur

[The Birth of Arthur and the Sword in the Stone]

Then Queen Igraine waxed[1] daily greater and greater.[2] So it befell after, within half a year, as King Uther lay by his queen, he asked her by the faith she ought[3] to him whose was the child within her body. Then was she sore abashed[4] to give answer.

1. Grew.
2. More and more pregnant.
3. Owed.
4. Ashamed.

'Dismay you not,' said the King, 'but tell me the truth, and I shall love you the better, by the faith of my body!'

'Sire,' said she, 'I shall tell you the truth. The same night that my lord was dead, the hour of his death, as his knights record, there came into my castle of Tintagel [5] a man like my lord in speech and in countenance, and two knights with him in likeness of his two knights Brastias and Jordanus, and so I went unto bed with him as I ought to do with my lord; and the same night, as I shall answer unto God, this child was begotten upon me.'

'That is truth,' said the King, 'as ye say, for it was I myself that came in the likeness. And therefore, dismay you not, for I am father to the child,' and there he told her all the cause [6] how it was by Merlin's counsel. Then the Queen made great joy when she knew who was the father of her child.

Soon came Merlin unto the King and said, 'Sir, ye must purvey [7] you for the nourishing [8] of your child.'

'As thou wilt,' said the King, 'be it.'

'Well,' said Merlin, 'I know a lord of yours in this land that is a passing true man and a faithful, and he shall have the nourishing of your child; and his name is Sir Ector [9] and he is a lord of fair livelihood [10] in many parts in England and Wales. And this lord, Sir Ector, let him be sent for for to come and speak with you, and desire him yourself, as he loveth you, that he will put his own child to nourishing to another woman and that his wife nourish yours. And when the child is born let it be delivered to me at yonder privy postern [11] unchristened.' [12]

So like as Merlin devised,[13] it was done. And when Sir Ector was come he made fiaunce [14] to the King for to nourish the child like as the King desired; and there the King granted Sir Ector great rewards. Then when the lady was delivered the King commanded two knights and two ladies to take the child, bound in a cloth of gold, 'and that ye deliver him to what [15] poor man ye meet at the postern gate of the castle.' So the child was delivered unto Merlin, and so he bare it forth unto Sir Ector and made an holy man to christen him and named him Arthur. And so Sir Ector's wife nourished him with her own pap.[16]

Then within two years King Uther fell sick of a great malady. And in the meanwhile his enemies usurped upon him and did a great battle upon his men and slew many of his people.

'Sir,' said Merlin, 'ye may not lie so as ye do, for ye must to the field, though ye ride on an horse-litter. For ye shall never have the better of your

5. On the north coast of Cornwall. There is still a ruined 12th-century castle there, high on the cliffs overlooking the sea.
6. Affair.
7. Provide, arrange for.
8. Nursing, upbringing.
9. Sir Ector de Maris, brother of Sir Lancelot.
10. Estates, possessions.
11. Secret, secluded side-door.
12. In peril of its soul. A child in the Middle Ages was often christened on the same day that it was born.
13. Arranged, set out.
14. Promise.
15. That.
16. Breast.

enemies but if [17] your person be there, and then shall ye have the victory.'

So it was done as Merlin had devised, and they carried the King forth in an horse-litter with a great host toward his enemies, and at Saint Albans [18] there met with the King a great host of the North.[19] And that day Sir Ulfius [20] and Sir Brastias did great deeds of arms, and King Uther's men overcame the northern battle [21] and slew many people and put the remnant to flight; and then the King returned unto London and made great joy of his victory.

And then he fell passing sore [22] sick, so that three days and three nights he was speechless; wherefore all the barons made great sorrow and asked Merlin what counsel were best.

'There nis [23] none other remedy,' said Merlin, 'but God will have His will. But look ye all barons be before King Uther to-morrow, and God and I shall make him to speak.'

So on the morning all the barons, with Merlin, came tofore [24] the King. Then Merlin said aloud unto King Uther: "Sire, shall your son Arthur be King after your days, of this realm with all the appurtenance?' [25]

Then Uther Pendragon turned him and said in hearing of them all, 'I give him God's blessing and mine, and bid him pray for my soul, and righteously and worshipfully [26] that he claim the crown, upon forfeiture of my blessing,' and therewith he yielded up the ghost.

And then was he interred as belonged to a king, wherefore the Queen, fair Igraine, made great sorrow and all the barons.

Then stood the realm in great jeopardy long while, for every lord that was mighty of men [27] made him strong,[28] and many weened [29] to have been king. Then Merlin went to the Archbishop of Canterbury and counselled him for to send for all the lords of the realm and all the gentlemen of arms, that they should to London come by Christmas upon pain of cursing,[30] and for this cause, that Jesus, that was born on that night, that He would of His great mercy show some miracle, as He was come to be King of mankind, for to show some miracle who should be rightly king of this realm. So the Archbishop, by the advice of Merlin, sent for all the lords and gentlemen of arms,

17. Unless.
18. In Hertfordshire. Perhaps a reminiscence of the first Battle of St. Albans, May 22, 1455, the first battle of the Wars of the Roses, when the sick King Henry VI was carried onto the battlefield and then defeated and captured by the Northern armies under the Duke of York.
19. The North in Malory is always enemy territory, as it was to the Lancastrian party, which found much support in the South, the West, and in Wales at the time of the Wars of the Roses.
20. The retainer of Uther Pendragon who had counseled calling in Merlin to work out a way for Uther to sleep with Igraine.
21. Army.
22. Extremely severely.
23. Is not.
24. Before.
25. Property rights, privileges belonging to an estate.
26. Honorably.
27. Having a large following.
28. Strengthened himself.
29. Expected.
30. Excommunication.

that they should come by Christmas even unto London; and many of them made themselves clean of their life,[31] that their prayer might be the more acceptable unto God.

So, in the greatest church of London—whether it were Paul's [32] or not the French book [33] maketh no mention—all the estates were long ere [34] day in the church for to pray. And when matins [35] and the first mass was done there was seen in the churchyard against [36] the high altar a great stone four square, like unto a marble stone, and in midst thereof was like an anvil of steel a foot on high,[37] and therein stuck a fair sword, naked, by the point, and letters there were written in gold about the sword that said thus: 'WHOSO PULLETH OUT THIS SWORD OF THIS STONE AND ANVIL IS RIGHTLY BORN KING OF ALL ENGLAND.' [38] Then the people marvelled and told it to the Archbishop.

'I command,' said the Archbishop, 'that ye keep yourselves within your church and pray unto God still; [39] that no man touch the sword till the high mass be all done.'

So when all masses were done all the lords went to behold the stone and the sword. And when they saw the scripture [40] some essayed, such as would have been king, but none might stir the sword nor move it.

'He is not here,' said the Archbishop, 'that shall achieve [41] the sword, but doubt not God will make him known. But this is my counsel,' said the Archbishop, 'that we let purvey [42] ten knights, men of good fame, they to keep this sword.'

So it was ordained, and then there was made a cry [43] that every man should essay [44] that would for to win the sword. And upon New Year's Day [45] the barons let make a joust and a tournament,[46] that all knights that would joust or tourney there might play. And all this was ordained for to keep the lords together and the commons, for the Archbishop trusted that God would make him known that should win the sword.

31. I.e. made confession.
32. St. Paul's Cathedral.
33. The *Suite de Merlin,* Malory's source for this section of his work; or, more generally, the French cycle of Arthurian romance on which he drew.
34. Before.
35. Morning prayers.
36. Opposite the spot where the high altar stood within the church.
37. In height.
38. The French version makes him the king of all the land, chosen by Jesus Christ.
39. Continually.
40. Inscription.
41. Obtain.
42. Appoint, choose.
43. Public announcement.
44. Try.
45. The turn of the year: part of the festivities during the great religious feast of Christmas.
46. By Malory's time a joust and a tournament were indistinguishable from one another. Twelfth-century tournaments were pitched battles between two sides of knights; the joust was originally a combat between two single knights. With the development of the theory and practice of chivalry, both were combined in one festival, lasting some days and including entertainments and dancing. Ladies looked on, and blunted or fragile weapons were used. (Fig. 50)

So upon New Year's Day, when the service was done, the barons rode unto the field, some to joust and some to tourney. And so it happened that Sir Ector, that had great livelihood about London, rode unto the joust, and with him rode Sir Kay, his son, and young Arthur, that was his nourished brother;[47] and Sir Kay was made knight at All Hallowmass[48] afore. So as they rode to the joust-ward Sir Kay had lost his sword, for he had left it at his father's lodging, and so he prayed young Arthur for to ride for his sword.

'I will well,'[49] said Arthur, and rode fast after the sword.

And when he came home, the lady and all were out to see the jousting. Then was Arthur wroth and said to himself, 'I will ride to the churchyard and take the sword with me that sticketh in the stone, for my brother Sir Kay shall not be without a sword this day.' So when he came to the churchyard, Sir Arthur alight and tied his horse to the stile, and so he went to the tent and found no knights there, for they were at the jousting. And so he handled the sword by the handle, and lightly and fiercely pulled it out of the stone, and took his horse and rode his way until he came to his brother Sir Kay and delivered him the sword. And as soon as Sir Kay saw the sword he wist[50] well it was the sword of the stone, and so he rode to his father Sir Ector and said, "Sire, lo here is the sword of the stone, wherefore I must be king of this land.'

When Sir Ector beheld the sword he returned again and came to the church, and there they alighted all three and went into the church and anon[51] he made Sir Kay to swear upon a book how he came to that sword.

'Sir,' said Sir Kay, 'by my brother Arthur, for he brought it to me.'

'How got ye this sword?' said Sir Ector to Arthur.

'Sir, I will tell you. When I came home for my brother's sword I found nobody at home to deliver me his sword. And so I thought my brother Sir Kay should not be swordless, and so I came hither eagerly and pulled it out of the stone without any pain.'

'Found ye any knights about this sword?' said Sir Ector.

'Nay,'[52] said Arthur.

'Now,' said Sir Ector to Arthur, 'I understand ye must be king of this land.'

'Wherefore I?' said Arthur, 'and for what cause?'

'Sire,' said Sir Ector, 'for God will have it so; for there should never man have drawn out this sword but he that shall be rightfully king of this land. Now let me see whether ye can put the sword there as it was and pull it out again.'

'That is no maistry,'[53] said Arthur, and so he put it in the stone. Therwithal[54] Sir Ector essayed to pull out the sword and failed.

47. Foster-brother, *frère-de-lait*.
48. All Saints Day, November 1, a major religious festival, hence suitable for assemblies of knights and receiving of knighthood.
49. I will, with pleasure.
50. Knew.
51. At once.
52. No, indeed.
53. Mastery, deed of prowess.
54. Thereupon.

'Now essay,' said Sir Ector unto Sir Kay. And anon he pulled at the sword with all his might, but it would not be.

'Now shall ye essay,' said Sir Ector to Arthur.

'I will well,' said Arthur, and pulled it out easily.

And therwithal Sir Ector kneeled down to the earth, and Sir Kay.

'Alas!' said Arthur, 'my own dear father and brother, why kneel ye to me?'

'Nay, nay, my lord Arthur, it is not so. I was never your father nor of your blood, but I wot [55] well ye are of an higher blood than I weened ye were.' And then Sir Ector told him all how he was betaken [56] him for to nourish him and by whose commandment, and by Merlin's deliverance.[57]

1468?–70 1485

[The Death of Arthur]

'Now tide me [1] death, tide me life,' said the King, 'now I see him yonder alone, he shall never escape my hands! For at a better avail [2] shall I never have him.'

'God speed [3] you well!' said Sir Bedivere.

Then the King got his spear in both his hands, and ran toward Sir Mordred, crying and saying, 'Traitor, now is thy death-day come!'

And when Sir Mordred saw King Arthur he ran unto him with his sword drawn in his hand, and there King Arthur smote Sir Mordred under the shield with a foin [4] of his spear, throughout the body more than a fathom.[5] And when Sir Mordred felt that he had his death's wound, he thrust himself with the might that he had up to the burr [6] of King Arthur's spear, and right so he smote his father, King Arthur, with his sword held in both his hands, upon the side of the head, that the sword pierced the helmet and the tay [7] of the brain. And therewith Mordred dashed down stark dead to the earth.

And noble King Arthur fell in a swoon to the earth, and there he swooned oftentimes, and Sir Lucan the Butler [8] and Sir Bedivere the Bold ofttimes hove him up. And so weakly betwixt them they led him to a little chapel not far from the sea, and when the King was there, him thought him [9] reasonably eased.

Then heard they people cry in the field.

'Now go thou, Sir Lucan,' said the King, 'and do me to wit [10] what betokens that noise in the field.'

55. Know.
56. Entrusted to.
57. Handing over.

1. Betide, befall.
2. Advantage.
3. Prosper.
4. Thrust.
5. Six feet.
6. Hand-guard.
7. Outer membrane.
8. Originally the knight who had charge of the wine for the king's table.
9. He seemed to himself.
10. Cause me to know.

So Sir Lucan departed, for he was grievously wounded in many places; and so as he yode [11] he saw and hearkened [12] by the moonlight how that pillours [13] and robbers were come into the field to pill and to rob many a full noble knight of brooches and bees [14] and of many a good ring and many a rich jewel. And who that were not dead all out [15] there they slew them for their harness [16] and their riches.

When Sir Lucan understood this work, he came to the King as soon as he might, and told him all that he had heard and seen.

'Therefore, by my rede,' [17] said Sir Lucan, 'it is best that we bring you to some town.'

'I would it were so,' said the King, 'but I may not stand, my head works [18] so . . . Ah, Sir Lancelot!' said King Arthur, 'this day have I sore missed thee! And alas, that ever I was against thee! For now have I my death, whereof Sir Gawain me warned in my dream.'

Then Sir Lucan took up the King the one part [19] and Sir Bedivere the other part, and in the lifting up the King swooned, and in the lifting Sir Lucan fell in a swoon, that part of his guts fell out of his body, and therewith the noble knight's heart burst. And when the King awoke he beheld Sir Lucan, how he lay foaming at the mouth and part of his guts lay at his feet.

'Alas,' said the King, 'this is to me a full heavy [20] sight, to see this noble duke so die for my sake, for he would have helped me, that had more need of help than I! Alas, that he would not complain him, for [21] his heart was so set to help me. Now Jesus have mercy upon his soul!'

Then Sir Bedivere wept for the death of his brother.

'Now leave this mourning and weeping, gentle [22] knight,' said the King, 'for all this will not avail me. For wit [23] thou well, and [24] I might live myself, the death of Sir Lucan would grieve me evermore. But my time passeth on fast,' said the King. 'Therefore,' said King Arthur unto Sir Bedivere, 'take thou here Excalibur,[25] my good sword, and go with it to yonder water's side; and when thou comest there, I charge thee throw my sword in that water, and come again and tell me what thou there seest.'

'My lord,' said Sir Bedivere, 'your commandment shall be done, and lightly [26] bring you word again.'

11. Went, walked.
12. Noticed.
13. Plunderers.
14. Neck chains, bracelets.
15. Completely.
16. Armor.
17. According to my advice.
18. Aches, hurts.
19. On one side.
20. Sad.
21. Because.
22. Noble, good.
23. Know.
24. If.
25. "Cut-steel"; the name was revealed to Arthur by the Lady of the Lake after she had given it to him.
26. Quickly.

So Sir Bedivere departed. And by the way he beheld that noble sword, and the pommel[27] and the haft was all precious stones. And then he said to himself: 'If I throw this rich sword in the water, thereof shall never come good, but harm and loss.' And then Sir Bedivere hid Excalibur under a tree, and so as soon as he might he came again unto the King and said he had been at the water and had thrown the sword into the water.

'What saw thou there?' said the King.

'Sir,' he said, 'I saw nothing but waves and winds.'

'That is untruly said of thee,' said the King. 'And therefore go thou lightly again and do my commandment; as thou art to me leve[28] and dear, spare not, but throw it in.'

Then Sir Bedivere returned again and took the sword in his hand; and yet him thought[29] sin and shame to throw away that noble sword. And so eft[30] he hid the sword and returned again and told the King that he had been at the water and done his commandment.

'What sawest thou there?' said the King.

'Sir,' he said, 'I saw nothing but waters wap[31] and waves wan.'[32]

'Ah, traitor unto me and untrue,' said King Arthur, 'now hast thou betrayed me twice! Who would ween that thou hast been to me so leve and dear, and also named so noble a knight, that thou wouldst betray me for the riches of this sword? But now go again lightly; for thy long tarrying putteth me in great jeopardy of my life, for I have taken cold. And but if thou do now as I bid thee, if ever I may see thee, I shall slay thee [with] my own hands, for thou wouldst for my rich sword see me dead.'

Then Sir Bedivere departed and went to the sword and lightly took it up, and so he went unto the water's side. And there he bound the girdle[33] about the hilt, and threw the sword as far into the water as he might. And there came an arm and a hand above the water, and took it and clutched it, and shook it thrice and brandished [it] and then vanished with the sword into the water.

So Sir Bedivere came again to the King and told him what he saw.

'Alas,' said the King, 'help me hence, for I dread me I have tarried over long.'

Then Sir Bedivere took the King upon his back and so went with him to the water's side. And when they were there, even fast[34] by the bank hove[35] a little barge[36] with many fair ladies in it, and among them all was a queen and all they had black hoods. And all they wept and shrieked when they saw King Arthur.

'Now put me into that barge,' said the King.

27. The knob at the top of the hilt (haft).
28. Beloved.
29. It seemed.
30. Again.
31. Presumably, lapping.
32. Presumably, darkening.
33. Belt of the sword.
34. Close.
35. Was waiting.
36. Flat-bottomed boat.

And so he did softly, and there received him three ladies with great mourning. And so they sat them down, and in one of their laps King Arthur laid his head. And then the queen said:

'Ah my dear brother! Why have ye tarried so long from me? Alas, this wound on your head hath caught overmuch cold!'

And anon [37] they rowed fromward [38] the land, and Sir Bedivere beheld all the ladies go fromward him. Then Sir Bedivere cried and said: 'Ah, my lord Arthur, what shall become of me, now ye go from me and leave me here alone among my enemies?'

'Comfort thyself,' said the King, 'and do as well as thou mayest, for in me is no trust for to trust in. For I must into the vale of Avylyon [39] to heal me of my grievous wound. And if thou hear nevermore of me, pray for my soul!'

But ever the queen and ladies wept and shrieked, that it was pity to hear. And as soon as Sir Bedivere had lost the sight of the barge he wept and wailed, and so took [to] the forest and went all that night.

And in the morning he was aware, betwixt two holts hoar,[40] of a chapel and a hermitage.[41] Then was Sir Bedivere fain,[42] and thither he went, and when he came into the chapel he saw where lay a hermit grovelling on all fours, fast there by a tomb [43] was newly graven.[44] When the hermit saw Sir Bedivere he knew him well, for he was but little tofore [45] Bishop [46] of Canterbury that Sir Mordred fleamed.[47]

'Sir,' said Sir Bedivere, 'what man is there here interred that ye pray so fast [48] for?'

'Fair son,' said the hermit, 'I wot [49] not verily but by deeming.[50] But this same night, at midnight, there came a number of ladies and brought here a dead corpse and prayed me to inter him. And here they offered a hundred tapers,[51] and they gave me a thousand besants.' [52]

'Alas!' said Sir Bedivere, 'that was my lord King Arthur, which lyeth here graven [53] in this chapel.'

37. At once.
38. Away from.
39. Avalon, the valley, sometimes identified with Glastonbury in Somerset, where Joseph of Arimathea is supposed to have brought the Holy Grail; and sometimes with the other world, the Earthly Paradise.
40. Bare woods.
41. The cell of a hermit, i.e. an ascetic religious living alone.
42. Glad.
43. I.e. grave.
44. Dug.
45. Before.
46. Archbishop.
47. Put to flight. The Archbishop had remonstrated with and excommunicated the usurper Mordred and Mordred had tried to kill him. The Archbishop fled, according to Malory, to Glastonbury, where Sir Bedivere finds him, guarding Arthur's tomb. The placing of Arthur's tomb at Glastonbury derives from Gerald of Wales (Giraldus Cambrensis, 1146?–1220?), who states that the tomb was found there in 1189.
48. Hard and frequently.
49. Know.
50. By guesswork.
51. Wax candles.
52. Bezant, gold coin first struck at Byzantium.
53. Buried.

Then Sir Bedivere swooned, and when he awoke he prayed the hermit that he might abide with him still,[54] there to live with fasting and prayers: 'For from hence will I never go,' said Sir Bedivere, 'by my will, but all the days of my life here to pray for my lord Arthur.' . . .

Thus of Arthur I find no more written in books that been authorised,[55] nor more of the very certainty of his death heard I never read, but thus was he led away in a ship wherein were three queens; that one was King Arthur's sister, Queen Morgan le Fay,[56] the other[57] was the Queen of North Wales,[58] and the third was the Queen of the Waste Lands.[59] Also there was Dame Nynyve,[60] the chief Lady of the Lake, which had wedded Sir Pelleas,[61] the good knight; and this lady had done much for King Arthur. (And this Dame Nynyve would never suffer Sir Pelleas to be in no place where he should be in danger of his life, and so he lived unto the uttermost of his days with her in great rest.)

Now more of the death of King Arthur could I never find, but that these ladies brought him to his grave, and such one was interred there which the hermit bare witness that sometime[62] was Bishop of Canterbury. . . .

Yet some men say in many parts of England that King Arthur is not dead, but had by the will of our Lord Jesus into another place; and men say that he shall come again, and he shall win the Holy Cross.[63] Yet I will not say that it shall be so, but rather I would say: here in this world he changed his life. And many men say that there is written upon the tomb this:

HIC IACET ARTHURUS
REX QUONDAM REXQUE FUTURUS.[64]

And thus leave I here Sir Bedivere with the hermit that dwelled that time in a chapel beside Glastonbury,[65] and there was his hermitage. And so they lived in prayers and fasting and great abstinence.

And when Queen Guinevere[66] understood that King Arthur was dead and all the noble knights, Sir Mordred and all the remnant, then she stole away with five ladies with her, and so she went to Amesbury.[67] And there she let

54. Always.
55. Perhaps: written or reliable.
56. Arthur's sorceress sister and opponent, who had imprisoned his knights, and tried to kill him.
57. Second.
58. Northgalys, i.e. North Wales; this queen was also a sorceress.
59. This queen was the aunt of Sir Perceval, one of the three knights admitted to the presence of the Holy Grail.
60. Vivian, the Lady of the Lake, who gave Excalibur to Arthur and befriended him in danger.
61. The lover, the dolorous knight, one of the knights in attendance on Guinevere, and her defender in battle.
62. Formerly.
63. I.e. shall liberate the Holy Land from the Turks.
64. "Here lies Arthur, the once and future king": i.e. who was once king and will come to be king again.
65. See note 47.
66. Arthur's Queen, Lancelot's mistress.
67. In Wiltshire, north of Glastonbury, where Lancelot arrives too late to see her before her death. He lives in holiness for the short remainder of his life.

make[68] herself a nun, and wore white clothes and black; and great penance she took upon her, as ever did sinful woman in this land. And never creature could make her merry, but ever she lived in fasting, prayers, and alms-doing, that all manner of people marvelled how virtuously she was changed.

1468?–70 1485

WILLIAM CAXTON

1415(-24)–1491

William Caxton, businessman and England's first printer, was born in Kent at some time between 1415 and 1424. After schooling, he was apprenticed to a member of the Mercers' Company, which dealt in cloth and silks and was one of the oldest and richest guilds of the City of London. Much of their trade abroad was with the Low Countries and, after Caxton had served his apprenticeship, some time in the 1440's he made Bruges the center of his activities. These included the selling of the manuscripts that were then produced in large numbers in Flanders. Having prospered and having become a bookseller on the side, he saw the opportunity in the English market offered by the new invention of printing. In 1469, he set himself to translate Raoul Lefèvre's French version of the *History of Troy,* continued the translation under the patronage of Margaret of Burgundy (sister of the English King Edward IV), and went to Cologne, the nearest town where printing was carried on, to learn the craft. Leaving Cologne late in 1472, he returned to Belgium, set up his press at Bruges, and issued the first book printed in English, his translation of Lefèvre, in 1473 or 1474. Before transferring his press to London in 1476, he had printed six books, four of them in French.

Like any printer, Caxton did a great deal of bread-and-butter work—official documents, school-books—in the next fifteen years. But he had always aimed at a noble and wealthy audience, and the bulk of his production consists of his own translations from French, Flemish, and Latin; of English poetry, especially Gower, Chaucer, and Chaucer's followers; and of works in English prose, such as Chaucer's translation of Boethius and Sir Thomas Malory's *Morte Darthur.* Caxton's aim was here not merely to make money: he set himself continually to raise the style of English language and literature as well as the style of English life itself, especially by the importation of French and Burgundian culture. The English authors whom he chose to print were those who had called in the help of Latin or French to enrich and refine their style and language. In his own translations he attempted to transfer some of the polish of the originals to the English tongue. But he was as much concerned to import into England some of the civilized spiritual and chivalric values of the late medieval Burgundian court, under whose patronage he had begun his literary career. He was always deeply concerned with the exemplary value of the works he printed, though sometimes, as in his translation of *The History of Reynard the Fox* (see above), the concern is allowed to slip a little and pleasure in the tale as tale takes over.

Caxton's deep involvement with the texts he prints comes out clearly in his habit of adding prologue and epilogue to almost all of them. In the Proem (preface) to his second edition of Chaucer's *Canterbury Tales* of 1484, he tells how, after he had printed the first edition (about 1478), he learned that his "copy" had been unsatis-

68. Had herself made.

factory and undertook another edition for the sake of an author whom he admired. His praise of literature and the written word at the beginning of the preface is a topos (see Glossary) of the emerging Renaissance, and so is his praise of Chaucer as laureate poet and philosopher; yet both represent a firm conviction. Chaucer's role as a refiner, embellisher, and rhetorician is given significant praise: Caxton's lament for the roughness and variety of English as against the smoothness, richness, and uniformity of Latin and French is, again, not merely a modesty topos, but a matter of real concern. Chaucer, too, is a poet from whom one may learn wisdom, and not an entertainer only. Caxton echoes Chaucer's own Retraction at the end of *The Canterbury Tales,* but it is not an empty echo.

In the second of the two prefaces here printed, that to his prose version of the *Aeneid,* Caxton justifies his own rhetorical practice in terms of his function and his audience, showing himself, in a famous passage, clearly aware of the influence toward uniformity and improvement of language that his principles and practice might have.

Both selections are modernizations, by the present editor, based on *The Prologues and Epilogues of William Caxton,* ed. W. J. B. Crotch (Early English Text Society, 1928).

The Proem to the Canterbury Tales

Great thanks, laud and honour ought to be given unto the clerks,[1] poets and historiographers that have written many noble books of wisdom of the lives, passions and miracles of holy saints, of histories, of noble and famous acts and feats; [2] and of the chronicles sith [3] the beginning of the creation of the world unto this present time, by which we be daily informed and have knowledge of many things; of whom we should not have known, if they had not left to us their monuments written.[4] Among whom and in especial tofore [5] all other we ought to give a singular [6] laud unto that noble and great philosopher [7] Geoffrey Chaucer, the which for his ornate [8] writing in our tongue may well have the name of a laureate [9] poet. For tofore that he by his labour embellished, ornated and made fair our English, in this realm was had rude [10] speech and incongru-

1. Learned men.
2. Deeds of arms.
3. Since. Medieval world chronicles always began with the Creation and the events of the Pentateuch, especially Genesis.
4. Caxton takes up the topos of the power of the written word, and the immortalizing function of the writer, a favorite idea among Roman authors and now being vigorously taken up by the emerging Renaissance.
5. Before.
6. Special.
7. Poets were held to be moral philosophers, hiding their lesson under the cloud of their story.
8. Polished and rich, a term of praise during the 15th century especially, when writers were trying to polish and enrich their rough vernacular and make it as fine and enduring a language as the Latin they wished it to replace.
9. Distinguished. Petrarch (1304–74) had given the word new currency and poetry a boost by having himself laureated in Rome in 1341. Laureate here means "worthy of laureation," i.e. of formal recognition of excellence.
10. Rough, unpolished.

ous,[11] as yet it appeareth by old books, which at this day ought not to have place ne be compared among ne to his beauteous volumes[12] and ornate writings, of whom he made many books and treatises of many a noble history as well in metre as in rhyme and prose, and them so craftily[13] made, that he comprehended his matter in short, quick[14] and high[15] sentences,[16] eschewing prolixity, casting away the chaff of superfluity, and showing the picked grain of sentence,[17] uttered by crafty and sugared[18] eloquence. Of whom, among all other of his books, I purpose to print by the grace of God the book of the Tales of Canterbury, in which I find many a noble history of every estate and degree; first rehearsing the conditions[19] and the array[20] of each of them as properly[21] as possible is to be said; and after, their Tales, which be of noblesse,[22] wisdom, gentilesse,[23] mirth[24] and also of very[25] holiness and virtue, wherein he finisheth this said book; which book I have diligently overseen and duly examined to the end that it be made according unto his own making. For I find many of the said books, which writers have abridged it and many things left out; and in some places have set certain verses that he never made[26] ne set in his book. Of which books so incorrect was one brought to me six years past, which I supposed had been very true and correct; and according to the same I did imprint[27] a certain number of them, which anon were sold to many and divers gentlemen, of whom one gentleman came to me and said that this book was not according in many places unto the book that Geoffrey Chaucer had made. To whom I answered that I had made it according to my copy, and by me was nothing added ne diminished.[28] Then he said he knew a book which his father had, and much loved, that was very true and according unto his own first book[29] by him made; and said more, if I would print it again, he would get me the same book for a copy,[30] howbeit[31] he wist[32] well that his father

11. Of all kinds and dialects; lacking both the uniformity and decorum that an educated single-speech standard, on the model of Latin, would confer.
12. Nor be put on a level with either his splendid volumes.
13. Skillfully.
14. Lively.
15. Exalted.
16. Statements, or perhaps approximating the modern sentences.
17. Sententia, didactic import, moral lesson.
18. Sweet, without any derogatory associations.
19. Social status, a paraphrase of Chaucer's General Prologue.
20. Dress.
21. Exactly, fittingly.
22. Noble, virtuous behavior.
23. "Courtesy," refinement.
24. Fun.
25. True.
26. The manuscripts and early editions of Chaucer, including Caxton's, contain tales and other verse by disciples and other poets.
27. Had printed. Caxton's first edition of *The Canterbury Tales* was published in 1478, the first printed English "classic."
28. Taken out, subtracted.
29. Chaucer's own fair manuscript copy. This is not likely and, in any case, it would have been written by a scribe.
30. "Copy" to print from.
31. Although.
32. Knew.

would not gladly part from it. To whom I said, in case that he could get me such a book true and correct, yet I would once endeavour me to print it again, for to satisfy the author, whereas tofore by ignorance I erred in hurting and defaming [33] his book in divers places, in setting in some things that he never said nor made and leaving out many things that he made which be requisite to be set in it. And thus we fell at accord.[34] And he full gentilly [35] got of his father the said book, and delivered it to me, by which I have corrected my book, as hereafter all along by the aid of Almyghty God shall follow, whom I humbly beseech to give me grace and aid to achieve and accomplish, to his laud, honour, and glory; and that all ye that shall in this book read or hear, will of your charity among your deeds of mercy,[36] remember the soul of the said Geoffrey Chaucer, first author and maker of this book. And also that all we that shall see and read therein, may so take and understand the good and virtuous Tales,[37] that it may so profit unto the health of our souls that after this short and transitory life we may come to everlasting life in heaven. Amen.

1484

From The Preface to the Aeneid

. . . And when I had advised me [1] in this said book I deliberated and concluded [2] to translate it in to English, and forthwith took a pen and ink and wrote a leaf or twain, which I oversaw [3] again to correct it. And when I saw the fair and strange [4] terms therein, I doubted that it should not please some gentlemen which late blamed me, saying that in my translations I had over curious [5] terms, which could not be understood of common people, and desired me to use old and homely terms in my translations. And fain [6] would I satisfy every man, and so to do took an old book and read therein and certainly the English was so rude and broad that I could not well understand it. And also my lord Abbot of Westmynster did do show to me late certain evidences [7] written in old English, for to reduce it into our English now used. And certainly it was written in such wise that it was more like to Dutch [8] than English. I could not reduce ne [9] bring it to be understood. And certainly our language now used varieth far from that which was used and spoken when I was born.

33. Harming.
34. Agreement.
35. Kindly.
36. The conventional formula at the close of a book: Caxton echoes Chaucer's Retraction.
37. Again echoing the Retraction: literature tends toward good.

1. Looked carefully through.
2. Decided.
3. Looked over, checked.
4. Foreign, difficult.
5. Far-fetched, artificial.
6. Gladly.
7. Documents.
8. Middle Dutch, the dialect of Caxton's day in the Netherlands.
9. Nor.

For we Englishmen be born under the domination of the moon,[10] which is never steadfast, but ever wavering, waxing one season and waneth and discreaseth another season. And that common English that is spoken in one shire varieth from another, insomuch that in my days [it] happened that certain merchants were in a ship in Tamyse [11] for to have sailed over the sea into Zealand,[12] and for lack of wind they tarried at the foreland, and went to land for to refresh them. And one of them, named Sheffelde, a mercer,[13] came into a house [14] and asked for meat,[15] and specially he asked after eggs. And the good-wife [16] answered that she could speak no French. And the merchant was angry, for he also could speak no French, but would have had eggs; and she understood him not. And then at last another said that he would have eyren.[17] Then the good-wife said that she understood him well. Lo, what should a man in these days now write, eggs or eyren? Certainly, it is hard to please every man, because of diversity and change of language. For in these days every man, that is in any reputation in his country, will utter his communication and matters in such manners and terms, that few men shall understand them. And some honest and great clerks [18] have been with me and desired me to write the most curious terms that I could find. And thus, between plain, rude [19] and curious I stand abashed; [20] but in my judgment the common terms, that be daily used, be lighter [21] to be understood than the old and ancient English. And forasmuch as this present book is not for a rude, uplandish [22] man to labour therein, ne read it, but only for a clerk and a noble gentleman that feeleth and understandeth in feats of arms,[23] in love, and in noble chivalry. Therefore, in a mean [24] between both, I have reduced and translated this said book into our English, not over rude ne curious but in such terms as shall be understood by God's grace, according to my copy. And if any man will intermit [25] in reading of it and findeth such terms that he cannot understand, let him go read and learn Virgil or the Epistles of Ovid, and there he shall see and understand

10. The moon, the quickest in motion of the planets, with its 28-day cycle of waxing and waning, was a byword for inconstancy. All things below the moon were considered transitory and subject to change.

11. Thames.

12. Province of the Netherlands, a regular trading area, especially for cloth, with England.

13. A dealer, often very wealthy, in wool and cloth; and possibly, like Caxton, a member of the guild or company of Mercers in the City of London.

14. Inn.

15. Food.

16. Hostess.

17. *Eyren* is the older Southern English plural form of *eye*, egg; *egg* was a Northern form, influenced by Norse, now on the point of ousting the other form throughout the country.

18. Learned men.

19. Rustic, rough.

20. Confused.

21. Easier.

22. Up-country, rustic.

23. Warlike deeds and tournaments. Caxton published *The Book of the Order of Chivalry* in 1484; and *The Book of Feats of Arms and of Chivalry* in 1489 or 1490. He is important for his part in the importing of Burgundian chivalric ideas and practices into England.

24. Middle.

25. Engage.

lightly all, if he have a good reader and informer.[26] For this book is not for every rude and uncunning[27] man to see, but to clerks and very[28] gentlemen that understand gentleness[29] and science.[30]

Thence I pray all them that shall read in this little treatise, to hold me for excused for the translating of it. For I acknowledge myself ignorant of cunning[31] to emprise[32] on me so high and noble a work.

1490

WILLIAM DUNBAR

c.1460–c.1520?

William Dunbar was born in Scotland, perhaps of noble parents, about 1460, perhaps attended the University of St. Andrews, and perhaps became a Franciscan friar. By 1500 he was in the service of James IV of Scotland, the first great Scottish patron of arts and letters. He died at an unknown date as a beneficed clergyman.

Dunbar's career follows the pattern of the court poet (or "makar," as he was called in Scotland). Unlike Chaucer, Dunbar was a cleric as well as a courtier and diplomat. (A good comparison would be Petrarch in Italy.) He moved in the atmosphere of a highly civilized and learned royal circle, receptive of the new learning, much under French influence, both directly and through England. Chaucer, whom he calls "reverend" (not "holy" but "to be revered") and "rose of rethoris" ("orators"), was his poetic master, along with John Gower and John Lydgate. He used the metrical and poetic forms that they had used, and he developed from them his elaborate, jeweled, Latinate, "aureate" language.

Dunbar's poetry—allegorical as in *The Golden Targe,* satirical as in *The Two Married Women and the Widow,* or elegaic as in the *Lament for the Makers*—is technically controlled and masterly, full of variety, rapid, exuberant, parodistic, wildly and often scabrously witty, as well as, when necessary, formally reverent or deeply moving.

26. Guide.
27. Unschooled, not knowledgeable.
28. True.
29. Noble, courteous behavior of all kinds.
30. Knowledge. The knowledge one would be expected to gain from the *Aeneid* would not be acquaintance with the story and characters, but with the moral lessons it carried. In Italy the poem was still in Caxton's day being presented as an allegory of human life, and continued to be so thought of throughout the Renaissance.
31. Knowledge, skill.
32. Enterprise, undertake.

Lament for the Makers°

I that in heill> was and gladness *health*
Am trublit> now with great sickness *afflicted*
And feblit> with infirmitie. *enfeebled*
Timor Mortis conturbat me.°

Our plesance> here is all vain glory, *pleasure*
This fals world is but transitory,
The flesh is bruckle,> the Feynd is slee.> *frail / wily*
Timor Mortis conturbat me.

The state of man does change and vary,
Now sound, now sick, now blyth, now sary,> *sad*
Now dansand> merry, now like to die. *dancing*
Timor Mortis conturbat me.

No state in erd> here standis sicker; *earth*
As with the wynd wavis the wicker°
So wavis this world's vanitie.
Timor Mortis conturbat me.

Unto the death> gois all estatis, *to death*
Princis, prelatis,> and potestatis,> *prelates / potentates*
Baith> rich and poor of all degree. *both*
Timor Mortis conturbat me.

He takis the knichtis> in to field> *knights / in battle*
Enarmit> under helm and scheild; *fully armed*
Victor he is at all mellie.°
Timor Mortis conturbat me.

That strong unmerciful tyrand> *tyrant*
Takis, on the motheris breast sowkand,> *sucking*
The babe full of benignitie.> *innocence*
Timor Mortis conturbat me.

He takis the campion> in the stour,> *champion / conflict*
The captain closit> in the tour,> *enclosed / tower*
The lady in bour> full of bewtie. *bower*
Timor Mortis conturbat me.

He sparis no lord for his piscence,> *power*
Na clerk> for his intelligence; *scholar*
His awful straik> may no man flee. *terrible stroke*
Timor Mortis conturbat me.

Lament for the Makers The title is traditional, not Dunbar's. Early printed versions end "Quod [said] Dunbar when he was sick." An *ubi sunt* poem, a dance of death, a statement of poetic indebtedness, this is a good example of the mixing of genres which makes Dunbar's poetry so difficult to categorize. *Makers,* or "makaris," means poets; etymologically the words are the same, "poet" coming from the Greek *poiein,* to make.

Timor . . . me "The fear of death confounds me." The refrain, from the Office of the Dead, had been used by Lydgate and others in the 15th century.

wicker strictly willow twig, so any living branch easily stirred by the wind

mellie French *mêlée*

Art magicianis° and astrologgis,> *astrologers*
Rethoris, logicianis, and theologgis,°
Them helpis no conclusionis slee.°
Timor Mortis conturbat me.

In medecine the most practicianis,
Leechis, surrigianis,> and physicianis, *doctors, surgeons*
Themself from Death may not supplee.> *beg off*
Timor Mortis conturbat me.

I see that makaris> amang the laif> *poets / rest*
Playis here their pageant,° syne> gois to graif;> *soon / grief*
Sparit> is nocht> their facultie.° *spared / not*
Timor Mortis conturbat me.

He has done petuously> devour *frighteningly*
The noble Chaucer, of makaris flour,
The Monk of Bury,° and Gower,° all three.
Timor Mortis conturbat me.

The good Sir Hew° of Eglintoun,
And eik Heriot, and Wintoun,
He has tane> out of this cuntrie.> *taken / country*
Timor Mortis conturbat me.

That scorpion fell> has done infeck> *terrible / infected*
Maister John Clerk, and James Affleck,
Fra ballat>-making and tragedie. *poem*
Timor Mortis conturbat me.

Holland and Barbour he has berevit;> *bereft*
Alas! that he not with us levit> *left*
Sir Mungo Lockart of the Lee.
Timor Mortis conturbat me.

Clerk of Tranent eik> he has tane, *also*
That made the Anteris> of Gawaine; *adventures*
Sir Gilbert Hay endit has he.
Timor Mortis conturbat me.

He has Blind Harry and Sandy Traill
Slain with his schour> of mortal> hail, *shower / deadly*

art magicianis masters of the magical art
Rethoris . . . theologgis masters of eloquence, logicians, theologians
conclusionis slee I.e. clever judgments. Conclusion is the technical term in logic for a proposition deduced by reasoning from two previous propositions, the last of the three propositions in a syllogism, what follows from the two premises. Dunbar uses it to mean a formal judgment or opinion arrived at by the academically correct deployment of acumen and learning.
pageant unsubstantial play of life on earth
facultie profession
Monk of Bury John Lydgate (*c.* 1370–*c.* 1449), prolific poet and monk of Bury St. Edmunds, one of Dunbar's acknowledged masters
Gower John Gower (1325?–1408), Chaucer's older London fellow poet and master, author of the *Confessio Amantis*. Gower, Chaucer, and Lydgate are regarded by the later 15th- and early 16th-century poets as the founders of their craft and models for imitation.
Sir Hew These Scottish poets are not equally well known. Sir Hugh (the title Sir, though here indicating knighthood, at least as often simply means a priest) Eglinton is not known as a poet; Heryot, Clerk, and Affleck (Auchinleck) are unknown; Andrew of Wyntoun wrote a chronicle of Scotland; John Barbour (d. 1395) is the author of the poem *Bruce*. The names are a roll call, not necessarily more.

Quhilk˃ Patrick Johnstoun might nocht flee. — *which*
Timor Mortis conturbat me.

He has reft˃ Merseir his endite,˃ — *bereft / poetry*
That did in luvė˃ so lively write, — *love*
So short, so quick, of sentence° hie.
Timor Mortis conturbat me.

He has tane Rowll of Aberdene,
And gentill Rowll of Corstorphine;
Two better fallowis˃ did no man see. — *companions*
Timor Mortis conturbat me.

In Dunfermline he has done roune˃ — *talked*
With Maister Robert Henrysoun;°
Sir John the Ross enbrast˃ has he. — *embraced*
Timor Mortis conturbat me.

And he has now tane, last of aw,˃ — *all*
Good gentil Stobo and Quintin Shaw,
Of quhom all wichtis hes pitie.°
Timor Mortis conturbat me.

Good Maister Walter Kennedy
In point of Death lies verily;
Great ruth˃ it were that so shuld be. — *pity*
Timor Mortis conturbat me.

Sen he has all my brether tane,°
He will nocht let me live alane;˃ — *alone*
Of force˃ I man˃ his next prey be. — *necessarily / must*
Timor Mortis conturbat me.

Since for the Death remeid˃ is none, — *remedy*
Best is that we for Death dispone,
After our death that live may we.
Timor Mortis conturbat me.
c. 1508

JOHN SKELTON

1460(-64?)–1529

Not much is known of Skelton's early life. About 1488 he received the "degree" of laureate (a graduate qualification in poetry and rhetoric) from Oxford. This, and two other such degrees from the universities of Cambridge and Louvain a few years

sentence Latin, *sententia*, i.e. morally profitable matter, knowledge: "So brief, so lively, of great pith."
Robert Henrysoun Henryson (1429–1508), schoolmaster of Dunfermline, the best Scottish poet, after Dunbar, of the century, author of fables (e.g. *The Uponlandis Mous and the Burges Mous*) and *The Testament of Cresseid*
Of . . . pitie whom all men regret
Sen . . . tane since he has all my brethren taken

later, would have formally established his fitness to practice Latin poetry, for the eternal glory of himself and those he wrote about. He had become a professional man of letters, in the style of Petrarch, who had set the fashion for Renaissance Europe by being laureated at Rome in 1341. Most such men supported themselves by going into the service of their ruler or the church: Skelton did both. He was tutor to the young prince who became Henry VIII, rector of Diss in Norfolk, and finally royal orator and cleric-courtier for the rest of his life.

Skelton was a translator (of historian Diodorus Siculus), a moralist and satirist, admired by his contemporaries for his learning, his ornate style, inventiveness, vigor, quickness, and pith. Knowing the works of Chaucer and of Langland well, he was sure of his own place in the English poetic tradition, and his responsibilities to the enrichment of the English language, as his *Garland of Laurel* makes clear.

Some of his satires use the dream-allegory form; some, like *Colin Clout* (Skelton also looks forward to Spenser), are much more rapid and direct statements of the complaints of ordinary Christians about their material and spiritual life. Here, and in *Speak, Parrot,* he is flaying his age and his church, but he is no Protestant reformer. *Magnificence,* an interlude or morality play, is also a "complaint" about the follies of the court and a mirror for princes: the magnanimous man, the prince, must display the virtue of fortitude against all branches of temptation.

These "satires" are often harsh, but they all have flashes of Skelton's quick, gay, inventive wit: his great poetic merits are his speed and metrical skill. In them and in other earlier poems he often uses the verse form (Troilus stanza; rime royal) and rhetoric of Chaucer's successors, reinforced by the long-lined alliterative tradition (of Langland as well as the Chaucerians). His best verse uses the "Skeltonic" meter—the rapid, two- or three-stressed lines, held together by single-rhyme patterns of up to fourteen lines. The stresses are often emphasized by alliteration, which may also hold together blocks of two or three lines, the helter-skelter controlled by Skelton's standard couplet or triplet, which gives a breathing space in the verbal and rhyming virtuosity.

Skelton is both an obviously difficult and a disarmingly simple poet. *The Tunning of Elinor Rumming* is a riot of words and rhymes, tossed off, almost, as the old bags toss off their ale. *Philip Sparrow* is perfectly and subtly structured: a mock-childish, mock-religious, mock-heroic poem built around the Office of the Dead. It looks forward to Alexander Pope's *Rape of the Lock* and Thomas Gray's *Ode on the Death of a Favourite Cat* as well as back to Catullus. The tone is of neither ridicule nor cosmic pathos; the seeming artlessness is poised between the observed innocence of the girl mourning the death of her pet sparrow (without knowing the connotations of lechery attached to the bird) and the conscious, aureate rhetoric which she is made to use as she invents a burial service and laments that her simple reading in romances and "historious tales" is not the right preparation to commemorate him suitably. In this early work, as always, Skelton shows himself inventive master both of the "high" style and of the simple. The two are most clearly differentiated in the long, ornate, *Garland of Laurel,* an elaborate, artificial, dream allegory, with its seven lyrics, building their praise of court ladies around simple, gentle rhyme, rhythm and refrain.

From Colin Clout°

. . . And if ye stand in doubt
Who brought this rhyme about,
My name is Colin Clout.
I purpose to shake out
All my cunning> bag, *learned*
Like a clerkly> hag.° *erudite*
For though my rhyme be ragged,°
Tattered and jagged,
Rudely rain-beaten,
Rusty and moth-eaten,
If ye take well therewith,
It hath in it some pith.
For, as far as I can see,
It is wrong with each degree:> *class*
For the temporalitie°
Accuseth the spiritualitie;
The spiritual again
Doth grudge and complain
Upon the temporal men:
Thus each of other blother> *gabble*
The one against the other:
Alas, they make me shudder!
For in hudder-mudder> *secrecy*
The Church is put in fault;
The prelates° be so haute,> *haughty*
They say, and look so high,
As though they would fly
Above the starry sky.

Lay men say indeed
How they take no heed
Their silly sheep° to feed,
But pluck away and pull
The fleeces of their wool
Unneth> they leave a lock *scarcely*
Of wool among their flock! . . .

c. 1523

Colin Clout The double name is Skelton's invention, later taken up by Spenser. Compare the earlier Piers Plowman, Jack Upland, the critics of their society: plain-spoken countrymen. Colin, a shepherd (see French poetry of the 15th and 16th centuries); Clout, either clod, rustic, or (patched) cloak or cloth. Colin Clout is either a shepherd or an itinerant academic, deeply concerned about the state of his church and about following the precepts and example of Christ.

hag applied to man or woman

ragged like my cloak; I am no fine orator—conventional modesty

temporalitie temporal men, laymen; as opposed to the spirituality, the clergy, whose jurisdictions and exactions were coming under attack, especially in matters of worldly wealth

prelates senior clergy, who have received preferment in the church

silly sheep poor, innocent flock

Philip Sparrow

Philip Sparrow is a mock elegy, like the Roman poet Catullus' (84–54 B.C.) elegy on Lesbia's sparrow. Jane Scroop, a young friend of Skelton's, mourns the killing by a cat of her beloved pet sparrow, Philip. Rhetorically, the poem is a re-working of the Office of the Dead, during which Jane officiates, inviting us and all bird-kind to share her grief, and begging for a suitable epitaph. This structural wit is complicated and reinforced by Jane's professions of modesty as she deploys her own elaborate rhetoric.

From Philip Sparrow

Pla ce bo,°
Who is there? Who?
Di le xi.°
Dame Margery?°
Fa, re, my, my.°
Wherefore and why, why?
For the soul of Philip° Sparrow,
That was late slain at Carrow,
Among the Nunnės Black,
For that sweet soulės sake
And for all sparrows' souls
Set in our bead-rolls,°
Pater noster qui,°
With an Ave Mari,°
And with the corner of a Creed,°
The more shall be your meed.> *reward*
When° I remember again
How my Philip was slain,
Never half the pain
Was between you twain,
Pyramus and Thisbe,°
As then befell to me.

Placebo the first word of the opening antiphon (psalm verse recited as a prelude and as a conclusion), and the title of the first section of the vespers of the Office of the Dead, Psalm 114:9 (Vulgate numbering used): "I will please [the Lord in the land of the living.]" Key words and phrases from the Office are used in the order in which they occur in the liturgy, their sense matching what Jane is saying at the time.
Dilexi the first word of the opening psalm of the Office, Psalm 114:1: "I have loved, [because the Lord will hear the voice of my prayer]"
Margery A Margery was superior at Carrow Abbey, the Benedictine convent (Black Nuns) near Norwich—see l. 8—where Jane Scroop was probably educated.
Fa . . . my the musical notes of the ending of the *Placebo*
Philip Philip, Phip, or Pip was a favorite name for a pet sparrow, in imitation of its chirping
bead-rolls the lists of persons for whom religious were bound to say prayers (*bedes*)
Pater noster qui "Our Father, who [art in heaven]"; the beginning of the Lord's Prayer
Ave Mari "Hail Mary, [full of grace]"; the angelic salutation to the Virgin, repeated as an act of devotion
Creed recited as an act of devotion. These three are the prayers that will be daily said for the soul of Philip Sparrow.
When Jane is beginning to use rhetorical devices —*demonstratio, exclamatio,* and *digressio*—to express her grief; and Skelton begins his variations on the monorhyme.
Pyramus . . . Thisbe young lovers, each of whom killed himself for grief in the belief that the other had been killed

I wept and I wailed,
The tearės down hailed,
But nothing it availed
To call Philip again,
Whom Gib,° our cat, hath slain.
  Gib, I say, our cat
Worried her> on that *choked herself*
Which I loved best.
It cannot be expressed,
My sorrowful heaviness,
But all without redress;
For within that stound,> *moment*
Half slumbering in a sound,> *swoon*
I fell down to the ground.
  Unneth> I cast mine eyes *scarcely*
Toward the cloudy skies;
But when I did behold
My sparrow dead and cold,
No creature but that would
Have ruėd> upon me, *had pity*
To behold and see°
What heaviness did me pang:
Wherewith my hands I wrang,> *wrung*
That my sinews cracked
As though I had been racked,°
So pained and so strained> *tortured*
That no life well nigh remained.
  I sighed and I sobbed,
For that I was robbed
Of my sparrow's life.
O maiden, widow, and wife,°
Of what estate ye be,
Of high or low degree,
Great sorrow then ye might see,
And learn to weep at me!
Such painės> did me fret> *tortures / torment*
That mine heart did beat,
My visage pale and dead,
Wan> and blue as lead;° *livid*
The pangs of hateful death
Well nigh had stopped my breath.
  Heu, heu, me,°

Gib short for Gilbert, the commonest medieval name for a cat
behold . . . see a popular rhetorical amplifying doublet in 15th-century English
racked tortured by being fastened to the rack and stretched
O maiden . . . wife perhaps a reminiscence of the Middle English laments of the Virgin Mary
Wan . . . lead like *black and blo* (l. 75): livid, lead-colored (with grief at or association with death)
Heu . . . me "Woe is me, [that my sojourning is prolonged]!"—opening of the second antiphon, Psalm 119:5

That I am woe for thee!
Ad Dominum cum tribularer, clamavi.°
Of God nothing else crave I
But Philip's soul to keep
From the marish> deep *marsh*
Of Acherontės'° well,> *pool*
That is a flood> of Hell; *river*
And from the great Pluto,°
The prince of endless woe;
And from foul Alecto°
With visage black and blo;
And from Medusa,° that mare,> *witch*
That like a fiend doth stare;
And from Megera's edders,
For ruffling of Philip's feders,> *feathers*
And from her fiery sparklings
For burning of his wings;
And from the smokės sour
Of Proserpìna's bower;°
And from the dennės> dark *dens*
Where Cerberus° doth bark,
Whom Theseus° did affray,> *frighten*
Whom Hercules° did outray,> *overcome*
As famous poets say;
From that hell-hound
That lieth in chainės bound
With ghastly headės three,
To Jupiter° pray we
That Philip preserved may be!
Amen, say ye with me!
   Do mi nus,°
Help now, sweet Jesus!
Levavi oculos meos in montes.°

Ad . . . clamavi "In trouble I cried to the Lord: [and he heard me"]—opening of the second vesper psalm, Psalm 119:1
Acherontes' Acheron was a bitter river that ran through the marshes of Hell, over which the souls of the dead were conveyed. Jane begins to pray that Philip's soul will be delivered also from the pagan Hades and its baleful guardians.
Pluto god of death, inexorable ruler of the underworld, father of the three Eumenides (Furies), who sat by his throne and hunted down wrongdoers on behalf of the gods
Alecto Alecto and Megaera (l. 78) were Eumenides; "edders" are adders, the snakes which these ladies had instead of hair.
Medusa One of the three snaky-locked Gorgons, whose look could kill or turn to stone; Medusa was killed by Perseus.
Proserpina's bower the underworld, to which Proserpina, daughter of Ceres, had been carried off by Pluto as his wife. She presided over the deaths of men.
Cerberus three-headed dog who guarded the entrance to the underworld
Theseus King of Athens. He went down into the underworld with his friend Pirithous to carry off Proserpina, but they were caught and Theseus was tied to the stone on which he was resting. Hercules tore him free, but so roughly that his skin was left behind.
Hercules The "whom" of this line may refer to Theseus, whom Hercules brought out of hell; or Cerberus, whom Hercules overcame and bound when he went down to the underworld to bring back Alcestis.
Jupiter king of the gods. The piled-up classical images are suddenly now confronted again with the Office of the Dead.
Dominus "The Lord [is thy keeper from all evil]"—the opening of the third antiphon, Psalm 120:7
Levavi . . . montes "I have lifted up my eyes to the mountains"—opening of the third vesper psalm, Psalm 120:1

Would God I had Zenophontes,°
Or Socrates the wise,
To show me their devise˃ *advice*
Moderately to take
This sorrow that I make
For Philip Sparrow's sake!
So fervently I shake,
I feel my body quake;
So urgently I am brought
Into careful˃ thought. *sad*
Like Andromach,° Hector's wife,
Was weary of her life,
When she had lost her joy,
Noble Hector of Troy;
In like manner also
Increaseth my deadly woe,
For my sparrow is go.˃ *gone*
  It was so pretty a fool;
It would sit on a stool,
And learned after my school,
For to keep his cut,°
With, 'Philip, keep your cut!'
  It had a velvet cap,°
And would sit upon my lap
And seek after small worms
And sometime white bread-crumbs;
And many times and oft
Between my brestės soft°
It would lie and rest—
It was proper and prest.˃ *active*
  Sometimes he would gasp˃ *gape*
When he saw a wasp;
A fly or a gnat,
He would fly at that;
And prettily he would pant
When he saw an ant;
Lord, how he would pry˃ *search*
After the butterfly!
Lord, how he would hop
After the gressop!˃ *grasshopper*
And when I said, 'Phip! Phip!'

Zenophontes Xenophon, *c.* 430–*c.* 355 B.C., a non-philosopher, but admirer and biographer of Socrates, many of whose sayings and actions he preserved
Andromach Andromache, the "type" of wifely devotion (to Hector, the Trojan hero, whose death she mourned in a famous lament)
keep his cut i.e. behave with propriety; cf. Sir Philip Sidney, *Astrophel and Stella*, Sonnet LXXXIII
velvet cap the brown-feathered top of the sparrow's head
Between . . . soft See Catullus II.1–2: "Sparrow, you my girl's delight / With whom she toys there in her lap / And gives you finger-tips to bite . . .". Sparrows were associated with lechery.

Then he would leap and skip,
And take me by the lip.
Alas, it will me slo˃ *slay*
That Philip is gone me fro!˃ *from*
  Si in i qui ta tes.°
Alas, I was evil at ease!
De pro fun dis cla ma vi,°
When I saw my sparrow die! . . .
c. 1505–7 *c.* 1545

From The Tunning of Elinor Rumming°

. . . Then Margery Milk-Duck
Her kirtle° she did uptuck
An inch above her knee,
Her legs that ye might see;
But they were sturdy and stubbed,˃ *thick*
Mighty pestles and clubbed;
As fair and as white
As the foot of a kite.°
She was somewhat foul,
Crook-nebbed° like an owl;
And yet she brought her fees:
A cantel˃ of Essex cheese,° *cut*
Was well˃ a foot thick, *fully*
Full of maggots quick;˃ *live*
It was huge and great,
And mighty strong meat˃ *food*
For the devil to eat.
It was tart and pungete!˃ *sharp*

  Another sort˃ of sluts: *company*
Some brought walnuts,
Some apples, some pears,
Some brought their clipping shears,
Some brought this and that,
Some brought I wot n'er˃ what, *know not*
Some brought their husband's hat,
Some puddings and links,˃ *sausage links*
Some tripes that stinks.

Si iniquitates "If thou, Lord, wilt mark iniquities: [Lord who shall stand it]"—the fourth antiphon, Psalm 128:3
De . . . clamavi "Out of the depths I have cried [to thee, O Lord]"—opening of the fourth vesper psalm, Psalm 128:1
The Tunning . . . Rumming *tunning* is pouring ale into barrels; here, "brewing"; Elinor Rumming was an actual Surrey ale-wife, in trouble for selling dear and short measure in 1525.
kirtle skirt or outer petticoat
As fair . . . kite "as yellow as a kite's foot" was a proverbial comparison
Crook-nebbed crooked-beaked, crooked-nosed
Essex cheese Essex ewe's milk cheeses were famous for their size and tendency to magotiness. The dirty ladies will bring anything to pay for their invitation and their drinks.

But of all this throng
One came them among,
(She seemed half a leech>), *doctor*
And began to preach
Of the Tuesday in the week
When the mare doth kick,
Of the virtue of an unset leek,°
Of her husband's breek;> *breeches*
With the feathers of a quail
She could to Bordeaux sail;
And with good ale-barm> *ale-froth*
She could make a charm
To help withal> a stitch: *moreover*
She seemed to be a witch. . . .
1517? *c.* 1521

The Garland of Laurel

The Garland of Laurel is a poetic, dream-allegory discussion of the function of the poet and the nature and dignity of his calling, between Queen Fame and Dame Pallas (reputation and learning). The upshot is that Skelton is received into the company of his great English predecessors (see Chaucer's envoi to *Troilus and Criseyde* below), who present him to Occupation (assiduity). Occupation takes him to the Countess of Surrey and her ladies, as they weave his poet's garland for him from the evergreen bay tree around which the Muses dance. Skelton, in gratitude, confers immortality on each lady in turn, by means of a lyric in style answering to her nature and condition.

From The Garland of Laurel

To Mistress Margery Wentworth

With margerain° gentle,
The flower of goodlihead,> *goodness*
Embroiderèd the mantle
Is of your maidenhead.°

Plainly (I cannot glose>), *flatter*
Ye be, as I divine,
The pretty primrose,°
The goodly columbine.°

leek the unset (young, untransplanted) leek was thought to be better medicinally than the set (transplanted and fully grown)
margerain Marjoram gentle, the best sort, symbolizes high-born excellence *(gentilesse)*. A warmer and comforter in scent and taste, it is like Margery in name and qualities.

maidenhead the maidenly qualities which clothe you
primrose the first flower of spring, exemplifying Margery's fresh, clear, young beauty
columbine again a flower image, with a hint of the innocence and faithfulness of the dove *(columba)*

With margerain gentle,
The flower of goodlihead,
Embroiderėd the mantle
Is of your maidenhead.

Benign, courteous, and meek,
With wordės well devised,
In you, who list˃ to seek, *pleases*
Be virtues well comprised.

With margerain gentle,
The flower of goodlihead,
Embroiderėd the mantle
Is of your maidenhead.

To Mistress Margaret Hussey

Merry Margaret,
As midsummer flower:
Gentle as falcon°
Or hawk of the tower.°
With solace and gladness,
Much mirth and no madness,
All good and no badness,
So joyously,
So maidenly,
So womanly
Her demeaning˃ *behavior*
In every thing—
Far, far passing
That I can endite,˃ *write*
Or suffice˃ to write *am fit*
Of Merry Margaret,
As midsummer flower,
Gentle as falcon,
Or hawk of the tower;
As patient and still
And as full of good will,
As fair Isaphill.°
Coliander,°
Sweet pomander,°
Good Cassander;°

falcon noble hunting bird. The emphasis is throughout on Margaret's good breeding and refinement (*gentle*), with a pun on *falcon-gentle*, the female and young of the goshawk.
hawk of the tower high-flying hawk that towers high in the air to swoop on the prey: again an image of lightness, beauty, and nobility
Isaphill Hypsipyle, legendary Queen of Lemnos, the perfection of womanly beauty and devotion to father and children; her story is told by Boccaccio in his *Of Famous Women*, Chap. 15
Coliander Coriander was a sweet, aromatic, comforting herb.
pomander ball of aromatics, carried or worn as a preservative against bad air and disease
Cassander Cassandra, the Trojan prophetess of doom, who had (the story is again in Boccaccio, Chap. 33) suffered for but adhered to her prophecies of Helen's coming and Troy's destruction: an *exemplum* of constancy

Steadfast of thought,
Well made, well wrought;
Far may be sought,
Erst that ye can find, *before*
So courteous, so kind,
As merry Margaret,
This midsummer flower:
Gentle as falcon
Or hawk of the tower.
c. 1495 1523

THE OTHER WORLD: PARADISE

In the beginning, when God had created all things, he made man lord of them all, and planted a garden eastward in Eden where man and woman could live in peace and joy. By disobedience and the Fall, they exchanged their happiness for misery (Fig. 56)—and their fault condemned us all to our condition.

This great myth of a Paradise lost to us was fact for the Middle Ages, firmly based on the biblical account. Was there a way to that happy garden state, so remote from us in time and place? Could we hope to reach it, in body or in soul?

For the church, there was one true answer. The only way a man could escape the misery of his life on earth was by living a truly virtuous life within the church, trusting that after death his soul would be numbered among the blessed. He must hope that the grace of God and the sacrifice of Christ would save him from passing out of the temporary torment of this world into the eternal torment of Hell. Then his soul might travel up to heaven through the concentric spheres of the universe (Fig. 55); despise the world, and see God face to face.

But the hope of even temporarily enjoying a place of rest and freedom from all things unpleasant while still in this life never quite died. Nor did the hope of coming, far off in the east on the mountain tops, upon the Garden of Eden itself. Columbus, when he discovered America, thought he must be near it; Marco Polo, journeying to China, felt he might find it somewhere out there. So "Sir John Mandeville," describing Paradise, has to say that he has never actually been there and must rely on hearsay. But the implication is that he believed in the possibility of someday traveling far enough—and his account has reminiscences of genuine descriptions of Eastern countries in the general area where he would look for it.

If Paradise were found, what would it be like? The word itself already gives a clue. It is known to derive from a Persian word meaning a walled park or pleasure ground and it passed into Greek in that sense. Its use in the Bible is decisive for its meaning throughout the Middle Ages; but the biblical description in Genesis 2 has much in common with Greek and Roman accounts of the conditions prevailing in Elysium, the abode of the blessed after death. All descriptions of Paradise, the *locus amoenus* (delightful place), and its literary-garden imitations, share certain features. They are secluded, shut off by a wall, often far-off in the East; inaccessible, because of being on a mountain top; they enjoy a perpetual sunny season which combines spring, summer, and autumn, with flowers and fruits always flourishing, evergreen trees, fountains, rivers, riches, jewels, perpetual abundance; the exclusion of all that is harmful in thought, word, or deed. All the features of "soft" primitivism are there, and they add up to a place of utter freedom from care.

These features are often elaborated or treated symbolically. The four rivers of the account in Genesis, for example, may be made to symbolize the four cardinal virtues—prudence, temperance, fortitude, and justice—and the whole turned into an allegory of man's soul. Or, at the other end of the scale, as in *The Land of Cokaygne,* they may merely signify fat plenty: oil, wine, milk, and honey, or sweet, soothing medicaments.

The selections given below are, first, the biblical text from Genesis on which all the later accounts are built; then two descriptions, from four centuries apart, where there is an allegorical tinge, sacred and implicit in the Old English ninth-century poem on the *Phoenix,* secular and explicit in the description of the garden from the thirteenth-century *Roman de la Rose.* Then comes a satirical, popular version, the fourteenth-century poem *Land of Cokaygne,* in which the description is stood on its head; then another, popular account of a journey from this wo**ı**ld to Elfland-Paradise, in the ballad of "Thomas the Rhymer"; then "Mandeville's" description of what Paradise actually looked like. Finally, there come the spiritual Paradises in the conclusions of the greatest medieval English poem, Geoffrey Chaucer's *Troilus and Criseyde,* and of the greatest poem of the whole European Middle Ages, Dante's *Divine Comedy.*

The ninth-century Old English *Phoenix,* from which our selection is taken, is based on a fourth-century Latin poem attributed to Lactantius (c. 270–340 A.D.), as much pagan as Christian in character. This happy land is a welcome relief from the glowering winter landscapes of most Old English poetry. The second half of the poem makes it an allegory of the perfection from which man has fallen and to which he will be restored by the phoenix, the symbol of a loving Christ.

The Paradise garden of *The Romance of the Rose* (Fig. 54) is the work of the first of its two authors, Guillaume de Lorris (fl. c. 1225–40). It is part of the dream-allegory vision which, by using the personified qualities of the true courtly lover, and their opposites, sets out the process by which noble and refined human love, free of all taint of lowness, can come to man and woman and be maintained. The garden wall excludes all base impediments to love: inside, all is pleasure, except for the threat of the God of Love's five discouraging arrows, which will, however, be used only in extreme cases. Cupid, the pagan god, and Narcissus, the pagan exemplar of self-love, accord quite naturally with the abstractions.

The Paradise of *The Land of Cokaygne,* written about 1315, is a down-to-earth reversal of such sentiments. It is part of a genre of fable that goes back to the Greek satirist Lucian of Samosata (b. 125? A.D.) and forward to the folk-ballad "The Big Rock-Candy Mountain." There is nothing refined and spiritual in this poor-man's satirical, anti-clerical presentation of the Paradise enjoyed by the monks who live on the fat of the land in jeweled luxury, without serfdom or toil, passing their time in eating, drinking, flying about, and tumbling the nuns. There is pleasure for them even in their religious observances.

The Paradise journey of Thomas the Rhymer is made to a far-off place: an elfin, sinister land, not a divine one, with echoes of sin and judgment, transformations of the Virgin Mary, of the waters of Paradise, of the prohibition on Adam and Eve (and of Proserpina, whose tasting of food in Hades condemned her to stay there half the year). Thomas seems to owe his return from the strange journey and his gift of prophecy to his refusal to accept the Queen of Elfland's gift.

"Mandeville's" Paradise has all the usual features in a much more recognizable form. His enormously popular book, first written in French, possibly at Liège in Belgium about 1357, was rapidly translated into other languages. Nobody knows who "Mandeville" was: the name is a fabrication. His book is one long traveler's tale, an account of the Holy Land and of the Marvels of the East as far as Cathay. It has elements of the hero's travels in chivalric romance, as well as of a popular encyclopedia, and it is full of "new things and new tidings" lifted and embroidered from genuine itineraries and from learned works.

The earthly Paradise one might reach, in dream or in fact, during one's lifetime: the celestial could be attained only when one had put off the encumbrances of the body and flown, in a vision or as a disembodied soul, up beyond the changeable spheres of the planets, to the eternal rest and harmony of heaven. The last two selections concern two different versions of this soul-journey, the literary source of which is Macrobius (see Chaucer's Nun's Priest's Tale, l. 353). In the first, Chaucer is bidding good-bye to his book, the story of the true love of Troilus for the false Criseyde, and telling how Troilus, having lost his love, who was his world, seeks death in battle to rid himself of a pointless life. Only when he is dead can he be carried up to a realization of the pettiness of earth and the joys of life after death. As a pagan he cannot enjoy the true love which Chaucer recommends to young lovers who are Christian—but he goes as far as he can.

The closing words of the final canto of Dante's *Paradiso* are the supreme medieval statement of the beatific vision, when Dante's dream-journey to heaven with Beatrice culminates in his realization of the nature of divine love. They have long passed the virtues of the active life on earth. Faith, hope, and charity have strengthened Dante until, finally reaching the abode of rest and stillness where God is, his will and divine love come together in the Paradise of the mind.

Genesis, 2:8–22 (Authorized Version)

8 And the LORD God planted a garden eastward in Eden; and there he put
the man whom he had formed.
9 And out of the ground made the LORD God to grow every tree that is
pleasant to the sight, and good for food; the tree of life also in the midst of
the garden, and the tree of knowledge of good and evil.
10 And a river went out of Eden to water the garden; and from thence it
was parted, and became into four heads.
11 The name of the first is Pison: that is it which compasseth the whole
land of Havilah, where there is gold;
12 and the gold of that land is good: there is bdellium and the onyx stone.
13 And the name of the second river is Gihon: the same is it that compasseth the whole land of Ethiopia.
14 And the name of the third river is Hiddekel: that is it which goeth
toward the east of Assyria. And the fourth river is Euphrates.
15 And the LORD GOD took the man, and put him into the garden of Eden
to dress it and to keep it.
16 And the LORD God commanded the man, saying, Of every tree of the
garden thou mayest freely eat:

17 but of the tree of the knowledge of good and evil, thou shalt not eat of it:
for in the day that thou eatest thereof thou shalt surely die.
18 And the Lord God said, It is not good that the man should be alone; I
will make him a help meet for him.
19 And out of the ground the Lord God formed every beast of the field,
and every fowl of the air; and brought them unto Adam to see what he would
call them: and whatsoever Adam called every living creature, that was the
name thereof.
20 And Adam gave names to all cattle, and to the fowl of the air, and to
every beast of the field; but for Adam there was not found a help meet for
him.
21 And the Lord God caused a deep sleep to fall upon Adam, and he slept:
and he took one of his ribs, and closed up the flesh instead thereof;
22 and the rib, which the Lord God had taken from man, made he a woman,
and brought her unto the man.

1611

From The Phoenix°

Lo! I have learned   of the loveliest of lands
Far to the eastward,   famous among men.
But few ever fare   to that far-off realm
Set apart from the sinful   by the power of God. . . .
The plain is winsome,   the woods are green,
Widespread under heaven.   No rain or snow,
Or breath of frost   or blast of fire,
Or freezing hail   or fall of rime,
Or blaze of sun   or bitter-long cold,
Or scorching summer   or winter storm
Work harm a whit,   but the plain endures
Sound and unscathed.   The lovely land
Is rich with blossoms.   No mountains rise,
No lofty hills,   as here with us;
No high rock-cliffs,   no dales or hollows,
No mountain gorges,   no caves or crags,
Naught rough or rugged;   but the pleasant plain
Basks under heaven   laden with bloom.
Twelve cubits° higher   is that lovely land,
As learned writers   in their books relate,
Than any of these hills   that here in splendour
Tower on high   under heavenly stars.
Serene that country   sunny groves gleaming;
Winsome the woodlands;   fruits never fail
Or shining blossoms.   As God gave bidding
The groves stand for ever   growing and green.

Phoenix The translation is by Charles W. Kennedy, in his *An Anthology of Old English Poetry*, New York, 1960.

cubits The cubit was either 18 or 21 inches.

Winter and summer the woods alike
Are hung with blossoms; under heaven no leaf
Withers, no fire shall waste the plain
To the end of the world. As the waters of old,
The sea-floods, covered the compass of earth
And the pleasant plain stood all uninjured,
By the grace of God unhurt and unharmed,
So shall it flourish till the fire of Judgment
When graves shall open, the dwellings of death.
  Naught hostile lodges in all that land,
No pain or weeping or sign of sorrow,
No age or anguish or narrow death;
No ending of life or coming of evil,
No feud or vengeance or fret of care;
No lack of wealth or pressure of want,
No sorrow or sleeping or sore disease.
No winter storm or change of weather
Fierce under heaven, or bitter frost
With wintry icicles smites any man there.
No hail or hoar-frost descends to earth,
No windy cloud; no water falls
Driven by storm. But running streams
And welling waters wondrously spring
Overflowing earth from fountains fair.
  From the midst of the wood a winsome water
Each month breaks out from the turf of earth,
Cold as the sea-stream, coursing sweetly
Through all the grove. . . .
  In that woodland dwelleth, most wondrous fair
And strong of wing, a fowl called Phoenix;° *bird*
There dauntless-hearted he has his home,
His lonely lodging. In that lovely land
Death shall never do him a hurt,
Or work him harm while the world standeth.
  Each day he observes the sun's bright journey
Greeting God's candle, the gleaming gem,
Eagerly watching till over the ocean
The fairest of orbs shines forth from the East,
God's bright token glowing in splendour,
The ancient hand-work of the Father of all.
The stars are hid in the western wave,
Dimmed at dawn, and the dusky night
Steals darkly away; then, strong of wing
And proud of pinion, the bird looks out

Phoenix Symbol of rebirth, a legendary, unique Egyptian bird associated with the sun. When, after many thousand years, it felt death approaching, it flew to Heliopolis, placed itself in a nest of spices on the altar of the sun and was burned to ashes, from which a new phoenix then rose. In the *Bestiary* (see Chaucer's Nun's Priest's Tale, l. 505) the phoenix signifies Christ and his resurrection, or the resurrection of mankind.

Over the ocean under the sky,
Eagerly waiting when up from the East
Heaven's gleam comes gliding over the wide water.
Then the fair bird, changeless in beauty,
Frequents at the fountain the welling streams;
Twelve times the blessed one bathes in the burn› *brook*
Ere the bright beacon comes, the candle of heaven;
And even as often at every bath
Tastes the pleasant water of brimcold° wells.
Thereafter the proud one after his water-play
Takes his flight to a lofty tree
Whence most easily o'er the eastern ways
He beholds the course of the heavenly taper
Brightly shining over the tossing sea,
A blaze of light. The land is made beautiful,
The world made fair, when the famous gem
O'er the ocean-stretches illumines the earth
All the world over, noblest of orbs.
When the sun climbs high over the salt streams
The grey° bird wings from his woodland tree
And, swift of pinion, soars to the sky
Singing and caroling to meet the sun. . . .

?9th century

From Guillaume de Lorris: The Romance of the Rose°

Short space my feet had traversed ere› *before*
A garden spied I, great and fair,
The which a castled wall hemmed round,
And pictured thereupon I found
Full many a figure rich and bright
Of colour, and how each one hight› *was called*
Clear writ beneath it; now will I
To you declare from memory
The semblance and the name of each,
And somewhat of their natures teach.

HATE

Amidmost stood Hell's daughter, Hate,
Malignant, base, and desolate
Of countenance; prime mover she

brimcold i.e. cool and brimming full
grey The phoenix is usually said to be brilliantly colored. Milton's picture of Satan sitting like an evil cormorant on the tree in the midst of Eden may be a deliberate evocation of the contrary of the good phoenix sitting on its palm-tree.

The Romance of the Rose Though Chaucer translated this part of the *Roman de la Rose*, and the translation here, by F. S. Ellis, makes it into a Pre-Raphaelite poem, Ellis's version is used as being more easily understandable.

Of quarrel, strife, and jealousy.
Her very being, as meseemed,
With black and treacherous poison teemed
Of evil passion, while her dark
And frowning visage bore the mark
Of frenzied madness. Heavenward rose,
As if in scorn, her camus˃ nose, *snub*
And round her head, as if with will
To make her foulness fouler still,
A filthy clout˃ had she enwrapped. *cloth*

. . .

ELD

To Sorrow next was pictured Eld:˃ *old age*
Time's hand all care for food had quelled
Within her, and a foot was she
Less than in youth she woned˃ to be, *used*
Bowed down by toil and drearihead.˃ *dreariness*
Her beauty, years long past, had fled,
And foul of face was she become.
And though old Time had left her some
Sparse, straggling locks, her head was white
As though 'twere floured: the loss were light
If that poor body, worn and waste,
The doubtful woe of death should taste;
For shrivelled were her limbs, and dry.
Faded her once bright lustrous eye;
Wrinkled the cheeks once soft and smooth;
And those once pink-shell ears, forsooth,
Now pendent hung; her pearl-like teeth,
Alas! had long since left their sheath,
And barely could she walk as much
As fathoms˃ four without her crutch. *six feet*

. . .

[The poet sees a gate in the wall.]

Full many a time with sounding blow
I struck the door, and, head bent low,
Stood hearkening who might make reply.
The hornbeam wicket˃ presently *small gate*
Was opened by a dame of air
Most gracious, and of beauty rare:
Her flesh as tender chicken's was;
Her blond locks bright as bowl of brass;
Radiant her brow; of arching due
Her eyebrows; and well spaced the two;
Neither too small, nor yet too great
Her nose, but straight and delicate.
No falcon, I would boldly swear,

Hath eyes that could with hers compare.
Her breath was sweet as breeze, thyme-fed;
Her cheeks, commingled white and red;
Her mouth a rosebud, and her chin
Well rounded, with sweet cleft therein.
Her tower-like neck, of measure meet,> *fitting*
The purest lily well might beat
For fairness, free of spot or wem.> *blemish*
'Twixt this and far Jerusalem
I trow> were found none other such, *believe*
So fair to sight, so soft to touch.
Her bosom would outshine the snow
New-fallen, ere it soil> doth show; *dirt*
And all her body formed and knit
So well, as nought might equal it.
Much doubt I, if since Time had birth,
A fairer dame hath trod dull earth. . . .

[Idleness/Leisure welcomes him and tells him what the garden is and to whom it belongs.]

No more I spake, but thanked kind fate,
When Idleness the garden gate
Threw open wide, and unafraid
To that sweet spot quick entry made.
Then burst on my astonished eyes
A dream—an Earthly Paradise:
And suddenly my soul seemed riven
From earth, to dwell in highest heaven;
Yet doubt I much if heaven can give
A place where I so soon would live
As this sweet garden, sacred haunt
Of birds whose soft melodious chaunt
Ravished mine ears; the nightingales
Here sang, and there the green wood-wales;> *orioles*
The bullfinch piped beneath, above,
I heard the crooning turtle-dove,
Near by, the sweet-voiced tiny wren,
While high in air, beyond my ken,
The skylark soared; the titmouse shrilled
The fauvette's> gentle treble trilled. *warbler's*
The merle> and mavis> seemed to shake *blackbird / song thrush*
The leaves in cadence, while each brake
With small fowl> rang, as they would try *birds*
Their throats in choral rivalry.
'Twould seem as all and each of these
Sweet birds sang joyance to the breeze,
And then, their hearts disburdened, flew
To keep some loving rendezvous.

[Idleness/Leisure having let the poet in, he wanders through the garden until he comes to the owner, Mirth, and his company, who are dancing to a tune and a song by Gladness. Courtesy comes to him, to ask him to join the dance. Then he sees the God of Love, with his companion Sweet Looking, who carries the quivers with the god's arrows of gold, whose wounds make happy and successful love: Beauty, Simplicity, Franchise (Generosity), Companionship, Fair Seeming; and his other arrows, symbolizing obstacles to love: Pride, Villainy (Base Behavior), Shame, Despair, and Fickleness. The god has, as his special companions, ladies called Beauty, Richesse (Wealth), Largesse (Gift-Giving), and Franchise. The poet now finally accepts Courtesy's invitation to join the dance.]

And next stood gracious Courtesy,
Who ne'er midst men can fail to be
Welcome: strangers to her are pride
And folly. Straightway to her side
She summoned me with kindly call
To join the gladsome dance withal.
Frank-eyed she was, and no deal˃ shy — *part*
Or timid, but most graciously
Spake forth to me in friendly wise,
With pleasant words and quaint˃ replies, — *ingenious*
Wherein one found no poison lurk.
Her form was nature's perfect work,
And e'en as stars like candles mean
Beside the moon's bright rays are seen,
So her companions showed beside
Her dazzling beauty's winsome pride.
Than this fair damsel who shall find
A nobler face or gentler mind,
Or one who would more worship gain
Should she as Queen or Empress reign?

Beside her stood a valiant knight,
Who knew to choose his words aright
Whene'er he spake; well loved seemed he
Of her who bare him company.
Well skilled in feats of arms, his grace
Showed forth alike in form and face.

Then, Idleness came near to me,
Whose hand I took most willingly
To join the dance. Erewhile˃ I've said — *before*
How fraught with grace and goodlihead
She was, and she 'twas raised the pin
That kept the wicket, and within
The close˃ through her I entrance gained, — *enclosure*
My trembling heart set free and fained.˃ — *gladdened*

. . .

[After the dance, the poet wanders through the garden, in some alarm because the God of Love is pursuing him with his bow.]

No thought had I to stay or rest,
But roved north, south, and east and west,
Desiring leisurely to view
The close, and all that 'longed> thereto. *belonged*

I noted that from side to side
The garden was nigh broad as wide,
And every angle duly squared.
The careful planter had not spared
To set of every kind of tree
That beareth fruit some two or three,
Or more perchance, except some few
Of evil sort. Among them grew
Pomegranates filled with seeds and thick
Of skin, most wholesome for the sick;
Strange nut trees, which in season bore
Rich fragrant nutmegs, good for store,
And nowise cursed with nauseous taste
But savouring well. Near by were placed
Almonds and gillyflower cloves,
Brought hither from hot Ind's> far groves, *India's*
Dates, figs, and liquorice which deals
Contentment while misease it heals. . . .
Moreover in this garden rare
Grew many a tree familiar,
As cherry, pear and knotted quince,
'Neath which a tender tooth will wince,
Brown medlars, plums both black and white,
Apples and chestnuts, peaches bright. . . .
And all around this pleasant close
Holly, and laurel, and holm° arose
With yew and hornbeam, fit I trow
For flitting shaft, and speeding bow;
The cypress sad, and pines that sigh
To soft south breezes mournfully,
Beech, loved of squirrels, olive dark,
And graceful birch with silvery bark;
The shimmering aspen, maple tall,
And lofty ash that topped the wall. . . .
But this I say, such skilful art
Had planned the trees that each apart
Six fathoms stood, yet like a net
The interlacing branches met,
Through which no scorching rays could pass

holm holly-oaks, evergreen oaks

To sear the sward, and thus the grass
Kept ever tender, fresh and green,
Beneath their cool and friendly screen.

Roebuck and deer strayed up and down
The mead, and troops of squirrels brown
The tree-boles scoured, while conies> grey *rabbits*
Shot merrily in jocund play
Around their burrows on the fresh
And fragrant greensward, void of mesh.°

Within the glades sprang fountains clear:
No frog or newt e'er came anear> *near*
Their waters, but 'neath cooling shade
They gently sourded.> Mirth had made *flowed*
Therefrom small channelled brooks to fling
Their waves with pleasant murmuring
In tiny tides. Bright green and lush,
Around these sparkling streams, did push
The sweetest grass. There might one lie
Beside one's love, luxuriously
As though 'twere bed of down. The earth,
Made pregnant by the streams, gave birth
To thymy herbage and gay flowers,
And when drear winter frowns and lowers> *scowls*
In spots less genial, ever here
Things bud and burgeon> through the year. *sprout*

. . .

[The poet comes finally to the Fountain of Narcissus, who scorned the love of Echo. She pined away and Narcissus was punished by being made to fall in love with his own reflection.]

Without the door
Of paradise the blest, I ween
No sight more beauteous may be seen
Than this bright well. The gushing source
Springs ever fresh and sweet. . . .
Fast in the fountain's pavement shone
Two sparkling spheres of crystal stone,
Whereon my gaze with wonder fell:
And, when the tale thereof I tell,
Your ears will tingle as I trow,
And pleasure unto marvel grow.
When that the sun, which searcheth all
The things that live on earth, lets fall
His rays within this fount we see
An hundred colours gorgeously

mesh i.e. clear of rabbit-net or snare

Shine forth within the water bright,
Vermilion, azure, silvery white,
And richest gold. Such virtuous power
These crystals have that every flower
And tree within this pleasaunce seen,
Reflection finds in their sweet sheen. . . .
By reason of the seed there sown,
This Fountain is to all men known
As that of Love: thereof is told
The tale full oft in many an old
Romance and song, but ne'er before
Hath any man so fully or
So truly set all forth as now
'Tis writ within this book I trow.

[Moving on, the poet finds the rose which is the object of his search, but before he can pluck it from behind its protecting hedge, the God of Love shoots him with all his golden arrows. He then anoints the poet's wounds and the poet acknowledges himself forever love's devotee.]

1225–40

The Land of Cokaygne°

Far in the sea, to the west of Spain,°
Is a country called Cokaygne.°
There's no land not anywhere,
In goods or riches to compare.
Though Paradise be merry and bright
Cokaygne is of far fairer sight.
In Paradise's happy bowers,
They've only grass and trees and flowers,
Though they've joy and pleasure great,
There they've only fruit to eat;
There's no boudoir, hall nor bench
And water only, thirst to quench.
And there are no men there but two:
Elijah° and Enoch° also:
Miserably must they roam,
When they live there all alone.
In Cokaygne there's meat and drink,

Land of Cokaygne This paraphrase by the present editor, in doggerel no worse than that of the original, has been made on the basis of the text in R. H. Robbins, *Historical Poems of the 15th and 16th Centuries* (1959).
Far . . . Spain a reminiscence of the Fortunate Islands of the ancients, and a reversal in position of Paradise, usually placed in the East
Cokaygne The origin of the name is obscure, but it has something to do with cakes and cookery.
Elijah the prophet, taken up to heaven by fiery chariot in a whirlwind (II Kings 2:11)
Enoch the righteous man, carried off by God (Genesis 5:24; Hebrews 11:5), who lived in heaven and—the story was—learned its secrets. He and Elijah were, according to the Bible, the only mortal men taken into Paradise.

Without trouble, fuss and swink.°
The food is fine, the drink is clear
At noon, at snack-time, at supper.
In truth—I say so without fear—
There's no land on earth its peer,
Nor under heaven a land—I hiss
To you—where there's such joy and bliss.

There are many sweetest sights,
All is day, there are no nights;
There's no quarrelling or strife
Nor is there death, but lasting life;
There's no lack of food or cloth
There's no man nor woman wroth.
There's no serpent, wolf or fox
Horse or hack or cow or ox
There's no sheep, or swine, or goat
No, nor filth there—God takes note—
Nor breeding stable, no, nor stud
The land is full of all things good.
There's no fly, no flea, no louse
In clothes, in town, in bed, in house;
There's no thunder, sleet or hail;
Nor any filthy worm, or snail;
Nor any storm, or rain, or wind;
Nor is there man or woman blind
But all is play and joy and glee
Happy he that there may be.

There are rivers broad and fine
Of oil and honey, milk and wine;
Water serves there for no thing
But looking at or washing in.
There are fruits of many sorts,
Endless pleasures, joys and sports.

There appears a fine abbèy
Of white monks and, also, of grey.°
There are bowers and there are halls,
All of pasties° are the walls,
Of rich food, of fish and meat
Which are delectable to eat.
Cakes of flour are the shingles all
Of church and cloister, bower and hall.
The roofing-pins are fat puddings—
Rich food for princes and for kings—

swink toil
white . . . grey white friars (Carmelites) and gray (Franciscans)
pasties meat pies

All he wants a man may eat
As of right and without threat.
All is common to young and old,
To brave and tough, to meek and bold.
There's a cloister, fine and light,
Broad and long, a splendid sight:
The pillars of that cloister all
Are fashioned out of pure crystàl,
Have their base and capital
Of jasper green and red coràl.
In the meadow is a tree
Most delicious to see:
The root is ginger and galingale,°
The shoots are all of cetewale°
And three maces are the flower;
Cinnamon bark makes sweet odour,
Cloves are its fruit, of spicy taste—
And cubebs° never go to waste.
There are roses, red in hue
And lilies lovely, just for you,
Never withering, day or night;
Sure this is the sweetest sight.
Four springs gush out from this abbèy
Of treacle and of halewey,°
Of balm° and also of spiced wine
Flowing freely, always fine;
And of those streams the èntire bed
Is precious stones and gold so red.
There are sapphires and uniunes
Carbuncles and astiunes
Emerald, ligure and prasine
Beryl, onyx, topazine
Amethyst and chrysolite
Chalcedòny, hepatite.°

There are so many birds they jostle:
Thrush and nightingale and throstle,°
Golden orioles, chalènders,°
And many others, of all genders,
Who never cease, by day or night,
Singing sweetly with all their might.
Another thing—I must tell it—
Geese, ready roasted on a spit.

galingale i.e. spice
cetewale zedoary, fragrant herb
cubebs spicy seeds
treacle . . . halewey Sweet, healing medicines, potions or lotions. Treacle was originally theriake, remedy for snakebite.
balm fragrant, healing medicine
sapphires . . . hepatite The rich gems are in imitation of the Heavenly Jerusalem. Uniunes are large pearls, carbuncles are garnets, astiunes are star sapphires, prasines are chrysopase, topazine is topaz, hepatite is bloodstone.
throstle song-thrush
chalènders larks

Fly to that abbey—God hear me talk—
And 'Geese, all hot, all hot,' they squawk.
They bring of garlic great supply
The best prepared that man may spy.
The larks, so tasty to every youth,
Flutter gently to man's mouth,
Cooked in a stew, upon the stove,
Flavoured with cinnamon and clove.
To drink there's need of no permission:
Just take your fill: no intermission.

And when the monks arrive at mass
All the windows, that are of glass,
Turn at once into crystal bright
So that the monks may have more light.
When the masses have been said
And the mass-books put to bed,
The crystal turns again to glass—
Back to the state it formerly was.

All the young monks every day
After food go off to play:
There's no hawk or bird, so high
Or swiftly flying through the sky,
As the monks in merry mood
Swooping on wings of sleeves and hood.

When the abbot sees them fly
Then with joy he winks his eye
But even so, and he's not wrong,
He calls them back to even-song.
But the monks will not come home.
They fly on: in a flock they roam.

When the abbot still can't spy
That his monks will back home fly
He takes a maiden, from a mass
And turning upward her white ass
He rattles the drum with his right hand
To make his monks come back to land.

When his monks that fine sight see
Back to the maid they quickly flee
And gather about her, with one mind,
To get a smack at her white behind.
And so they quietly, after the session,
Go off home in a procession
And from their food they do not shrink,
As long as they're given enough to drink.

Another abbey lies nearby:
It is a fine great nunnery,
Beside a stream of sweetest milk,
Where there's also plenty of silk.
When the summer's day is hot
The young nuns get themselves a boat
And launch it out and make it shudder
So fast they handle oars and rudder.
When they are safely behind the bluff
And hidden, they quickly strip to the buff.
They slip down into the waters brimming
And happily pass their time in swimming.
When the young monks cast their eye
On this, they get up fast and fly
And reach the nuns' pool at the run.
Then each and every monk takes one
And quickly carries off his prey
As far as his fine and great abbèy
And teaches the nuns an orison°
With jigging up and jigging down.

The monk who'd be a stallion good
And knows how to arrange his hood
He shall have, without refusal
Twelve wives a year (the number's usual),
As of right, not special grace,
So as to give him his solace.
And the monk of all that nation,
Who orders best his recreation
It's hoped that he, by help of God,
Will soon be chosen new abbòt.

Whoever wants to reach that land
Must do great penance at command:
In a pig-pen seven long years
He must wade, up to his ears
In muck—perhaps just up to the chin
Will do—on the way that land to win.

Gentlemen good and gentlemen gay
May you never go from this world away
Until you see and grab your chance,
Perform completely this penance
So that you may that land see plain
And nevermore come back again.
Let's pray God that so it be
Amen, for holy Charity.

c. 1315

orison prayer

Thomas the Rhymer°

True Thomas lay on Huntly bank,
  A ferlie> he spied wi' his e'e;> — *marvel / eye*
And there he saw a lady bright
  Come riding down by the Eildon Tree.°

Her shirt° was o' the grass-green silk,
  Her mantle o' the velvet fyne;
At ilka tett> of her horse's mane — *every braid*
  Hung fifty siller> bells and nine. — *silver*

True Thomas, he pull'd off his cap
  And louted> low down to his knee: — *bowed*
'All hail, thou mighty Queen of Heaven!°
  For thy peer on earth I never did see.'

'O no, O no, Thomas,' she said,
  'That name does not belong to me;
I am but the Queen of fair Elfland
  That am hither come to visit thee.

Harp and carp,> Thomas,' she said, — *sing*
  'Harp and carp along wi' me,
And if ye dare to kiss my lips,
  Sure of your bodie I will be.'

'Betide me weal,> betide me woe, — *happiness*
  That weird> shall never daunton> me.' — *fate / daunt*
Syne> he has kissed her rosy lips — *at once*
  All underneath the Eildon Tree.

'Now ye maun> go wi' me,' she said, — *must*
  'True Thomas, ye maun go wi' me;
And ye maun serve me seven years
  Thro' weal or woe, as may chance to be.'

Thomas the Rhymer Child, no. 37. Air: Blaikie ms. (National Library of Scotland, ms. 1578). Thomas Rymour, Thomas the Rhymer (i.e. Minstrel), Thomas of Erceldoune, True Thomas, is spoken of as a poet during the 14th century and in the 15th acquired a reputation as a seer, a kind of Scots Merlin, which lasted until the 19th. He seems to have been a historical person of the late 13th century. A 15th-century romance of Thomas of Erceldoune exists, relating his gift of prophecy to his visit to the Queen of Elfland. It and the ballad are other-world journeys, with features that go back to the earliest of such tales, to other romances such as *Ogier the Dane,* to Merlin stories, to St. Patrick's Purgatory, and the like.

Eildon Tree Also in the romance; the Eildon Hills are near Melrose, in Berwickshire, Scotland. Woods and trees are the natural habitat of fairies and supernatural beings.

shirt i.e. skirt

Heaven i.e. the Virgin Mary

She mounted on her milk-white steed,
  She's ta'en True Thomas up behind;
And aye> whene'er her bridle rung *always*
  The steed flew swifter than the wind.

O they rade> on, and farther on— *rode*
  The steed gaed> swifter than the wind— *went*
Until they reached a desert wide
  And living land was left behind.

'Light> down, light down now, True Thomas, *dismount*
  And lean your head upon my knee;
Abide and rest a little space
  And I will show you ferlies> three. *wonders*

O see ye not yon narrow road°
  So thick beset with thorns and briars?
That is the path of righteousness,
  Though after it but few enquires.

And see ye not that braid,> braid road *broad*
  That lies across that lily leven?> *lovely plain*
That is the path of wickedness,
  Though some call it the road to heaven.

And see not ye that bonny> road *fine*
  That winds about the fernly brae?> *hillside*
That is the road to fair Elfland,
  Where thou and I this night maun gae.> *go*

But Thomas, ye maun hold your tongue
  Whatever ye may hear or see,
For if you speak word in Elflyn land
  Ye'll ne'er get back° to your ain> countrie.' *own*

O they rade on, and farther on,
  And they waded through rivers aboon> the knee, *above*
And they saw neither sun nor moon
  But they heard the roaring of the sea.

It was mirk,> mirk night and there was nae stern> light *dark / star*
  And they waded through red blude> to the knee; *blood*
For a'> the blude that's shed on earth *all*
  Rins> through the springs o' that countrie. *runs*

Syne> they came on to a garden green° *then*
  And she pu'd> an apple frae a tree: *plucked*

road Thus begins the supernatural knowledge which Thomas acquires and which allows him to prophesy truly on his return to earth.
Ye'll . . . back But he does get back; in the romance, the Queen sends him back after three years to avoid his being captured by the Devil.
garden green Paradise; the Queen repeats Eve's gift of the apple to Adam, but the fairy gift gives him the gift of true speech and prophecy, rather than causes him harm or permanent residence in the lower world. Perhaps this is because of his rather churlish, but independent, reply in the next stanza.

'Take this for thy wages, True Thomas,
 It will give thee the tongue that can never lee.'˃ *lie*

'My tongue is mine ain,'˃ True Thomas said, *own*
 'A gudely gift ye wad gie˃ to me; *give*
I neither dought˃ to buy nor sell *dare*
 At fair or tryst˃ where I may be; *market*

I dought neither speak to prince or peer
 Nor ask of grace from fair ladye.'
'Now hold thy peace, the lady said,
 For as I say, so must it be.'

He has gotten a coat of the even˃ cloth *smooth*
 And a pair of shoes of velvet green;°
And till seven years were gane and past
 True Thomas on earth was never seen.

From Mandeville's Travels°

. . . Of Paradise [1] ne can [2] I not speak properly, for I was not there. It is far beyond, and that forethinketh [3] me, and also I was not worthy. But as I have heard say of wise men beyond,[4] I shall tell you with good will. Paradise Terrestre, as wise men say, is the highest place of earth that is in all the world, and it is so high that it toucheth nigh to the circle of the moon,[5] there as the moon maketh her turn. For she [6] is so high that the Flood of Noah ne might not come to her that would have covered all the earth of the world all about and above and beneath, save Paradise only alone. And this Paradise is enclosed all about with a wall, and men wit [7] not whereof it is, for the walls be covered all over with moss, as it seemeth. And it seemeth not that the wall is stone of nature nor of no other thing that the wall is. And that wall stretcheth from the south to the north, and it hath not but [8] one entry that is closed with fire burning,[9] so that no man that is mortal ne dare not enter.

green fairy, forest color

1. "Mandeville" gives a color of truth-telling to his tale: *properly* means "in my own person."
2. Double negative intensifies.
3. Grieves.
4. In addition.
5. In the so-called Ptolemaic universe, with the earth at the center and the planets arranged in concentric spheres outward, the lowest sphere was that of the moon, the quickest in orbit and the most changeable. All below the sphere of the moon was subject to mutability. Paradise is far to the East, at the edge of the world, where the moon dips below it.
6. I.e. Paradise.
7. Do not know of what material.
8. Only.
9. Genesis 3:24. God placed fiery cherubims and a flaming sword at the gates of Eden after the expulsion of Adam and Eve. "Mandeville's" account is based ultimately on Genesis.

Mandeville's Travels The text used is a modernization by M. C. Seymour, *Mandeville's Travels.*

And in the most high place of Paradise, even in the middle place, is a well [10] that casteth out the four floods that run by diverse lands; [11] of the which the first is cleped [12] Pison or Ganges, that is all one, and it runneth throughout Ind [13] or Havilah,[14] in the which river be many precious stones and much lignum aloes [15] and much gravel of gold. And that other river is cleped Nile or Gihon, that goeth by Ethiopia and after by Egypt. And that other is cleped Tigris, that runneth by Assyria and by Armenia the Great. And that other is cleped Euphrates, that runneth also by Media and by Armenia and by Persia. And men there beyond say that all the sweet waters of the world above and beneath take their beginning of that well of Paradise, and out of that well all waters come and go.

The first river is cleped Pison, that is to say in their language 'assembly,' for many rivers meet them there and go into that river. And some men clepe it Ganges, for a king that was in Ind that hight [16] Gangeres and that it ran throughout his land. And that water is in some [17] place clear and in some place troubled, in some place hot and in some place cold.

The second river is cleped Nile or Gihon, for it is always troubled and Gihon in the language of Ethiopia is to say 'troubled' and in the language of Egypt also.

The third river that is cleped Tigris is as much for to say as 'fast running,'—for he runneth more fast than any of the other, and also there is a beast that is cleped tiger that is fast running.

The fourth river is cleped Euphrates, that is to say 'well bearing,' for there grow many goods upon that river, as corns, fruits, and other goods [18] enough plenty.

And ye shall understand that no man that is mortal ne may not approach [19] to that Paradise. For by land no man may go for wild beasts that be in the deserts and for the high mountains and great huge rocks that no man may pass by for the dark places that be there and that many. And by the rivers may no man go, for the water runneth so rudely [20] and so sharply because that it cometh down so outrageously [21] from the high places above that it runneth in so great waves that no ship may not row nor sail against it. And the water roareth so and maketh so huge noise and so great tempest that no man may hear other in the ship, though he cried with all the craft [22] that he could in the

10. Spring that gives rise to the four rivers (floods).
11. Genesis 2:10–14, where the rivers are named. "Mandeville" does not, as many medieval writers do, allegorize the rivers into the cardinal virtues. Where he can, he identifies them with real rivers and gives a derivation of their names.
12. Called.
13. Literally, India; but often the Far East in general.
14. "Sandy," i.e. Arabia.
15. Aromatic wood, used in pharmacy, thought to be carried down by the Nile.
16. Was called.
17. One . . . another.
18. Good things.
19. Men still hoped to discover Paradise as late as the 16th century. Marco Polo carried a copy of "Mandeville."
20. Roughly and quickly.
21. Excessively. These details may derive from a genuine account of the cataracts of the Nile.
22. Power.

highest [23] voice that he might. Many great lords have assayed with great will many times for to pass by those rivers toward Paradise with full great companies, but they might not speed [24] in their voyage. And many died for weariness of rowing against those strong waves. And many of them became blind and many deaf for the noise of the water. And some were perished and lost within the waves. So that no mortal man may approach to that place without special grace of God, so that of that place I can say you no more. And therefore I shall hold me still [25] and return to that that I have seen.

c. 1375

From Geoffrey Chaucer: Troilus and Criseyde

From Book 5: The Finale°

Go, litel book, go litel myn tragedie,
Ther> God thy maker yet er that he° dye, *where*
So sendė might to make° in som comedie!
But litel book, ne making thou n'envye,°
But subgit> be to allė poesye; *subject*
And kis the steppes, wheras thou seëst pace> *pass*
Virgile, Ovyde, Omer, Lucan, and Stace.

And for> ther is so greet diversitee *since*
In English and in wryting of our tonge,
So preye> I God that noon miswrytė thee, *pray*
Ne thee mismetre for defaute of tonge.°
And red> wherso thou be, or ellės songe, *read*
That thou be understonde> I God beseche! *understood*
But yet to purpos of my rather speche.°

The wrathe, as I began yow for to seye,
Of Troïlus, the Grekes boughten dere;> *paid for dearly*
For thousandės his hondės> maden deye,> *hands / die*
As he that was withouten any pere,> *equal*
Save Ector,° in his tyme, as I can here.°
But weylaway, save only Goddės wille!°
Dispitously him slough the fiers Achille.°

23. Loudest.
24. Succeed.
25. Silent.

Finale Chaucer slips in and out of this *envoi* or conclusion, in which he gathers up and seals his story, claims kinship with the poetic masters of past and present, and sums up the "morality" to which his whole poem has been leading. Like Troilus, he surveys his doings in the world below the spheres: imperfect as they are, his tenderness cannot quite condemn them.
he i.e. Chaucer, the "maker" of this book
make match with, not turn into; the pun is intended
n'envye Do not be envious, take your place below the Roman and Greek poets Virgil, Ovid, Homer, Lucan (author of the *Pharsalia,* 39–65 A.D.) and Statius (author of the *Thebaid, Achilleid,* and *Silvae,* 61–96 A.D.). The reputation of the last two was higher in the Middle Ages than it is today.
defaute of tonge Chaucer recognizes the effect of dialect and linguistic change.
But . . . speche Back to the purport of my earlier words—i.e. back to my story of Troilus.
Ector Hector, the Trojan champion
as I can here as I understand
But . . . wille alas for everything, unless God wills it
Achille Achilles, the Greek hero: without mercy, the fierce Achilles slew him.

And whan that he was slayn in this manere,
His lightė goost ful blisfully is went
Up to the holownesse> of the eighth spere.° *concavity*
In convers letinge> every element; *leaving behind*
And ther he saugh,> with ful avysėment,> *saw / in full view*
The erratik sterrės, herkeninge armonye> *hearing harmony*
With sownės> fulle of hevenish> melodye. *sounds / heavenly*

And down from thenės> faste he gan avyse> *thence / did consider*
This litel spot of erthe, that with the see> *sea*
Enbracėd° is, and fully gan despyse
This wrecched world, and held al> vanitee *everything*
To> rèspect of the pleyn> felicitee *in / absolute*
That is in hevene above; and at the laste,
Ther> he was slayn, his loking doun he caste; *to where*

And in himself he lough> right at the wo *laughed*
Of hem that wepten for his deeth so faste;
And dampnėd> al our werk> that folweth so *damned / doings*
The blindė lust,> the which that may not> laste, *pleasure / cannot*
And sholden al our herte on hevene caste.°
And forth he wentė, shortly for to telle,
Ther> as Mercùrie° sorted> him to dwelle. *where / allotted*

Swich fyn> hath, lo, this Troïlus for love, *ending*
Swich fyn hath al his gretė worthinesse;> *valiance*
Swich fyn hath his estat reäl above,°
Swich fyn his lust,> swich fyn hath his noblesse;> *pleasure / nobility*
Swich fyn hath falsė worldės brotelnesse.> *brittleness*
And thus bigan his lovinge of Criseyde,
As I have told, and in this wyse> he deyde.> *manner / died*

O yongė fresshė folkės, he or she,
In which that love up groweth with your age,
Repeyreth> hoom from worldly vanitee,° *return*
And of your herte up casteth the visage
To thilkė> God that after his image *that same*
Yow made, and thinketh al nis> but a fayre> *is nothing / show*
This world, that passeth sone as flourės fayre.

And loveth him, the which that right for love
Upon a cros, our soules for to beye,> *redeem*
First starf,> and roos,> and sit in hevene above; *died / ascended*
For he nil falsen no wight,> dar I seye, *will deceive no-one*
That wol his herte al hoolly> on him leye.> *wholly / set*

spere Troilus' insubstantial soul travels joyfully from the earth up through the concentric spheres of the planets (erratic, i.e. moving, stars), until he can hear the perfect music they make as they pass on their courses. Sitting in heaven, leaving behind all the elements of which matter is composed (air, fire, earth, and water), he can see the true nature of things.
Enbraced i.e. encircled; see Fig. 55
And . . . caste i.e. when we ought to set our whole heart on heaven
Mercurie Mercury, messenger of the gods, who led souls where they were to live henceforth
estat . . . above i.e. exalted, royal condition
Repeyreth . . . vanitee The repudiation of earthly love for heavenly was a literary convention, but one that was also deeply felt.

And sin> he best to love is, and most meke, *since*
What nedeth feynėd> lovės for to seke? *false*

Lo here, of payens corsėd> oldė rytes, *pagans cursed*
Lo here, what alle hir> goddės may availle; *their*
Lo here, these wrecched worldės appetytes;
Lo here, the fyn> and guerdon> for travaille> *end / reward / toil*
Of Jove, Appollo, of Mars,° of swich rascaille!> *riff-raff*
Lo here, the forme of oldė clerkės> speche *learned men*
In poetrye, if ye hir bokės seche.

O moral Gower,° this book I directe
To thee, and to thee, philosophical Strode,°
To vouchensauf, ther nede is, to corecte,
Of your benignitees and zelės gode.
And to that sothfast> Crist, that starf on rode,> *true / cross*
With al myn herte of mercy ever I preye;
And to the Lord right thus I speke and seye:

Thou oon, and two, and three,° eterne on lyve,> *eternally living*
That regnest ay in three and two and oon,
Uncircumscript, and al mayst circumscryve,> *embrace*
Us from visìble and invisìble foon> *foes*
Defende: and to thy mercy, everychoon,> *everyone*
So make us, Jesus, for thy gracė, digne,> *worthy*
For love of mayde and moder> thyn benigne! Amen. *mother*

Explicit Liber Troili et Criseydis.°
1380–86

From Dante: The Divine Comedy: Paradise[1]

. . . As is he who dreaming sees, and after the dream the passion remains imprinted, and the rest returns not to the mind, such am I; for my vision almost wholly fails, while the sweetness that was born of it yet distils within my heart. Thus the snow is by the sun unsealed; thus on the wind, in the light leaves, was lost the saying of the Sibyl.[2]

O Supreme Light, that so high upliftest Thyself from mortal conceptions, re-lend a little to my mind of what Thou didst appear, and make my tongue so powerful that it may be able to leave one single spark of Thy glory for the

Jove . . . Mars Jupiter, ruler of the gods; Apollo, god of the sun, of music and poetry; Mars, god of war
Gower John Gower (1325?–1408), Chaucer's senior and—in a sense—poetic master, author of the *Confessio Amantis* (Lover's Confession)
Strode probably the Oxford philosopher Ralph Strode
three an adaptation of Dante, *Paradiso* XIV. 28–30
Explicit . . . Criseydis Here ends the book of Troilus and Criseyde.

1. Canto xxxiii, ll. 58–145. The translation is by Charles Eliot Norton.
2. The Cumaean Sibyl wrote her prophecies on leaves which the wind scattered at the opening of her cave.

future people; for, by returning somewhat to my memory and by sounding a little in these verses, more of Thy victory shall be conceived.

I think that by the keenness of the living ray which I endured, I should have been bewildered if my eyes had been averted from it. And it comes to my mind that for this reason I was the more hardy to sustain so much, that I joined my look unto the Infinite Goodness.

O abundant Grace, whereby I presumed to fix my eyes through the Eternal Light so far that there I consumed my sight!

In its depth I saw that whatsoever is dispersed through the universe is there included, bound with love in one volume; substance and accidents and their modes, fused together, as it were, in such wise, that that of which I speak is one simple Light. The universal form of this knot [3] I believe that I saw, because in saying this I feel that I more at large rejoice. One instant only is greater oblivion for me than five and twenty centuries to the emprise which made Neptune wonder at the shadow of Argo.[4]

Thus my mind, wholly rapt, was gazing fixed, motionless, and intent, and ever with gazing grew enkindled. In that Light one becomes such that it is impossible he should ever consent to turn himself from it for other sight; because the Good which is the object of the will is all collected in it, and outside of it that is defective which is perfect there.

Now will my speech be shorter, even in respect to that which I remember, than an infant's who still bathes his tongue at the breast. Not because more than one simple semblance was in the Living Light wherein I was gazing, which is always such as it was before; but through my sight, which was growing strong in me as I looked, one sole appearance, as I myself changed, was altering itself to me.

Within the profound and clear subsistence of the lofty Light appeared to me three circles of three colours and of one dimension; and one appeared reflected by the other, as Iris by Iris,[5] and the third appeared fire which from the one and from the other is equally breathed forth.

O how short is the telling, and how feeble toward my conception! and this toward what I saw is such that it suffices not to call it little.

O Light Eternal, that sole dwellest in Thyself, sole understandest Thyself, and, by Thyself understood and understanding, lovest and smilest on Thyself! That circle, which, thus conceived, appeared in Thee as a reflected light, being somewhile regarded by my eyes, seemed to me depicted within itself, of its own very colour, by our effigy, wherefore my sight was wholly set upon it. As is the geometer [6] who wholly applies himself to measure the circle, and finds

3. The unity of all being and all modes of being in the Creator, bound as leaves in a book, or as in an inextricable knot, by his power.

4. The shadow of Argo, ship of Jason and his Argonauts, seeking the Golden Fleece, and the first ship ever to sail, astonished Neptune, god of the sea, as it sailed over him. This happened 2500 years ago. Dante's vision was so splendid that the minute which elapsed after it had faded seemed like 2500 years.

5. Iris is the rainbow. The rainbows reflected in and begotten of each other represent the Trinity.

6. An impossibility topos. The geometrician cannot find the principle on which the circle can be measured, and Dante cannot find the measure of God, who is immeasurable, or tell the immensity of his infinite vision in the finite medium of words, however infinite his will.

not by thinking that principle of which he is in need, such was I at that new sight. I wished to see how the image accorded with the circle, and how it has its place therein; but my own wings were not for this, had it not been that my mind was smitten by a flash in which its wish came.

To my high fantasy here power failed; but now my desire and my will, like a wheel which evenly is moved, the Love was turning which moves the Sun and the other stars.

1318?–21

Glossary

A Commentary on Selected Literary and Historical Terms

Airs (1) Songs, or tunes in general. (2) The songs for solo voice with lute accompaniment, as opposed to the polyphonic madrigals (*q.v.*) of the late 16th and early 17th centuries. Airs were strophic, and the successive strophes, or stanzas, of a poem were set to the same melody.

Alchemy The predecessor of chemistry, based upon classical and medieval mythological notions of the structure of matter; it was a study that nevertheless produced a great deal of practical chemical knowledge. Believing in the ancient notion of the relative nobility of metals—for example, from gold down to "baser" substances like lead—alchemists sought to discover a mysterious *philosopher's* (i.e. "scientist's") *stone* enabling them to perform transmutations of baser metals into gold. Since it thus constituted reversing a natural order, it could be thought of as theologically subversive. Alchemists themselves were by way of being practitioners of a hermetic (*q.v.*) religion, and transmuting metals was by no means their sole aim. Alchemical theory employed what would be today regarded as poetic concepts: e.g. sexual combination for chemical compounding, where today one might think of valence or charge. During the 17th century, when chemistry evolved as a science, alchemical lore and language, alluded to in poetry, became part of the body of myth, like Ptolemaic astronomy and the astrological theory it supported.

Allegory Literally, "other reading"; originally a way of interpreting a narrative or other text in order to extract a more general, or a less literal, meaning from it, e.g. reading Homer's *Odyssey* as the universal voyage of human life—with Odysseus standing for all men—which must be made toward a final goal. In the Middle Ages allegory came to be associated with ways of reading the Bible, particularly the Old Testament in relation to the New. In addition, stories came to be written with the intention of being interpreted symbolically; thus e.g. the *Psychomachia* or "battle for the soul" of Prudentius (b. 348 A.D.) figured the virtues and vices as contending soldiers in a battle (see *Personification*). There is allegorical lyric poetry and allegorical drama as well as allegorical narrative. In works such as Spenser's *The Faerie Queene* and Bunyan's *Pilgrim's Progress* allegory becomes a dominant literary form. See also *Dream Vision; Figure; type.*

Alliteration A repeated initial consonant in successive words. In Old English verse, any vowel alliterates with any other, and alliteration is not an unusual or expressive phenomenon but a regularly recurring structural feature of the verse, occurring on the first and third, and often on the first, second, and third, primary-stressed syllables of the four-stressed line. Thus, from "The Seafarer":

> hréran mid hóndum hrímcælde sǽ
> ("to stir with his hand the rime-cold sea")

In later English verse tradition, alliteration becomes expressive in a variety of ways. Spenser uses it decoratively, or to link adjective and noun, verb and object, as in the line: "Much daunted with that dint, her sense was dazed." In the 18th and 19th centuries it becomes even less systematic and more "musical."

Amplificatio, Amplifying The rhetorical enlargement of a statement or dilation of an argument, especially used in tragedy or epic (*q.v.*) poetry or in mock-heroic (*q.v.*). Language and stylistic ornament are deployed so as to increase the importance of a subject or to raise the level of its treatment.

Assonance A repeated vowel sound, a part-rhyme, which has great expressive effect when used internally (within lines), e.g. "An old, mad, blind, despised and dying king,—" (Shelley, "Sonnet: England in 1819").

Astronomy and Astrology Astrology may be regarded as an earlier phase or state of the science of astronomy—with an added normative provision in the notion that the *apparent* positions of the heavenly bodies, when viewed from a central earth about which all were thought to move, determined the shape of human life. (See *Zodiac.*) The geocentric astronomy of Ptolemy, wrong as it was about the relation between what was seen by an observer on earth and what caused him to see what he saw, nevertheless enabled men to predict with some accuracy events such as eclipses. In the microcosmic-macrocosmic world-view of the Middle Ages and the Renaissance, in which perspective the microcosm, or little world of man, constituted a miniature version of the whole cosmos, the relations between patterns discernible in the heavens and those of the four elements (*q.v.*), or the humors of the human constitution (*q.v.*), came to have great meaning. Specifically, the stars (meaning sun, moon, planets, fixed stars) were thought to radiate non-material substances called influences (literally, "in flowings") that beamed down to earth and affected human lives. Although the new astronomy of Copernicus, Kepler, and Galileo helped to destroy the conceptual basis for the belief in stellar influence, it is improper to think of a 16th- or 17th-century intellectual (and far less, a medieval man of letters and learning) as being superstitious in his use of astrological lore that was losing its centrality only with acceptance of the new ideas.

Aubade The French form of the Provençal *alba* ("dawn"), the morning song complementary to the evening *serenade;* it took its name from the word *alba* in the refrain (e.g. that of a famous anonymous poem, *L'alba, l'alba, oc l'alba, tan tost ve* ("the dawn, the dawn, o the dawn, it comes too soon"). In English such a song as Shakespeare's "Hark, hark, the lark / At heaven's gate sings" (from *Cymbeline*) exemplifies this tradition.

Aureate Literally, "golden"; used of the poetic and sometimes the prose language of 14th- and 15th-century England and Scotland; an idiom highly wrought and specializing in vernacular coinages from Latin.

Baroque (1) Originally (and still), an oddly shaped rather than a spherical pearl, and hence something twisted, contorted, involuted. (2) By a complicated analogy, a term designating stylistic periods in art, music, and literature during the 16th and 17th centuries in Europe. The analogies among the arts are frequently strained, and the stylistic periods by no means completely coincide. But the relation between the poetry of Richard Crashaw in English and Latin, and the sculpture and architecture of Gianlorenzo Bernini (1598–1680), is frequently taken to typify the spirit of the baroque. (See Wylie Sypher, *Four Stages of Renaissance Style*, 1955.)

Balade, Ballade The dominant lyric form in French poetry of the 14th and 15th centuries; a strict form consisting of three stanzas of eight lines each, with an *envoi* (*q.v.*), or four-line conclusion, addressing either a person of importance or a personification. Each stanza, including the *envoi*, ends in a refrain.

Ballad Meter Or *common meter;* four-lined stanzas, rhyming *abab,* the first and third lines in iambic tetrameter (four beats), and the second and fourth lines in iambic trimeter (three beats). See *Meter.*

Blazon, Blason (*Fr.*) A poetic genre cataloguing the parts or attributes of an object in order to praise it (or, in its satirical form, to condemn it). The first type, most influential chiefly on English Renaissance poetry, had its origin in a poem by Clément Marot in 1536 in praise of a beautiful breast. The English verb, *to blazon,* thus came to mean to catalogue poetically.

Bob and Wheel The bob (usually consisting of a two-syllable line) and the wheel (a brief set of short lines) are used either singly or together as a kind of *envoi* (*q.v.*) or comment on the action of the stanza preceding them. See *Sir Gawain and the Green Knight* for a prime example.

Calvin, Calvinist John Calvin (1509–64), French organizer of the strict religious discipline of Geneva (Switzerland), and author of its *Institutes* (1st ed., 1536). Calvin's teachings include among other things, the doctrine of Scripture as the sole rule of faith, the denial of free will in fallen man, and God's absolute predestination of every man, before his creation, to salvation or to damnation. There are Calvinist elements in the Thirty-Nine Articles (1563) of the Church of England, but the English (as opposed to the Scottish) tradition modified the rigor of the doctrine; Milton passed through a phase of strict Calvinism into greater independence and a rejection of absolute predestination.

Carol, Carole Originally (apparently) a song sung to an accompaniment of dance, and often set out in ballad meter and uniform stanzas of which the leader probably sang the verse and the dancers a refrain; later, generally, a song of religious joy, usually rapid in pace.

Carpe Diem Literally, "seize the day"; from Horace's Ode I.xi, which ends, *Dum loquimur, fugerit invida / aetas: carpe diem, quam minimum credula postero* ("Even while we're talking, envious Time runs by: seize the day, putting a minimum of trust in tomorrow"). This became a standard theme of Renaissance erotic verse, as in Robert Herrick's "Gather ye rosebuds while ye may."

Cavalier Designating the supporters of Charles I and of the Anglican church establishment, in opposition to the Puritans, or Roundheads, during the English Civil War. In a literary context, the lyric poetry of some of these so-named soldier-lover-poets (e.g. Thomas Carew, Richard Lovelace) is implied with its elegant wit (*q.v.*) and grace. (See *Civil War.*)

Chanson d'aventure A French poetic form describing a conversation about love or between lovers, and represented as overheard by the poet.

Civil War The struggle between Charles I and his Parliament came to a head in 1641, when the King tried forcibly to arrest five dissident members of Parliament. He failed, and in April 1642 raised his standard at Northampton, intending to advance on London. For some time there was a military deadlock, but in January 1644 the Parliamentary forces, allied with the Scots, defeated the King at Marston Moor. The Parliament men now controlled the North, but not until they instituted major military reforms did they overcome the King decisively at Naseby in June 1645. Charles became the captive of Parliament in January 1647 and was executed two years later. In 1653 Oliver Cromwell expelled the "Rump" of the Long Parliament (*q.v.*), which had survived since 1640, and became Lord Protector.

The terms "Cavalier" and "Roundhead," implying respectively aristocratic dash and middle-class puritanism, are not wholly misleading as descriptive of the Royalist and Parliamentary sides in the war; but the fact of new money and religious fervor on the winning side was not the whole story. The split between "Presbyterian" and "Independent" in the Parliament faction was partly religious, partly a division between the affluent and the enthusiastic; and with the victory of the "monied" interest the Revolution itself became conservative. But the execution of the King was an event that for a century or more resonated throughout the course of English history, and, as Marvell understood (see his "Horation Ode"), ended a whole phase of civilization.

Complaint Short poetic monologue, expressing the poet's sorrow at unrequited love or other pains and ending with a request for relief from them.

Complexion See *Temperaments.*

Conceit From the Italian *concetto,* "concept" or "idea"; used in Renaissance poetry to mean a precise and detailed comparison of something more remote or abstract with something more present or concrete, and often detailed through a chain of metaphors or similes (see *Rhetoric*). In Petrarchan (*q.v.*) poetry, certain conceits became conventionalized and were used again and again in various versions. The connection between the Lady's eyes and the Sun, so typical of these, was based on the proportion *her gaze : love's life and day :: sun's shining: world's life and daylight.* Conceits were closely linked to emblems (*q.v.*), to the degree that the verbal connection between the emblem picture and its *significatio,* or meaning, was detailed in an interpretive conceit. See also *Personification.*

Contemptus Mundi Contempt for the world, i.e. rejection of temporal and transitory pleasures and values in favor of the spiritual and eternal.

Contraries See *Qualities.*

Courtly Love Modern scholarship has coined this name for a set of conventions around which medieval love-poetry was written. It was essentially chivalric and a product of 12th-century France, especially of the troubadours. This poetry involves an idealization of the beloved woman, whose love, like all love, refines and ennobles the lover so that the union of their minds and/or bodies—a union that ought not to be apparent to others—allows them to attain excellence of character.

Dance of Death Poem accompanied by illustrations on the inevitability and universality of death, which is shown seizing men and women of all ranks and occupations, one after the other.

Decorum Propriety of discourse; what is becoming in action, character, and style; the avoidance of impossibilities and incongruities in action, style, and character: "the good grace of everything after his kind" and the "great masterpiece to observe." More formally, a neoclassical doctrine maintaining that literary style—grand, or high, middle, and low—be appropriate to the subject, occasion, and genre. Thus Milton, in *Paradise Lost* (I.13–14), invokes his "adventurous song, / That with no middle flight intends to soar. . . ." See also *Rhetoric*.

Digressio Interpolated story or description in a poem or oration, introduced for ornamentation or some structural purpose.

Dissenters In England, members of Protestant churches and sects that do not conform to the doctrines of the established Church of England; from the 16th century on, this would include Baptists, Puritans of various sorts within the Anglican Church, Presbyterians, Congregationalists, and (in the 18th century) Methodists. Another term, more current in the 19th century, is *Nonconformist*.

Dream Vision, Dream Allegory A popular medieval poetic form. Its fictional time is usually Spring; as the poet falls alseep in some pleasant place—a wood or garden—to the music of a stream and the song of birds, he dreams of "real" people or personified abstractions, who illuminate for him the nature of some aspect of knowledge, mode of behavior, or social or political question. See also *Allegory*.

Elegy Originally, in Greek and Latin poetry, a poem composed not in the hexameter lines of epic (*q.v.*) and, later, of pastoral, but in the elegiac couplets consisting of one hexameter line followed by a pentameter. Elegiac poetry was amatory, epigrammatic. By the end of the 16th century, English poets were using heroic couplets (*q.v.*), to stand for both hexameters and elegiacs; and an elegiac poem was any serious meditative piece. Perhaps because of the tradition of the pastoral elegy (*q.v.*), the general term "elegy" came to be reserved, in modern terminology, for an elaborate and formal lament, longer than a *dirge* or *threnody*, for a dead person. By extension, "elegiac" has come to mean, in general speech, broodingly sad.

Elements In ancient and medieval science, the four basic substances of which all matter was composed: earth, water, air, fire—in order of density and heaviness. They are often pictured in that order in diagrams of the universe. All four elements, being material, are below the sphere of the moon (above, there is a fifth: the quintessence). The elements are formed of combinations of the

Qualities (*q.v.*) or Contraries: the union of hot and dry makes fire; of hot and moist, air; of cold and moist, water; of cold and dry, earth.

Emblem A simple allegorical picture, or *impresa,* labeled with a motto to show its significance, and usually accompanied by a poetic description that connects the picture or "device" with the meaning, frequently by means of elaborate conceits (*q.v.*), sometimes with more obvious moralizing. Many Renaissance paintings are emblems, without the text. The first Renaissance emblem book was that of the Venetian lawyer Andrea Alciati, in 1531; for the next century and one-half, the pictures and verses were copied, translated, expanded upon, added to, and adapted in French, Dutch, Spanish, German, and Italian as well as his original Latin. Famous English books of emblems were those of Geoffrey Whitney (1586), Henry Peacham (*Minerva Brittana,* or *A Garden of Heroical Devices,* 1612), George Wither (1635), and Francis Quarles (1635). Based originally on classical mythography, an interest in ancient coins and statuary, as well as "hieroglyphics" in all ancient art, emblem traditions generally divided, in the 17th century, into "Jesuitical" types (involving precise and intense images such as tears, wings, hearts, and classical Cupids signifying not *amor,* but *caritas*), and more pragmatic Protestant emblems (particularly in the Dutch tradition), which tend toward genre scenes of everyday life illustrating proverbs in the text. In the Renaissance, pictures were to be *read* and understood, like texts; and this kind of reading of hieroglyphics extends, in a writer like Sir Thomas Browne, to all of creation:

> The world's a book in folio, printed all
> With God's great works in letters capital:
> Each creature is a page, and each effect
> A fair character, void of all defect.

These lines of Joshua Sylvester are a commonplace. See also *Conceit; Symbolism;* and Figs. 16–21 in illustrations for the Renaissance section of this Anthology.

Enjambment The "straddling" of a clause or sentence across two lines of verse, as opposed to closed, or end-stopped, lines. Thus, in the opening lines of Shakespeare's *Twelfth Night:*

> If music be the food of love, play on!
> Give me excess of it, that, surfeiting
> The appetite may sicken and so die . . .

the first line is stopped, the second enjambed. When enjambment becomes strong or violent, it may have an ironic or comic effect.

The Enlightenment A term used very generally, to refer to the late 17th and the 18th century in Europe, a period characterized by a programmatic rationalism—i.e. a belief in the ability of human reason to understand the world and thereby to transform whatever in it needed transforming; an age in which ideas of science and progress accompanied the rise of new philosophies of the relation of man to the state, an age which saw many of its hopes for human betterment fulfilled in the French Revolution.

Envoi, Envoy Short concluding stanza found in certain French poetic forms and their English imitations, e.g. the *ballade* (*q.v.*). It serves as a dedicatory postscript, and a summing up of the poem of which it repeats the refrain.

Epic Or, *heroic poetry;* originally, oral narrative delivered in a style different from that of normal discourse by reason of verse, music, and heightened diction, and concerning the great deeds of a central heroic figure, or group of figures, usually having to do with a crisis in the history of a race or culture. Its setting lies in this earlier "heroic" period, and it will often have been written down only after a long period of oral transmission. The Greek *Iliad* and *Odyssey* and the Old English *Beowulf* are examples of this, in their narration mixing details from both the heroic period described and the actual time of their own composition and narration. What is called *secondary* or *literary* epic is a long, ambitious poem, composed by a single poet on the model of the older, primary forms, and of necessity being more allusive and figurative than its predecessors. Homer's poems lead to Virgil's *Aeneid,* which leads to Milton's *Paradise Lost,* in a chain of literary dependency. Spenser's *Faerie Queene* might be called *romantic epic* of the secondary sort, and Dante's *Divine Comedy* might also be assimilated to post-Virgilian epic tradition.

Epic Simile An extended comparison, in Homeric and subsequently in Virgilian and later epic poetry, between an event in the story (the *fable*) and something in the experience of the epic audience, to the effect of making the fabulous comprehensible in terms of the familiar. From the Renaissance on, additional complications have emerged from the fact that what is the familiar for the classical audience becomes, because of historical change, itself fabled (usually, pastoral) for the modern audience. Epic similes compare the fabled with the familiar usually with respect to one property or element; thus, in the *Odyssey,* when the stalwart forward motion of a ship in high winds is described, the simile goes:

> And as amids a fair field four brave horse
> Before a chariot, stung into their course
> With fervent lashes of the smarting scourge
> That all their fire blows high, and makes them rise
> To utmost speed the measure of their ground:
> So bore the ship aloft her fiery bound
> About whom rushed the billows, black and vast
> In which the sea-roars burst . . .
>
> (*Chapman translation*)

Notice the formal order of presentation: "even as . . .": *the familiar event, often described in detail;* "just so . . .": *the fabled one.*

Epicureanism A system of philosophy founded by the Greek Epicurus (342–270 B.C.), who taught that the five senses are the sole source of ideas and sole criterion of truth, and that the goal of human life is pleasure (i.e. hedonism), though this can be achieved only by practicing moderation. Later the term came to connote bestial self-indulgence, which Epicurus had clearly rejected.

Exclamatio Rhetorical figure representing a cry of admiration or grief.

Exemplum A short narrative used to illustrate a moral point in didactic literature (especially sermons) or in historical writing. Its function is to recommend or dissuade from a particular course of conduct.

Fabliau A short story in verse, comic in character, its subject matter often indecent, and the joke hinging on sex or excretion. The plot usually involves a witty turn or practical joke, the motive of which is love or revenge. See The Miller's Tale of Chaucer.

Fathers of the Church The earliest Christian theologians and ecclesiastical writers (also referred to as "patristic"), flourishing from the late 1st century through the 8th, composing severally in Greek or Latin. Well-known "Fathers" are St. Augustine, St. Jerome, Tertullian.

Feudal System The system of land tenure and political allegiance characteristic of Europe during the Middle Ages. The king, as owner of all land, gives portions of it to his vassals, by whom it can be passed on to heirs, in return for their pledge of loyalty and of specified military service. These nobles divide their land among their followers, the subdivision continuing until it reaches the serfs, who cultivate the land but must hand over most of their produce to the lord.

Figurative Language In a general sense, any shift away from a literal meaning of words, brought about by the use of tropes (*q.v.*) or other rhetorical devices. See *Rhetoric*.

Figure As defined by Erich Auerbach in his essay "Figura," a mode of interpretation establishing a connection between two events or persons, the first of which signifies both itself and the second, while the second encompasses or fulfills the first—e.g. the Eucharist, which is the "figure" of Christ. See *Allegory*.

Free Verse, Vers Libre Generally, any English verse form whose lines are measured neither by the number of 1) stressed syllables (see *Meter* §3, accentual verse), 2) alternations of stressed and unstressed syllables (§4, accentual-syllabic verse), nor syllables alone (§2, syllabic verse). The earliest English free verse —that of Christopher Smart in *Jubilate Agno* (18th century)—imitates the prosody of Hebrew poetry (reflected also in the translation of the English Bible), in maintaining unmeasured units marked by syntactic parallelism. While many free-verse traditions (e.g. that of Walt Whitman) remain close to the impulses of this biblical poetry, yet others, in the 20th century, have developed new *ad hoc* patternings of their own. *Vers libre* usually refers to the experimental, frequently very short unmeasured lines favored by poets of the World War I period, although the term, rather than the form, was adopted from French poetry of the 19th century.

Gothic Term (originally pejorative, as alluding to the Teutonic barbarians) designating the architectural style of the Middle Ages. The revival of interest in medieval architecture in the later 18th century produced not only pseudo-Gothic castles like Horace Walpole's "Strawberry Hill", and more modest artificial ruins on modern estates, but also a vogue for atmospheric prose romances set in medieval surroundings and involving improbable terrors, and known as Gothic novels. The taste for the Gothic, arising during the Age of Sensibility (*q.v.*), is another reflection of a reaction against earlier 18th-century neoclassicism (*q.v*).

Hermetic, Hermeticism, Hermetist Terms referring to a synthesis of Neoplatonic and other occult philosophies, founded on a collection of writings attributed to Hermes Trismegistus ("Thrice-greatest Hermes"—a name given the Egyptian god Thoth), but which in fact date from the 2nd and 3rd centuries A.D. An important doctrine was that of correspondences between earthly and heavenly things. By studying these correspondences, a man might "walk to the sky" (in the words of Henry Vaughan) in his lifetime. Hermetic tradition favored *esoteric* or forbidden knowledge, over what could be more publicly avowed.

Heroic Couplet In English prosody, a pair of rhyming, iambic pentameter lines, used at first for closure—as at the end of the Shakespearean sonnet (*q.v.*)—or to terminate a scene in blank-verse drama; later adapted to correspond in English poetry to the elegiac couplet of classical verse as well as to the heroic, unrhymed, Greek and Latin hexameter. Octosyllabic couplets, with four stresses (eight syllables) to the line, are a minor, shorter, jumpier form, used satirically unless in implicit allusion to the form of Milton's "Il Penseroso," in which they develop great lyrical power. (See *Meter.*)

Humors The combinations, in men and women (the *microcosm*) of the qualities (*q.v.*), or contraries. In primitive physiology, the four principal bodily fluids in their combinations produce the temperaments (*q.v.*) or "complexions" These "humors," with their properties and effects—at least in the Middle Ages—are, respectively: Blood (hot and moist)—cheerfulness, warmth of feeling; Choler (hot and dry)—a quick, angry temper; Phlegm (cold and moist)—dull sluggishness; Melancholy (cold and dry)—fretful depression. The Renaissance introduced the concept of "artificial" humors—e.g. scholars' and artists' melancholy, creative brooding. The humors, the temperaments, and the four elements (*q.v.*) of the macrocosm, or universe, were all looked upon as interrelated. See *Renaissance Psychology.*

Irony Generally, a mode of saying one thing to mean another. *Sarcasm,* in which one means exactly the opposite of what one says, is the easiest and cheapest form; thus, e.g. "Yeah, it's a *nice day!*" when one means that it's a miserable one. But serious literature produces ironies of a much more complex and revealing sort. *Dramatic irony* occurs when a character in a play or story asserts something whose meaning the audience or reader knows will change in time. Thus, in Genesis when Abraham assures his son Isaac (whom he is about to sacrifice) that "God will provide his own lamb," the statement is lighted with dramatic irony when a sacrificial ram is actually provided at the last minute to save Isaac. Or, in the case of Sophocles' *Oedipus,* when almost everything the protagonist says about the predicament of his city is hideously ironic in view of the fact (which he does not know) that he is responsible therefor. The ironies generated by the acknowledged use of non-literal language (see *Rhetoric*) and fictions in drama, song, and narrative are at the core of imaginative literature.

Judgment In Catholic doctrine, God's retributive judgment, which decides the fate of rational creatures according to their merits and faults. Particular judgment is the decision about the eternal destiny of each soul made immediately after death; General (Last) Judgment is at the Second Coming of Christ as God and Man, when all men will be judged again in the sight of all the world. See Fig. 50 in illustrations for the Medieval section of this anthology.

Kenning An Old Norse form designating, strictly, a condensed simile or metaphor of the kind frequently used in Old Germanic poetry; a figurative circumlocution for a thing not actually named—e.g. "swan's path" for sea; "world-candle" or "sky-candle" for sun. More loosely, often used to mean also a metaphorical compound word or phrase such as "ring-necked" or "foamy-necked" for a ship, these being descriptive rather than figurative in character.

Lancastrians See *Wars of the Roses.*

Locus Amoenus Literally, "pleasant place"; a garden, either Paradise, the most perfect of all gardens, or its pagan equivalent, or the later literary garden that was a figure (*q.v.*) of Paradise. See *Topos.*

Long Parliament The Parliament summoned by Charles I on November 3, 1640; the last remnant, not dissolved until 1660, opposed the King and brought about his downfall and execution. See *Civil War.*

Macaronic Verse in which two languages are mingled, usually for burlesque purposes.

Machiavelli, Niccolò Italian diplomat, historian, and political theorist (1469–1527), whose chief work, *Il Principe* (*The Prince,* 1513), based in part on the career of Cesare Borgia, outlines a pragmatic rule of conduct for a ruler; thus, politics should have nothing to do with morality; the prince should be an exponent of ruthless power in behalf of his people. In England his theories were put into practice by Thomas Cromwell in the reign of Henry VIII; his writings, however, were not translated until the 17th century, and his image in England, based on rumor and the reports of his adversaries, fostered a myth of the evil "Machiavel" as he appears in Marlowe (*Titus Andronicus*) and Shakespeare (*Richard III*).

Madrigal Polyphonic setting of a poem, in the 16th and 17th centuries, for several voice parts, unaccompanied or with instruments. Because of the contrapuntal texture, the words were frequently obscured for a listener, though not for the performers.

Meter Verse may be made to differ from prose and from ordinary speech in a number of ways, and in various languages these ways may be very different. Broadly speaking, lines of verse may be marked out by the following regularities of pattern:

1. *Quantitative Verse,* used in ancient Greek poetry and adopted by the Romans, used a fixed number of what were almost musical measures, called *feet;* they were built up of long and short syllables (like half- and quarter-notes in music), which depended on the vowel and consonants in them. *Stress accent* (the *word* stress which, when accompanied by vowel reduction, distinguishes the English noun "*con*tent" from the adjective "con*tent*") did not exist in ancient Greek, and played no part in the rhythm of the poetic line. Thus, the first line of the *Odyssey: Andra moi ennepe mousa, polytropon hos mala polla* ("Sing me, O muse, of that man of many resources who, after great hardship . . .") is composed in *dactyls* of one long syllable followed by two shorts (but, as in musical rhythm, replaceable by two longs, a *spondee*).

With six dactyls to a line, the resulting meter is called *dactylic hexameter* (*hexameter*, for short), the standard form for epic poetry. Other kinds of foot or measure were: the *anapest* (◡ ◡ –); the *iamb* (◡ –); the *trochee* (– ◡); and a host of complex patterns used in lyric poetry. Because of substitutions, however, the number of syllables in a classical line was not fixed, only the number of measures.

2. *Syllabic Verse,* used in French, Japanese, and many other languages, and in English poetry of the mid-20th century, measures only the *number* of syllables per line with no regard to considerations of *quantity* or *stress.* Because of the prominence of stress in the English language, two lines of the same purely syllabic length may not necessarily sound at all as though they were in the same meter, e.g.:

> These two incommensurably sounding
> Lines are both written with ten syllables.

3. *Accentual Verse,* used in early Germanic poetry, and thus in Old English poetry, depended upon the number of strong *stress accents* per line. These accents were four in number, with no fixed number of unstressed. Folk poetry and nursery rhymes often preserve this accentual verse, e.g.:

> Sing, sing, what shall I sing?
> The cat's run away with the pudding-bag string

The first line has six syllables, the second, eleven, but they sound more alike (and not merely by reason of their rhyme) than the two syllabic lines quoted above.

4. *Accentual-Syllabic Verse,* the traditional meter of English poetry from Chaucer on, depends upon both numbered *stresses* and numbered *syllables,* a standard form consisting of ten syllables alternately stressed and unstressed, and having five stresses; thus it may be said to consist of five syllable pairs.

For complex historical reasons, accentual-syllabic groups of stressed and unstressed syllables came to be known by the names used for Greek and Latin feet—which can be very confusing. The analogy was made between *long* syllables in the classical languages, and *stressed* syllables in English. Thus, the pair of syllables in the adjective "con*tent*" is called an *iamb,* and in the noun "*con*tent," a *trochee;* the word "classical" is a *dactyll,* and the phrase "of the best," an *anapest.* When English poetry is being discussed, these terms are always used in their adapted, accentual-syllabic meanings, and hence the ten-syllable line mentioned earlier is called "iambic pentameter" in English. The phrase "high-tide" would be a *spondee* (as would, in general, two monosyllables comprising a proper name, e.g. "John Smith"); whereas compound nouns like "highway" would be *trochaic.* In this adaptation of classical nomenclature, the terms *dimeter, trimeter, tetrameter, pentameter, hexameter* refer not to the number of quantitative feet but to the number of syllable-groups (pairs or triplets, from one to six) composing the line. Iambic pentameter and tetrameter lines are frequently also called *decasyllabic* and *octosyllabic* respectively.

5. *Versification.* In verse, lines may be arranged in patterns called *stichic*

or *strophic,* that is, the same linear form (say, iambic pentameter) repeated without grouping by rhyme or interlarded lines of another form, or varied in just such a way into *stanzas* or *strophes* ("turns"). Unrhymed iambic pentameter, called *blank verse,* is the English stichic form that Milton thought most similar to classic hexameter or *heroic* verse. But in the Augustan period iambic pentameter rhymed pairs, called heroic couplets (*q.v.*), came to stand for this ancient form as well as for the classical elegiac verse (*q.v.*). Taking couplets as the simplest strophic unit, we may proceed to *tercets* (groups of three lines) and to *quatrains* (groups of four), rhymed *abab* or *abcb,* and with equal or unequal line lengths. Other stanzaic forms: *ottava rima,* an eight-line, iambic pentameter stanza, rhyming *abababcc; Spenserian stanza,* rhyming *ababbcbcc,* all pentameter save for the last line, an iambic hexameter, or *alexandrine.* There have been adaptations in English (by Shelley, notably, and without rhyme by T. S. Eliot) of the Italian *terza rima* used by Dante in *The Divine Comedy,* interlocking tercets rhyming *aba bcb cdc ded,* etc. More elaborate stanza forms developed in the texts of some Elizabethan songs and in connection with the ode (*q.v.*).

Microcosm Literally, "the small world"—man. For fuller explanation see selections of Walter Ralegh and Thomas Browne on this theme. See also *Astronomy, Astrology; Humors; Qualities.*

Mirror for Princes A treatise setting out the education necessary to make a ruler and the modes of mental, moral, and physical activity that befitted him.

Mock-heroic, Mock-epic The literary mode resulting when low or trivial subjects are treated in the high, artificial literary language of classical epic (*q.v.*) poetry. The point of the joke is usually to expose not the inadequacies of the style but those of the subject, although occasionally the style may be caricatured, and the joke made about decorum (*q.v.*) itself. Alexander Pope's *The Rape of the Lock* is a famous example.

Music of the Spheres The ancient fiction held that the celestial spheres made musical sounds, either by rubbing against the ether, or because an angel—the Christian replacement for the Intelligence which in Plato's *Timaeus* guided each one—sang while riding on his charge. The inaudibility of this music was ascribed by later Platonism (*q.v.*) to the imprisonment of the soul in the body, and by Christian writers, to man's fallen state. Frequent attempts were made to preserve some meaning for this beautiful idea: thus, Aristotle's conclusion that the continuous presence of such sounds would make them inaudible to habituated ears (a sophisticated prefiguration of the modern notion of background noise). And thus the belief of the Ptolemaic astronomy that at a certain point the ratios of the diameters of the spheres of the various heavenly bodies were "harmonious" in that they would generate the overtone series. Even Kepler, who demonstrated that the planetary orbits, let alone non-existent spheres, could not be circular, suggested that the ratios of the angular velocities of the planets would generate a series of melodies; he then proceeded to put them together contrapuntally. See *Astronomy and Astrology.*

Myth A primitive story explaining the origins of certain phenomena in the world and in human life, and usually embodying gods or other supernatural forces, heroes (men who are either part human and part divine, or are placed between an ordinary mortal and a divine being), men, and animals. Literature continues to incorporate myths long after the mythology (the system of stories containing them) ceases to be a matter of actual belief. Moreover, discarded beliefs of all sorts tend to become myths when they are remembered but no longer literally clung to, and are used in literature in a similar way. The classical mythology of the Greeks and Romans was apprehended in this literary, or interpreted, way, even in ancient times. The gods and heroes and their deeds came to be read as allegory (*q.v.*). During the Renaissance, *mythography*—the interpretation of myths in order to make them reveal a moral or historical significance (rather than merely remaining entertaining but insignificant stories)—was extremely important, both for literature and for painting and sculpture. In modern criticism, mythical or *archetypal* situations and personages have been interpreted as being central objects of the work of the imagination.

Neoclassicism (1) In general the term refers to Renaissance and post-Renaissance attempts to model enterprises in the various arts on Roman and Greek originals—or as much as was known of them. Thus, in the late Renaissance, the architectural innovations of Andrea Palladio may be called "neoclassic," as may Ben Jonson's relation, and Alexander Pope's as well, to the Roman poet Horace. The whole Augustan period in English literary history (1660–1740) was a deliberately neoclassical one.

(2) More specifically, neoclassicism refers to that period in the history of all European art spanning the very late 18th and early 19th century, which period may be seen as accompanying the fulfillment, and the termination, of the Enlightenment (*q.v.*). In England such neoclassic artists as Henry Fuseli, John Flaxman, George Romney, and even, in some measure, William Blake, are close to the origins of pictorial and literary Romanticism itself.

Neoplatonism See *Platonism.*

Nonconformist See *Dissenters.*

Octosyllabic Couplet See *Heroic Couplet; Meter.*

Ode A basic poetic form, originating in Greek antiquity. The *choral ode* was a public event, sung and danced, at a large ceremony, or as part of the tragic and comic drama. Often called *Pindaric ode,* after a great Greek poet, the form consisted of *triads* (groups of three sections each). These were units of song and dance, and had the form *aab*—that is, a *strophe* (or "turn"), an *antistrophe* (or "counter-turn"), and an *epode* (or "stand"), the first two being identical musically and metrically, the third different. In English poetry, the Pindaric ode form, only in its metrical aspects, became in the 17th century a mode for almost essayistic poetic comment, and was often used also as a kind of cantata libretto, in praise of music and poetry (the so-called *musical ode*). By the 18th century the ode became the form for a certain kind of personal, visionary poem, and it is this form that Wordsworth and Coleridge transmitted to Romantic tradition. A second English form, known as *Horatian ode,* was based on the lyric (not choral) poems of Horace, and is written in *aabb* quatrains, with the last two lines shorter than the first two by a pair of syllables or more.

Oral Formula A conventional, fossilized phrase common in poetry composed as it was recited, or composed to be recited, and repeated frequently in a single poem. It serves as either a means of slowing or even stopping the action momentarily, or of filling out a verse: e.g. "Beowulf, son of Ecgtheow," or "go or ride"—i.e. "whatever you do."

Paradox In logic, a self-contradictory statement, hence meaningless (or a situation producing one), with an indication that something is wrong with the language in which such a situation can occur, e.g. the famous paradox of Epimenedes the Cretan, who held that all Cretans are liars (and thus could be lying if—and only if—he wasn't), or that of Zeno, of the arrow in flight: since at any instant of time the point of the arrow can always be said to be at one precise point, therefore it is continually at rest at a continuous sequence of such points, and therefore never moves. In literature, however, particularly in the language of lyric poetry, paradox plays another role. From the beginnings of lyric poetry, paradox has been deemed necessary to express feelings and other aspects of human inner states, e.g. Sappho's invention of the Greek word *glykypikron* ("bittersweet") to describe love, or her assertion that she was freezing and burning at the same time. So too the Latin poet Catullus, in his famous couplet

> I'm in hate and I'm in love; why do I? you may ask.
> Well, I don't know, but I feel it, and I'm in agony.

may be declaring thereby that true love poetry must be illogical.

In Elizabethan poetry, paradoxes were frequently baldly laid out in the rhetorical form called *oxymoron* (see *Rhetoric*), as in "the victor-victim," or across a fairly mechanical sentence structure, as in "My feast of joy is but a dish of pain." In the highest poetic art, however, the seeming self-contradiction is removed when one realizes that either, or both, of the conflicting terms is to be taken figuratively, rather than literally. The apparent absurdity, or strangeness, thus gives rhetorical power to the utterance. Elaborate and sophisticated paradoxes, insisting on their own absurdity, typify the poetic idiom of the tradition of John Donne.

Pastoral A literary mode in which the lives of simple country people are celebrated, described, and used allegorically by sophisticated urban poets and writers. The *idylls* of Sicilian poet Theocritus (3rd century B.C.) were imitated and made more symbolic in Virgil's *eclogues;* shepherds in an Arcadian landscape stood for literary and political personages, and the Renaissance adapted these narrative and lyric pieces for moral and aesthetic discussion. Spenser's *Shepheardes Calendar* is an experimental collection of eclogues involving an array of forms and subjects. In subsequent literary tradition, the pastoral imagery of both Old and New Testaments (Psalms, Song of Songs, priest as *pastor* or shepherd of his flock, and so on) joins with the classical mode. Modern critics, William Empson in particular, have seen the continuation of pastoral tradition in other versions of the country-city confrontation, such as child-adult and criminal-businessman. See *Pastoral Elegy*.

Pastoral Elegy A form of lament for the death of a poet, originating in Greek bucolic tradition (Bion's lament for Adonis, a lament for Bion by a fellow poet, Theocritus' first idyll, Virgil's tenth eclogue) and continued in use by Renaissance poets as a public mode for the presentation of private, inner, and even coterie matters affecting poets and their lives, while conventionally treating questions of general human importance. At a death one is moved to ask, "Why this death? Why now?" and funeral elegy must always confront these questions, avoiding easy resignation as an answer. Pastoral elegy handled these questions with formal mythological apparatus, such as the Muses, who should have protected their dead poet, local spirits, and other presences appropriate to the circumstances of the life and death, and perhaps figures of more general mythological power. The end of such poems is the eternalization of the dead poet in a monument of myth, stronger than stone or bronze: Spenser's *Astrophel,* a lament for Sir Philip Sidney, concludes with an Ovidian change—the dead poet's harp, like Orpheus' lyre, becomes the constellation Lyra. Milton's *Lycidas* both exemplifies and transforms the convention. Later examples include Shelley's *Adonais* (for Keats), Arnold's *Thyrsis* (for Clough), and Swinburne's *Ave Atque Vale* (for Baudelaire).

Penance In Catholic doctrine, the moral virtue by which a sinner is disposed to hate his sin as an offense against God; and the sacrament, of which the outward signs are the acknowledgment of sin, self-presentation of the sinner to priest to confess his sins, the absolution pronounced by the priest, and the satisfaction (penance) imposed on the sinner by the priest and to be performed before the sinner is delivered from his guilt. See Figs. 32 and 52 in illustrations for the Medieval section of this Anthology.

Peroration Final part of an oration, reviewing and summarizing the argument, often in an impassioned form. (See also *Rhetoric.*)

Personification Treating a thing or, more properly, an abstract quality, as though it were a person. Thus, "Surely *goodness* and *mercy* shall follow me all the days of my life" tends to personify the italicized terms by reason of the metaphoric use of "follow me." On the other hand, a conventional, complete personification, like *Justice* (whom we recognize by her *attributes*—she is blindfolded, she has scales and a sword) might also be called an *allegorical figure* in her own right, and her attributes *symbols* (blindness = impartiality; scales = justly deciding; sword = power to mete out what is deserved). Often the term "personification" applies to momentary, or *ad hoc,* humanizations.

Petrarch, Petrarchan Francesco Petrarca (1304–74), the Italian founder of humanistic studies, with their revival of Greek and Latin literature, was influential in Renaissance England chiefly for his *Rime sparse,* the collection of love sonnets in praise of his muse, Laura. These poems, translated and adapted in England from the 1530's on, provided not only the sonnet (*q.v.*) form but also many devices of imagery widely used by English poets of the 16th and 17th centuries.

Physiognomics The "art to read the mind's complexion in the face." From ancient times to the Renaissance, it was believed possible to gauge a person's character precisely from his outward appearance and physical characteristics.

Platonism The legacy of Plato (429–347 B.C.) is virtually the history of philosophy. His *Timaeus* was an important source of later cosmology; his doctrine of ideas is central to Platonic tradition. His doctrine of love (especially in the *Symposium*) had enormous influence in the Renaissance, at which time its applicability was shifted to heterosexual love specifically. The *Republic* and the *Laws* underlie a vast amount of political thought, and the *Republic* contains also a philosophical attack on poetry (fiction) which defenders of the arts have always had to answer. Neoplatonism—a synthesis of Platonism, Pythagoreanism, and Aristotelianism—was dominant in the 3rd century A.D.; and the whole tradition was revived in the 15th and 16th centuries. The medieval Plato was Latinized, largely at second-hand; the revival of Greek learning in the 15th century led to another Neoplatonism: a synthesis of Platonism, the medieval Christian Aristotle, and Christian doctrine. Out of this came the doctrines of love we associate with some Renaissance poetry; a sophisticated version of older systems of allegory and symbol; and notions of the relation of spirit and matter reflected in Marvell and many other poets.

Prayer Book The Book of Common Prayer, containing the order of services in the Church of England. Based on translations from medieval service books, it first appeared in 1549, under the direction of Thomas Cranmer (1489–1556), Archbishop of Canterbury. It was much revised, partly to meet Puritan complaints, but in 1662 achieved the form it has since kept, with only slight alteration.

Purgatory According to Catholic doctrine, a place or condition of temporal punishment for those who die in the grace of God, but without having made full satisfaction for their transgressions. In Purgatory they are purified so as to be fit to come into God's presence.

Quadrivium The second division of the seven liberal arts, which together with the trivium (*q.v.*) comprised the full course of a medieval education and fitted a man to study theology, the crown of the arts and sciences. The quadrivium consisted of music, arithmetic, geometry, and astronomy.

Qualities Or **contraries**; the properties of all material things, the various combinations of which were held to determine their nature. They were four in number, in two contrasting pairs: hot and cold; moist and dry. See *Elements; Humors; Temperaments.*

Recusant Literally, "refuser"; in the Elizabethan period, anyone who refused to join the Church of England—although now the term is commonly used to allude to "popish recusants," i.e. Roman Catholics, and "recusancy," to English writings of certain Catholics during the late 16th century.

Renaissance Psychology Poetic language, particularly that of lyric poetry, is always implicitly raising assumptions about inner states of people who have feelings and who wish to express them. In the Renaissance, several informal ways coexisted of talking about the relation which we now see as one of mind and body. From Aristotelian tradition the concept of three orders of soul was maintained: in ascending order these were the *vegetable* (the "life," immobile and inactive, of plants), the *animal* (accounting for the behavior of beasts), and the *rational* (the power of reason, often associated with language as well as thought, in men). On the other hand, *wit* (*q.v.*) meant intellect, and in Elizabethan language, the conflict of *wit* and *will* correspond roughly, but not precisely, to a modern opposition of reason and emotion. Physical, as well as psychological, human diversity was explained by the theory of the humors and temperaments (*qq.v.*). On the other hand, there were mysterious entities called *spirits* (associated with the Latin root, meaning "breath," and its application to alcoholic fluids: waters that "breathe" and "burn"). Spirits were fine vapors mediating between the body and the soul, and patching up a connection which scientific psychology is still trying to make. *Natural spirits* came from the liver and circulated through the veins. *Vital spirits* came from the heart and circulated arterially. *Animal spirits* were distilled from the vital spirits (which can be associated with blood) and went to the brain through the nerves, which were thought to be conducting vessels. (See the selection from Burton's *Anatomy of Melancholy.*) Other faculties of the soul included the power of *fancy* or *fantasy* (the word "imagination" most often referred to something imagined, rather than to a faculty).

Reverdie Old French dance poem imitated in other languages, usually consisting of five or six stanzas without refrain, in joyful celebration of the coming of Spring.

Rhetoric In classical times, rhetoric was the art of persuading through the use of language. The major treatises on style and structure of discourse—Aristotle's *Rhetoric,* Quintilian's *Institutes of Oratory,* the *Rhetorica ad Herrenium* ascribed for centuries to Cicero—were concerned with the "arts" of language in the older sense of "skills." In the Middle Ages the *trivium* (*q.v.*), or program that led to the degree of Bachelor of Arts, consisted of grammar, logic, and rhetoric, but it was an abstract study, based on the Roman tradition. In the Renaissance, classical rhetorical study became a matter of the first importance, and it led to the study of literary stylistics and the application of principles and concepts of the production and structure of eloquence to the higher eloquence of poetry.

Rhetoricians distinguished three stages in the production of discourse: *inventio* (finding or discovery), *dispositio* (arranging), and *elocutio* (style). Since the classical discipline aimed always at practical oratory (e.g. winning a case in court, or making a point effectively in council), *memoria* (memory) and *pronuntiatio* (delivery) were added. For the Renaissance, however, rhetoric became the art of writing. Under the heading of *elocutio,* style became stratified into three levels, *elevated* or high, *elegant* or middle, and *plain* or low. The proper fitting of these styles to the subject of discourse comprised the subject of decorum (*q.v.*).

Another area of rhetorical theory was concerned with classification of devices of language into *schemes, tropes,* and *figures.* A basic but somewhat confused distinction between figures of speech and figures of thought need not concern us here, but we may roughly distinguish between schemes (or patterns) of words, and tropes as manipulations of meanings, and of making words non-literal.

Common Schemes

anadiplosis repeating the terminal word in a clause as the start of the next one: "Pleasure might cause her read; reading might cause her know; / Knowledge might pity win, and pity grace obtain" (Sidney, *Astrophel and Stella*).

anaphora the repetition of a word or phrase at the openings of successive clauses, e.g. "The Lord sitteth above the water floods. The Lord remaineth King forever. The Lord shall give strength unto his people. The Lord shall give his people the blessing of peace."

chiasmus a pattern of criss-crossing a syntactic structure, whether of noun and adjective, e.g. "Empty his bottle, and his girlfriend gone," or of a reversal of normal syntax with similar effect, e.g. "A fop her passion, and her prize, a sot," reinforced by assonance (*q.v.*). Chiasmus may even extend to assonance, as in Coleridge's line "In Xanadu did Kubla Khan."

Common Tropes

metaphor and simile both involve comparison of one thing to another, the difference being that the *simile* will actually compare, using the words "like" or "as," while the metaphor identifies one with the other, thus producing a non-literal use of a word or attribution. Thus, Robert Burns's "O, my love is like a red, red rose / That's newly sprung in June" is a simile; had Burns written, "My love, thou art a red, red rose . . .", it would have been a metaphor—and indeed, it would not mean that the lady had acquired petals. In modern critical theory, *metaphor* has come to stand for various non-expository kinds of evocative signification. I. A. Richards, the modern critic most interested in a general theory of metaphor in this sense, has contributed the terms *tenor* (as in the case above, the girl) and *vehicle* (the rose) to designate the components. See also *Epic Simile.*

metonymy a trope in which the vehicle is closely and conventionally associated with the tenor, e.g. "crown" and "king," "pen" and "writing," "pencil" and "drawing," "sword" and "warfare."

synecdoche a trope in which the part stands for the whole, e.g. "sail" for "ship."

hyperbole intensifying exaggeration, e.g. the combined synecdoche and hyperbole in which Christopher Marlowe's Faustus asks of Helen of Troy "Is this the face that launched a thousand ships / And burned the topless towers of Ilium?"

oxymoron literally, sharp-dull; a figure of speech involving a witty paradox, e.g. "sweet harm"; "darkness visible" (Milton, *Paradise Lost* I.63).

Rhyme Royal See *Troilus stanza.*

Right Reason A natural faculty of intelligence in man, his capability of choosing between moral alternatives. In the humanism of the Renaissance, Aristotle's term, *orthos logos,* associated with the Latin word *ratio,* was thought of as having preceded the fallen knowledge acquired in Paradise by Adam and Eve's first sin.

Romance (1) A medieval tale of chivalric or amorous adventure, in prose or verse, with the specification that the material be fictional. Later on, there developed cycles of stories, such as those involving Arthurian material or the legends of Charlemagne. Many of these, particularly the Arthurian, came to involve the theme of courtly love (*q.v.*)

(2) In the Renaissance, romance becomes more complex and literary, involving some degree of consciousness on the part of the author that he was reworking medieval materials (Spenser's *Faerie Queene,* of Arthurian legends; Ariosto's *Orlando Furioso,* of Charlemagne's heroic knight; Tasso's *Gerusalemme Liberata,* of stories of the Crusades).

(3) Prose romance, the 19th-century outgrowth of earlier essays into the

Gothic (*q.v.*) tale, represents a poetic kind of narrative to be clearly distinguished (in England if not in America) from the mode of the novel (e.g. Mary Shelley's *Frankenstein* and Hawthorne's *The Scarlet Letter* are both prose romance).

Rondeau, Roundel A strict French poetic form, thirteen lines of eight to ten syllables, divided into stanzas of five, three, and five lines, using two rhymes only and repeating the first word or first few words of line one after the second and third stanzas. The two terms are used interchangeably in the Middle Ages.

Satire A literary mode painting a distorted verbal picture of part of the world in order to show its true moral, as opposed merely to its physical, nature. In this sense, Circe, the enchantress in Homer's *Odyssey* who changed Odysseus' men into pigs (because they made pigs of themselves while eating) and would have changed Odysseus into a fox (for he was indeed foxy), was the first satirist. Originally the Latin word *satura* meant a kind of literary grab bag, or medley, and a satire was a fanciful kind of tale in mixed prose and verse; but later a false etymology connected the word with *satyr* and thus with the grotesque. Satire may be in verse or in prose; in the 16th and 17th centuries, the Roman poets Horace and Juvenal were imitated and expanded upon by writers of satiric moral verse, the tone of the verse being wise, smooth, skeptical, and urbane, that of the prose, sharp, harsh, and sometimes nasty. A tradition of English verse satire runs through Donne, Jonson, Dryden, Pope, and Samuel Johnson; of prose satire, Addison, Swift, and Fielding.

Scholasticism, Schoolmen Scholasticism is the term used for the philosophy and theology of the Middle Ages. This consisted of rational inquiry into revealed truth; for it was important to understand what one believed. This technique of disposition was developed by the Schoolmen over a long period, reaching its perfection in Peter Abelard (1079–1142). In the 13th century it absorbed the newly discovered Aristotelian philosophy and method. In this phase its greatest exponent was St. Thomas Aquinas (*c.* 1225–74), who became the chief medieval philosopher and theologian; his authority, challenged in the 16th century, was more seriously contested in the 17th century by the adherents of the "new science."

Seneca Lucius Annaeus Seneca (4 B.C.–65 A.D.) was an important source of Renaissance stoicism (*q.v.*), a model for the "closet" drama of the period, and an exemplar for the kind of prose that shunned the Ciceronian loquacity of early humanism and cultivated terseness. He was Nero's tutor; in 62 A.D. he retired from public life, and in 65 was compelled to commit suicide for taking part in a political conspiracy. He produced writings on ethics and physics, as well as ten tragedies often imitated in the Renaissance.

Sensibility (1) In the mid-18th century, the term came to be used in a literary context to refer to a susceptibility to fine or tender feelings, particularly involving the feelings and sorrows of others. This became a quality to be cultivated in despite of stoical rejections of unreasonable emotion which the neoclassicism (*q.v.*) of the earlier Augustan age had prized. The meaning of the word blended easily into "sentimentality"; but the literary period in England characterized by the work of writers such as Sterne, Goldsmith, Gray, Collins, and Cowper is often called the Age of Sensibility.

(2) A meaning more important for modern literature is that of a special kind of total awareness, an ability to make the finest discriminations in its perception of the world, and yet at the same time not lacking in a kind of force by the very virtue of its own receptive power. The varieties of awareness celebrated in French literature from Baudelaire through Marcel Proust have been adapted by modernist English critics, notably T. S. Eliot, for a fuller extension of the meaning of *sensibility.* By the term "dissociation of sensibility," Eliot implied the split between the sensuous and the intellectual faculties which he thought characterized English poetry after the Restoration (1660).

Sententia A wise, fruitful saying, functioning as a guide to morally correct thought or action.

Sestina Originally a Provençal lyric form supposedly invented by Arnaut Daniel in the 12th century, and one of the most complex of those structures. It has six stanzas of six lines each, folllowed by an *envoi* (*q.v.*) or *tornada* of three lines. Instead of rhyming, the end-words of the lines of the first stanza are all repeated in the following stanzas, but in a constant set of permutations. The *envoi* contains all six words, three in the middle of each line. D. G. Rossetti, Swinburne, Pound, Auden, and other modern poets have used the form, and Sir Philip Sidney composed a magnificent double-sestina, "Ye Goat-herd Gods."

Skepticism A philosophy that denies the possibility of certain knowledge, and, although opposed to Stoicism and Epicureanism (*q.v.*), advocated *ataraxy,* imperturbability of mind. Skepticism originated with Pyrrhon (*c.* 360–270 B.C.), and its chief transmitter was Sextus Empiricus (*c.* 200 B.C.). In the Renaissance, skepticism had importance as questioning the power of the human mind to know truly (for a classic exposition see Donne's *Second Anniversary,* ll. 254–300), and became a powerful influence in morals and religion through the advocacy of Montaigne.

Sonnet A basic lyric form, consisting of fourteen lines of iambic pentameter rhymed in various patterns. The *Italian* or *Petrarchan* sonnet is divided clearly into *octave* and *sestet,* the first rhyming *abba abba* and the second in a pattern such as *cdc dcd.* The *Shakespearean* sonnet consists of three quatrains followed by a couplet: *abab cdcd efef gg.* In the late 16th century in England, sonnets were written either independently as short epigrammatic forms, or grouped in sonnet sequences, i.e. collections of upwards of a hundred poems, in imitation of Petrarch, purportedly addressed to one central figure or muse—a lady usually with a symbolic name like "Stella" or "Idea." Milton made a new kind of use of the Petrarchan form, and the Romantic poets continued in the Miltonic tradition. Several variations have been devised, including the addition of "tails" or extra lines, or the recasting into sixteen lines, instead of fourteen.

Stoicism, Stoics Philosophy founded by Zeno (335–263 B.C.), and opposing the hedonistic tendencies of Epicureanism (*q.v.*). The Stoics' world-view was pantheistic: God was the energy that formed and maintained the world, and wisdom lay in obedience to this law of nature as revealed by the conscience. Moreover, every man is free because the life according to nature and conscience is available to all; so too is suicide—a natural right. Certain Stoics saw the end of the world as caused by fire. In the Renaissance, Latin Stoicism, especially that of Seneca (*q.v.*), had a revival of influence and was Christianized in various ways.

Strong Lines The term used in the 17th century to refer to the tough, tense conceit (*q.v.*)-laden verse of Donne and his followers.

Style See *Decorum*.

Sublime "Lofty"; as a literary idea, originally the basic concept of a Greek treatise (by the so-called "Longinus") on style. In the 18th century, however, the *sublime* came to mean a loftiness perceivable in nature, and sometimes in art—a loftiness different from the composed vision of landscape known as the *picturesque,* because of the element of wildness, power, and even terror. The *beautiful,* the picturesque, and the sublime became three modes for the perception of nature.

Symbolism (1) Broadly, the process by which one phenomenon, in literature, stands for another, or group of others, and usually of a different sort. Clear-cut cases of this in medieval and Renaissance literature are *emblems* or *attributes* (see *Personification; Allegory*). Sometimes conventional symbols may be used in more than one way, e.g. a mirror betokening both truth and vanity. See also *Figure; Emblem.*

(2) In a specific sense (and often given in its French form, *symbolisme*), an important esthetic concept for modern literature, formulated by French poets and critics of the later 19th century following Baudelaire. In this view, the literary symbol becomes something closer to a kind of commanding, central metaphor, taking precedence over any more discursive linguistic mode for poetic communication. The effects of this concept on literature in English have been immense; and some version of the concept survives in modern notions of the poetic *image,* or *fiction.*

Temperaments The balance of combinations of humors (*q.v.*) which in the medieval and Renaissance periods was believed to determine the psychosomatic make-up or "complexion" of a man or a woman. See *Renaissance Psychology.*

Topographical Poem A descriptive poem popular in the 17th and 18th centuries and devoted to a specific scene or landscape with the addition (in the words of Samuel Johnson in 1799) of "historical retrospection or incidental meditation." Sir John Denham's "Cooper's Hill" (1642) is an influential example of the tradition (which includes also Pope's "Windsor Forest") and sometimes blends with the genre of a poem in praise of a particular house or garden.

Topos Greek for "place," commonplace; in rhetoric (*q.v.*), either a general argument, description, or observation that could serve for various occasions; or a method of inventing arguments on a statement or contention. It is often used now to mean a basic literary topic (either a proposition such as the superiority of a life of action to that of contemplation, or vice versa; of old age vs. youth; or a description, such as that of the *locus amoenus* (*q.v.*), the pleasant garden place, Paradise, which allows many variations of thought and language.

Trivium The course of study in the first three of the seven liberal arts—grammar, rhetoric, and logic (or dialectic): the basis of the medieval educational program in school and university. See also *Quadrivium*.

***Troilus* stanza** Or *rhyme royal;* iambic pentameters in stanzas of seven lines, rhyming *ababbcc*, popularized by Chaucer in his poem *Troilus and Criseyde* and called *rhyme royal* supposedly on account of its use by James I of Scotland, king and poet.

Trope (1) See *Rhetoric*. (2) In the liturgy of the Catholic Church, a phrase, sentence, or verse with its musical setting, introduced to amplify or embellish some part of the text of the mass or the office (i.e. the prayers and Scripture readings recited daily by priests, religious, and even laymen) when chanted in choir. Tropes of this second kind were discontinued in 1570 by the authority of Pope Pius V. Troping new material into older or conventional patterns seems to have been, in a general way, a basic device of medieval literature, and was the genesis of modern drama.

Type, Typology (1) Strictly, in medieval biblical interpretation, the prefiguration of the persons and events of the New Testament by persons and events of the Old, the Old Testament being fulfilled in, but not entirely superseded by, the New. Thus, the Temptation and Fall of Man were held to prefigure the first Temptation of Christ, pride in each case being the root of the temptation, and a warning against gluttony the moral lesson to be drawn from both. The Brazen Serpent raised up by Moses was held to prefigure the crucifixion of Christ; Isaac, as a sacrificial victim ("God will provide his own Lamb," says Abraham to him) is a *type* of Christ. The forty days and nights of the Deluge, the forty years of Israel's wandering in the desert, Moses' forty days in the desert are all typologically related.

(2) In a looser sense, a person or event seen as a model or paradigm. See also *Figure*.

Ubi Sunt . . . A motif introducing a lament for the passing of all mortal and material things: e.g. "*Ubi sunt qui ante nos in mundo fuere?*" (Where are they who went before us in this world?), or "Where are the snows of yesteryear?" (Swinburne's translation from the French of Villon's *ballade*).

Virelay A French poetic form, a dance song; short, with two or three rhymes, and two lines of the first stanza as a refrain.

Wars of the Roses Series of encounters between the house of Lancaster (whose emblem was the red rose) and the house of York (whose emblem was the white), which took place between 1455 and 1485 to decide the right of possession of the English throne. At the Battle of Bosworth Field in 1485 the Lancastrian Henry Tudor defeated the Yorkist Richard III and was proclaimed king as Henry VII. He married Elizabeth of York, daughter of King Edward IV.

Worthies, Nine Nine exemplary heroes, three from the Bible (Joshua, David, Judas Maccabaeus); three from pagan antiquity (Hector of Troy, Alexander the Great, Julius Caesar), and three from "Christian" romance (King Arthur, the Emperor Charlemagne, and Godfrey of Bouillon, a leader of the First Crusade and King of Jerusalem). They were favorite figures for tapestries (see Fig. 46 in illustrations for the Medieval section of this Anthology) and pageants.

Wit (1) Originally, "intellect," "intelligence"; later, "creative intelligence," or poetical rather than merely mechanical intellectual power. Thus, during the age of Dryden and Pope, a poet might be called a wit without any compromising sense. In the 19th century, "wit" came to mean verbal agility or cleverness, as opposed to the more creative powers of the mind. (2) More specifically, in literary history, as characterizing the poetic style of John Donne and his 17th-century followers. The Augustan age would contrast this with the "true wit" of *neoclassical* (*q.v*) poetry.

Yorkists See *Wars of the Roses.*

Zodiac In astrology, a belt of the celestial sphere, about eight or nine degrees to either side of the ecliptic (the apparent orbit of the sun), within which the apparent motions of the sun, moon, and planets take place. It is divided into twelve equal parts, the signs, through each of which the sun passes in a month. Each division once coincided with one of the constellations after which the signs are named: Aries (Ram)—in Chaucer's time the sun entered this sign on 12 March; Taurus (Bull); Gemini (Twins); Cancer (Crab); Leo (Lion); Virgo (Virgin); Libra (Scales); Scorpio; Sagittarius (Archer); Capricornus (Goat); Aquarius (Water-Carrier); Pisces (Fishes). Each zodiacal sign was believed to govern a part of the human body. See *Astronomy and Astrology.*

Suggestions for Further Reading

This reading list is deliberately summary: it cites the books most immediately helpful in providing a text or an introductory study. From the bibliographies and footnotes contained in these, the student can find his way to the more elaborate text editions and the more extended critical and historical studies.

General Backgrounds: Europe Medieval English literature is part of a larger European unit: its relations with both the classical and the medieval vernacular literatures of the Continent should always be kept in mind. The themes and modes of these literatures are splendidly treated in the first ten essays—three of them concerned with Antiquity—of Erich Auerbach, *Mimesis: The Representation of Reality in Western Literature* (trans. Willard R. Trask), 1957. Auerbach's long paper "Figura," in his *Scenes from the Drama of European Literature*, 1959, is also important. An older work, well worth reading, on European literature from the sixth century to the twelfth, is W. P. Ker's *The Dark Ages*, 1904.

For the wider context of medieval thought, Gordon Leff's *Medieval Thought: St. Augustine to Ockham*, 1958, is informative. The most stimulating general introduction oriented toward literature is C. S. Lewis's *The Discarded Image: An Introduction to Medieval and Renaissance Literature*, 1964.

The interrelations of European literature, thought, and art during the medieval period are treated by George Henderson in his lively companion volumes *Early Medieval*, 1972, and *Gothic*, 1967, in the series Style and Civilization.

For the intellectual and material conditions of life in Europe during the later Middle Ages, with their antecedents, the classic study is Johan Huizinga's *The Waning of the Middle Ages*, 1924. The best preliminary account of medieval daily life is Eileen Power's *Medieval People*, 1924.

Backgrounds: England The best introduction to the literature of England from Anglo-Saxon times to the end of the Middle Ages is still W. P. Ker's *Medieval English Literature*, 1912. Longer and more exhaustive is A. C. Baugh, ed., *A Literary History of England*, 1948; a useful survey, with bibliographies, is W. L. Renwick and H. Orton, *The Beginnings of English Literature to Skelton*, 3rd ed., revised by M. F. Wakelin, 1966.

The social and political background is treated in companion volumes by C. N. L. Brooke, *From Alfred to Henry III, 871–1272*, 1961, and George Holmes, *The Later*

Middle Ages, 1272–1485, 1962. G. M. Trevelyan's *Illustrated Social History of England,* 1949, is less satisfactory on the Middle Ages than on other periods, but is useful.

For the artistic achievement of England in the Middle Ages, consult Margaret Rickert, *Painting in Britain: The Middle Ages,* 2nd ed., 1965; Lawrence Stone, *Sculpture in Britain: The Middle Ages,* 1955; and G. F. Webb, *Architecture in Britain: The Middle Ages,* 1959—all valuable and fully illustrated volumes in the Pelican History of Art.

Anglo-Saxon England and Old English Literature A classic study is H. M. Chadwick's *The Heroic Age,* 1912; but the best and fullest general history is Sir Frank Stenton's *Anglo-Saxon England,* 3rd ed., 1971, one of the finest volumes in the Oxford History of England. P. Hunter Blair's *An Introduction to Anglo-Saxon England,* 1956, is a useful shorter survey, with illustrations, but the best introduction is Dorothy Whitelock's *The Beginnings of English Society,* 1952. For art and archaeology this can be supplemented by the best preliminary study of the subject, David M. Wilson's *The Anglo-Saxons,* 1960.

Of primary sources, *The Anglo-Saxon Chronicle* has been well translated by G. N. Garmonsway, 1953; and Venerable Bede's *Ecclesiastical History of the English People,* by L. Sherley-Price, 1955.

For Old English literature, the best survey is C. L. Wrenn's *A Study of Old English Literature,* 1967; while S. B. Greenfield's *A Critical History of Old English Literature,* 1965, is useful.

BEOWULF

Editions The standard edition of the text is F. Klaeber, ed., *Beowulf and the Fight at Finnesburh,* 3rd ed., 1950; but C. L. Wrenn, ed., *Beowulf, with the Finnesburh Fragment,* 3rd ed., 1973, is more up-to-date and often easier to use. Neither edition has a translation, but both are very fully annotated. There are prose translations by J. R. Clark Hall, with introduction and notes by C. L. Wrenn, and preface by J. R. R. Tolkien, 1950; and by E. Talbot Donaldson, 1966 (excellent). Besides the verse translation by Charles W. Kennedy used in this volume, there is a fine poetic version by Kevin Crossley-Holland, with helpful introduction and notes by Bruce Mitchell, 1968.

Critical Studies R. W. Chambers's *Beowulf: An Introduction,* 3rd ed., with Supplement by C. L. Wrenn, 1959, is the basic and encyclopedic work on *Beowulf.* Good selections of critical essays are Lewis E. Nicholson, ed., *An Anthology of Beowulf Criticism,* and Donald K. Fry, ed., *The Beowulf Poet: A Collection of Critical Essays,* 1968, which both include the most important and influential article so far published on the poem, J. R. R. Tolkien's "Beowulf: The Monsters and the Critics," from *Proceedings of the British Academy* XXII, 1936. J. C. Pope's *The Rhythm of Beowulf,* 1942, is the most elaborate study of the meter; and Dorothy Whitelock's *The Audience of Beowulf,* 1951, the best study of its social and cultural setting.

Recordings Readings from *Beowulf,* in the original Old English, are available in recordings by Jess B. Bessinger, Jr., *Beowulf, Cædmon's Hymn,* and *Other Old English Poems,* Cædmon TC 1161; by Nevill Coghill and Norman Davis, *Beowulf,* with introductory material, Spoken Arts 918; by Charles W. Dunn, *Early English*

Poetry, Folkways FL 9851; and by J. C. Pope and H. Kökeritz, *Beowulf and Chaucer,* Lexington 5505.

Shorter Old English Poems In addition to C. W. Kennedy's *Anthology of Old English Poetry,* translated into alliterative verse, 1960 (used in this Anthology), there are verse translations by Michael Alexander, *The Earliest English Poems,* 1966 (made on different principles from Kennedy's), and by Kevin Crossley-Holland, *The Battle of Maldon and Other Old English Poems,* ed. Bruce Mitchell, 1965. *The Dream of the Rood* has recently (1970) been edited by Michael Swanton, with excellent introduction and notes.

Middle English Literature Exhaustive general surveys are E. K. Chambers, *English Literature at the Close of the Middle Ages,* 1945, and H. S. Bennett, *Chaucer and the Fifteenth Century,* 1947, both volumes in the Oxford History of English Literature. George Kane, *Middle English Literature,* 1951, and the later sections of W. P. Ker, *Medieval English Literature,* 1912, are the best short introductions. For the 14th century, D. S. Brewer, *Chaucer and His Times,* 1963, is a good general survey; and J. A. Burrow, *Ricardian Poetry: Chaucer, Gower, Langland and the Gawain Poet,* 1971, a stimulating study of these poets and their milieu. The background is usefully treated in Gervase Mathew, *The Court of Richard II,* 1968.

GEOFFREY CHAUCER

Editions Still basic is W. W. Skeat, ed., *The Works of Geoffrey Chaucer,* in six volumes and a further collection, *Chaucerian and Other Pieces,* 1894–97, with extensive commentary; but the most informative single-volume edition is F. N. Robinson, ed., *The Complete Works,* 2nd ed., 1957, with explanatory notes and glossary. The most helpful substantial selection is E. Talbot Donaldson, ed., *Chaucer's Poetry: An Anthology for the Modern Reader,* 1958.

Critical Studies and Handbooks The best collection for the history of Chaucer criticism is J. A. Burrow, ed., *Geoffrey Chaucer,* in the Penguin Critical Anthologies series, 1969 (excerpts). Collections of modern critical essays ed. by E. C. Wagenknecht, *Chaucer: Modern Essays in Criticism,* 1959; by R. J. Schoeck and Jerome Taylor, *Chaucer Criticism,* two vols., 1960–61; and by C. J. Owen, *Discussions of the Canterbury Tales,* 1961, all give a representative selection. The most rewarding group of essays by a single author and the best guide to the character of Chaucer's poems is E. Talbot Donaldson, *Speaking of Chaucer,* 1970.

Among monographs, John Livingston Lowes, *Geoffrey Chaucer,* 1934, remains the best introduction, especially to Chaucer's reading and his thought world. Useful additional materials are Charles Muscatine, *Chaucer and the French Tradition: A Study in Style and Meaning,* 1957, and Walter Clyde Curry, *Chaucer and the Medieval Sciences,* 2nd ed., 1960, the standard account of this special aspect. D. W. Robertson, Jr., *A Preface to Chaucer: Studies in Medieval Perspectives,* 1969, is the most lively and controversial of modern studies on Chaucer. A thorough and interesting introduction to the General Prologue of the *Canterbury Tales* is Muriel Bowden's *Commentary on the General Prologue to the Canterbury Tales,* 1967.

R. D. French, *A Chaucer Handbook,* 2nd ed., 1947, is a handy reference book; but for up-to-date essays, with excellent bibliographies, on all aspects of Chaucer, the most useful manual is Beryl Rowland, ed., *Companion to Chaucer Studies,* 1968.

The best short work on Chaucerian speech is Helge Kökeritz's *A Guide to Chaucer's Pronunciation,* 1954. *Chaucer's World,* ed. E. Rickert, C. C. Olson, and M. M. Crow, 1948, is excellent background reading, with contemporary accounts of events and many documents. Roger S. Loomis, ed., *A Mirror of Chaucer's World,* 1965, is a handsome picture book.

Recordings Readings on records are given in Chaucerian pronunciation by Nevill Coghill, Norman Davis, and J. A. Burrow, of the General Prologue, Argo RG 401; by the same, with L. Davis, of the Nun's Priest's Tale, ll. 1–625 and some shorter poems, Argo RG 466; and by N. Coghill and N. Davis, the Pardoner's Tale, ll. 739–894, Spoken Arts 919.

SIR GAWAIN AND THE GREEN KNIGHT

Editions The best old-spelling edition for the beginner is *Sir Gawain and the Green Knight,* ed. J. A. Burrow, 1972, in which obsolete letters and usages have been modernized and, wherever possible, a single spelling has been adopted for the same word spelled in different ways by the scribe. Notes and glossary are included. The standard old-spelling edition, however, is *Sir Gawain and the Green Knight,* ed. J. R. R. Tolkien and E. V. Gordon, revised by Norman Davis, 1967, with full notes and glossary.

In addition to that by Brian Stone, 1972 (used here), there are verse translations by Theodore Howard Banks, Jr., 1929; by Marie Borroff, 1968; and by John Gardner, in his *Complete Works of the Gawain Poet,* 1965.

Critical Studies The most important critical essays are collected in R. J. Blanch, ed., *Sir Gawain and Pearl: Critical Essays,* 1966; Denton Fox, ed., *Twentieth Century Interpretations of Sir Gawain and the Green Knight,* 1968; and D. R. Howard and C. K. Zacher, eds., *Critical Studies of Sir Gawain and the Green Knight,* 1968. The book-length studies by Marie Borroff, *Sir Gawain and the Green Knight: A Stylistic and Metrical Study,* 1962, and L. D. Benson, *Art and Tradition in Sir Gawain and the Green Knight,* 1965, are full and careful; but the most stimulating is J. A. Burrow, *A Reading of Sir Gawain and the Green Knight,* 1965.

PIERS PLOWMAN

Editions Standard for all three texts is *The Vision of William Concerning Piers the Plowman,* ed. W. W. Skeat, two vols., 1886, reissued with additional bibliography, 1954. It is copiously annotated, and though textually superseded for the A text by the edition of George Kane, 1960, its notes are still essential for an understanding of any of the three versions. Useful selections from the C text have been edited by Elizabeth Salter and Derek Pearsall in *Piers Plowman,* 1967.

There are verse translations by H. W. Wells, *The Vision of Piers Plowman,* 1935 (complete), and by Nevill Coghill, *Visions from Piers Plowman,* 1949 (selections). The most accurate is the complete prose version of the B text by J. F. Goodridge, 1959.

Critical Studies The best short account of the poem is still that of R. W. Chambers, in his volume of essays *Man's Unconquerable Mind,* 1939, chaps. 4–5. *Piers Plowman:*

Critical Approaches, ed. S. S. Hussey, 1969, usefully collects major articles, and Elizabeth Salter's *Piers Plowman, An Introduction,* 1962, is an excellent brief study.

Medieval Drama Good collections, with annotations, are A. C. Cawley, ed., *Everyman and Medieval Miracle Plays,* 1960 (modernized spelling), and R. G. Thomas, ed., *Ten Miracle Plays,* 1966. The standard edition of the *Second Shepherds' Play* is that of A. C. Cawley, in *The Wakefield Pageants in the Towneley Cycle,* 1958; and the handiest single edition of *Everyman* is by the same editor, 1961.

E. K. Chambers's *The Medieval Stage,* two vols., 1905, is still standard, though dated; Hardin Craig, *English Religious Drama of the Middle Ages,* 1955, is somewhat old-fashioned, but informative. *Christian Rite and Christian Drama in the Middle Ages,* by O. B. Hardison, Jr., 1965, is among the most important recent contributions; and V. A. Kolve, *The Play Called Corpus Christi,* 1966, is a first-rate study. The best introduction is Arnold Williams, *The Drama of Medieval England,* 1961. Karl Young's *The Drama of the Medieval Church,* two vols., 1933 (corrected reprint, 1951), is one of the great and exhaustive works on medieval sacred drama.

Middle English Lyrics Standard collections are: *Medieval English Lyrics: A Critical Anthology,* ed. R. T. Davies, 1963 (little annotation); *A Selection of English Carols,* ed. Richard Leighton Greene, 1962, with excellent introduction and annotation; *The Oxford Book of Medieval English Verse,* ed. Celia and Kenneth Sisam, 1970, not annotated, but with helpful vocabulary at the end of each poem, and including extracts from longer poems as well as lyrics; and *Medieval English Lyrics,* ed. Theodore Silverstein, 1971, with good introduction and annotation. A fuller collection is James J. Wilhelm, trans. and ed., *Medieval Song: An Anthology of Hymns and Lyrics,* 1971, which begins with late Latin poetry. On records there is *Medieval English Lyrics,* with notes on texts by E. J. Dobson and on music by F. L. Harrison, Argo 443, 1965.

The best inclusive study is Peter Dronke, *The Medieval Lyric,* 1968, which includes Continental lyrics and deals with the English material in relation to them. Best on the English religious lyric is Rosemary Woolf's *The English Religious Lyric in the Middle Ages,* 1968. Douglas Gray's *Themes and Images in the Medieval English Religious Lyric,* 1972, is a splendid illustrated survey.

Popular Ballads The monumental collection of F. J. Child, ed., *The English and Scottish Popular Ballads,* five vols., 1882–98, is still standard, and gives variant versions. The student's one-volume edition, with texts and headnotes, ed. H. C. Sargent and George Lyman Kittredge, 1904, is the fullest of its kind. More inclusive and entertaining is M. J. C. Hodgart, ed., *The Faber Book of Ballads,* 1965, with a good introduction and a broad additional selection of modern ballads. James Kinsley, ed., *The Oxford Book of Ballads,* 1969, includes tunes, but has no introduction and confines itself to the older ballads. The most exhaustive work since Child (not yet complete), Bertrand H. Bronson, ed., *The Traditional Tunes of the Child Ballads,* four vols., 1959–70, collects the ballad tunes of the British Isles and the U.S.A. The best short introduction is M. J. C. Hodgart's study, *The Ballads,* 1950.

There are recordings as well—e.g. *The Child Ballads,* Topic 12T160–161 (taken down in the field); and Ewen MacColl and A. L. Lloyd, *English and Scottish Popular Ballads,* Riverside RLP12-624.

SIR THOMAS MALORY

Editions The standard is *The Works of Sir Thomas Malory,* ed. Eugène Vinaver,

2nd ed., three vols., 1967, which prints the Winchester MS., with the necessary supplements and variant readings from Caxton, and a full commentary. There is also a one-volume edition without commentary, 2nd ed., 1970. The Caxton version is most easily available as *Morte d'Arthur,* in Everyman's Library, 1906, without annotation.

Critical Studies Still the best general study is Eugène Vinaver, *Malory,* 1929, reissued 1970; and the same author's chapter in R. S. Loomis, ed., *Arthurian Literature in the Middle Ages: A Collaborative History,* 1959, is the finest short introduction. The essays in J. A. W. Bennett, ed., *Essays on Malory,* 1963, are all useful, but especially P. E. Tucker's "Chivalry in the *Morte*" and Sally Shaw's "Caxton and Malory." The most recent collection is that of R. M. Lumiansky, *Malory's Originality: A Critical Study of Le Morte Darthur,* 1964.

WILLIAM CAXTON

The best study of all aspects of Caxton is also a recent one: N. F. Blake's *Caxton and His World,* 1969.

WILLIAM DUNBAR

A one-volume edition of the poems, without notes, is W. Mackay Mackenzie's *The Poems of William Dunbar,* 1932; but the best way to begin on Dunbar is through the selection of *Poems,* with appreciations by various critics, and introduction, notes, and glossary by James Kinsley, 1958.

JOHN SKELTON

The standard edition is still that of Alexander Dyce, *The Poetical Works of John Skelton,* two vols., 1843, with notes. This is the basis of the unannotated, modern-spelling edition by Philip Henderson, 2nd ed., 1948. The best introductory selection is *Poems,* ed. Robert S. Kinsman, 1969, with introduction and commentary.

THE OTHER WORLD: PARADISE

Two treatments, the first more exhaustive, the second more perceptive, are H. R. Patch's *The Other World According to Descriptions in Medieval Literature,* 1950, and A. Bartlett Giamatti's *The Earthly Paradise and the Renaissance Epic,* 1966.

Author and Title Index

First-Line Index